Early California Commentaries

Rose Marie Beebe & Robert M. Senkewicz
Series Editors

Volume II

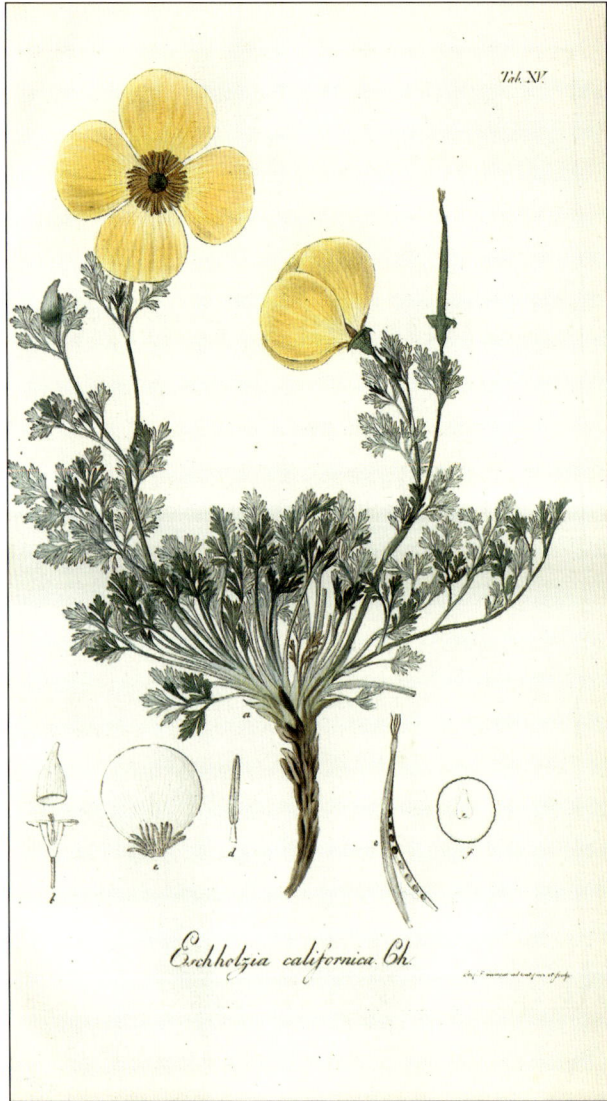

Louis Choris, *The California Poppy (Eschscholzia californica)*, 1818, watercolor. *Courtesy of the LuEsther T. Mertz Library of The New York Botanical Garden, Bronx, New York.*

California Through Russian Eyes
1806–1848

Compiled, translated, and edited by
JAMES R. GIBSON

With the assistance of
ALEXEI A. ISTOMIN

THE ARTHUR H. CLARK COMPANY
An imprint of the University of Oklahoma Press
Norman, Oklahoma
2013

*Publication of this book is made possible
through the generosity of Edith Kinney Gaylord.*

Library of Congress Cataloging-in-Publication Data
Gibson, James R.
    California through Russian eyes, 1806–1848 / compiled, translated, and edited
by James R. Gibson ; with the assistance of Alexei A. Istomin.
        pages cm. — (Early California commentaries ; volume II)
    Includes bibliographical references and index.
    ISBN 978-0-87062-421-6 (hardcover : alkaline paper) 1. California—Description
and travel—Sources. 2. California—History—To 1846—Sources. 3. Russians—
California—History—19th century—Sources. 4. Visitors, Foreign—California—
History—19th century—Sources. 5. Travelers' writings, Russian—California.
6. Hispanic Americans—California—History—19th century—Sources. 7. California—Ethnic relations—History—19th century—Sources. 8. California—Relations—Russia—Sources. 9. Russia—Relations—California—Sources. I. Istomin,
A. A. II. Title.
    F864.G53 2013
    305.8009794—dc23
                                    2012046841

California Through Russian Eyes, 1806–1848
is Volume 2 in the Early California Commentaries series.

The paper in this book meets the guidelines for permanence and durability
of the Committee on Production Guidelines for Book Longevity
of the Council on Library Resources, Inc. ∞

1 2 3 4 5 6 7 8 9 10

In memory of
those Russians who visited Spanish and Mexican California,
and those Californios who hosted them

And to Peter Gerhard (1920–2006), W. Michael Mathes (1936–2012),
and David J. Weber (1940–2010), whom I regrettably
never met but whose admirable scholarship
has informed my own work

Contents

Illustrations

Acknowledgments

I am indebted to the following archives and libraries for access to written and pictorial sources: the Archive of the Foreign Policy of the Russian Empire (Moscow); the Archive of the Russian Geographical Society (St. Petersburg), especially Mariya Fyodorovna Matveyeva; The Bancroft Library of the University of California–Berkeley; the Estonian Historical Archive (Tartu); the Hamilton Library of the University of Hawaii–Manoa; the LuEsther T. Mertz Library of The New York Botanical Garden; the Museum of the Russian Academy of Fine Arts, St. Petersburg; the Elmer E. Rasmuson Library of the University of Alaska–Fairbanks; the Peter the Great Museum of Anthropology and Ethnography (Kunstkamera), St. Petersburg; the Russian State Library (Moscow); the Russian State Historical Archive (St. Petersburg); the Russian State Naval Archive (St. Petersburg); the Scott Library of York University, especially its Resource Sharing Department; and the State Archive of Perm Kray (Perm).

I am especially thankful to a colleague, Alexei Istomin, for his careful transcriptions and annotations of several of the longer documents.

For assistance in a variety of matters I am grateful, too, to Katherine Arndt, Mia D'Avanza, Glenn Farris, Natalia Gubina, Lyn Kalani, John Middleton, Pat Polansky, Will Ryan, Rachel Seale, Leonid Shur, Lyudmila Spiridonova, Sarah Sweedler, and Valery Tishkov.

Last, for their numerous and helpful corrections and suggestions I thank three readers—Michael Mathes, Kenneth Owens, and Robert Senkewicz—as well as my editors at the University of Oklahoma Press, particularly Jessica Mitzner, and freelance copy editor Sally Bennett. The manuscript benefited, too, from the advice about Spanish linguistic oddities on the part of my wife, Gail, not only my longtime support system but also a onetime teacher of Spanish whose offer to teach me the language's fundamentals I so foolishly declined during a sabbatical many years ago in picturesque Pátzcuaro, Mexico. *Mi culpa!*

Editor's Note on the Translations

All of the dates in the documents have been left in the Old Style (Julian calendar), putting them twelve days behind the New Style (Gregorian, or modern, calendar) in the nineteenth century in the Eastern Hemisphere but eleven days behind in the Western Hemisphere (including Russian-American), as the International Date Line had not yet been demarcated.

Transliteration of the Russian documents follows the system of the American Council of Learned Societies, a system that renders historical and geographical literature more phonetically in English than that of the U.S. Library of Congress. In translating the documents, I have adhered faithfully to the originals in all respects except, occasionally, paragraphing and punctuation (in the interests of comprehension and readability); this adherence sometimes produces inconsistencies both within and among documents in terms of the treatment of numbers as cardinals, numerals, or ordinals, for example. Also, the variable spacing and centering of subheads, salutations and closings, and columnar information in tables in the documents have been standardized.

Interlinear additions to the originals are enclosed within forward slashes in bold type; deleted text is shown in strikeout, missing text as four bracketed blank spaces, and illegible text as four bracketed hyphens. Numbered footnotes are mine; asterisked notes are those of the original authors; and my notes within the asterisked footnotes are bracketed and initialed. In the tables, the word "ditto" is indicated by the double prime (that is, the "inches") symbol, consisting of two very short, straight lines, as follows: ".

Introduction

Russian America came about as a result of expeditions of exploration and discovery undertaken in 1725–29 and 1733–42 under Vitus Bering northward and eastward from the Pacific Coast of Siberia on the orders of Peter the Great, the tsar (and, from 1721, emperor) who was determined to make his country more modern and less isolated. His reforms were costly, so his interest in the waters and lands between northeastern Asia and northwestern America was more commercial than scientific. Siberia's chief source of wealth for the Russian conquerors (apart from the southern strip of arable land for runaway and deported serfs from European Russia) was not salt or hard gold but "soft gold"—furs, especially lucrative sables, which were hunted and trapped by Russian *promyshlenniks*,[1] with the state exacting a percentage of their take in taxes, as well as fur tribute from the natives.

Thanks to the high value of sables (upon which Siberia had a virtual monopoly), the ubiquitous navigable river network, the weak opposition from the disunited, scattered, and backward natives (once the Tatar khanate of Western Siberia had been defeated, at least), and the lack of intervention on the part of China or Japan, Russian entrepreneurs advanced very rapidly from the Ural Mountains to the Pacific Coast (a distance of some 2,500 miles in about fifty years), hunting out and trapping out one river basin after another as they went. By the beginning of the 1700s, in the middle of Peter's reign, the furbearers of the Russian Far East had been depleted, too. New sources of wealth had to be sought, and again to the east, a direction dictated by the pack ice of the north and isolationist and formidable Manchu China and Tokugawa Japan to the south.

Bering's second expedition returned without its leader (he died on his eponymous island in the Commander archipelago) but brought news of a "great land" (Alaska) across the ocean to the east and, more important, samples of fresh

---

[1]Originally the term *promyshlennik* (from *promyshlyat*, meaning generally "to earn one's livelihood" or, specifically, "to hunt") denoted a freelance hunter/trapper in Siberia, but in Russian America the term came to be applied to a Russian-American Company common worker, one without any authority.

peltry—this time not sables but the even more lucrative "sea beavers" (sea otters), whose fur proved so valuable in the nearby (and large) Chinese market that it was used primarily for trim, not whole garments. So from the middle 1740s, the Russians launched another "fur rush" across the northernmost Pacific, aided again by weak native resistance (until they met the Tlingits on the Northwest Coast), an absence of interest from rival powers (the British Hudson's Bay Company and the Canadian North West Company had not yet crossed the Rockies, and the Spaniards had yet to venture north of the Californias). The continental Russians, who had much experience in riverine and coastal navigation but very little in oceanic voyaging, were helped, too, by the existence of the stepping-stones of the Aleutian Islands and the Alaska Peninsula across the stormy and foggy Bering Sea.

It was not long before the promyshlenniks had depleted the sea otter (and fur seal) rookeries of the islands and coasts of what came to be known as Russian America and were eyeing the untapped Northwest Coast. Meanwhile, the several rival Russian fur trading companies were coerced in 1799 to merge into a chartered monopoly—the Russian-American Company (1799)—by the Russian government, which was alarmed by both the ruthless competition among them (at the expense of both the traders and the natives) and the increasing likelihood of foreign entanglements as Spanish ships out of San Blas began to probe the Northwest Coast from the 1770s to monitor the Russian advance, British explorers such as James Cook on his third voyage (1776–80) and George Vancouver on his survey of North America's Pacific Coast (1792–94) breached Russian coastal waters, and from the late 1780s first British and then American shipowners, alerted by the publication in 1784 of Cook's findings, outfitted trading vessels to the Northwest Coast, where for sea otter skins (which they later exchanged at Canton for teas, textiles, and chinaware for the Yankee market) they bartered sundry goods, including guns and grog, to the formidable Tlingits, Haidas, and Tsimshians, even inciting them against the Russians. So no longer did the Russians have a monopoly on the sea otter trade and no longer did they enjoy the twin luxuries of ineffectual resistance from the indigenous inhabitants and nonexistent opposition from imperial rivals. At the same time, they had to cope with longer and longer supply lines from the motherland (the imperial capital was half a world away) and the costlier and riskier requirements of maritime operations (seagoing vessels and trained mariners). These unfamiliar conditions took the Russians to California— or rather, the Spanish colony and later Mexican province of Alta California.

They were attracted initially by California's nutrias. Admittedly, the southern sea otter's pelt was not as large, dark, or lush as that of its northern relative, which had to survive in colder climes and colder waters; however, sea otter fur was so highly valued on the seemingly insatiable Chinese market that even inferior pelts fetched handsome prices. Besides, the Russians had little choice; the rookeries of the Kuriles, Kamchatka, and Aleutians had been exhausted, while the Northwest Coast otters to the south of New Archangel (Sitka), the Russian-American Company's colonial capital, had become the preserve of mostly American "coasters," with their superior trade goods, higher prices, and better ships. The Californian rookery was the last reserve of sea otters, and it had been tapped only halfheartedly by the Spanish missionaries of both Baja and Alta California.

The Russians, however, lacked the requisite vessels and sailors for accessing this reserve, although they did possess the world's best hunters of sea otters in the Aleuts (modern Unangans) and Konyagas, or Kodiakers (modern Alutiiqs), whom they consequently more or less enserfed (and therefore did not have to hunt or trade for the otters themselves). The result was a series of joint hunting ventures "on halves" in 1803–12 from New Archangel to the Californian coast in American ships with American captains and crews and Aleut or Konyaga hunters with their kayaks and harpoons and Russian overseers, the catch being shared equally. During these forays the Russians came to know not only the coast's rookeries and fisheries but also its islands, harbors, shoals, rocks, winds, currents, and weather—knowledge that was to serve them well when they finally began in 1806 to send their own ships down the coast to hunt and to probe, resulting eventually in the founding of their own base of Fort Ross in 1812. Thereafter they hunted on both their own account (while poaching in Spanish California's waters, including San Francisco Bay, whenever possible) and from the early 1820s until the middle 1830s periodically on halves with Mexican traders. Fur seals, sea lions, and even sea birds were taken (especially on the Farallones), but the chief prize remained the sea otter until its virtual extirpation by the middle 1840s.

The sea otter, however, was not the only Californian magnet for the Russian-American Company. The firm also saw the province as a site for an agricultural colony that could provision its Alaskan settlements, whose undersupply reached the starvation point by 1805 (prompting Nikolay Rezanov's desperate voyage in the *Yunona* [*Juno*] to San Francisco, where he gained not only a load of precious wheat but also the lovely hand of Concepción Argüello, the teenaged daughter of the commandant of the presidio).[2]

What the company called its "colonies" (colonial subdivisions such as Unalaska, Kodiak, and New Archangel) received some provisions from Eastern Siberia but at high cost and much risk, given the enormous distance from Irkutsk, the rugged terrain of the Yakutsk–Okhotsk route from the Eastern Siberian interior

---

[2] In Spanish a presidio was, strictly speaking, a prison, but on the northern frontier of New Spain it meant a garrisoned fortification or simply a garrison (and figuratively even a citadel, fortress, or fort, depending on its strength). The meaning of the term "garrison" was derived from the fact that military service on the frontier was often an alternative to a prison sentence for minor crimes.

to the North Pacific coast, and the flimsy vessels plying the foggy, rainy, windy seaway between Okhotsk and New Archangel. So with the advent of American fur trading vessels on the Northwest Coast from the late 1780s the company turned to them as a more dependable and more economical source of supplies, including provisions, which they bartered to the Russians for fur seal skins from the Pribilofs. This strategy, however, made the company reliant upon its principal competitor in the sea otter trade for the necessities of life—hardly a desirable position. The Russians did enjoy an abundance of fish, especially salmon, as well as game, and they did try to grow grain and vegetables and to rear livestock, but the cool, damp climate and the thin, patchy soils of coastal Alaska were not conducive to bumper crops or plump cattle. Knowing that grain and cattle thrived in Alta California at its missions and ranchos, they decided to found a colony on California's unoccupied northern frontier that would exploit both the sunny, fertile land and the southern sea otter rookery. The result was the establishment in 1812 of Fort Ross, plus a port at Bodega Bay and, eventually, several nearby farms, as well as a shipyard, a brickworks, and a tannery.

This newest member of the company's "colonies"—the "counter" (district) of Ross, or simply Russian California—proved agriculturally disappointing, however. Founded right on the foggy and windy coast against the Coast Ranges with a view more to defense and hunting than to farming, it lacked the extensive and fertile land and warmer, sunnier climate of the Spanish missions and ranchos to the south, and it lacked the means to expand into the much more promising inland valleys. The colony did not even have a decent harbor, Bodega Bay being an exposed roadstead. Some wheat and barley, butter and beef, and vegetables and fruit were produced (as well as hides, shingles, and bricks) but not enough for the colony to feed even itself, let alone the other colonies, in some years.

In the meantime, the colony's existence had diplomatic repercussions, first with Spain and then (from 1821) with Mexico. Spain, still smarting from its retreat from Vancouver (Quadra) Island under the Nootka Sound Convention of 1790 and having to cope with both political instability at home in the aftermath of the Napoleonic Wars and revolutionary unrest in its American colonies, including Mexico, was sensitive to Russian encroachment on the *frontera del norte*. The Russians were regarded as trespassers, even though the Nootka Sound Convention nullified Spanish sovereignty over the coast north of the Golden Gate, and not until 1819 under the Transcontinental Treaty did the United States (but not Russia) recognize Spanish dominion over the Pacific slope south of 42° N. What mattered, however, were realities on the ground, not lines in treaties. And in Alta California the reality was that Spain was weak in manpower and firepower and thus could do little about Russian encroachment except inspect, protest, and report—which it began to do within a month of the founding of Fort Ross (when Ensign Gabriel Moraga made the first of his two visits) and sporadically thereafter.[3] It also resorted to the mission stratagem; San Rafael (1817) and Sonoma (1823) at least discouraged, if not forestalled, Russian expansion into the agriculturally more promising interior and the northern seaboard and superior anchorage of San Francisco Bay. The balance of power was not changed by Mexican independence; in 1822 a Mexican envoy, Agustín Fernández de San Vicente, visited Fort Ross and demanded its abandonment within six months, but the threat was hollow and nothing changed. The fledgling republic was preoccupied with political stability in Mexico proper, and Alta California remained a peripheral province that, moreover, suffered from its own brand of political factionalism as well as mounting pressure from the 1830s from foreign traders and settlers. For their part the Russians failed to take advantage of these circumstances. A few, such as the young radical Dmitry Zavalishin and Governor Ferdinand von Wrangell, advocated expansion of the Fort Ross and Bodega Bay footholds, but St. Petersburg lacked the desire to do so. California was even more marginal in importance to Russia than it was to Spain and Mexico, the tsar's primary foreign concerns being other European powers and the Ottoman Empire. The Russians were already overextended in Alaska, let alone in even more remote Alta California, where, moreover, prospective opposition from an expansionist United States promised to be even more formidable. Besides, action might disrupt the Russian-American Company's trade with the Californios, who were able to supply the abundant provisions that its Fort Ross colony failed to deliver.

Commerce, then, represented Alta California's remaining attraction for the Russians. The commercial incentives were mutual—the Spaniards had an abundance of wheat and beef, which the Russians needed, and a lack of manufactures, which the Russians could provide. Rezanov had secured a cargo of grain in 1806 but not a trade pact; His Catholic Majesty's Laws of the Indies prohibited foreign trade with Spanish colonies, and the Russians succeeded only occasionally in persuading the province's governors and missionaries to exchange provisions for goods, plus "presents." Then in 1821, alarmed by American commercial inroads, Russia "cut off its nose to spite its face" by banning foreign shipping—including American coasters—from the waters and ports of the Russian Far East and Russian America, thereby depriving the Russian colonies of one of their chief sources of supply (although the ban was nullified in 1824 and 1825 by conventions with the United States and Great Britain, the damage had been done). In the same year Mexico became independent and the Laws of the Indies no longer applied to the Californias. Thereafter the company sent two or three ships annually to San Francisco and Monterey to trade a variety of goods (textiles, metals, utensils, implements, coffee, tea, sugar) for mostly wheat, dried and salted meat, and tallow and

---

[3]See Mathes, *Russian-Mexican Frontier.*

lard (as well as to Baja California for lake salt), just as Yankee shipowners sent ships round the Horn for hides and tallow from the same source. These exchanges continued, despite periodic harvest failures and mounting duties and charges, until the secularization of the missions in 1833–36 sharply reduced agricultural production.

By then, too, the southern sea otter had been largely hunted out and farming in the colony of Ross had reached its modest limits. So when at the end of the decade the Hudson's Bay Company offered to supply New Archangel reliably for ten years with superior provisions from its Oregon Country farms and manufactures from England in return for moderate delivery charges and hunting rights to the mainland Alaskan panhandle, the Russian-American Company accepted, rendering Russian California redundant. In 1841 it was sold for $30,000 (payable in wheat) to John Sutter of New Helvetia.

Meanwhile, the Russian navy had also been drawn to Alta California. Founded by Peter the Great, the navy had long confined itself to the defense of Russia's shores and the support of land-based operations in the Baltic and Black Seas, usually against Sweden and Turkey. In fact, as a continental power par excellence and a largely self-sufficient empire Russia had little need of either a merchant or a military marine; besides, the short stretches of its lengthy coastline that were not obstructed by ice all or much of the year were found in embayments of the world ocean, such as the Baltic and Black Seas, whose outlets were ultimately controlled by foreign powers (in the case of the Black Sea doubly so). The sole part of the Russian coast that was unfrozen year-round was the remote Murman Coast of the Kola Peninsula.

By the end of the eighteenth century, however, circumstances had changed in the navy's favor, thanks to the Enlightenment's promotion of empirical scientific enquiry (abetted by "enlightened despots" such as Peter the Great and Catherine the Great). Grandiose maritime expeditions of exploration and discovery were launched, especially to the Pacific Ocean, notably those of James Cook for England, Jean Lapérouse for France, and Alejandro Malaspina for Spain. It was incumbent upon Russia, as a great power and a Pacific nation, to enter the lists and gain knowledge for science and glory for the country, as well as to train seamen. The result was Russia's first voyage around the world in 1803–1806 by Captain-Lieutenant Ivan Kruzenstern (with Rezanov) on the *Nadezhda* (*Hope*) and Captain-Lieutenant Yury Lisyansky on the *Neva*; even so, both vessels had been bought in England, both captains had apprenticed in the English navy, and the voyage was belated, coming almost three hundred years after the world's first circumnavigation (Magellan's) and fifteen years after the first by the young United States (under the command of Captain Robert Gray). But Russia made up quickly for lost time, following its first with thirty-three more—mostly on navy but some on Russian-American Company ships—before the sale of Russian California in 1841 (and another thirty-one, mostly in company and chartered vessels, before the sale of Russian America in 1867).[4]

Some of these voyages undertook considerable scientific investigation in such fields as oceanography, meteorology, mineralogy, botany, zoology, and ethnography.[5] The very first Russian voyage to San Francisco, that of the company's *Yunona* by Nikolay Khvostov and Rezanov in 1806, also bore the physician and naturalist Georg von Langsdorff, although his attempts to collect floral and faunal specimens were frustrated by his superiors. This scientific curiosity was especially noticeable (and more successful) in the voyages of the Russian navy, whose objects were not commercial and whose backers could afford to employ scientists and artists (many of whom were foreign, notably German and French). These efforts were exemplified by the round-the-world voyage in 1815–18 of the brig *Ryurik* [*Rurik*] under Otto von Kotzebue.[6] The expedition was financed by Count Nikolay Rumyantsev, a wealthy patron of the arts and sciences, and its purpose was to find the Northeast Passage. En route it stayed a month in San Francisco Bay, where two naturalists, Ludovik von Chamisso and Johann von Eschscholtz, assisted by the artist Louis Choris, collected a herbarium of seventy species of plants (including the California poppy [*Eschscholzia californica*], the state flower)[7] as well as the seeds of many plants for botanical gardens, while Choris sketched and painted the local natives, plants, and animals in a realistic fashion.[8] Such work continued on subsequent naval voyages, including Kotzebue's second voyage to Alta California (again with Eschscholtz) in the *Predpriyatie* (*Enterprise*) in 1824, when two months were spent at San Francisco and Monterey.

The mere existence of the company's overseas colony (Russia's first and only) from the late 1700s was another factor that favored the navy, for the possession had to be supplied and defended in part, at least, by sea. Russian America and the Russian Far East were entangled in the North Pacific sphere of international rivalry among Spain, Great Britain, the United States, and Russia (China and Japan were marginalized by their self-imposed isolationism), but the contiguous Russian Far East could at least be reinforced overland from Siberia. Overseas Russian America was more vulnerable. And the navy was obviously better equipped than the company to protect its colony. Such was especially the case during the first half of the 1820s, when Russia's ban on foreign vessels from what it deemed to be Russian North Pacific waters was enforced by naval cruisers.

At any rate, whether exploring and discovering or transporting and protecting,

---

[4]See Ivashintsov, *Russian Round-the-World Voyages*. For general background, see Barratt, *Russia in Pacific Waters*.

[5]See Smith, *Science Under Sail*.

[6]See Kotzebue, *New Voyage of Discovery*.

[7]See Rogers, *Trodden Glory*. California officially designated the poppy the state flower in 1903 to symbolize its wealth of gold and abundance of sunshine. The poppy's golden floral display along the coast caused passing Spanish seamen to exclaim "¡tierra del fuego!" ("land of fire"); one of the common Spanish names for the flower is "copa de oro" ("cup of gold"). California's natives used the poppy's juice as a mild narcotic.

[8]See Choris and Eyries, *Voyage pittoresque*; Choris, *Vues et paysages*; and Chamisso, *Voyage around the World*; and Mornin, "Adelbert von Chamisso."

these ships, before reaching and after leaving the North Pacific and during the winters between patrols of those waters, had occasionally to put into a safe and open port in a balmy climate with surplus supplies and to wood, water, and provision, make repairs, and rest and restore the crews. There were two choices: the Hawaiian Islands (Honolulu) or Alta California (San Francisco). The Russian ships usually chose the latter, which, although less balmy (and less exotic), was sunny and warm enough and had a larger and safer harbor and—most importantly—the wheat and beef that the Russians wanted (as well as, incidentally, less promiscuity, no doubt to the relief of the ships' physicians but to the chagrin of their crewmen). For hungry, weary, and sickly Russians in the North Pacific the reputed abundance and salubrity of Arcadian California were irresistible.

After the 1820s, however, ships of the Russian navy disappeared from Californian waters. In 1824 and 1825 Russia signed conventions with the United States and Great Britain, respectively, that readmitted American and English vessels to Russian America's waters and ports, so Russian warships were no longer needed to patrol the coast. Moreover, the round-the-world voyages of supply of the Russian-American Company proved costly, prompting reliance upon other sources, especially Alta California's missions from 1821, when the province's ports were opened to foreign trade under Mexican independence, as well as American coasters, which returned to New Archangel from 1824. Consequently, thereafter most Russian impressions of California came not from the officers, scientists, and artists aboard naval ships but from company officials—the governors, managers, and agents who had to deal directly with the Californios.[9]

The varied motives, activities, and impressions of all of these Russian visitors to colonial California who wrote records that have survived—military and civilian—are reflected in their articles, letters, reports, orders, memoranda, memoirs, charts, plans, and views. Some aspects of the province and its inhabitants especially caught the attention of the Russian writers: the deep, spacious, sheltered, and ice-free harbor of San Francisco Bay ("one of the best ports in the world"), with its balmy climate and ready access to plenty of fresh water, fresh provisions, and firewood (Russia lacked any harbor with such a combination of assets); the religious and economic importance of the chain of Catholic missions, with their devout friars and neophyte workers (the Russian Orthodox Church was not an especially evangelical faith, and, notwithstanding Ivan Veniaminov's exceptional work in the Aleutian Islands and at Sitka, missionization did not

---

[9]The Russians also left even more records about Russian California—its scattered settlements (Fort Ross, Port Rumyantsev [Bodega], several farms, and an *artel* [a cooperative enterprise] on the Farallones) and its various activities (sea otter hunting, farming, fishing, logging, shipbuilding, brick making, tanning, trading). These documents have been published in Russian and English editions. The Russian edition has appeared in two volumes as Istomin, Gibson, and Tishkov, *Rossiya v Kalifornii* and the English edition in three volumes as Gibson and Istomin, *Russian California*.

loom large in Siberia and Russian America); the receptiveness and corruptibility of the Franciscan missionaries, who were very keen to swap their surplus produce for the Russians' goods that they so sorely lacked and were quite ready to accept "presents" (one even showed himself to be "a great *beggar*"); the sorry plight of the mission Indians ("the Spaniards lasso them in the mountains and bring them to the missions . . . where they are kept as slaves and . . . half of them are infected with venereal disease"); the agricultural productivity of the mission and rancho plowlands, pastures, orchards, and gardens, whose yields—"the usual [grain] harvest is 20-fold, 25-fold, and 30-fold the seed"—were much higher than those of Russian farmlands, which faced much longer and colder winters, shorter growing seasons, and more frequent droughts; the delightful climate of the Alta Californian coast, with mild winters ("there are neither stoves nor fireplaces in the houses") and sunny skies (which, combined with the easygoing lifestyle of the Californios, spawned runaways from Fort Ross and deserters from both Russian-American Company and Russian navy vessels); the Californios them- selves, whose religion, language, dwellings, cuisine ("corn, frijoles, and meat"), dress (such as serapes), pastimes (including bull and bear baiting), and customs ("hospitality is an alien virtue to them, but they like to be treated") were novel to Russians, who had little contact with either Old or New Spain, the former at the opposite end of Europe and the latter halfway around the globe; the filth and stench around dwellings as a result of the frequent *matanzas* ("the heads of bulls and the bones and carcasses of dead horses scattered everywhere; the foul smell from them and the flocks of crows, seagulls, and various hawks devour- ing all of this carrion"); the military weakness of Spanish/Mexican California, which boasted only a few underpaid soldiers and no warships (the presidio of San Francisco sometimes even had to borrow gunpowder for its decrepit can- nons from visiting vessels in order to salute them); the persistent instability of the province's government, stemming from factionalism between clerics and soldiers, civilians and officials, royalists and *independenistas, peninsulares* (motherlanders) and *coloniales*, monarchists and republicans, Californios and Mexicanos, and so forth; the exotic flora and fauna, especially poison oak ("those who grasp it in their hands, or fall asleep under it, or . . . burn it, soon become swollen and their face, extremities, and genitals become enlarged to such a degree that I have never actually seen [before]"), coyotes, and California quail ("the tastiest dish of local game"); the ethnographic peculiarities of the Californian Indians, particularly the Pomos, Miwoks, and Costanoans ("bows and arrows, which they wield very skilfully," "a talent for needlework," "baskets of various kinds so tightly woven . . . that they hold water"); the economic and social changes in Alta California following Mexican independence ("the seizure of free Indians has . . . ceased, and the elderly [mission] Indians are even being freed," "the Mexican leadership is

trying to introduce European customs, beginning with dress, dances, and food");
despite the productive missions and ranchos, the slight degree to which the province (particularly its interior) had been populated and developed by Spain and
Mexico, for example, the dearth of manufacturing (hence the market for articles
made at Fort Ross) and the primitive transport—and consequently the opportunity for the Russian-American Company to expand its colony of Fort Ross
eastward and southward to San Francisco Bay (hence Captain-Lieutenant Gleb
Shishmaryov's survey and Navigator Mikhail Rydalev's chart of San Pablo Bay in
1821); and the designs and intrigues of foreign, especially American, traders and
settlers designed to draw the province away from Mexico and toward the United
States ("the Americans employ every measure to kindle hatred of the Mexicans
by the Californios, and they seem to hope that a California independent of Mexico will at least come under the protection of the United States if not join it").

Owing to the language barrier, it is unlikely that much of the data contained
in these Russian records was provided by Californio informants; communication
was undoubtedly problematic, especially for the Russians. Most likely none of
Alta California's bureaucrats and missionaries could speak or read Russian (or any
tongue other than Spanish), whereas many of the Russian visitors were conversant in French (the vernacular of the Russian upper class at the time), some were
conversant in German (Kotzebue and Wrangell, for example), and a few knew
Latin and even some Spanish (Kirill Khlebnikov and Zavalishin, for instance).

This disparity helps to explain why the Spanish accounts of Russian California
are not only less numerous but also less substantive than the Russian accounts of
Alta California. Another reason is the fact that it behooved the Russians to know
more about the Californios than vice versa because they needed what the Californios possessed (sea otters, provisions, and salt [from Baja], which were not accessible elsewhere in the North Pacific, save salt in Hawaii) more than the Californios
needed what the Russians possessed (manufactures, which were also obtainable at
similar prices but of higher quality from foreign, notably American, smugglers and
traders). Besides, generally speaking, to the Californios the Russians were a threat
to their vulnerable province, while to the Russians the culturally unfamiliar Californios were a curiosity, so the inquisitive Russians were inclined to visit while the
suspicious Californios were inclined to stay home, unless they wanted intelligence.

Nevertheless, the two sides had not a little in common: both were European
invaders and colonizers on the margin of a remote New World, both were patriotic subjects and Christian believers, and both had sizable mixed-blood popula-
tions. These commonalities undoubtedly helped to keep their relations friendly
and pacific throughout four decades of personal and business contact.

DOCUMENT I

Excerpt from Nikolay Rezanov's Report about a Voyage to Alta California, 1806

EDITOR'S INTRODUCTION

Nikolay Petrovich Rezanov (1764–1807), a high state official and one of the founders of the Russian-American Company in 1799, accompanied the multipurpose round-the-world voyage of 1803–1806 (Russia's first) in the company ships *Nadezhda* (*Hope*) and *Neva* as ambassador to Japan. In the summer of 1805 he and his personal physician, Georg von Langsdorff, reached the recently refounded outpost of New Archangel (Sitka), which faced not only hostile Tlingits but also a critical shortage of supplies, especially provisions. So Rezanov bought the visiting American trading vessel *Yunona* (*Juno*) with its cargo of goods and foodstuffs and in early 1806 sailed in it with Langsdorff to San Francisco, where he spent six weeks. He held trade talks with the Spanish officials and missionaries and toured the vicinity, paying particular attention to the missions and their surplus output, goods in demand, and military strength. In addition to acquiring considerable intelligence, he succeeded in procuring a small cargo of wheat—thanks to the friendship and compassion of the local authorities—but not an agreement for regular exchanges, since the Laws of the Indies forbade foreign trade on the part of Spain's colonies. Barring smuggling as a means of tapping Alta California's productive agriculture, the Russian-American Company was left with the option of founding its own colony there—the option that Rezanov was to recommend after his departure and that was implemented in 1812 in the shape of Fort Ross.

Rezanov also obtained, ostensibly by means of both affection and diplomacy, the hand of the daughter of the presidio's commandant, Concepción Argüello, reputedly the prettiest maiden in the entire province. The romance of the teenaged

Conchita, a devout Roman Catholic, and the middle-aged Russian Orthodox widower (which began with their betrothal and ended with his death eleven months later from pneumonia while hurrying across Siberia to report to St. Petersburg, while she remained celibate and eventually took vows) has become a Californian legend. It has been immortalized in, for example, Bret Harte's poem "Concepcion de Arguello," Gertrude Atherton's novel *Rezánov*, Andrey Voznesensky's poem "Avos," and Voznesensky's and Aleksey Rybnikov's rock opera *Yunona i Avos*. In considering Rezanov's opportunism, recall that in both Russia and Spain at that time girls not infrequently married while in their early teens (Rezanov's first wife, Anna Shelikhova, daughter of the Irkutsk merchant Grigory Shelikhov, one of the founders of the Russian-American Company, was at most fifteen years of age when she married him).[1]

IMPERIAL CHAMBERLAIN NIKOLAY REZANOV, A REPORT TO MINISTER OF COMMERCE NIKOLAY RUMYANTSEV[2] ABOUT A VOYAGE TO ALTA CALIFORNIA IN THE *YUNONA*,[3] NEW ARCHANGEL, 17 JUNE 1806

To His Highness, the Minister of Commerce. Secret.

Dear Sir, Count Nikolay Petrovich!

From my recent reports to you, gracious sire, and to the Board of Directors of the Company Your Highness is already sufficiently aware of the disastrous condition in which I found the Russian American territory; you know that we suffered starvation all winter and that, moreover, even the provisions bought with the ship[4] *Yunona* scarcely supported the men; and you have been informed of the diseases, the wretched condition into which the entire territory had been plunged, and the resolution with which I perforce undertook a voyage to New[5] California, setting to sea with inexperienced and scorbutic men at the risk of either saving the territory or perishing. Now, with God's help, our voyage—rendered difficult

---

[1]For more biographical information on Rezanov, see Grinëv, *Kto yest kto*, 449–50; and Pierce, *Russian America*, 418–20. Also see Iversen, *Romance of Nikolai Rezanov*. For more documentation of Rezanov's visit, see Farris, *So Far from Home*, 20–43.

[2]Count Nikolay Petrovich Rumyantsev (or Rumyantsov) (1754–1826) was an influential statesman, serving under three rulers in a series of high posts, including minister of foreign affairs (1807–14). He was also a patron of the arts and sciences, and as minister of commerce (1802–10) he promoted the first Russian circumnavigation of 1803–1806. See Grinëv, *Kto yest kto*, 462; and Pierce, *Russian America*, 435–36.

[3]AVPRI, f. 161 (Sanktpeterburgsky Glavny arkhiv I-7), op. 6 (1802), d. 1, pk. 34, fols. 20–62v. Original, duplicate, and holograph.

[4]A ship (in the nongeneric sense) was a sailing vessel with a bowsprit and three masts, all square-rigged and each with a topmast and a topgallant mast.

[5]The word "New" is lacking in the RGIA variant.

by circumstances—has been accomplished, and so it is a pleasure for me to give Your Highness a report on the first step [taken] by Russians in this land [of California].

Having set out on my journey on 25 February on the ship *Yunona*, which I had bought from the Bostonians,[6] my crew soon began to falter. Scurvy had weakened the men, and scarcely half of them could man the sails. Our scorbutic condition forced us to land. I had already intended to examine the Columbia River, about which I have submitted enough comments to the Board of Directors, and so I refer you to my last reports in order to avoid repeating myself. We came in sight of its mouth on 14 March, but contrary winds forced us to withdraw. Holding a course to the south, we returned the next day and thought of entering, as our observations indicated another latitude and we saw that the strong current had taken us 60 miles closer and that we were opposite Gray's Harbor, whose northern shore closely resembled the mouth of the Columbia. The seaward breeze allowed us to lie at anchor, and we sent a kayak[7] with Doctor Langsdorff to the harbor. A lead indicated a depth of 4 to 5 *sazhens*[8] on the bar at low tide, and according to him it is not at all as impassable as it has been described, but perhaps it has since been eroded by the current. He saw a lot of smoke at the end of the bay and for that reason concluded that it was inhabited. The haven itself is good; it is quite sheltered from the wind, and the bottom is sandy. Here I [merely] repeat the doctor's words to Your Highness; but I [myself] saw a fairly gently sloping, sandy shore covered with trees. During the night, taking advantage of the breeze, we moved offshore, and finally strong contrary winds drove us out to sea. The number of sick increased daily, and our sufferings had already claimed one victim. The scurvy spared no one, even the officers, including myself, and, having sought to enter the Columbia River as the sole harbor before California in order to recover, we approached the latter on 20 March in the evening and dropped anchor. The next day we considered entering [San Francisco Bay], but the strong current and the high breakers in the channel [Golden Gate] hampered us. On the hilltops the Indians lit fires, which invited us to enter, but it was obvious that the wind was too fresh to let them be our guides. Finally, we set out to find ourselves a haven, stopping in such surf that we barely managed to

---

[6]Specifically, Captain John D'Wolf of Bristol, Rhode Island, who commanded the brig *Juno* on its second voyage to the Northwest Coast in 1804–1805. See D'Wolf, *Voyage.* All American shipmasters were called "Boston men" or "Bostonians" (and British shipmasters "King George's men") in the Chinook jargon of the Northwest Coast, and the Russians adopted and modified this usage.

[7]Kayaks (*baidarkas,* literally, "little *baidaras* [umiaks, q.v.]") were one-, two-, or three-hatched hide boats used by the Russian-American Company's Aleuts and Konyagas for hunting (especially sea otters), fishing, and travel. See Brinck, *Aleutian Kayak;* Dyson, *Baidarka;* Lister, "The Kayak and the Walrus"; and Zimmerly, *Qayaq.*

[8]1 *sazhen* = 7 feet or 2.13 meters.

drop anchor and hold our ground in four sazhens. Here I saw a test of the skill of Lieutenant Khvostov,[9] for I must do justice to his determination, it being only through it [i.e., such determination] that we saved ourselves and thus successfully escaped the place, which was surrounded by rocky ledges. The fresh north wind, and even more the sickness of the men, forced us to take advantage of the former, and we, thanks to God, taking a prolonged favorable wind with the new moon, made San Francisco Bay by the night of 24 March, although pale and half-dead, and on account of fog we dropped anchor to await the morning.

The next day the wind and the current afforded us the means of entering the port, and we took advantage of them. Knowing the suspicious nature of the Spanish government, I deemed it pointless to make contact in order to request permission [to enter], for in case of a refusal we must perish at sea, and so, figuring that two or three cannon balls would make less difference to us than a refusal, I decided to go straight through the [Golden] gate and past the fort—such was our situation. Unfurling all sails, we ran for the harbor. Upon nearing the fort we saw much commotion among its soldiers, and when we drew abreast of it one of them inquired through a hailer, "What sort of ship are you?" "Russian," we said. They shouted to us repeatedly to drop anchor at once, but we answered: "Si señor, si señor," and meanwhile, feigning being busy, we passed the fort and, distancing ourselves a cannon shot away from it, we then complied there with their demand.

Soon twenty men on horseback, including the commandant and a missionary, demanded the [surrender of the] ship, but we made bolder, for this cavalcade was within range of our grapeshot. I sent Midshipman[10] Davydov[11] to say that I was the person about whom, I hoped, they had been informed by their government, that I had been bound for Monterey,[12] but fierce equinoctial [mid-March] storms had damaged our ship and forced me to take refuge in the first port, and that I would be on my way after having had repairs made. The answer was that an order had already been received from the king to render me assistance, that the commandant had asked me to dine at the presidio, and that all of my wishes would be accommodated with exactitude. Gratitude compelled me to go ashore, where

---

[9]Lieutenant Nikolay Andreyevich Khvostov (1776–1809), who captained the *Yunona*, had been invited by Rezanov in 1802 to enter the company's service under the terms of an imperial decree that permitted naval officers to transfer from the navy's to the company's fleet. He and his friend Midshipman Gavriil Davydov were hired at the same time, and they both accompanied Rezanov to New Archangel and then to San Francisco. See Grinëv, *Kto yest kto*, 567–68; and Pierce, *Russian America*, 234–35.

[10]Midshipman (*michman*) was the lowest commissioned rank in the Russian navy, equivalent in the nineteenth century to a lieutenant in the Russian infantry.

[11]Midshipman Gavriil Ivanovich Davydov (1784–1809) had joined the company's fleet at the same time (1802) as Lieutenant Nikolay Khvostov, the *Yunona*'s captain, and they became close friends. See Grinëv, *Kto yest kto*, 145; and Pierce, *Russian America*, 112–15. Also see Davydov, *Two Voyages*.

[12]The provincial capital and governor's seat.

I met Don Luis de Argüello,[13] the commandant's son, who had taken his father's place in his absence. We were given saddle horses, but as the presidio stood no more than a *versta*[14] from the shore, we went there on foot, accompanied by the commandant and the missionary, Father José de Uría;[15] the former's amiable family showered us with cordiality and treated us to dinner, and after staying until the evening we returned to the ship, to which beef, greens, bread, and milk had already been sent in the meantime, and our men, whose exhausted strength was restored the same day, felt as pleased as we did.

Don Luis told me with special courtesy that he was obliged to send a courier about my arrival to the governor and that for that reason he found himself compelled to ask the whereabouts of our ships, the *Nadezhda* and the *Neva*, about which they had been forewarned. I replied that I had sent them back to Russia and that, having been given command of all of our American territories by His Imperial Majesty, I had inspected them last year, wintered at Norfolk [Sitka] Sound, and finally decided to see the governor of New California in order to talk with him, as the head of a neighboring country, about mutual benefits.

Do not think, gracious sire, that it was from ambition that I announced myself as Commandant Général, head of our northern territories; rather, it was done solely in order to lend weight to them in the eyes of the Spaniards and to put our business on the best course. The interests of our fatherland demanded it. However, it seems that even here I did not err in the slightest, for I really do have the overall command by both the will of the Emperor and the trust of all of the shareholders,[16] and I did not abuse it at all but sacrificed myself constantly for the common good. With the same courier I sent a letter to the commandant thanking him for his initial tokens of hospitality and informing him that, after the ship had been repaired, I would proceed forthwith to Monterey.

The next day the missionaries of San Francisco invited me to dinner. The mission was an hour's ride from the presidio. We mentioned trade, and their strong desire for it was very noticeable. I will have the honor to explain to Your Highness in the proper place the situation of all of the missions and presidios, trade, and the surpluses and shortages of this province, but now permit me to

---

[13]Lieutenant Luis Antonio Argüello (1784–1830), a *colonial* (a Californian of Spanish extraction [Californio] born in New Spain), was a career soldier. He became captain of the San Francisco garrison in 1818 and governor of Alta California in 1822–25. [Bancroft], *California Pioneer Register*, 41–42. Also see Morrison, "Luis Antonio Arguello," 193–204 and 347–61.

[14]1 *versta* = 0.66 miles or 1.06 kilometers.

[15]José Antonio Uría (1769–1815), a *peninsular* (a Californio born in the Iberian Peninsula), left Spain in 1796 and did not arrive in Alta California until 1799. Already in poor health, he served at Mission San José until mid-1806, and in 1812 he retired. See Geiger, *Franciscan Missionaries*, 259.

[16]Earlier during the round-the-world voyage, the question of supreme command of the expedition had become a bone of contention between Rezanov and Captain-Lieutenant Ivan Kruzenshtern of the flagship *Nadezhda*.

occupy you, gracious sire, with what are perhaps trifling circumstances in order to show you how I imperceptibly—to them—achieved my aims, in what critical situations I found myself, and what means I employed. We returned from the mission, and after dinner I sent splendid presents to both the commandant and the missionaries, being generous to everyone in order to conceal from the Spaniards our poverty and shortages, about which the Boston ships had told them beforehand to our detriment. I completely succeeded in doing so, for in the end there was not one person who had not received something that he needed, and the universal pleasure was expressed to us from the hearts of all of the residents, so that favorable rumors of the Russians drew missionaries from afar, and those nearby were already offering their services to supply me with a cargo of grain.

Perceiving the possibility of soon obtaining grain from this port, I decided to go by land to Monterey, which was 80 miles away. I sent a courier to the governor with a letter explaining that as the repairs to the ship might detain me here a long time, I begged to be allowed to visit him. He replied with complete cordiality that he would not suffer me such trouble and would on the following day take this route himself, confident that the confirmation of his orders would assist me in everything, and at the same time he sent the commandant to ceremoniously congratulate me on his behalf on my arrival. I sensed the suspicion of the Spanish government, which everywhere hinders foreigners from becoming acquainted with the interior of their lands and from observing the weakness of their forces.[17]

Meanwhile, the fine climate of California, the abundance of grain by comparison with our shortage, and the prospect of additional starvation in the future were the constant subjects of conversation among our men. We noted their inclination to remain here altogether, and we took our own measures [to prevent desertion]. On the third day after our arrival our three Bostonians and one Prussian, who had entered the company's service as sailors with the purchase of the *Yunona*, declared to me that they wanted to stay here. I told them that I would speak to the commandant, and when he refused [to accept them], I ordered them taken to a barren island [Alcatraz or Angel Island], where they were kept during our sojourn until our very departure.[18] Meanwhile, we erected pickets and established rounds on shore, and the Spaniards provided mounted patrols, but although all measures were utilized, two of our best and most closely guarded men, Mikhailo Kalyanin and Pyotr Polkanov, went to the river to wash clothes and fled without a trace.[19] Subsequently, however, the Spanish government gave

---

[17]Ironically, Russian officialdom had the same reputation.

[18]This may be the first instance of the use of Alcatraz as a place of confinement, although the natives or Californios may, of course, have already used it for that purpose.

[19]Kalyanin and Polkanov set an example that Russian sailors from naval and company ships and Russian employees from Fort Ross were to not infrequently follow.

me its word to ship them [if caught] to Russia via Veracruz, and I will ask that they be punished and returned to America for life. Without making a severe example of these traitors to the men, it will be impossible to contain them.

Awaiting the governor, we spent every day in the home of the hospitable Argüellos and came to know them fairly quickly. Of the beautiful sisters of the [acting] commandant, Doña Concepción[20] is reputed to be the beauty of California, and so, Your Highness, you will deign to agree with me that we were sufficiently rewarded for our sufferings and that time passed joyfully. Forgive me, gracious sire, that I have included something romantic in such a serious letter. Perhaps I should [not] be too candid. Meanwhile, the constant reports in our favor to Monterey from this port had already closely ingratiated me with the governor himself, who fortunately for us had since his boyhood been the best friend of this household.

Finally, on 7 April [in the evening], Don José de Arrillaga,[21] the governor of both Californias [Alta and Baja],[22] arrived. The fort saluted him with 9 cannons, and a battery hidden behind our ship beyond a point [Fort Point?] fired the same number of its guns. As weak as the Spaniards are, they have augmented their artillery since the time of [Captain George] Vancouver's visit [in 1793]. Subsequently, we secretly examined this battery, which has five 12-pound brass cannons, and it is said that they have seven guns in the fort, but whether more or fewer is unknown because I myself was never there and, in order to remain completely above suspicion, did not allow others [to go there]. I immediately sent an officer to congratulate him on his arrival, and he replied with gratitude and informed me that his leg was ailing and that he was tired from the journey but that he hoped to see me soon. Indeed, this old man, with white hair [he was fifty-six years of age], was extremely fatigued from horseback riding, for there is no other form of travel in all of California.

The next day I was expecting him or at least one of his officers when I noticed a great commotion at the presidio among the soldiers, and toward noon two missionaries came to the ship to tell me that the old commandant, Don José de Argüello,[23] who had arrived with the governor, had invited me to dinner. I

---

[20]María de la Concepción Marcela Argüello (1790–1857). According to Bancroft, she was the "spoiled darling" of the commandant's large family. See [Bancroft], *California Pioneer Register*, 41.

[21]José Joaquín de Arrillaga (1750–1814), a peninsular, had served as acting governor of the Californias in 1792–94 and 1800–1802, and upon their separation in 1804 he became the first governor of Alta California until his death. See [Bancroft], *California Pioneer Register*, 43.

[22]In fact, at this time he was governor of Alta California only.

[23]José Dario Argüello (1753–1828), a native of New Spain (colonial Mexico), arrived in Alta California in 1781 as the military officer in charge of the overland expedition that founded the pueblo of Los Angeles. He served as the commandant of the presidios of first San Francisco and then Monterey. He became acting governor of Alta California in 1814–15 and the governor of Baja California in 1815–22. According to Bancroft, he was for a long time "the most prominent, influential, and respected man" in Alta California. See [Bancroft], *California Pioneer Register*, 41.

extended my thanks to him for his kindness and answered the missionaries that courtesy demanded that I thank him personally for the daily kindnesses of his family but that because the governor, with whom I was having political relations, was now in his house he must forgive me for having to postpone the fulfilment of my obligations. One of the missionaries, Father Pedro,[24] with whom we had become very closely acquainted, told me, "You have not understood me correctly, the governor ordered that you be invited, too; everyone is already at the presidio and dressed in full parade uniform in order to receive you properly." I gave him to understand that it would have been possible to send an officer, but the cheerful Pedro replied, "Are the holy fathers really worse than the officers? We live in America [i.e., the New World] and, truly, know nothing but openness." I thought that perhaps they figured that they had already complied with etiquette by sending the commandant several days ago. Thus, in order not to injure our business I decided to go. Saddle horses were brought, and we set off. Dropping behind with Father Pedro, I asked him, "Do you have permission to sell grain?" "I will tell you in confidence," he said, "before his departure [from Monterey] the governor received a report from Mexico that if we are not already at war with you, then we soon will be." "What nonsense," I said laughingly; "In such a case would I have come here?" "That is just what we said," he replied. It became quite clear from this that they were more afraid of us than we were of them, and that they suspected that we had come with other intentions, supposing, perhaps, that those two ships [*Nadezhda* and *Neva*]—which they expected—would arrive soon. In the meantime, on the pretext of having forgotten my kerchief, I sent a note to the ship [telling the officers] not to let the men go ashore and calmly resumed my route. We rode into the presidio, the officers having met us outside the gates, and the pickets formed a guard; the governor in full-dress uniform came into the courtyard to meet us. Crossing the plaza and noticing the cheerful faces of the beautiful Spanish women, my suspicions evaporated, for otherwise they would have been absent, of course.

After having greeted the governor and thanked Mr. Argüello for the kindnesses of his family, I explained to them frankly that it was in their name that the missionary gentlemen had invited me and that, not knowing their relations with the holy fathers, I had decided not to tarry and to subordinate all etiquette to the benefits that had drawn me to this territory, desiring impatiently to become acquainted with the authorities. The governor, who spoke French fairly well, became confused and apologized for the impetuosity of the missionaries. "It is

---

[24]Probably Pedro de la Cueva (1776–18??), a peninsular, who arrived in California in 1804 and served at Mission San José from that year until 1806, when he was recalled to Mexico. See Geiger, *Franciscan Missionaries*, 57–61.

true," he said, "that I wanted to have the honor of inviting you, but I did not make bold to do so without having forewarned you of my arrival, for, although everything here in California is under my command, my right leg"—on which he could barely stand—"refuses to obey me, and in this quandary my missionaries, already having your favor, undertook to inform you but instead of that assignment fulfilled quite another." "In that case," I said, "I am even more grateful to the missionaries for having brought us together sooner." The governor's open nature, the exchange of courtesies at the table, and my familiarity with the Argüello household soon gave rise to a genuine closeness between us. The commandant of Monterey, Don José de la Guerra y Noriega[25] (who had come with the governor, an artillery officer, and several cadets), anticipated me with every civility, and very quickly that day we became very closely acquainted with the chief authorities of California. I asked the governor for a meeting about my business; he suggested the morrow, but I prevailed upon him not to delay, and thus we busied ourselves that very evening.

"Do not be surprised," I said, "at my impatience. I hope that you have already noticed from my letters how precious time is to me." Explaining myself, I continued that my visit had as its object the welfare of the American territories belonging to both powers, and, launching into the matter, I gave him to understand all of the wants of California and the needs of our settlements, which only a mutual trade could dispel, and that only in this way could a permanent alliance of friendship be established between both courts, would their colonies flourish, and would our coasts, forming a mutual bond between us, always be equally defended by both powers, nobody daring to settle between us. I explained to him further that the possessions of His Catholic Majesty in the New World were so extensive that it was impossible to defend them, that sooner or later they would fall victim to adventurers having seen their weak forces, and that perhaps [only] the war in Europe [the Napoleonic Wars] was saving them [now]; as to the longstanding suspicion of the Russians on the part of the [Spanish] court, which thinks that we ourselves want to settle these places, I assured him that even if they were to give us California, then because of the expense of upkeep it could not bring us such benefits as we—or as many as they themselves—could expect from mutual trade. "Dismiss this false notion," I said to him; "The possessions of my monarch in the north contain inexhaustible sources of wealth in furs, which, on account of the growing demand for them on the part of northern peoples as a necessity as well as

---

[25]Captain José de la Guerra y Noriega (1779–1858), a peninsular, arrived in Alta California in 1801. He served at Monterey until 1806, and in 1815 he became commandant at Santa Bárbara. He was also a successful merchant and an influential politician, as well as a ranchero. Noriega retired from military service in 1842. See [Bancroft], *California Pioneer Register*, 172–74. Also see Pubols, *Father of All*.

a luxury, would never permit us to abandon places that enrich us and that because of their vastness can be tapped for centuries. Thus, Russia's situation and its own interests should assure you that it does not need the southern parts of America, for if it were otherwise you would agree that such a strong power would not disregard its goals and that you would not be able to impede it at all. I tell you frankly that we need grain, which we can obtain from Canton, but as California is closer to us and has surpluses that it cannot sell anywhere, I have come to talk to you as the head of this country, convinced that we can take preliminary steps and submit them for approval and ratification by our [royal] courts. This is the real reason why I have come, and I most humbly beg you to make a decision on my proposal quickly so that I do not waste time." I perceived that the governor was listening to me with much pleasure. "We have already been informed," he said, "of your monarch's trust in you with regard to America, and we are equally well aware of your mission with respect to all commercial aims, and for that reason I am extremely pleased to come to know you personally; but my situation is quite different, and for many reasons I cannot answer you quickly and definitely. Meanwhile, permit me to ask you, have you had letters from Europe recently?" "Ten months ago," I replied untruthfully, for before his arrival I had fortunately managed through the missionaries to fortify myself with the latest political news. "Do you know," he said, "that you are at war with Prussia?" "Perhaps," I replied, "on account of the purchase of Pomerania." "But the latest news that I received from Europe five and a half months ago," [he rejoined,] "shows that Russia's relations with France and therefore with the other powers of the [Anglo-Russian] coalition [against France] are no longer so close." "That may be so," I said, "but the threats of European cabinets should not always be taken at face value. You will agree that we are [found] now in such a remote corner of the world that we might hear of war when peace has [already] been concluded." "True," he said, "but you take it too coolly!"[26] "Men like us," [I replied], "who are conversant with all dangers, should not have much respect for rumors." I returned him to our earlier conversation, and he asked me to give him until the next day to think about it, and in the meantime he told me cordially that although he did not doubt my character, formality demanded that I should furnish him with my plenipotentiary documents, so that he could submit them to the viceroy. "Most gladly," I said, "and then we will busy ourselves a little more seriously tomorrow morning."

The next day, having connections in the Argüello household [i.e., Doña Concepción], I knew everything—word for word—that they had said upon my departure. He [the governor] liked my frank explanation; he acknowledged the

---

[26]The RGIA variant has *vosprinimayete* ("you perceive" or "you interpret") instead of *prinimayete* ("you take" or "you accept" or "you receive"), and without the exclamation mark.

correctness of my conclusions regarding their country's shortages, consulted with the missionaries—who in the meantime were all on my side—and revealed to them the unpleasant situation of our European cabinets, and confessed that he wanted nothing more than to somehow rid himself quickly of such guests, for whose kindly or unkindly reception he could innocently suffer on account of the suspicion of his government. Meanwhile, they had spent all evening writing down what I had said.

Finally, I appeared. The governor received me cordially, and I immediately engaged him on my subject; I handed him credentials for various powers, having them in duplicate, and said that I had given the Spanish versions to the ships returning to Russia, not intending then to visit California. He copied only the credentials for the French court and the accreditation from the company and then returned everything to me.

"Your conversation yesterday," he said, "was extremely interesting to me. I confess that with all my heart I wish you success, but I cannot hide from you the fact that I am hourly expecting a complete rupture between us and that I am at a loss as to how to approach your project, and I tell you frankly that I greatly desire that you leave us amicably before the arrival of the courier that I am expecting." "I am surprised at your haste," I replied; "You have orders concerning my reception, and—unless you have received others—as I have come with honorable intentions, it seems to me that the laws of nations give you the right of always parting from me in a pleasant manner, setting me only a time when I am able to leave." "Oh! Of this you can be certain," [rejoined the governor]. "Then," I said, "let us dismiss these unpleasant thoughts, when now nothing hinders us from occupying ourselves with the interests of both powers." "You want to buy a cargo of grain, but tell me" [he asked], "why such an amount, for you do not have such a need for ship's provisions?" "I will explain my reasons to you forthwith," [I answered.] "First, the ship needs to be repaired and the ballast unloaded, and in place of the latter I would like to embark grain; and second, I wish to buy the grain itself in order to learn—having delivered a little to our enterprises in America as well as Kamchatka—whether the prices are reasonable, and to determine more accurately—having decided the needs of each place—the total amount required in the general plan, now knowing in detail how much of what surpluses California can supply. You yourself, however, will admit that five thousand *puds*[27] of cargo is by itself not an [enormous] article of trade." "I agree with that," he said, "but I have heard that you brought goods." "None whatever," I replied, "although my supercargo has some that I allowed him to take, but I will not hide from you the

---

[27] 1 *pud* (40 *funts*) = 36.11 pounds or 16.38 kilograms.

fact that to that end it would give me pleasure to trade them with your permission." "All that I can do to oblige you," responded the governor, "is to permit you to buy grain with piasters,[28] but with respect to trade you will forgive me that, on account of the government's strict injunction,[29] I cannot consent to it; regarding the former [grain selling], while it is not difficult for me, I ask you to give me a statement of your requirements without explaining your purposes, and in it I most humbly beg you to briefly relate everything about your voyage from [St.] Petersburg." "I am sorry," I said, "that you will not resolve the latter [trade]; as the inhabitants have said, the things that we have brought are sorely needed by them, and I would like my supercargo to sell them in order thereby to make more room in the ship; however, it does not matter to me whether I pay the missionaries or the supercargo for the grain; it is just a pity that my visit will not satisfy the former's wants, but you could easily agree to satisfy general needs. The missionaries would bring grain, I would pay in piasters and take receipts from them, and you would submit the original receipts to the viceroy; it seems to me that where the holy fathers spend the money will trouble neither you nor me." "No, no," he said, "that is trade, too, and, having lived 60 years without reproach, I cannot have that on my conscience." "But," [I replied,] "it is not self-interest but a desire to benefit your countrymen that obliges you to bend the rules somewhat. Here you see the territory's needs better than they see them in Madrid, so I really see no harm in it, especially," I said with a smile, "when all of the clerics will genuflect for you." "Oh, I see very well that they have already kneeled for you," the governor answered me with a laugh, "but, joking aside," he continued, "you cannot imagine how strictly trade is prohibited here, and I will give you an example: five years ago a Boston ship wintered here, ran into debt, and, it not having any cash, I decided to take needed goods as payment but not before reporting to the viceroy, who replied that it was quite all right this time but never again, for it would give foreign ships occasion to visit our ports." "In order to convince you," I said, "that I am far from wanting you to be blamed for anything, I will drop this conversation and only ask you to reassure me—may I obtain the needed amount of grain?" "You will get it." "Then, in order not to lose time, I will order the ship to unrig?" "Good luck," answered the governor. In his presence I sent an order to the ship, pleased with the beginning [I had made], and I had time to complete my commercial attempts, being very sure of their fulfilment.

The next day I presented a statement, but five days passed and no grain was supplied. Meanwhile, rumors of war between us and the French were growing

---

[28]Piasters were Spanish silver dollars. 1 *piaster* = 8 *reals*.

[29]Spain's Laws of the Indies prohibited foreign trade by its colonies, although necessity spawned clandestine transactions; also, enforcement of the laws was being weakened at the time by independence movements throughout the Spanish American colonies.

daily, and in addition they were expecting a frigate from San Blas[30] for patrol duty. I learned that part of the Monterey garrison had been stationed at Mission Santa Clara, a distance of one day's journey [on horseback] from the port. The inclination of our men to betray us, and the desertion of two men at this same time, rendered our situation even more critical. Meanwhile, the respect [shown] to me especially did not diminish in the least; I always had a dragoon as a guard of honor, the Spanish pickets saluted, the governor greeted and attended me every day, and the universal cordiality removed any suspicion on my part.

Day by day, however, although in an imperceptible way to the governor, the kindness to me of the Argüello household was drawing him closer and closer to me. He apologized for not having come to my ship. "Let us drop pointless formalities," I said; "I know the ways of your government, and I am sure that if you had followed your heart you would have visited me long since, but then I am with you every day." "You have accustomed us to you," said Don José de Arrillaga, "and I guarantee that the good family of my friend Argüello appreciates the pleasure of seeing you in their home just as much as it is grateful for your benevolence to them." Here I should make a confession to Your Highness of my personal adventures. Seeing that my situation was not improving, daily expecting much unpleasantness, and having little confidence in my own men, I decided to change from being cordial to having a serious bearing. Courting the Spanish beauty every day, I noticed her venturesome character and her unlimited ambition, which had already at the age of fifteen made her—alone among her family—unsuited to her fatherland. She always referred to it jokingly: "A beautiful country, a warm climate, a lot of grain and cattle, but nothing else!" I portrayed Russia to her as more severe [climatically] but at the same time abounding in everything; she was prepared to live there, and finally I imperceptibly implanted in her an impatience to hear something serious from me until I had only to offer her my hand and she accepted.[31] My proposal shocked her parents, who had been raised amidst [religious] fanaticism; the difference in religion and the prospective separation from their daughter were a crushing blow to them. They resorted to the missionaries

---

[30]San Blas was the Nayarit port that served as Spain's chief naval base (and supply point for Nueva Galicia and the Californias) from 1768 until 1810. See Thurman, *Naval Department*.

[31]In the RGIA variant of Rezanov's letter the portion beginning with "Seeing my situation" and ending with "she accepted" has been replaced by the following sentence, which draws a considerably different picture of the relationship between him and Concepción Argüello: "The beautiful Concepción daily increased her cordiality to me, her interest in my situation, her services, and her openness—all of which I regarded with indifference for a long time, until they began imperceptibly to fill the emptiness in my heart; we were drawn daily closer by our declarations, which finally ended with her giving me her hand."

Rezanov seems to have confessed his actual attitude toward Concepción in a letter that he wrote at Irkutsk five weeks before his death to the director of the Russian-American Company: "Concepción is sweet, like an angel, beautiful, good-hearted, and she loves me; I love her, but I weep that there is no room in my heart for her, and here I am my friend, like a sinner at confession, tormenting myself, but, as my good shepherd, keep the secret" (Avdyukov, Olkhova, and Surnik, *Komandor*, 645–46).

(who did not know what to do), took poor Concepción to the church, heard her confession, and urged her to recant, but her determination finally reassured everyone. The holy fathers left a resolution [of the difference in religion] to the [papal] throne of Rome, and although I could not finalize my marriage, I made a conditional agreement to that effect and forced our betrothal, to which they consented on the condition that, pending the pope's decision, it be kept a secret. Thereafter, having positioned myself as a close relative of the commandant, I managed the port of His Catholic Majesty as my interests dictated, and the governor was utterly astounded to see that he had very inopportunely persuaded me of the openness of his household and that he himself, so to speak, had come to be my guest.

He was obliged by some thirty years of friendship with the commandant to consult him in everything. Every paper that he received passed through Argüello's hands and consequently through mine. But soon the governor was disarmed, and he placed a like trust in me; finally, no mail held the slightest secrets from me. Hour by hour I spoke more and more Spanish, from morning until evening I was in the Argüello home, and the officers, noticing that I had become semi-Hispanicized, vied with each another to forewarn me of everything beforehand, so that I had no fear of any ominous courier of theirs.

Meanwhile, I was surprised that the missionaries were not bringing grain, and I let the governor know of my dissatisfaction. He told me frankly that the holy fathers expected a courier and thought by delaying to enjoy the ship's entire cargo gratis [through seizure]. I answered him just as frankly that he was the cause by keeping the garrison at [Mission] Santa Clara, and that when he order[ed] it to return to Monterey, the rumors would disappear by themselves. The governor was astonished that his secret orders were known to me and, recomposing himself with a joke, immediately ordered the detachment to return, and he repeated to the missions that those that wanted to supply grain were to deliver it, otherwise he would be obliged to take [punitive] measures; at the same time, at my request he ordered the first shipment from a pueblo of veterans [*ivalidos*], where grain had been stocked for me with the help of Concepción's brothers. As soon as this [grain] was on its way, the missions began to vie with each other, bringing so much grain that I begged them to stop carting it, for after accommodating the ballast, artillery, and trade goods my ship could not take more than 4,500 puds, including the 470 puds of lard and tallow and the 100 puds of salt and other items that I had obtained.

Our account was done in piasters. The prices, set by the government in California, were known to me, and so on that basis I made my purchase without errors. I will speak about the prices in their proper place, but I wanted without fail to make a trading experiment. I prodded the governor in every possible way, promising him the favor of my sovereign. This old man hesitated a long time before deciding one day to ask my frank advice as to how to fulfil my wish and at the same time remove himself from any suspicion. "It is very easy," I said; "Let the missionaries and the inhabitants submit petitions to you, appeal to me, detail your officers to inspect the goods for quality and to learn their prices, which I will set as agreeably as I can [in accordance] with the interests of the inhabitants, whereupon you will order that the original invoices—according to which they came to you from Mexico—be shown to me, and then I will transfer the payment in piasters [for the grain] to my supercargo, from whom you will receive the goods and divide them among the inhabitants in accordance with the number of their demands." This was put into effect, the goods checked for quality, and the transfer made; my name did not appear at all in the transaction, except that in the general invoice of goods bought by them I signed that these goods belonged to supercargo Panayev,[32] that to satisfy the needs of the inhabitants of California and to please the Spanish government I had permitted him to sell them, and that I had left a document with them at the port authority.

This, gracious sire, is the first trial with trade with California; at least a million rubles' worth of it could be conducted annually. Our American territories would not be in want; Kamchatka and Okhotsk could be supplied with grain and other provisions; the Yakuts, who are now burdened with grain transport [from Yakutsk to Okhotsk on packhorses], would be placated; the treasury would lessen its expenses on the provisioning of military ranks; Irkutsk would be relieved of the dearness of grain when the sizable proportion that is annually shipped to remote regions is used for itself; the customs duties would provide new revenue to the crown; and domestic industry in Russia would be noticeably encouraged when factories have to multiply on account of the California trade only; and meanwhile the means would be found of rerouting the trade of India through Siberia. Be assured, gracious sire, that with a good and carefully considered beginning this could be accomplished in a very short time. In my latest reports to the Board of Directors I have written enough about the ways of expanding trade here to an extent that is appropriate to the dignity of an empire, and I am referring to them especially here to again say frankly that it is too early, or rather, unprofitable for us to return ships to Russia via Canton. First I would contemplate strengthening New Archangel and dispatching ships from there to Canton and back and directing them to Siberia and America, whither their voyages will be more expeditious, more dependable, and more profitable. Unless they are to remain here, ships should not be sent from St. Petersburg with needed goods. Then America

---

[32]Fyodor Arefyevich Panayev, a Siberian merchant, arrived in Russian America in 1805 on the brigantine *Sv. Mariya Magdalina* (*St. Mary Magdalene*) and served as a supercargo; in the 1810s he was employed at the company's headquarters in St. Petersburg as an auditor's assistant. See Grinëv, *Kto yest kto*, 404.

will be fortified and its fleet enhanced and Siberia will be revived by trade, and when it becomes impossible to sell all of the goods, then time will of its own accord indicate that period when it will be useful to undertake round-the-world trade; otherwise, you will admit that everything will be only empty glitter, with few benefits. But forgive me, gracious sire, for again theorizing and digressing. I am obliged to give Your Highness a true idea of the California trade, and so I will start to explain California's measures, weights, and coinage, and then continue.

All grain is sold there in *fanegas*.[33] In Russian weight a fanega is estimated to contain sometimes 3 puds, 30 *funts*[34] and sometimes 3 puds, 25 funts but never fewer than three and a half puds [3 puds, 20 funts] of grain.

The arroba[35] is a weight containing 24 Russian funts.

The *quintal*[36] is a liquid measure. It seems to be measured in bottles.

The vara[37] is [roughly equivalent to] an *arshin*,[38] exceeding the Russian measure by five inches.

The piaster is divided into 20 reals in Europe but into 8 in America.

The prices decreed by the Spanish government for Californian products are [as follows]:

1	fanega	of wheat	2	piasters
1	"	garbanzo beans [chickpeas]	3	"
1	"	plain[39] [green] peas	1¾	"
1	"	frijoles [kidney beans]	2½	"
1	"	large [green?] beans	1¾	"
1	"	barley	1½	"
1	"	corn or maize	1½	"
1	"	hemp see[d]	2½	"
1	arroba	butter	2	piasters
1	"	lard	2	"

---

[33]The *fanega* was a dry measure of capacity that varied considerably with place, time, and crop. In Alta California, according to Bowman, 1 fanega equalled 1.64 bushels or approximately 125 pounds (Bowman, "Weights and Measures," 31, 319); according to Kirill Khlebnikov, the company's commercial agent in Alta California in the 1820s, 1 fanega comprised 3.75 puds (135.42 pounds) of wheat, 4 puds (144.45 pounds) of peas, and 3 puds (108.34 pounds) of barley (Gibson, "Russian America," 7).

[34]1 *funt* = 0.90 pounds or 409.5 grams; there are 40 funts (old Russian pounds) to 1 pud.

[35]According to Bowman, 1 arroba = approximately 25 pounds (Bowman, "Weights and Measures," 315, 318) or 11.3 kilograms; according to Khlebnikov, 1 arroba = 25 Spanish pounds or 28 funts (25.28 pounds or 11.47 kilograms) (Gibson, "Russian America," 7).

[36]According to Khlebnikov, 1 *quintal* = 101.47 pounds or 46.01 kilograms (Gibson, "Russian America," 7–8).

[37]According to Bowman, 1 vara = 33 inches (Bowman, "Weights and Measures," 315, 334); according to Khlebnikov, 1 vara = 33.24 inches or 84.66 centimeters, since, according to him, 84 varas equalled 100 arshins (233.33 feet or 71.12 meters) (Gibson, "Russian America," 7).

[38]1 *arshin* = 28 inches or 71.79 centimeters.

[39]The RGIA variant has the word "ordinary" (*obyknovenny*) instead of the word "plain" (*prostoy*).

1	"	mustard seed	½	"
1	"	capsicum [hot or sweet peppers]	1½	"
1	"	washed wool	3	"
1	"	unwashed wool	1½	"
1	"	white flour	2	"
1	"	fine flour of the 2nd grade	1½	"
1 bull			4	"
1 horse			from 4 up to 15 piasters, depending upon the quality	
1 ram			2	"
1 chicken			½	"
1 unsheared sheepskin			½	"
1 sheared sheepskin			¼	"
1 oxhide			¼	"
1 red deerskin			1¾	"
1 white chamois			1½	"
1 Mexican serape [poncho] of the best grade			7–8	"
1 ordinary Mexican serape			4	"

Moreover, transport costs 1 piaster by boat or for each packhorse, plus half a piaster per fanega.

Here I will explain all of the [above] items to Your Highness in detail.

Wheat. Assuming a piaster to be 1 [ruble], 80 ko[pecks][40] and a *chetvert*[41] to be 7¼ puds, it [a chetvert of wheat] would cost the company 10 rubles, including spillage. Figuring the upkeep of ships, insurance, and agents, the company could sell it for 20 rubles [per chetvert] in Kamchatka, where, as well as in America, a private person [sells] rye flour for [no] less than 8 rubles per pud and consequently [no] less than 60 rubles per chetvert—or rather, he needs an amount that he could never obtain—and where the state itself now obtains rye flour for no less than 30 rubles, accompanied by scarcity, exhaustion of the Yakuts, expenses for ships, and spoilage in damp storehouses, and part of it is moldy, so that the state would gain 10 rubles from each chetvert, apart from the advantage that in Irkutsk grain would then be plentiful and the treasury would receive income from customs duties. Speaking of this initial provisionment, New California could annually provide up to 100,000 fanegas or up to 50,000 chetverts of various grains.

[40]The silver ruble coin was the standard Russian monetary unit, consisting of 100 kopecks.

[41]A *chetvert* was an old Russian dry and liquid measure of varying capacities, but the dry measure commonly contained 5.77 Imperial bushels (346.2 pounds of wheat) or 5.96 American bushels (357.6 pounds of wheat) or 210 liters.

Thus, this article only would constitute up to one million rubles' [worth] of trade, and the lowering of prices would relieve the inhabitants and spread abundance.

Butter and lard would cost the company 6 [rubles], 75 kopecks per pud. Very little butter—and more bad than good butter—is brought to Kamchatka, where it is sold for no less than 40 rubles, and often more, but there is none at all in America. At Okhotsk [it costs] from 21 up to 26 rubles per pud. If it were sold for double [*sic*: half], that is, for 13 [rubles], 50 ko[pecks] per pud, the inhabitants would be relieved of their scarcity, and Okhotsk would benefit just as much, and for that reason the annual cost of up to 4,000 puds of both of these articles would be 54,000 rubles.

Flour of a fine grade, assuming an arroba to cost 1½ piasters, would cost 5 [rubles], 25 ko[pecks] per pud, but it would be cheaper for both the company and the inhabitants to receive wheat as grain, establish their own gristmills, and profit from the extra flour [*primol*];[42] with that I will leave this article.

Hemp seed is very necessary to the company. Its fleet requires the annual painting of ships to preserve them, but there is no oil. Now the company will be able to make its own and avoid the necessity of importing it. Perhaps mustard seed would serve the purpose, if experiments are successful.

Hemp has also begun to be prepared by them [the Californios]. The governor told me that they made their first experiment last year and that he had sent 700 arrobas to San Blas. The missionaries have promised to pursue this industry, if there is a demand. It would be very convenient if the company were to obtain hemp, always have fresh seed, and make its own experiments, for it will grow in northern climes. I regret that I did not find any seeds, for all of them had been sown.

Sheepskins are ½ a piaster, or 90 ko[pecks], for the very best [sort]. Assuming 8 sheepskins in a fur coat, the latter would cost 7 [rubles], 20 ko[pecks], but at present fur coats of the lowest grade, made of Vyatka[43] sheepskins, are imported into America for 20 rubles. By selling those of the best wool for 15 [rubles] we could be certain that 10,000 sheepskins would be sold annually in our northern districts, and so here again is a 20,000-ruble article.

Sheep's wool, washed, resembles silk and costs 9 rubles per pud. On account of the small population of our territories, I cannot determine the demand for it, and I will leave it [i.e., the determination] for the future, when in accordance with my plan people will one day constitute the first object of concern of the company and all of the [native] Americans will derive benefit from [sea] otters, but with profit and welfare combined and not at the expense of humaneness. Meanwhile,

---

[42]*Primol* refers to the amount of flour that is obtained in excess of what is expected from grinding a certain quantity of grain.

[43]A town in northeastern European Russia (renamed Kirov in the Soviet period).

I will take these 25 arrobas of wool so that the home for girls, which I am proposing, will benefit from the spinning of wool and the making of stockings and caps from it, whose softness will undoubtedly be beneficial to them. This and like experiments should, according to my plan, pay for the upkeep of the home and promote other forms of charity. I have the honor to attach herewith, Your Highness, a sample of the wool.

Cattle, sheep, and goats[44] can be obtained from California, but they are already reared by us. If there are economic regulations, then we can expect success from it [cattle rearing], but in the present situation there is no hope of it. Meanwhile, salted [corned] and dried [jerked] beef, which cost 1 piaster per arroba, could be obtained from California, and they would constitute a very good supply of seafaring provisions.

Horses are absolutely necessary for America. They would be a substitute for men, who are few, and they would relieve the poor native slave workers [*kayuras*],[45] who now carry logs from the forest to the seashore and from the seashore up the beach—and all other heavy objects—on their shoulders. But for this it is necessary to build special ships [for transporting horses], and then with the rearing of this animal all of our establishments in America would be greatly bolstered. Cattle, horses, and sheep are incredibly numerous in California. In support of this I will tell Your Highness two anecdotes that occurred during my short stay. The missionaries had complained that the herds of horses had multiplied to the point of damaging plowland. The governor ordered several detachments of dragoons to shoot some and showed me the order, which prescribed the killing this summer of 8 to 10 thousand, and when I expressed [my] astonishment to him, [he] replied, "Do not be surprised, for in order to maintain a balance at least 50,000 of them should be killed, but the shortage of men deprives me of the means." The other instance: sacks for bringing grain to me were lacking at Mission San José. The missionaries immediately ordered that horses be caught, and up to 70 were killed solely in order to skin them for sacks. This is the degree of abundance of everything that is needed by, and close to, so to speak, our territories.

Sheep seldom propagate as much [as cattle and horses]. I took 4 rams and 2 ewes with me to Sitka. The harsh climate might degrade their soft wool, but I hope to propagate their breed nevertheless.

---

[44]In Russian, *rogaty skot*, literally, "horned cattle (or livestock)," referring to cattle, sheep, and goats. *Skot* denotes domesticated livestock in general (horses, camels, reindeer, etc.) or cattle in particular; *krupny rogaty skot* literally means "large horned cattle (or livestock)," i.e., cattle, and *melky rogaty skot* means "small horned cattle (or livestock)," i.e., sheep and goats. *Melky skot* ("small cattle (or livestock)") includes pigs.

[45]A native slave worker of the company who had come from the ranks of the slaves (*kalgas*) of the Aleuts, Eskimos, or Tlingits.

Hides, on account of the large number of cattle that are slaughtered in California, are mostly buried. I again refer to the growth of population in our territories, and then, having obtained oxhides for 45 kopecks [each], it would be possible to make yuft [Russia leather] from them in America and ship it to Canton and India. At the port of San Francisco up to 10,000 hides from only three missions could be obtained annually, but it is not possible to get them from everywhere in California. This article could provide occasional income, and when the trade has been established, can it and all of the others hardly not be profitable?

Serapes are two woolen fabrics 2½ arshins wide and 1½ arshins long that are sewn together on the shoulders and worn over the head instead of cloaks; they are usually striped. They are durable, soft, warm, and very easy to use. The best are double ones brought from Mexico and sold in California for 7 to 8 piasters [each], but in California ordinary ones, which are made just as soft and durable but without bright colors, are sold for 4 piasters each. Serapes would constitute a considerable branch of trade for the company, for there is no doubt that the Koloshes[46] and other American natives would barter for fine cloth, which they prefer; a cloak takes no less than three arshins of it.

Woolen blankets are very soft and sell in California for 10 and 12 reals each. I took 25 of them for the infirmary, and I am sure that it would be an absolute blessing for the men to sell them for 5 rubles each—when they pay 10 rubles for a worthless Tyumen[47] cowhide carpet—because they would obtain an article that is very useful and durable, for these blankets are washable.

Various woolen fabrics are made in California and are sold for 3 to 4 reals per vara. Although they are not very well made, it can be assumed that in the northern districts they would be used to line clothing.

Wine. Red wine, similar in taste to wine from the valley of the Don River but much better, is made at [Mission] Santa Clara. A quintal costs half a piaster, but this year at [Mission] San José they began to make a wine much superior to [Mission] Santa Clara's. Grapevines are cultivated at the missions in great abundance and with particular success. It is hoped that their vineyards will soon supply plenty of wine. Although this article cannot loom very large in trade, it would serve to satisfy the inhabitants of distant places, where everyone is prepared to sell everything in order to satisfy their taste; in short, wherever there are fancy delicacies, worthy people are more readily drawn to those places. Our [Russian] America could also obtain oranges, figs, apples, and other fruits, both fresh and dried, from California.

---

[46]The Russian ethnonym (probably derived from a term for "labret") for the natives of the northernmost part of the Northwest Coast in general (Tlingits, Haidas, Tsimshians) but in particular the Tlingits. For Russian-Tlingit relations, see Grinëv, *Tlingit Indians;* and Kan, *Memory Eternal*, chaps. 1–4.

[47]A town in western Siberia.

[*Sea*] *otters,* which now constitute the company's chief object, proliferate in California. According to the information that I collected, the company could obtain from 2 to 3 thousand from the port of San Francisco alone. The bay abounds in them as much as the coast. The missionaries use their neophytes to hunt them and, not having other means of selling them, await the Boston ships, which annually smuggle along the coast and trade contraband to them, but now they have been deprived of this means, and the [sea] otters can bring them no benefit whatever, and because of this [stoppage] they have foregone hunting to the extent that during my entire six-week sojourn supercargo Panayev bought only five [sea] otters at 7 piasters each. I will have the honor to report to Your Highness elsewhere on the reasons why this hunting is being hampered.

There are bears, wild [feral?] goats, many chamois [deer], and foxes, as well as a species of tiger [cougar], which they call a [mountain] lion (Leo) [*Felis concolor*], but all of these furbearers are of no use, their fur and color being unattractive. I am supplying a stuffed [specimen] of the last animal [mountain lion]. Evidently the best land animals are found in the natural environment of the North!

Such, then, Your Highness, are the great sources of trade in California, and they promise the company very important benefits, as well as the inhabitants of the northern districts lower prices on supplies of the first necessity. Although the selling prices that I set are far lower than current prices, they should not be permanent and would decrease noticeably year by year. I think that in the first two years they would be such as to let the company acquire ships and build the necessary storehouses and warehouses everywhere, but already in the third year the prices ought to decrease noticeably, with great advantages to the company. Here I will state the means of this beneficial trade. First: the company, having acquired ships, could certainly make two voyages in them annually to California, if not three or two and a half, for I am assuming two months to voyage there and back and a month to load and unload, and, with contrary winds and ship repairs increasing this by twenty-five percent, the ship could then make three voyages, on the understanding that the ships are sound and not those that are at present merely occupying space; consequently, the annual upkeep of the ships and the agents would then be defrayed by three or, say, two cargos, and thus the transport would on its own accord become cheaper. Second: I made the estimates in piasters, but in bartering goods they become quite different. For example, a pud of iron is bought in St. Petersburg for 2 [rubles], 25 ko[pecks] and, assuming transport and insurance to be 50 percent (it cannot be higher), costs the company in America 3 [rubles], 37½ kopecks. In California a pud is sold for 4 piasters, 1 real or 7 [rubles], 42½ ko[pecks]—thus there is already a net profit of more than one hundred per-cent on the 3 [rubles], 37½ ko[pecks]. Now, selling 2½ puds for 10 piasters, 2½ reals and getting for them 4 fanegas plus, or 14 puds, 25 fun[ts], of wheat, which equals two chetverts minus 15 funts, and selling a chetvert in the northern parts of Siberia for 20 rubles, yields a gain of 39 rubles, and thus a pud of iron falls to just over 15 rubles. The very same profit has already been derived from trials with other goods, and this [result] will assure Your Highness that in the whole world there could be no other trade more useful to us than the California trade.

Forgive the verbosity of my letter, gracious sire. How I have tried to shorten it, but the interest of the subject imperceptibly captivates me, and so, even if you are vexed, consider it with patience.

Broadcloth, twilled woolen fabrics, calico, Flemish linen, duck, sackcloth,[48] everyday clothing, tablecloths, variegated or striped cloth [*pestred*],[49] printed cotton fabrics, stockings, silk, cotton, and printed shawls, Moscow taffeta, hats, coarse blue cotton cloth [*dabba*],[50] flannel skirts, ribbons, needles, pins, Pavlovo knives,[51] scissors, razors, iron, cast-iron pots, various iron implements, various glass and wooden tableware, locks, and nails—all of these are abundant in Russia but wanting in California. Clocks, earrings, rings, buckles, muslin, muslin shawls, printed cottons, half-printed cottons, and similar articles could be transported there with great profit, and porcelain is needed, including small items, primarily chocolate-colored cups.

Finally, I will explain to Your Highness my attempts to confirm how severely strained is domestic industry in our fatherland and how many articles could be supplied via Okhotsk. In order to demonstrate the benefits more correctly, I will leave transport by sea and consider now transport in Siberia, whose scale makes it arduous.

Flemish linen is obtained from Mexico for 31 piasters, 3 reals per piece.
Assuming a piece of Flemish linen
bought at Irbit[52] to cost .... 20 [rubles],
and transport from Irbit to Okhotsk to cost
11 [rubles] per pud and the weight of a piece
25 fun[ts] 7,
and assuming the cost, per piece, of agents
and transport to America to be 3,
then one piece would cost .... 30 [rubles] or 16⅔ piasters.

---

[48]A coarse cotton or linen cloth; sackcloth was the traditional garb of penitence.

[49]*Pestred*, or *pestryad*, was a coarse fabric of hemp or linen, usually variegated or blue striped, also called *zatrapeza*.

[50]*Dabba*, or *daba*, was a coarse and durable cotton fabric made in China and used to make workers' clothing.

[51]Presumably knives made at the metalworks founded by the Counts Sheremetev in the village of Pavlovo at the junction of the Oka and Tarka Rivers in Nizhny Novgorod Province.

[52]Irbit on the eastern slopes of the Ural Mountains in Yekaterinburg Province was the site of Siberia's main fair every February.

They bought Flemish linen from us in California for 31 piasters or 55 [rubles], 80 ko[pecks], so that the net profit was 25 [rubles], 80 ko[pecks] in cash. But as no more than 20 thousand piasters in money can be put into unrestricted circulation now in California, goods have to be bartered, and so for 31 piasters it would be possible to buy more than 12 fanegas—or 5 chetverts, 2 puds—of wheat. Assuming a chetvert to sell for 20 [rubles], then 105 [rubles], 30 ko[pecks] would be received. The transport of the grain and the upkeep of agents and storehouses take 1 ruble per pud, making 5 [rubles], 15 ko[pecks], or a total of 35 [rubles], 15 ko[pecks]. It eventuates that from one piece of Flemish linen the company would receive a net profit after expenses of 70 rubles.

Duck was sold for 25 piasters or 45 [rubles] per piece. Its weight is also 25 funts. After having estimated all expenses for transport and agents, a net profit of one hundred percent would be received from a piece, but more than three hundred percent through barter.

Nizovsk[53] sackcloth was sold for 2½, Lyskovo[54] for 2, Ivanovo[55] for 1½, and Lalsk[56] for 1 real per arshin. Moreover, they were not of very good quality, so this light article promises much profit. Sackcloth would replace *manta*[57]—a kind of thick, white calico with a width of an arshin—that they obtain from Mexico. They pay 3½ reals for a vara.

Scarlet "oil cloth"[58] was sold for 3 and blue for 2 piasters per arshin. According to the invoices, that which they obtain from Mexico costs 1 piaster, 7 reals per vara for blue and 2 piasters, 1 real per vara for scarlet. Mexican cloth does not have such a pile as European cloth, but it is very durable and does not lose its color.

They bought Aleksandrovsk[59] variegated cloth for 3 arshins per piece. I sold it to them for less in order to introduce them to this article. Afterwards the price was raised.

Patterned flannel at 5¼ reals or 1 [ruble], 18 ko[pecks] per arshin would be fairly profitable in barter, but other articles could bring more profit.

Stockings: men's felt are 1½ piasters; women's felt, 1 piaster; cotton striped, 1 piaster; and linen, 3 piasters per pair.

Shawls: cotton are 2, 1½, and 1 piaster each; shawls in a batch of nine are 1 piaster each, small shawls are 6 reals each, and sackcloth shawls are 2 reals each.

---

[53]"Nizovsk" refers to the middle reaches of the Volga River's right bank in general and to the Moscow-Vladimir region in particular; the latter was the heart of what became the Central Industrial District of Moscow-Ivanovo, tsarist's and Soviet Russia's chief region of light industry, especially textile manufacturing.

[54]Lyskovo was a village in Nizhny Novgorod Province near the junction of the Sundovik and Volga Rivers.

[55]Ivanovo was an industrial town of Vladimir Province that was to become known as the "Russian Manchester."

[56]Lalsk was a town in Vologda Province just to the east of Veliky Ustyug.

[57]Coarse cotton cloth, used for blankets and large shawls.

[58]A heavy, dense cloth produced at Klintsy in western Russia and designed especially for the China trade.

[59]The Alexandrovsk textile mill was founded in 1799 on the left bank of the Neva River on the outskirts of St. Petersburg to introduce mechanized spinning to Russia.

German needles are 4 piasters per thousand. They obtain needles from Mexico for 3 to 5 piasters per thousand.

They bought embroidered yuft boots for 5 piasters per pair.

For ordinary combs they paid 1½ piasters each. Our combs were of horn and of the lowest grade. According to the Mexican invoices, ivory combs—regardless of size—are sold to them for 3 to 5 reals each.

They bought awls from us for 20 piasters per thousand.

For twilled woolen fabric they paid 1 piaster per arshin.

For hats with narrow lace they paid 4 piasters each.

Razors: for plain razors or, rather, razors of the lowest grade they paid 1 piaster each. They obtain ordinary ones from Barcelona for 8 piasters each.

Ordinary penknives are 4 piasters each.

Ordinary pocketknives are 2 piasters each.

Hand knives are 2 reals each.

Ordinary small scissors are 3 piasters per pair.

Large locks are 1 piaster each.

Medium locks are 1 piaster each.

Small locks are 6 reals each.

Onion-shaped medium locks are 2 reals each.

Large and small chisels are 1 piaster each.

Crosscut saws are 15 piasters each.

Files are 2 reals each.

Ordinary gimlets are 2 piasters each.

Ordinary iron spoons are 2 piasters each.

Bright buttons are 4 reals per set.

They bought large axes for 1½ piasters each. For the same price they obtain axes from Europe via Mexico.

Ticking, *deburet*,[60] and dyed linen are sold for 4 reals or 90 ko[pecks] per ar[shin]. Ivanovo and Karetnikovsk[61] printed fabrics are 5 reals and 5½ reals per arshin, respectively.

Although the price of dabba has been set at 3 rubles each [bale?] by the Okhotsk agency [of the company], I ordered it sold for 1 piaster. My reasons were [as follows]: 1st, that they obtain them from Mexico for no more than this; 2nd, in order to secure the trade in this article to ourselves in the future; and 3rd, that the company can still sell it at a profit at this price. I will again explain the cost of dabba with a calculation.

---

[60]A colored linen fabric designed for the China trade.

[61]After the merchant Pyotr Karetnikov, who began to make printed calico at his factory in the village of Teykovo in Vladimir Province in 1765.

Assuming it is bought for..90 [kopecks],
and its transport to Okhotsk costs 18,
then it costs .... 108 kopecks [1 ruble, 8 kopecks].

Formerly (I do not know about the present), dabba was bartered for 60 to 90 kopecks. Fifty dabbas are called a *bakla* [bale?], which weighs 2 puds, 10 funts, and so the transport of each is not great, but for this [amount] three rubles are charged at Okhotsk, since the prices of all goods have been abruptly and excessively raised (nobody knows this), and so, according to my estimate, it would be very profitable to sell it for 1 piaster or 1 [ruble], 80 ko[pecks], especially when in barter it goes for just over 3 rubles (and besides, it would be even cheaper to trade it at Canton).

In addition, the Californios[62] asked about [the following]:

Foulard, but we did not have any. I saw in their invoices that a piece of 15 varas supplied from Mexico was priced at 15 piasters. This light article would be very suitable, and it would be just as profitable for us to transport it from Kyakhta.

Silk shawls? We had none of them either. In their invoices the smallest sort were supplied to them for 1 piaster, 1 real or 2 rubles [each]. I have sent one shawl to the Board of Directors, and you will deign to infer from this how our Moscow factories would be stimulated by this trade.

Ribbon? But we had none. According to the Mexican invoices, ribbon with satin on one side was supplied to them for 3 reals per vara, and their taste is for striped ribbon. Glossy black silk ribbon a *vershok*[63] in width is 1 real per vara. Men wear them in bunches in their braids.

Yellow uniform buttons? From Mexico they obtain large ones for 2½, and small ones for 1½, reals each.

Glass tableware, as well as large [*shtofnie*],[64] medium, and small bottles? After having written the Board of Directors, I realized how useful it would be to establish a glass factory in America. The ships going for grain could supply all of California with glass.

Here I will tell Your Highness about the extent to which the Mexicans fleece them [the Californios]. Argüello showed me six gilded cut-glass glasses, nestled inside each other in a case; they are known to us as caesars in St. Petersburg, and before my departure I bought them for 1 [ruble], 50 ko[pecks] each for my Japanese mission. I asked him the price. "Seven piasters," he replied, showing me the invoice, and when I offered to supply them for 3½ piasters [each], they were prepared to pay the money in advance.

---

[62] The Californios were the Hispanic residents of California, as the Tejanos were the Hispanic residents of Texas.

[63] 1 *vershok* = 1.75 inches or 4.4 centimeters.

[64] A *shtof* was a Russian bottle with a capacity of 1.30 quarts or 1.23 liters.

Kegs, tubs, buckets, and every sort of wooden vessel could be very profitable. I brought such with me, and they would willingly have paid me half a piaster for a bucket, but I gave everything to the royal garrison. They have plenty of timber, but there are no craftsmen, and so a master cooper could support himself at the New Archangel shipyard or at least incur a saving to the regional administration.

Wheels would also produce unbelievable revenue. They transport everything on packhorses, although they do have a four-wheeled cart called a *carreta*, but it is pitiful to see how flour is moved. Eight strapping oxen cart barely 50 puds, and a pair pull an empty cart with difficulty. Their wheels are made of a single, imperfectly rounded piece of wood, mounted on an axle, on which it barely rotates, and the weight of the cart exceeds the weight of the load.

I am sure that they would like our *droshkies*,[65] if only they could be delivered to them with full harness. But in Old Mexico there is a luxury of everything, including carriages. The governor told me that the capital of New Spain [Mexico City] can accommodate up to five thousand carriages. With only walrus hides, which are now wasted, our company could form a substantial branch of trade, shipping them to California, whence they could be taken to San Blas on the two corvettes that arrive from there annually and that always return empty. I dare to assure Your Highness that, having opened trade with California, we will reach Mexico.

For trade with California it is necessary to say something about women's clothing. They greatly favor cotton print skirts that are wide at the bottom and have a hem six vershoks in width, such as used to be sewn by us. It is de rigueur that the upper part of the skirt be striped lengthwise in bright shades or soft colors, with a border of the same or another color and with a garland. All of them also wear a kind of shawl, called a rebozo, which mantles them from their heads, around which it is wound. It is 3½ arshins long and 1½ arshins wide; its ends are hemmed or fringed and usually striped in dark blue, pale blue, orange, or other bright colors but always with white. Each stripe is more than half a vershok in width. Silk, cotton, and sackcloth rebozos are equally valued, for all Spanish women, regardless of position, wear this garment, and on account of the hotness of the climate it is not possible to devise a better one. They wear nothing, except a blouse, under a rebozo, and, wrapping themselves in it artfully, they always seem to be fully dressed and very neat, and besides their head is protected from the hot sun. This article is convenient and economical to transport.

Black taffeta and satin of superior quality will fetch a high price. This is the apparel in which all Spanish women receive communion. Thus, those who can, own a black dress and a white muslin veil.

---

[65]A *droshky* was an open, low-slung, four-wheeled Russian carriage with a long transverse bench, on which the passengers sat with their feet resting on bars near the ground.

I will inform Your Highness of the number of iron implements that the three missions of Santa Clara, San José, and San Francisco asked me to supply annually. From this you will deign to infer what the expenses of all of California can be.

Shears, 5½ vershoks, for shearing sheep 1,200
Plows, half an arshin 300
Sickles 500
Hand knives 5,000
Wire carders (pairs) 300
Axes 360
Shovels 500
Indoor locks of various sizes 200
Large saws 12
Medium saws 12
Small saws 24
Large pots of various capacities 20

In addition, hinges, braces, augers, awls, hammers, tongs, anvils, and nails of 10 inches and less. Such is the need for the last that when their roofs need to be reinforced with nails, they bind them with rawhide thongs, which they are obliged to replace frequently.

Having explained to Your Highness all of the items of trade and California's needs, or at least as much as my brief stay allowed me to observe, I will now direct you, gracious sire, to the political state and administration of this province. They are already known to you, of course, but my recent information will prove useful for comparison.

California is divided into Old and New. Old [Baja] California includes all of the peninsula from Cabo de San Lucas to the port of San Diego and is itself mountainous, hot, and barren. New California begins at the port of San Diego and stretches at present to the port of San Francisco, for the Spaniards have not yet settled farther north. I have already had the honor of explaining its abundance to Your Highness and recounting its surpluses—which Old California does not utilize, however, satisfying its needs from San Blas and the district of Sonora, which lies across the Crimson Sea, or Gulf of California (Vermilion Sea) [Sea of Cortez], and is so productive that usually the harvest of grain is from 70- to 100-fold [the seed], and sometimes up to 130-fold is produced, as the Spaniards who were once there assured me, and it can easily be believed, having seen this province [New California].

The administration of both Californias has been entrusted to a single governor, but this year at the request of Don José de Arrillaga there will be separate governors, and both will be subordinate to the viceroy of New Spain in Mexico

City. The administration has military ceremony but no courts or penalties at all. The salary of the governor is 4,000 piasters per year. At present the viceroy of New Spain is Don José de Iturrigaray,[66] a lieutenant general, who receives a salary alone of 60,000 piasters per year for serving in this post, which is also accompanied by great benefits. The viceroy is usually appointed for two and a half years and may last for 20 years, but the government reserves the right to recall him at any time.

New California is divided into five presidios: Monterey, San Francisco, San Diego, Santa Bárbara, and Loreto[67] on the coast of the Crimson Sea. Three of them have ports.

A presidio is a place where soldiers have their barracks and which administers the surrounding area under its jurisdiction. Each has a garrison or company and some artillery. Monterey's company comprises 1 captain, 1 lieutenant, 2 ensigns, 2 cadets, 2 sergeants, 8 corporals, 86 dragoons, 1 artillery officer, 1 artillery sergeant, 2 artillery corporals, and 12 gunners. At the other presidios, as well as at the port of San Francisco, the companies are smaller, comprising 1 captain, 1 lieutenant, 1 ensign, 1 cadet, 2 sergeants, 6 corporals, 48 dragoons, 1 artillery sergeant, 2 artillery corporals, and 6 gunners. Thus, New California's entire military strength comprises fewer than 400 men. In support they have tried to settle veterans [superannuated soldiers] in the interior of the country, calling such settlements *Pueblos de los Inválidos*. Two miles from Santa Clara there is such a settlement, consisting of 30 families, and they try to establish these villages within the jurisdiction of each presidio. They give them [native] Americans as help, and the state does not spare expenses attracting settlers from Mexico and even from Europe itself. The governor told me that in [Spanish] America revenue from agriculture in the hands of the clergy is distributed the following way. Five-tenths of the harvest is allotted to the bishopry [diocese] and four-tenths to the clergy [parish], and one-tenth is left in possession of the farmer; but the king, who is encouraging migration, takes only a tithe [one-tenth] from the veterans, leaving nine-tenths to them, and pays the clergy in money. Meanwhile, many people have migrated from Mexico to Loreto, which is fairly populous, except for the garrison. The fine climate, the fertile soil of Sonora on the other side of the gulf, and the close contact with Mexico attract settlers. The road from Loreto to San Diego, running through dreadful mountain ranges, is very difficult, and for that reason the Spanish are trying to find a route much farther north to Santa Fe, which is the capital of New Mexico and which lies no more than 200 [*sic*: 1,000] miles from

---

[66]Iturrigaray (1742–1815) was viceroy of New Spain from 1803 until 1808, when he was removed for supporting Mexico's colonials against the Napoleonic puppet on the Spanish throne.

[67]Actually, the presidio of Loreto was in Baja, or Old, California.

the port of San Francisco. Having searched the interior of the country constantly, the Spanish last year laid a hundred-mile section and, [upon] meeting some savages, learned from them that at the distance of a two-day ride these very same savages had seen men in uniforms identical to theirs and that the route thither was good, and for that reason they concluded, and very rightly, that the savages were speaking of the garrison at Santa Fe. This information caused the viceroy to order an expedition under the command of a keen officer to discover a route. Don Luis de Argüello has been appointed leader; he has been given a sergeant, a cadet, 20 dragoons, and one missionary,[68] and they will set out the day after my departure. His instructions include a survey of the land, the peoples, and, most of all, the route to New Mexico. Don Luis must try to make Santa Fe, and when he succeeds in doing so he will receive help from the local viceroy to build a road and to found missions on the route, so that in the event of the passage of an army settlements and grainfields will have been established and storehouses constructed everywhere, and then New California will always have the necessary reinforcements for its military forces.[69]

This, gracious sire, is how the government, notwithstanding its fanaticism, takes care to improve its territories. It is true that all of their measures are still weak, but at least there is a beginning, there are laws, and there is order, management, and discipline, and already external appearances alone assure everyone that this country is the possession of an enlightened power, but the unhappy parallel of our establishments—to the shame of our fatherland—is the one disgrace of our time, and it is painful to describe what is happening there. Forgive me, gracious sire, I was speaking of the presidios, and so I shall return to them immediately. The garrison is maintained on salaries alone. A captain receives 1,500 piasters per year, a lieutenant 500, an ensign 300, a sergeant 250, a corporal 225, and a cadet and a private 217½. Every private must supply his own uniform, food, carbine, saber, lance, pistols, horses (not one but eight), and a saddle, and the state provides nothing except gunpowder. Each presidio provides the missions with 2 dragoons, who live at the missions and escort the missionaries on their outings, and for that reason the presidios are being weakened, as you will judge.

[68]Father José de Uría was appointed from the missionaries. He and Father Martín de Landaeta are greatly respected by the governor. Both are utilized in all important matters and councils. [JRG: José Antonio Uría (1769–1815), a peninsular from the Basque region, became a Franciscan in 1789, left Spain in 1796, and arrived at Monterey from San Fernando College in the summer of 1799. Despite painful physical ailments, he served at Mission San José for seven years and then at Mission San Fernando (1806–1808) and Mission San Juan Capistrano (1808–12), whereupon he retired to Mexico. See Geiger, Franciscan Missionaries, 259. Martín de Landaeta (1760–1809), a peninsular, arrived in California in 1791 and served chiefly at Mission San Francisco. See Geiger, Franciscan Missionaries, 135–36.]

[69]Don Luis told me that when he has succeeded in opening this route, California will be transferred to the viceroyalty of New Mexico. The viceroy of New Spain has striven more to that end in order to rid his jurisdiction of such an extensive territory, which brings no benefits at all, only trouble.

With respect to layout, the presidio is a square, with each side up to 60 sazhens [long]. It has two gates. There is a church in the middle opposite the main facade and barracks along the sides; on the right side are the quarters of the commandant, officers, administration, and shop, and on the other sides are the barracks and storehouses. They are built of adobe [unfired brick] and roofed with grass [tule reeds?]. Nobody has glass, and for that reason there are very few windows for more protection from the wind during cold spells. If we were to build a glass factory, it would be recompensed by means of California within a year.

I will describe to Your Highness the presidio of the port of San Francisco, but I heard that all of the others are somewhat better.[70] It lies under a hill more than a versta from the fort. Concerning the fort, I will tell you that it has nothing other than a small earthen wall, behind which there are 12- and 24-pound cannons. By making a landing a mile away with 50 men with two regimental guns, it would be very easy to seize this port.

With the presidio taken, the number of men in the fort, who are stationed there for a single purpose, would be unable to operate such heavy artillery, and besides, they would be forced to surrender even more quickly by the fact that their families live in the presidio. They are now at war with England, which, if California were to contain something other than grain and cattle, would not fail to profit from it, and I think that piasters, which are circulating plentifully in Chile, will quickly attract the enemy there. In addition, the northern shore of the entrance to the port of San Francisco is not fortified in the least, and it is itself twice as high as the southern shore, and a single cannon mounted on it could command all of the fort on the opposite shore.

I will repeat here, gracious sire, that the coast of New Albion,[71] which I myself passed, is not occupied by anyone. The port of Bodega, which Vancouver described, is also not occupied by the Spaniards; in short, they have not settled beyond the port of San Francisco. On the other side of this broad bay, which extends more than 70 miles inland, there is not a single Spaniard. They do not have any boats at the port, although timber is sufficient, and they could obtain prefabricated ships from San Blas, where there is a shipyard, but evidently they are prevented from having them for political reasons—the weakness of their forces. The soil on the other side [of the bay], as the Spaniards themselves admitted to me, is more fertile than that of San Francisco. Lieutenant Khvostov went there on the pretext of seeking our deserters and brought me a lot of laurel [bay]

---

[70]I have the honor, Your Highness, to enclose with this a map of the port of San Francisco. [JRG: This map, signed by Rezanov, is in AVPRI, f. 161 (Sanktpeterburgsky Glavny arkhiv I-7), op. 6 (1802), d. 1, fol. 65. It is reproduced in Istomin, Gibson, and Tishkov, *Rossiya v Kalifornii*, I, 143.]

[71]The toponym "New Albion," conferred by Francis Drake, referred loosely to that uncolonized stretch of the Pacific slope between the mouth of the Columbia River and the entrance to San Francisco Bay.

leaves; the timber is fine, and he saw oak trees, chestnut trees, whose fruit he brought, and many other unknown trees, as well as standing wheat, which, evidently, had been planted formerly or sown as an experiment or brought by the savages, who in fleeing the missions sometimes cross [the bay] in reed boats. There are many wild [feral?] goats, as well as bulls; amphibians and fish abound. The savages, or Indians, are numerous; they are much more submissive than the northern ones.[72] Mr. Khvostov met four who were fishing among the rocks; he treated them kindly, and his trifling presents immediately prompted them to follow him. They came to the ship in their reed boat and stayed overnight. Bird-skin cloaks were their clothes, and their food, which they had with them, consisted of finely ground seeds and roots and was quite tasty and nutritious. I ordered that they be dressed and presented to the governor.

It seems to me that present circumstances will not become more favorable for the implementation of my project—about which I wrote to you—for moving us quickly to the south. England, of course, will [not] consent to let us occupy the lands that it utilizes and to which it has common rights with the Spaniards in accordance with the [Nootka] convention of 1790. However, it would unquestionably be possible to undertake the matter, but it would be safer at a later time, when the will of this power has been marked by some sort of action.

I have thought to make the first settlement on the Strait of Juan de Fuca at Port Discovery at 49° [N], where, as Vancouver says, the soil promises to be very fertile and where, besides, [sea] otters and black bears are hunted. Having placed 50 men at this place, Gray's Harbor is to be occupied with 50 men and the Columbia River with 100 men and, having indulged the natives and made settlements, then, when the last two settlements—on account of their closeness to one another—are able to help, it will be possible to move imperceptibly farther south and make the port of San Francisco itself our neighbor, and the advantageous situation of the northern shore will without fail make it a common port.[73] Of all individuals, there could scarcely be anyone who would feel such satisfaction as I when, living with relatives cheek by cheek, I would be able to see her [Doña Concepción] every day.

But joking aside, gracious sire, if you obtain permission to trade with California, then on that account the company could establish granaries, and in the proposed southern colony, having treated the numerous savages kindly, it would at the same time commence grain growing and stock rearing, and, having organized trade with Canton, it could settle Chinese there. Your Highness will perhaps deign to

---

[72]By "northern" Indians are meant those of the Northwest Coast, where at the beginning of the 1800s there was deadly conflict between the Russians and the Tlingits in particular.

[73]Rezanov did not know that Lewis and Clark had just staked an American claim to the Columbia by erecting Fort Clatsop at its mouth and wintering there.

laugh at the expense of my far-reaching ventures, but I adamantly insist that my proposals are the very crux of the matter and are very feasible and that if men and means were provided, then all of this territory could be secured to Russia forever without any substantial sacrifice by the treasury, and then, only when you are pleased to consider and investigate all of the circumstances, you yourself will deign to agree that trade will make momentous and gigantic strides. All large-scale plans seem ridiculous on paper, but when they are calculated correctly, their execution evokes surprise. Only in this way, and not through petty trade, do commercial bodies attain their greatness. If the government had thought earlier of this part of the world, if it had valued it [i.e., this region] as it should have, and if it had constantly pursued the perspicacious aims of Peter the Great with the few resources that the Bering[74] expedition had for mapping anything, then [one] can positively say that New California would never have become a possession of the Spaniards, for only after 1760 did they pay attention to it, and this better tract of country was secured forever only through the enterprise of the missionaries. There still remains at present an unoccupied section that is just as advantageous and very necessary to us, and thus if we overlook it, then what will our descendants say? It seems to me that I, for my part, will not be arraigned by them.

It should be assumed that the Spaniards, fanatical as they are, will advance farther, and however much I diverted their suspicion from us, their government will hardly believe my soothing words. I am as sure of success in these pursuits as I am [of the fact] that if we do not value these benefits in the reign of Alexander I, then we must never expect them, and the moment will have been missed, and then it will be seen that the Russians, with all of the enterprise and overcoming of difficulties that are associated with their national character, must have surrendered to circumstances and subsided into inactivity, and that their heart for the significant and the grandiose must have disappeared. In short, we will become like a worn steel from which a spark can barely be struck until the hand tires and then is idle and can ignite nothing, a steel that [once] did have fire but was not used.

For God's sake, gracious sire, examine patriotically the circumstances of this territory that promises the fatherland vast trade benefits, for which only you, Your Highness, can plead at the throne, and present to the Tsar Emperor my proposals, which will remain immortal in subsequent centuries. In England Queen

---

[74]The Danish mariner Ivan Ivanovich (Vitus Jonassen) Bering (1681–1741) was one of the many skilled foreigners recruited by Peter the Great in an attempt to forcibly modernize his lagging country. At the end of 1724 Bering was called to lead the First Kamchatka Expedition (1725–29), which probed the uncharted waters between northeastern Siberia and northwestern North America. The inconclusive findings prompted the much more ambitious Second Kamchatka Expedition (1733–42) in two ships under the command of Bering and Aleksey Chirikov; both reached as far as the coast of the Gulf of Alaska, but on the homeward voyage Bering's vessel was shipwrecked, and he died on his eponymous island in the Commander archipelago. See Grinëv, *Kto yest kto,* 62–63; and Pierce, *Russian America,* 53–55. Also see Frost, *Bering.*

Elizabeth is the architect of its present strength, and her name is hallowed by the people, but the name of our monarch will be more blessed when during his happy reign Russians will have shed enslavement by foreign nations and tasted the abundant fruit of their great deeds. In my latest reports to the company I have been content to explain that my experiments will be nothing more than the confirmation of those prospects, which nature itself in every way so rightly offered us long ago, and my voyage to California has seemed not only to justify them but equally should also attest to Your Highness that they, like my other endeavors, are not at all chimerical.

As I have already had the honor to explain to Your Highness, the governor, having become my close friend, hid nothing from me, being certain that I had the means of learning everything through Mr. Argüello. He admitted to me frankly that their court feared Russia more than anybody else and that Shelik-hov's[75] settlements had given them cause to expect further enterprise, but that the past twenty years had completely pacified them. "Please," I said, "divest your court forever of any suspicion and explain to it my earlier conversation with you on this subject." "Do not ask me," he said; "It is my pleasure to inform the viceroy of your so agreeable and sincere assurances, which will help even more to advance trade; dispose me to the common good of the people entrusted to our care and you will see with what heartfelt participation I am ready to help you." And in fact every day I had new proofs of their friendship; everything was at my complete command; the garrison was constantly on the move, forcing the faster delivery of grain; their people procured water for us—in short, everyone was competing to please us, and I, with no difficulty whatever, was engaged solely in giving orders, and despite the many rumors of war, I gave the Spaniards feasts and din-ners, and those who were kept in the presidio I always occupied in an agreeable manner with my missions. To demonstrate his sincerity the governor, with his weak legs, danced with me, and we did not spare the gunpowder [for firing guns in celebration] either on the ship or in the fort. Spanish guitars combined with Russian singers, and notwithstanding the wants of my Californians, I think that they will long remember the coming of the Russians with their gifts, for I admit

---

[75]Grigory Ivanovich Shelikhov (or Shelekhov) (1748–95), a native of Rylsk in southern European Russia, went to Siberia in 1772 and joined the Irkutsk firm of Ivan Golikov. In 1781 Shelikhov and two Golikovs formed the Northeastern American Company in an attempt to dominate the trade and curb the ruinous competition. In 1783 the company launched an expedition of three ships from Okhotsk to found a colony in Alaskan waters; a year later it reached Kodiak Island, where Three Saints Harbor, perhaps the first per-manent Russian settlement in the New World, was founded. He also founded a settlement on Urup Island in the Kuriles in 1794. His sudden death in 1795 disrupted his plans, but his astute widow, Natalya, and her influential son-in-law, Nikolay Rezanov, successfully continued his enterprise. His company became the basis of the Russian-American Company. See Grinëv, *Kto yest kto*, 604–605; and Pierce, *Russian America*, 454–59. Also see Andreyev, *Russian Discoveries;* Black and Petrov, *Natalia Shelikhova;* and Shelikhov, *Voyage to America.*

to Your Highness that I spared nothing in order to direct the due respect of this part of the world to the greatness of the Russian nation.

I often talked to the governor about trade. I was surprised that California was in so much need while it had so close at hand the means of satisfying its wants. "It seems to me," I said, "that with a little encouragement of trade all of your shortages here would be averted." "Do not wonder," he replied, "that trade has been neglected by us, but now the government is opening its eyes to this matter, although it still sees it dimly. The diversity of strong voices at court and the meddling of private interests do not afford the means of reconciling everyone for the common good. It is true that trade has been greatly protected; the class of men pursuing it is now so respected that the king, contrary to the rights of the nobility, has given many of them the title of marquis, and such [recognition but] never occurred before in Spain. Also, the Caracas Company[76] had completely collapsed, but three years ago it was buttressed in an unprecedented manner. Its directors are now in Madrid, and suddenly fifteen million piasters have been deposited with it, including a million and half piasters from the king himself for six thousand shares; it has been given ships with the royal standard and the right to demand in his name the necessary officers and crewmen from the fleet. It conducts trade with the East and West Indies, but poor California is forgotten. I regret to tell you—but it is the absolute truth—that our government is too sluggish, and for that reason it does not have, or does not want to have, a correct notion of it [i.e., California]. When the company wanted to help us trade, private individuals who have long been sending galleons from Manila to Acapulco protested that [this offer] was an infringement of their rights, and it eventuated that the king forbade it [i.e., the company] from touching the western coast of America. The Manilans send their galleons partly with Chinese goods, which do reach us, but we do business with the Mexicans, who by means of two naval corvettes that annually ply our coast from San Blas supply us with our wants at immoderate prices, and we give them piasters in advance in order to have what we need—and without which we cannot manage—sent the next year."[77]

Once, turning him to the Philippine Islands, I asked him with what nations they traded and whether it was true that for remitting their piasters to Europe the Manilans lent them at two or three percent [interest]? "Manila," he replied, "is a free port to us; as regards the money, perhaps it used to be so, and it happens that the greed of the English and others trading in India has raised prices in

[76]The Real Compañía Guipuzcoana de Caracas, or Caracas Company (1728–84), was a Basque corporation established by the Spanish crown as a monopoly on Venezuela's lucrative cocoa trade to counteract smuggling of this quasi-narcotic source of chocolate, which was the colony's most profitable export for two centuries. See Hussey, *Caracas Company*.

[77]For the "China ship" trade from 1565 to 1815 between Acapulco and Manila, see Flynn, Giráldez, and Sobredo, *European Entry*; and Schurz, *Manila Galleon*.

favor of the Manilans, but I know for sure from one of our San Blas officers that the English paid them no less than 25 percent, and, believe me, this made them rich, when they make more than 200 percent on goods bought with someone else's money in Canton, Bengal, and elsewhere, but now, I think, the Bostonians will profit from the breach in our friendship, for upon England's declaration of war they immediately renewed their former requests for permission to trade in our American territories. The government refused, but when the United States minister to Madrid left in displeasure, the evidently critical situation of our court prompted the dispatch after him of a satisfactory response, which gave them four ports on the eastern coast, namely, Buenos Aires, Veracruz, Caracas, and Cartagena, and, having the province of New Orleans ceded to them by France and having Pensacola close to New Mexico, they had already begun to trade with them [i.e., the Bostonians], so that Santa Fe is beginning to use their goods. Having myself witnessed the enterprise of this republic in our waters, I am not surprised at its success; it flourishes in trade, and it has come to know its value, and everybody knows this save only us, who pay from our purses for such negligence, and while, as they say, the whole world is hustling, we are content merely to amuse ourselves with dried fish."

"I will tell you frankly," continued the governor, "that your emperor need only to insist firmly and it will be done quickly; otherwise, the slowness of our government will cause you anguish. The Bostonians are an example for you: for a long time they made requests unsuccessfully, but their crucial question was persuasive, and the very same ministers who several years earlier would not agree have now found that it is extremely useful and that in wartime piasters can always be transported safely from America to Europe via trade with a neutral power."

"Rest assured," I said, "that when my monarch deigns merely to concur with my project, then I will consider that it has already been implemented, but it is necessary that you, for your part, make an equally strong representation to your viceroy." "Certainly," he answered, "and I will tell you my plan; three missions have already submitted their petitions to me, but after returning to Monterey I will receive others, and I will submit all of them in the original with my conclusion, in which I will explain all of the benefits that you have so correctly fathomed and that I will supplement with my heartfelt feeling that the shortages of the territories to which I have devoted my whole life will be averted. Meanwhile, I beg you to support my letter to the viceroy with one of your own." "Most gladly," I replied, and the next day I gave it to him.[78]

[78]See "Resanow—José de Yturrigaray, 5/17 may 1806 g.," AVPRI, f. 161 (Sanktpeterburgsky Glavny arkhiv I-7), op. 6 (1802), d. 1, pk. 34, fols. 63v–64. The bulk of this letter was published as a Russian translation in Narochnitsky, *Vneshnyaya politika,* 692–93; for an English translation, see Dmytryshyn, Crownhart-Vaughan, and Vaughan, *Russian-American Colonies,* doc. 17, 109–10.

During all of this time by means of his friends and the missionaries I tried in every possible way to instill more enthusiasm in the old man in order to make his submission utterly convincing. My daily suggestions turned him frequently to this matter. "I am very thankful for your coming," he told me once. "You have given me the means of renewing my frequent representations on the necessity of trade, representations that were never respected because of the remoteness of this place, and sometimes they even caused me grief when my friends told me of this disagreeable opinion of the ministers: 'California is surely an accursed country, affording nothing save trouble and losses!' As if I were to blame for its useless establishments." "Tell me," I asked, "what does its upkeep cost per year?" "No less than half a million piasters." "And its income?" "Not a real." "But you told me once about a grain tithe?" "It is collected from the superannuated soldiers only, and it is reserved for the missions in case of a crop failure, and for that reason they have policemen at their storehouses; in short, the king maintains the garrisons, the warships, and the missions and is obliged to contribute to the construction and beautification of the churches, for his sole object is to propagate the true faith and to safeguard the people, and for that reason, as the true defender of the faith, he donates all of his profits to religion." Listening to such a panegyric, I nearly burst from laughter. "This is very commendable and edifying," I replied in a pious mien, "but unfortunately we see such moral corruption that already there are entire peoples who do not see the true goal of bliss and who are so deluded as to prefer temporary to eternal happiness, and your most heartwarming intentions and your priests' passionate supplications do not have the power to protect either your religion or you yourselves from such scum of the earth." "You are right," he said; "Several times I have requested an increase in military strength, but after you mollified us by confining yourselves to the north, my representations elicited only promises. Now, however, the effrontery of the Bostonians has aroused us, and this year they promised to send me a naval frigate to blockade the ships of the American states that constantly smuggle along our shores and conduct a clandestine trade, but this is still not enough; they [American ships] sometimes leave ten or fifteen men here, absolute brigands, who on account of the smallness of our garrisons disturb the peace and corrupt our morals. They land with women and insolently seek the means of settling among us."

"Earlier I spoke of the Bostonian Captain O'Cain,"[79] the governor said to me

---

[79]Captain Joseph O'Cain (17??–1807), a genuine Bostonian from the suburb of Dorchester, made several voyages to the Northwest Coast in the last decade of the eighteenth and the first decade of the nineteenth century, twice as a shipmaster, and for a time he served aboard Spanish transports at San Blas. In 1803–1804 he became the first American skipper to hunt sea otters in southern waters on halves with the Russians, each side providing what the other side lacked—the Russians, hunters (Aleuts or Konyagas) and the Americans, vessels. See Grinëv, *Kto yest kto*, 392; and Pierce, *Russian America*, 388–89. Also see Engstrom, *Joseph O'Cain*.

once; "He came here in 1803 from Unalaska with 40 islanders [Aleuts and Konya-gas] with kayaks and passed the whole winter hunting [sea] otters, and it is not known where they went; you will oblige me greatly by recounting this matter, which I may have to explain to the viceroy." Here it is my duty to inform Your Highness of this event. Captain O'Cain came to Kodiak in a ship of the same name; he made a contract with Mr. Baranov, who gave him 40 kayaks for hunting [sea] otters on halves on a new island[80] that he [i.e., O'Cain] had found, promis-ing—in case he were to call at places for provisions—to allow the [company's] agent to buy some on behalf of the company without himself sharing in the pro-ceeds; having obtained men, he straightaway landed them in California. Whether O'Cain deceived Mr. Baranov or the latter was to profit from his deception, I leave to Your Highness to judge, adding that at that time they were dying from hunger and that several barrels of flour brought by O'Cain revived them. Now a similar contract, which I was unable to control, has been made with [Captain John] D'Wolf, and, having bought his ship, I have done likewise in a large amount without any reproach, but I gave the Spaniards the following version of this affair. "I am very glad," I said, "that you have reminded me of this event. The Bostonians do more harm to us than to you. They are landing men here, but they are taking them from us. Besides trading in our waters, this scoundrel of whom you speak seized a remote party of our [native] Americans for hunting, taking up to 40 Konyagas with their families; the next year the good Captain Barber[81] brought 26 of these men to us on Kodiak, saying that he had ransomed them from captivity on the Queen Charlotte Islands and that he would return them for 10,000 rubles, which humanity obliged us to pay, but we still do not know where O'Cain put the others. The returnees asserted that they had been in various places and on vari-ous ships, but on account of their ignorance we were unable to learn from them exactly whom they had met and where they had landed. I can assure you that this and similar actions have taught us to be more careful and that we will also take steps to evict these guests, but the numerous channels in our waters deprive us of effective means." "And I," he said, "will answer you that I have now issued orders such that, it seems, they will soon be driven away. I have established mounted patrols along the coast, and when from a height they sight a ship on the horizon, they will inform the nearest presidio, and meanwhile they will not lose sight of its course, and as soon as a boat lands it will, I am sure, be seized."

[80]Probably one of the Channel Islands off Mission Santa Bárbara.

[81]Captain Henry Barber (17??–1807) was an English skipper, born in Hamburg, who commanded four trading voyages to the Northwest Coast. During his third (1801–1803) aboard the *Unicorn* he rescued more than two dozen survivors of the Tlingit destruction of Archangel St. Michael, the precursor of New Arch-angel, in late June 1802 and took them to St. Paul's Harbor on Kodiak Island, where they were ransomed for furs by Governor Baranov. See Grinëv, *Kto yest kto,* 46; and Pierce, *Russian America,* 25–28.

Indeed, within five days the governor showed me a report from San Diego about the Anglo-American brigantine[82] *Peacock* of 108 tons with 6 cannons and 4 falconets under Captain Oliver Kimball,[83] who had approached the coast and landed a boat with four men, who were captured, and the ship left. Navigator Thomas Kilvain from Boston, second quartermaster Jean Pierre from Bordeaux, and two sailors were seized. They asserted that they had departed Boston in September 1805 and reached the Sandwich [Islands][84] directly on 12 February, that their cargo consisted of ordnance and various goods that they were taking to the Russian-American possessions to barter for furs, and that they had come ashore only to refresh themselves. The next day they found on the beach a letter to the navigator in which the captain assured him that he would ply the coast for several days in order to rescue him. But in the meantime they [the captives] had already been shackled, and they will be taken to San Blas. I congratulated the governor on the happy success of his orders, and this greatly pleased the kind old man.

From Mexico they finally received dispatches, which, however threatening, did not frighten me in the least. With them were sent newspapers, in which it was said that Napoleon had routed the Germans and that our armies had withdrawn, and one very disagreeable article of 4 October 1805 from Hamburg said that an unexpected rebellion had occurred in St. Petersburg but that no mention of it had been dared until definite confirmation had been received. I was crushed by this news, and hard as I tried to hide my grief, it was noticed. The Spaniards were unanimous in saying that it was not possible to expect this to refer to our tsar in particular, being loved not only by his own [subjects] but by all peoples, for all of the newspapers describe his kind heart and perforce envy the happiness of his subjects. Such impartial praise, not often heard from foreigners, was especially pleasing to me, but on this occasion my heart was rent all the more. "My God!" I thought to myself; "What has become of my fatherland?" I could not stay calm, and as the governor had not shown me the viceroy's letter, I figured that he had withheld the last issue of the newspaper from me; however, since nothing was hidden from me, I soon had it [the letter] in my hands. He [the viceroy] described to him [the governor] in detail the desperate battle of the allied and English fleets, sent him 4 issues of the newspaper, added an extract from letters from France [to the effect] that Napoleon had taken Vienna and forced the

---

[82]A brigantine (from "brigand" because they were the favorite craft of Mediterranean pirates) was a two-masted sailing vessel, square-rigged on the foremast and fore-and-aft rigged on the mainmast.

[83]This was the only voyage that Oliver Kimball (17??–18??), Joseph O'Cain's brother-in-law, made to the Northwest Coast. Following the Tlingit destruction of the Russian settlement of Yakutat in the fall of 1805, he ingratiated himself with Baranov by ransoming a Chilkat Tlingit chief for two of the Aleut survivors. On its way home in early 1808 the *Peacock* was damaged by a gale in Sunda Strait and condemned and sold at Batavia.

[84]The Sandwich Islands was the name given by Captain James Cook to the Hawaiian Islands in honor of the Earl of Sandwich, First Lord of the Admiralty.

[Holy] Roman Emperor to retire to Moravia, and concluded with a caustic joke at the expense of the allies. I found nothing else, and it seemed to me that the newspaper accounts did not warrant such secrecy.

I asked the governor how often they received news from Europe. "Officially, orders are received once every month from Cádiz by a packet boat established for this purpose, but news is received more frequently by means of trade, and from Mexico, apart from the usual monthly couriers, everything of interest is communicated to all places by express messengers." I envied this system and thought it was as if our poor possessions did not really exist in the New World. With the expansion of trade we could receive news twice a year. "But should your packet boat be seized in wartime," I said, "then your dispatches will be in enemy hands?" "Never," he said; "The trunk with the letters is always tied to a leaden weight and in case of an attack is thrown into the sea, and they are received by the next ship, for in wartime not only dispatches but even all letters are sent in duplicate and triplicate." "If you wish to write to Europe," he added, "you may be sure that your letters will reach their proper destination." I took advantage of his offer and sent a report to His Imperial Majesty, a copy of which, as well as a copy of my letter to the viceroy, I have the honor to attach herewith for Your Highness.

Once I turned to the matter of [sea] otter hunting. "Tell me," I asked the governor, "why do you not make use of sea otters, when they abound in this bay and along the entire coast?" "We are unable to prosecute this trade," he replied, "and truly this commodity is awaiting you. Ten years ago the king presented a project to make substantial revenue from this by sending them to Canton; it was approved,[85] and I received orders to pay nine piasters for each [sea otter skin]. Several thousand of them were amassed at San Blas and sent from there to Canton, but—blame it on faulty dressing, clumsy handling, or our warm climate—all of the [sea] otters rotted and the crown received nothing but pointless losses. Subsequently, private individuals also tried several times but likewise to no account, and this trade has been completely abandoned. Every year officers coming on the ships from San Blas take several of them, trading various things for them and so cheaply that they do not complain if half of them spoil, but the quantity is negligible, for those that the inhabitants get they sell to the Bostonians, but when the prohibition of clandestine trade by them came to be enforced more strictly year by year, then they stopped engaging in this traffic altogether, except those who wanted to get themselves a saddle blanket or the trimming for a greatcoat." Although their [sea] otters are inferior to ours in color, [the skins] are nevertheless fairly good and densely furred. They do not wash [the skins], and [the] pelt is very greasy, and so it is not surprising if they spoil, especially in

---

[85]The governor may have been referring to Viceroy Revilla Gigedo's decree of February 1794 that removed export duties on pelts. See Ogden, *California Sea Otter Trade*, 30–31.

such a hot and dry climate as that of San Blas, which lies at 22° of latitude. One can be confident that with permission to trade our company could easily obtain six or seven thousand [sea otter skins] for no more than 7 or at most 10 piasters [each] at the three ports [San Francisco, Monterey, and San Diego], and they would cost half this price in goods.

But I promised Your Highness to talk about the missions. I saw Mission San Francisco, and both the governor and all of the Spaniards assured me that having seen one I had, so to speak, seen all of them, the only difference being that in accordance with the number of neophytes some had more buildings and facilities and others fewer. The mission that I visited resembled a small town, but then it was built thirty years ago. The chief building is the residence of the missionaries, which on one side adjoins a spacious church with all of its appurtenances. This building is 70 sazhens in length and 20 in width, with many compartments or dwellings arranged in a circle in the center. Boys live in one, girls in another, a lard works is in a third, and weaving and other industrial facilities are in still others. Opposite this building there is a square [plaza], and beyond it there are 16 buildings in parallel rows, two buildings per row of 25 sazhens, where the married [native] Americans live, with each family having its own quarters. All along the sides of these buildings stands a long block containing kitchens, smithies, workshops, storehouses, and other facilities. All of the structures are made of adobe and roofed with tiles. The streets are unparalleled in their cleanliness. Gardens adjoin the buildings, and beyond them lie extensive fields that surround the entire mission and are cultivated by the neophytes. They number 1,200 here, 1,800 in Mission Santa Clara, and 800 in Mission San José, but in all of New California there are up to 26,000 American converts. This [enumeration] I know from the governor.

The Americans [mission Indians] are fed three times daily: in the morning, at noon, and at sunset. At twelve o'clock a bell was rung and the neophytes returned from the fields in the hundreds, and I asked the missionaries to afford me the pleasure of watching them eat. After they had assembled, the missionaries arrived and said three prayers, which the kneeling neophytes repeated. Very clean tureens were brought with a very tasty and nutritious soup of beef with peas and greens. Each American came with his reed pot, into which was poured one large ladleful of soup with a piece of meat for bachelors and two ladlefuls for married men. In addition, they are given wheat, from which they themselves make flour that they eat lightly grilled. The missionaries examine the sick and send them to the physician and the pharmacist.

Regarding the physician, I will tell you, gracious sire, that there is only one in all of California at Monterey, and the governor admitted to me that it would be better without him, for he causes only trouble for the missionaries, who are more able than he. His salary is set by the state at 300 piasters, so one cannot expect to have a skilled and knowledgeable man for such pay. Here I am reminded again of our territory, which is still in a grievous state, for we have none whatsoever.

All of their neophytes are naked, wearing only loincloths woven from wool and above them woolen serapes, which are enough for them on account of the warm climate. All of their fields are irrigated by canals from springs, and so they are never afraid of droughts. At San Francisco the soil is a sandy mixture and the worst in all of California, and so some of its fields yield no more than 12-fold [the seed] and others 20-fold and 30-fold, but they yield 30-, 40-, 50-, and even 70- and 80-fold at the missions of Santa Clara and San José, such harvests being common at the other missions, too. Last year Father José de Uría planted 150 arrobas at Mission San José and reaped 12,000. Never having heard of such yields, I would not have believed them if they had not been attested by the inhabitants and confirmed by the governor.

Fruit trees—namely, fig, peach, quince,[86] and others—never grow at Mission San Francisco, on account of the piercing northern winds from the surrounding mountains. There are some that we saw in full bloom, but they are enclosed by stone fences and require much tending. At Missions Santa Clara and San José, which lie inland only a day's ride away, such precautions are not necessary. There the grape and every fruit abounds, except the orange, which begins at Santa Bárbara. We ate the latter at the port of San Francisco, and they were fairly tasty. Santa Clara's apples are also pleasing to the taste.

Their Indians, or Americans, are fairly tall and dark-skinned but weak and sluggish, and they must be inferior to our northern inhabitants. Their customs, dances, and way of life resemble those of our natives. Every tribe has its own tattoo mark. Their clothes are of feathers and grasses; household utensils are plaited from roots; their weapons are bows and arrows with points of jasper; their food is dried fish, mussels, and ground seeds and roots; their ornaments are feathers, bones, and shells. They, like our natives, paint their faces and wear feather helmets, as well as shells and round pits in their ears and sometimes in their noses. Their boats are [made] of several long bunches of reeds [tule (bulrushes)] tied together, and although their sea lions and seals are more numerous than ours, they do not utilize them and do not have umiaks.[87] Thus, in their level of understanding, handicraft

---

[86]Russ., *memerilly;* unidentified, perhaps Sp., *membrillo?*

[87]Here Rezanov may be confusing umiaks with kayaks, which were used primarily for hunting and traveling. Umiaks (Russ., *baidaras,* possibly derived from the same term for a type of Dnepr riverboat) were much larger hide boats used by the Aleuts and Konyagas for freighting. One seen by the German scientist Adolf Erman in December 1829 at San Francisco measured forty feet in length and twelve feet in width and boasted sails and ten thwarts and a crew of thirty men; pulled ashore, tipped onto its side, and propped with its oars, it served the crewmen as a shelter for a week on the beach below the presidio (Erman, "Zusats-Bemerkungen über Neü Californien," 254–55). Also see Arima, "Building Umiaks," 139–57.

skill, dexterity, and strength itself they must be inferior to our northern natives. From ours it is possible to have good warriors but never from these locals.

Roaming the world, gracious sire, not for my own pleasure but for the good of the fatherland, I again appeal to your authority and present to Your Highness an unbiased parallel with the treatment of our local Americans. The crown's heavy expenses and the government's care, however weak it is, give California great capacities. All of the missionaries are educated men, unlike our holy men, who become the shepherds of our souls from the [ranks of] barely literate peasants. I have written enough in my reports about what is practiced in our [Orthodox] mission here, and I think that I have put it in order, but it is necessary that the character of the clergy should likewise be appropriate. In California the missionaries, having finished their courses of study in European or Mexican colleges and having been awarded their [clerical] rank through examinations, are sent to their appointments at state expense. The Franciscans receive a salary of 400 piasters and the Dominicans 300 piasters per year. They are highly respected, and this [respect] is merited by their qualities and conduct. Over all of the clergy stands a superior [*padre presidente*], who lives in Monterey and is required to report on all of the missions to the archbishop of Mexico. At present the superior is Father Estevan Tapis.[88] After 10 years have passed, the missionaries are free to return to Europe, where upon the recommendation of the [church] administration they are given clerical posts or benefices[89] in preference to others, but having become accustomed to, and domiciled in, California, they willingly end their lives there— proof that man's freedom in any position brings benefit to the state. Their buildings are fairly good, the cleanliness is unparalleled, the care of the neophytes is extraordinary, the food of the Indians is exceptional, and their clothing is warm; in short, every foreigner, [upon] having seen their settlements and ours, will say that there is charity there [in Alta California] and inhuman oppression here [in Russian America], but this would be too severe, and I would never agree, although I more than anyone am aware of the depravity in our America. It can happen that sometimes two travelers describe one and the same place quite differently but nevertheless are both veracious because they have viewed the object from different points of view. Mr. Vancouver was attracted by superficial splendor. Knowing the merit of the man and having read him, my imagination here was already prepared. Curiosity generates impatience; a happy exterior suddenly rewards waiting with pleasantness, so can there be anything stronger than this impression? On the first day I myself was enraptured and would have remained biased my entire

---

[88]Estevan Tapis (ca. 1756–1825), a peninsular, arrived in Alta California in 1790 and served chiefly at Mission Santa Bárbara. He was president of the province's missions from 1803 until 1812. See Geiger, *Franciscan Missionaries*, 253–56.

[89]Russ., *plebendy;* unidentified, perhaps Sp., *prebendas?*

life if I had not been obliged to go into more detail, but in examining everything impartially and comparing their possibilities with ours I found that not all that glitters is gold. Thus, in the very unorganized administration of our territory I still find much that seems to me to be better than there [Alta California], and if the government were to attend to it [Russian America], then our settlements, despite the severity of the climate, would soon make a more positive impression upon every traveler—to the true glory and honor of the fatherland, besides—than those of California. Permit me, Your Highness, to explain my parallel.

1. Their climate in itself gives them a great advantage over ours; already in March we had fresh beans and wild strawberries. They have winters with early morning frost, but by midday there are at least 8 degrees [Réaumur][90] of heat, and thus what a palpable difference! But northern residents like ourselves cannot fear the severity of our climate. One need only develop the economy, create order, and test everything, and trade will replace whatever does not succeed.

2. Regarding the missionaries, I have already said above that when our clergy sends enlightened and well-behaved men, and with the same freedom to return and to be rewarded for their work—and, besides, sends white [i.e., married] clerics and not unmarried monks [i.e., black clerics], who are very out of place here preaching chastity—then it is possible to be confident that their economic activities, good family examples, industry, and wise counsel will make Christians of the present savages and provide the territory with useful citizens.

However, it seems that /**at this time**/ neither the Spaniards nor we can boast of the spread of the true faith in America. Our [native] Americans have learned to make the sign of the cross correctly, and the Californians have memorized the three sacred prayers,[91] but the success of both peoples in religion is the same. Its true moral code is forgotten, so of what use is it? But after the priests have been given complete instructions for the education of true Christians, they can at the same time instruct them [the natives] in agriculture, supplying them with directions such that they will undertake it gently but surely, acquiring a taste for kindness but never losing sight of man's freedom. Then, when the cultivators find that it is to their own advantage to acquire a taste for industry, success will be more certain and each individual as much as everyone as a whole will promote the welfare of the entire territory.

By contrast, the missionaries in California have completely enslaved their neophytes. It is true that they maintain them well, giving them drink and food,

[90]René Antoine Ferchault de Réaumur devised his thermometric scale around 1730. On his thermometer 0° marks the freezing point, and 80° the boiling point, of water; its readings are converted into Celsius by multiplying them by 5⁄4 and into Fahrenheit by multiplying them by 9⁄4 and adding 32.

[91]These prayers presumably refer to the three prayers of the Rosary: the Paternoster (Lord's Prayer), the Ave María, and the Gloria Patri, which all Catholics would be expected to know.

tending and watching them to the utmost, and this is the exterior that strikes the eye! But I admit to Your Highness that I look at it differently, and in a moral sense I see only a pure and tidy cattle yard in which the thrifty master tends them like bulls. They derive not the slightest benefit from their work; they perceive that they are condemned to a monotonous exercise for their whole lives; their hearts are consumed by melancholy, and they flee, leaving their wives and children, but they are returned and so must patiently endure their fate. And is this still praiseworthy? This is called making people happy? Is mankind astonished by this charity? My God! What false conclusions, when man's rights are flouted, his advantages are forgotten, the brawn and brain of his kin are converted to cattle, his spirit is killed forever, and, notwithstanding all of his innate upsurges of spiritual strength, he can never raise himself, and against his will he must crawl![92]

Of our [native] Americans, only the kayuras are burdened by labor, but I composed a resolution on their behalf and presented it to the company. However, all of our Americans are utilized quite freely; their needs are satisfied by nature itself, and they go hunting of their own free will[93] in order to sell furs to the company and to please their fancy. *Man everywhere is like an ape;* he wants everything that others have. Our Americans have been drenched with a kind of luxury; they love sackcloth, silk shawls, and the like, and this has caused them to be industrious. Each of them seeks every means of getting furs, and when he has bartered something for foppery that he needs, then he is rapturously happy and consequently as gratified as we are in our enlightened state after we have attained an object. He immediately dresses himself like a Russian in order to feel the superiority of the nation that encroached upon him; he imitates because it raises his spirits. He is proud of his success, and at the same time his character converges with ours. Now, I ask, which of the two American peoples [Russian American natives or Spanish Californian natives] is happier? Give our Americans good examples and then another question will arise: what prospects lie ahead for both peoples?

3. Their buildings catch the eye, but the time and labor expended on them are immense. Our buildings are hewn from wood, using perhaps no more than one hundred men annually, and they are under armed guard besides. I have issued special orders about buildings that I have explained in detail in my reports, and after they have been executed I will again be confident that our establishments will soon be equal [to those of Alta California], and after horses have been reared and a sawmill built they will be able to surpass California's within five years.

---

[92]The missionary zeal of the Franciscan friars and their forcible recruitment and nominal conversion of the Indians greatly affected Rezanov and other Russian visitors, for the Russian Orthodox Church was not especially evangelical, and its relatively few missionaries in Siberia and Russian America did try to proselytize in the vernacular and to gain voluntary converts. Not that Russian America's natives were not enserfed—indeed they were, but strictly for economic, not religious, reasons.

[93]Rezanov is dissembling here; Aleuts and Konyagas, for example, were more or less enserfed by the Russians.

4. The unparalleled cleanliness. In this we have to give them their due, but bear in mind [that there are] 1,200 people living placidly in one spot, any one of whom can always move away, and the climate [is better], too. Our small population, however, does not excuse us, and with good order this part of our governance will soon be secured.

5. The care of humanity. Leaving aside the sham system of well-being of the neophytes, the good conduct and self-interest of the missionaries are conducive to this, for by losing neophytes they lose workers and hence their income. With us, by contrast, the sole object is the [sea] otter, and *humanity has been forgotten*. But such is the position of the company itself, such is the consideration of the government, and such are its limited means. The Russian newcomers consist of unruly and corrupt men, and they exhaust themselves during their four [contracted] years on half shares. The company's overseers are also shareholders. Their *object* is *furs and not Americans,* whom they will never see again after the expiration of their terms and *whom they have not been responsible for* at all. If fate had not provided the ranks of the company's officials in this territory with Aleksandr Andreyevich Baranov, who has unselfishly and resolutely restrained the promyshlenniks, then it cannot be imagined what monstrosities would have occurred long ago. They would have smashed the heads of the Americans, who would then have avenged themselves. But now even worse monstrosities can be expected in the future, when there are officials who, being totally out of control, feather their nests even more and worse, but also only for the present because they are unable to consider the future, and there will be the same victims—and Russia will lose the territory. In California the governor and the commandants of the presidios travel their districts and send annual reports to the viceroy; but it fell to my lot to be the first [inspector] since the very beginning of our [colonial] administration to be sent, and until my arrival in America neither the government nor the company itself had the slightest information. But eliminate shares, establish personnel, and organize the company as a political body in all of its parts, [and] then here, too, as with other independent companies, everything will fall into its proper place; *humanity will always be the first, not the last, concern of administration;* the profits of the stockholders will increase; laws will preserve the safety of each and every one [of them]; the territory will have the necessary protection, commerce will strengthen, and the reformers of an entrenched and ruinous system, apart from priceless pleasure for their soul, will earn the satisfaction of the reputation of a friend of mankind for posterity.

6. The clothes of the neophytes consist of one serape and a woolen loincloth, which they themselves weave, but they have innumerable sheep; other livestock are similarly abundant, but I did not see boots on [a single] one of the neophytes. By contrast, our Americans are [fully] clothed and shod; some have heavy,

coarse cloth and duffel capotes and frock coats, wide trousers and boots made of the throat skin of sea lions, dabba shirts, and undergarments, and the poor have marmot-skin and bird-skin (instead of heavy, coarse cloth) parkas, which the company, notwithstanding all of the shortages, supplies them on credit in exchange for hunting, and in this case our natives are better clothed, despite the absence of cattle rearing.

7. Food. It is true that it is good, but while there might be surpluses from cattle rearing in our America, I would never allow it. A heavy annual toll is taken of their neophytes, except the epidemically sick, for example, those with measles, of whom I will speak below, and the reason for this is their aversion to the food, which is not as tasty as formerly, but they are used to it and are raised on it. The governor frankly admitted to me that in Old California all of the Indians perished and the missions were deserted and that this must be expected here, too, for according to his observations, since the establishment of missions in New California two-fifths of the Indians have died, besides the more than 3,000 who have died from measles alone, as I saw in his reports. Measles is a kind of fever whereby a person f[eels] pangs for four or five [days] and at that time a rash appears and then passes, but two weeks later severe bloody diarrhea occurs, often entailing death. This disease was unknown to them and was brought from Mexico. But Old California was deserted even without measles. Thus, I think that our Americans should always be maintained on *yukola*,[94] [fresh] fish, whale blubber, fat, *burduk*,[95] berries, and the like, not departing at all from their traditional food, not discarding their putrid drinks, and not raising their children differently. But I will say some more about the means of subsistence of the Californian [natives] and ours. They have numerous feral bulls, which roam in herds, and so, by [simply] throwing a lasso, food is readied; but we have yukola, whale blubber, berries, *sarana*,[96] and others that have to be *stocked with much labor;* consequently, at present we are condemned to much labor and care in the feeding of our Americans, and I would like to see the economy of the Californian missionaries in our north! I succeeded in winning the friendship of their Father Martín de Landaeta, who in 1791 was sent to Nootka Sound and wintered there. Despite all of the means provided by the government (ships were sent with grain, provisions, cattle, and seeds, and they were even supplied with luxuries), he did not succeed at all but said—speaking to me in exactly these words—this is a climate for devils to inhabit, not people, and upon their return the Spaniards explained the impossibility such that the court forever abandoned the attempt on the north.

---

[94] *Yukola* was dried fish, a staple ("Kamchatkan bread") of Russian America and the Russian Far East.

[95] *Burduk*, or *burda*, was a Siberian thick soup of rye flour and water, first soured and then boiled.

[96] *Sarana*, or "tsar's curls," was the dried and pounded bulb of the Kamchatka lily (*Fritillaria camschatcensis*).

In fact, for a migrant from the torrid zone to endure it is impossible, but to Russians born in the north—besides the fact that the overcoming of every difficulty is innate to them—the climate of our America *seems* very *mild*. Only the downpours of autumn are monotonous and intolerable, and it rains until January, but the cold is moderate. This winter [of 1805–1806 at New Archangel] until 7 January it was always 2, 4, and 6 degrees [R.], snow falling one day and melting the next, but on the 7th the first frost struck and for a week it [the thermometer] stood at only 12 to 16½ degrees, and snow fell and lay [on the ground] until May, but until 25 February, when I put to sea, there were 4, 5, and 6 degrees of frost in the mornings but less by noon, and often the thermometer was not only at the freezing point but sometimes up to three degrees above [zero]. Notwithstanding the moderate cold, owing to the high, snow-covered mountains, at the end of February 5 or 6 times every day it was gusty with whirlwinds of strong hail, which often interrupted work. However, right from January the season was fine, and both spring and summer were accompanied by uninterrupted fair weather.

These, gracious sire, are all of my observations and comparisons regarding California [that I made] for Your Highness during my six weeks' sojourn in that land. Forgive me if I have anywhere bared my feelings perhaps too much—ascribe it to a weakness common to man. Having seen things here as they should be seen, I cannot speak indifferently after they cost me such labor and the sacrifice of my strength, and I can assure Your Highness that scarcely a man is to be found who would brave them in the future. I have gone considerably into the customs of both the native inhabitants and their foreign guests. Being accustomed to both, I have proposed a reorganization of the territory, indicated the ways of eradicating the evils that are shameful in our time, spoken of trade, the economy, industry, the avoidance of shortages, and the establishment of order, laws, obligations, and humane charity, and explained what fruits are in store for the remote regions of Siberia from the facilities here, and I have not omitted a single subject; in short, I have outlined a whole approach to the political organization of our commercial institution [the Russian-American Company], I have fought prejudices here, I have persuaded with the obvious, and I have written reams of paper here, albeit not in a fine, moving style but perhaps from the soul and heart, and I have sent just as many to the Board of Directors, and does not all of this deserve respect? If my discussion of matters in the present and in the future from their bad and good sides does not merit their attention, then I will be bitter about the distrust of my work, and I will feel even more painfully that the unhappy consequences will compel them to agree when irretrievable time has been lost. Please be assured, gracious sire, that if the inhabitants of Kamchatka and [Russian] America are not to be condemned to annihilation, which has already happened to the deserted Kurilian, Aleutian, and Fox [Fox Aleutian] chains of islands, where the inhabitants are memorialized now by human traces only, then there are no other means than trade to extricate these semipopulated regions from their disastrous circumstances, and in that case access to California's [trade] is so important that I can safely congratulate you on it already. Will this happy beginning have a happy ending? It should be added that the governor of California during my representations designated three ports for us, namely, Monterey, San Diego, and San Francisco. However, from these new labors of mine I personally derived this benefit for myself—that as in Kamchatka, here, too, I saved my countrymen from starvation, ensured them a surplus for a year, opened new prospects for the fatherland, and justified myself in my conclusions. I am overjoyed, gracious sire, when my conscience allows me to say that I was unsparing of myself for the good of my neighbor and did everything that my powers and meager means afforded.

Forgive me, gracious sire, that in my letter I have conflated many different matters as I encountered them and that I have so inopportunely, perhaps, included my personal adventures. I truthfully do not have time to put in the necessary order each of the special letters that I wrote to Your Highness, and so I am candidly describing the chain of all events in the form in which they occurred. If fate is pleased to end my romance, which was motivated not at all by ardent passion—which has no place in [a man of] my years—but by completely different considerations, and perhaps as much by remnants of feelings that once made my life happy, I have made—out of consideration for circumstances, distance, and my duty—a very careful and conditional beginning, and in that case I can render a new service to the fatherland by personally inspecting Havana, Veracruz, and Mexico and by traveling throughout the interior of America—and because of the suspicion of the Spanish government hardly anyone but I can succeed—and I will give you my thorough observations on all of their trade, surpluses, shortages, etc.; I can derive new benefits for my countrymen and, having become acquainted with the viceroy, attempt the ports of the eastern coast of America with our ships. Perhaps during the reign of our solicitous sovereign some Russians will open trade from St. Petersburg in our natural surpluses and industrial products, which foreigners can use to our account; at the same time I can cast my eyes on the trade of the American states, visiting them and securing trade in our company's interest. Here, gracious sire, is a new sacrifice for you of a man who has devoted himself totally to the good of his fellow men and wants nothing more in life than that his strength might match his zeal.

But I am equally obliged to report to Your Highness on our [return] voyage from California, as well as on all local [Sitkan] circumstances.

We left the port of San Francisco on 10 May at 6 o'clock in the evening. The governor and all of our friends came to the fort to see us off. We saluted with 7 guns and they answered with 9. At our departure we set out by longitude, and having traversed 10 degrees, we found a favorable wind, with which we reached Kaigan[i] (Prince of Wales) Island.[97] Here we were becalmed for ten days. During this time many of our shrouds broke, and after cutting up a cable [to make repairs], we barely had time to fasten them with stoppers before a high wind arose that could, of course, have carried away all of our masts. We arrived in Norfolk Sound on 8 June and saluted the fort with our guns, but the delayed response, besides our not meeting any kayaks or seeing anybody, worried us, for it was fresh in our minds that we had left nearly all of them on their deathbeds. Having 10 good cannons, we had already begun to ready ourselves for hostilities when toward nightfall some kayaks arrived, and we, having been reassured of the well-being of New Archangel, were towed during the night into the harbor and at 9 o'clock in the morning we dropped anchor at the port. . . .[98]

[97]Actually, Dall Island. Kaigani was a popular rendezvous of American "coasters" (fur trading vessels on the Northwest Coast).

[98]The rest of Rezanov's report, which concerns what he calls "local events" at New Archangel, is omitted here.

DOCUMENT 2

Excerpt from Semyon Yakovlevich Unkovsky, "Voyage around the World," 1815

Editor's Introduction

Little seems to be known about Semyon Yakovlevich Unkovsky (1788–1882). A native of Novgorod Province, he graduated from St. Petersburg's Naval Academy as a cadet in 1803 and in the same year was assigned to the English navy as a volunteer. During the Napoleonic Wars he took part in several battles and was captured by the French but released after the Treaty of Tilsit (1807).

In 1813 Unkovsky sailed on the Russian-American Company's French-built, 337-ton merchantman *Suvorov* (at the invitation of its commander and his long-time colleague, Lieutenant Mikhail Lazarev) to New Archangel via Portsmouth, Rio de Janeiro, the Cape of Good Hope, and Port Jackson (Sydney). The voyage had two official aims: to deliver supplies to Russian America and to open trade with Alta California. The supplies were unloaded at New Archangel in the fall of 1814, and the next summer a cargo of mostly peltry was embarked at the colonial capital for delivery to St. Petersburg. However, the *Suvorov* left New Archangel prematurely and stealthily (and even under fire from the fortress) after Lazarev had disagreed strongly with Governor Baranov's seizure of the American brig *Pedler* for smuggling, with Baranov threatening to remove Lazarev from command.[1] Lazarev had to stop at San Francisco to augment his stock of water and provisions, as well as to try to open trade on behalf of the Russian-American Company. He failed to open trade but did exchange goods for some wheat and beef from the missions—the customary, if illicit, transaction that the Russians

---

[1] These are the "unforeseen circumstances" mentioned in N. A. Ivashintsov's guarded account of the voyage (Ivashintsov, *Russian Round-the-World Voyages*, 22).

would employ until Spain's prohibition of foreign commerce by its colonies was voided by Mexican independence in 1821.

The *Suvorov* returned to Kronstadt with a cargo worth two million rubles (mostly furs) via San Francisco, Callao, Cape Horn, and Portsmouth again, whereupon Lieutenant Unkovsky resigned his commission, married, and retired to his Kaluga estate. One of his sons, Ivan Semyonovich (1822–86), commanded the frigate *Pallada* (*Pallas*) in Admiral Putyatin's squadron in 1852–54 in the Far East and later became an admiral himself.[2]

Lieutenant S. Ya. Unkovsky, "A Voyage around the World in the Ship *Suvorov*, 1813–16,"[3] New Archangel–San Francisco, 25 July–18 August 1815

Thus did we leave Sitka without money, and our supply of provisions was very slight, so we had to stop in [Alta] California at the port of San Francisco to stock provisions there for the entire voyage to Russia and to sail from there to Lima on the Peruvian coast. We had many articles left on the ship that had been sent from Russia by the R[ussian]-A[merican] Company for trade with the surrounding inhabitants of the coast of America adjoining our colonies and for Kamchatka and Okhotsk, where we had not stopped. Consequently, some of these goods were designated by Mr. Baranov for sale and barter in Peru, where, in accordance with a recent decision, we had to stop on our return voyage to Russia, and some of these goods we had to leave at Bodega or Fort Ross, lying at 38° North latitude, where our hunting of [sea] otters was permitted by agreement with the Spanish government. Adhering literally to the instructions of Mr. Baranov, we decided to sell some of these goods at the port of San Francisco.

Our voyage was directed southward, so that we did not leave the coast of northwestern America in order to visit the port of Bodega without wasting time and to reach the port of San Francisco as soon as possible.

August

5th. At 10 o'clock in the morning in gloomy weather we saw Cape Mendocino in 40° 19' W [*sic:* N] latitude to the north-east-north of us about 10 miles distant.

---

[2] See Grinëv, *Kto yest kto*, 547. Also see Ivashintsov, *Russian Round-the-World Voyages*, 20–23.

[3] S. Ya. Unkovsky, *Zapiski moryaka*, 129–36. This account was originally scheduled for publication in 1934, but the closure of the publishing house by the Soviet authorities prevented its appearance. It was finally published—with some abridgements and different paragraphing—as part of "Iz 'istinnykh zapisok moyey zhizni' Leitenanta S. Ya. Unkovskovo" [From "The True Memoirs of My Life'" of Lieutenant S. Ya. Unkovsky] in Samarov, *M. P. Lazarev*, doc. 12, pp. 11–60. For another (although incomplete) account of the *Suvorov*'s voyage, see Fyodorov, "Puteshestvie Alekseya Rossiiskavo."

6th. At midnight I had just replaced M. P. [Lazarev][4] on the watch, and a half hour had not passed when a sailor shouted from the forecastle, "Breakers ahead." We were running with a northeasterly wind about 6 knots per hour with standing rigging under the topsail and studding sails on the port side. At the same instant I yelled "To port" in order to direct our ship away from the breakers and toward the sea. With 15 men on the watch I marveled at the speed of work—they lowered the studding sails. Within ¼ of an hour the entire command was already above, and we lay close-hauled to starboard. From time to time the moon appeared from behind thick clouds, the waves became noticeably higher, and the wind changed from a topgallant to a topsail wind; they lowered the topgallant sail and dropped a large spare lead—the depth was 20 sazhens. After an hour the bow men again shouted, "Breakers." We turned the ship into the wind and soon realized that we were among the underwater rocks at the spit of Barro de Arena, which juts rather far out to sea. Evidently the underwater rocks are not marked on Vancouver's map and protrude much farther seaward. We found ourselves in a very frightful

------

[4]Mikhail Petrovich Lazarev (1788–1851) was the second of three seafaring sons of a landowner of Vladimir Province. After the death of both parents, the three boys were enrolled in St. Petersburg's Naval Academy at the beginning of 1800. Upon graduation in 1803 Mikhail went to England to apprentice for five years in the Royal Navy, reaching the rank of midshipman in 1805. He returned to Russia in 1808 and served with distinction in the naval campaigns of the Napoleonic Wars, being promoted to lieutenant in 1811.

In 1813 Lazarev was given command of the Russian-American Company vessel *Suvorov* to take supplies to New Archangel, where in the summer of 1815 he sided with John Jacob Astor's agent, Wilson Price Hunt, whose ship, *Pedler* (Captain Samuel Northrup), which had been given sanctuary by Governor Baranov until the end of the War of 1812, was seized by Baranov for allegedly trading firearms to the Tlingits. The angry governor threatened to remove Lazarev from the command of the *Suvorov*, and the captain made a premature and unauthorized departure under cannon fire from the fort (the ship's physician and supercargo, respectively, Dr. Georg Schäffer and German Molvo, who had sided with Baranov, were left behind). Upon his return to Russia Lazarev defended himself successfully against a denunciation from Baranov.

In 1819–21 Lazarev commanded the sloop *Mirny*, which with the flagship *Vostok* (Captain [of the second rank] Faddey Bellingshausen) undertook the first Russian expedition to Antarctica; at the same time, the venture's second division, comprising the two sloops *Otkrytie* (Captain-Lieutenant Mikhail Vasilyev) and *Blagonamerenny* (Captain-Lieutenant Gleb Shishmaryov), probed the North Pacific for a northwest passage. Bellingshausen and Lazarev circumnavigated the unknown continent and established the extent of the ice pack. Upon their return Lazarev was promoted to captain of the second rank.

In 1822–25 he commanded the frigate *Kreiser* (and his brother, Captain-Lieutenant Aleksey, the sloop *Ladoga*) on a round-the-world voyage to New Archangel, where the two warships relieved the *Apollon* in cruising Russia's North Pacific shores to enforce the 1821 ban on foreign shipping. The frigate's company included Lieutenant Ivan Kupreyanov, future governor of Russian America, and Midshipman Dmitry Zavalishin, future Decembrist and Siberian exile.

Upon his return to Russia, Lazarev was promoted to captain of the first rank in 1825, and in 1826 he was placed in command of a new ship-of-the-line, the *Azov*, in which he distinguished himself in naval campaigns against the Turkish-Egyptian axis. He was promoted to rear admiral in 1827 and to vice admiral in 1833, when he also became commander of the Black Sea Fleet. Lazarev worked long and hard to strengthen Russia's naval presence on its southern frontier, and in 1843 he was promoted to admiral. He died in Vienna, where he had gone for medical treatment, and was buried in Sevastopol, his fleet's home base. See Grinëv, *Kto yest kto,* 289–90; and Pierce, *Russian America,* 298–300.

situation, the night grew darker and darker, and the moon was completely hidden behind clouds. The sounding continued and indicated between 25 and 26 sazhens, we turned every half hour, and all the while the crew worked with amazing speed. The waves pounded. At 4 o'clock in the morning the ship was turned not into but with the wind on the starboard, and we expected that at any minute it would strike an underwater rock. About 5 o'clock, before sunrise, there was a dreadful fog, we lay close-hauled to starboard, the depth increased to 50 sazhens, and finally the lead did not register. With this our terror passed; Divine Providence had clearly saved us from destruction. If the ship had been wrecked and if it had been fated that we would be saved from death, then, of course, none of the three of us[5] would have returned to the fatherland—[or] so we had decided.[6]

7th. At dawn with the appearance of the sun the sky became clear of fog and the wind was still northwesterly but had strengthened to a strong reefed topsail wind. At 3:45 we approached Fort Ross and hove to. Kayaks had been sent from the port of Bodega, and we transferred our dispatches from Mr. Baranov, and then we immediately raised the grapnel[7] and went to the port of San Francisco. During this voyage we saw many whales swimming around the ship; how glorious it would be to go hunting on a whaler!

9th. At 4 o'clock we saw the Farallon Islands, and at 5 o'clock the flag at the presidio of San Francisco came in sight. We prepared the anchor and unwound 40 sazhens of cable. At 8 o'clock in the evening with the illumination of the passage itself by porters ashore and by the fort's lanterns we entered the port and dropped anchor at a depth of 8 sazhens. We took the bearings of the fort at 80° West [latitude] and of the barracks, where the commandant lived, at 35° South [longitude]; the distance to the fort was ¾ of a versta.

Here stood the R[ussian]-A[merican] Company's schooner *Chirikov*, Cap[tain] Benzeman[8] (a Prussian subject).

10th. The next morning we saluted the fort with 7 guns and received a like reply. I went ashore and received permission to water and to prepare the necessary provisions for the command. It was strictly forbidden, of course, to speak of our unilateral departure from Sitka. Otherwise, the Russian colony could communicate

---

[5]Presumably the three ranking officers: Lieutenants Lazarev, Unkovsky, and Platon Stepanovich Nakhimov (a brother of Pavel S. Nakhimov, a hero of the Crimean War and one of Russia's most celebrated admirals).

[6]The meaning of this last phrase is uncertain; perhaps Unkovsky means that in that case they would be too ashamed to return home.

[7]A grapnel (*drek*) is a small boat anchor weighing fifteen to twenty pounds.

[8]Khristofor Martynovich Benzeman (Christof Benzemann) (1774–1842), a shipbuilder and navigator from Danzig, joined the RAC in 1807 after arriving on the Northwest Coast on the American ship *Peacock*. He became one of the company's best skippers, despite losing one or both of his legs when one of his ship's cannons burst during firing. In 1824 he became a Russian subject, as well as a convert to Russian Orthodoxy. See Grinëv, *Kto yest kto*, 58–59; and Pierce, *Russian America*, 50–51.

with the commandant and we could be detained. Nowadays [after 1850] with the construction of the telegraph it is not always possible to act so [furtively].

A Sojourn at the Port of San Francisco

The locale of the port of San Francisco can be called unique in the world. The climate is fine and the soil is fertile, although still little cultivated. This territory gives promise of a large population in the future; at the present time under Spanish ownership this beautiful land is in almost a semiwild state. The population of the Spanish colony is negligible, with one mission [Mission San Francisco de Asís] of two Franciscan friars; this small colony is completely under the influence of the savage Californians [Indians]. One has to marvel at how the Spaniards have in the course of 300 years from Chile to California—along the entire western coast—managed to populate so many colonies, some of which have already become populous and wealthy cities with magnificent missions, and how the Catholic faith has become firmly entrenched in pagan soil. Such a small country as Spain, with a population of some 7,000,000 inhabitants, has seized nearly all of the southern coast of America and in the west has ascended as far as 40° Nor[th] latitude, after having taken the best part of the Philippine Islands and many other parts of the Pacific Ocean. Thus one can judge the might of Spain as a naval power during the sway of Carlos V. But there is an end to everything, and this formerly powerful state began to decline from year to year, and its colonies in all parts of the world that were so rich came close to defection on account of the complete collapse of its naval power. New, fearsome possessors of the seas from the Saxon tribes* have destroyed the naval power of Spain and other states and now control all of the seas, and with their influence and commerce they have come to be dreaded by the coastal settlements of other countries. England's turn has come, but it, too, will decline as the sea power of the New World—[the United States of] America—surpasses it in might. Another one hundred years and perhaps the same thing that is now happening to Spain will happen to England.[9]

Our sojourn at the port of San Francisco was most pleasant. The hospitality of the commandant, Don León [sic: Luis] Argüello, and the two monks, Father Ramón[10]

---

*I have in mind the English—the descendants of the Germanic Saxon tribe who migrated in the middle of the 5th century [B.C.] from the regions of the Elbe and Weser Rivers and the Jutland Peninsula to Britannia.

---

[9]The twentieth century would confirm Unkovsky's prescience.

[10]José Ramón Abella (1764–1842), a peninsular, arrived in Alta California with seven other priests in 1798. His first posting was Mission San Francisco, where he served with distinction until 1819. Following Mexico's attainment of independence from Spain in 1821, Abella, like many of his Franciscan brothers, declined to swear an oath of allegiance to the republic's 1824 constitution. At his death he had served longer than any other missionary in the province. See Geiger, *Franciscan Missionaries*, 3–6.

and Father Juan,[11] afforded us much and varied pleasure. For visiting the vicinity some excellent riding horses of the Andalusian breed with escorts were offered, and during the time that we were freed from our work we did not fail to take advantage of this offer. We replenished our provisions with an excellent supply, buying it all with some insignificant Russian articles that we gave in exchange, such as coarse, colored cotton fabric, sailcloth, samovars, and axes, which went at prices double their cost. We bought some steers of 18 to 20 puds each for no more than two Spanish talers[12] [piasters] apiece, and we prepared an excellent supply of salted beef; the wheat, which we likewise bought from the monks, was very cheap.

The company brig *Chirikov* raised anchor the day after our arrival and sailed back to Sitka with a supply of wheat[13] and salt.

On the 12th we rode to dine with the friars at their mission 9 verstas from the port. The road went through woods on dry ground crossed here and there by small streams, and, galloping on the beautiful Andalusian horses, we made the journey quickly. Fathers Ramón and Juan met us with customary courtesy. First of all, they showed us their small church, which was kept fairly tidily but was evidently not rich, and then we ate a filling dinner, for which they gave us a very ordinary wine made from the native vineyards, tasting like Spanish wine. . . . After dinner they took us to see their supply of wheat, excellent in quality and stored in the loft of their rather spacious residence. We saw their fields, cultivated by oxen with a very simple implement consisting of two plowshares of wood and harrowed by meek native Mexicans [Californian Indians], half naked, quite dark, and long haired. This race of people is very weak, and syphilis is strongly developed among them. The dwellings of these savages consist of [wattle] huts of interlaced brushwood, similar to the huts of our drivers of timber rafts. After examining the fields and vineyards, we were taken by the friars to see the barracks of the new converts to Christianity. These quarters were built of earth [adobe] near the church, about 25 sazhens long and up to 3 arshins high. Light was admitted upstairs by skylights. Each family had a compartment, consisting of a plank bed covered with matting made by the new converts themselves. We could not understand how these friars were able to explain the Christian religion to their neophytes when they hardly understood Spanish and the Catholic service is performed in Latin. But it is evident that it is all done for one purpose, and

---

[11]Juan Sáinz de Lucio (1771–18??), a peninsular, was assigned to Mission San Francisco upon his arrival in the province in 1806. His health failing, he departed a decade later. See Geiger, *Franciscan Missionaries,* 212.

[12]"Talers," or "thalers," which devolved into "dollars," were large silver coins issued by various German states from the 1500s.

[13]The *Chirikov* obtained 1,245 fanegas (2,041 bushels) of wheat, plus 432 fanegas (708½ bushels) more from Fort Ross (ARGO, raz. 99, op. 1, d. 18, fol. 33).

mainly to have free workers for their small colony because the friars themselves told us that the Californians are very weak and that very few of them are able to live 5 years in such a disciplined state as that established by the Franciscan friars. The savage Californians never come voluntarily; mounted Spanish soldiers catch them with lassos and bring them to the missionaries, and the latter give the neophytes—already somewhat used to the established order and to labor—to their brethren.

Passing through the barracks, we saw only the sad faces of these pitiful savages, emaciated in the extreme, and several of them were sick and lying on their beds. One of them seemed close to death. Father Ramón approached him, knelt, covered him with his cassock, and began to hear his confession, but the friar himself was too sluggish from the local wine at dinner; meanwhile, he wanted to give the appearance of solicitude and compassion for the dying man. [He] began to hear his confession: "My good son, tell me everything that troubles your conscience, I have come to forgive thy sins and to counsel thee in passing to the other and better world." Thus, after having stayed on his knees several minutes and not having waited for any answer from the dying man, who was groaning loudly, he began to talk and to ask to whom he was leaving his belongings—Father Juan or Father Ramón; the friar uttered the former word [name] softly but the latter much more loudly and then started to repeat incessantly, "Father Juan or Father Ramón?" We were unable to hear what the dying man finally answered, but Father R[amó]n was convinced that the sick man had promised his belongings to him. All this time Father Juan kept silent and, being quite sober, seemed embarrassed by the suasive behavior of his colleague. After having thanked the good friars for the fare and settled the accounts for the purchased wheat, we returned by the same road to our ship.

15th. M. P. [Lazarev] and I set out to see the locale of the magnificent bay of San Francisco; in a longboat[14] under sail we took our course toward the island of St. Ángel. After tacking in all directions through the bay and taking regular soundings of the depth, we finally landed on the eastern side of the island of St. Ángel and settled ourselves there on the beach to dine. The day was clear with a very moderate west-south-west wind. While the rowers saw to the erection of a tent and to [the preparation of] dinner, the two of us walked to the summit of the island in order to view all of the bay from there, even though we were somewhat acquainted with its surrounding shore. Not expecting any encounter

---

[14]A longboat, or launch (Russ., *barkaz*), was the largest boat carried aboard a fully rigged ship. Both a rowing and a sailing vessel, it had a full bow and high sides, up to twenty oars, and two masts and sails for short cruises. A ship's gun could be mounted in its bows. It was used primarily for lightering (wooding, watering, provisioning) but also served as a ship's principal lifeboat.

on the island, which is separated from the mainland by a distance of ¾ of a versta and has a circumference of about 2½ verstas, we did not take our double-barreled muskets with us but only paper, pencils, and a telescope. By a small path apparently made by human feet and running between small copses and shrubs, we clambered to the very summit of the island. From it we were presented with a picture of the splendid expanse of the bay, bordered by picturesque shores, and we sat for more than half an hour on a boulder, perfunctorily sketching everything that came into view on the horizon. Then we crossed the volcanic plain, about 200 sazhens long, of the island's summit and, gazing at this marvelous natural scene to our hearts' content, we chose one of the draws for the descent to our landing. I picked up a goat horn, saying, "This is evidently a watering place for wild goats." At that moment we heard the loud rustle of a kit (*kumovnik*)[15] in the thick shrubbery nearby. We stopped to see what it could be. The crackling began to resound more loudly, and suddenly an infuriated bear of a blue-gray color burst forth, running straight at us on his hind legs. We were 10 sazhens away, and we threw ourselves headlong down the hillside, shouting the danger to our sailors. At this point we were not yet running but rolling helter-skelter. Lazarev's patent-leather hat fell off his head, and the bear snatched it in his front paws and stopped, looking at the hat in amazement. At the same instant shot followed shot below the hill, and the sailors ran noisily to meet us. The bear, after immediately abandoning the hat, disappeared into the bushes. All of our crew of 8 rowers, including the brave young Komov, who wielded a dagger very well and was a very strong and adroit fellow, set off with us in search of our enemy, who had so suddenly and so boldly attacked the unarmed two of us. But after searching for more than an hour, we did not discover a trace of our foe, and we returned to our dinner.

At 5 o'clock in the afternoon, moving under sail along the shore of the mainland, we again saw a bear on a hillock, calmly munching herbs—probably the same one that had charged us on the summit of the island. This time we, for our part, prepared ourselves to give him a scare. Four loaded falconets and 8 muskets were ready to loose a volley at the word "fire." As soon as a loud salvo followed, our bear, finding himself 400 sazhens from us, stood on his hind legs and looked with surprise to one side and then the other and finally lowered himself and galloped headlong uphill. At this point we fired another volley from the longboat and he again stopped, looked back, and then started to run without glancing backward, and we soon lost sight of him.

At 9 o'clock in the evening we returned safely to the ship.

---

[15]On the assumption that *kumovnik* is a diminutive form of *kuma*, a conventional epithet for a fox in Russian folklore.

16th. The next day, when we recounted our encounter with the bear, the commandant said that such a lucky event occurred very rarely and that usually an unarmed man who meets a Californian bear falls certain victim to it. They watch a man in the bush and attack suddenly. We ascribed our rescue to Divine Providence through the hat falling from the head of M. P. [Lazarev] and halting the surprised bear, giving us time to roll down the hill somewhat farther away from it. If we had found ourselves on the hill a little above the bear, then one of us, of course, would have been torn to pieces. This event has long remained in my memory, and I will never forget that I owe my rescue solely to the will of God.

18th. Bidding the inhabitants of the port of San Francisco farewell, we raised anchor and went to sea, taking a course to the southwestern coast of America.[16]
. . .

---

[16]Unkovsky's description of the rest of the *Suvorov's* homeward voyage via Callao, Peru, Cape Horn, and Portsmouth, England is omitted here.

Otto von Kotzebue, "Voyage from Unalaska to California," 1816

EDITOR'S INTRODUCTION

Otto von Kotzebue (Otto Yevstafyevich fon Kotsebu) (1788–1846) was born in Reval (Tallinn) into an affluent noble family of Baltic Germans as the second son of the noted dramatist August von Kotzebue (and a distant relative of the celebrated mariner Ivan Kruzenshtern, who commanded Russia's first round-the-world voyage, in 1803–1806). Otto entered St. Petersburg's Naval Academy at the age of seven, and as a young teenager he accompanied the first Russian circumnavigation, apprenticing on the *Nadezhda* under Captain Kruzenshtern and Lieutenant Ratmanov. From 1806 until 1815 he commanded small ships in the Baltic and White Seas.

Upon Kruzenshtern's recommendation, Kotzebue was appointed commander of an expedition financed by the wealthy foreign minister, Count Nikolay P. Rumyantsev, with the purpose of finding an Arctic seaway from the Pacific to the Atlantic northeast from Bering Strait. He sailed on the 180-ton brig *Ryurik (Rurik),* named after the putative Norse founder of the first Russian state and built at Abö (Turku), from the naval base of Kronshtadt on Kotlin Island at the head of the Gulf of Finland in the midsummer of 1815 with thirty-four men, including the poet and naturalist Ludovik-Charles-Adelaid von Chamisso (Adalbert Loginovich de Shamisso), the artist Louis, or Ludwig, Choris (Login Andreyevich Khoris), and the naturalist Johann Friedrich Gustav von Eschscholtz (Ivan Ivanovich fon Eshsholts). After sailing around Cape Horn to what the Russians logically termed the Eastern (Pacific) Ocean, the expedition discovered several islands in the South Pacific, sojourned at Petropavlovsk in Kamchatka, and probed Bering Strait in the summer of 1816 (and reached and named Kotzebue Sound in the Chukchi Sea).

At summer's end Kotzebue sailed south to replenish his provisions in Alta California prior to a winter cruise in the equatorial Pacific, including Hawaii. He returned north to seek once more an Arctic waterway in the summer of 1817, but again unsuccessfully, and sailed home via Manila and the Cape of Good Hope.

LIEUTENANT OTTO VON KOTZEBUE, "A VOYAGE FROM UNALASKA TO CALIFORNIA,"[1] UNALASKA–SAN FRANCISCO, 14 SEPTEMBER–1 NOVEMBER 1816

14 September [1816]. Work on the ship *Ryurik* was finished, water was stocked, and all of us were in a state of readiness to leave Unalaska the next day; only Doctor Eshgolts,[2] who had gone botanizing yesterday evening, had not yet returned. At my request Mr. Kryukov[3] sent a large number of men with lanterns to the mountains, and fortunately they found him before sunrise. Darkness had overtaken him during his excursion, and he had not dared to descend the steep cliffs and had decided to calmly await daybreak at the summit, where he was found. It is impossible to describe the joy that we felt upon the happy return of our amiable and skilled doctor. As soon as he boarded the ship, we raised anchor, and a fair wind took us out of the harbor. During our stay on Unalaska the weather was fairly warm, and the approach of winter was proclaimed only by the snow covering the peaks of the mountains. At Unalaska I was assured that the safest route to the ocean was the passage [Unimak Pass] between the islands of Akun and Unimak; therefore, I directed our course thither.

At daybreak on 15 September we rounded the end of Akun Island and found ourselves in the strait, which seemed open and safe. There was a clear view of Unimak Island ahead of us, and the majestically high and cone-shaped peaks in the middle of the island were free of clouds; according to our reckoning they were 5,525 English feet in height. A contrary wind held us here; the fine weather, allowing us to make observations of the latitude and longitude, also afforded us

---

[1] [Kotzebue], *Puteshestvie v Yuzhny okean*, 3–15.

[2] Johann Friedrich von Eschscholtz (Ivan Ivanovich fon Eshgolts) (1793–1831) was born in Dorpat (Tartu or Yuryev). He graduated from the University of Dorpat in 1815 with a medical degree and opted to sail as ship's doctor on the *Ryurik* rather than go to the Urals as a physician. Chamisso was the expedition's official naturalist, but he and Eschscholtz agreed to share the role, with the latter concentrating on insects and sea animals. Kotzebue named a bay in Kotzebue Sound after Eschscholtz, and Chamisso named a perennial herb, the California poppy (*Eschscholtzia californica*), for his colleague. In 1823 Eschscholtz accepted Kotzebue's invitation to accompany him on his third round-the-world voyage as physician and naturalist on the warship *Predpriyatie*. During the expedition Eschscholtz described 2,400 species of animals and collected numerous specimens. Upon his return, he was in frail health, thus unable to spend much time studying and publishing the results of his findings, and he died of "neural fever" (typhus). See Eschscholtz, "Descriptiones plantarum novae Californiae" for an account of the results of his botanizing in Alta California in 1816.

[3] Ivan Vasilyevich Kryukov (ca. 1773–1823), a veteran seafarer and promyshlennik, served as manager of Unalaska Counter from 1813 to 1820. See Grinëv, *Kto yest kto*, 272; and Pierce, *Russian America*, 268–69.

the means to compile an accurate map. This strait seemed so safe and wide to me that I can recommend it to every navigator. On the 16th at 8 o'clock in the morning we found ourselves in the open sea. . . .

1 October. A strong wind from the N and NW, becoming almost a storm at times, enabled us to make a very rapid voyage from Unalaska to California. About midnight we saw Point Reyes in the moonlight, and at 4 o'clock in the afternoon we cast anchor in the port of San Francisco opposite the structure of the presidio. It seemed that our small ship threw the presidio into considerable confusion, for when we approached the fort of San Joaquín, which was built on a spit composed of high cliffs and constituting the southern entrance to the port, we saw many infantry and cavalry soldiers; at the fort itself they were busy loading cannons. The entrance to the port is so constricted that it is necessary to pass within musket shot of the fort. Inasmuch as the Russian naval ensign is unknown here, as we neared the fort they asked us through a hailer to what nation we belonged. We replied that we were Russians and their friends, and I ordered the firing of five guns, and the fort saluted with an equal number. We cast anchor, and a whole hour later nobody had concerned themselves with us; all of the soldiers had left the fort and were standing along the beach opposite our ship. Finally I remembered that [Captain George] Vancouver had not found a single boat here, and for that reason I sent Lieutenant Shishmaryov with Mr. Shamisso[4] ashore to announce my arrival to the commandant. The commandant, Don Luis Argüello,[5] a cavalry lieutenant, received my two emissaries with particular friendliness and promised to supply the *Ryurik* with fresh provisions. He immediately sent me a basket of fruit, of which I had been long deprived, so this present was very gratifying to me. As he already had orders from his government regarding us, today he sent a courier to Monterey to inform the governor of California of our arrival.

3 October. This morning I was visited by the commandant's emissary, an artillery officer of the presidio, who came with one priest from the mission [San Francisco de Asís]. The former in the name of the commandant offered every

[4]Adelbert Loginovich Shamisso (Ludovik-Charles-Adelaid de Chamisso) (1781–1838) was a poet and naturalist. He was born into a noble French family, which during the French Revolution emigrated to Berlin, where he became first a royal page and then a Prussian soldier. Proving unsuited to military life, he resigned to travel, teach, and study languages and the sciences, as well as to write. He was invited to serve as the naturalist for Kotzebue's expedition, which afforded him many opportunities for linguistic, ethnographic, geological, botanical, zoological, and climatic studies. During the voyage of the *Ryurik* his scientific endeavors were allegedly hindered by Kotzebue, and his findings were not published in full until 1836 as part of his collected works. See Grinëv, *Kto yest kto*, 597; and Pierce, *Russian America*, 83–84. Also see Mornin, "Adelbert von Chamisso"; and Chamisso, *Voyage around the World*, xi–xxiv.

[5]Luis Antonio Argüello (1784–1830) was the son of the commandant of San Francisco, José Darío Argüello, during Rezanov's visit and the brother of Doña Concepción, Rezanov's fiancée. He rose rapidly through the army's ranks and, like his father, became commandant of San Francisco (1818) and then acting governor (1822–25). See Bancroft, *California Pioneer Register*, 41–42.

possible assistance, and the priest did likewise on behalf of the mission. After having gratefully accepted such gracious offers, I expressed only the desire to obtain fresh provisions daily for all of my crew. They found my request very modest and repeated their promise to supply us with all of the province's products; in the afternoon of the same day we received two plump bulls, two goats, cabbages, pumpkins, and plenty of fruit. After a long want of everything, we now lived in abundance, and I truly rejoiced that my men were enjoying such healthful food, and they had a chance to renew their strength for the long voyage ahead of us. Although all of them appeared to enjoy complete health, some of them might nevertheless be hiding the beginnings of scurvy, for the labor endured by them in Bering Strait, the utter lack of fresh provisions, and the damp weather could really have sown the seed of this disease in them. To avert this evil as much as possible, I ordered the daily issuance of a large number of watermelons and apples (which are very good here) to the men after dinner.

The next day the mission celebrated the name day of St. Francis, and the priest invited all of us to dinner. Today after dinner, accompanied by all of my assistants, I took a walk to the presidio; the commandant, Don Luis Argüello, received us at the gates and saluted us with 8 guns, and then he conducted us to his residence. I found the presidio in the very same condition as that described by Vancouver; the garrison consists of one company of cavalry, whose head is the commandant, who has only one artillery officer under his command.

4 October. At 8 o'clock in the morning all of us proceeded ashore to the presidio in order to go with the commandant to the mission in compliance with our agreement. The horses were already saddled, and we set off on our route with 10 cavalrymen in our convoy, themselves fine and adept men who wielded carbines and lances as skillfully as our Cossacks. They have acquired such skill from constant practice, for it is well known that the army in California serves only to protect the missions against attacks from the savages; moreover, they also help the clergy to convert the savages to Christianity and to hold the converts to their new faith. We kept our journey to an hour in very fine weather, although more than half of the route went through sandy places and hills. Here and there the barren heights were adorned with only small shrubs, and not until the vicinity of the mission did we encounter delightful country and recognize the luxuriant nature of California. After having passed a road settled by Indians,* we halted before a large building alongside the church housing the missionaries. Five clerics emerged to meet us; three of them belonged to this mission [San José], and two had come here from Mission Santa Clara for the celebration of the name-day festivities. These missionaries conducted us to a large, simply furnished, and

---

*The Spaniards call the local savages *los Indios,* and so I have retained this name.

rather untidy room, where they received us respectfully. At exactly 10 o'clock we entered a spacious and well-appointed stone church, where we found several hundred half-naked Indians already kneeling; from the time of their conversion they are not allowed to miss a single mass, although they understand neither Spanish nor Latin. As the missionaries do not bother to learn the language of the Indians, it was incomprehensible to me how they had instilled the Christian religion in them. The deepest gloom must rule the minds and hearts of these poor people, who can only mimic the external ceremonies by eye and then copy them. The conversion of savages is now spreading throughout the South Sea [Pacific Ocean], but it is a pity that the missionaries do not contemplate transforming them into human beings before converting them into Christians; thus, that which should afford them happiness and serenity provides grounds for bloody wars. For example, on the Friendly [Tonga] Islands the Christians and heathens continually try to exterminate each other. It seemed strange to me that the converts were not permitted to rise from their knees during the entire service; after this exertion they were rewarded with church music, which seemed to give them much pleasure and which was probably the only part of the entire liturgy that they understood. The orchestra comprised one cello, one violin, and two flutes; these instruments were played very discordantly by young half-naked Indians.[6] From the church we went to dinner, where there was no lack of food or wine, which the missionaries themselves had made. After dinner they showed us the dwellings of the savages, consisting of long, low houses built of brick [adobe] and forming several streets. The filthiness of these barracks was frightful and is probably the cause of the great mortality here, for of the 1,000 Indians found at San Francisco, 300 die annually. The Indian girls, who number 400 at the mission, live separately from the men in similar barracks, and all are compelled to work hard. The men cultivate the fields; the missionaries gain the harvest and keep it in storehouses, and the Indians are given only that which is necessary to keep them alive. The soldiers of the presidio also eat this grain, but they do not receive it gratis, having to pay a high price for the flour. The women spin wool and from it weave a coarse cloth, which is partly used for their common clothing and partly sent to Mexico to be traded for other necessary goods. The clothing of the local Indians is clearly depicted in the drawings of Mr. Khoris.[7] Owing to the

---

[6]California's natives had their own musical instruments; flutes were favored, but whistles and rattles were also played. Mission San José was famous for its neophyte orchestra and choir, developed and conducted by Father Narciso Durán. For more on music at the missions of Alta California, see Russell, *From Serra to Sanchez.*

[7]Login Andreyevich Khoris (Ludwig [or Ludovik or Louis] Choris) (1795–1828) was the artist on Kotzebue's first round-the-world voyage. During Kotzebue's voyage Choris made hundreds of drawings and paintings illustrating—in an original and realistic rather than idealistic style—the native peoples and natural history of the *Ryurik*'s destinations. From 1819 until 1827 he lived in Paris and published his illustrations in two works (Choris and Eyries, *Voyage pittoresque* [1822]; and Choris, *Vues et paysages* [1826]).

name-day holiday, the Indians had been freed from work, and they had divided themselves into various groups and were amusing themselves with all sorts of games, including one that required special skill. It consists of the following: two of them sit on the ground opposite one another, and in their hands each holds many small sticks, which one of them suddenly flings into the air very quickly, and the other must guess immediately whether the number of sticks is odd or even; beside each player sits a recorder, who tallies the wins and losses. Never playing for nothing, and not owning anything except clothing, which they do not dare to stake, they laboriously and skillfully polish white shells [dentalia],[8] which serve them in lieu of money.

The coast of California is inhabited by such a variety of tribes that at the mission there are often people from more than 10 different tribes, each of which speaks its own particular language. After leaving the mission, we met two Indian throngs, also from different nations. They were in battle dress, i.e., completely naked and painted in motley colors; the heads of most of them were adorned with feathers and other ornaments, and some of them had covered their long, tangled hair with down and daubed their faces in a frightful manner. There is nothing remarkable in their war dances, and I regretted only that I did not understand the lyrics of their songs. The faces of these Indians are vile, and they express stupidity and brutishness; however, they are well proportioned, fairly tall, and dark complexioned. The women are short in stature and very ugly; their faces bear a great resemblance to those of Negros, which, however, can be called pretty beauties by comparison with the locals. They are distinguished from Negros principally by the fact that they have extremely long, straight, and very black hair. The missionaries assured us that it was very difficult to teach these savages because of their stupidity, but I think that these gentlemen do not take many pains over it; in addition, they told us that the Indians come from the remote interior of this land and voluntarily submit to them (which we also doubted, however), that immediately after their arrival they [i.e., the friars] begin to instruct them in Christianity, and that some are baptized sooner and others later in accordance with the knowledge that they have acquired. California occasions much expense on the part of the Spanish government and does not bring it any gain, except the conversion of several hundred heathens into Christians, who, however, die soon after their conversion, being unable to become accustomed to a new way of life. Twice a year they receive permission to visit their homeland; this short time is

---

[8]Dentalia shells (*Dentalium indianorum* or *D. pretiosum*), or *haiqua,* are short snail shells, milk white and very hard but fragile. They were one of the most popular native trade items on the entire Northwest Coast, outranked only by Monterey, or abalone, "ear shells" (*Haliotis cracherodii*), noted for their colorful lining of mother-of-pearl. Both were used as a form of currency by coastal natives and were especially prized by the Yuroks of the northwesternmost corner of California.

for them the happiest, and I myself saw how they hurried home in throngs with joyous outcries. The sick, who are unable to make the journey, at least accompany their fortunate compatriots to the shore [of the bay], where they embark, and afterwards they sit for whole days on the beach, fixing a sorrowful gaze on the faraway mountain peaks surrounding their abode; they pass several days on this spot, often without any food, so much does a look at their lost homeland captivate these newly converted Christians.[9]

Two large rivers flow into San Francisco Bay, the largest of which flows farther north and is called the Río Grande [Sacramento River] by the Spaniards. According to the account of the missionaries, there is no other river like it in the whole world; the largest ships can ply it conveniently, and its banks are fertile, the climate pleasant, and the population extremely large. The missionaries often take trips on this river in large, well-armed rowboats in order to convert the people to Christianity.[10] After drinking another cup of chocolate and thanking the missionaries for their friendly reception, we set out on our return journey; in the evening we reached the *Ryurik* at the same time as a courier arrived from Monterey from Don Pablo Vicente de Solá,[11] governor of Old [*sic:* New] California. He handed me the governor's letter, in which the latter extended his courtesy, congratulated me upon my safe arrival, and promised to come himself to San Francisco as soon as his duties permitted in order to assure himself that all of my wishes were not only fulfilled but even anticipated. At the same time, at my request I received the commandant's permission to send a courier to Mr. Kuskov.* I immediately wrote to him about supplying me with certain necessities that he could readily obtain, having trading relations with American ships.

5 October. It was necessary to caulk the *Ryurik,* mend the sails, and change the rotten rigging; the fine weather favored us in executing these necessary tasks.

---

*Mr. Kuskov, manager of a counter of the Russian-American Company, has on the orders of Mr. Baranov, governor of all of its possessions in America, established his [temporary] residence at Bodega in order to supply the company's settlements with provisions from there. Bodega is found north of San Francisco at a distance of a half day's journey by sea from the latter town and is called Port Bodega by the Spaniards. Only small ships can enter its harbor; Mr. Kuskov's more important holding [Fort Ross] is found somewhat farther north of the port of Bodega.

---

[9]At this point the paragraph in the first English edition concludes with the following sentence, which is absent from the Russian edition: "Every time some of those who have the permission, run away; and they would probably all do it, were they not deterred by their fears of the soldiers, who catch them, and bring them back to the Mission as criminals; this fear is so great, that seven or eight dragoons are sufficient to overpower several hundred Indians" (Kotzebue, *Voyage of Discovery,* 1:284).

[10]In the first English edition this sentence ends with the following phrase, which is absent from the Russian edition: "in which, however, they seldom succeed, as the Indians there are valiant and well-armed" (Kotzebue, *Voyage of Discovery,* 1:284).

[11]Solá (1761–1826), a peninsular from Spain's Basque Country, was the last Spanish governor (1815–22) and briefly (1822) the first Mexican governor of Alta California.

Lieutenant Shishmaryov took these upon himself, and I occupied myself with the instruments, which were moved to a tent pitched on the beach, where I checked the movement of the chronometers daily. Our apprentice naturalists also practiced their profession energetically, especially since it was possible to make a variety of new discoveries in this country, which is visited so rarely by scientists. Mr. Khoris diligently made drawings. With all of these undertakings, the day passed very quickly, and in the evening in the company of the officers of the presidio we gathered to delight in the serenity of the splendid climate. The soldiers seem dissatisfied with both the government and the mission, and one cannot be surprised by this inasmuch as for 7 years running they have not received their pay and suffer much want, even of essential clothing; in addition, the residents do not have any European goods whatsoever, for trading vessels are not allowed to enter any harbor in California. It has to be regretted that this beautiful and fruitful country is not utilized at all.[12]

17 October. Today, to our great joy, there arrived a large umiak loaded with everything requested by us and sent by Mr. Kuskov.[13] We also had the pleasure of entertaining the hon. governor with his entourage at dinner in our tent. His noble, courteous, and relaxed behavior pleased us greatly and made us want to see him more often; and as he apparently also seemed pleased to talk to us, we met daily either in the presidio or at my quarters. He even anticipated all of our wishes, and we are very obliged to him for our having passed a pleasant time in that province.[14]

18 October. Taking advantage of the umiak's departure to return to the port of Bodega, I communicated to Mr. Kuskov the governor's wish to meet him here to discuss face-to-face the [Russian-]American Company's settlement here. I was astonished to learn from the governor that a considerable number of Russians are held captive in California; one of the [Russian-]American Company's ships had approached the coast to trade; but because this is against Spanish law, some of the crew who had gone ashore unaware of any danger were seized by soldiers and confined in a dungeon. Upon the strict orders of the viceroy of Mexico [New

---

[12]In the first English edition this paragraph is followed by the following paragraph, which is absent from the Russian edition: "On the 16th, at five o'clock in the evening, seven guns from the fortress announced the approach of the Governor; and soon after, eight guns from the Presidio, his arrival there" (Kotzebue, *Voyage of Discovery,* 1:286).

[13]Ivan Aleksandrovich Kuskov (1765–1823), Governor Baranov's right-hand man and the manager of New Archangel Counter from 1806, was instrumental in the Russian-American Company's campaign to hunt sea otters and found a settlement on the coast of Alta California. In 1812 he established Fort Ross, and he remained its first manager until 1822, when he was replaced by Carl Schmidt.

[14]Kotzebue is being less than candid here, understating serious problems in Russian-Spanish relations in California arising from the existence of the colony of Ross (which he does not once mention by name in his book). A comparison of Kotzebue's and Chamisso's narratives shows that the former omits many episodes and details. See Mahr, *Visit of the "Rurik,"* 39, 47–49; and Chamisso, *Voyage around the World,* 104–105, 108–109.

Spain], the governor was unable to return these men to Mr. Kuskov, but he wanted to deliver them to me, provided that I would take them with me. Unhappily, however, the smallness of the ship did not allow me to do so; I could take only three men.[15] In addition, I accommodated Mr. Elliot [de Castro] on the ship in order to land him, at his request, on the Sandwich [Hawaiian] Islands, where he could find an occasion to leave on a North American ship bound for Sitka and return to Mr. Baranov. John Elliot de Castro, a native of Portugal, arrived at Sitka on an American ship and was invited by Mr. Baranov to accompany as a supercargo a trading vessel assigned to California, and there he was taken prisoner together with the other crewmen.

23 October. Today the governor provided us with an interesting spectacle, having arranged a fight between a bull and a bear; the latter are so numerous here that one need go no farther than a mile from the residences into the woods to meet many of them. The local bears are distinguished from ours by their pointed head and gray fur; they are also livelier and bolder than ours. Despite this, the dragoons here are so skilled and brave in catching them that it is customary to send them to the woods on horseback for a bear just as we would send a cook to the barnyard for a goose. Three mounted dragoons, equipped only with lassos, can very readily overpower a bear, which they try to keep in the middle between them during the pursuit and constantly irritate. As soon as the exasperated beast wants to rush one of the horsemen, another throws a lasso—which is fastened by a strong thong to his saddle—around its foreleg, spurs his horse, and thus throws the bear to the ground; one of the other dragoons, seizing this moment, lassos the beast's hind leg and halts his horse on the opposite side, and while the bear is sprawled the third dragoon binds all of its legs and conveys it home in this state without any danger. Thus did the dragoons get a bear today. At the same time, they fetched another wild bull in the same manner. Even the domestic cattle remain at pasture the whole year without any tending and thereby become so wild that when one of them is needed for milking, it has to be lassoed by a mounted soldier. The wild bull's fight with the bear was rather interesting, and although the former often hoisted his infuriated opponent on its horns, it was nevertheless finally defeated.

29 October. After the arrival of Mr. Kuskov, the governor talked to him,[16] and when he had seen that all of our wishes had been satisfied and that the *Ryurik* was

---

[15]In a receipt in Spanish of 28 October 1816 given by Governor Solá to Kotzebue the three Russians are called deserters from "the establishment that the Russian-American Company has at the port of Bodega" and are named as Juan (presumably Ivan Stroganov), Diego, and Grigory (Mahr, *Visit of the "Rurik,"* doc. 5, 120–23).

[16]Kuskov arrived on 25 October; the talks ("conference"), with the participation of Chamisso and Argüello, took place on the 26th; and the protocol was signed on the 28th. In response to the signing of the protocol Solá solemnly gave his word not to undertake any forcible measures against the Russian settlement before the question had been resolved at the highest level (Mahr, *Visit of the "Rurik,"* 46–47). The result of the talks was a protocol in both Spanish (ibid., doc. 4, 116–21) and Russian.

ready to sail, he went back to Monterey, accompanied by our heartfelt gratitude. Ivan Stroganov, one of the Russians who had been a prisoner here and who was taken on board by me, had been maimed to such a degree while hunting when gunpowder had caught fire accidentally that he died, despite all of the efforts of our skillful and solicitous physician.[17]

1 November. The *Ryurik* was now in perfectly good condition again, the movement of the chronometers had been checked, and all of the instruments had been brought on board. The residents had supplied us abundantly with provisions, and all of the sailors were healthy; so, taking advantage of a NW wind and the outgoing tide, we raised anchor at 9 o'clock, saluted the fort, and found ourselves already out of the bay at 10 o'clock. After having gone two miles out to sea, we still heard the howling of the sea lions lying on the coastal rocks. Sea otters abound on the coast of California; as they were formerly not seen at all, it can be supposed that they have moved here from the Aleutian Islands and the northern part of America to avoid being hunted there.[18]

From frequently repeated observations on shore, I made the following determinations:

The latitude was 37° 48' 33" N. The longitude, calculated from the distance of the moon from the sun,[19] was 122° 12' 30" W.

The declination of the magnetic needle was 62° 46'.

The variation of the compass was 16° 5' east.

The mean of our observations at the port of San Francisco of high tide and low tide gave a high-tide duration of 1 hr. 50'. The greatest difference between high tide and low tide was 7 feet.

After leaving the coast, we caught a strong NW wind, which commonly prevails on this coast, and we made rapid progress.

---

[17]According to Chamisso, Stroganov was an old man who rejoiced at being among fellow Russians again. In the evening before sailing, his powder horn exploded while he was hunting. He wanted to die among his compatriots, and he expired on the third day and was buried at sea (Mahr, *Visit of the "Rurik,"* 44–45; Chamisso, *Voyage around the World,* 107).

[18]Kotzebue was mistaken, of course. Sea otters had long inhabited the coast of California, where they constitute a distinct subspecies (*Enhydra lutris nereis*). They were nearly extirpated by Russian and American traders and Konyaga hunters in the nineteenth century and were considered extinct, and Kotzebue himself hunted them (Mahr, *Visit of the "Rurik,"* 48–49; Chamisso, *Voyage around the World,* 109). A pod of survivors was discovered in 1938, and conservation measures have since increased their number, although not to eighteenth-century levels (their federal U.S. status is "threatened").

[19]The following phrase appears in the first English edition but not in the Russian edition: "of which 125 were taken on different days" (Kotzebue, *Voyage of Discovery,* 1:289).

Vasily Golovnin's Report about a Voyage to Alta California, 1818

Editor's Introduction

Vasily Mikhailovich Golovnin (1776–1831) entered the Naval Academy in St. Petersburg at the age of twelve, and within two years he was a midshipman and participating in naval battles against the Swedes. After being promoted to lieutenant and serving as a volunteer on English warships in the Atlantic for four years, he was given command of the 300-ton sloop *Diana* on its voyage to the North Pacific, where he visited Petropavlovsk in Kamchatka and New Archangel. While surveying the Kuriles, he and six of his men were seized by the Japanese authorities on Kunashir Island and held captive until 1813.[1]

Golovnin became one of the Imperial Navy's most experienced officers. In 1817, although engaged to be married, he accepted command of the 900-ton, 32-gun sloop *Kamchatka* with a crew of 130 with orders to supply Kamchatka and Okhotsk, inspect the Russian-American colonies (especially with respect to the behavior of company employees toward the natives), and determine the geographic positions of some islands and locales in Russian America and survey the Northwest Coast between 60° and 63° N (provided that the *Ryurik* under Captain Kotzebue had not already done so). Sailing via Cape Horn, he again visited Kamchatka and Russian America and then Alta California and Hawaii, returning to Kronshtadt via the Cape (and St. Helena, where Napoleon Bonaparte was imprisoned).[2] During the 1820s Golovnin was active in the upper levels of the naval bureaucracy, especially in shipbuilding. In 1827 he was appointed head of

---

[1]Golovnin's account of the voyage was published as *Puteshestvie rossiiskavo shlyupa "Diana."* It has yet to be translated into English, but his account of his Japanese captivity has been translated and reprinted as Golownin, *Memoirs of a Captivity in Japan.*

[2]Golovnin's account of this voyage was published as *Puteshestvie vokrug Sveta;* it has been translated into English as *Around the World on the Kamchatka.*

the Naval Ministry, and in 1830 he was promoted to vice admiral. A year later the imperial capital's great cholera epidemic took his life.

A REPORT FROM CAPTAIN OF THE 2ND RANK VASILY GOLOVNIN
TO THE STATE ADMIRALTY COLLEGE ABOUT A VOYAGE TO
ALTA CALIFORNIA,[3] [SLOOP *KAMCHATKA* AT PORT RUMYANTSEV?],
24 SEPTEMBER 1818

We remained 21 days at the port of New Archangel to discharge company cargo, to investigate the conduct of the promyshlenniks, and to wood and water, and in a calm on 19 August with the help of kedges[4] we left the harbor in the space between the islets, and during the night with a rising favorable wind we set out on our route.

I did not send reports to the State Admiralty College from either Kodiak or New Archangel because this year the company's vessels have not gone to Okhotsk yet, as one had left before our arrival, and for that reason my report will arrive in [St.] Petersburg much later (at least half a year) than I had hoped. From New Archangel I set my course to the company settlement called Slavyano Ross, located on the coast of New Albion in latitude 38° 33' N, where I arrived on 13 September, but as this place is completely exposed I stayed [only] a few hours under sail, and after having taken aboard some fresh provisions, I set out for the port of Monterey, where, I had been informed, the [acting] governor of the company's colonies, Captain-Lieutenant Hagemeister,[5] with whom I needed to talk about the state of the company in this region, was found. On 17 September I reached Monterey, and at its very entrance I met Mr. Hagemeister, who returned there with me. The Spanish governor, Don Pablo Vicente de Solá, received us very well; meanwhile, Captain-Lieutenant Hagemeister informed me of business and told me that the claim of the Spaniards that our [Russian-] American Company had occupied places in New Albion that belonged to them was incorrect because they are inhabited by independent Indians who do not suffer the Spaniards and make constant war with them—and by contrast are

---

[3]RGAVMF, f. 212, op. 9, d. 276, fols. 294v–96 (original).

[4]A kedge (*zavoz*) was an anchor with long ropes for hauling a vessel against the current.

[5]Leonty Andreyevich Gagemeister (Ludwig von Hagemeister, or Hagenmeister) (1780–1833), a Baltic German from Livonia, commanded three round-the-world voyages: in 1806–10 in the *Neva*, in 1816–19 in the *Kutuzov* (with the *Suvorov*), and in 1828–30 in the *Krotky* (*Gentle*). During the first voyage Hagemeister reconnoitered the Hawaiian Islands, established friendly relations with King Kamehameha I, and launched trade; during the second he inaugurated the new colonial regime at New Archangel of management by naval officers, replacing Governor Baranov, and opened regular trade with Alta California; during the third he nearly lost his ship and his life at Tahiti during stormy weather. He was appointed to the command of a fourth on the *Amerika* in 1833 but died of a stroke before its departure.

attached to the Russians and ask us to settle among them and supply them with
European goods—and because in these places there never have been any Spanish
settlements, and even the Spaniards have no knowledge of the location of these
places, and for that reason Mr. Hagemeister asked me to go to Port Rumyantsev
(so-called by the company but named Bodega Bay by foreigners), lying in latitude
38° 18' [N], so that I can assure myself of everything that he said for reports to the
government. Assuming that this matter was of no small importance, I decided
to call there, so I set off from Monterey on 18 September and arrived on the 21st
of the same month at Port Rumyantsev, where the company has a storehouse
and a vessel that had been built there. I stayed two days and had a meeting with
the independent Indians, all of whom declared through an "Aleut"[6] interpreter
living among them that these lands are theirs, that the Spaniards have never
visited them or settled there, and that they [i.e., the Indians] do not recognize
their [i.e., the Spaniards'] authority at all and always kill them when they [i.e.,
the two groups] meet to the north of San Francisco Bay, which they consider
the ultimate Spanish border in that quarter. But they ask the Russians to settle
among them, for they [i.e., the Russians] treat them honorably and do not enslave
them. In conclusion, their [Coast Miwok] leader by the name of Valenila asked
me for a Russian flag that he could raise upon the arrival of Russian vessels as
a sign that he considers the Russians his friends. He was with me on the sloop
and repeated the same request, which I fulfilled, after giving him and some of
his countrymen various useful things.

In the morning of 24 September I set out from Port Rumyantsev to go to
Fort Ross, which we now (at 10 o'clock in the morning of 24 September) have in
sight, in order to leave my reports there for sending at the first opportunity to
[St.] Petersburg; after having delivered them I will go directly to the Sandwich
Islands and from there to Manila and then to Europe. Until now the sloop and
its crew (with the exception of the deceased seaman Markov,[7] mentioned above)
have been well and in the very best condition. I have the honor to report this to
the State Admiralty College.

Fleet Captain of the 2nd rank and Cavalier Golovnin.

P.S. At midday on 24 September, before I had time to send this report, a strong
wind rose from the NW that prevented rowing vessels from not only making
a landing but even nearing the coast; this wind continued nearly two days and

---

[6]After about 1800 most, if not all, of the "Aleuts" reported in the Russian documents were actually
Konyagas, owing to the high toll exacted by exploitation of the former after initial contact with the Russians
a half century earlier.

[7]The first-class seaman Yevdokim Markov, who had suffered from internal pain during almost the entire
voyage, died en route from Kodiak to New Archangel between 20 and 28 July.

moved us such a distance away from the coast that until the evening of 26 September we were unable to approach it at Bodega Bay, where I now made ready to send my reports with the "Aleuts" who were with me. At this time the sloop and the company are well, and I have the honor to report this to the State Admiralty College.

Captain of the 2nd rank Golovnin.

DOCUMENT 5

Vasily Golovnin's Report about the Frontera del Norte of Alta California, 1818

CAPTAIN OF THE 2ND RANK VASILY GOLOVNIN, A REPORT ABOUT
RUSSIAN INTELLIGENCE OF THE SEACOAST AND INTERIOR OF THE
FRONTERA DEL NORTE OF ALTA CALIFORNIA,[1] [SLOOP *KAMCHATKA*
AT PORT RUMYANTSEV?], SEPTEMBER 1818

On 13 September 1818 the hunters sent from Fort Ross to hunt [sea] otters toward
Cape Mendocino were in the first bay [Humboldt Bay] to the north of it at an
approximate distance noted by them of 20 verstas, and they speak of it as follows:

"Samoilov[2] and several [other] Konyagas note that this bay is divided into two
arms, the first situated in the direction of Trinidad Bay, which will be to the
NW, and the other to the E or even the NE; they are unable to determine its
circumference, but it is not small. Besides two large rivers, three small ones also
enter it, and in the bay and the rivers they saw sturgeon, large king salmon, and
many of another, unknown kind of fish riffling the surface of the water. They
saw many ringed [*sic*] or harbor seals in both large rivers, and the shore of the
bay and the banks of the large rivers were covered with trees. The best [timber]
for construction is the fir but mostly what appears to be that which we call *chaga*
[coast redwood], large alder, and others that are found in places lying near our
settlement of Ross; the locality inland from the bay is treeless, and there is a large
expanse of mainland stretching as a plain to the NW toward Trinidad Bay, and
they suppose that there is a small neck of land between this [bay] and Trinidad
Bay. The entrance from the sea to the bay is not very wide; during the stay of our

---

[1]RGAVMF, f. 7, op. 1, d. 19, fols. 7–7v (original).

[2]Ivan Samoilov was a Konyaga chief from Mysovsk; his son, Dmitry, was also employed at Ross. See
Grinëv, *Kto yest kto*, 471.

[hunting] party under Samoilov's leadership in 1817 they noticed and assumed a great depth but now they have found a projecting sandbank with shallow water."

Our promyshlenniks who have been in S[an] Francisco Bay speak of its northern part [San Pablo Bay] as follows: that it stretches to the north as far as the parallel [of latitude] of the entrance to Great Bodega [Bay, i.e., Tomales Bay] and that two large rivers enter it; one [Petaluma River or Napa River?] flows from the northwest and the other [Sacramento River?] from the northeast. The first, according to the Indians, flows from the same very large lake [Clear Lake?] that the Slavyanka [Russian] River issues,[3] and our [men] ascended the second for 100 verstas and found there a large volcanic peak [Mount Shasta or Lassen Peak?] that even the Spaniards did not know; the Indians are certain that a third large river [Eel River?] flows from the same lake to the west, and that, judging from their words, must be one of those falling into the bay [Humboldt Bay?] lying 20 verstas to the north of Cape Mendocino that Samoilov reported.

Between the said bay of Samoilov's and Trinidad Bay there is another large bay [Arcata Bay?]—larger than the former—into which flow two large rivers that our promyshlenniks plied, and in the expanse from Cape Mendocino to Trinidad Bay there are 4 large and 3 small rivers; only one is designated on Spanish maps, under the name Río de las Tórtolas. This [fact] clearly shows how little this [northern] side [of San Francisco Bay] is known to the Spaniards, who had no knowledge of the aforesaid volcano until we told them.

---

[3]In fact, the Petaluma, Napa, and Russian Rivers do not originate in Clear Lake.

DOCUMENT 6

Russian-American Company, "About the Arrival on the Sitkan Coast of a Spanish Vessel," 1821

Editor's Introduction

This document concerns a little-known sidelight of the well-known raid on Monterey and Mission San Juan Capistrano in late 1818 by the French-Argentine seaman and corsair Hipólito Bouchard. Before leaving Alta California in early 1819 to raid Spanish ports in South America, he captured a Spanish schooner off Santa Bárbara. He manned it with some Hawaiians, who later became separated from their leader's frigate. They tried to sail to Hawaii but lost their way and drifted to New Archangel, where they were rescued by the Russians, who salvaged the cargo, repaired the ship, and engaged the survivors.

[The Board of Directors of the Russian-American Company], "About the Arrival on the Sitkan Coast of a Spanish Vessel with a Sandwich Islander Crew,"[1] [St. Petersburg], 14 January 1821

In the month of June of this year [1819] a schooner was seen at sea from the fortress at Sitka. Immediately a pilot was sent, and then a longboat was sent, too, in order to tow it. The next day it was brought to the roadstead. Upon its arrival, to everyone's surprise, only 7 Sandwich Islanders and not a single European were

---

[1] ARGO, raz. 99, op. 1, d. 20, unpaginated. A notation at the bottom of the first page reads, "Read on 14 January 1821 to a general meeting of shareholders." For more details on this episode, see ARGO, raz. 99, op. 1, d. 14: doc. 6, Semyon Yanovsky to New Archangel Counter, 8 June 1819; doc. 387, Yanovsky to New Archangel Counter, 8 June 1819; doc. 3, New Archangel Counter to Yanovsky, 10 June 1819; doc. 4, New Archangel Counter to Yanovsky, 12 June 1819; and doc. 397, Yanovsky to Khlebnikov [New Archangel Counter], 31 July 1819.

found on it. They declared unanimously that [Hipólito] Bouchard, the captain of the rebel Spanish frigates *Argentina* and *Santa Rosa,* had taken them aboard as sailors from the Sandwich Islands.[2] From there these frigates went directly to New [i.e., Alta] California and burned the ports of Monterey, the governor's seat, and San Francisco;[3] then they stopped at Seres [Cedros?] Island, and after having returned to Monterey, they found this schooner there and seized it as a prize, the captain and Spaniards on it escaping ashore. Three Europeans and the said Sandwich Islanders were put on it to be conducted to any rebel port, but a mutiny erupted aboard the frigates. Captain Bouchard and the other officers were killed,[4] and some saved themselves by fleeing ashore. The mutineers chose new captains. When the Europeans on the schooner left in the frigates, they took with them as much of the cargo as they could and ordered the Sandwich Islanders to follow the frigates, which went to sea. The place of the schooner's captain was taken by one of the Sandwich Islanders who had sailed before on American ships but scarcely knew the use of a compass, and thus did they set out after the frigates. But the frigates did not want to wait for the schooner, and the Sandwich Islanders devised another plan: instead of following the frigates they went to the Sandwich Islands with the intention of giving the schooner to their king, Tomi-omi [Kaumualii].[5] After sailing 82 days, they arrived at Sitka instead of the Sandwich Islands. They had half of a barrel of water and provisions for only two days. Everything in the hold was in disarray, and the schooner had a very large leak. Judging from its construction and equipment, it was not Spanish but American. Now it is at Sitka, and its small cargo, consisting of cotton, has been transferred to the local storehouses. The captain of the schooner and his assistant are also being detained at Sitka, and the others have been sent on a company vessel to the Sandwich Islands; the schooner itself is called the *Fortuna* [*Fortune*], and until the owner is found it will be used in the service of the company.[6]

---

[2]See Uhrowczik, *Burning of Monterey.* The *Fortuna* is not mentioned in this book.

[3]San Francisco was not, in fact, attacked by Bouchard.

[4]Actually, Bouchard was killed by servants on his estate in Peru in 1837 (Uhrowczik, *Burning of Monterey,* 96).

[5]Kaumualii was the ruler of Kauai and the last holdout against the hegemony of King Kamehameha I; in 1817 he had briefly allied himself with the Russians at the urging of Dr. Georg Schäffer, a Bavarian in the employ of the Russian-American Company who had accompanied Lieutenant Unkovsky to Russian America on the *Suvorov* as the ship's surgeon.

[6]Later the Russians learned that the schooner was actually the *Nuestra Señora de Guadelupe,* alias *El Gallardo* (*The Elegant*); its owner was identified, but he was unable to retrieve it (RRAC, roll 33, doc. 474, fol. 315v).

Russian-American Company, "About the Inhumane Treatment of Promyshlenniks by the Spaniards," 1821

EDITOR'S INTRODUCTION

One of the problems that arose between the Russians and the Spaniards was poaching.[1] By the beginning of the 1800s the coast of Alta California afforded the last undepleted population of sea otters on North America's Pacific Coast. Their pelts were not as large or as dark as those of their Northwest Coast relatives, but they still fetched a high price in the Chinese market. So the Russians were willing to risk poaching the Spanish rookeries, especially on the Channel Islands, which were unoccupied by the Spaniards, who, moreover, lacked patrol vessels. It was only when the Russian hunters went ashore on the mainland that they risked capture by mounted patrols. Such a case is recounted in this document, which also describes the torturing to death of one of the Konyaga captives.

[THE BOARD OF DIRECTORS OF THE RUSSIAN-AMERICAN COMPANY], "ABOUT THE INHUMANE TREATMENT OF RUSSIAN PROMYSHLENNIKS BY THE SPANIARDS,"[2] [ST. PETERSBURG], 14 JANUARY 1821

The company promyshlennik [Ivan] Kyglaya [or Kykhlaya or Kegli], a native of the island of Kodiak, who was taken prisoner by the Spaniards in 1815 and

---

[1] For early Russian poaching on the coast of California "on halves" with American shipmasters, see Farris, "Otter Hunting."

[2] ARGO, raz. 99, op. 1, d. 20, unpaginated. A notation at the bottom of the first page reads, "Read on 14 January 1821 to a general meeting of shareholders." For more documentation on this incident, see Farris, *So Far from Home*, 128–32.

returned to our settlement of Ross and then to our chief colony on the island of Sitka in 1819, has provided information about the following inhumane treatment of one of its [i.e., the company's] promyshlenniks.

In [September] 1815 the company employee [Boris] Tarasov was the leader of a party of [twenty-five] promyshlenniks hunting on the [Santa Barbara Channel] island of Ilmen [San Nicolás], which belongs to nobody, and, not foreseeing any success, decided to set out from there with 15 islanders of our Kodiak colony under him for the other islands of Santa Rosa and Santa Catalina. Finding a leak in his kayak on the way, he had to hug the coast of California. They put in to a bay under Cape St. Peter [San Pedro], where they were detained another day by the weather. There a Spanish soldier came to him from the mission of San Pedro [Gabriel?] and told Tarasov that in return for presents he could bring to him two of our Kodiak-ers who had earlier fled from another of Tarasov's [hunting] parties and were now at the mission. After the soldier's departure it would have been possible for them to set off on their intended route, the weather having eased; however, the desire to see and to free their compatriots kept them there for a while. On the fourth day up to twenty armed riders suddenly galloped up to them at this place, bound all of them, and wounded many of them with their drawn sabers; they cut the head of one of the Kodiak islanders by the name of Chunagnak. In the meantime they looted their belongings and all of the company's trade goods, and then they conducted the captives to the mission of San Pedro, where they actually did find the aforesaid two Kodiakers, who had fled from another party of hunters on San Clemente Island. Upon their arrival at the mission the chief missionary[3] proposed that they accept the Catholic creed, and the captives replied that they had already long since adopted the Christian faith of the Graeco-Russian creed and did not want to make the proposed change. After several days Tarasov and nearly all of the Kodiakers were taken to Santa Bárbara; only two of them, Kyglaya and the wounded Chunagnak, were thrown into a prison containing some Indians and languished several days there without food or drink. One night the runaway Kodiakers were sent to these two by the chief missionary with an order to accept the Catholic creed, but on this occasion they remained steadfast in their faith. At dawn a cleric accompanied by many Indians approached the prison, and he ordered them to form a circle around the captives after they were led out of it. With the formation of the circle he gave the order to cut off all of Chunagnak's fingers and then both of his hands, and finally—not content with this tyranny— he ordered the opening of his insides. Tortured thusly, Chunagnak's soul left him with this last act. The same punishment awaited the other Kodiaker, Kyglaya,

---

[3]If this was indeed the mission of San Gabriel, then the missionary would likely have been José María Zalvidea, one of the most zealous of Alta California's friars.

if the holy father had not just then received some sort of written message. After reading it, he ordered the burial of the dead man, and Kyglaya was again thrown into prison, from which after several days he was sent to Santa Bárbara. There he found none of the comrades who had been taken captive with him; all of them had already been sent to Monterey. He was put to work, like the company pro-myshlenniks who had been captured earlier by the Spaniards. Wanting to free themselves from such a life of torment, one of them and Kyglaya resolved to flee. They stole a kayak and set off toward the cape of San Pedro Bay, from which they decided to go to Santa Catalina Island and then cross to Santa Bárbara Island, and finally to Ilmen Island, where one of them died; the other, Kyglaya, was taken from there on the company brig *Ilmena* to the settlement of Ross. The others with whom he had been imprisoned were freed at the insistence of our Captains Hagemeister and Kotzebue.

This occurrence is one of many acts against Russian promyshlenniks by the Spaniards, albeit more striking as well as inhumane. Many of those taken captive were exhausted by their labor and so mutilated by beatings that their coffins will feel the results. And it is impossible to imagine what the poor Indians suffer from them without heartfelt shuddering. Not only do they [i.e., the Spaniards] not consider them human beings but even rank them lower than beasts. A Spaniard's chief pleasure consists of beating an innocent Indian and boasting of the blows in front of his compatriots. The company's Board [of Directors] brought such conduct on the part of our Spanish neighbors to the attention of the Foreign Minister on 28 October 1819.[4]

---

[4]In early 1820 Governor Yanovsky had suggested to the board of directors that it petition the Spanish government to see that the Californios not mistreat captured "Aleut" hunters (out of "inhumanity and igno-rance")—but he reminded the board that the company had little leverage because "the colonies of the RAC cannot manage without the grain obtained from the Spaniards" (RRAC, roll 27, doc. 26, fol. 6).

Semyon Ivanovich Yanovsky (1788–1876), a graduate of St. Petersburg's Naval Academy, joined the company as a lieutenant in 1816 and reached New Archangel in the summer of 1817 aboard the *Suvorov* under the command of Lieutenant Zakhar Panafidin. There he married Governor Baranov's daughter, Irina, at the beginning of 1818, and several days later her ageing and ailing father was formally replaced as governor by Lieutenant Leonty Hagemeister, who had arrived in the autumn on the *Kutuzov*, the *Suvorov*'s flagship, to investigate Baranov's management. When Hagemeister sailed to Alta California in the summer of 1819 for supplies, he left Yanovsky in charge at New Archangel, and when Hagemeister returned from California in early autumn in failing health, he appointed Yanovsky acting governor and left with Baranov aboard the *Kutuzov* for Russia. Although Yanovsky fulfilled his duties diligently, as a lame-duck governor he was eager to return home, and in 1821 he and his family left the colonies via Okhotsk and Siberia for his estate in Chernigov Province. In 1824 Irina died, and two years later Yanovsky remarried. Following a long stint (1834–52) as a school principal in Kaluga, he entered a monastery there in 1864, becoming a member of the white (married) clergy as Monk Sergey. See Grinëv, *Kto yest kto*, 634; and Pierce, *Russian America*, 197–99.

DOCUMENT 8

Excerpts from Aleksey Lazarev's Visit to [Alta] California, 1820–1821

EDITOR'S INTRODUCTION

Once Kruzenshtern and Lisyansky had accomplished Russia's first circumnavigation in 1803–1806, the Russian navy hurried to recoup lost time by showing the flag, training seamen, flexing naval muscle, and exploring and discovering in the world's oceans, especially in the North Pacific, where it could also supply the tsar's maritime possessions on both the Asiatic and the American sides. English, French, Spanish, and Portuguese navigators, as well as traders, had already revealed the major islands and coasts to non-native eyes, but the Arctic and Antarctic Oceans were still largely unknown seas.

Moreover, a northern passage had yet to be found through the Arctic Ocean between the Pacific and Atlantic. Kotzebue had managed to get as far as the Chukchi Sea in 1816 but no farther than St. Lawrence Island in 1817. So in 1819–22 Russia undertook an ambitious expedition of exploration and discovery in the polar waters of both the Northern and Southern Hemispheres: the "southern division" under the command of Captain (of the second rank) Faddey Bellingshausen in the flagship sloop *Vostok* (*East*) and Lieutenant Mikhail Lazarev in the sloop *Mirny* (*Peaceful*) explored to the Antarctic Ocean and sought the legendary "southern continent" (and succeeded in discovering and circumnavigating Antarctica), while the "northern division" under the command of Captain-Lieutenant Mikhail Vasilyev[1] in the flagship sloop *Otkrytie* (*Discovery*) and

---

[1] Mikhail Nikolayevich Vasilyev (1770–1847), from a noble Serbian family, was educated in the Naval Academy and trained in both the Baltic and Black Sea Fleets. Upon his return from the North Pacific in the *Otkrytie*, he rose steadily through the ranks, and in 1831 as a rear admiral he succeeded Vasily Golovnin as intendant-general of the fleet. In 1835 he was promoted to vice admiral. See Bolgurtsev, *Morskoy biograficheksy spravochnik*, 43; Grinëv, *Kto yest kto*, 92; and Pierce, *Russian America*, 520.

Captain-Lieutenant Gleb Shishmaryov[2] (who had served with Kotzebue) in the sloop *Blagonamerenny* (*Benevolent*) probed the Arctic Ocean and sought a northern passage to the Atlantic Ocean from Bering Strait. The two ships penetrated Bering Strait in the summers of 1820 and 1821 but were then stymied by pack ice. They had been outfitted for only two years, so supplies had to be replenished (and crewmen refreshed) at San Francisco, where they anchored for three months in the winter of 1820–21. This lengthy sojourn allowed the two captains and two of their officers, Lieutenants Aleksey Lazarev[3] (Mikhail's younger brother) and Nikolay Shishmaryov[4] (Gleb's nephew), to explore the vicinity at their leisure and to record their impressions in detail. As usual, San Francisco Bay especially attracted the attention of the Russian navigators, as did the Franciscan missions.

---

[2]Gleb Semyonovich Shishmaryov (1781–1835) was born in Vyshnevolotsk, Tver Province, into a family of minor gentry. He entered the Naval Academy as a young teenager and upon graduation in 1801 apprenticed on several vessels in the Northern Fleet in the Baltic and Barents Seas. Despite the loss of a ship under his command in the Gulf of Finland in 1809, he was promoted to the rank of lieutenant the next year. In 1815–18 he served as Captain Kotzebue's senior officer on the *Ryurik* during its round-the-world voyage, and after his return he was promoted to the rank of captain-lieutenant in 1819.

In the same year Shishmaryov was appointed to the command of the sloop *Blagonamerenny*. Upon his return to Russia in 1822, he was promoted to the rank of captain of the second rank and awarded double pay for the voyage. Thereafter he served in St. Petersburg and Kronshtadt, reaching the rank of rear admiral in 1829. See Grinëv, *Kto yest kto,* 611; and Pierce, *Russian America,* 464–65.

[3]Aleksey Petrovich Lazarev (1791–post 1851) was the youngest of three brothers; all three visited Alta California, and all three became noteworthy navigators. Aleksey's route to a naval career was more tortuous, however, because he combined it with court service that risked disfavor and delayed his progress through the naval ranks. He served in the Adriatic Sea from 1806 until 1810, when he was promoted to midshipman and transferred to the Baltic Fleet. Following his promotion to lieutenant in 1815, he served until 1819 on royal yachts out of St. Petersburg in the Gulf of Finland. Upon learning that the imminent round-the-world voyage of the *Blagonamerenny* would be commanded by his close friend Gleb Shishmaryov, Lazarev succeeded in obtaining permission to join the expedition and was transferred from the Guards to the fleet.

Upon his return he resumed his court service, becoming a captain-lieutenant in the Guards and in 1825 an aide-de-camp to Grand Duke Nikolay Pavlovich, soon to succeed his brother as Tsar Nicholas I. But with the latter's accession Lazarev's court and naval career—for unknown reasons—temporarily declined, and he was sent on a two-year mission to the Black and Caspian Seas and Olonets Province. In 1828 he was reassigned to the fleet and served in the Black Sea under his brother Mikhail. In 1839 he was promoted to rear admiral and appointed commandant of the Astrakhan Regiment and the Caspian Fleet. He retired from the navy in 1842 but returned in 1848 to serve in the Black Sea Fleet with his brother Mikhail, whose death in 1851 was soon followed by Aleksey's final retirement. See Grinëv, *Kto yest kto,* 288–89.

[4]Nikolay Dmitriyevich Shishmaryov (1797–1843) was born into a noble family and attended the Naval Academy in 1804–12. In 1815 he was promoted to the rank of midshipman and enrolled in the Baltic Fleet, which he left in 1818 to join Vasilyev's round-the-world expedition. Upon his return he was promoted to lieutenant. In 1824–26 he took part in the round-the-world voyage of the *Yelena* under the outbound command of Pyotr Chistyakov, the new governor of Russian America, and the homeward command of Matvey Muravyov, his predecessor. Shishmaryov was reassigned to the Baltic Fleet, where he served until his death. He was promoted to captain-lieutenant in 1831 and captain of the second rank in 1839, when he became commandant of Kamchatka for two years. See Bolgurtsev, *Morskoy biografichesky spravochnik,* 208; Grinëv, *Kto yest kto,* 611; and Pierce, *Russian America,* 465.

LIEUTENANT ALEKSEY LAZAREV, EXCERPTS FROM NOTES OF A
ROUND-THE-WORLD VOYAGE IN THE SLOOP *BLAGONAMERENNY*
IN 1819–22: A VISIT TO [ALTA] CALIFORNIA,[5]
8 NOVEMBER 1820–11 FEBRUARY 1821[6]

During the night of the 8th [of November] we saw *cachelots* [sperm whales] and
pelicans, and at 6 o'clock in the morning we sighted the coast of New California
stretching from the N to the NEE. At first, because of the distance, Point Los
Esteres [Reyes?] could not be distinguished, but soon it revealed itself together
with the rocks of the Farallones.

9 November. At midday we had the said point 6° NE, Point Roca [?] 10° NE,
and the southern Farallon rock 80° NE at 15 miles. We lay to the ENE and were
very vexed by the unbroken calm that slowed our passage; only from time to
time did a light wind blow from the coastal valleys, and we took advantage of
it to advance toward the port of San Francisco. At 8 o'clock in the morning [of
the 10th] a breeze began to blow from the east, and [after] hoisting the flag, we
began to tack into the strait [Golden Gate]. At our approach the fort raised the
Spanish flag. At half past 9 o['clock] the wind began to blow more freshly from
the east-northeast and the current became favorable; this was so advantageous
for our tacking that we quickly entered the strait, where we were becalmed. The
current pulled us strongly into it, and at half past 12 o'clock in the afternoon we
dropped anchor at a depth of 10½ sazhens on a sandy bottom. The commander of
our sloop immediately commissioned me to go ashore to [see] the commandant
for talks about salutes and fresh provisions for the men. At 2 o['clock] a breeze
blew from the southeast and a current began [to flow] out of the bay, whereupon
our sloop moved closer to the settlement and to a depth of 6½ sazh[ens] on a
sandy bottom, and we again cast anchor. Upon my return from the commandant's we saluted the fort with 9 guns and were answered with an equal number.

---

[5]Lazarev, "Zapiski o plavanii," RGAVMF, f. 213, op. 1, d. 111, fols. 193v–202v (published with variations in
Lazarev, *Zapiski o plavanii*, 241–47). The extracts are taken from Lazarev's original manuscript, whose text
has been collated with the published version of 1950 for variant readings; there are only nine, and they do not
affect the interpretation of the text. The leather-bound manuscript of 325 folios is very well preserved, having been prepared for presentation to the tsar and for subsequent publication, which—again for unknown
reasons—did not occur. Many phrases and words have been underlined in pencil, but the author and the
date of these underscorings cannot be established, with the exception of one in ink in Lazarev's hand, so it
is the only one reproduced here.

[6]The description of the voyage of the *Otkrytie* and the *Blagonamerenny* from Kronshtadt through the
Atlantic, Indian, and Pacific Oceans (with stops at Copenhagen, Portsmouth, Rio de Janeiro, and Port
Jackson) and through the Pacific to Unalaska, Bering Strait, and Kotzebue Sound and back to Unalaska and
then to New Archangel, of their stay at New Archangel, of the parting of the two ships, and of the *Blagonamerenny*'s voyage to Alta California is omitted here.

Upon entering the bay we were very surprised not to find the *Otkrytie* here, and we now feared that it had met with some misfortune; afterwards, however, we learned that after parting from us it had stayed farther out to sea. In the evening provisions were sent to us from ashore.[7] In the morning, just before noon, the sloop *Otkrytie* arrived and stood at anchor near us.

11 [November]. The leader of the expedition intended to use the period of his sojourn at the port of San Francisco to examine and repair the rigging, the masts and spars, the sails, and the rowing vessels—in short, to put both sloops in the best condition for the subsequent voyage. For this, after having unfurled the sails and lowered the top[m]ast and yards, without losing time we began to examine the ships and make all necessary repairs. Ashore we pitched a tent for an observatory and solicited rooms for quarters for our navigators, taking the chronometers and all of the astronomical instruments to them from both of the sloops. Also, we unloaded the bricks brought from Kronshtadt and on a spot allotted to us began to build a stove for preparing rusks [biscuit or hardtack].[8] Because the latter would be insufficient for all of the forthcoming voyage, Captain Vasilyev arranged to obtain baked bread daily from the Spaniards for feeding the men during our stay at the port of San Francisco and to buy flour for rusks at the missions.[9] In order not to overlook anything during our stay at this port, the leader of the expedition commissioned Mr. Rydalev,[10] the navigator of his sloop, to chart all of the bay, giving him an assistant for this, and he [the expedition's leader] assigned a midshipman and a naval cadet to observe the tides. With everything

---

[7]In the *Blagonamerenny*'s logbook, Navigator Vladimir Petrov records that on 11 November the commandant of the presidio sent one steer (weighing 14 puds, 16 funts), 24 heads of cabbage, 20 heads of lettuce, 375 onions, and 68 radishes to the sloop (Navigator Vladimir Petrov, "Putevoy zhurnal shlyupa *Blagonamerennavo* . . . v 1819 i 1820 godakh" ["Logbook of the sloop *Blagonamerenny* . . . in the years 1819 and 1820"], 11 November 1820, RGAVMF, f. 870, op. 1, d. 3473a/8).

[8]Petrov's logbook notes that on 22 November a bathhouse was contrived of sails ashore for the sloop's company, which also washed their linen there (and again a week later), and that the next day bricks were sent ashore to make a stove for baking rusks (Petrov, "Putevoy zhurnal . . . 1819 and 1820," 22, 23, and 29 November 1820).

[9]On 14 January 1821 the sloop's rusks and peas were inspected, and 62 puds, 31 funts of rusks and 5 puds, 17 funts of peas were found unfit for consumption and discarded overboard (Navigator [Vladimir] Petrov, "Putevoy zhurnal *Blagonamerennavo* . . . v 1821 i 1822 godakh" ["Logbook of the *Blagonamerenny* in the Years 1821 and 1822"], RGAVMF, f. 870, op. 1, d. 3473b/9). The missions ground flour for themselves but traded whole grain to the Russians, who had to mill it at New Archangel. The *Blagonamerenny* received (and stored on its cutter) a total of 126 sacks of wheat in January–February 1821 but only 20 sacks of flour (Petrov, "Putevoy zhurnal . . . 1821 and 1822," 21, 24, 25, and 26 January and 2 and 4 February 1821).

[10]Mikhail Trofimovich Rydalev (ca. 1785–ca. 1835) had two decades of navigational experience with the Russian navy in the Baltic, White, and Caspian Seas before he took part in the voyage of the *Otkrytie* under Captain-Lieutenant Vasilyev in 1819–22. He charted the eastern coast of the Chukchi Sea and the Pribilof Islands before making the first accurate Russian chart of San Pablo Bay. Upon his return to Russia he was promoted to the rank of navigator, eighth class and awarded a lifetime pension of 600 rubles a year. In 1828 he was posted to the Caspian Fleet at Astrakhan, where he later died at the rank of colonel in the Corps of Fleet Navigators. See Bolgurtsev, *Morskoy biografichesky spravochnik*, 167; and Grinëv, *Kto yest kto*, 464.

thus put in order, it remained for us to engage in astronomical observations and manage the sloops, which we commenced forthwith.[11]

While we performed these labors, which lasted 3 months, the weather was mostly fair, and the winds were light, blowing almost always from the northern quarter. Often there was little wind, and sometimes calms, and only eight times during this whole period did a rather strong wind blow, and rarely did it rain.[12]

On 12 December we celebrated the birthday of the Tsar Emperor. On this occasion both sloops were bedecked in topgallant mast flags, and they made a 21-gun salute. Again during the dinner given by the leader of the expedition, who invited all of the Spanish officers from the presidio, we fired 31, then 21, and finally 11 cannons. The fort even took part in this celebration, but only after having asked us for gunpowder to do so, for it had none. In the evening we provided a small display of fireworks.[13]

We greeted the new year agreeably and cheerfully, quite unlike that of a year ago. On 16 January, as a result of an order from the leader of the expedition to compile a map of the port of San Francisco, our captain gave the command of the sloop to me, and, taking provisions for 10 days, he set out with Midshipmen Hall[14] and Gellesem[15] in an armed longboat to examine and describe the bay [San Pablo Bay] and make astronomical observations, ranging from the eastern cape of Mission San Rafael to the north.[16] Upon his arrival at the port of San Francisco Mr. Shishmaryov found the commandant to be Don Luis Argüello, his former acquaintance from Lieutenant Kotsebu's expedition, who was also in this harbor, and he was very glad to see this good Spaniard. Without the slightest difficulty our officers became acquainted with the other officials, especially with the missionaries, who on account of their extreme poverty always accept presents.

---

[11]The words "November 1820" are written in the margin of the manuscript opposite this paragraph.

[12]The phrase "[From] 11 [November 1820] to 10 February 1821" is written in the margin of the manuscript opposite this paragraph. During this period there were usually 1–1½ feet of water in the ship's hold and one crewman on the sick list.

[13]This paragraph was omitted from the published version of 1950, undoubtedly for ideological reasons.

[14]Roman Romanovich Gall [Robert R. Hall] (17??–1822) was the son of Roman Romanovich Gall (1761–1844), an Englishman who joined the Russian navy at fifteen and remained in Russia, becoming a Russian citizen and rising steadily through the ranks to admiral. The son, who charted Bodega Bay, died at Rio de Janeiro on the *Otkrytie*'s homeward voyage. See Grinëv, *Kto yest kto*, 117.

[15]Baron Karl Karlovich von Gellesem, or Gilsen (Karl von Hüllessem) (17??–18??), who had graduated as a naval cadet in 1813, was promoted to the rank of midshipman on the *Blagonamerenny* in early 1820 during its outbound voyage. Upon his return to Russia he wrote an incomplete account of the voyage ("Puteshestvie na shlyupe *Blagonamerenny*," 213–38. In 1825 he was promoted to the rank of captain. See Grinëv, *Kto yest kto*, 122; and Pierce, *Russian America*, 167.

[16]The logbook records that on 16 January, in compliance with Shishmaryov's order "to compile a map of the port of San Francisco," Captain-Lieutenant Lazarev left the sloop in an armed longboat with Navigators Hall and Gellesem and provisions for ten days to survey the bay "from the eastern point of Mission San Rafael to the north" (Petrov, "Putevoy zhurnal . . . 1821 and 1822").

These men do not request them from visiting mariners but simply expect them, considering it an obligation on the part of the latter. Particularly one priest showed himself to be, as we say, a great *beggar*. However, these messrs. also give in their turn but with the difference that they demand money for their presents. Our acquaintance with them afforded us the advantage of going several times to the nearest missions, namely, San Francisco, Santa Clara,[17] and San José. The second has been built on a beautiful, extensive plain that, it seems, is never flooded, and the third is situated on a rather large hill.

Sizable gardens are cultivated at these missions, but they are not well tended; there they grow watermelons, muskmelons, peaches, and other fruits that are valued dearly in our cold climate. They also cultivate grapes, from which they began to make wine during our visit, and they plant wheat, beans, peas, and such. The soil is extremely fruitful. At the poorest mission of San Francisco, wheat yields 50-fold [the seed] and at the others, 120-fold.

With such fertility it is incomprehensible where they can market the grain, for the Spanish government has prohibited all trade with California. It is true that the missions supply the presidios, but this [outlet] means almost nothing when one considers that there are not a hundred men in each of them. The soldiers in this province have [access to] 4 missions, and from 100 to 800 savage Indians work in each of them. Our warships that stop in California for a certain amount of flour and wheat for their own rations, plus our [Russian-]American Company,[18] buy annually up to 3 t[housand] pud[s], and sometimes more; but all of this amounts to very little compared with the amount of grain that is gathered at the 5 or 6 missions. As regards the trade of this company with California, it can be said that it is essential to our colonies, but as it is conducted in the form of the provisionment of ships calling there and is not regulated at all by the government, it is indefinite and irregular; the sale of grain depends upon the wishes of the Spaniards, and when they do sell they take in exchange things of their choosing. If this trade were arranged otherwise by mutual agreement of both governments, then our American colonies, as well as Kamchatka and Okhotsk, would not want for grain and would obtain it very cheaply. One should not take flour in California, for it is sold dearly there, but simply buy wheat and then grind it at our own mills.

California's climate is so good that the livestock there have pasture year-round; only in January and February do they become thin from hunger. However, this

---

[17]The two captains and their officers left their ships on 3 January to visit Mission Santa Clara and returned on 8 January (Petrov, "Putevoy zhurnal . . . 1821 and 1822").

[18]Upon the *Blagonamerenny*'s return to New Archangel, it unloaded in May 1,060 puds (265 sacks) of wheat, 10 sacks and 10 barrels of flour, 2 barrels plus 26 puds, 35 funts of groats, 20 barrels plus 88 puds of rusks, 10 barrels plus 10 puds of peas, and 6 barrels of butter for the Russian-American Company (Petrov, "Putevoy zhurnal . . . 1821 and 1822," 21, 22, 23, 26, and 27 May 1821).

[leanness] stems from the laziness of the Spaniards, for not one of them takes it into his head to make hay for only these two months. Neither the soldiers nor the officers have gardens.

The port of San Francisco is very spacious, and it can be said that in size there is no other like it in all of California. The entrance to it is convenient and visible to ships of all classes; there are no shoals at all in it, apart from a few rocks lying near the shore. The current in it runs up to 3 knots, but faster around the fort of San Joaquín, from which the water seems turbid; because the current runs from various quarters, it makes sand like that seen on sandbanks. Upon entering the bay it is convenient to stand at anchor anywhere; only near the presidio is the bottom sandy, and in the middle there is silt everywhere.

It was stated above that the captain of our sloop went with his officers to chart the northern part of the port of San Francisco at the point where a river [the Sacramento River?] enters it. Although he took chronometers and instruments for this [task], the cold at this time of year, the foul weather, and the short days greatly impeded him, and so he soon returned to the sloop; the remainder of the charting was done by Navigator Rydalev. It seems that this was the first charting of San Francisco Bay by a European.[19] La Pérouse in his atlas copied a Spanish map very inaccurately, and evidently he drew it with eyeball, not geodetic, measurements. Vancouver wanted to chart it, as he ought to have done, but the Spaniards did not let him; and Lieutenant Kotsebu intended to do so but met the same fate. We were very lucky not to have encountered any hindrances.

The port of San Francisco abounds in oaken timber for firewood, and if you cut it yourself they do not demand payment for the wood (unless, perhaps, you are a trader), but it is poor in [fresh] water. To water one must go to a marsh, where water flows from the hills, a distance of about ¾ of a versta from the shore where ships land, dig a hole, surround it with a wattle fence in order to protect it against dirt, pump out the accumulated water several times in order to make sure that it is not dirty, and then pour it into barrels and casks, which are carried or rolled across the marsh with much difficulty. And for this purpose it is necessary to make a [corduroy] road, covering it with branches, boards, and the like, as we had to do. However, despite the fact that this water was nasty and dirty, it kept very well and had not spoiled when we reached Sitka a second time, which took about 3 months. In stocking the aforesaid firewood we always had to peel the bark, which harbored various vermin.

The interior of California is little known to the Spaniards themselves, who from time to time send detachments of soldiers there to catch Indians for work at the missions, and sometimes even the priests also go there under escort.

---

[19]Lazarev was unaware of Lieutenant Khvostov's charting of the bay in 1806 while sojourning with Rezanov.

On 21 January the Russian-American Company brig *Golovnin* arrived at the port of San Francisco from the settlement of Ross to buy wheat. It saluted the fort and the sloop *Otkrytie* with 7 guns, to which the former answered with the same number and the latter with 5 guns.

On 23 January our commander, G. S. Shishmaryov, returned to the sloop. He had determined the width of the bay's entrance to be one Italian mile[20] and its depth 13 and 15 sazh[ens], its latitude 37° 59' N, and its longitude 3' west of the meridian of the presidio of San Francisco. The northern shore is generally lower, marshy, and overgrown with ru[s]hes and in higher places with trees; inland there are hills. The southern shore is elevated, cleared, and hilly; in places there are lowlands and woods. At the entrance [to San Pablo Bay] is found the Spanish settlement of San Pablo, where horses and cattle graze. At the end of the bay a half-mile-wide river [the common estuary of the Sacramento and San Joaquín Rivers] runs to the east, and its depth is 1½ [sazhens?] at its mouth, then 7, and after 5 miles [upstream] again 1½. Its banks are low, marshy, and covered with rushes. The river's mouth is at latitude 38° 4' [N] and at longitude 23' east of the meridian of the presidio of San Francisco. Here Mr. Shishmaryov ended his charting.

On 5 February, when nearly all of the work was finished, three sailors failed to make an appearance on our sloop, but they were found in the hills by Spanish soldiers who had been sent after them and brought them back on the 7th.[21]

On the 9th, when everything was ready for our departure, the Spanish officers came to say goodbye and spent a rather long time with us. In the evening our captain received orders from the leader of the expedition regarding the impending voyage. In them, incidentally, it was stated that our sloop was to keep to the starboard of the *Otkrytie* so that we could observe the signals of the latter and better see both sides of the new route.

In the morning [of the 10th of November] at 6 o'[clock] with a light north-northeast wind, clear weather, and a current from the bay we began to raise anchor. At noon it became calm, and both sloops, having raised their topgallant yards, awaited only a wind in order to get under way; soon it blew again from the north-northeast, and we, having set our sails, went through the channel to the WN½W. The wind in the meantime begin to shift to the north; when we were near the fort of San Joaquín—almost in the strait itself—it suddenly blew from the west-southwest rather freshly, and the current came from the sea. We

---

[20]An Italian mile equals 1.15 English miles or 1.85 kilometers.

[21]The desertion of Russian crewmen from visiting ships was a chronic problem. Sailors were occasionally allowed shore leave or sent ashore to cut firewood, draw water, bake rusks, wash laundry, make besoms, fetch ballast, etc. On 6 February able seamen Khariton Salnikov, Yefim Kosourov, and Aleksey Rozov went ashore on leave and did not return; they were caught in the hills by Spanish soldiers and returned to the *Blagonamerenny* on 8 February (Petrov, "Putevoy zhurnal . . . 1821 and 1822").

began to tack, but having noticed that we were being borne away, we had to drop anchor in a depth of 11 sazh[ens] on a sandy bottom. The *Otkrytie*, staying on a kedge anchor only, also had to come to a halt.

At 8 o['clock] in the evening, with a continuing calm, we noticed 20° over the western horizon a small comet that was turning to the west and nearly forming with Jupiter and Saturn an equilateral triangle; it shone very dimly. We had looked through the telescope the day before but had not seen this comet and had noticed only a bright, shining spot.

At 6 o['clock] in the morning [of the 11th of November] with a breeze from the NEN both sloops raised anchor and, taking the previous compass bearing, left port. Our loaded sloop drew 14 f[eet], 1 i[nch] of water on an even keel, but it should be noted that the firewood and the water had to be taken from the bow for their first use. At half past 7 o'clock we passed the fort, over which a flag had already been raised, but there was nobody to be seen. Then we lay to the west-southwest. After exchanging salutes with the fort and the brig *Golovnin*, the *Otkrytie* at 10 o'cl[ock] took a course to the southwest.

For two more hours the Farallon rocks were visible in the west-southwest, and at midday we found ourselves at an observed latitude of 37° 45' 14" N, bearing south of these rocks 67° SW (and by the true compass 82° SW) at an estimated distance of 11 miles, and at a longitude of 237° 15' 48" E by the chronometer. We took this spot as our point of departure. The barometer registered 30° 38' and the thermometer 9¼[°]. . . .[22]

---

[22]The description of the voyage of the *Blagonamerenny* and the *Otkrytie* in the North Pacific (to the Hawaiian and Aleutian Islands, New Archangel, Bering Strait, and Kamchatka) and of the return voyage to Kronshtadt, with a stopover at Rio de Janeiro, is omitted here.

Excerpts from Nikolay Shishmaryov's Journal of a Visit to [Alta] California, 1820–1821

LIEUTENANT NIKOLAY SHISHMARYOV, EXCERPTS FROM A
JOURNAL OF A VISIT TO [ALTA] CALIFORNIA DURING THE
ROUND-THE-WORLD VOYAGE OF THE SLOOP *BLAGONAMERENNY*
IN 1819–22,[1] NOVEMBER 1820–FEBRUARY 1821

9/21 [November]. . . .[2] At 6:45 [AM] we saw the coast of New Albion from the
N to the right to the NEE, stretching from Cape Mendocino to Point Reyes,
and soon the rocks of the Farallones were revealed to the EN½E. At this time
we lowered the studding sails and took a course to the ENE. At 9 o'clock there
was a light wind, which soon died. . . .[3]

On the 10th/22nd at one o'clock [in the morning], with a NW wind following
the calm, we hove-to to the NEE. At 4 o'clock the rocks of the Farallones were
in a line 68" to the NE and Point Reyes 10° to the NE. By 4:30 the northern rock
of the Farallones was abeam to the right at 3 miles. At 5:30 we hove-to to the
ENE½E. At 6 o'clo[ck] Point Reyes, according to the [magnetic] compass, lay

---

[1]RGAVMF, f. 203, op. 1, d. 7,306, fols. 79v–97 (original holograph). Shishmaryov's manuscript comprises
twenty-four folders bound as a single thick volume with a leather spine and cardboard cover. Besides the
archival label of the Naval Ministry at the top of the cover, in the center there is an earlier label, and on it is
written, apparently, the author's title of his manuscript: "A Journal of 1819, 1820, 1821, and 1822 on the Sloop
Blagonamerenny." The circumstances surrounding the archive's acquisition of the manuscript are unknown.
The text is written in red ink, with few emendations; the handwriting, although generally clear, is peculiar
and not easy to decipher. In the second half of the nineteenth century a proposal to publish the journal
under the editorship of Sergey Vasilyevich Maksimov, a Russian ethnographer, folklorist, and writer, was
abandoned for unknown reasons.

[2]A description of the voyage to the coast of Alta California is omitted here.

[3]Observations of the ship's coordinates and position relative to California's capes are omitted here.

30" to the NW, and to the E of it was a high double cape at 40° NE. The south-ernmost of the rocks of the Farallones was 7 miles to the S. At 8 o'clo[ck] in the evening the depth, according to the lead, was 28 sazh[ens], and the bottom was fine, gray sand with shells. By 10 o'clock the foresail and mainsail had been made ready. Before midnight the depth gradually decreased, and at midnight it was 20 sazh[ens], and the bottom was silt and the finest sand. All night it was clear and calm. The moon illuminated the coast. The high double cape was 4 miles to the NE½E of Point Reyes, according to the [magnetic] compass. At 3:30 in the morning, being fairly close to the SW point of the entrance [to San Francisco Bay], with a light wind between the S and E and a contrary current on the port tack, we turned to port, and at 4 o'clock we hove-to under a maintopsail, the depth at this time being 10 sazh[ens] and the bottom sand. At 5 o'clock in the morning in a depth of 8½ sazh[ens] we close-hauled to starboard. At 7 o'clock they raised a flag over the fort of St. Joaquín. From 9 o'clock in the morning there was a very light breeze from the E and a favorable current. So we began to tack toward the entrance. At 9:30, having the SW point of the northern shore of the entrance ½ a mile to the NE at 40°, we turned to port in a depth of 6 sazh[ens]. At 10:30, having Sea Lion Rocks ¾ of a mile to the SEE, we turned to starboard. The depth was 16 sazh[ens]. Toward 11:30 near the SE point of the N shore we turned to port and soon passed the fort of St. Joaquín. Approach-ing it, we saw officers and soldiers in full-dress uniform, and with a very large hailer they—probably the watch—shouted questions at us. Although we had Lieutenant [Aleksey] Lazarev, who ~~was fluent in~~ understood Spanish, he could hear nothing but a rumble. After we had passed the aforesaid fort, Lieutenant Lazarev was sent ashore with congratulations and an explanation of our coming here and our needs. At noon the barometer stood at 30.08 and the thermometer at 12° [Réaumur]. The wind was very light between the S and E.

11th/23rd. At 12:30 in the afternoon we approached a spit running eastward from the SE point of the entrance. The depth was 10¼ sazh[ens] and the bottom was sand. We set the starboard sheet anchor ½ a mile from shore. At 2 o'clock in the afternoon, with the ebb tide, we raised anchor and moved to the southern point of the spit in a depth of 6½ sazh[ens] and a sandy bottom, where we set the starboard sheet anchor, with the position of the presidio being 22° to the SE. The fort of San Joaquín was 80° to the SW, and after a while it saluted us with 9 guns, which were answered with an equal number. The loaded sloop drew 14 fe[et] at the sternpost and 14 f[eet] at the stem; the lading at the stern was 2 times that at the bow.

Arriving in San Francisco Bay, we expected to see the *Otkrytie* but were very surprised not to meet her. Toward nightfall a bull of 14 p[uds], 16 f[unts], 24 heads of cabbage, 375 onions, 20 heads of lettuce, and 60 radishes were sent to us by the commandant of the presidio, Don Luis Antonio Argüello. At 10 o'clock in the morning [on the 12th], having lowered the longboat and cutter, we took the kedge anchor 1½ cable lengths to the SW of the bow and took in another notch [of the windlass]; at 2 o'clock in the afternoon we raised it again and took it ENE to a depth of 10½ sazh[ens], with a bottom of silt and sand. At 11:30 [AM] the *Otkrytie* entered from the sea with a favorable wind and current and dropped anchor ahead of us closer to the fort, and at 1:45 it saluted the fort with 9 guns, which were answered by an equal number. At 10 o'clock in the evening, having raised the starboard sheet anchor and hauled ourselves ~~several~~ 45 sazhens toward the kedge anchor, we set the port sheet anchor to the W. The night was clear and calm, and the wind blew from the NW and W. At noon the barometer stood at 30.16 and the thermometer at 6.1[°].

13th/25th. The ship drifted and the wind blew from the WNW, but during the night it shifted to the NE, and by morning it had almost completely died; throughout these twenty-four hours the weather was fine. Today we unfurled the sails and lowered the topgallant mast. At midday the barom[eter] [read] 30–35 and the thermometer 6½[°].

14th/26th. From midday the wind blew from the NE. From 8 o'clock in the evening rain began to fall ~~continued~~ and came down harder and harder. During the night it poured. There were 3 men on the sick list; by midday [of the 15th] the rain had stopped, and it became clear, the barom[eter] [reading] 29.94 and the therm[ometer] 27°.

15th/27th. The wind, from the NE, was variable and light. Fresh snow fell on this date, and it was fairly cold. The thermometer showed 1½°. In the afternoon the kedge anchor that had been taken to the ENE was raised and the starboard sheet anchor was put in its place. We lowered the [----] topmast and the lower yards and began first of all to caulk the ship. At 9 o'clock there were 4 men on the sick list and 17½ [barrels?] of water [left], and at noon the barometer [read] 30.26 and the thermom[eter] 8.2°.

16th/28th. The same NE wind. Fine weather. There were 3 men on the sick list, and at noon the barometer stood at 30.39 and the thermometer at 5½°.

After our arrival in San Francisco Bay, toward 13 November before noon the captain [Gleb Shishmaryov] with some officers went ashore, where the Spanish officers were invited to dine with us. At the same time the *Otkrytie* arrived at a very opportune moment for eating together, for its crew had [neither] fresh meat nor greens. The commandant, Don Luis Antonio Argüello, a captain in rank; Lieutenant Ignacio Martínez;[4] a [San] Francisco ensign; and another (recently

---

[4]Ignacio Martínez (1774–185?), a native of Mexico City, enlisted as a cadet in 1799 and arrived in Alta California in 1800 to serve first at Santa Bárbara and then at San Diego. He was promoted to the rank of lieutenant in 1817 and was mistakenly posted to San Francisco, where he served as commandant from 1822 to 1831. See [Bancroft], *California Pioneer Register,* 241.

a sergeant) from a cavalry company, Don [José Antonio] Sánchez,[5] came to dine with us [on board]. All of them were with their families and in full-dress uniform. A priest (formerly of the presidio) came with them. His name was Juan [Vicente Cabot],[6] or Ivan to us; from the very beginning he brought apples and chickens to us as gifts. They were all glad to spend time with us, especially the ladies, who, it seems, had never managed to attend a decent dinner with foreigners. One could notice this at the table. They did not know that one should eat with knives and spoons. After dinner, in order to enjoy the fine weather, we went ashore, where it was more interesting to see their presidio.

First of all, it took not a little trouble to go ashore, for the breakers hampered our moving the sloop closer, and there was no landing anywhere. The Spaniards [Californios] have no need of one (for they never leave their dwellings, unless someone invites them; then they are prepared, it seems, to sacrifice everything except their lives, the reason likely being their penury). During the sojourn here of our envoy Rezanov (who had been sent to Japan) on a ship with Khvostov and Davyd[ov], they constructed a landing and a fairly decent road to the presidio, and if they [i.e., the Spaniards] had maintained it even a little, then it would not have deteriorated. This [negligence] demonstrates their carelessness and laziness.

Somehow we got ashore, and from there we hoped to go the 1½ verstas to the presidio. The road was sinking into the surrounding marshes, and for that reason it was necessary to take flagsto[n]es [?] with us and walk on them; after 150 sazhens the shore became slightly higher and the going better. Finally, we had to climb to the top of a sandy and clayey hill; it has been known to be impassable after rain. Having thus ascended the hill, we saw the presidio. It stands on a flat plain covered in verdure year-round. There are no large trees along the road, [only] bushes.

Approaching the presidio, we came upon endless horse and cattle droppings, as well as the heads and hoofs of bulls, offal, and all sorts of filth;[7] here is another [demonstration] of their neglect of neatness and cleanliness.

A place where officers and soldiers live is called a presidio. It is built as a square and surrounded by a brick [adobe] wall just over 3 sazhens high. There is a wicket on each side and gates on 2 opposite sides. ~~Passing any of these wickets,~~

---

[5]José Antonio Sánchez (1775–1843), a native of Sinaloa, soldiered mostly at San Francisco from 1791, becoming commandant in 1829 and retiring in 1836. See [Bancroft], *California Pioneer Register*, 318.

[6]Juan Vicente Cabot (1781–185?), a peninsular from the Balearic island of Mallorca, joined the Franciscan order in 1796. In 1804 he sailed from Cádiz for Veracruz and entered San Fernando College in Mexico City; volunteering for the California missions, he reached Monterey in 1805. Cabot served at several missions, mainly San Miguel (1807–19 and 1824–34), as well as Mission San Francisco from the spring of 1819 until late 1820. He accompanied military expeditions to the Tulare Country in the Central Valley in 1814, 1815, and 1818. His health failing, Cabot left for Spain in 1835. See Geiger, *Franciscan Missionaries*, 32–34.

[7]These were the leavings of a matanza.

~~one reaches a courtyard, from which a fairly wide [----]~~. In the middle of the presidio is a large plaza; a kind of gallery, 2 arshins wide and paved with slabs, has been built around the four barracks, or, rather, sheds. But all of the presidio's interior space re[p]resents a plaza. In one wing, that is, on one side, live the commandant, lieutenants, ensign, 2 details for the visiting priest, and 1 large detail for the church. The other 3 sides are occupied by soldiers, who total 75 me[n] here, including cavalrymen and infantrymen. There are fewer of the former, i.e., of cavalrymen, [than of] infantrymen.

If you meet a Spanish offic[er] on the road, he will gladly invite you to his home. You will enter an apartment or house [*saray*], fo[r] they closely resemble our houses, except that theirs are much more untidy; it is a large, very high room with 2 small, barred windows and four big doors. The windows lack glass; [when] it is fairly cold in the months of January, February, and March—especially when it is windy—then they close the shutters and doors against the hard frost and sit thus in the dark, [the men] in greatcoats and the women lying on the floor by a brazier under sheepskins made expressly for this purpose, and they drink [hot] chocolate frequently in order to warm themselves somewhat. The interior is whitewashed, and some worthless pictures hang on the walls. In ½ of the apartment there are benches, where they usually ask you to sit; in some [of these apartments] there is a plain table, but I saw one at the lieutenant's only (at the commandant's benches were the whole of the room's furniture). To the right and to the left there are even smaller compartments, which serve them as bedrooms. Here even the floor is stone, and so it is colder still for them [there]. In these compartments there are chests, a table, and an inferior bed (curtained without fail) covered with a *sarape* [poncho] or blanket made at the mi[s]sions; the floors in these apartments are never washed, and for that reason they are always dirty. There are also horses and cows at the presidio. This is what it was possible to notice the 1st evening.

Toward 6 o'clock we went home, going not via the clayey steep slope that we had climbed to the presidio but via another, much less steep and less rough slope, and for that reason it [i.e., the footing] was firmer. The wind blew from the NE, by the evening from the N, and at 1:30 [on the 17th] from the W, and then it rained but stopped by 3 o'clock. There were 3 me[n] on the sick list and 14 [barrels?] of water [left], and at noon the barometer [read] 30.7 and the thermometer 9½°.

18th/30th. At 9 o'clock in the morning the commander [Vasilyev], with a detachment of only those officers who could go, having obtained saddle horses at the presidio, rode with the Spanish officers to the mis[s]ion 3 leagues distant from the presidio. The road to the mission was very bad, mostly sand, and the frequent hills that had to be crossed greatly tormented the horse[s], and it was rather difficult to walk. No very large trees were growing, but we came upon some of a fairly decent size; in riding along the road it was necessary to be careful lest the entangled branches and twigs put out one's eyes. Thus did 20 men, all on horseback, pass the last hill, from which the mission called San Francisco is visible. it comprises several stone We arrived there in a few minutes, and 2 priests in gray caftans met us in the gallery, where about 25 or perhaps more Indians stood, all naked (except for the requisite covered [private parts), and they played various sacred hymns rather agreeably. The first room that we entered was exactly the same size as the presidio's, the difference being that here it was somewhat cleaner and its windows had glass; otherwise the furniture was the same, comprising a large table and 2 benches around it. In the middle of the wall there was a small cupboard, where cups, spoons, knives, forks, glasses, plates, and such were stored.

From the hall there were several doors to small rooms that serve them as bedrooms. Here the furniture was much better: a bunk,[8] a bed[9] or a mattress, pillows with clean linen, a table clock, and various [other] items. After seeing their rooms, we went into the garden. It was fair[ly] extensive and had fruit trees and vegetables, but they were arranged without any taste; the helter-skelter paths were choked with leaves. Then we saw the entire establishment, for example, the barracks for workers (which here numbered about 2 thousand men, all Indians), the joinery, the blacksmithy, and the tannery (they dress the hides of their sheep, not their bulls, for soldiers' boots). There were storehouses for peas, wheat, beans, and various vegetables. The place where they scatter [----][10] wheat Although they have a gristmill, it had been broken before our arrival, and for that reason the priests were forcing several hundred girls to grind on a stone slab made just like that which we use for pulverizing paints, and from [knowing] this work one can judge their progress. Then they sift the ground flour. We inspected

Afterwards we walked to the Church of St. Francis, where the priests showed us their sacristy, which certainly merits attention. In their churches we admired one picture more [than any other]. It was painted by a rather bad artist, was not very large, and was hung high on the wall. A woman, crucified by her arms and legs, is being trampled by animals for, they say, adultery. In the same picture a man is having his nostrils slit for taking snuff—but not for smoking, for the priests themselves all smoke, and some even take snuff. Of course, such depictions are displayed, perhaps, for [the sake of] the completely dependent Indians, and they [i.e., the priests] want them to believe that in the afterlife such pleasures will be punished thusly. Finally, we seated ourselves to dine; it [i.e., dinner] was

---

[8]Russ., *krovat*.

[9]Russ., *postel*.

[10]Illegible word: "ground"?

prepared to their liking and was a fairly decent meal. The tableware might kill anyone else's appetite; the knives and forks were very small and very dirty. The spoons, mostly tin, were also dirty; nothing had its proper appearance. At 6 o'clock they served tea. The large teapot, in which they boiled a very great deal of tea, acted as a samovar; they offered 3 or 4 cups, including chipped ones, and we drank by turns, first the oldest, then the youngest, and they themselves had to wipe everything dry without fail. However, the hospitality was quite good. At this time the commander of our detachment, upon a request from the priests, promised to repair their gristmill; but it seems that they wanted Mikhail Nikolayevich [Vasilyev] to do more than make it right. He had seen their unsuccessful work in grinding wheat, and so the next day 3 carpenters and 2 blacksmiths were sent to the mission [in order to make hand mills]. While the sun was setting we rode to the presidio and went from there to our sloop.

19 Novem[ber]/1 December. On the morning of the next day, that is, the 19th, we moved our chronometers and instruments to the presidio to the 2 rooms where we had met the visiting priests. They had put glass in the only window in each room and an iron stove in both rooms, a stovepipe leading to the window in one room and to the door in the other (front) room; these rooms were always warm. The Spaniards liked this very much, and they came very often to warm themselves in the evening and regaled us with something [all] the while.

21 Novem[ber]/3 Dec[ember]. There was no work today because of the sabbath. After dinner the crew went ashore to go walking and riding; since only the soldiers have horses, they leased them for a taler[11] for an evening [of riding], and now they were spurring the horses to the utmost.

The first concern of the commander of the detachment was to see that every day on both ships there was fresh meat, greens, and baked bread instead of rusks, not much of which would remain for us without economizing. Moreover, usually the crew made tea every morning and sago wine[12] twice a week. Those days were Wednesday and Friday.

On the 22nd, too, there was no work, and the crew were permitted to go to a bathhouse that we had made from a tent and to wash their linen and bedding, for which cauldrons, tubs, washtubs, and the like were issued.

The Spaniards themselves do not make stoves, and they do not even know how to make them. They cook their food on a hearth, where instead of bread they bake flatcakes [tortillas?], and they make some of them not from [wheat] flour but from

---

[11]A taler, or thaler, was a silver coin issued by various German states. Here it is equated with a piaster, or silver dollar.

[12]Presumably an alcoholic beverage (like kava) made from the starchy pith (sago) of the sago palm (genus *Metroxylon*, especially *M. laeve* or *M. rumphii* of the East Indies).

corn, or maize, as it is called. However, stoves had been made at the lieutenant's and the recently promoted ensign's, where our sailors baked bread. It is said that these stoves were built by an Englishman during [Captain] Vancouver's stay.[13]

23 Novem[ber]/5 Decem[ber]. Of the 1,000 bricks that we had ordered at Kronshta[d]t, 500 usable ones remained, and they were moved ash[ore] to the presidio in order to make a Russian stove and bake rusks from the flour supplied by the Spaniards. Clay was extracted from the soil, which is clayey. Within 1½ weeks it was built at the presidio between 3 walls protruding from the roof, and a cover was made of sails over the stove atop poles set in the ground so as to shelter it from the rain and keep the rusks dry. During the construction of our stove the Spaniards watched with surprise; I even showed the ensign how to lay bricks, but [even] with ready-made bricks and clay he could not make one in his own home. This further demonstrates their laziness. They would rather sit behind the cooks at home, not working and complaining of their fate, than do some work for a little while and be free of the hard frost. Today we dragged the longboat and the pinnace onto the beach opposite the sloop for repairs. Meanwhile, having calked the outside [of the ship], we began to caulk the decking, which on the way from Sitka had been loosened a great deal, even the skylights[14] having been dislodged; consequently, the decking had to be relaid.

On Sunday the 28th/10th there was no work. The crew went ashore and walked everywhere.

29th/11th. The crew went to the bathhouse to bathe and wash their linen, and for that reason there was no work.

30 Novemb[er]/12 Decemb[er]. Today there was work of every kind. About 5 o'clock in the afternoon the Spaniards held vespers in the presidio for the Virgin of Guadalupe's holy day on the morrow, that is, 1 December, and afterwards, following a procession with her icon, they fired the cannons in the plaza of the presidio. The icon was adorned with ribbons, beads, and foil and carried by 4 maidens, who were all in black silk dresses.* Yesterday the commandant, Don Luis Antonio Argüello, invited our commander and all of his officers to dine and attend church with him tomorrow.

1st/13th. So the next day, that is, the 1st, about 8:30 we all rode to the presidio. I did not have the pleasure of seeing them dine and sitting at the table. The reason for this [absence] was my watch duty. About 7:30 in the morning after prime song

---

* The Spaniards attribut[e] their liberation and the renewal of their faith to the Virgin of Guadalupe [the patroness of the Mexican *independistas*].

[13]Vancouver does not verify this assertion in his journal.
[14]Russ., *lyuminatory*.

they carried the icon and cross in the same way [i.e., in procession], and the fort of San Joaquín had already heralded [saluted] the holiday.

Our officers arrived at the presidio at dinner time, but not everyone had come, and so it was not very pleasant for the Spaniards, especially the priests.

After dinner, too, they carried the icon and fired the cannons in the presidio. After all of this [festivity] there was a parade in the plaza. This was the only [parade] day during the whole of our stay here of 3 months, but, not having a convenient opportunity to see the parade, I cannot describe it. The commandant's dinner was quite good but [eaten] in the same way. It concluded with dancing in their style, that is, hopping in one spot and drumming with one's feet [as a fandango]; the music at this time was regimental, that is, the soldiers played—one on the violin and another on a balalaika [guitar?], and a third whistled.

During the holiday the commandant gave his soldiers wine to drink (called *aguardiente*),[15] which was even sold in a very strong form by the ensign and one of the soldiers), and it was customary for each drunken soldier to arrive at his superior's (commandant's) and sit as long as he wanted and even dance with some of the lieutenant's daughters—3 eligible [postpubescent and/or unmarried] girls and 1 12-year-old. Such behavior on the part of subordinates toward their superior in the presence of foreign officers was not very agreeable to us. Finally, it reached a point where a tall, drunken drummer approached the commandant holding a knife behind his back; seeing this, some told the Spanish officers, but their manners did not allow anyone to remove him, and for that reason the déclassé guests were obliged to leave with the knife and return early to the ship. In the evening after vespers they again carried the icon to the presidio under several volleys, which marked the end of the holiday.

By 12 December all of the outside of the ship had been scraped, as well as the deck; passing along the yards, they [i.e., the crewmen] hoisted the rigging into place. They extended the lower shrouds, stays, backstays, and main *ulingi*[16] and, after raising the topmast and extending the jib boom, they spread the rigging. The longboat and pinnace that had been hauled onto the beach were quite ready; they were waiting only for the paint to dry.

11th/23rd. In the evening, namely, the evening of the 12th, the commander of the detachment suggested that tomorrow, weather permitting, flags be flown at daybreak and after the prayer service 31 guns be fired from both ships. This evening all of the officers, ours as well as the Spanish, were invited to the dinner table.

12th/24th. The next day, namely, the 12th, having finished the prayer service on our sloop, we all went in full-dress uniform to the *Otkrytie;* but because a fresh

---

[15]Literally, "fiery water," meaning brandy or rum (note the similarity to the native term "firewater").

[16]Presumably another element of the rigging, probably some sort of stays.

wind had arisen by midday, the commander did not order the flying of flags at daybreak and [instead] ordered their raising on the flag[s]taffs one by one. Thus, after a thanksgiving service in the open for the birthday of His Imperial Majesty, following the *Otkrytie* we fir[ed] 31 guns and raised flags on the flagstaffs—the Spanish on the front, the flagship's[17] on the middle, and the jack on the rear flagstaff. We were very sorry that the wind had not allowed us to show our daybreak [flag display] to the Spaniards. At 2 o'clock in the afternoon we took our places at the tables, one in the captain's cabin and the other at the officers'. During dinner the sloop *Blagonamerenny* fired 21 guns to the health of the Tsar Emperor. Afterwards the same number [were fired] to the health of the Spanish king; finally, our sloop fired 11 guns to the health of their governor of California (his name was Don Pablo Vicente de Solá) ~~and in the evening it was terminated~~. The attending commandant and his officers, wanting to share our rejoicing, ordered the fort to fire an equal number for our tsar; but on account of their slowness they were unable to get ready, and for that reason, when they drank to the health of our tsar, the fort did not fire, but it had to salute their king. Toward evening their families and children were invited; the eligible girls danced and sang songs. The holiday ended with fireworks and rockets.

14th/26th. On 14 December, having removed our sloop's rudder, we took it ashore at high tide; and then it was slowly dragged a little farther so as to be out of reach of the water. Its hard use, especially in fresh crosswinds, forced our captain to decide to shorten the rudder; for this 1 reason it was dragged ashore.*

16th/28th. Today it was quite cold, especially early in the morning. On land all streams, pools, and marshes froze. At 4 o'clock in the morning the thermometer fell to 0.5° [Réaumur]. The Spaniards said that they had not had such cold weather for a long time before the arrival of our ships; however, although the atmosphere and the sky were clear and the air was fresh, the ice on the puddles surprised them and forced them to dress warmly. By midday the thermometer indicated 3°.

17th/29th. For the next twenty-four hours, namely, [until] the morning of the 17th, the thermometer indicated 0° with clear and fair weather.

6 December was my name day, and all of the officers, and especially I, wanted to spend the day together and have dinner on the sloop, and for that reason in the evening we invited all of the Spanish officers and their wives and children to dine with us. Today's weather was fair, and so, after having pitched a tent ~~and having cleared the cannons from the quarterdeck~~ and cleared the quarterdeck of

---

*The lower part was shortened abo[ut] 5 inches, and the upper part was levelled, so that the middle became 7 i[nches].

[17]The first admiral's flag, i.e., St. Andrew's ensign.

flags and cannons, we laid a table. But owing to the poverty of our kitchen, it was impossible not only to bake a large pastie[18] or patty [or pâté][19] but even to toast [or grill] a good piece [of bread], and for that reason the *Otkrytie*'s cook (being better than ours) was sent ashore to the recently promoted sergeant's, where he made large apple pasties and patties in his stove and roasted lamb [or mutton] that had been sent by the priests. However, when everyone had assembled, it was necessary to wait for the large pasties and roast, and it was about 4 o'clock at least before we sat down to eat. We passed these twenty-four hours very enjoyably. My 1 cask[20] of wine from Port Jackson [Sydney] was taken for madeira, so I did not dampen the holiday in the least.

On the 18th and 19th it was also cold in the morning, the thermometer indicating ½°, but by midday it was indicating no less than 5[°].

25th/6th. Nothing had yet been stocked for our officers, and so Lieut[enant] Lazarev, as the keeper of our company, went at noon today in the launched longboat to Mission San Rafael, which was 60 miles distant[21] from the presidio to the N. In the longboat there were 13 m[en] with sufficient provisions and some rum.

27th/8th. From this date we began to review the rusks, and for that reason all of the men were put to it [i.e., the task]. Moldy rusks were discarded and the rest dried thoroughly and repacked in barrels and stored in their place in the stern hatchway.[22]

29th/10th. Today the longboat returned safely, and they [i.e., the crewmen] had not only been unable to get provisions but even any for themselves, for the mission had been founded [only] recently [in 1817], and for that reason it still had nothing; the Indian residents and the priest himself, Estevan [Tapis],[23] still live in huts.

1/13 Janu[ary]. After a prayer service for the new year, the commander gave a dinner, and all of the Spaniards ashore came to it.

3rd/15th. Today in the evening, namely, at 2 o'clock at night, the commander sent a notice to our captain. Tomorrow morning, weather permitting, he would set off about 6 o'clock; for that reason, having risen early and seen the fair weather, we quickly began to prepare ourselves. The longboat was ready, and so we had only to dress for travel and to breakfast. At 6:30, as soon as the longboat pushed

---

[18]Russ., *pirog.*

[19]Russ., *pashtet.*

[20]Russ., *ankerok,* or *anker:* a cask with a liquid capacity of about 3 *vedros* (pails), or about 36 liters or 38 quarts (9–10 ½ American gallons).

[21]The actual distance is some twenty miles.

[22]Russ., *akhterlyuk.*

[23]Estevan Tapis (1756–1825), a peninsular from Catalonia, was a longtime missionary, having arrived in Alta California in 1790. He served as president of the province's missions from 1803 to 1812. During Shishmaryov's sojourn Tapis was actually stationed at Mission San Juan Bautista, and presumably he was visiting Mission San Rafael at the time.

off from the *Otkrytie*, we quickly pushed off, too (having given instructions to Midshipman Gellisem [Gillsen], who remain[ed] on the sloop), and we boated along the shore to the E. At first the wind was favorable.

The reason for our journey was the de[s]ire of our ow[n] commander and all of the officers to see the other missions, especially Santa Clara, which had been praised by all of the Spaniards, and we directed our course thither; Midshipman Stogov,[24] the astronomer, and the navigat[or] were left on the *Otkrytie*. The pilot, who had recently been promoted to sergeant, sat beside the commander in the longboat.

The commander had wanted to set out before the 3rd, but the rainy weather was the reason why he had not succeeded in doing so, and therefore the trip to Santa Clara was known to everyone. The lieutenant, who had also been invited to accompany us, said that he would go not in the longboat, fearing its rolling, but on horseback along the shore, and he invited those of us who wished to do so [to go] with him, promising a good horse and assuring us besides that the road was excellent. At first I was determined [to go], but the whole distance from the presidio to Santa Clara—judged to be 18 leagues—would have to be [traveled] on horseback, and for that reason I feared that illness might befall me (which would be very easy) from my unaccustomedness [to such riding], or, one could say, from my initiation. Finally, however, at his request I decided [to go]. So when the captain and his officers began to prepare themselves, I, taking a bottle of rum and a bottle of wine, set off to the presidio. Awakening my companion, I said that our men had already gone. But he, after arising, drank some chocolate, and they readied 2 horses, and it was already 9:30 before we set out. With us there was a soldier armed with a rifle, a shield, and a lasso against Indian attacks. ~~The reason why they travel everywhere armed, especially afar, is this: it has happened that the Indians have shot arrows at them, often killing them.~~ An officer or a priest never travels without a soldier. Thus did the three of us ride the designated route. Within ½ an hour we passed the nearest mission of San Francisco, and from there right to Santa Clara the road is really excellent—level and green, and we constantly encountered high laurel and various other trees. /**Of animals, there were many**/ coyotes, geese, and ducks. Passing the halfway mark, where they pasture horses, cattle, and sheep and where they have built a small shack for the soldier who guards them, we stopped, drank a glass of wine and ate some turnovers[25] [empanadas?] brought by the lieutenant, and meanwhile the soldiers went to catch 2 horses to replace mine and the soldier's, which were quite tired,

---

[24]Ivan Petrovich Stogov, who was later (1840–50) to serve as the vice director of the Shipbuilding Department of the Russian Admiralty. See Grinëv, *Kto yest kto*, 512.

[25]Russ., *pirogi*.

and within an hour we were ready to continue. The closer we approached our destination, the worse the road became, for before we had begun our journey rain had spoiled [it], and we often had to ride through marshes, which were not, however, very boggy. Three-quarters of the way from the presidio there is a stone building with 2 decent rooms, and one can overnight there from high wind or rain. We encountered a great many geese, ducks, and animals resembling our wolves (which they call coyotes).[26] Finally, on a level place there appeared a white stone building, which proved to be Mission Santa Clara. Until now the longboats had been visible to us everywhere, and if the wind had favored them, maybe they would have arrived before us, of course.

For clothes the soldier who had come with us wore a leather shirt (used for defense against Indian arrows), and he bore a shield on his arm and wielded a rifle in order to show the thousands of Indians everywhere that they [i.e., the Spaniards] were always prepared to repulse them.

Thus did we arrive at Santa Clara before sunset about 4 o'clock, so we had ridden a little more than 6 hours. The work of the mission is supervised by 2 priests, the younger of which [José Viader][27] was absent [at] Mission San José; here the older one, named Father Magín [Matías Catalá],[28] met us. He immediately treated us to chocolate and various kinds of apples and tried to receive us as courteously as possible.

His first question to the lieutenant was, who was I and why was I here; and when he learned that, besides myself, other Russian officers were coming in two longboats, the displeasure in his face was noticeable. He wondered why those Spaniards who knew our intentions and were even coming themselves had not informed him of our visit well in advance, [thereby] making it necessary [for him] to try to render his services. From me he tried to learn what we, as well as the men [in the longboats], needed; but I explained to him as far as I was able in Spanish that we did not need anything and that until the arrival of our commander I knew nothing. I only asked the old man that he send a rider to see where the longboats were and whether they would overnight here; not knowing

---

[26]In North America, coyotes came to also be called "prairie wolves" or "bush wolves," as opposed to "timber wolves."

[27]José Viader (1765–18??), a Catalan peninsular, joined the Franciscan order in 1788. In 1795 he left Spain for Mexico, and a year later he reached San Francisco, whereupon he was assigned to Mission Santa Clara. He remained there for thirty-seven years. As early as 1820 he requested permission to retire, but he did not leave Alta California until 1833, when all of the Franciscan missions north of San Miguel were transferred to the Zacatecans. See Geiger, *Franciscan Missionaries*, 263–65.

[28]Magín Matías Catalá (1761–1830), a peninsular from Catalonia, was ordained in the Franciscan priesthood in 1785. The next year Magín sailed from Cádiz for Mexico, where he trained for six years at Mexico City's San Fernando College. He arrived in Alta California in 1793 and was assigned as chaplain to the *Aránzazu* on its voyage northward to Nootka Sound. Upon his return Catalá served at Mission Santa Clara from 1794. See Geiger, *Franciscan Missionaries*, 42–46.

the language, it cost me much effort to talk to him, yet he came to like me and tried by every means to please me.

At teatime a soldier came and said that they [i.e., those in the longboats] were far away and would not be overnighting; I pitied them then because during the night it would become quite cold and everything would be covered with hoarfrost, and in the cramped longboats they would not, of course, be as comfortable as I.

Later, after dinner, the entertaining old man turned the conversation with me toward political affairs, for examp[le], he asked how many princes and princesses we had, which were married to whom, and such; to tell the truth, I wanted to leave him quickly, but I had to meet his wishes as far as possible, and I noticed that he liked very much to talk to me, although [I] knew no more, perhaps, than 30 or more common [Spanish] words.

I slept in the same room as the lieutenant; a bed, a mattress with 4 blankets, and 2 pillows with clean bed linen constituted my berth, and from the journey that I had made on horseback I slept very well, which would have been impossible in the longboats that night.

5th/17th. The next day early in the morning the old man sent 18 horses there [to the longboats], and they were much needed by them, especially because several times they had foundered on a sandbar, thanks to the inept pilot not knowing the channel, and he did not even know a suitable landing place, and they had to land quite far from the mission. The road hither was very poor. Finally, toward 10 o'clock the commander and all of the officers reached the mission, having left the longboats at the landing place. The men, who had all likewise been left there, were ordered to pitch tents on the bank and to cook themselves food from the salted beef and fresh English meat that they had brought and to use tea in the morning and in the evening; moreover, they shot geese and ducks with their muskets and ate rather well all of the time.

On the 5th, having all dined together at Santa Clara, we rode to Mission San José, 6 leagues distant from Santa Clara. Father Magín had sent a soldier there beforehand to announce our visit, and so at San José they kn[e]w about our visit of it. In saying goodbye to the old man we were asked [by him] to come again the next day to dine at his mission, and the commander gave his word to [honor] his request.

Thus did a whole troop of cavaliers set off. The road was not as level as that to Santa Clara, and sandier. However, there were sufficient plains meadows with grazing herds of livestock; and all the places that we encountered were very interesting.

Toward 6 o'clock in the evening we reached the aforesaid mission. Its 2 priests and a third [Viader] from [Santa] Clara met us in the gallery with music and showed us other signs of respect.

The building in which they live is the same everywhere, and therefore a table had been laid the length of the large hall and set with various fruits, grapes, and wine (made here). Our interpreters suff[ic]ed, and so we were able to converse with them. After a while, with the permission of the oldest of the priests, named Narciso [Durán],[29] we went at the urging of all of them to examine the establishment.

The mission, which had been founded very recently [in 1797], had not yet succeeded in building [very much]. The Church of San José, various storehouses, and the dwellings for the soldiers (who totalled 8 me[n]) and themselves [i.e., missionaries] were of stone; however, not all of the residents, or workers, who numbered 4,000 here, lived in them yet, and most of them lived in hu[t]s that had been very well built.

The organization of agriculture soon became evident. A water mill, which had been very skillfully made, deserves attention.

Water from various places runs into a basin, where it is impounded by valves and cannot flow anywhere. A wooden chute leads from the basin to the mill some distance away. The mill is activated [with] the help of millstones under a wheel with paddles. Water leaving the basin runs along the chute and strikes downward on the paddles, thereby activating the wheel, which sets the millstones in motion.

Paths, beds, and flower plots have been quite artfully made in the garden, where all kinds of apples, peaches, and grapes grow in very good order.

The mission stands on a low hill from which the sea and nearly the whole establishment (which is very extensive) are visible. There are various workshops, a tannery, and establishments for processing wool and manufacturing blankets and serapes (like blankets but with a hole in the top and used by both officers and soldiers instead of cloaks in cold weather).

We all overnighted at the mission in one room, the 2 captains sleeping on beds and all of the other 11 men side by side on blankets sp[r]ead on the floor. By nightfall a wind was blowing and snow was falling, so that it was quite cold. Because they had not made stoves in the rooms, they ordered the fetching of braziers, which were brought with hot coals; it seemed very good at first, but after some time they did [not] feel the coals at all, and in the morning they all had headaches. After having a drink of tea here, the commander, in spite of the

---

[29]Narciso Durán (1776–1846), a native of Catalonia, arrived in Alta California in 1806 with his fellow Catalan Buenaventura Fortuny, and both were assigned to Mission San José. In May 1817 Durán accompanied a two-week expedition up the Sacramento and San Joaquín Rivers under Commandant Luis Argüello of San Francisco (see Chapman, *Expedition on the Sacramento*). Durán and Fortuny served together at Mission San José until 1826, when Fortuny was transferred to Mission San Francisco Solano and was succeeded by Durán, who remained until 1833. Their charge, like Mission Santa Clara, flourished. Durán became president of all of the province's missions in 1825. See Geiger, *Franciscan Missionaries*, 68–75.

snowstorm and the slush, wanted to go, and he was prompted to leave all the more by the fact that he had given his word to be at dinner; but the priest here from [Santa] Clara by the name of Viader took everything upon himself, and instead they persuaded [him] to dine with them, and so the commander stayed.

At this time Father Narciso, as the host, gave all of us gifts of Indian arrows, bows, and various curios. The wine that he presented from his own garden proved quite good, and so we asked him to give us a supply, and he willingly consented and promised to send it with the curios in a longboat.

6th/18th. After we had dined with them at 12 o'clock, the horses were ready, and so we were able to leave at one o'clock in the afternoon. The weather was very foul; the snowstorm and slush forced some of us to buy serapes and to lose 3 talers each in order to cover ourselves against the snow, all of our greatcoats having been left in the longboats.

Thus did we set off to Santa Clara. After riding a while, the weather improved and soon became quite fair. Not far from Santa Clara—I recko[n] a distance of 1 league or more—there is a pueblo, or village, and as it was still fairly early the commander bent his way there in order to examine it. This village comprises a small stone building and several huts that are encountered on the route; we saw rather many livestock of various kinds. Its head is an old sergeant, and 3 soldiers form his guard or garrison.

A small stone house of 2 rooms is his dwelling; he had nothing with which he could treat us, and poverty was evident in the rooms, which were very dirty. From here to Santa Clara there is a fairly good trail, with large maple trees on both sides; we reached Santa Clara at 6 o'clock in the evening.

The naturalist Shtein[30] had already been gone 1½ weeks to examine all of the missions; his guide was an armed Spanish soldier, with our sailor Kharlam Salnikov,[31] also armed. They arrived at the village at the same time as we did, and from there they set out for Santa Clara with us. He had been in Monterey, the chief place in all of California, and had been given a cordial reception by the governor and all of the officers there.

Upon our arrival at Santa Clara, Father Magín began to make a fuss about beds and tried, as it were, to provide us with a good rest; meanwhile, we needed to warm ourselves against the wet weather, and as much as we tried to order tea or vodka, the friar, from his fussiness and stinginess, paid little attention. However, after urgent requests they gave us supper, and after eating we went to sleep; rooms with beds, each with a pillow and a decent number of blankets, had already been prepared for everyone; 3 m[en] slept in each room, and 2 in several rooms.

---

[30]Fyodor Shtein, a German naturalist, was the expedition's physician.
[31]Unidentified.

On the 7th/19th, having taken a proper breakfast, all of the officers set off in the longboats, and we, namely, the lieutenant, Lieutenant Boil [Boyle?],[32] and I, wanting to tr[a]vel on horseback, stayed to dine; especially the lieutenant wanted to stay, and, it seemed, with Father Magín. We wanted to ride after them, but the lieutenant responded that there were no horses, and he sent for some to be caught; although we saw his ruse, it was necessary to meet his wish. As soon as we had dined and the horses were readied, we bade farewell to the friar and thanked him for his favor and cordial reception, and all three of us, with the soldier, set off. The farther we went, the fresher the wind blew, especially toward evening, and there was even frost, and combined with the headwind, it afforded us little pleasure, to tell the truth. About 5 o'clock we reached the [stone] building with 2 rooms. Here we halted, and the soldier caught 2 fresh horses, and after drinking a glass of rum, we proceeded. We saw that the lieutenant was reluctant to continue, and several times he urged us to remain and overnight, but we firmly refused and decided that it was better to proceed, despite the wind and frost. The route seemed very long to me, and I even reprimanded the lieutenant for losing our way; finally, about 8 o'clock in the evening we reached Mission San Francisco. From fatigue I could barely move my legs; I was frozen from the cold, and after having had [so much] exercise, I was very hungry, but Father José and the other friar, Blas,[33] immediately realized [our plight] and gave us potluck to eat and wine to drink and left us to overnight here, which we were very glad to do. We slept better here than anywhere else; each man was allotted a room with a mattress and 2 pillows with clean pillowc[a]ses and sheets; our fatig[u]e correspondingly affected our sleep, and we awakened at 8 o'clock in the morning. Having drunk some tea, we rode to the presidio, where we arrived at 10 o'clock in the morning.

8th/20th. The longboats set off ½ a day before us and because of a strong headwind had to overnight en route; at 4 o'clock in the afternoon they reached the sloop, and although it was not raining, everyone was drenched and frozen.

In going from the sea into San Francisco Bay the course is NE and the depth gradually decreases, but more to the S, or right, side, so one keeps very close to it. The fort of San Joaquín has been built on the right side atop a fairly high and isolated headland.[34] The left side is much lower and is right at sea level.

---

[32]Roman Platonovich Boil (Boyle?) (1794–1854) later (1851) became a vice admiral. See Grinëv, *Kto yest kto*, 70.

[33]Blas Ordaz (1792–1850) was a peninsular who arrived in Alta California in 1820 from Mexico City's San Fernando College. While serving at Mission San Francisco, he joined a month-long military expedition to the north under Captain Luis Argüello to check rumors of intrusion by English or American settlers. Subsequently Ordaz served at a variety of missions, and he was the last of the Fernandinos to die in Alta California. See Geiger, *Franciscan Missionaries*, 171–74.

[34]Russ., *kekur*, which in Russian America denoted a rocky promontory—often an islet—that was used as a site for a fort, as in the case of New Archangel.

It is more advantageous to enter [the bay] after waiting for a favorable current, even without a wind; with a contrary current from the E—always very strong and lengthy—it is impossible to enter, especially without a fair wind. Just inside the entrance the right side runs more to the E and is lower and sandy; the left side extend[s] a little toward the N and then the NE, where it [i.e., the entrance] has a width of about 3 miles.

Ships going from the sea into San Francisco Bay, after approaching Point Rey[e]s (in latitude 38° 00' N and longitude 122° 37' W on Vancouver's map), must take a course between the northern group of the Farallon rocks and the aforesaid point and [sail] 77° SE straight to the fort of San Joaquín 26½ miles away.

Point Reyes is revealed as fairly precipitous and protuberant and pale yellow in color; it becomes lower from W to E. From this point the Farallon rocks, consisting of 3 groups, are visible, and the northern group lies 13½ miles and 37° SW of Point Rey[e]s.

The N side of the bay is generally high, mountainous, and in places [slopes] steeply to the water, and the mountains are fairly wooded. The S side of [San] Francisco Bay is low, although [as far as] Poi[n]t Lobos, or the SW cape of the entrance, it is sandy for some distance to the S. At Point Lobos itself there are rocks [i.e., Seal Rocks], one of which has been carved into a gate by breakers, and there are sea lions there.

The cape [Fort Point] at the fort is fairly high and gradually rises steeply to the SW.

One must not approach the fort of San Joaquín close to this cape but try to round it at a distance, especially if there is not a fair wind. Otherwise, from the strong current that always rushes or flows here one can hug the fort's cape during a light wind and the outgoing tide; an underwater rock runs from it to the channel, and for that reason to avoid anything it is better to keep ENE to the middle of the channel (the width of the chan[nel] is about 3 miles) and, passing the fort's cape W of the underwater rock (which runs 75 sazh[ens] from the shore), drop anchor at the sandy spit. The depth is 7 sazh[ens] and the bottom is fine sand where our sloop stood at anchor a short distance from both said rock and the shore.

Inside the bay closer to the N side there is a small isle that the Spaniards call Ángel Island. Beyond it a mountain range on the N side of the bay is visible in the distance.

One can enter the bay on the right [southern] side of the Farallon rocks, namely, between the SW cape of the entrance and the southern rocks of the Farallones. The width of this passage is 17 miles and very safe.

Since 1776 all of New California has belonged to the Spaniards, and now it is administered by Governor Colonel Don Pablo Vicente de Solá, ~~New Albion is divided~~ who has his seat at Monterey as the chief place in all of California.

It is divided into several missions, or districts, ~~several~~ each of which belongs to a certain presidio or its commandant. For example, the missions of San Francisco, Santa Clara, Santa Cruz, San José, and San Rafael are under the command of Don Luis Antonio Argüello. The commandant of Monterey administers San Juan Bautista, San Carlos (nearby lies the presidio of Monterey), Soledad (where the senior bishops reside), San Antonio, San Miguel, and San Luis Obispo. Close to Mission Santa Bárbara lies the third presidio, and Santa Bárbara, Purísima, San Buenaventura, and San Fernando Rey belong to it.

The fourth presidio, called Santiago [San Diego], lies near the mission of the same name. Santiago, San Gabriel, San Juan Capistrano, and San Luis Rey belong to it. In all of these missions there are 39 priests, and in the presidios 20 officers (including the governor).

The priests at the missions are obliged to grow grain, all kinds of greens, and fruit, to rear livestock, and to oversee various enterprises, such as the processing of hides, wool, and various other articles. For this purpose each mission has numerous workers, male and female, and as all of them are Indians, 6, 8, or 10 soldiers from the presidios are assigned to the priests to protect them, as well as to guard against possible revolts by the Indians; although it seems very improbable that 10 soldiers could defend against 1,000 or more Indians, this [disproportion] is what we, at least, were able to observe [during] our trip to 3 missions.

All of the Indians yield very unwillingly to the Catholic fathers, who, besides exacting their labor very strictly, teach them to pray to God; several times [daily], wherever they may be, if the bell starts to ring in the morning, at midday, or in the evening, then all of them kneel, and whoever is reluctant to obey them is immediately flogged and beaten rapidly with a belt or a lash. In order to have more workers at the missions the priests send soldiers on horseback to catch them with lassos, which they use very skillfully, and after they have been fetched they are shackled and restrained so that they will be [----][35] obedient. Before our arrival at San Francisco a very important event occurred. A priest going to his appointed post was killed en route by Indians;[36] they were caught and brought to the presidio of San Francisco, and we saw them completely fettered. During the day they worked without shackles but at night they were locked in a cellar; every morning at the rise of the ☉ [sun] the commandant [gave] each of them 25 lashes. The same fate befalls Indians who have fled and are caught or who have stolen livestock or who have [committed] any crime. The malevolence of the Indians toward the priests forces them [the latter] to be vigilan[t] everywhere, especially

---

[35]Undecipherable word fragment (*neza*[----]*ym*, possibly *nezabvennym*, meaning "unforgettably" or "forever").

[36]Shishmaryov may be referring to the assassination of Father Andrés Quintana at Santa Cruz Mission in 1812. See Castillo, "Assassination of Padre Andrés Quintana," 117–25.

on the road, and for that reason no priest and not even an officer travels anywhere without an armed soldier, even a very short distance from the presidio; and
finally, the priests force these people to take up arms against their fellow Indians.

The priests and all of the Spaniards in general are reputed to be very hospitable,
but in fact they were very impertinent and discourteous. One instance will serve
as an example. When we visited the missions, at San José we requested wine,
which they soon sent in a longboat; Father Narciso, who had come to the same
place, demanded for the wine (which had just been made)* rigging, sails for their
longboat, glass, rope, an anchor, and many other things that we did not have in
great abundance, although we did have twice as much [as we needed].

And so the commander, who usually very courteously relinquished such things
but was displeased with the demand, wanted them to take money [instead]. But
Father Narciso, with much annoyance and various unpleasantries, departed without visiting the commander at the request of the latter, who had tarried especially
in order to invite him to dinner. Another example will serve as further proof.
When the ships were ready to leave San Francisco, the commander, wanting to
settle accounts with all of the Spaniards, forthwith requested statements for this,
and—as had been the case when their demand for our things was refused—Mission San Franc[isco] set very high prices on everything; moreover, Father José,
who was with the commander on the occasion of the accounting, rebuked him
for not having included in the account the dinner that he had fed us. To tell the
truth, who would not be infuriated by such beastliness, and the commander was
very displeased, especially as it was not his own but the state's business.

All of the [Spanish] officers think very badly of their own government because
it sends no ships whatever to them, and for that reason they have nothing at all,
not even their salaries; during our stay at San Francisco they said that they had
not been paid for about 10 years.

As a captain the commandant receives a salary of 1,500 talers, a lieutenant 500,
an ensign 400, a sergeant 235, a corporal 225, and a soldier 217. Those who receive
neither clothing nor money live in still more abject poverty; this [penury] even
prompts them to talk to visiting officers.

The priests do not receive salaries but content themselves with income from
their missions—not all of it, of course, giving part to the governor and to other
functionaries upon whom they depend somewhat; moreover, they are obliged
to improve their missions, and for that reason they must spend money on the

---

*Afterwards it was found that the wine was not ready at all. Of our captain's 76 bottles, only 1 remained;
a great many of the others would have been guzzled [?]. [JRG: In the original the ending of the verb (*per-
etre*[----]) is illegible; presumably *peretreskal by* ("would have been guzzled") was intended.]

adornment of the churches, the making of appropriate music in the churches, vestments, and such.

They are also obliged to maintain their numerous workers well; but they feed them rather modestly and do not clothe them at all, and we rarely saw an Indian in a shirt, most of them being naked and protected from the cold by [only] a serape. The priests themselves live much better than the officers. The ordinary seems very strange to them. They say that they are not allowed to have gold and silver, even things made of these metals, although they are always prepared to take them if only the opportunity arises. For this reason priests sitting at a table have spoons ~~knives~~ and forks of bone, and their iron knives are not used at all or very little; in order for them to eat beef it is boiled to a pulp, and generally any dish can be eaten with a fork.

The cavalrymen in California are very good, and although there are very few of them, their agility on horseback and the daring with which they ride and lasso offsets their [small] number. With lassos they catch not only horses and cows but even people if necessary. We had one such example. On Sunday, the 6th of February, a hut was given to the crew, who had been granted shore leave. In the evening, after the sun had set, three sailors (Kharlam Salnikov, Yefim Kasaurov, and Aleksey Rozov), having taken the guard's rifle from the tent and paid for horses at the presidio, left, following their noses. On the 7th early in the morning the boatswain was sent to seek them at the presidio, thinking that the drunks had stayed somewhere to overnight. Not finding them, he informed the commandant, who immediately sent 2 cavaliers in pursuit; during the night the runaways had already passed Mission San Francisco. But by the evening of the 8th they had all been captured without any losses; before they were brought to the sloop, the commandant, who was aboard the sloop at that time, ~~appealing to their conscience~~ said that he feared that they had fled again, because the infantry was not dependable (and in fact they are not a very manly people). The aforesaid cavaliers overtook them not far from Mission Santa Clara, and they were behind a hill slaughtering a bull that they had caught for food, and when they saw that they were in peril they at first began to indicate that they would shoot, but the Spaniards quickly captured them with their [i.e., the Spaniards'] lassos and muskets, and for that reason [the runaways] had to surrender and accompany the Spaniards; it is more [likely], perhaps, that they were forced to surrender by the fact that they did not have any gunpowder or cartridges (they did have one [of the latter] but had to use it to kill the bull).

It is clear that the reason for their flight was their intention to escape to Monterey. For that reason Salnikov had accompanied the naturalist everywhere. And Shtein subsequently said that meanwhile at Monterey he [i.e., Salnikov] had become acquainted with one of Kuskov's deserters, who had probably promised to hide them and afford them an opportunity to gain the governor's trust; but such did not happen. They said explicitly that the cause of their desertion was Lieutenant Lazarev's painful and unjust punishment of them, although this was completely untrue, for Salnikov, who was quite a good helmsman, had been praised by Lazarev; the other two, Rozov and Kasaurov, had never been flogged and had behaved quite well (many of the crew were worse than they). For this act the commander demoted them to seamen, 2nd class, and ordered them kept under surveillance. The commander exhibited a great deal of magnanimity. The deserters deserved severe punishment, especially as they had been chosen from all of Russia's sailors.

The Indians or inhabitants of ~~California~~ America are of medium height and have dark skin and black hair, which always hangs loose and long; from living at the missions some of them part their hair in the middle and braid it. Generally they are unshapely and slender, and they have large feet. They do not have clothes and are always naked, [while] covering the necessary [private] parts. They do not have dwellings and live anywhere. They use everything for food, [including] spiders, worms, and reptiles. However, being at the disposal of the priests, they are abandoning [their customs] and are trying to clothe themselves. Some of them are quite good people. Their weapons are bows and arrows, which they wield very skillfully. They have a talent for needlework. We saw baskets of various kinds so tightly woven (from reeds and grass) that they hold water, and they decorate them with little shells and hair [or wool]; the Spaniards use these baskets to carry water, milk, and every [other] sort of liquid. When dancing they adorn themselves with capes made from the feathers of various birds, moccasins, belts, and wings, all very well made.

With dyes that they get from the mountains they color their things tastefully, and when gaming they daub themselves with dyes. The females are the very same as the males, but at the missions they are clothed; they are given shirts, and they sew skirts from the blankets that they make. They are employed mostly in the processing of wool and cotton, the manufacturing of blankets, and similar work. Ma[l]es do all of the other work, for example, working the land, digging the [garden] beds, dressing hides, and various other [tasks]. Moreover, with a soldier or a noncommissioned officer authorized by the priests they are sent with provisions to the presidio or elsewhere. They all go together to church, and the women kneel on the left side and the men on the right side, and they sing in turn after the priests.

The priests oversee both the ma[l]es and the females very closely, but especially the latter, and for this [reason] they are subject to strict obedience.

The Indian boats merit much attention. They are made from several bunches of reeds, which are tied together very tightly to resemble a boat. They [i.e., the Indians] kneel in them by twos or threes and propel them with paddles 1½ arshins [long]; they cannot, of course, move as well as wooden boats, and they sit very high in the water. So it can be supposed that they [i.e., the Indians] cannot navigate very far, for these boats on their own accord age very rapidly and become unusable. One instance will serve as proof that these Indians are clever and not at all bestial. The ensign, Don Sánchez, related an anecdote: in 1816 he was sent with a detachment of soldiers to the village of Livanta Liomi[37] [or Liooni] (lying to the right [east?] of the settlement of Ross) to annihilate the Indians who had supposedly attacked some soldiers on the road. During the ensuing battle with the Indians one soldier was wounded in the shoulder by an arrow, and the blood flowed not from the wound but from his throat. An Indian who was accompanying the aforesaid Sánchez as an interpreter forthwith examined the wound and said that he would survive and be robust; he immediately gave him a herb mixed with rice groats and ordered him to sip warm water, and within 3 days the blood stopped flowing from his throat and the wound healed very quickly. And now that soldier is a corporal.

The peninsula of California was discovered in 1537 by Hernán Cortés;[38] all of it has a temperate climate, and so it produces everything possible with minimal working of the land. Grain grows very well here; we heard that at Mission San Francisco it yields 30- to 50-fold and at others 80-fold [the seed]. In addition, there are fruits, grapes, various vegetables, all kinds of greens, many cattle, horses, and pigs—all in abundance. Having given the Spaniards plenty, nature makes them live idly. Here there is grass in the fields year-round; we were at San Francisco during the worst months but there was suffi[ci]ent pasture.

Their cattle, horses, cows, and sheep are in the fields all year, and when the lean months—namely, January, February, and [the first] ½ of March—occur, the grass withers and shrinks and becomes scanty for the livestock; but the Spaniards do not worry at all about their feed, which they could prepare in large amounts. Consequently, in winter the livestock become very lean, especially the horses, and for that reason at this time, i.e., when there is no pasture near the presidio, they dispatch more horses to places with a little more grass.

Grapes, which are fairly abundant at the distant missions, provide the priests with white and red wine, which is very weak, and only the priests have it, not the officers. Game is also abundant—geese, ducks, and grouse—and there are

---

[37]Unidentified.

[38]In fact, the first European to enter Baja California was the pilot Fortún Jiménez (1533), whose ship had been sent by Cortés.

beautiful birds called *codornizes* [California quail (*Callipepla californica*)], which have pale gray feathers, an even lighter breast, and a small, black beak. The males are distinguished from the females by a topknot of 2 or three black feathers. They are found, it seems, only in California and often fly in flocks between bushes. Their flesh is very white and tasty and resembles that of our partridge; and around marshes there are a great many sandpipers. Rare was the day when we sat to dine without eating fowl, and we even managed to salt some for the voyage. Black crows flock around the presidio for the carrion found there. Of animals, there are coyotes [*Canis latrans*], which have long, bushy tails, a rather pointed muzzle, and long ears and are reddish all over. They come very close to the presidio, especially at night, and they take sheep and various carrion for food; at night they usually howl, and they are very timid, especially when they meet a person on the road.

There are also bears and foxes but far away from San Francisco. During the stay of the *Ryurik* here Commandant Luis Antonio Argüello showed them [i.e., the crew] the baiting of a bear by a bull; but now, of course, either he did not want to do so or he was afraid to send for a bear because of the lateness of the season. The Californians also catch bears like people. They train their horses for this and ride them very recklessly [*otchayano*].

The Spaniards relate that 50 leagues from the presidio of San Francisco they allegedly saw unicorns[39] and buffalos,[40] and according to the Indians there are supposedly [mountain] lions, but this seems unlikely.[41]

There are a lot of fish of various kinds, as well as sea animals: ringed seals [*Phoca hispida*], sea lions, and [sea] otters. During our stay in San Francisco Bay there arrived from Bodega (or the settlement [Ross] belonging to the Russian-American Company) the Russian-American [Company's] brig *Golovnin*, whose Captain Benseman[42] with some "Aleuts" caught a goodly number of [sea] otters. And Kuskov, too, the manager of Bodega, catches various animals and sends their skins to Sitka. But the Spaniards do not occupy themselves with anything, and they never have anything except meat, of course. All of this [idleness] must

---

[39]Presumably pronghorn "antelopes" (*Antilocapra americana*), or prong bucks, are not true antelopes but the sole survivors of a species of artiodactyl mammal endemic to North America, which harbors several subspecies.

[40]Bison (*Bison bison*) were present in Alta California during the contact period. They were identified in the vicinity of Monterey in the 1600s and inhabited the Sacramento Valley as late as the 1800s.

[41]Actually, cougars were widespread in Alta California, and they are still found in parts of the state.

[42]Khristofor Martynovich Benzeman, or Benseman (Christof Benzemann) (1774–1842), was a Prussian shipbuilder and shipmaster. Born in Danzig, where his father was a master shipbuilder, Benzeman arrived in Russian America in 1807 from Boston as navigator of the *Peacock* (Captain Kimball). He entered the service of the Russian-American Company and became one of its ablest skippers. See Grinëv, *Kto yest kto*, 58; and Pierce, *Russian America*, 50–51.

be attributed to laziness, for when they ate our cooked fowl or fish they praised it, but they themselves did not have the energy to hunt and fish.

The fort has been built on the S shore of the entrance to the bay not far from the presidio of San Francisco. The road to it through the hills is quite bad. It is [built of] stone and stands on a small crag; cannons of a large caliber are in place, but they are seldom serviceable, because they are all blistered [from rust] and very old. They total 13 or 16, and the best are emplaced at the entrance. A guardhouse has been built in the middle of it, and it is very dirty, although quite large. It is divided into 2 halves, and gunpowder in boxes is found in one and an old soldier—who constitutes the fortifi[c]ation's garrison—in the other. In the event of the entry of ships or of firing from the fort a flag is raised on a short pole. The fort was built by an American seaman. The timber under the mountings in the parade ground is good but already very old, and it would be a lot of work for the Spaniards to repair it. And so it can be supposed that it will exist until it collapses, and then they will have to resort to none other than foreigners. Because they themselves will not fetch a flag or a flag rope anywhere, they will ask a ship [for them].

14/26 January. We finished examining the rusks and all of the dried provisions, finding 62 p[uds], 31 f[unts] of rusks and 5 p[uds], 17 funts of peas unfit to eat, and [according to] the inspection commission, they merited being thrown overboard, but as we had quite a few livestock on board it was ordered that they [i.e., the spoiled provisions] be used for them [i.e., the livestock].

16th/28th. In compliance with an order from the commander to our captain, today at 9 o'clock in the evening an armed longboat* with Midshipmen Hall and Gel[l]esem set off to survey the N part of San Francisco Bay. The [following] instruments were taken: sextants, an artificial [or false] horizon, leads, a compass, and a small pocket chronometer, no. 880. A total of 12 men were taken, and pistols in accordance with the number of men. At this time the sloop and the crew were entrusted to Lieutenant Lazarev, who was the senior [officer] after the captain. Upon the departure of the longboat from the sloop all of the crew shouted "hurrah." The wind was fair and fresh; the weather, after the rain (which prevented them from leaving earlier), was clear.

23rd/4th. Today the Russian-American [Company] brig *Golovnin* arrived from Bodega [Bay]; passing the fort, it saluted with 7 guns, which were answered with an equal number, and its [additional] salute of 7 guns upon reaching the anchorage was answered with 5. The reason for its coming here was trade with the

---

*[Armed] with 4 12-*lot* brass falconets, muskets, and naval provisions for 15 men for 10 days. In addition, fresh butter in jars [or tins], tea, and granulated sugar were taken. [JRG: A *lot* is an old Russian measure of weight equal to 12.78 grams, or 0.45 ounces, so 12 lots = 153.36 grams, or 5.41 ounces (about ⅓ of a pound); 1 funt = 32 lots, and 1 lot = 3 *zolotniks*.]

Spaniards; it had various goods from Sitka, such as coarse cloth, linen, taffeta, a variety of shawls, mirrors, and various other things that had to be exchanged for wheat. But the commandant of the presidio of San Francisco could not allow it to trade until he had received permission to do so from the governor at Monterey; and although trade is forbidden here, circumstances [i.e., shortages] have probably forced them to permit it. Before our arrival, insurgents [in 1818 under Hipólito Bouchard] had destroyed a great deal at Monterey and surroun[d]ing places; consequently, they [i.e., the Californios] had lost everything that they owned. Although a very high price was set on the goods, these circumstances forced them to give 5,000 puds of grain.

One had to see the anxiety of the Spaniards [to believe it] when the brig *Golovnin* entered [the bay].[43] The commandant and all of the officers, as well as all of the guards, went to the fort from the presidio, leaving only womenfolk there; not knowing the flag, they did not know the nationality of the ship, and each of them shouted in Spanish in a long, broken hailer that was constantly passed from hand to hand, but all in vain. Being with them at this time in the fort, I told them whose ship it was and where it was from, and I satisfied several of their requests; I shouted into the hailer and was understood. After this they were visibly calm.

24 Janu[ary]/5 Febr[uary]. At 1 o'clock in the afternoon the captain arrived safely with everyone; while surveying [the bay] they had experienced considerable difficulties and obstacles because the rain and overcast that prevailed during most of their absence had prevented them from landing and making observations. The cold also hindered their overnighting. He nevertheless ~~mapped the N part of [San] Francisco Bay~~ succeeded in describing the N part of [San] Francisco Bay [San Pablo Bay] and making a chart. During their trip they saw numerous deer, but [----]ev,[44] a good marksman, was unable to bag even one. They also saw [sea] otters, ringed seals, and sea lions. The locale of the shore was attractive, and there was plenty of grass for pasturing livestock.

The Spaniards told us the following important news: 4 days on foot to the N of Mission San José the Indians had encountered a new fort, hitherto unkn[o]wn, and they asserted that there were up to 1,000 residents [there]. They saw some in full-dress uniforms like those of the Spaniards, and they were white [skinned] and very rich; they bought fish from the Indians for shirts and piasters, and they said that they did not have grain. These neighbors, it seems, have greatly alarmed the Spaniards.[45]

---

[43]The vulnerable Californios were understandably alarmed by the presence of several Russian ships, including warships, at the same time in the bay.

[44]The first part of the name is illegible.

[45]This report was likely an exaggerated description of Fort Ross, perhaps deliberately embellished by the Indians to frighten their Spanish enemies.

The governor of New California, Don Pablo Vicente de Solá, intends to dispatch an official with a suitable number of armed men in April or May to investigate. They say that the river [Petaluma or Napa River?] that runs past this new fort toward Mission [San] Rafael on San Francisco Bay has steep banks and much depth everywhere except near the aforesaid Mission [San] Rafael, where it is shallow and very swift; moreover, inland this river allegedly has a considerable number of small islands.

1/13 Febr[uary]. Today we moved all of our instruments and belongings from the presidio to the sloop, and having struck our tent, we also moved it to the sloop. The latitude of the presidio, according to our observations, was found to be 37° 47' 48" N, and the longitude, taken as the true mean of 2,100 observations of the distanc[e] between the ☉ [sun] and the ☾ [moon], was 122° 27' 24.4" W.

8th/20th. Today we hoisted the longboat and the cutter onto the booms, and the commander could have left, of course, but for the 6 runaway sailors, who were led into the presidio in the afternoon. I was sent to bring them to the sloop. It should be said that when I saw them on shore, Salnikov was in great despair; during the whole time before boarding the sloop he demanded the knife that the Spanish soldiers had taken from them, and I was very glad when we finally reached the sloop safely and they were immediately placed bound in the forecastle. The commander was vindicated within a day by what happened in the presence of the whole crew on the 9th. That very day was his [i.e., Salnikov's] name day, and such was his impertinence and his insensitivity to the commander's magnanimity after having committed a grave act that he asked to take a walk on shore again; the captain had to release him from surveillance, but he returned in a good mood by the designated time.

9th/21st. Today we were quite ready and awaited the order to raise anchor. Our sloop had been very well painted and cleaned on the outside, and the masts and spars, too; everything had been completely caulked. The sails and all of the rigging had been totally repaired. About 40 sazh[ens] of firewood had been cut, and all of the water had been drawn. [The] overhaul having been [conducted] thusly, it is necessary to mention the water and firewood that we procured, as well as the wheat, having taken 528 puds, 32¼ fun[ts] of flour [and] 76 pud[s], 12 fun[ts] of threshed [whole grain].*

The Spaniards have a well in the presidio, but it is so dirty and so neglected that to call it such is impossible. They also have small lakes, where they usually wash their linen and draw water, but [these are] not [used by] ships arriving at San Francisco, owing to the great distance to the lakes, and besides it would be very

*During our anchorage here from 12 November to 9 February we ate 15 bulls, or 158 p[uds], 56 f[unts] of beef, 195 p[uds], 28 f[unts] of bread baked from the grain, and about 15 puds of various greens.

difficult (for it would be necessary to carry casks over the hills), [so] it is not possible to water there. For that reason during our stay we had to clean the wells, or rather the pits—which had likely been used by earlier seafarers—near the shore. Having dug them deeper, we lined them inside with brushwood and always kept them covered. Most of the water that accumulated in them was rainwater, and so if it did not rain, nothing was drawn, but we were so fortunate on this score that in a very short time both ships were watered. There is sufficient firewood [i.e., timber] here, but it is small and mostly spruce. Before felling the trees, we scorched the outside of them in order to rid them of insects, which were quite numerous; then we felled and barked them. We preferred to cut firewood close to the landing on the other side of a small, dirty stream.

It was certainly not impossible to construct a landing where the sloop stood for 3 months. So we built one as soon as we arrived in the bay. At low tide the site was above water, and piles were embedded around it, except on the shore side, in order for it [i.e., the landing] not to remain on sand [only], and atop everything were laid rock and sand; throughout our stay here it served us very well.

The flour that we obtained from Mission San Francisco was supplied very slowly, although their mill had been repaired very quickly; for that reason the commander decided to take wheat and have it ground or exchanged for flour after reaching Sitka.

It is impossible to describe the festive occasion when the mill was ready. The first desire of the commander in inviting all of the officers (ours [the *Blagonamerenny*'s] as well as those ashore [the *Otkrytie*'s]), to Mission San Francisco was to ask everybody to grind flour. The mill was activated by a hinny[46] and was very simple, but each of us had to grind a little after the example of the commander (after they had put blinders on the hinny). It is tethered or harnessed to a lever affixed to a winch, which turns an axis that activates the millstones. After all of this [activity], in the rooms of the priests the commander drank with his own wine to the successful operation of the mill, and he expressed the wish that it would succeed in grinding the flour and that they would deliver it, but the negligence of the Spaniards, who look after their own [interest] more than the public good, took effect. We baked 162 puds, 0 funts of rusks in the stove that we had built here; afterwards it [i.e., the stove] was left for the Russian-American Company skipper Benseman, who also baked bread and rusks.

The wheat and flour were delivered to us on donkeys, which were as lazy as their owners. They usually haul flour and such like, wheat, peas, and the like.

---

[46]A hinny is a hybrid offspring of a female donkey and a male horse. It differs from a mule (a hybrid issue of a male donkey and a female horse) in its bushier tail, a disproportionately larger body relative to its legs, and a gentler disposition.

The bags are made of deerskin; they never brought to us on the sloop at the landing more than 10 to 15 of these bags (or sacks, each weighing no more than 2 puds) per day. The commandant and his officers were with us on the sloop on the 10th[/22nd] in the evening, and Midshipman Hall had been sent by the commander so that we could raise anchor tomorrow at dawn, and so the wind perforce became a parting wind. ~~Besides punch, which they usually drink after tea~~ The punch, wine, and captain's liquor (rum, infused with apples and sweetened) took effect on the Spaniards, and after supper not one of them was able to stand, and all of the Spanish officers, except the commandant, had to stay overnight with us. At 6 o'clock in the morning, having raised the port sheet anchor, we lowered the cutter and took the small anchor 1½ cable lengths NNE into 10½ sazhens. Then, having raised the starboard sheet anchor, we hauled up the small anchor and again dropped the starboard sheet anchor. We hoisted the cutter and the small anchor to their places and awaited the signal. The loaded sloop as usual drew 14 f[eet], 1 i[nch] at the sternpost and at the stem. Until 3 o'clock in the afternoon the wind blew NNE. Thereafter it blew WSW and became calm.

18th/30th. After cruising for 1 hour on the 11th, following the *Otkrytie*, we took in our topgallant yard. At 1 o'clock we raised anchor, set all sails, and got under way to the WN½W. But at 2 o'clock with a WSW wind we had to close-haul and tack. Meanwhile, the nearer we approached the fort of San Joaquín, the stronger became the current, and we began little by little to draw near the islands in the bay. So at 2:30, having tacked to the starboard and reached a depth of 11 sazh[ens], we had to drop the starboard sheet anchor, and we let go up to 50 sazh[ens] of the chain. . . .[47]

By 9 o'clock in the evening it was clear, and we saw a comet in the W at a height of 20°. The brightness of its tail was weakened by the constellation of Cassiopeia. The comet almost formed an equilateral triangle with Jupiter and Saturn, and the L [tail?] of the comet was turned to the N. The night was calm and clear. . . .[48]

---

[47] The *Blagonamerenny*'s bearings at its temporary anchorage are omitted here.

[48] The account of the departure of the two sloops through the Golden Gate and of the remainder of their round-the-world voyage is omitted here.

DOCUMENT 10

Karl Gillsen's Account of a Visit to Alta California, 1820–1821

MIDSHIPMAN KARL GILLSEN,[1] "AN EXCERPT FROM AN ACCOUNT OF
THE ROUND-THE-WORLD VOYAGE OF THE *BLAGONAMERENNY*
IN 1819–1822,"[2] [SLOOP *BLAGONAMERENNY* IN SAN FRANCISCO BAY?],
25 OCTOBER 1820–8 FEBRUARY 1821

. . . .[3]

On 25 October [1820] we raised anchor [at New Archangel] and went to sea
via Mayak [Lighthouse] Strait. The [flagship] *Otkrytie*, standing directly opposite
the middle of the sound, wanted to cross it but the wind shifted and [the ship]
had to abandon this plan and follow the same route that we had taken. So it
left for the sea, and we hove to and awaited it; by the evening it had entered the
ocean, and we set all sails and took a course to the S.

---

[1]Karl Karlovich Gellesem (Gillesem, Gillsen, or Gilsen) (1801–18??) was born into an old Lutheran gentry
family in Kurland, where his father was an assessor. Educated in German, French, and Russian, he entered
St. Petersburg's Naval Academy in 1813, graduated as a cadet in 1815, and became a midshipman in 1818, when
he sailed aboard the *Blagonamerenny*. Upon his return Gellesem was promoted to lieutenant and granted a
leave of nine months to recover his health. In mid-1825 he was transferred to a communications construction
detachment with the rank of captain. He was living in Riga as a retired major in 1830, when he requested
permission to publish in German an account of the round-the-world voyage of the *Blagonamerenny*. Despite
a favorable report by one referee (who found the contents "deserving of the curiosity and attention of many
readers"), it was not published (although three chapters did eventually appear in a Russian periodical). The
rest of his life is a blank.

[2][Karl Gillsen], "Puteshestvie na shlyupe *Blagonamerenny* dlya izsledovaniya beregov Azii i Ameriki za
Beringovym Prolivom s 1819 po 1822 god," part 2, *Otechestvennie zapiski* 66, no. 11 (November 1849): 6–24.
This excerpt is taken from the second of three articles by the author about the *Blagonamerenny*'s voyage of
1819–22, the first (*Otechestvennie zapiski* 66, no. 11 [October 1849]: 213–38) describing the outbound passage
via the Cape of Good Hope and Port Jackson (Sydney) to New Archangel and the third (*Otechestvennie
zapiski* 66, no. 11 [December 1849]: 215–36) the homeward passage from Alta California via Hawaii to Kamchatka. Presumably they were published three decades after the event in order to take advantage of the
worldwide interest in California sparked by the gold rush.

[3]Gillsen's description of his sojourn at New Archangel is omitted here.

At daybreak on the 26th we saw the *Otkrytie* on the horizon to the NW. On account of the wind we set every possible sail, and knowing that the *Otkrytie* sailed much better than our sloop, we did not shorten [sail] one bit. By midnight the wind had shifted to the SW and strengthened; we lowered the topgallant sail and reefed the topsail and tacked to the SE. Only then did the *Otkrytie* overtake us, and by the morning it had disappeared from view. To describe the rest of the voyage would be easy because it presented nothing remarkable. The whole time we had strong winds from the NW and W, with the help of which by the 10th [of November] we had already passed the rocks called the Farallones lying off the entrance to the port of San Francisco. Here we were becalmed, and it was not until the next day with the help of the flood tide that we could enter the bay and drop anchor. The *Otkrytie* was not yet there; so the captain sent Lieutenant Lazarev ashore to arrange a salute with the commandant, Cavalry Captain Don Luis Argüello. He [Lazarev] returned before sunset, and then we saluted with nine guns and received as many in reply.

The voyage from Sitka to San Francisco was unusually fortunate, considering the time of the year and the fact that we were plying the stormiest ocean.

In 15 days we had traveled a direct distance of more than 3,000 verstas like magic, going from late fall to the finest summer. Never before or after did we feel so keenly the effect of such a rapid change. At Sitka and during the voyage we had cold, damp weather—and then suddenly we found ourselves under an Italian sky and in a land endowed lavishly by nature with all of the delights of southern countries and without enervating heat.

The outer coast of California near the port of San Francisco presents a picture of infertile, sandy mountains and bare cliffs, behind which a chain of high mountains [Sierra Nevada] is visible in the distance. The entrance to the bay is clearly marked by two high capes, between which in the distance appears a shore covered with the most beautiful verdure and bordering the enormous bay. On the southern cape a redoubt has been built and armed with eighteen cannons of various calibers, of which only five were fit for use, and even they lay in embrasures on logs, not on mounts; the Spanish flag was still flying here at that time. [After] passing this redoubt, we entered an extensive, nearly circular basin [San Francisco Bay] bounded by green hills covered with groves of oak and laurel [bay] trees, the green leaves of which were not in the least faded, despite the fact that it was the middle of November. At a distance of two or three verstas from the southern shore on a flat height there arose before our eyes the only building on this side, called the presidio of San Francisco by the Spaniards; it is the residence of the commandant, two officers, and forty soldiers. On the northern shore the scattered buildings of the mission of San Rafael are visible. Lying in the middle of the bay is the small, high, conical island of San Angel, which hides from our eyes the strait to another basin [San Pablo Bay], about which I will speak below.

The port of San Francisco, especially at our anchorage, was not far from the entrance under the presidio—which is rather troublesome. With a SW or W wind the ocean swells go directly into the bay, and although the waves break on the Farallones and then on the capes that confine the flood tide and become weaker, they are still so great, however, that with such winds we were obliged twice to deploy an anchor in the sea on another hawser; because we had double anchored,* the breakers nearly always continued to the sandy shore and against the presidio, and sometimes they did not allow us to put in to it [the shore] at all, and they threw rowing vessels ashore; thus, the navigation of these waters by means of such vessels was very difficult and slow, if not completely impossible. To avoid this inconvenience our captain ordered the construction of a large cobblestone embankment extending two sazhens from the shore at low tide; but despite the fact that the embankment was made of large rocks, it was washed away twice before its completion.

On 12 November we went ashore to visit the commandant here; there we learned that the sentries from the fort had sent word that another Russian warship was approaching. Assuming that it was the *Otkrytie*, we hurriedly returned but still had not managed to cast off by the time it actually entered the bay. It anchored alongside our sloop. From our comrades we learned that they had parted from us and kept more to the S, whereas we had continued our direct course to the SSE and therefore arrived earlier. After having double anchored and saluted the fort's flag, Captain Vasilyev went ashore; the next day we were conveyed to the presidio, where the commandant allotted us one room. We took our astronomical instruments and chronometers with us to establish an observatory in this room.

The chief purpose of our coming to California was to prepare the necessary number of rusks, very few of which we had left, and even those had almost become unfit for consumption. They had all become moldy from the dampness, and most of them were maggoty; for that reason they had to be thrown overboard, but they were still suitable for pig feed. In the hold there was considerable space, and although we still did not have any of these animals, it had been proposed to stock some on the Sandwich (or, more correctly, Hawaiian) Islands, and so the [spoiled] rusks were stowed [in the hold] in empty barrels. Immediately orders were given to buy the requisite amount of wheat at the missions of San

---

*To double anchor [*fertoing*] means to stand on two anchors that are dropped on opposite sides [of the ship] at a distance of a hawser's length or more, i.e., 100 and 150 sazhens, so that the ship is anchored between them. This method is usually used in those places where there are flood tides and ebb tides, and then the anchors are placed in the direction of the current.

Francisco, Santa Clara, and San Rafael; but now there appeared the difficulty of how to convert the wheat into flour, for the only gristmill in operation was damaged, and the Spaniards ground wheat for their own use in hand mills, which for the amount that we needed would be virtually unfeasible or at least too slow. For this reason we sent our carpenters to the mission, where they soon repaired the gristmill. But then another shortcoming appeared: in all of the presidios there were no suitable stoves. We overcame this obstacle, too: we found enough bricks (unfired, of course), and there was no want of clay, and in one week behind the walls of the presidio we assembled two huge ovens and made a roof over them from boards. From the crews of both sloops we detailed eight men as bread makers, and the matter took its course with the desired success; in two months they baked all of the rusks that were required for the remainder of the voyage, not counting the provisionment of the crew with fresh bread during the three months of our voyage to California. Meanwhile, aboard the sloops they mended the rigging, caulked the deck and sides, and painted the sides on the outside. In the makeshift observatory they checked the chronometers and the longitude of the port; an average of $122°\ 27'\ 24''$ W was deduced from numerous moon and star distances and the passage of Jupiter's satellites. The [difference between] high tide and low tide at the full moon reached up to 8 feet.

Having mentioned the very uninteresting pursuits during our three-month stay in California, I will now turn to the remarkable occurrences in the course of this period and to a description of the state of this land at that time, the manners and customs of the inhabitants, both white-skinned and red-skinned, and the products of this beautiful province.

The presidio of San Francisco, as has already been noted, lies on a flat eminence and consists of an enormous brick building with an extensive rectangular courtyard [plaza], which all of the windows and doors face; the outside of the wall is blind, except for two gates and rifle embrasures. One wing is occupied by a church, the empty room that had been allotted to us (a former apartment of one of the friars who had gone to Santa Clara Mission), and the apartment of the commandant, Cavalry Lieutenant Don Ignacio Martínez. In the other wing were found a common hall, where ceremonial festivities were held, and the apartments of the artillery lieutenant, Don Luis Pancho,[4] and two sergeants (one in the cavalry and one in the infantry). The two remaining [rooms] accommodated soldiers and an armory. The church was very fine, and even the altar was richly adorned; it was the only building in all of the presidio that had glass windows. The living quarters for both officers and soldiers were nothing other than large rooms furnished like Russian *izbas* [peasant cabins] with scattered benches and

---

[4]Unidentified.

a large table in the front corner; not one had a window frame with glass, and the windows had movable grating that blocked the sun and wooden slides instead of shutters against hard frosts.

The mission of San Francisco is found five leagues inland from the presidio. Two Franciscan friars, Father José [Altimira] and Father Blasius [Blas Ordaz], manage the mission. It comprises the friars' residence, which is just like the apartments of the presidio's officers (described above); a large church, very richly appointed, standing separately without a bell tower; then a number of buildings housing some cavalrymen and the natives who have been converted to Christianity and who number up to 800 of both sexes; and granaries, other storehouses, and workshops where the various labors of the Indians take place. In the smithies and joineries they fashion agricultural implements, shoe horses, make very good saber blades, and bore rifle barrels—all by hand, not by machine. They also curry good suede (red and white) from deerskin and sheepskin, as well as [make] shoe uppers and calf leather from oxhide; they imprint the suede with designs, not all at once by machine but [individually] with a stencil, a cutter, and a mallet. The tooled leather is used by the Spaniards in footwear in place of boot tops. The [Indian] women spin and weave wool for blankets, ponchos (a kind of cloak an arshin in width with a lengthwise hole in the middle for inserting one's head, so that the ends overhang the chest and the back, leaving the arms free), and heavy, coarse cloth, which they dye blue, black, and red.

New California, or New Albion, lies on the western coast of North America and stretches from the 25th degree of North latitude to an indefinite boundary in the north; at that time it constituted a province of the Viceroyalty of Mexico [New Spain]. It was administered by a governor who had his residence at Monterey (in the words of the Spaniards, a "presidio," like San Francisco's) and was divided into eleven missions. In each of these missions were found two, three, or five Franciscan friars, who, in conformity with the mission's size, were defended by cavalry, which, however, never exceeded 40 soldiers, so that California's entire garrison consisted of only 500 men of this kind of army. In addition, at San Francisco and Monterey, where there were forts, up to 150 infantrymen and artillerymen were found. The number of Indians settled at the missions reached 10,000; of them, very few had voluntarily become settlers, and all of the rest had been taken by force by the cavaliers, who catch them like animals with lassos and lead them to the missions. There they are gradually accustomed to a sedentary existence and are always treated very affectionately and well. When an Indian has been acculturated, then they send him back to his tribe to fetch his wives and children, if he has any; it does happen that they escape the Europeans and remain in the forest, but this is very rare, and most of them come back with some of their relatives. For this reason they not only prefer but even fear the sedentary existence, for if a runaway is settled again, then he is shackled, forced to do the hardest work, and generally treated very cruelly; for a second escape he is hanged. It is difficult to reconcile how six or seven hundred Europeans can not only keep up to 10,000 settled Indians obedient but also increase their number daily. For this [task] the government commits only cavalrymen who are born locally and whose calling and skillful horsemanship and fearlessness are imbibed from their fathers from childhood; this army can be compared to our Cossacks. But for all that it is not possible to consider the infantry of much help to the cavalry; marking time in the presidios and not taking part in the administration of the province, it performs only garrison service. The cavaliers are dressed in the following manner: their uniform consists of a blue jacket, with a red collar and red cuffs, that reaches and covers the knees; variegated blue and white worsted stockings; and short boots that cover only the feet. These short boots are made of black and red suede with thick soles; they have heels more than half an inch high to support the enormous spurs, which hang from the saddle when the rider is not on the horse and which he dons before he mounts the horse with uncommon swiftness and deftness. The calves [of his legs] are doubly wrapped from the knees down to the boot tops with imprinted suede made from kidskin. The cavalier's armament consists of a suede shirt without sleeves, sewn from seven deerskins, one laid over the other; this shirt, which reaches from the shoulders to the knees, serves as armor that cannot be pierced by the savages' arrows, which are often tipped with poison. On his head he has a felt hat with a round crown and a wide brim; he protects his face with a small shield with an image of the Spanish coat of arms. When he sets out to catch one of the natives for a mission or to seek a runaway, his horse is covered with a saddlecloth of imprinted oxhide such that its head, neck, and entire body are covered against arrows. This saddlecloth is decorated with steel or copper rattles, so that from the clatter of this ornamentation he is heard from afar.

He has a lance, a short carbine that hangs from his shoulder, a pistol in a holster, and a saber whose scabbard is attached securely to the saddlecloth, so that it always remains with the horse. His chief weapon is a lasso, which the natives fear more than a gun; indeed, they have [good] reason [to do so], because the Spaniards are able to wield it with uncommon adroitness and swiftness, as proof of which the following can serve. The horses and cattle that are exported from California roam the hills and woods in huge, wild herds, and from them the Spaniard selects whatever horse he needs for himself. When such a need arises, he sets out on a good tamed horse to find a herd. After having found a herd, he rushes at the chosen horse, giving his own horse its head, with a lasso in his right hand and a coil of fifty sazhens of rope in his left; the lasso, made of horsehair, is half an inch thick and very strong. After having overtaken the wild horse, he throws the lasso at one of its rear legs, snaring it, and circles around, entangling and bringing down the horse by its legs; then in an instant he jumps off his own horse, on the captive horse puts a readied bridle to which he has affixed a wide, movable leather strap that covers the horse's eyes, untangles its legs, and with the lash of a whip raises the animal, which, confused by the sudden blindness, stands as if rooted to the ground; then the Spaniard takes the saddle from his own horse and puts it on the new horse, cinching it to the utmost, mounts [the captive horse], and removes the band from its eyes. The horse, feeling the unaccustomed weight, makes every effort to unburden itself—it jumps, whirls, and throws itself onto the ground, but all in vain. The Spaniard sits as if rooted to the spot. Finally, the horse starts to run; the Spaniard not only gives it free rein but in addition also goads it with his spurs and whip until it tires and halts. Then he begins to inure it to the bridle and again make it feel the enormous sharp spurs until it has exhausted itself. After having done so, he removes the saddle and with the lasso leads it home, where he breaks it in by the rule book. This breed of horse is excellent: it runs easily and is obedient, stately, and of medium size. Stallions, especially those that have recently been caught, are extremely bad-tempered; having this trait in common with nearly all wild adult horses, they bite and strike everyone except their master, whom they fear such that they move their ears back at the sight of him and dutifully obey only his voice. It runs so lightly that while the rider overtakes a deer on it and lassos its antlers, the horse, as if it knows that his master never misses the mark, stops at the moment that the lasso flies from his hand and sits almost like a dog on its hind legs and props itself firmly on its forelegs. The deer continues its flight but is shortly brought to a halt by the [tautly] extended lasso, whose other end is fastened to the saddle, and falls, whereupon the hunter shoots it with an arrow and stabs it to death with a lance or severs the major veins behind the head with a saber. After having gutted it on the spot, he loads the deer on the horse behind his saddle, provided it is not too big, otherwise he drags it behind the horse on the ground, for one ought not to leave a kill in the field for even a very short time because it is sure to be eaten immediately by the innumerable jackals [coyotes] that live here.

When we needed fresh meat for the crews, the Spaniards provided live bulls that they caught among the many herds roaming the woods. For this [purpose] they dispatched five men on horseback, four of whom were armed with lassos and the fifth with a long whip. After having chosen a victim, two of them, after passing it on different sides, throw a noose over its horns, and the other two riders, who are following them, throw a noose around its forelegs, while the fifth drives the bull with his whip. Sensing the impediment and feeling the whiplashes of the driver, the animal furiously rushes at one of his captors, but at the same instant they pull its forelegs out from under it and against its will it has to follow their lead. Then it starts to tear the ground with its horns and yields only to the heavy and ceaseless lashes of the whip.

The daring and skill of these horsemen will seem unbelievable if I say that two of them will not only catch but also bring home a live bear, which are enormous and fierce there. After finding a bear, they separate, and one of them throws sticks of wood at it in order to irritate the beast, which rears and runs with open jaws at its tormentor; the other horseman, seizing the moment when the bear raises one of his hind legs, lassos it, turns his horse around, and throws the bear down onto its front legs. The bear then turns to this rider, but it cannot take even one step because its other leg has already been ensnared by the lasso of the second Spaniard. Then one of them, after having described a semicircle, rejoins his comrade and together they drag the unfortunate creature while trying to grasp its front paws should any opportune situation present itself. But it is all to no avail; if they see that it is not possible to drag the bear any farther, they slacken the lasso, letting the bear have a chance to grab them, and once more it is enticed. Everything described here serves not only to obtain the bearskin and the meat but to derive amusement, too, for rarely is this hunt accompanied by danger. The Spaniards exhibit the same skill and daring when they hunt a native or a runaway from the missions, despite the fact that then the danger is incomparably greater. Armed in the aforesaid manner, one or no more than two mounted Spaniards confront an entire throng of savages who shower them with a whole swarm of poison-tipped arrows; but the Spaniards, protected by their leather armor, pay no attention to this [fusillade], draw close, lasso the nearest [native] around the neck, and drag him behind them. If they need only a runaway, then after having moved some distance away, they halt and begin to parley with the aim of exchanging the captive for the fugitive; but the Indians seldom produce the latter, and in his stead the unlucky victim must go to the mission. If they do hand over the runaway, then the Spaniards immediately release their captive so as to keep the Indians' trust.

Here is a description of the local cavalrymen (there is nothing to be said about the infantrymen, who dress nearly the same as the cavalrymen, but they are weaker and lazier); however, the former are not free of the latter's vice, which is common to all Spaniards who spend all of their time without work in *dolce far niente* [delightful idleness]). There are no other inhabitants of California, except the above; the entire colony is populated by servitors [*slyuzhashchie*] and friars. There was not a single genuine colonist of European birth, and therefore

I assume that a province that does not yield any revenue but on the contrary costs the Spanish government dearly is completely neglected. California has never had direct communication with Europe, only via Mexico; the governors are appointed by the viceroy, and the friars, the soul of the Californian administration, are sent from there [i.e., Mexico], and they are chosen mostly from among Mexican mestizos. Therefore, their ignorance was incredible; many of them did not even know how to write, not to mention their ignorance of the sciences. Of Latin, so necessary for the Catholic priesthood, they knew only the liturgy from memory; to such people had been entrusted the education of the savages! Their sole contribution consisted of the fact that they were able to impart a superficial understanding of the faith; but even here their learning was full of various superstitious dogmatisms, and they misrepresented Christianity to the point where it was unrecognizable. Moreover, their contribution [also] consisted of the fact that they taught the neophytes various skills with respect to agriculture and the requirements of a sedentary existence. Here, too, however, they did not work very hard. [Given] the blessed climate and the virgin nature of this land the agriculturalist can produce all of the necessities of life almost without a care. The sole kinds of sown grain—wheat and corn—yield one-hundred-fold and more the seed, in spite of the fields being badly plowed and generally carelessly worked. After having reaped a bountiful harvest, they abandon the fields for several years, firstly in order to indulge their indolence and secondly because they have occasion to sell the surplus to our [Russian-]American Company only, and if they were to harvest regularly every year they would not know what to do with it. Of garden vegetables here, which grow almost wild, potatoes and cabbages are grown; there are no cucumbers at all, but then superior watermelons and muskmelons are grown without any watching and tending. As to manuring the soil, they have no knowledge of it here; and as for the improvement of varieties of fruit by means of grafting, they do not bother. The local apples are small and sour, and so are the cherries. Grapes grow on the slopes of the hills and creep along the ground but nonetheless provide superior wine that after standing several years greatly resembles port. Generally speaking, much could be made of California after having settled it with an industrious people. The climate is capable of producing all of the products of southern countries; the cultivation of silkworms, sugarcane, and even coffee would yield substantial income; and oranges, lemons, and other fruits would afford an agreeable and healthful variety of food. Besides, how readily could all of this work be done for California's settlers by the Indians without the necessity of having to buy black slaves to do so. Now the natives are imitating the indolence of their mentors and are living better on whatever nature offers them than [do] those who want to toil. But the present

Spanish administration is much to blame for this [situation], for all nations have been forbidden to trade with the colonies [of Spain] except our company, and even it is only permitted to buy wheat and cattle on site for cash. But then the inhabitants of California are in need of all kinds of luxury goods, so that they have asked us to pay for the provisions not in money but in goods. They lack not only tea but even the products of the other American colonies that then belonged to Spain, such as sugar, coffee, rum, and spices. Absolutely nothing was supplied by sea because there was nothing to take from here in return, and conveyance from Mexico by land was accompanied not only by great difficulties (because it could be done only by packmules) but also by dangers during the crossings of the Andes [*sic*, Sierra Madre Occidental] and from the savage Indians thereabouts. For the same reason, communication with Mexico usually occurred only once or no more than twice a year, and the Spaniards lived in complete ignorance of the rest of the world. They learned of the insurrection in Peru [i.e., in 1813 at Cuzco] only the year before our arrival [i.e., in 1819], and that from two [rebel] frigates [under Hipólito Bouchard] coming to Monterey from Lima. These frigates burned the presidio, seized payments consisting of wheat and money, and sailed back. The local Spaniards, all of them very devout, nonetheless do not observe fasting, and I assume that the reason for this [omission] is the utter want of any other food than meat. Although they do have cabbages and potatoes, they are not fond of vegetables and rarely consume them; there is no vegetable oil whatever, and although there are fish in the rivers and bays, out of indolence they do not catch them. All of their food consists of various grains, nearly all of which are prepared the same way. Many times during our stay at the port of San Francisco, we were treated to dinner at both the mission and the presidio, and in order to give an idea of all of these entertainments I will describe one of them. Soon after our arrival the friars of said mission on the occasion of examining their mill invited us to dinner. Horses were readied for us at the presidio, and escorted by Spanish officers we set off. Descending the height atop which the presidio is located, we rode across a wide sandy plain bordered by a series of beautiful green hills; along them ran our road or, rather, path, no wider than was necessary for a single rider, between low bushes that gradually changed to trees. Here the woods were primarily oaks, which ended half a mile before the mission, which lay on a treeless and extensive plain; on the edge of a deep and long gully, at the bottom of which flowed a stream that became a swift, deep river in January and February, when rain prevails here. After having examined the mission and heard the Catholic mass in the church, we went to the dining hall, i.e., a long, huge room, quite like that described above. In the middle stood a table, without a tablecloth, set with numerous clay dishes of food and clay plates; there were no knives, forks, or spoons, but we, who already knew about this [lack] from the stories of Captain Shishmaryov, who had been here [in 1816] aboard the brig *Ryurik,* had previously supplied ourselves with these items and thereby delivered ourselves from the necessity of having to use our fingers instead. Long benches stood in place of chairs around the table; we sat, and as the first dish they served us a Spanish favorite, *olla podrida,*[5] filled beforehand with chili peppers, which made it impossible to eat. Then came boiled cubes of beef swimming in melted butter; overboiled mutton; overboiled venison; grilled wild goose and *codornices* [California quail] (a kind of grouse, about which I will speak below); and at the end watermelon, muskmelon, and dried grapes [raisins] appeared. Nearly all of the dishes were heavily peppered. This is an example of the local Spanish dinners to which we were treated by the friars, the commandant, and the officers by turns; at some [of the dinners] there were only vegetables, such as boiled cabbage and boiled corn on the cob.

On 1 December, Old Style, on the day of the patroness of North America, Holy Mother Maria Guadaloupe, are held the festivities of all of the Catholic lands of this part of the New World, and here they last for two days. On the first day a statue of the Mother of God, covered with various materials and adorned with a golden crown, is carried in a procession around the plaza and the walls of the presidio; at this time five guns—the only ones fit to use—were firing continuously, followed by [the cannons of] our sloop, which was highly appreciated by the Spaniards. The dinner that followed this [firing], however, was just the same as that described above, where the officers, friars, soldiers, and guests, i.e., us, sat at a common table and drank champagne (which we had provided) to the health of His Majesty Emperor Alexander [I] and King Ferdinand VII. Dancing began after dinner, with guitar playing and female singing taking the place of music. The favorite Spanish dance, the fandango, was almost the only one that they danced. With this the first day ended. The second began with the same procession, after which horsemen began to demonstrate their skill in riding, rearing the horse, and throwing the lasso. The most skillful is awarded the prize of a complete outfit, namely, deerskin armor, a shield, a horse, and a lasso; this prize was won by a young soldier by the name of Bernardo Gilo [or Jilo]. After these games they started to dance, as on the preceding day, and then they performed some sort of play, after which they danced again until the morning. We participated in all of these festivities because we had been received with honor, not only as guests but also as hosts, for through common effort we donated to this holiday a lot of rum and wine, nearly all of which they drank by the evening without our having had an opportunity to taste it. This day did not end as happily as the first:

---

[5]Spanish stew, a potage of mixed vegetables and meat (literally, "rotten pot").

with the commandant, Don Luis Argüello, lived his sister and her daughter, a very pretty girl of fourteen years of age who had two admirers, one of which was preferred by her uncle and the other by the niece herself. It seemed to the latter [admirer] that she treated the uncle's favorite too affectionately, and—inflamed by jealousy—he drew a knife, which is usually carried instead of a dagger in one's belt, and inflicted a deep wound (fortunately, not fatal) on his rival's neck. Our doctor, Mr. [Grigory] Zaozyorsky, came and bandaged it, so that the suitor recovered completely before our departure. This incident somewhat dampened the merriment of the others, and when it was reported to the commandant he said quietly, "Let them, the dogs, bite; it doesn't matter to me."

On 12 December, the birthday of the Tsar Emperor Alexander Pavlovich, our sloops were decorated with flags, and we saluted with all of our guns. In reply the Spaniards demonstrated their courtesy on the holiday by also firing uninterruptedly while our cannonading continued. On this day we entertained on our ship—its quarterdeck and the stateroom were more spacious than those of the *Otkrytie*—all of the local aristocrats with their wives and daughters. After dinner all of the husbands and wives began to dance and sing. The songs of the maidens with their very sweet voices were extremely agreeable; especially the youngest daughter of Lieutenant Martínez, Doña Incarnación, distinguished herself, as did the commandant's niece, Doña Josefa de Solá.[6]

Several days later the friars of San Rafael Mission arrived and invited us to some sort of holiday there, and we set off with them. This mission, as has already been mentioned, lies on the northern shore of the bay, not right by the water but at a distance of half a league from it, and is situated on the slope of several hills. The road thither from the bay shore is very difficult: it runs across barrens [*tundry*] and marshes as an extremely narrow path, so that traveling it on horseback is not even possible. Here again are seen in all of their glory the indolence and the unconcern of the Spaniards: having almost daily to walk this route, they somehow force their way along it and do not even want to exert a little effort to improve it. All of us, muddy from the marsh and tired, finally reached our goal; there we were met by the entire population of the mission, comprising four or five hundred Indians of both sexes, under the command of five Spanish cavalrymen.

From our sloops one large building—very fine from afar—was visible; so we assumed that what was found there was nothing like that of San Francisco Mission, but we were badly mistaken. The said building, which accommodated a church, was very insignificant in terms of richness and adornment, and the living quarters of the friars and the Spanish horsemen were built of wood and closely resembled sheds. Around this residence were scattered up to fifty thatched

---

[6]The daughter of Governor Pablo Vicente de Solá.

shacks. Here there are neither skilled workers nor a mill, and the settlers engage only in grain growing. Extensive fields stretch between the mission and the bay shore for a considerable distance. It [i.e., the mission] was established only three years before we [arrived,] by order of Governor Don Pablo Vicente de Solá, the brother of the local commandant [of the presidio of San Francisco]. The soil of the land along the sea is less productive [than that inland], and we could not understand why the mission was founded just here, separated from the other parts of California by a wide bay marred by inadequate means of unrestrained communication. To our questions [about this matter] they [i.e., the Spaniards] did not reply at all; but from what we were told [*ponamskam*] we were able to conclude that the reason was the nearness of our colony in California called the "Ross Settlement" and the fear that it would expand to San Francisco Bay. The Spaniards said that it was no more than 40 leagues by land to this settlement, and they intended to extend their own settlements even farther to the north.

The Spaniards often mentioned two bays [San Francisco Bay and San Pablo Bay], which were connected by the basin in which we had anchored, and a river, the Rio Grande (Great),[7] that flowed into them. They related that this river really did merit its name, that it was more than a league wide, and that nobody had yet reached its source. In order to check these stories Captain Vasilyev [on 14 January] ordered Captain[-Lieutenant Gleb] Shishmaryov to set out in our sloop's longboat [or launch] with two officers and survey these bays, provided they did exist, as well as to find the mouth of the Great River.[8] The rains and the strong winds that prevail from the end of December did not allow us to begin the exploration until 17 January [1821]. On that day the weather cleared, and although it was winter, we again had warm, even hot, days. We outfitted the longboat, and the captain, accompanied by me, Midshipman [Roman] Hall,[9] twelve sailors, and one noncommissioned officer, started the cruise, taking provisions for ten days, a pocket chronometer, two sextants, two mercury [artificial] horizons [for observing altitude], a chain [for linear measurements], a surveying compass [*okruzhny instrument*], an azimuth, and two ordinary compasses; in addition, we provided ourselves with warm clothing and two tents. We did not forget hunting and fishing gear, of course.

After pushing off from the sloop at ten o'clock in the morning, with a moderate wind from the SE we took a course to San Rafael Mission, trying to reach it

---

[7] This river was actually the Sacramento and not, of course, today's Rio Grande.

[8] For Shishmaryov's rather technical and spare report, see "A Journal of a Survey of the Northern Bay [San Pablo Bay] of the Port of San Francisco, Made in a Longboat in 1821 from the 17th to the 25th of January [28 January–5 February] by Fleet Captain-Lieutenant Shishmaryov, the Survey Beginning at the Islet [Red Rock] Designated on the Map by the Letter A," RGAVMF, f. 213, op. 1, d. 89, fols. 1–10.

[9] Hall and Gillsen were instructed to draw views and keep a journal.

before midday in order by observation to determine its latitude and to take the starting point of the subsequent survey; but the wind began to abate and the heavily loaded longboat advanced very slowly, so that we were unable to reach our destination in time and had to put in to a small island [Tesoro, now Red Rock] in order not to lose such a clear day for taking the midday height [of the sun]. After having determined its latitude to be 37° 57' 17" N and finished dinner, we proceeded. When we neared the strait between the two capes [Point San Pedro and Point San Pablo], a frightful squall from the NE came upon us, and we saved the masts and furled the sails just in time. This squall was accompanied at first by pouring rain and then by thick snow, which in one minute filled the hot air such that we, soaked to the skin, had to grab warm clothing. Fortunately, the squall lasted no more than half an hour, at the end of which the former temperature was restored. Knowing that nothing is more harmful than such a sudden change, we hurried to land in order to dry ourselves and to take cover from the sultriness in the tents. After having chosen a suitable site, we went to the northern shore of the cape [Point San Pedro] at five o'clock in the afternoon. The depths from the little island to the cape where we landed extended from one and a half to fifteen sazhens, with a bottom of silt near the shore and of fine sand in the middle [of the passage].

After having made fast the longboat on the shore itself beyond the surf foam, we pitched the tent on the edge of a laurel grove, made a fire, and began to dry ourselves out. Immediately behind the grove towered quite high rock faces of sandstone, and farther beyond rose sizable mountains [Coast Ranges] that ran for some distance from the bay shore to the north and then formed a semicircle of blue hills. The sandy soil between the grove and the shore was our overnight camp. The night was warm, as is usual in these latitudes, especially in winter, although there was not a cloud in the sky, and the stars shone brightly in the almost black firmament. Not the slightest breeze rustled the leaves of the nearby grove; on the southern bay shore, fires were visible, and we ascribed them to some native tribe, although the Spaniards had told us of some sort of fort on the side where we saw the fires. They said that unknown persons lived in this fort—whites, but not Spaniards, presumably because they were not dressed at all like those who had seen them. During the day from a high point on the cape and with a good telescope we saw nothing on that side, and as we were aware that at such a distance it is not possible to distinguish between native huts and the surrounding bushes, we reckoned that our assumption was correct. We knew from experience that the green resinous leaves of the laurel tree burn with a crackle and a clear, bright flame; in order to learn what effect is produced by the igniting of this tree, we lit one that stood a little apart from the others. Instantly all of its branches caught fire and lit up all of the vicinity; with this we fired our falcon-ettes all together, and the fires on the opposite bay shore vanished.

High tide occurred at a quarter before eleven [in the evening] and reached a height of seven feet, four inches.

On the 18th we had clear weather and light breezes from the NW. The cap-tain ordered me to again climb to the top of the neighboring mountains and to examine all of the bay shore, which presented itself to us in the form of a circular lagoon, to see whether the mouth of some river is visible. The southern shore was high and wooded, the eastern shore also, and among the cliffs to the NE was seen the fairly broad arm of a river that I took to be its mouth. Several miles from that spot a height extended northward into the interior, leaving a low, marshy expanse between it and the bay shore, which described a semicircle almost to the site of our overnight camp. Toward the SE on the very edge of the horizon I had seen yesterday an unremarkable large, white structure that we took to be the fort of some unknown inhabitants; but, as will be seen below, we were mistaken. As to the fires that we had seen last night, they could not have been fires at this fort, because they were too clear and burned over a much greater distance than the length of the structure.

After having taken the midday altitude and the angles [of the sun] for the determination [of the location] of the most conspicuous places, we left our over-night camp and set out for the opposite cape. The depth here was from 13 to 15 sazhens, the bottom sandy, and the compass variation at the cape 13° 30' E. After having taken the appropriate angles, we immediately set off. At first we hugged the shore in order to better determine its bends; but the depth rapidly decreasing to only several feet, we were obliged to abandon this intention and take a straight passage to the more distant cape [Point San Pablo]. About halfway between both capes the captain ordered the dropping of a grapnel in order to [be able to] draw views. While this [task] was being performed, a young sea otter surfaced alongside the longboat, and one of the sailors, holding an oar in his hands, gave it a moderate blow to the head; this blow stunned it, and we pulled it out [of the water]. After a few minutes it regained consciousness and began to bite everyone who approached it, so we killed it. On the shore, which at first was low-lying and then elevated, we saw an innumerable multitude of wild cattle and horses. After having drawn views, we raised the grapnel and about five o'clock put in to the new cape, where we composed ourselves for the night. The cape's shore was high with a gentle surface, so that we could scarcely find a suitable site for the tents. Generally this place was very unsuitable; the men had to go rather far for firewood, and there was no fresh water at all, but we had brought a supply for just such an occasion. During the night there arose a strong wind [from the

WNW] with snow and rain, which sometimes fell so hard the tents could not stem it; this downpour did not let us close our eyes all night. Toward morning the wind died and let us fall quietly asleep for a few hours; then in order to limit our activities we extended a base line along the shore for 250 sazhens, and after taking angles at both ends, we were preparing ourselves to sail away when we saw two horsemen galloping directly toward us. When they approached, we recognized them as the two Indians whom I had seen one morning coming to the habitation belonging to the mission of San Francisco and called San Pablo. They had seen our fireworks and heard the firing of our falconettes; as to the fires that we had seen, they said that they indeed belonged to one of the nomadic Indian tribes that had been staying a while thereabouts and that they had undoubtedly taken fright at our firing and had left the same night.

About ten o'clock we left the cape and had not had time to sail a few hundred sazhens when an awful squall came upon us from the W with hail, snow, and rain. Because it was completely favorable to our course, we were gladdened by it more than by the initial calm; the squall lasted a full hour and a half and then began to abate. From the racing clouds fell such thick snow that the sailors barely managed to bail the meltwater, and we were unable to discern objects as far as the length of the longboat. But it did not last long, and the sky totally cleared. With the help of this squall we flew like a bird, and we only glimpsed the shore in front of us. Passing yet another cape, we entered a mile-wide strait [Carquinez Strait], which we took at first to be the Great River, the more so as we met here a strong countercurrent; but soon, from the taste of the water, we convinced ourselves of our mistake. The water was salty, as at sea. Farther [along,] the banks came closer together. The southern bank was high, rugged, and wooded and the northern, although also rugged, totally treeless, and on it were grazing many deer, which quickly ran off at our approach.

Meanwhile, the wind had died completely, and we had to work the oars so as not to be swept away by the current. Now we came upon a whirlpool formed by eight strong competing currents, one of which went absolutely its own way and another, parting from it, struck the inlet's bank, where, rebuffed, it returned toward a cape and, meeting another current, formed a vortex so strong that the longboat instantly began to rotate, and [only] with difficulty were we able to row out of it. Here many [harbor] seals had composed themselves on an islet, but they did not let us approach them and quickly cast themselves into the water.

By three o'clock we had neared the cape, and finding it very suitable for an overnight stay, we pulled into a river flowing into the bay here and pitched the tents. This cape rose 250 feet above the level of the water as a sheer cliff supporting the end of a chain of mountains running from the interior toward the seacoast. We ascended the first mountain with the telescope and, finally, sighted the goal of our trip, i.e., the Great [Sacramento] River. Its mouth was found at the eastern end of the strait, from which a wide blue strip of water is visible disappearing beyond the horizon and bordered by (as it seemed to us) treeless green meadows. To the right [southeast] of the cape for a distance of five to seven miles stretched the aforesaid mountains, from which flowed the river that served as a harbor for our longboat; on its banks not far from its mouth we saw for the first time several huts of the savage Indians and on the river itself three or four boats of fir bark. From the movement around the huts we concluded that the savages had already noticed us and, fearing an attack, wanted to abandon their camp. The captain did not wish to alarm them but did want to make contact with them, so he ordered Midshipman Hall with three sailors to go to them and try to detain them there. He succeeded in fulfilling the captain's desire without any difficulty; the savages, seeing that we were not Spaniards and hoping to obtain various trifles and rum (which they liked very much) from us, remained. Seeing the friendly relations of our envoys with the Indians, we went to [see] them. The village (or, rather, temporary camp) consisted of seven huts built from tree bark and just like those that we had seen among the Koloshes [i.e., Tlingits] at Sitka; in them lived twenty persons of both sexes.

The Californians [i.e., Indians] are of medium height, broad shouldered, and muscular; they are dark chestnut in color, and their features, although somewhat sullen, are not at all unpleasant. They clothe themselves in blankets interlaced with black and white feathers; across their shoulders as far as their knees they wear a kind of cloak. Around the middle of their body they wind bast-like matting of their own making, and the rest is bare. The disposition of the savages seemed gentle to us; but the Spaniards asserted that they are crafty and vicious. Among the women, who dress just like the men, we saw several young ones whose appearance was rather agreeable. The weapons of the savages consist of bows and arrows, very skillfully made from some sort of porous and flexible wood. The outside of the former is covered in deerskin sewn with sinews; they [the bows] are extremely elastic and capable of shooting arrows—some with heads of stone and others with just the sharp wooden points—fifty and more paces; in addition, they use clubs and spears. We exchanged rum and various trifles for all of these weapons and clothes. [When we were] returning to our tents, it was already after sunset, and the captain, despite the fact that the Spaniards had described the Indians as cowardly, ordered the posting of sentries with loaded rifles and falconettes at the longboat and by the tents; but the night passed peacefully, and after having taken angles, we set out to explore the river.

At six o'clock in the morning we left the site of our overnight stay, and not having a breeze, we rowed in fine weather toward the strait's northeastern end, where we had seen the mouth of the river, trying to reach it before noon with the intention of taking the midday height of the sun for the determination from it of the latitude of the river's mouth. Of the three large bays connected by narrow straits and constituting the port of San Francisco, this last bay [Junta de los Cuatro Evangelistas, now Suisin Bay] is surrounded on the east and the west by high hills; the northern shore has the appearance of a boundless plain stretching across the southern bank of the river as far as the chain of hills running from the site of our last overnight camp toward the east for a distance of nearly seven or more miles.

The change in the taste of the water, going gradually from bitterly salty to fresh, indicated to us the proximity of a large river. About 11 o'clock we entered it, forcing its way and revealing itself clearly between sandy banks with a channel from one to six sazhens deep. Near the southern bank was found a small island on which several seals had disposed themselves, and upon our approach they threw themselves noisily into the water with a roar. At first the captain wanted to put in to this island in order to take the midday height [of the sun], but taking into account that for this [task] it would be necessary to wait about two hours and thereby lose precious time for further exploration of the river in such fine weather, he conceived the idea of taking the height later on the river itself. We continued, uninterruptedly measuring the depth, which we found to be from seven to three sazhens and less on a sandy bottom. The banks were marshy, overgrown with reeds [tule], and so low that nowhere did we find it possible to put in to take the height; finally, we found several logs lying together in the reeds, and we came alongside them and installed the mercury horizon—but in vain, [for] the mercury continually fluctuated, so that we were forced to abandon our attempt and satisfy ourselves with a determination of the height of the river from the distance covered and the angles from a certain point.

The captain ordered that we return from here because, firstly, the depth had begun to decrease and, secondly, seeing the endlessness of these marshy and low banks, we could not hope to come to the end of them for several days, which would be too grueling for the men; besides, we did not have enough provisions. By five o'clock we had gone back to the last overnight site and composed ourselves there to spend another night, which was quiet and warm. We did not find our friends, the Indians, here now; they had withdrawn to the northern shore. I concluded this [withdrawal] from the fact that there we had seen their boats and the bundles of reeds that they use in place of boats when there are not enough of the latter for fast crossings.

Here at 35 minutes past midnight we observed the height of the high tide and found it to be 8 feet, 4 inches; the next day from the noontime height [of the sun] we calculated the latitude of the cape [Point San Pedro] to be 38° 2' 29" N and the variation of the compass to be 13° 59' E.

At thirty minutes past midnight we left this cape for the second time, and in order to measure the depth we rowed to the opposite cape [Point Pinole]; there we found the depths to be 7 sazhens at the southern shore, 7 again toward the northern shore, and 14 in the middle. From here we took angles and set off to the nearest island [Seal Island?], near which we dropped the grapnel in order to measure the current and found that it reached up to three and half knots. Here we shot two seals. After overnighting here, the next day we set off toward a peninsula. After having explored a bay [the mouth of Napa Creek?] between this peninsula and the shore and seeing there a huge herd of wild deer, the captain, wanting to get venison for the crew, ordered the best four hunters among the men to land; we ourselves made for the isthmus connecting the peninsula to the mainland in order to drive the deer to the landed hunters. The detail of four hunters had been ordered at an agreed signal, namely, the firing of a falconette, to hide under the cliffs at the very edge of the water. After having landed, we connected both beaches with a chain of hunters and, advancing on the prey, gave the agreed signal. The deer, having heard the gunshot, rushed swiftly to the end of the peninsula, where, meeting the other hunters (who killed one deer), they turned back, where the same such reception awaited them, and another was felled, but the rest flung themselves from the steep bank into the water and, after swimming across the bay, vanished into the mountains. After having loaded the catch onto the longboat, we set off again to the northern shore of the bay and then toward the cape [Point San Pedro] where we had overnighted the first time. The next day, after having described the cove and overnighted, we returned to our sloops, where we arrived by the evening of the 24th. During our final overnight we almost lost three of our sailors. Being short of water, the captain sent them with [ten-gallon] casks[10] to a hollow in the mountains to find a spring or a stream. They left long before sunset, and after sundown we awaited their return in vain. The captain began to worry that they had lost their way in the mountains, and after night fell he ordered the lighting of a laurel tree atop the highest mountain near our camp and the firing of falconettes every five minutes. But all was to no effect; the night passed and the men did not come back. Then we detailed all of the remaining crewmen, except two sentries, to find the missing, first posting markers in the nearest mountains. The detail had not yet set off when we saw our men descending the mountains toward us, each of them dragging a cask of water. They recounted that they had sought a spring for a long

---

[10]Russ., *ankera*s (derived, like many Russian naval terms, from the Dutch): 1 ankera = 3 *vedros* ("pails") of 3¼ gallons each.

time and had finally found it; meanwhile, by the time they had filled the casks it was quite dark, whereupon not expecting to find their track in the dark and fearing getting lost, they had decided to overnight at the spring. Although they had heard the shots, a rumble echoing from the mountain tops was refracted in the hollows and reached their ears first from one side and then from the other; and they did not see the fire signal at all. Thus did they pass the night, cold and damp, with no food and no fire under the open sky.

We named the northern shore of these bays the San Rafael Shore after the mission lying on them, the southern shore already having been named St. Paul (or San Pablo in Spanish).

Having described this land and the people inhabiting it, it remains to add only a few words about its products.

California abounds in timber, both deciduous and coniferous species. It brings no benefit because the Spaniards use it only for trifling articles and for rafters under roofs, which are usually thatched with straw or reeds and very rarely with tiles or shingles. Of deciduous trees, the noteworthy are oak, maple, beech, ash, laurel, poplar, and various kinds with colored wood; of conifers, cedar, pine, and larch [tamarack] are noteworthy. All of these varieties grow either mixed with each other or form separate groves and immense forests. The trees are huge in size and could provide excellent material for shipbuilding.

The Spaniards say that there is copper in the interior mountains, but it is not mined.

The seas and rivers abound in fish characteristic of the Pacific Ocean in these latitudes. Moreover, in the waters washing the coast of California there are sea lions (with their rookeries found especially on the rocks of the Farallones), seals, and sea otters. Beavers and [land] otters live in the rivers and lakes.

The bears are black and silver gray; the latter [i.e., grizzlies] are very large and fierce to the extent that they often attack people, even if not wounded, and are anxious only in their dens. The Spaniards catch them with lassos, as described above, both for their coats—which they use instead of beds—and for their meat, which when smoked is very tasty and forms their [i.e., the Spaniards'] favorite food when traveling.

The jaguar, or American tiger, lives in the mountains; but it often descends into the valleys for prey, sometimes even approaching dwellings, where they savage flocks of sheep, the sole domestic livestock of the indigenes. The jaguar is almost the only beast against which the Spaniards use the gun, and against all others they use the lasso, not only primarily because the inhabitants, as has been described, wield it with amazing skill but also because of the shortage of gunpowder and lead, which are conveyed overland from Mexico.

The jackal [i.e., coyote], an animal midway between a wolf and a fox [in size], roams in numerous packs near habitations and in the forests. At night their howling is heard for several miles, and by this time they are so bold that they approach the very settlements and from the enclosures steal sheep in the presence of watchmen. During our trip to survey the northern bay we had occasion to convince ourselves of their daring; they came so close to our tents, despite the fires that were usually lit in several places, that their howling gave us no rest, and we were able to escape these uninvited guests only by shooting several times in the direction from which the howling came.

Besides these thieving creatures, there were deer living together in large herds; in the low-lying woods and on the hills there were rabbits, martens [weasels?], anteaters [skunks?], and others.

Of birds, we saw [the following] (and had occasion to shoot some of them): eagles of various sizes and kinds, and that encountered most often of all was a huge white-headed [bald] eagle living on high seaside cliffs; and kites [vultures?] with bare necks no shorter than the birds themselves. After them in size came an owl with long ears, and a multitude of other large and small hawks and owls.

Besides these birds, there are some that live here permanently and some that fly here and nest here: cranes, storks, raptors [?],[11] and an innumerable multitude of small birds, most of them pretty, among which the beautiful hummingbird and various sandpipers distinguish themselves. Finally, the California quail, a very pretty bird whose size and taste are like those of our hazel grouse, is found only in California. Its back and wings are brown in color, and its breast and belly are gray; the head is black, with two little topknot feathers, and its tail is black. The quail lives in flocks and runs very fast in the grass, but on the other hand it flies heavily and noisily. Shooting or catching it is very easy. At night they fly up into the trees. Noticing this [habit], we put a net over a tree and then pulled it off suddenly after a fairly large number of them had gathered [to roost]; thus, in the morning we counted up to a hundred captive quail. They become tame very fast.

On our arrival here we saw a countless multitude of wild geese and bagged so many of them that we did not know what to do with all of them. Toward the end of our moorage they became timid and allowed us to approach, of course on high ground, and then they flew away. And various kinds of wild ducks, pelicans (or "old woman" birds), and other sea birds were numerous here.

At last, all of our work on the sloops and the baking of rusks were finished; on 8 February we moved from the shore but it was only on the 12th at 9 o'clock that we were able to leave the port, on account of the contrary winds. We were

[11]Russ., *traffy*, which does not seem to exist; however, *travlya* can mean "hawks" or "falcons" and may connote "raptors" (Dal, *Tolkovy slovar*, 819).

very glad that the tedious three-month anchorage at the port—albeit in a good climate—had ended, but nonetheless the small population did not offer a sailor any amusement. The unbroken monotony of life so bored us that when the day ended we thanked God and wished to endure a storm at sea and foul weather rather than stay here [any longer]. Indeed, we were right; the unenlightened, half-wild, sleepy, and indolent Spaniards of that land at that time could not offer us a satisfactory conversation, only astronomical observations, daily hunts, and horseback riding that bored us unimaginably, and we rejoiced when we raised anchor and, leaving the port, saluted the Spanish flag, which was destined soon after us within a lifetime to be lowered hereabouts. Knowing that we were going to the Hawaiian Islands further increased our joy at our departure.

Excerpts from Mikhail Vasilyev, "Remarks on [Alta] California," 1821

Captain-Lieutenant Mikhail Vasilyev, "Remarks on [Alta] California" (from fragments of draft notes on the round-the-world voyage of the sloops *Otkrytie* and *Blagonamerenny* in 1819–22),[1] [Sloop *Otkrytie* on the Northwest Coast?], no earlier than 11 February 1821[2]

On 11 February 1821 we weighed two anchors at the port of [San] Francisco. . . .[3]

---

[1] RGAVMF, f. 213, op. 1, d. 105, fols. 1, 2v.–8v., d. 107, fols. 1–22 (original, draft, and autograph). The sequence of Vasilyev's two notes (I and II) on California does not reflect the chronological order of their writing, a question that remains open. Essentially they are two independent works, the information, subjects, and topical elements coinciding in some cases but sometimes repeated; this inconsistency reflects some irregularity in their writing. The decipherment made by Leonid Shur in the early 1970s—checked and amended against the original in accordance with the principles of publication of Russian documents—has been used in the preparation of the notes. A collation of the differences, especially in orography, between Shur's decipherment and that in this collection confirms the high professional level of Shur's text, which serves as a valuable guide for the study of the peculiarities of Vasilyev's handwriting. At the same time (besides differences in the approach to transliteration), the collation reveals more than 150 variant readings of individual letters; sometimes the complete form of a word depends upon them, and in some cases Shur's reading of a word rendered its full form incorrect (e.g., *shchit* ["shield"] instead of *yashchik* ["box"], *vsyaky* ["any" or "every"] instead of *chast[n]oy* ["private" or "particular"], and others). Also, nearly all of the words that Shur did not succeed in reading have been deciphered (thirteen cases).

The text of this collection basically follows the paragraphing done by Shur (the notes are nearly lacking in paragraphs), as well as his punctuation in part and some of his words of explanation. At the same time, as far as possible Vasilyev's peculiar language with its grammatical and orographical mistakes, nonagreeing words (in terms of case, number, or gender), etc., have been preserved. There are numerous mistakes or slips of the pen in the writing of consonants, e.g., *pyut* ("they are drinking") instead of *byut* ("they are beating"), the repeated writing of *l* instead of *r*, and others, some of which have been removed during the editing of the text (in those instances when a correct understanding of their meaning is otherwise completely or substantially prevented).

[2] Dated in accordance with the time of departure of Vasilyev's squadron from San Francisco. Judging from their content, Vasilyev's remarks were written soon after he left Alta California.

[3] A description of the raising of the anchors and the departure of the sloops from the port, as well as of the prevailing currents and winds in San Francisco Bay, is omitted here.

[I]

Allow me to relate some information about Nueva [New, or Alta] California. The Spaniards, fearing that some European power would occupy the [northwestern] coast of North America, began to establish missions to the north of Vieja [Old, or Baja] California in order to shield its possessions as far as the Arctic Ocean. First they occupied the port of San Diego in 1768 [*sic:* 1769] on the orders of the viceroy of Mexico, and then Monterey, the port of San Francisco, and Santa Bárbara. The concern of the missionaries was the conversion of the savage Indians to Christianity and the cultivation by them of the land.

The port of [San] Francisco was the northernmost settlement of the Spaniards. Its fort, on the southern cape at the entrance to the bay, comprises a battery of stone with 15 embrasures. The guns in it are two old, long brass cannons, 6-pounders apparently, brought from Mexico and cast at least 146 years ago, in 1671 and 1673, and five iron siege cannons brought from Manila, a little smaller, and there is no date stamped on them, but judging from the rusting of their exteriors over time, they must have been cast very long ago, and I do not know [whether] balls have been fired from them. Altogether in the battery there are seven cannons on bad gun carriages and gun mountings, and another cannon lies on blocks, part of the barrel corroded by rust. This battery was built on the most advantageous site against an attack from the sea, and it is one Italia[n] mile from the opposite high shore; this is the narrowest part of the entrance to the bay. A rocky reef runs 70 sazhens from the batteried cape, and in general it is shallow along the southern shore but deep along the opposite shore—from 45 to 60 sazhens. The current is very fast on both sides of this entrance. Formerly there was another battery on the cape where the bay runs southward past the presidio, but it has crumbled since the time of the stay of the ship *Ryurik* in 1817 [*sic:* 1816] at the port of [San] Francisco and its guns have been moved; two brass cannons were mounted almost against the presidio on the edge of the high shore and another brass cannon below the battery, which from this cape could fire far into the bay if a ship were to enter it. At the battery on the cape they raise the Spanish flag when any ship enters or leaves. They call the batter[y] a *castillo*.

Past the batteried cape is found the presidio, opposite which one lies at anchor. The presidio is a quadrangular structure, and it cannot be called stone, although it is similar to it. The walls are made of clay [adobe], similar to that used in bricks but unfired. The roof is tiled, and there is a courtyard [plaza] inside this structure. The presidio would be about a versta in circumference. Here live all of the soldiers of the port of [San] Francisco. Its commandant, Captain Don Luis Antonio Argüello, is in charge of everyone, and below him is the senior officer,

First Lieutenant[4] Don Ignacio [Martínez,][5] head of the cavalry, the[n] Ensign
Don Francisco [   ], head of the infantry, and Don [José] Antonio Sánchez,
recently promoted from ensign to sergeant; there is no officer of the artillery,
which is commanded by a sergeant. The soldiers are, it seems, [as follows]: up to
15 artillerymen, up to 20 infantrymen, and up to 40 cavalrymen, for a total of up
to 75 men, who can be armed. They live in the presidio with all of their families,
and there is also a church, /**one workshop,**/ and a bad blacksmithy. ~~Several~~ Four
three-pound cannons—one brass one on a gun carriage and three iron ones on
gun mountings—stand in the courtyard by the artillerymen. The artil[l]erymen
stand guard at the battery, and the infantrymen at the presidio. There are no
glass panes or stoves in any of the rooms, although it is fairly cold in winter. I
saw them put hot coals on a tile, which the women sit beside to work; otherwise
they feel the cold.

In general it can be said [that] they pass all of their time in id[l]eness. A soldier
is offered a salary of only 19 piasters per month by the king and nothing more.
Against his salary he gets bread of wheat or maize, i.e., corn, from the commandant. The commandant obtains all of this [grain] on credit from the mis[s]-
ionaries, but the soldiers take little wheat because it has to be milled. They have
not established a mill, and it [i.e., grain] is ground by others on a stone; they say
that this [task] is a lot of work, and that corn can be boiled or baked. They also
have many cattle, and they [i.e., the cattle] graze year-round in fields; /**the owners do not stock feed for them in winter, and they become gaunt/**.[6] Bulls are
caught by lasso with horses and driven to the presidio; they [the Californios] eat
only pure meat and discard the head, legs, and all of the guts on the ground. All
are sated—people, birds of prey, dogs, and /**sometimes**/ even wolves, which they
call coyotes, intermediate in size between a dog and a wolf.

They live very slovenly; they throw the heads and bones of butchered cattle
outside the presidio, and everyone dumps all of the filth from his room in front
of the barracks, and the carrion lies there and rots. In summertime the air around
the presidio must be foul, and it must be mucky in the rainy season. They do not
have gardens, although the soil is good. None of the officials even has a garden,
no fruit trees have been planted, and they grow no flowers; everything grows in
its own time in the care of nature.

[4]Sp., *teniente.*

[5]Ignacio Martínez (1774–185?), a native of Mexico City, entered the army in Alta California in 1799 as a
cadet and in 1817 was promoted to lieutenant and stationed at San Francisco. There he served as commandant or acting commandant from 1822 until his retirement from the military in 1831. He owned the large
rancho of Pinole in Contra Costa, the eastern shore of San Francisco Bay. See [Bancroft], *California Pioneer
Register,* 241.

[6]This phrase is written in the margin of the manuscript.

It seems that all of them, once they are sated, devote themselves to sleeping, and sometimes they gamble for piasters ~~or drink~~, otherwise they stand for several hours at the door of their barracks, apparently bored with their lives. The commandant is also a great lover of doing nothing, and each of our requests was fulfilled very slowly. They like to lie and to boast.

Everyone in the presidio has a duty to protect the missions, which have been entrusted to them, and the missions supply them with bread. The sole laborers are Indians, and they are regarded as slaves. I was curious as to how the priests procure savage Indians and convert them to Christianity, and they answered me that they [i.e., the Indians] are found and sent to them by God. Later we learned [that] in fact the Spaniards [Californios] lasso them in the mountains and bring them to the missions. The friars, who already have some Indian believers [neophytes], send [them] to the mountains to try to persuade the other savages; otherwise they try to capture the father or mother of a family, and the children follow them. At present at Mission San Francisco, Father Blas told me, the priests intend to go to the savages in the mountains with cavalrymen to preach the word of God. Every friar, wherever he goes, is accompanied by an armed cavalryman as a bodyguard, for the savage Indians detest the priests and once killed one; but they greatly fear the Spaniards, who are very skilled at catching them with lassos.

The Spaniard who hunts savage Indians dons armor similar to a vest, made of five layers of deerskin and sewn without sleeves, and on his arms and legs he wears special thick leather inscribed with various designs, and in his left hand [he carries] a shield of thick leather, well curried, ¼ of an inch thick, shaped like two ovals, linked to each other, up to two feet long and a little less wide, convex, and etched with the Spanish coat-of-arms on the outer side. He always wears boots of a peculiar style, pointed, with slitted sides, /**[made from] weasel skin, half black and half yellow, trimmed/** with deerskin [thongs] twisted with white rabbit fur, around the calf, one end [of the thongs] inscribed with a design, forming boots. The horse's saddle blanket of thick hide is inscribed with various designs. He takes a rifle, which he places across the saddle, two pistols in spaces in the saddle blanket, a saber hanging from the left side of the saddle blanket, and a lance in his right hand. He passes his left arm through two loops made on the shield. When he attacks a savage Indian, his shield screens his face and all other parts of his body against arrows shot by the savages. The arrows cannot pierce the hide covering him. They [i.e., the Californios] kill or wound the Indians defending their liberty, and this [outcome] is considered the wrath of God for not heeding the true faith. They lasso the timid ones who have hidden themselves, throwing a noose of hide thong over their necks and taking them to the missions, where they are immediately baptized and converted to Christianity, whereupon they become the property of the missions. Some of them, given the opportunity, escape to their former abodes and are deemed fugitives. The friars, of course, seek these Indians as their laborers.

At [Mission] San José I also saw many [Indian] youngsters, who had, of course, been captured in order that they could learn the ways of the missionaries better and forget their former way of life faster. As far as I was able to observe, the education of the Indians who had been living at the missions a long time was slight; it seems that they know a few prayers and perhaps the church rites, and the friars say that it is difficult to teach anything to an adult Indian. Indians of both sexes having been procured, they marry with the mission's consent, and from them are chosen elders who oversee the others. Some Spanish soldiers—a kind of manager, called a *mayordomo* [steward]—are executors, it seems, of the orders of the priests.

There are many Indians in the mountains, and as far as those places are known, they number five tribes, so that they do not understand each other's language; they live in families in huts built in the likeness of a nightcap,[7] covered with rushes; the men go completely naked but the women cover themselves with either sewn animal or bird skins. None of their rituals has been observed, except that they express their grief at the death of relatives by scratching their bodies. They burn the bodies of their dead to ashes.

They live on various fruits and nuts, and the coastal ones on fish, and they hunt deer, which are numerous. It was amusing to be told how they hunt these timid and swift animals. An Indian dons a deerskin and ties deer antlers to his head. Resembling the deer, he goes on all fours and locates them. When he spots them, he acts as if he were grazing. Going closer, he kills them with an arrow. They hunt wild sheep. Numerous birds abound. They have one weapon—a bow with arrows of very good workmanship. The bow is made from animal sinew, tightly strung to one side of [a haft of] hard wood or, rather, from [a haft of] flexible wood affixed to sinew. A three-foot bowstring is made from sinew, and the arrows are made from reeds [rushes] about half an inch in circumference, /soft/ ~~weak~~ inside, and up to three feet long, and an arrowhead of transparent ~~stone or~~ flint [obsidian?] is fashioned with the very same stone and affixed to one end and feathers are tied to the other end. Other Indians have sharpened arrows of wood only without arrowheads. They always hold the bow to bend against the wooden haft, and when they have to shoot an arrow they draw the bow very dexterously ~~they draw the bow~~ on the inside of the wooden [haft] and shoot very accurately without aiming at all. It is said that in battle they do so with a cry. I was unable to learn reliably whether they imbue the arrows with poison, but it seemed to me more likely that they do not do so. The Indians have a medicine for wounds.

---

[7]Russ., *kolpak*.

They told me that they know a plant that they chew to heal wounds. Because of it the arrow leaves the body and the wound cleanses itself and then closes; but the Spaniards told us that they do not know this herb.[8] The Indians carry their bow and arrows in some sort of animal skin that serves them as a quiver. They know an herb, called ch[i]a,[9] that makes them sweat. We tried it; it is a useful plant that grows everywhere in the fields. They use saunas, forming a kind of oven from clay, heating it as much as possible, and sweating in it; this serves to mitigate their diseases ~~known to them~~. They start a fire by rubbing wood on wood that is known to them to ignite quickly; they cook everything on stones piled on the coals, and they bake or fry meat and fish. They either pluck their beard or remove it by rubbing it with hot stones. They are brown in color, their countenance is not disagreeable, their hair is black and wiry on their heads, they are well built, and they are medium in stature, although there are tall ones.

We saw their dances at Mission San Francisco. They sing and clap; some beat time with a split stick and some dance and pose, marking time by striking the ground hard with their /**right**/ foot, and in their mouth they have a whistle made from a bird's foot, with which they also keep time. They stain themselves in stripes of black and red, strew white bird down on their entire chest and face and in stripes on their arms, and around their head wear bands of small reeds, dyed red, with small black feathers on the ends. They also stick a feather in their hair and a crow's tail feathers in a stick, and ~~they hang~~ they tie crow's feathers either to their back or to an entire waistband. /**They told us**/ that in the mountains the women also dance naked and on their head wear a kind of helmet of black feathers /**or a headband of down**/, and they mark time, swinging and flicking their arms. We saw another kind of dance: at a signal from a conductor,[10] apparently, two come running, dressed alike except that on one's head there is a hat of black feathers and on his lips there is a long beak like a crane's made of feathers. In both of their mouths there is a whistle made of pelican feet, and both run back and forth, whistling, with sticks in their hands, and the others sing. Having finished running, the crane gestures threateningly at all of the spectators, and then one behind the other they run quietly to the side. At a si[g]nal they again come running and do as before and retire.

The savage Indians tie a reed band, dyed red, around their head and pass black

---

[8]This plant was probably the California, or wavyleaf, barberry (*Mahonia pinnata*, syn. *Berberis pinnata*), which was widely used by Californian natives for medicinal purposes. Miwok hunters inserted a piece of chewed bark or root of barberry into a wound to prevent swelling. See Mead, *Ethnobotany*, 71; and Strike, *Aboriginal Uses*, 27–28.

[9]Chia (*Salvia columbariae*) is a species of sage. Its highly nutritious seeds, one of the ingredients of pinole, were eaten by California's natives, as well as used to make a soup, a porridge, a beverage, an oil, and flour. See Mead, *Ethnobotany*, 377–78; and Strike, *Aboriginal Uses*, 139–40.

[10]The manuscript has *derifor*, presumably a corruption of *dirizhyor* ("conductor").

feathers under it from above and below. In their hair they stick two or three sticks or bones, around which are tied red feathers from some sort of bird that has red feathers on its neck and part of its wings and black feathers elsewhere, and on the very ends they tie several condor feathers. Around their neck they wear several round bones, cut cleanly from fish, and pearl [abalone?] shells, and white fish bones [dentalia shells?] these bones serve them as money and pieces of pearl shell are strung on a string. They pierce their ears with bones [shells?] with designs and similar [----], and they have large waistbands of bones [shells?].

They play at sticks, like the Koloshes [Tlingits], and they have another game: apparently it is necessary to guess whether one has an even or uneven number of pebbles in one's hand. White bones [dentalia shells?] serve as currency, and the more they have the richer they are. To their bowstrings they tie the skins of young birds so that in shooting arrows their hand does not become sore and the shot cannot be heard, for without the skin the bowstring twangs.

The coastal [Indians] make boats by tying several bunches of reeds together, and they kneel in them and hold in both hands a long paddle with two blades, and they stroke two, three, or four times on each side in calm weather only and until the reeds are waterlogged. They catch fish with nets. They weave baskets fairly skillfully from small white withies, and they adorn the outside with red feathers, white bones [dentalia shells?], and feathers from a condor's head. They obtain firewood [thusly]: they set fire to a tree and then shatter [it].

The Spaniards say that their Indian neighbors are unman[l]y, timid, and good-tempered. They live far from the missions and stay mostly in the mountains. They say that /sometimes/ wars are waged between their tribe[s]. No special talents on their part have been observed. The Spaniards have not yet investigated thoroughly how numero[u]s they are, what places they [inhabit], what their origin is, and other details about these people.

II

Although the presidio of San Francisco is utterly lacking in everything, the missions can be called rich in every kind of grain and livestock; it seems that only the priests are engaged in tireless pursuits. Mission San Francisc[o] was found[ed] in 17[76] on a good site one Spanish league from the presidio. In all of the missions the first concern was to build a church [and to have] a good set of utensils and a rich sacristy; although they lack organs, they have the music of several violins and cellos, and it can be said that the Indians have learned to play the psalms respectably. Near the church stands an annex where the prie[s]ts live; there are two of them from the Franciscan order at each of the missions of Santa Clara, San José, and San Rafael. They dress in gray cassocks with many pockets and a hat of light yellow with a wide brim. Behind this building, and linked to it, are all of the workshops and storehouses. Opposite this building is a kind of barracks for the Indians, who live there. Between the church and the Indian residence is a square [plaza], where a tall pole topped by a cross has been erected.

An orchard also adjoins the first building from the church, and there are fruit trees (apple, pear) and flowers in it; in the garden they plant cabbage, pumpkins, pota[toes], onions, garlic, radishes, peppers, and watermelons. We found the orchard at Mission San José in the best order; although it was wintertime, the farming could be judged. They grow grapes, from which they make red wine. We drank this year's vintage, made in September, and we cannot say how it is after it ages but now it is rathe[r] sweet. They have planted olive trees, whose fruit has the best taste of all. They do not seem to exert much effort on garden vegetables, for we did not find enough food at the four missions for both sloops. At first we got some, but then it was impossible to get any at all, except apples, which were abundant at Santa Clara and San José. Even the best kind had little taste and were mostly coarse and woody.[11]

Although Mission San Francisco is older than the other surrounding [missions], it is poorer than the others; clearly it does not have good managers. Upon our arrival the senior friar, Juan [Vicente Cabot], was summoned during our stay to another mission, Soledad, not far from Monterey. Two friars remained: José [Altimira],[12] who had been there one year, and Blas [Ordaz], who had arrived several months ago. The friars are sent from Spain to Mexico [City], where there is a college [San Fernando College, est. 1734], whence they are [graduated and] assigned to the missions. Two priests are posted to each mission, and they receive a salary of 400 piasters a year; but because they do not need money, the [cost] of things that they need is deducted [from their salary], and they told me that they are punctually supplied with everything. By contrast, those serving the king at the presidio have not received any salary for seven to ten years. The bishops and clerical officials live better and richer than everyone else, receiving large incomes and salaries from the king.

They told us that all of the revenue received from Mexico for Old and New California is divided into three parts. One goes to the upkeep of the king's servitors and all royal fortifications and establishments, another to the clerics,

---

[11]Russ., *oderevenelie.*

[12]José Altimira (1787–1860s), a peninsular from Barcelona, arrived in California in 1820 and was assigned to San Francisco. He was instrumental in the illegitimate (but subsequently legitimized) establishment in 1823 of Mission San Francisco Solano at Sonoma, the last of the twenty-one missions and the only mission founded under Mexican auspices. He remained there until 1826, when the mission was burned by Indians. Altimira declined to swear allegiance to the Mexican constitution of 1824, and in early 1828 he fled Alta California before he could be subjected to the terms of a decree of late 1827 that stipulated the expulsion of all Spaniards from the country. See Geiger, *Franciscan Missionaries,* 6–10.

and the third to the king, but it is also left to the priests. It seems to me that the Spaniards, having completely entrusted themselves to their priests, are totally dependent upon them, and this makes them very indolent and negligent toward everything in the community. Also, seeing themselves as necessary, they [i.e., the priests] hold sway over them [i.e., their compatriots]; without them nothing can be begun, and their advice and opinion are necessary for everything.

In examining these two different classes of people, priests and citizens, it would seem that the obligation of the former is to teach religion to the young, correct their ~~morals~~ manners, and encourage them to be industrious. The latter, respecting their masters, ensure their proper upkeep. By contrast, the missionaries nourish everything; they recruit Indians by their own effort, and they operate everything that is needed in the community. They strictly honor the church rites and strive to inspire everyone to that [end]. It seems that in order not to miss the most sacred church rite of the Spaniards—the hour of prayer—a priest will drop everything. When we visited Mission San José, the priest showed [us] his establishment. A bell announced the hour of prayer, and he kneeled on the ground where we stood, and at the end of the prayer all of the Indians and Spaniards resumed what they had been doing. I do not have faith in the sincerity of this prayer; it is just hypocrisy. Every Spaniard and Indian knows all of the prayers by heart, but their morals, as far as we could tell, were very bad. The prie[s]ts rarely preach in church, and they attend to the decent existence of the parishioners in their congregation even less. Adultery and stealing on their part are not, it seems, major vices, and all others are even more minor.

It merits regret that none of their youngsters has been educated. There is a school in the presidio; one sergeant teaches reading and writing to the young children of the soldiers. I saw a 16-year-old boy who does [not] yet write in straight lines but who rides and lassos expertly. It is strange that the [holy] fathers do not oversee the behavior of the children at all (boys up to 20 years of age they call lads),[13] so that they are great thieves, at home always stealing eggs from the hens and milk from the cows, crawling under their udders and sucking their teats. Few of us were not robbed. From our observatory, erected in the presidio, they stole a hygrometer, which had been hung behind a window to measure the humidity of the air and went missing during the night; they [i.e., the Californios] were unable to find it, although all of the officials and friars seemed to take part [in the search]. [They] said indifferently that the muchachos had stolen it. Once we arrived at the presidio from Mission San Francisco at dusk. Our doctor, Mr. [Ivan] Kovalyov, was in the l[e]ad, and at the presidio in the courtyard his horse stumble[d] and fell

---

[13] Sp., *muchachos*.

with him. A purse with *chervonetses*[14] and piasters, as well as some medicinal powders that he always took with him just in case, fell out of his pocket. At this time
he did not think to examine his pockets, but after a while, having gone calmly to
the commandant's, he remembered the purse. Immediate[ly] they sent [someone]
to search the spot, [but] they found nothing. Afterwards they brought the lost
powders and later even the purse to him, but the chernovetses and piasters were
missing, and they all reckoned that finding them would be impossible.

Those living at the presidio were all born in the Americas, and the Spaniards
who are sent from Mexico and Old California, [as well as] from Monterey, to the
port of [San] Francisco—as the northernmost Spanish settlement in America—
are badly behaved. The commandant [Luis Antonio Argüello] was also born in
America. His father, [José Darío,] from Europe, was formerly commandant of
the presidio and is now governor of Old California. The other officers are derived
from soldiers, and I do not know the origin[s] of [Don] Francisco.

Of the furniture in the commandant's quarters, there are four benches in the
hall, and in his bedroom and office there are two plain wooden tables covered
with thick blue cloth, two broken wooden armchairs, one bench, a mirror, and
a picture of the Battle of Kiel [1814] presented by Lieutenant Lazarev during his
stay at this port in 1815 aboard the *Suvorov*. There are a few more rooms, similar
to storerooms, where his relatives live. The cavalry officers are somewhat neater;
on their walls there are some old pictures and gilded frames, in which there used
to be, apparently, small mirrors.

Don Sánchez, having a large family, lives more crowdedly than the others;
when the opportunity offers, he trades liquor, and he is, apparently, the richest of
them all, having numerous cattle, sheep, and horses. All of the officials—except
[Don] Francisco, who is as poor as a church mouse—have their own livestock.
During our stay he [i.e., Don Francisco] was given a room that had been repaired
with adobe where it had crumbled and provided with a door. His furniture is one
table and a bench; he sleeps at the commandant's.

Usually hay is not stocked in winter for livestock either at the presidio or the
missions, and during our stay meat was fairl[y] good at first, but later the livestock
became so thin that it was not possible to eat either beef or mutton, which afterwards spoiled on our cruise, [and we] had to throw [it] overboard. [The meat] had
a peculiar disagreeable taste, although the bulls had been young but not castrated.

They told us that in summer their horses add so much weight [that] it is difficult
to control them, and as they are very fond of horseback riding there are not many
of them who have not been thrown by their horses. Riding seems to be their only
form of exercise.

---

[14]A *chervonets* was a tsarist gold coin of three, five, or ten rubles' denomination.

It is not possible to admire very much Europeans who, living in the climate of the paralle[l] of latitude of 37° [N], suffer a lack of the most necessary things of life. They do not have their own shirts or boots and no dresses or dishes. At the missions the most coarsely made shawls [serapes] are woven by Indians from sheep's wool, although the wool is excellent. They cut [an opening] in the center of the shawl and wear it over the head, and it covers the entire body and serves as a cloak; the Spaniards and the Indians wear them.

All of the things that they have—coarse cloth, linen, and other textiles and articles—are brought from Mexico or bought from visiting ships. Although com[mer]ce with foreign powers is forbidden in Spanish America, out of necessity—for want of its needs being met—they buy from foreigners. The [Spanish] Americans seek silver and our [Russian-]American Company grain.

They told us that the climate here is fine, except in the months of June, July, and August, when there is fog on the coast. Spring and autumn are beautiful. We were there in the month[s] of November, December, January, and half of February. Apart from January, the season was fine, and sometimes—when the wind was from the S or SW—the weather was foul, but most of the time it was fine, the temperature from 7 to 15 degrees Réaumur. In January snow sometimes fell with a north wind, but it did not last on the ground. The weather was cold and overcast, and often it rained; apparently spring arrives in the middle of February.

In December we went to Mission San Rafael. It was founded [in] 1817 and is the most recent. There is one priest there, Friar Juan Amorós,[15] and up to 250 Indians altogether at the whole [mission], [which] is situated on a hillside; a church, quarters for the friar, storehouses, and a workshop have been built. There are buildings where the women and young children live. The other Indians [live] in huts covered in rushes, [just] as they usually live in the hills. A better location would be north of San Francisco on the other side of the [entrance to the] bay. There is a small garden.

They showed us the Indian dance, [which] is the same everywhere: they sing and clap their hands or slap their chest, and the others stomp affectedly in one spot; the women, waving their hands overhead, snap their fingers. We saw their stick game and another—odds or evens. Bleached [dentalia?] shells, strung on a string, are their currency. The men are almost naked, except that they cover their genitals, and the women have woolen blouses and skirts.

We had to go to within a mile of Angel Island and then to the N. From deep water it is possible to enter a stream [San Rafael Creek?] and land near the

---

[15]Juan Amorós (1773–1832), a Catalán, arrived in Alta California in 1804 and served at Mission San Carlos until 1819 and then at Mission San Rafael until his death. He was noted for his religious zeal, administrative skill, and practicality. See Geiger, *Franciscan Missionaries,* 11–13.

mission, but we arriv[ed] in shallow water and landed on the bank at a distance of two leagues from the mission.

The church is always seen first. After having lunched with the friar, we returned in the sloop toward evening.

At the beginning of January we went in longboats to Mission Santa Clara, a distance of up to forty Italian miles at the very end of the southern bay [San Francisco, as opposed to San Pablo Bay]. We were advised that it was better to go by land on horseback, there being a fine road and a shelter halfway—a hut where sentries live and the commandant's herd grazes. But it was my wish to examine the bay. At 8 o'clock in the morning on the 4th of January, Tuesday, we set out. The wind from the N and the current were favorable. We took as a guide Sánchez, who assured me that he knew the way. After midday we came abreast of an island [Blair Island?] lying at the end of the bay. The weather was beautiful. Here sandbanks began, and the dept[h], which was up to 7 sazhens at a point [Redwood or Ravenswood Point?] abreast of us, gradually decreased, and soon we were sailing in a depth of 1½ sazhens. We approached the sandbanks in very shallow water. Our guide said that he did not know the channel, and it was impossible to proceed and necessary to await the incoming tide, as the mission's *lanchas* [longboats] usually navigate shallow water but have run aground several times. [We] withdrew to deeper water and dropped the grapnel to await the tide. Evening was nigh, and this spot was only halfway. The longboat from the *Blagonamerenny*, which was taking soundings, found enough [depth] for a passage, and we followed it, continuing to go I knew not where. Night fell. Having touched bottom several times and [passed] the whole day in a longboat in the cold rendered our situation unpleasant. Perhaps there is a channel in the shallowest water; sometimes [we] found depths of 4 and 7 sazhens, but I think that neither he [i.e., Sánchez] nor the Indians themselves knew any indications whatever, and they usually plied the shallow water at high tide.

At last we saw a low shore and the mouth, apparently, of a stream [Guadalupe Slough/Creek?]. The tide was already running. After having passed several creeks, I wanted very much to land on the bank. At 10 o'clock in the evening we found a suitable spot, where we decided to overnight in the longboat. It was a cold but clear night. The next morning we decamped and went to find a real landing. This stream **/has salt water from the sea and does not have a freshwater source in the mountains, and there are marshes along both sides of it;/** [it] meanders unbrokenly and has many branches, and it ends two leagues from Mission Santa Clara. We halted in one branch to test whether or not it was possible to reach the mission on foot.

A cavalry officer left for Santa Clara by land on the very day that we did. He arrived the same day and reported our **/trip/** ~~arrival~~. The next day horses were sent for us. After going ashore, we heard the voices of Indians awaitin[g] us; we arrived at Santa Clara on horseback.

This mission is situated on a level place and has the usual layout of all the others; [it] is fairly extensive, has 1,400 Indians, was founded in 1775 [*sic:* 1777], and has José Viader and Joaquín[16] as friars. They have been at this mission 25 years, and [both] are /48 [?]/ elderly. We found only Father Magín at home, and the other was at Mission San José. We examined all of the facilities and the farming. The church was very well appointed, with a rich sacristy; [here], too, there are no organs but they have music. In the workshops they only ~~make~~ weave women's serapes from wool, and all of the Indians wear these, and they also make blouses and skirts from wool. The women dress leather, and they inscribe it with various designs. The work is very simple: they make designs on iron bars, with which they stamp the soft leather, inscribing design to design. The bars must have been brought from either Mexico or Europe. There is a small joinery and a blacksmithy. All of the missions are greatly in need of tools for their workshops. The gristmill is simila[r] to a hand mill but has a larger millstone and is worked by a mule. There is considerable wheat, beans, peas, and corn, some garden produce (onions, peppers, garlic, apples), and some dressed leather and handmade serapes in the storehouse. The orchard is fairly large, with ~~many~~ whole av[e]nues [i.e., rows] of apple and pear [trees] and some beds for garden vegetables.

After having lunched, we went to Mission San José, a distance of 5 or 6 leagues from Santa Clara by a good road. We arrived there toward evening. It is situated in the mountains NE of Santa Clara; it is also two leagues from it to the bay, and there is a stream [Coyote or Mission Creek?] flowing into the bay. It would have been shorter to go to this mission by sloop, and they say that there are fewer sandbars, but our guide did not know the way.

We were met with music, and fruit (apples, pears, grapes) had been laid on a table. This mission is administered by Father José Narciso [Durán] and Father [   ].[17] The mission was founded only 23 years [ago],[18] and the priests have been here fourteen years.

---

[16]A mistransliteration of "Magín," referring to Magín Catalá.

[17]There is a blank in the manuscript, but the friar is presumably Buenaventura Fortuny (1774–1840), a peninsular from Catalonia. After joining the Franciscan order in 1792, he had gone to New Spain in 1803 with Narciso Durán, and they proceeded together to Alta California in 1806 after three years at Mexico City's San Fernando College. Both, too, were assigned to Mission San José, where they remained together for twenty years. In 1826 he succeeded José Altimira at Mission San Francisco Solano, which had been temporarily abandoned in the face of Indian attacks. In the same year Fortuny, like Durán, refused to take the oath of allegiance to Mexico, and both were among the thirteen missionaries exempted by Governor José María de Echeandía when the decree expelling all Spaniards from Mexico became law in 1827. From 1833 until 1837 Fortuny served at both Mission San Luis Rey and Mission San Diego, and thereafter at Mission San Buenaventura until his death. See Geiger, *Franciscan Missionaries,* 89–91.

[18]Actually, 25 years previously.

Examining their farming, we found [it] better than that of all of the other missions that we had visited. There are 1,700 Indians here; the church is not as good or as richly appointed as that at Santa Clara, [however,] on account of its newness. There is a water mill that grinds very well and works very simply. A stream descends between the mountains, and a dam has been made and the water blocked, as if in a small lake. A pipe has been made in this dam, and water exits through it and flows along a chute that overlies the millstones. The mill has been built at the foot of the mountains. [It is] a small stone building; a beam has been installed in it, and affixed to its underside is a horizontal wheel with teeth protruding vertically right to the edge. A millstone has been placed on the topside of the beam and another under it in the floor of the building. Water from the chute accumulates in a small stone ba[s]in alongside the mill. A pipe runs from this basin at a gradient of more than 45°, so that the water descending the pipe strikes the wheel and teeth, thereby forcing the beam to turn the upper stone. The beam rotates on a pinion,[19] and above the upper millston[e] there is a box into which the wheat is poured. The rush of the water forces the millstone to rotate quickly. Fine flour emerges, and this mill works well but operates only 4 months of the year, there not being enough water the rest of the year.

At this mission more than at the others we saw young Indians; although they are not yet laborers, it was more feasible to teach them a new way of life. [Because] few barracks have been erected for the Indians, some live in huts that they themselves have built.

This mission is more extensive and more affluen[t] than the others, as far as we could see. The workshops are as poor. The stock of grain is large. Praising the goodness of the soil, Father Narciso told us that wheat yielded no less than 30-fold and sometimes up to 50-fold [the seed] and that the rest of the land yielded superlatively. The orchard is fairly extensive, [with] al[l]eys [i.e., rows] of apple and pear [trees], and they grow grapes, from which they make a rather sweet red wine, which they give to Santa Clara, [San] Francisco, and [San] Rafael. There are also two olive trees, many flowers, and garden vegetables, but as we examined them in wintertime, it was not possible to see everything properly. In the storehouse there is considerable dressed leather, woolen serapes, and so on. We saw only waxen candles at this mission, and they say that they [i.e., the candles] are supplied from Manila for the church. Everywhere [i.e., elsewhere] they burn tallow for want of waxen candles.

Having examined all of the missions situated around the port of [San] Francisco, [one can] conclude [the following]: the productivity of the soil is generally good, especially where fog does not harm growth some distance from the sea.

---

[19]Russ., *pyatka*.

The output of the soil more or less [depends upon] the number of Indians, i.e., laborers, that the missions have. Of course, much depends upon management. We saw that San Francisco is, in fact, neglected because all of the friars have been changed. The wealth of the missions consists of grain and cattle, and they ~~are in need of~~ suffer a lack of everything else. Although the sheep's wool is fine, they ~~do not know to work it and~~ are unable to make anything better from it save serapes, blouses, and skirts of crude workmanship. They make no linen whatever, although it seems that the land could produce flax and hemp. They also dress crude leather ~~as well as~~ and boil poor soap. They dip mediocre candles from the blended tallow of bulls and deer. They have no meta[l]s whatever and are greatly in need of iron, copper, and so on, especially tools for blacksmithing, locksmithing, and joinering, as well as many other things necessary to a communit[y]. For example, they do not have wire for making brushes for combing wool, and they comb with some difficulty. They do not have wicks for candles, and they make some by pulling threads from old shirts and similar rags. They are greatly in need of all European things necessary to housekeeping, and they get them partly from Mexico and partly from visiting foreign ships.

Wanting to thank them for their hospitality, I gave to each mission some presents that we ha[d], such as waxen candles, wicks, a few tools of every sort, and so on. Nevertheless, I could not satisfy a[l]l of the needs of these fathers, especially [those of] Mission San Francisco. They liked every article that we had on the sloops, and they would have liked to have taken everything. It can be said that in showering them as much as possible with things of importance to them, their requests increased daily in order to get something else, and they would not take money for the trifles that we received from them, and everything that we gave cost me dearly. It would be incomparably cheaper to acquire the ornaments and weapons of the savage Indians from the Indians themselves than from these greedy friars.

On the eve of our departure from the port of [San] Francisco, Father Blas came to bid us farewell. Scrutinizing his cassock, we detected seven pockets in it—four in the wide sleeves and three in the round collar. In addition to these, there is a large space between the neck and the waist [where it is possible] to put something.

In accordance with his feigned liking for us, [he] promised at our departure to say a prayer in the church of his mission and to free 20 Indians from work and drive them into the church to pray for our safe voyage. He offered this with such pomposity and goodness that we were obliged to humbly thank him. /**On the eve of**/ ~~On the day of~~ his name day this same priest wrote to me, "See how generously God bestows His blessing on us, how with the care of the Almighty we have such a happy lot." And for that he sent an empty bottle, the largest I have ever seen, to be filled with rum. After I had sent him the rum with a not[e] similar to his, he sent on his name day two goats as a gift, and then he billed us and accepted the money.

We overnighted at Mission San José. The next day the weather was foul, wet snow fell, and the wind was from the N. After lunching and thanking our hosts, we ro[d]e to a *pueblo*—a Spanish village on the road to Santa Clara. This settlement, which is under the supervision of the commandant of the port of [San] Francisco, comprises Spaniards who were born in America; there are up to 250 of them, mostly juveniles. As at the mission, they have nothing except grain and cattle. From this settlement the road runs a league to Santa Clara as an ave[n]ue [i.e., tree-lined], made and tended by the priest Magín. Toward evening we arrived at Santa Clara, where we spent the night.

Early the next day, our longboat having arrived, we proceeded homeward with the tide. During our trip to Santa Clara I had observed that our guide did not know the way. At Mission San José I asked Father Narciso to give us an Indian who was experienced in plying the shallow water.

At 8 o'clock we cast off, and the current was favorable and the wind rather fair. We soon left the stream and passed the sandbanks; the wind blew fresh from the N, and the current, which had helped us until now, flowed adversely, and rowing against both the contrary current and the headwind was difficult. The day yielded to evening. The cold wind from the north was pa[l]pable, the breakers lapped over us, and the rowers were exhausted. It was necessary to land. The western shore of the bay seemed high, but at low tide a sandbank stretched a long way offshore. So it was not possible to land there. Withdrawing to a depth of one sazhen, we lay at anchor and decided to spend the night in the longboat. The wind blew stron[g]ly from the N and created ~~considerable~~ breakers that quite often lapped over us. Sheltering under a tarpaulin, we waited until the current became favorable. Fortunately, the ~~weather~~ night was ~~fair~~ clear with a full moon; however, the cold was app[r]eciable. The [s]plashes of the breakers froze on the tarpaulin and the sheepskin coats of the sailors. Toward morning with a change in the current we raised anchor. After we had neared Salt [Hunters?] Point in less than two hours, the current beca[m]e contrary, and with a fresh N wind we landed near Salt Point. After going ashore, we warmed and dried ourselves; after midday the current became favorable, and we set out again, and at 3 o'clock in the afternoon we reached the sloop on Sat[u]rday, the fifth day.

Having learned the situation of this bay and the distances along its shores, [we found that] it is necessary to enter the shallow waters or the sandbanks at high tide. They told us that the [mission] Indians in their boats, when they thus encounter a contrary wind, either land on the shore, the depth permitting, or stop at anchor close to the bay's shore. Some of them stay on guard, and the rest swim ashore to await a favorable current or fair weather. Their boats, which can be called launches with 20 and more oars, are crudely made, very heavy, and poorly operated. There are two at Mission San José and two at Mission San Francisco, and the commandant has one.

Being short of rusks, which in Russia we were able to load to suffice for two years only, I had intended to go from Sitka to the port of [San] Francisco in Californi[a], where I kn[e]w that the missions were rich in wheat. I hoped to stock it for the subsequent voyage. The other reason [that] induced me to choose the port of [San] Francisco was the fact that I had heard that the English sloop *Raccoon* /**of 22 guns and a crew of 126 men/**,[20] [under] Captain Black, having been damaged on the shoals of the Columbia River, had been careened at that port. At Sitka, while coming to anchor, we had touched the front of a rock. We had the hull below the waterline inspected by a diver, and a sheet of copper was [found to be] missing from the port side opposite the yardarm near the second girdle from the keel. It was not possible to lose a sheet from such a light blow, which had not occurred right at the sternpost, where crumpled lead and some mossy wood were visible. I thought it more likely that the sheet had been torn off by an anchor cable in Kamchatka. During high winds we had often seen the sheathing, and it was found to be worn in many places. At the port of [San] Francisco I intended to examine it properly and, if necessary, to careen [the ship].

However, upon examining the hull below the waterline after the high winds and severe rolling that we had had during our passage from Sitka to the port of [San] Francisco, we found [that] only that sheet was missing. Moreover, I was satisfied that it had been torn off by a cable in Kamchatka and that more copper had not been damaged by the passage and the tossing. I abandoned my intention to careen; thinking, too, that it would be safer to anchor at this port than at Monterey, I remained here, having resolved to rest the men and to repair everything properly at our leisure. Ashore they allotted a room to us at the presidio for the astronomer and his assistants. We took all of their instruments and chronometers there and lowered the rigging [in order to] repair it. At my request the commandant had bulls driven to the landing and baked bread issued. We were able to obtain greens at first [only], and even then not many. But as we were in vital need of rusks, and in order to stock them for the voyage, I appointed Lieutenant Lazarev to ride to Monterey to explain to the governor, as the overlord of the province, and to rely upon every assistance from him, especially as all of the Spanish ports in America had been forewarned by Spain to supply us with everything necessary in the event of our arrival.

---

[20]In the manuscript this phrase is written in the margin.

To my surprise, the commandant refused, saying that without [the permission of] the governor he could not allow a foreigner to travel into the interior. After having prepared a letter explaining the reason for my arrival in California, [I] asked the governor's assistance in supplying me with rusks, flour, and wheat, as well as permission for the naturalist to satisfy his curiosity in the interior of New California as far as Monterey. The governor replied that he would be very pleased if I were to remain and obtain everything that I needed for the expedition, and he offered to order everything that I required, and he again ordered the commandant to satisfy the naturalist's desire. He said nothing about my reques[t] for his consent to allow Kuskov to come [from Fort Ross] to [see] us at the port of [San] Francisco. Then he explained to me that the governor [commandant] here has nothing of his own and cannot order that we be supplied with what we need. The commandant promised to furnish us as much flour as he could for baking rusks, as well as wheat. They themselves never bake rusks and do not stock them.

With up to 1,000 of the bricks that we took from Russia on the *Blagonamerenny,* we built an oven at the presidio, and with as much flour as they could supply we baked up to 260 puds [of rusks], which sufficed us on both sloops for two months. We took flour—[what] we were able to get here—and wheat for three months. Figuring that we would have enough baked bread for two months, we provisioned ourselves for eight months. After reviewing all of our casked and sacked rusks, we found that 20 of the 500 puds were unfit for consumption, and on the *Blagonamerenny* 60 of 1,000 puds proved unfit, mostly in those casks that were stored alongside water barrels. Of course, either moisture got in them or they were damp [when filled]. After having opened some casks on the bottom, [we found that] the rusks on the surface had spoiled. Of course, the old casks were not strong, but most of the rusks were as good as when they were stocked, albeit not after a year and a half. It is far better to put all sea provisions in stout casks. So far we have had up to 300 puds of rusks spoil, mostly those that were put in sacks and that lay in the watery hold, the afterhatch, and the mess deck, [where] it was not possible to save them from spoilage; in the hold and in the bread room, where they were strewn, it was damp. We were t[o]ld [that] the rusks bought at Sitka from American ships from Boston (seven years after they were baked) are preserved best in rum casks. Altogether we acquired about one and a half years' worth of grain, figuring that this stock would suffice us for my intended voyage.

My choice of the port of [San] Francisco to rest the crews of the ships was guided further by the fact [that] it was known to me that north of this port at [   ]²¹ in Bodega Bay and somewhat to the north of i[t] the Russian-American Company had established the settlement of Ross, which was managed by Commercial

---

²¹Presumably the latitude and longitude of Ross were intended to fill this gap in the manuscript.

Counsellor Ivan Aleksandrovich Kuskov. In 1806 Nikolay Petrovich Rezanov, the plenipotentiary of the [Russian-]American company, travelled from Kodiak to California on the ship [   ],[22] whose commander was Lieutenant Khvostov. They were at the port of [San] Francisco, and [Rezanov] went to Monterey. After becoming acquainted with the governor, [Rezanov] desired to marry his daughter.[23] The outcome of this [voyage] was the fact that in the following year, 1807, Mr. Kuskov was sent with some Russian promyshlennik[s] and some Konyaga and Aleut fa[m]ilies to settle at Bodega [Bay].[24] It was reckoned that the advantage of this [venture], of course, was the fact that this place abounds in timber for shipbuilding and ships could be built here.[25] The climate of 38° [N] latitude is far better than Kodiak's or Sitka's; the soil produces everything in abundance; the savage Indians are a well-behaved people and timid compared with the Koloshes; [and] there is [sea] otter hunting along the coast of California, as well as in [San] Francisc[o] Bay. On the largest rock of the Farallones [Southeast Farallon] there is a sea lion rookery and fur seal hunting. It seems that for all of these very advantageous reasons the company founded the settlement of <u>Ross</u>, and Mr. Baranov, the governor, sent his assistant, Kuskov, there. Before the governor at Monterey was replaced [in 1814], we enjoyed all of these advantages, and we caught [sea] otters at the port of [San] Francisco its[elf] and on the coast toward Monterey, neither the Spaniards nor the Indians engaging in such hunting. Upon the ascension [to office] of the present governor, Don Pablo Vicente de Solá, he enquired by what right the Russians had settled in California on land belonging to Spain. Although the Spaniards had never settled north of the port of [San] Francisco, the governor did not want to have such neighbors. [He] prohibited hunting by us along the coast of California and halted all contact with Kuskov. But Kuskov stayed at his post and the governor did not hound him any more.

Being now so close, I wanted to see Mr. Kuskov, as an old-timer, to obtain trustworthy information about his settlement and about California, and as I had been told that the Indians were favorably disposed toward us and were related to the Konyagas and Aleuts through intermarriage, [to learn whether] he had [heard through them] any rumors of Europeans residing to the north. But for him it was a difficult p[a]ss[a]ge to us by kayaks in the open sea—a four-day trip in winter— and neither the governor nor even Kuskov himself seemed to want this, and we did not meet. [I] satisfied my curiosity partly through correspondence with him:

---

[22]*Yunona.*

[23]Vasilyev is mistaken. Rezanov did not travel to Monterey, and he hoped to marry the daughter of the commandant of San Francisco, not the governor's.

[24]Vasilyev is again mistaken. Kuskov's first expedition to Alta California occurred in 1808–1809, and its purpose was not the founding of a settlement on Bodega Bay.

[25]Vasilyev is mistaken once more. Shipbuilding was not a factor in the founding of Ross, not being undertaken until later in its development; moreover, timber was lacking near Bodega Bay.

three times he sent kayaks to us with various green vegetables, for which I was extremely grateful to him.

The settlement of Ross lies at latitude 38° in a small cove on the very ocean; there are up to 20 Russian promyshlenniks, who are engaged in shipbuilding. So far they have built the two-masted ships *Ilmena, Chirikov, Rumyantsev,* and *Buldakov* and are building one more [the brig *Volga*].[26] The shipwright [is] one of the promyshlenniks [Vasily Grudinin], who learned shipbuilding from an American [named Lincoln] serving the compan[y] at Sitka after leaving an American ship out of dissatisfaction. After five years he [i.e., Lincoln] went to Canton, and his apprentice continued his shipbuilding experimentally. I know not whether they have been built properly—only that they sail, one in the spring to Okhotsk and the other to the Aleutian chain and the Fur Seal [Pribilof] Islands, as well as to Kodiak and California year-round. For several years already [they] have been so fortunate that not a single vessel has been wrecked. Then just last year, 1820, in the month of June the ship *Ilmena* [*Ilmen*] under the command of the navigator [Charles Stevens], with the manager of Sitka Counter, Kirilo[27] Timofeyevich Khlebnikov, on board, bound for grain at Monterey, was wrecked on 19 June on Point Arena, running aground under topsail with a favorable wind. All of the cargo and men were saved, and then the ship was dismantled.[28] This ship, the *Ilmena,* ought to have stopped earlier at Bodega to take from Kuskov the newly built two-masted ship *Buldakov* and go together to Monterey for wheat. Owing to the accident, they went to Monterey for wheat in one ship, the *Buldakov.* After having exchanged their goods for up to seven thousand puds of wheat—paying the governor 25 percent, they say—they set out to sea on 22 September from Bodega, but their [   ] was damaged by strong winds, and they went down to Santa Bárbara. After having made repairs, they reached Sitka on 24 November.

From hearsay and correspondence with Mr. Kuskov I learned that at the settlement of Ross the Russians are engaged in shipbuilding. One of the promyshlenniks, with three or four Konyagas, lives on the largest rock of the Farallones to hunt sea lions and fur seals. Hunting is the duty of the other Konyagas and Aleuts living at Ross; but as Monterey's present governor has forbidden them to hunt [sea] otters at the port of [San] Francisco and on the coast of California (and there are none at Bodega), these men remain, as it were, on ho[l]iday, although they hunt sea lions, dress rawhides,[29] and sew rain capes [*kamleikas*][30] from gut. The[y] catch a variety

---

[26]Vasilyev is partially mistaken; the *Rumyantsev* and the *Buldakov* were built at Ross but the *Ilmena* was bought from an American shipmaster and the *Chirikov* was built at Sitka.

[27]"Kirilo" is a diminutive form of "Kirill."

[28]For more details on this incident, see [Khlebnikov], *Khlebnikov Archive,* 41–52.

[29]Russ., *lavtaki.*

[30]A *kamleika* (the diminutive form of *kamleya*), derived from the Chukchi word *kemilyun,* is a waterproof cape made from the intestines of sea mammals and used as outerwear when hunting at sea and as everyday attire in the summer.

of fish, and sometimes they help to fetch timber for construction; but this is not considered their real work, and they are given none of the grain and meat that the Russian promyshlenniks enjoy. The Konyagas and Aleuts are paid for their hunting, but as there is no hunting, the company gives them nothing. Some of them have gardens, and some are hired by Russians and subsist somehow.

Here I want to note something: in my opinion, Mr. Rezanov's best service to the company was his occupation of the site of the settlement of Ross.[31] Perhaps it was establish[ed] for hunting, which was then the company's primary source of profit. But when the company took upon itself the right to resettle Konyagas and Aleuts arbitrarily to places that were profitable to it, then it would have been better, it seems, if it had put itself in the position of these poor native inhabitants, who, it can be said, afford the company its sole income or purpose. Before their management by the company, three times as many Konyagas and Al[e]uts went hunting. By resettling them and by taking everything that they have, it [i.e., the company] has eradicated 2 thirds of these people; hunting is decreasing annually, and if such management continues several years more, it will have to stop completely. The [Russian-]American company has no humanity. Its sole idol is the hunting of [sea] otters, foxes, fur seals, and [s]uch, regardless of what this entails and what will result. Of course, a pri[v]ate individual sees to his own advantage and exploits that which has been granted to him. The term of the [first charter of the] company was fixed at 20 years; it behaved such as to not regain it. But now that the government has let [the company] have all of the American settlements in perpetuity, it is necessary to compel it [i.e., the company] to take some humanitarian measures for its own good.

Every animal killed by the Aleuts and Konyagas belongs to the company. The company pays 10 rubles for a [sea] otter [pelt] and sells it at St. Petersburg for about 400 rubles. These were the prices in 1819; he [i.e., the seller] receives ten rubles from the company's store in goods, which are surcharged at 50 percent, and in addition the seller keeps his account at the store, which is run by the company. This price was fixed for the first time [in] 1820; before then an otter

---

[31]Vasilyev contradicts himself here, having said earlier that the settlement was founded by Kuskov. Rezanov had the idea of establishing a Russian settlement, but it was not realized until five years after his death. In a set of secret orders to Governor Baranov dated July 20, 1807, on the eve of his departure for Okhotsk, Rezanov proposed six possible sources of provisions for Russian America: trade with Alta California ("a trustworthy and inexhaustible source"), trade with Japan (especially for millet [rice?], "in which Japan abounds"), trade with the Philippines, trade with the "Bostonians" (American shipmasters, whose grain "always costs one-half of that from Okhotsk"), trade with China at Canton, and—"the most promising"—agricultural colonization in New Albion (Library of Congress, Manuscript Division, Yudin Collection, Box I, Item 12, "A copy of secret instructions by Nikolai Rezanov for Alexander Baranov" [digital id: mtfms yoo10035], pp. 21–22). Baranov, for his part, after founding Archangel Michael, the precursor of New Archangel, in 1799 resolved to advance southward and occupy the Queen Charlotte Islands and Nootka Sound (Library of Congress, Manuscript Division, Yudin Collection, "Draft of report to Alexander I, [1800] (Reports to Alexander I by the Board of Directors of the Russian-American Company)" [digital id: mtfms yoo10044], p. [4]).

was fixed at 5 rubles, and other furs in proportio[n]. They also try to incur debts, advancing tobacco, *kamleika*s, and other garments. Half of [every] whale belongs to the company, too. They also catch sea lions and fish for the provisionment of everybody. A really Christian payment[32] is exacted for everything, so that the poor Aleuts and Konyagas can get nothing for themselves and are hungry. They told me that they never lived better than before, that this was their usual way of life, and that now they are even compelled to stock food for themselves for the winter (fish, sea lions, whales, and so on). I believe that the company, employing ever[y] means, forces them to supply themselves with food; but the Aleuts and Konyagas understand the company well and understand that they are its slaves, and they lead their lives regardless. Before, enjoying freedom, he [i.e., the Aleut or Konyaga] was altogether different. If they sometimes suffered from hunger, they endured it with indifference. Going along the seacoast, [they] gathered sea kale and mussels [and] used [them] as food. But then, when they killed a whale and shared it, having considerable whale blubber, they considered themselves the happiest of anyone in the world. Merrymaking, games, and dances were everything to them, and they were content with their lot. Now oppression has killed their spirit, and whole settlement[s] have been eradicated by hunger and disease.

I think that the Konyagas and Aleuts who have been taken to the settlement of Ross live better than elsewhere; because of the good climate they are afforded vegetable gardens and live more tolerably. It seems to me that if the company were to engage them in grain growing, they would supply themselves with better food and make a profit. There is something strange about the company's dominion over the Aleuts and Konyagas and their independence. It is as if in hunting it [i.e., the company] has the right to direct them as it wishes but not in anything else.[33]

Hunting along the American coast proved profitable, [and in] 1805 [*sic:* 1804] they [i.e., the Russians] [re]occupied Sitka; but on account of their weakness, the Koloshes, as they had done [   ][34] years earlier, captured the fort. They say that most of the men had gone hunting, leaving only seven Russians. [They] could not hold the fort, several were killed, and the others were taken captive, and later an American ship either ransomed them or exchanged them for a captive Kolosh elder and took them to Kodiak. Now the fort is on a rocky point. They said that this site was bought for a frock coat from a Kolosh chief [Katlean], who apparently lived there.

Almost every annual hunt costs several Konyagas and Aleuts their lives from Kolosh attacks. These [native] Americans are steadfast and courageous. Having

---

[32]Presumably "Christian payment" is sarcasm on Vasilyev's part.

[33]This "strangeness" stemmed, of course, from the fact that the hunting and trading of sea otters was the company's primary concern and the Aleuts and Konyagas were peerless (and hence priceless) hunters of them.

[34]The blank should read "two," i.e., in 1802.

firearms, they defend themselves against interlopers, and the [sea] otters that the company gets are steeped in the blood of the innocent Konyagas and Aleuts. In [   ][35] two hundred umiaks[36] were lost, and the Aleuts were accused of becoming overheated in a fight with the Koloshes; this occurred in Cross Sound.[37] In 1818 a French ship [   ][38] arrived to buy furs, and its master [Captain Camille de Roquefeuil] struck a deal with Mr. Hagemeister to obtain twenty Konyagas and Aleuts from him for hunting on halves; as security he left up to 200 piasters' [worth] of goods for each man. But he did not take any real precautions against the Koloshes, lost the Konyagas, furs, his men, and his deposit, and departed at a loss.

An American [shipmaster] also took several Konyagas from Kuskov to hunt [sea] otters on halves along the coast of [Alta] California. The governor [of Alta California] ordered that they be apprehended on the frontier. Some managed to escape, but the others were caught.[39] On several occasions they have been drowned while crossing in large umiaks[40] from Kodiak to Chuvash Sound, and going to the Fur Seal [Pribilof] Islands, and they have perished while pursuing sea lions. The native inhabitants are decreasing annually, and venereal disease—brought by the Russians—also plays a part in the toll. The company does not tend at all to the welfare of the inhabitants or to their health. The sick are left without any care, and in 20 years not one physician has visited the islands; they are all Christians, but in the same period no priest has visited them. On Kodiak there is one dissolute *hiermonk*,[41] and the other, a pious monk [Father German],[42] leads a life in seclusion. There has been a white [i.e., married] priest at the church in Sitka since [   ].

During our stay at the port of [San] Francisco the commandant, the other officers, and the priests told us that in December [*sic:* November] of 1819 the frigate *Argentina* of 32 guns and the corvette *Santa Rosa* of 20 guns arrived at Monterey. They were insurgents from Buenos Aires. The captain of the frigate, a Frenchman, called himself Hipólito Bouchard; on the corvette was the American

---

[35]This blank should probably read "1802."

[36]Here Vasilyev is confusing umiaks with kayaks, which both the Aleuts and the Konyagas used for hunting.

[37]Vasilyev is likely referring to the killing of 165 Konyaga hunters (in 83 two-man kayaks) in Ivan Urbanov's "Sitka party" in mid-June 1802 near Frederick Sound by Tlingit warriors.

[38]This blank should read "*Le Bordelais*."

[39]Vasilyev is mistaken here, too. He is referring to the company brig *Ilmena*, which was commanded by an American, William Wadsworth, but which was hunting not on halves but solely for the company.

[40]Here again Vasilyev is confusing umiaks with kayaks.

[41]A monk who has been ordained as a priest, as opposed to a lay brother.

[42]German (Yegor Ivanovich Popov) (1751–1836), a peasant's son from Voronezh Province, was one of the eight monks of the first Russian Orthodox spiritual mission to Russian America sent in 1794 by Empress Catherine II to proselytize the natives. He labored on Kodiak and nearby Spruce Island, where he founded the settlement (with a school and orphanage) of New Valaam and acquired a reputation for sanctity, charity, and humility. His good works (especially his championing of the natives against exploitation by the Russian-American Company) earned him canonization in 1970 as German of Alaska, the first saint of the Orthodox Church of America. See Grinëv, *Kto yest kto*, 124; and Pierce, *Russian America*, 164–66.

[   ].[43] Earlier they had cruised at Manila and then in the Sandwich Islands, where they had seized several Sandwich Islanders as sailors. They arrived at Monterey at night, and the corvette stood under the presidio and in the morning opened fire on it. The corvette was damaged by gunfire from the presidio; the frigate, not lying under the guns of the presidio, landed up to 500 armed men, they said. At that time there were only 30 armed Spaniards at Monterey, the rest being on assignment. The governor sent for help to the other presidios at San Francisco, Santa Bárbara, and San Diego, and he himself retreated six leagues. The insurgents captured the battery, spiked the cannons, and looted and burned the presidio. The Spaniards mustered up to 200 men [but] were unable to attack, saying that the weather was very foul (constant rain). Bouchard, after having repaired the corvette, set out to sea on the fifth day. Four of his men deserted. Then he went to Santa Bárbara but did not land any men. At one place on the coast three of his officers were captured, but at his request they were returned on the condition that he not ravage the place; yet afterwards he did so [anyway]. Going out to sea, he seized a Spanish schooner. After putting several Sandwich Islanders and his rebels on it, he ordered that it keep behind the frigate. The same day there was a mutiny aboard the frigate, and the revolutionary flag was lowered. The insurgents moved from the schooner to the frigate, leaving 5 Sandwich Islanders on the schooner. The wind became strong, and they could not keep pace with the frigate and were left behind. Not knowing where to [go] where they were, they wanted to sail to the Sandwich Islands but did not find them. One of these islanders had been at Sitka, and they decided to seek it; fortunately, they arrived safely in the month of [   ][44] and gave the schooner to the company's governor, Lieutenant Yanovsky. The schooner was repaired, coppered, armed, and returned, and [   ] rubles had to be paid for its repairs, but only if its owner were found. Three Sandwich Islanders were set free, and two were kept as witnesses, and the schooner was given the name *Fortuna* [*Fortune*].[45]

In 1819 and during our stay the Indians spread rumors that some sort of people with families, numbering up to 1,000 souls and heavily dressed and armed, had reached and settled within a four-day march of Mission San José and had built a fort.[46] They say that three years ago several indentured Spanish families arrived from Mexico, and perhaps [it was] they, for they do not know what happened to them. In May the commandant of the port of [San] Francisco with 40 cavalrymen tried to verify this.

We did not find proper dis[c]ipline in the command at the presidio of the port

---

[43]Vasilyev is again mistaken here. The captain of the *Santa Rosa* was an Englishman, Peter Corney.

[44]This blank should read "June."

[45]For a fuller account of this entire episode, see Uhrowczik, *Burning of Monterey*.

[46]This rumor likely refers to Fort Ross.

of [San] Francisco; it is true that many are exiles and all of them are dissatisfied with the government. The soldiers come to the commandant in their hats and without any respect talk to him about what they need. Their violent character [manifests itself] when [they] drink until drunk the foul liquor that they have obtained and that each of them has the right to sell. Often their arguments lead to knifings. Many are drunk on their major holidays. Throughout New California there is only on[e] doctor, at Monterey, and he is not competent. There are many sick everywhere; it seems that venereal disease holds sway over all others, plus bloody flux [diarrhea], common fever, light fever,[47] and various external ailmen[ts] [i.e., fractures, dislocations, and rashes]. All of them doctor themselves somehow, appealing for help to Saints Cosmas[48] and Damien,[49] as well as [La Virgen] María [de] Guadalupe, the patron saint of all of Spanish America. And the friars exert themselves in order that the sick man dies after he has fulfilled his Christian duty [i.e., confessed]. They say that before the very end all of his friends, in order to be certain of reading his burial service in time, seize prayer books and read, one louder than the other, about his absolution in the next world. Then the deceased is taken the same day to the mission and buried. It seems that, as [f]ar as we could tell, the church ceremony is their holiest.

The anchorage at the port of [San] Francisco is opposite the presidio. They say that to anchor elsewhere is forbidden, but we were not told of this prohibition. Moreover, I think that they anchor there so that fresh meat, water, and firewood can be received [at that point]. But it seems to me that it would be calmer to anchor past the presidio and beyond the point toward the mission in a depth of 7 and 8 sazhens with a soft, sandy bottom and without ocean swells. [There] it is also possible to receive meat, bread, or wheat from the mis[s]ions, and there is water and timber for firewood along the shore. But I think that it would be even better for a voyager to an[c]hor where the English ship *Raccoon* was careened between the mainland shore and Angel Island on its northern side. There is considerable timber on the island, and opposite there is a freshwater stream, [although] sweet water has to be fetched from somewhat farther away. The port of [San] Franci[sco] can supply only bulls, rams, and cocks, and the missions, whea[t]. They have very few greens. On the other hand, on a fine spot not far from the ship it is possible to erect an observatory and workshops and peacefully attend to one's business. Being anchored near the presidio, our ship was visited constantly by the Spaniards, who distracted [us] from our business, and the soldiers and the boys pilfered and the ladies sought banquets, and everyone solicited presents, so that it became burdensome.

---

[47]Russ., *likhoradka*.

[48]Russ., *Kuzma*.

[49]Saints Cosmas and Damien, fourth-century Christian martyrs and physicians who took no fees, are the patron saints of physicians and apothecaries, respectively, and they were remembered daily in the Mass.

They get water near the presidio beyond a marsh that extends from the shore. At the foot of the mountains they dig holes that collect water from the mountains. The water is good, but it tastes swampy and is dis[c]olor[ed]. I used it boiled. Sometimes the boiled water is as condensed as lamp oil [i.e., inferior olive oil]. There is enough timber for firewood everywhere, but our ignorant sailors sometimes cut shrubbery.

There is a plant called *yedro*[50] [*Rhus diversiloba*, poison oak]; the stalk is reddish and long, and inside there is a liquid resembling milk. To touch or hold it is enough [to produce blisters, and] it causes tumors on one's face and makes one's genitals swell, with extreme itchiness. They [i.e., the Californios] doctor themselves, and after several days [the effects] pass or leave scars.[51]

It is inconvenient to put in to the shore, [for] there are always swells; during rains the road to the presidio is very muddy, and it is necessary to go around the mountain, a distanc[e] of half a mile. **/On the shore by the landing there are many mice./**[52]

Sometimes for our amusement we went horseback riding, renting horses from the soldiers for a taler per ride. Often we rode to the mission, about a league from the presidio.

During our three-month stay at the port of [San] Francisco we were engaged in describing [i.e., charting] the extensive bay, although not all of it with absolute accuracy, but heretofore nobody had described it as much as we did. We verified the chronometers, and we determined the latitude and longitude of the presidio according to the distance of the moon from the su[n], the variation of the compass, the magnetic inclination of the needle (we found an additional hour), the incoming and outgoing tides, and the current. We rearmed the sloops, reexamined the dry provisions, and redried the rusks in the barrels. **/The peas in the barrels proved to be moldy, but none—as well as none of the rusks—had spoil[ed]./**[53]

Here we bought a bull [for] four piasters, a ram [for] two piasters, two hens for a piaster, and 48 eggs or onions for a piaster. When it was possible to find wheat, [we paid] 2½ piasters for one fanega or six arrobas, each arroba comprising 28 of our funts. Flour was 2 piasters per arroba and baked bread 3 piasters per arroba. A large hide for uppers was 4 piasters, and the washing of linen [was] very expensive. But it would still have been possible to buy these things much more cheaply, for they are greatly in need of clothes, linen, shoes, glassware, and all housewares, and they can do nothing with piasters, and for that reason they are very cheap. In their best homes there are no water glasses, wine glasses, plates, knives, or forks. If

---

[50]In Spanish, *yedra* or *hiedra*.

[51]The northern Californian Indians, thanks to regular ingestion of the buds of poison oak, enjoyed a high degree of resistance to the effects (itchy rash, oozing sores, even death) of its toxins. The plant is not a true oak but a member of the cashew family (Anacardiaceae).

[52]In the manuscript this sentence is written in the margin.

[53]In the manuscript this sentence is written in the margin.

these [items] are present, then they are either very ordinary or inferior. After having seen such poverty, it was impossible for us not to give them [the Californios] gifts, although we had little surplus and nothing to sell. The presents cost me dearly.

There is another plant in the fields of the port of [San] Francisco that they use for cuts. After having cut their hand, they sprinkle this herb in the wound, which stings and then begins to heal; [the plant] is fragrant.[54] Our naturalist travelled into the interior of California as far as Monterey and collected much of interest in his field, and he sketched animals.

The Indians of the missions, where they are kept as slaves and have only a shawl, are to be pitied. However, they are fed corn and are sometimes given wheat, peas, beans, and meat. Worst of all, half of them are infected with vene-real disease, and this disease has even been taken to the savages in the mountains, so that already they are being born with the infection. And at Missions San José and [Santa] Clara they are annually dying by the hundreds from bondage, their new way of life, and disease. The friars do not improve their lo[t] at all, as though it were their [i.e., Indians'] Christian duty to die.

They told us that when a Spanish ship arrives, it stands beyond the point with the battery and moors close to shore. I saw this spot; swells also come there, but they say that they [i.e., the swells] are not strong. There has been no ship from [New] Spain for ten years; the last to arrive was the frigate *Princesa* [*Princess*].

Fish, crayfish, shrimp, [sea] otters, and seals are caught in the bay. Sea lions lie on the rocks near the [bay's] entrance at the S point.

In January of this year there was an earthquake at Santa Bárbara, and the church collapsed.

During our stay at the port of [San] Francisco a company ship, the brig *Golov[n]in* under the command of Benseman, arrived on Sunday, January 23, from Sitka for wheat after having given part of the cargo received from the *Boro-dino*[55] to Mr. Kuskov at Bodega.

From Bodega Bay two bays go to the N and S; the former is called Great Bodega [Bodega Harbor] and the latter Little Bodega [Tomales Bay].[56] Great Bodega can only be entered at the new moon and the full moon, when there are

---

[54]This plant was probably milfoil, or yarrow (*Achillea millefolium*), whose aromatic leaves were used by the Miwoks (and other tribes) to poultice cuts and wounds. See Mead, *Ethnobotany*, 7–8; and Strike, *Aboriginal Uses*, 3.

[55]The 600-ton Russian-American Company supply ship *Borodino* under Lieutenant Zakhar Panafidin (or Ponafidin) had reached New Archangel in October via the Cape of Good Hope after a long voyage plagued by constant leakage, frequent calms, contrary winds, and much sickness (at least six crewmen, including the physician, had died). The return voyage via Cape Horn was likewise marked by calms, storms, adverse winds, and sickness, with about half of the crew on the sick list and many deaths by the time Rio de Janeiro was reached. See Ivashintsov, *Russian Round-the-World Voyages*, 56–60.

[56]Here Vasilyev confuses the two Bodega bays; what he says about Great Bodega refers to Little Bodega, and vice versa.

up to 11 feet [of depth] at the entrance at high tide and 4 feet at low tide, and it is fairly deep—3 and 4 sazhens—in the bay itself, where the compan[y] has built a warehouse for the storage of goods. Ships do not enter Little Bodega; the bay is ordinary[57] and exposed. In [Great] Bodega there is an island with a stony reef, beyond which ships stand at anchor. [The bay] is open to the S and SW, and the strong winds cause much choppiness.

During our stay we received permission from the governor to buy wheat or to trade goods for it; the price of a fanega of wheat with duty was set at 23 reals— twenty, or 2½ piasters, for the wheat and 3 reals for the duty. We bought a fanega of wheat for 2½ piasters. The company imposed [a surcharge of] 350 to 450 percent on its goods, which is what it cost it [i.e., the company] to import them to Sitka, or just the same as what it cost in pape[r] rubles to sell for Spanish piasters. Blue cloth costing 25 ru[bles] at Sitka here fetched 25 talers and ordinary tobacco 1 pias[ter], 2 reals, which was worth 1 [ruble], 30 k[opecks], and other things in like proportion. However, the supercargo, Mr. Benseman, was allowed to raise or lower the price of any good, regardless of need, in order that a ruble equalled a piaster in round figures. Such absurd pricing astonish[ed] everyone; it was possible to buy much more cheaply at Monterey than here on the spot. During our stay the missions' friars, who have wheat, did not see our goods and did not bargain, even after three weeks had passed.

Benseman obtained one two-hatched kayak with two Konyagas from Kuskov. In their spare time they hunted [sea] otters at night in the bay, and during our stay they bagged eight large ones, having requested the governor's permission to shoot ducks.

It must be said that there are many wildfowl on the land and in the water, and the best tasting of all are *codornices* [California quail (*Lophortyx californica*)] and others that they call grouse or partridge;[58] there are many wild geese, ducks of various species, sandpipers, and other birds. Throughout our anchorage we enjoyed wildfowl daily, and we bagged or stuffed them for the naturalist. There were also many deer and numerous coyotes, and bears came close [to us].

It is necessary to go from the sea into the port of [San] Francisco from the N or the S; off it are found the rocks of the Farallones. . . .[59] Leaving the port of [San] Francisco, we left the large Farallon rock to the N, passed close to it, and sketched it.

---

[57]Russ., *pryamoy.*

[58]Vasilyev is probably referring here to the masked bobwhite (*Colinus ridgwayi*) of the American Southwest, as the meat of the blue grouse (*Dendragapus obscurus*) of the Sierra Nevada has an unpleasant taste.

[59]A description of the best route to the port of San Francisco for ships is omitted here.

[Mikhail Vasilyev?], "About the Environment, Population, Economy, and Political Situation of [Alta] California," ca. 1821

Editor's Introduction

An unpublished transcription of this document by Leonid Shur (and now in his possession) entitles it "Notes in the Form of Questions and Answers about the Environment, Population, Economy, and Political Situation of California" and ascribes its authorship to Ivan Kuskov, referring to his correspondence with Vasilyev. However, there is nothing in the correspondence to indicate this authorship; moreover, the document's sources are obviously heterogeneous and include information obtained in all likelihood from the Spaniards. Finally, the mention in the document of "our hon. naturalist" unconditionally identifies the author as a member of the Vasilyev-Shishmaryov expedition. A comparison of the document's facts and style with Vasilyev's account of his sojourn in California strongly suggests that he is the author. The question-and-answer format may have been provided by the Ministry of the Navy or the Academy of Sciences or may simply have been Vasilyev's own device.

[Captain-Lieutenant Mikhail Vasilyev?], Answers to Questions about the Environment, Population, Economy, and Political Situation of [Alta] California,[1] [Sloop *Otkrytie* in San Francisco Bay?], no later than the beginning of February 1821[2]

[1]. Who occupied New [Alta] California and when, and by force of arms or without any opposition from the native inhabitants [?].

The Spaniards occupied New California on 12 July 1767, and at the same time the viceroy [of New Spain], the Marqués de Croix, separated Old [Baja] and New [Alta] California, and at this time the Spanish king expelled the priests of the Jesuit order and installed those of the Franciscan order; first they occupied the place now cal[led] Mission S[an] Diego in 1768.

[2]. Where are New California's fortified places, how many are there, and what forces do they have [?].

In New California there are 19 missions, and a 20th—S[an] Rafael—is considered only partly a mission.[3]

The missions [are as follows:]

1. S[an] Diego [de Alcalá], 2. S[an] Luis Rey, 3. S[an] Juan Capistrano, 4. S[an] Gabriel, 5. S[an] Fernando [Rey], 6. S[an] Buenaventura, 7. S[anta] Bárbara, 8. S[anta] Inés, 9. [La] Purísima Concepción, 10. S[an] Luis Obispo, 11. S[an] Miguel, 12. S[an] Antonio [de Padua], 13. La Soledad, 14. S[an] Carlos, 15. S[an] Juan Bautista, 16. S[anta] Cruz, 17. S[anta] Clara, 18. S[an] José, 19. S[an] Francisco [de Asís,] and [20.] S[an] Rafael.

[3]. Where are New California's boundaries, according to the Spanish government [?].

The boundaries of New California have not been determined.[4]

[4]. How many harbors or good roadsteads for anchorage for visiting ships are there, and which of the best of them are suitable for possible wintering [?].

The ports of New California are [as follows]:

---

[1]RGAVMF, f. 213, op. 1, d. 114, fols. 1–14v (original). The transcription deciphered by Shur has been checked against the original, resulting in numerous corrections.

[2]Dated in accordance with the time of the departure of Vasilyev's squadron from San Francisco (11 February 1821) and the mention of General Riego's rebellion and the restoration of the constitution of 1812 in Spain (January–March 1820), as well as the events of the previous year.

[3]Mission San Rafael was founded in 1817 as a so-called *asistencia,* or satellite, of Mission San Francisco de Asís to succour ailing neophytes from the less healthful mother mission and to block Russian expansion southward to San Francisco Bay.

[4]In fact, Alta California's northern boundary had been demarcated along the 42nd parallel of north latitude by the Adams-Onís, or Transcontinental, Treaty of 1819.

1. S[an] Francisco.
2. Monterey.
3. S[an] Luis Rey.
4. [San Luis] Obispo.
5. S[anta] Bárbara.
6. S[an] Diego.
7. S[an] Juan Capistrano.

S[an] Diego, which has a presidio two miles away, is considered the best port for the moorage of ships. After it Monterey is 2nd and S[an] Francisco is 3rd.

The fortresses [citadels] in New California are [as follows]:

1. S[an] Francisco, 2. Monterey, 3. S[an] Diego, and 4. Santa Bárbara, under construction.

[5]. What soldiery—infantry, cavalry, and artillery—is there in New California, and did it come expressly from Europe or Mexico or were the previous soldiers local natives [?].

The army consists of 400 (hundred [*sic*]) cavalrymen, infantrymen, and artillerymen with officers. Some of the soldiers' sons study and others farm. None of the Indians is a soldier, but they are used for various tasks.

[6]. What period of military service to the king is fixed for a soldier, and when it ends does he have the right to return to Spain [?].

It is fixed that a soldier serve the king for 10 years, but they [also] serve 20 and 30 years. They never return anywhere from New California.

[7]. What pay is fixed for a military servitor [?].

A soldier receives 19 (nineteen) and a half talers per month and nothing more.

[8]. Are children begot by a soldier here or [elsewhere?] in America free to choose their own kind of life [?].

All of the children of soldiers are free to choose their own kind of life.

[9]. Besides soldiers and Indians, what settlers are there in [New] California (Spaniards or other nationalities), and what are they taxed [?].

The Spanish inhabitants and the soldiers call themselves people (people of reason [*gente de razon*]), or Spaniards who speak Spanish. The other people at all of the missions are Indians. There are no other nationalities, except a few Englishmen who are staying by chance.

New California is further divided into 3 towns.[5] The first town is called San

---

[5]Instead of *gorod* ("town") the Russian text has *narod* ("people"), a translation of *pueblo*, which can mean either "people" or—as it should here—"town."

José, the second <u>Nuestra Señora de Los Angeles</u>, and the third <u>Villa de Branciforte</u>. The first is at [Mission] S[anta] Clara, the second at [Mission] S[an] Gabriel, and the third at [Mission] <u>S[anta] Cruz</u>.

[10]. Who is now the viceroy of Mexico [New Spain] and how long has he served, and who is the governor of New California [?].

The viceroy in Mexico is now Señor Don José Ruiz de Apodaca. His title is Conde de Venadito.

[11]. What does New California produce through cultivation [?].

New California produces field, garden, and orchard crops. They plant wheat, barley, and beans in winter in the m[on]ths of November, December, January, and February and corn, <u>garbanzos</u> ([chick]peas), and frijoles in the m[on]ths of April and May; they harvest at the end of July and in August. New California also produces heavy, coarse cloth, and in some places—namely, at S[an] Gabriel—sackcloth is woven, and at S[an] Luis Obispo leather, blankets, and other articles, house soap, cheese, and such are made.

[12]. What trees grow [?].

Redwood, willow,[6] oak, various kinds of willow, pine, spruce, laurel, poplar, "populus,"[7] and nut trees similar to walnut grow, as well as tea, a fruit-bearing tree thus named by the Indians, with fruit like that of the chestnut but rounder, the Indians using it as food, boiling it many times and making a watery blancmange[8] of a milky color. The <u>grape</u> grows wild in the south, and the wild rose abounds.

The poison oak[9] is a low bush, and at this time [i.e., winter] it has no leaves; those who hold it in their hands, or fall asleep under it, or—even more ignorantly—burn it, soon become swollen and their face, extremities, and genitals become enlarged to a degree that I have never actually seen among my countrymen. The naturalist calls this bush *Rhus Tocsicadendron* [*Toxicodendron diversiloba*].

Fruit trees, such as apple, pear, peach (which the Spaniards [Californios] call *durazno, Persicum duratinum,* which they say is quite another species of this plant), cherry, fig, olive, grape, capulín [*Prunus capuli*] (which the Spaniards call a species of cherry), plum, and tomatoes grow in the orchards, and there is a red fruit [persimmon?] with a sweet-and-sour taste that I did not see; there are watermelons, muskmelons, pumpkins, potatoes, onions, garlic, cabbage, peppers, lettuce, celery, parsley, and other garden plants. The governor[10] also grows aloe,

---

[6]Exactly which species of *Salix* Vasilyev had in mind is unknown; it was distinct enough not to be included under "various kinds of willow."

[7]*Populus* is a genus of trees that includes poplar, as well as aspen and cottonwood, either (more likely the latter) probably being what Vasilyev had in mind.

[8]Russ., *kisel.*

[9]The manuscript has *yedra*, a transliteration of the Spanish *hiedra* [i.e., *hiedra venenosa*].

[10]The manuscript has *regist*, presumably derived from the Spanish *regir*, "to govern."

rose, marsh mallow, mint, anise, elderberry, and mango.[11] They did not have any
other plants because it was late winter, and if there were stalks it was very difficult, even impossible, to identify them.

[13]. What animals are there [?].

Mule deer [*Odocoileus hemionus*] abound, and there is another kind of deer,
black-tailed deer[12] [*Odocoileus hemionus columbiana*], wild goats, wild sheep,
bears, leopards [jaguars?], tigers [cougars?], wolves (coyotes), wolverines, foxes,
rabbits, various species of rats, mice, moles, forest cats [bobcats?], and hedgehogs
[porcupines]. Of marine animals there are sea otters, river otters, seals, and sea
lions. There are snakes, too; I saw one *coluber*.[13]

[14]. What minerals occur, or are there no signs of any [?].

According to the Spaniards, such minerals as gold, silver, iron, lead, and others
occur. Twice the Spaniards have tried to mine traces in the mountains between
San Juan Bautista and Soledad, and they found excellent silver but little of it.

[15]. What kinds of birds are there [?].

There are geese, swans, various ducks, also various sandpipers, grouse, [Cali-
fornia] quail, cranes, thrushes (*chanates* [blackbirds] or *tordo*), larks, pelicans,
seagulls, loons, eagles, hawks, kites [or condors or turkey vultures?], crows, magpies, species of sparrows, owls, and herons, as well as oth[er] songbirds that are
seldom seen in winter.

[16]. Are there rivers or lakes, and what kind of fish abound [?].

There are no large rivers in New California,[14] but there are shallow <u>streams</u>, as
they call them. One at the site of Rancho [del] Rey[15] is cal[led] the Monterey;
[it] abounds in fish, mostly red fish—salmon and *testudo* [rainbow trout?]. In
it, too, are found herring [or sardines], which they cal[l] *truchas* [trout], eels of
a special kind [lampreys?], and *barbus* [catfish?], whose Russian name I do not
know. All of these fish are tasty. There are round crabs [crayfish?]—similar to
marine ones—that they call *cangrejo* [crab], and shrimp.

<u>Another</u> river is cal[lled] the Pájaro (which means "bird" in Spanish)[; it is
located] one league [from] San Juan Bautista, and it is also fishy, like the above.

A <u>third</u> river, the Coyote, is found at Santa Clara, and it, too, is fishy.

The <u>fourth</u> [river,] at S[an] José, is cal[lled] the Alameda; there are fish in it.

The <u>fifth,</u> at S[an] Buenaventura, is named after that place; its water is very
hard and salty.

[11]The manuscript has *kanapel*, presumably a corruption of the Spanish *canabal*, a Mexicanism for "mango."
[12]The manuscript has the Spanish *venado*.
[13]Sp., *culebra*, "snake."
[14]The Sacramento and San Joaquín Rivers were evidently unknown to Vasilyev.
[15]The grazing land attached to Monterey's presidio.

The <u>sixth</u> large river is ca[lled] the <u>Santa Ana</u>, [and it] flows between two missions, S[an] Gabriel and S[an] Juan Capistrano, and [thence] into the sea; its water is sweet and very fishy.

The <u>seventh</u>, whose source is unknown, is grand; it runs near S[anta] Cruz [?] and is ca[lled] the S[an] Lorenzo [Sacramento]. Its water is very sweet, and it teems with fish of all kinds; it enters the ocean near S[an] Rafael and forms a kind of lake [San Pablo Bay]. The savages catch fish in this river.

There are lakes in New California during the rainy season from December until the m[ont]h of May, and then they dry up and are called lagoons because of their small size; there are really none larger.

[17]. What is the climate during the four seaso[ns] of the year, th[at] i[s], spring, summer, autumn, and winter [?].

All of the seasons of the year are different; the cold begins in November, December, and January, but in the m[on]th of February the warm [weather], i.e., spring, commences. It is summer in May, June, July, and August, and in this season there are fogs, little rain but more humidity, and strong winds; this season is also very lean[16] compared with the other m[on]ths.

[18]. Who owns what the missions have, does the government—as well as the commandants of the presidios—have the right to demand what they need, and do they pay for it or not [?].

The missions belong to the crown, and—as the priests say—they are not assessed any taxes; the property of the Spanish settlers belongs to them as owners, and the church property belongs to the bishop, named <u>Bernado de Espíritu Santo</u>, who lives in the province of Sonora and is the bishop of Sonora and both Californias. Now the [New] California governor collects money from the missions (100 talers from each of S[an] José and Santa Clara and 50 talers from S[an] Francisco, as I heard) for repairs to the cannon and battery at Monterey in the hope that Spain will pay the debts to the missions; such contributions from the missions have not been made before.

The <u>league</u> (*liga* [*sic: legua*] in Spanish) contains 7,500 geometrical paces [i.e., 37,500 feet, or about 7 miles].

[19]. What can be said about the Indians, their manners, customs, trades, handicrafts, way of life, ceremonies, worship, weapons, and origins, and how many generations are there [?].

The Indians differ greatly, even at the same mission, being of various stocks or so-called peoples, and they have various languages, so that one [tribe] does

---

[16]Russ., *khudoy.*

not understand what the other speaks. The Spaniards call the habitations or the tribes of the savage Indians rancherías; at the present time many thousands of Indians have been baptized into the Christian faith, and they live and work at the missions under the principal supervision of the priests.

The Indians have many rancherías, which (as well as districts or habitations) have their own names. These Indians commonly or generally call them[selves] kauntos;[17] they live within the missions. Others, called Huchunes,[18] live 9 miles from Mission S[an] Francisco. To the south, on the other side of the bay opposite a mission on the same mountain [Diablo Range] (where redwood grows, so it is called Los Palos Colorados), the Indians customarily call them[selves] huchunes agvastos;[19] 15 miles from the mission there are others by the name of Saklanes,[20] and on the same mountain to the north are others [who call themselves] Talkvines.[21] Farther to the south they call themselves bolbones,[22] and others farther to the north on this mountain who speak differently call them[selves] tazkanes.[23] In the vicinity of the S[an] Juan Capistrano River and beyond it they call them[selves] chuskanes.[24] I cannot remember all of the places where the savages are located, but according to hearsay their names are said to be the following:

Rargvines-Svizuntes.[25]
Malakas-Subkanes.[26]
Gvalaktas-.[27]

Closer to the presidio and on the other side of the bay are the guimenes[28] and gvalanes,[29] and on the mountain [Marin Peninsula] opposite the presidio they call them[selves] Tamales,[30] and on the other side of this mountain they call them[selves] omiomi.[31] Most of the neophytes at this mission are from the agvostos.

[20]. From what materials do the Indians make their bows and arrows, and are their various wares decorated [?].

---

[17]Unidentified.
[18]Unidentified.
[19]Kroeber's "Huchiu-n" (Kroeber, *Handbook,* 465).
[20]Kroeber's "Sakla-n" (Kroeber, *Handbook,* 463, 466).
[21]Unidentified.
[22]According to Kroeber, a Costanoan village (Kroeber, *Handbook,* 895).
[23]Unidentified.
[24]Unidentified.
[25]Unidentified.
[26]Unidentified, although Kroeber lists a Wintun village named "Malaka" (Kroeber, *Handbook,* 356).
[27]Unidentified.
[28]Unidentified.
[29]Unidentified.
[30]Kroeber lists a Coast Miwok village named "Tomales" (Kroeber, *Handbook,* 897).
[31]Unidentified.

The wood from which the Indians make bows and arrows the Spaniards ca[ll] *jaral* [reed, i.e., tule], but the ends in which the arrowheads are set are of another wood they ca[ll] *mirten* [*sic: mirto,* "myrtle"]. Both grow as bushes, not tall trees. The arrowheads are made from flint-like and crystal-like stones. They fashion the arrows sometimes with a flint-like stone but more often with a glassy stone [obsidian?], and neither has any form whatever.

[21]. If possible, obtain the implements with which the Indians cut firewood, catch fish, and make fire for cooking their food.

The Indians do not cut firewood, but they burn wood and catch fish. They make fire by rubbing wood on wood very rapidly and by means of an arrow without an arrowhead, and with another wood, namely, elder (*Sambucus* [*mexicana*]) by means of a hand-held tinder. They catch fish with nets, which they weave from nettles, as well as with hooks of bone from quadrupeds. They do not have any vessels for cooking, and they place meat directly on the fire, with water among the stones, and afterwards put it in bowls plaited by the women.

The feathers that adorn the Indians are taken from crows, hawks, and many other birds; sometimes they catch the birds with snares but more often they kill them with arrows. They make necklaces in different forms from various shells, and they make clothing from fox and rabbit skins and the women from deerskin (*venado*). Female adults cover their private parts with plait[ed] small reeds or sedge, similar to mats, and loincloths but girls go quite naked; they also make girdles two hands in width from grass in which grasses and feathers are stuck. For holding seeds the women make baskets from roots and decorate them variously; they work skillfully.

[22.] Are there any precious stones in New and Old California [?].

They [i.e., the Spaniards] say that precious stones, with the exception of diamonds, do occur, but they do not know what kind and how much; there is a lot of black marble, and our naturalist [Fyodor Shtein] told them that [precious] stones are extant—and they believed him more than he believed himself.

[23]. What does the new constitution in Sp[a]in comprise, and is there any official information about it [?].

People assembled from throughout Spain for the enactment of a new constitution, called the *Cortes*,[32] which restored the country's laws. It was reinstated in the m[on]th of September 1820. It was begun in 1812 [at Cádiz] in the absence of the king, who was a prisoner in France, but it was not renewed, and in 1814, when the king [Ferdinand VII] returned to Spain, royal decrees prevailed, even until

---

[32]In fact, the Cortes was the legislature, not the constitution.

September of last year (1820), and in March of that year the king dispatched 21 thousand soldiers against insurgents, who, despite this, made a plot against him. They wanted to kill the king if he did not accept the constitution, and thereby the constitution was reinstated, and now there is a national government; 148 members, chosen by the people, govern and have designated a national constitution, for the laws are made by the people themselves.

The Supreme Council consists of 5 men from the *cortes*, of whom three are Castilians [metropolitans] and two are Americans [colonials]. *Cortes* [comes] from the word *cor,* "heart."[33]

The king has the right to test any matter in the Council three times, and if after three times he does not agree, then the *cor*[*tes*] or the popular Council itself decides, and the power of the king without the popular [Council] is weak.

[24]. Are gold, silver, and other items now sent from Spain, or do they send them from Europe?

Last year from Mexico they sent clothing for the soldiers in New California, as well as silver [dollars] for salary; some say forty thousand and others thirty thousand piasters, but the soldiers did not receive anything except clothing; only the governor knows about the silver. Many iron weapons, such as cutlasses, lances, some muskets, [cannon] balls, grapeshot, and bullets, as well as gunpowder, were also sent.

Spain received no metals from New California.

[25]. Do the Spaniards of Old and New California have any trade with foreign powers [?].

They remit tallow, wheat, beans, peas, and frijoles from New California to Spain for sale in [Spanish] America. At present they do not trade with any power except Russia, and Americans [of the United States] sometimes buy wheat for goods by necessity, they say.

[26]. What are the boundaries of Old and New California to the east [?].

They [i.e., the Californios] are unaware of Old or New California's boundaries but guess that [they go] as far as the Icy Sea [Arctic Ocean] in America [i.e., the New World].

[27]. How many inhabitants do they reckon there are in Old Mexico and Old and New California, as well as Spaniards from Europe [*peninsulares*], Spaniards born here [*coloniales*], and subject Indians [?].

The number of inhabitants of New and Old California, as well as Mexico, is

---

[33]In fact, *Cortes* is the plural of *cort,* meaning "court" in both Spanish and Portuguese. *Corazón* means "heart" in Spanish.

unknown here, but they put the total [population] of all of Spanish California at ten to twelve million.[34] About. . . .[35]

In New California near Mission S[an] Francisco on the land of S[an] Mateo they obtain salt from the ocean in June, July, and August.

[28]. From what is the term "insurgent" taken, and what is the origin of these people [?].[36]

The term "insurgent" comes from the [Latin] word *insurgo*—"I am rising up."

All of the insurgents here are sons of Spain. They began to secede from Spain in 1809 in South America at <u>Santa Fe de Quito</u> [Ecuador]; in North America at the town of Dolores (Costilla), Hidalgo [y] Costilla, a priest of the Catholic faith, was the first insurgent. Now, from fear or belief, there are even Indians among the insurgents.

[29]. How numerous are the insurgents now, what provinces are occupied by them, who are their leaders according to the latest information, and what is the condition of their land and naval forces [?].

The insurgents are very numerous, such that they [i.e., their numbers] cannot be estimated, and they have occupied the provinces of Valladolid [Morelia] near Mexico [City] and S[an] Blas, where a bishop is found, but he is not an insurgent, [although] others are. Valladolid does not contain many insurgents, but there are more in South America and in many other places. They do not have a leader now; they are split into various parties and are factious, and there is news that the insurgents are fighting among themselves, for they dispute their leadership.

The head of the insurgents is [José] Artigas in [the viceroyalty of] Buenos Aires and the Río de la Plata. This faction has more naval power and many ships.

[30]. Is it true that three years ago up to 1,000 insurgents, disavowing the king, left Mexico and have now entrenched themselves not far from the port of [San] Francisco [?].[37]

I have heard that many secessionists have left the province of <u>Texas</u> with their wives and children. Their number is unknown, and where they have settled is not known.

---

[34]This figure is a gross exaggeration, of course. A much more plausible population for both Californias at the time of Vasilyev's visit would be some 31,000, of whom about 6,000 would have been non-Indians (Gerhard, *North Frontier*, 295, 309).

[35]This word probably marks the beginning of a variant that should have been struck.

[36]It is interesting to note the amount of attention given by the questionnaire to the revolutionary movements in Spanish America. The autocratic and conservative regimes of Europe, including Alexander I's Russia, were nervous in the wake of the democratic ideals and revolutionary ardor unleashed by the French Revolution.

[37]Russia was presumably interested in this question insofar as any insurgency in Alta California might render that province less resistant to possible Russian expansion there.

[31]. What is related about the insurgents who arrived last year at Monterey in two ships [?].

> What kind of ships were they, i.e., how many cannon did they have [?].
> What were they [i.e., the ships] called, and who were the leaders [of the insurgents?].
> What was the object of their coming [?].
> What did they do [?].

From what places did these ships come and who commanded them [?]. Did they have any assignment and where did they sail [?]. From where did these ships obtain insurgents and how [?]. What destruction did they wreak and what harm did they do [?]. Is it true that one ship ran aground and was damaged, so that it filled with water and lay on its side and all of the people moved to the other large ship, where the leader of the expedition was found, [who] lowered the flag and was in captivity for 24 hours, and then the frigate apparently moved to the side [of the bay] where the battery could not harm it, landed armed men, seized the battery, burned the presidio, repaired another ship, and after 4 days went to sea with both ships [?].[38]

First, two ships arrived—the frigate [La] Argentina with Captain Hipólito Bouchard, a native of France, and another that the Spaniards called Negra,[39] whose captain the Spaniards do not know.

The insurgents arrived at Monterey under the guise of friendship, and first they asked about meat and other provisions via a longboat sent by them. But the hon. governor of New California, Pablo Vicente de Solá asked about their papers and who they were and why they had come; the [insurgents'] messengers replied that they did not have any papers, and the governor said that he did not have any provisions and that if they would not bring papers and had none, then they must sail away. The messengers returned and told their leader what they had heard; then they sent another, much larger longboat with more men to the hon. governor. This was sent by [the insurgents] with the reply that if they were not given provisions, then they would make war. Meanwhile, the small frigate, called Negra [Santa Rosa], approached the presidio little by little, and at night it came very close; when the presidio called "Who goes, and why?" the insurgents replied that they [i.e., the Californios] would see the next day, and in the morning they [i.e., the insurgents] answered the first such question from the presidio with cannon and bombs. For its part the presidio also fired shot and with greater success than the frigate; during the brief action with the presidio the frigate lost 9 or 10 men and was damaged and lay on its side. Now the frigate's insurgents

---

[38]For a comprehensive treatment of this episode, see Uhrowczik, *Burning of Monterey*.

[39]The other ship was the corvette *Santa Rosa;* the Californios referred to *La Argentina* as the *fragata negra* ("black frigate").

began to appeal for pity or mercy, and the commandant of the presidio told his soldiers to stop fighting.

Meanwhile, the large frigate stood at a distance, so that shot could not damage it. It sent all of its rowboats—7 or 9—with many armed men to make a landing; the first time they could not reach the shore, but after some effort they found a suitable place for landing the men.

Before this [event] the governor had written to the priest Felipe [Arroyo de la Cuesta][40] (at S[an] Juan Bautista) in order that he arm his Indians and write to the other priests in his name to do the same, and this [action] was taken. Soon the Indians were properly armed and readily went to fight, but from their ignorance of cannon fire they took fright and soon scattered. Without missing their chance the insurgents burst into the presidio. The commandant of the presidio told his men to cease fighting, and he said to the insurgents that they [i.e., the Californios] had always been friends of the Spaniards and that he himself had been born a Spaniard. They had ceased fighting because the insurgents outnumbered the Californios, and then the governor, seeing that the enemy was stronger, had withdrawn with his men and the insurgents had burst into the presidio, training their cannons on it; they looted all of the houses, beginning with the governor's home, and seized everything that they needed for themselves. They spent 4 or 5 days at Monterey, and during this time their other ship succeeded in reaching and helping to repair their damaged ship.

Heavy rain fell during this period, but in spite of it the insurgents managed to burn Monterey, and they began the fire at the governor's house. Then they proceeded to S[anta] Bárbara to an outlying settlement cal[led] Rancho de la Remedia,[41] which they also looted and torched; on this occasion two of the insurgents' officers were captured and taken to Sant[a] Bárbara. Then both frigates approached S[anta] Bárbara and demanded the return of the two captive officers; they promised not to harm S[anta] Bárbara. Their demand was met, and they went to S[an] Juan Capistrano, but the soldiers and Indians there were already armed. Despite this [opposition], the insurgents landed their men. The Californios, seeing such a small number, began to retreat with the intention of cutting them off; this time they [i.e., the insurgents] succeeded in burning several Indian huts but did not have time to loot, only smashing a barrel of vodka [wine?]. On this occasion four men from the insurgents' command went over spontaneously to the Californio side; then both frigates went to sea and appeared no more.

[40]Felipe Arroyo de la Cuesta (1780–1840), a native of Spain, served zealously at Mission San Juan Bautista for twenty-five years from 1808, despite severe rheumatism and mental distress. He paid particular attention to linguistics and music. See Geiger, *Franciscan Missionaries*, 19–24.

[41]No such rancho existed; Vasilyev is presumably referring to Rancho Nuestra Señora del Refugio, or El Refugio, which was granted to José María Ortega in 1797.

The frigate [*La*] *Argentina* was larger than the *Negra*, but the Californios do not know how many cannons they had.

These ships arrived from Saint Ludovik, N.B., <u>where Cook died</u>.[42] An American had told the governor of New California about the imminent arrival of the insurgents, but he [i.e., the governor] did not believe him.

The insurgents were on the Philippine Islands about 4 months, but they did not manage to seize any prizes; they also cruised off <u>Manila</u>.

The first ship came from <u>Buenos Aires</u>, or the <u>Río de la Plata</u>, and the other joined it in <u>Chile</u>. The commanders of these frigates call themselves Generals of the Pacific. The frigate that fought with the presidio at Monterey flew a flag of truce at first and then the insurgents' flag, which was never struck.

[32]. Where do the names "presidio" and "missionizing" come from, and just what do they mean [?].

"Presidio" in Latin means "fortress," "defense," or "protection."[43]

"Missionizing" means the sending of someone to spread the Word of God.

The <u>Cathol[ic]</u> priests say that the Franciscan Order has more priests than any other, both in New California and in the whole world; however, in New California and in [Spanish] America there are many other orders, and they differ among themselves in their ordainments.

Here there are [the following orders]: (1) <u>Saint Francis Assisi</u> [Franciscans]; (2) <u>S[aint] Basil</u> [Basilians]; (3) <u>Sai[nt] Bernard</u> [Bernardines, an offshoot of the Cistercians]; (4) <u>Holy Trinity</u> [Trinitarians]; (5) <u>Carmelites</u>; (6) <u>Dominicans</u> of S[aint] Dominic; (7) <u>Capuchines of S[aint] Johannes de Paul</u> [?]; (8) <u>S[aint] Benedict</u> [Benedictines]; (9) <u>S[aint] Hieronymus</u> [Jerome] (<u>Capuchines</u>); [(10)] <u>Jesuits</u>.[44]

In [Spanish] America there are likewise many [orders] with differing ordainment[s].

In [Spanish] America there are [the following orders]: <u>S[aint] Francis, S[aint] Augustine, Mercedarians, S[aint] John the Baptist</u>—S[aint] Ioanni de Deo, and <u>S[aint] Hippolytus</u>. But most of all there are Franciscans.

---

[42]This reference is unclear. Captain James Cook was killed at Kealakekua Bay on the island of Hawaii.

[43]In Spanish, *presidio* means "garrison."

[44]Vasilyev is mistaken here; there were only Franciscans in Alta California and Dominicans in Baja California.

DOCUMENT 13

Excerpt from Akhilles Shabelsky's Journal of a Visit to Alta California, 1822–1823

EDITOR'S INTRODUCTION

The twenty-eight-gun warship *Apollon* under Captain (of the first rank) Irinarkh Tulubyev and the brig *Ayaks* (*Ajax*) under Lieutenant Nikandr Filatov were dispatched from Kronshtadt at the beginning of the autumn of 1821 to convey supplies to Kamchatka and Russian America, whereupon the *Apollon* was to patrol the Northwest Coast in defense of Russian trade. Outbound the two vessels were battered by a week-long storm in the North Sea; the *Ayaks* was wrecked among the West Frisian Islands but was recovered, repaired, and returned to Kronshtadt a year later, while the *Apollon* was refitted at Portsmouth and at the end of the year proceeded to Rio de Janeiro. Now the lateness of the season precluded sailing round the Horn, so Tulubyev took a course to the Cape of Good Hope and then Port Jackson (Sydney), but he died of tuberculosis on the way and was succeeded by the senior officer, Lieutenant Stepan Khrushchov. The sloop made Petropavlovsk in late August and New Archangel in late October 1822 but had to winter at San Francisco for four months to recover the health of its crew and to replenish its provisions. In the spring of 1823 it cruised the Northwest Coast until it was relieved by the frigate *Kreiser* at the end of the summer, when it returned to Russia with the sloop *Ladoga*.

TITULAR COUNSELLOR AKHILLES SHABELSKY,[1] AN EXCERPT FROM A
JOURNAL OF A VISIT TO CALIFORNIA DURING THE ROUND-THE-WORLD
VOYAGE OF THE SLOOP *APOLLON* [*APOLLO*] IN 1821–24,[2]
[SLOOP *APOLLON* IN SAN FRANCISCO BAY?],
13 NOVEMBER 1822–27 MARCH 1823

Various circumstances not permitting us to winter at Sitka, we were forced to
proceed to California, and on 13 November we left the port of New Archangel.
During the voyage cold winds changed our course and tore several of our sails; in
the night of 26 [25] November with a favorable wind we entered the port of San
Francisco.

At dawn the next day we hoisted our flag, and in the center of the Spanish
settlement we saw an unfurled flag that was absolutely new to us. At this time
[Agustín] Iturbide ruled in Mexico; politically California was dependent upon
the Mexican government because it had sworn an oath of allegiance to this so-
called emperor.

During the four months that we passed in this country, having the opportunity
to travel around the district between San Francisco and Monterey, to spend a
month at the mission of Santa Clara, and to make an excursion from San Francisco to the port of Bodega [Port Rumyantsev], I was able personally to assess
the state of affairs, although the Spaniards took care to hide it from foreigners;
I offer a short form of my observations.

After the separation of California from Spain the former order of things did
not change; as before it is divided between presidios, or military establishments,
and missions. The former are occupied solely by soldiers under the command of
military officers, and the missions are populated by Indians under the surveillance of monks [*sic:* friars] of the Franciscan order.

New California is under the jurisdiction of a governor [Luis Argüello] residing at Monterey. In accordance with new laws, a junta has been established at
Monterey; its deputies are chosen from California's inhabitants and recognize
the governor as their president.

---

[1]Akhilles Pavlovich Shabelsky (Achille Schabelski) (1802–56), a titular counsellor (the ninth rank in the
civil service list), was a scion of Polish gentry who had received Russian citizenship in 1686 and settled in
South Russia. He worked as a translator/interpreter in the Ministry of Foreign Affairs and volunteered
to serve aboard the *Apollon* in the same capacity. Upon his return he was posted to the Russian mission at
Philadelphia as second secretary in 1824–26. After returning to Russia his failing health forced him into
retirement at his estate in Kharkov Province. See Grinëv, *Kto yest kto,* p. 596.

[2]Schabelski, *Voyage aux colonies russes,* 80–95. An excerpt from this French edition (excluding the California visit) was published in Russian in the same year (see [Schabelski], "Prebyvanie v koloniakh." For another
English translation of this account of the *Apollon*'s visit to Alta California, see Farris, "Visit of the Russian
Warship," reprinted in Farris, *So Far from Home,* 106–13; also see Farris, "Russian Sloop *Apollo.*" For the
captain's concise account of the *Apollon*'s voyage, see [Khrushchev], "Plavanie shlyupa Apollona."

When this province formed part of the Spanish monarchy, the king sent large sums here. The object that he envisaged—the conversion of the indigenes of California—was laudable, but did the Spanish government know how this task was executed?

The manner of conversion of the Indians being the same today as it was before [independence] and, besides, having occasion to see it practiced with my own eyes, one can judge from a description of it that it does not conform at all to the principles of Christianity.

When the commandant of the presidio wants to increase the number of mission residents, he sends a detachment of soldiers there, and the missionaries provide them with acolytes who have long since adopted Christianity, speak Spanish well, and serve as guides and interpreters for the soldiers.

Leaving the mission, they range the country, and as soon as they see a sign of any settlement [of natives] they stop to await nightfall and send the cleverest Indians to reconnoiter the locale. Having assured themselves of the existence of a village, they swoop down upon it during the night with loud cries. The savages, the most timid of the indigenes of America, with only a bow for a weapon, rush from their dwellings and are driven back by gunfire, which they hear for the first time. Gripped by a panic of terror, they do not seek safety in flight; the Spaniards, taking advantage of the disarray, rush upon them and throw lassos over them. As soon as an Indian is roped, he is dragged to the ground and tied to a horse, whereupon the soldier rides at a gallop until the Indian is weakened by the loss of blood flowing from his wounds, and then he is bound and entrusted to the Indian acolytes.

If the soldiers, after having caught several dozen wretched Indians, see that their holy zeal will not gain more captives, they return to the mission. The reverend Franciscan fathers receive their new children and make them accept Christianity. Such is the method used in California to make new converts to Catholicism.

The savages taken thusly to the Spanish settlement gradually accustom themselves to their new way of life under the threat of punishment and become suitable for all kinds of work.

The missions of California are built quite uniformly, the only difference being that those to the south of Monterey are richer. The church occupies the best site; beside it is found the house for the friars and nearby a barracks to house the soldiers and a kind of convent in which the fathers lock the unmarried Indian women at nightfall.

The [Indian] village comprises several square houses made of adobe, and each room is occupied by one family. A large cross always stands in the space between the lodgings [of the friars and soldiers] and the Indian village.

Such a mission, which sometimes contains more than a thousand Indians, is usually supervised by two friars, who are guarded by only a squad of three or four soldiers; this number more than suffices to keep order among the timid Indians.

The way of life that the indigenes of California lead in the missions is very uniform. Upon arising they have to go to church; after attending Mass, of which they do not understand a single word, they assemble in the public square [plaza], where they are given a light breakfast, which is followed by hard work until midday, when the church bell peals and the Indians have to stop working, fall to their knees, and appear to be praying deeply: this is heard when they are in the presence of the friars. After this act of devotion each of them, a basket in hand, goes to the common kitchen, where he receives his dinner of boiled wheat flour [atole]. These baskets are made of tree roots so skillfully that they hold water; [mussel] shells serve in place of spoons. After dinner they work until sundown, when they go to church and from there to the kitchen for supper, and then they disperse to their quarters.

The Indians are always subject to the heavy work, and they have no possessions; only rarely did I find a little salt or some seeds among a few of them. A shirt and a woolen blanket, which they wrap around their body, are the sole items that they receive from the fathers, and even they are made at the missions by the Indians.

Earlier only the friars enjoyed the fruits of their [i.e., the Indians'] labor, but for the past dozen years Spain's troubles [i.e., the Napoleonic Wars] have no longer permitted the king to send money for the upkeep of California, and the governor and the commandants of the presidios are obliged to demand from the friars the provisions and the supplies necessary for the maintenance of the soldiers. The friars argued in vain that all divine and human laws were on their side. Their greed had to yield to the force of necessity, and now the soldiers are clothed and nourished by the missions. The money that comes from the sale of trade goods is shared between the fathers and the officers.

Such an administration of California produces the most harmful consequences for the country. The Indians, deprived of all possessions and having no motive that might encourage them to become more industrious, lead an extremely miserable existence. The soldiers, who are inclined to indolence, consider labor to be the greatest misfortune. Only the friars and the officers possess something, yet the soldiers do not want to do any work.

The presidio is a large square building of adobe, divided into several rooms and having more the appearance of a stable than a European establishment.

It is difficult to imagine the state of misery in which the Spaniards of California live. When an observer finds himself among them, he thinks that he has been transported to the sixteenth century; the construction of their houses, their clothing (including that of their wives), their weapons, and their opinions and prejudices

make them appear to be contemporaries of Cortés and Pizarro. [Despite] possessing a country that enjoys an excellent temperature and an extreme fertility, they
do not exert the slightest effort to profit from their fortunate situation.

The forts built at both San Francisco and Monterey are falling into disrepair
and are provided with cannons on old gun carriages that will shatter with the
first discharge; I noticed one at San Francisco dated 1740. Visiting Monterey's, I
found just one soldier, and he was asleep. It is true that in order to put this presidio in a state of defense it would be necessary to establish many fortifications,
but San Francisco's, because of its position, has a site that could be defended very
successfully against a superior enemy force, for at the port's entrance, which is
extremely narrow, batteries could be built on the opposing two sides.

It is with the same negligence that they have attended to matters suited to the
improvement of the condition of the inhabitants of this country. No school exists
in either San Francisco or Monterey, and one so-called doctor,[3] a worthy student
of Sangrado,[4] relieves all of California's sick.

In passing through the village [i.e., pueblo] situated on the road from Santa
Clara to San Juan [Bautista] I was surrounded by a large number of sick who,
with tears in their eyes, begged me to visit them and give them some medicines.
These same people do not know that less than six leagues[5] from their village,
very near the mission of San José, there are thermal springs saturated with sulfur
that would be of much benefit to most of them. It was the Indians of this mission
who showed them to me. Having returned to San José, I did not fail to represent
to the friars the necessity of building some sort of dwelling near these waters for
providing the sick with the means of recovery; I doubt very much, however, that
my advice will have any effect.

It is wrong of [Captain George] Vancouver [in 1792] to describe the Indians
as savages totally without reason and quite resembling overgrown children. This
judgment is so decisive as to have been perhaps suggested to him by the friars,
who want to keep them under their absolute supervision, as was formerly done
by the Jesuits in Paraguay. A more impartial examination shows us that these
Indians are not only suited to all agricultural labors but will in time even become
artisans, and it is to them that California is indebted for its few manufactures.

It is pleasant and even comforting to find in works such as Chateaubriand's[6]
sublime descriptions of the sacrifices made by the missionaries of the New World

---

[3]Probably the surgeon at the presidio of Monterey, Manuel Quijano, who served from 1807 until his death
in August 1823 ([Schabelski], "Visit of the Russian Warship," 12).

[4]Sangrado is a physician in Alain René Le Sage's picaresque romance *Gil Blas de Santillane* whose methods of treatment are confined to the letting of blood and the drinking of warm water.

[5]Throughout his narrative Shabelsky seems to be equating a league with two miles.

[6]François René de Chateaubriand (1768–1848) was a French statesman and romantic writer.

in propagating Christianity. But upon examining what actually happened, one is forced sometimes to consider them sparkling illusions and to accept the opinion of La Rochefoucauld[7] and Pope[8] that conceit also governs the actions of men. These verses of the English poet—

> Two Principles in human nature reign;
> Self-love, to urge, and Reason, to restrain;
> Self-love, the spring of motion, acts the soul;
> Reason's comparing balance, rules the whole.
> Reason rules the whole, not self-love alone[9]—

are only too applicable to the missionaries of California, who, speaking only of eternity and their contempt for passions, are thinking solely of satisfying their [own] eager desire.

The [political] changes occurring in Mexico have to affect California. The first act of power that they [i.e., the Californios] should exercise is the abolition of the military government, whose rule of the province is quite contrary to their interests. Its trade, which is too limited by the existence of the missions, requires reforms suited to the improvement of the condition of the Indians and to their acquisition of the means of acquiring property. They must also encourage agriculture among California's [indigenous] inhabitants.

Wanting to see the Russian establishment near the port of Bodega, I crossed San Francisco Bay and arrived at the mission of San Rafael. After having declared my intention to the missionary [Juan Amorós], from him I received horses and a young Indian guide who also knew Spanish and could serve as my interpreter.

Because I had to cover more than thirty-five leagues across country completely uninhabited by Europeans, prudence demanded that I take some weapons with me, and it was with only two pistols and a saber, without any soldier for a guard, that I decided to cross this expanse. The extreme timidity of the Indians reassured me of my security.

The first day I crossed some country of a very pleasant appearance, but the lack of trees rendered it marginally suitable for habitation. Meanwhile, I saw only a few dozen wretched runaways from the mission of San Rafael, who took me for a Spaniard and fled into the mountains.

The next day toward noon I was stopped by a river [the Russian River] that I had to ford; having decided to await the ebb tide, I was pleasantly surprised toward nightfall to see some thirty Indians of Mission San Rafael approaching me, led by

---

[7]The French moralist writer François de la Rochefoucauld (1613–1680), whose maxims stressed the importance of self-interest.

[8]The English poet Alexander Pope (1688–1744).

[9]From Pope's "Essay on Man."

a chief of their tribe who had been dispatched a week ago to catch fugitives. They immediately felled a large tree, whose trunk served as a launch and its branches as oars. As they accompanied me as far as the establishment [of Ross], I had occasion to see how they pursued the natives, from whom they differ only in their cruelty and their knowledge of some superficial Catholic ceremonies.

In the morning of the third day I saw the Russian flag flying in the middle of the New Albion establishment. The fort, which contained within its walls the manager's house and the storehouses, forms a square fortified with four bastions having twenty-four cannons. Everything that I encountered was in the greatest order. Their foresight even went so far as to dig a well near the manager's house—even though a stream runs a few steps from the walls—so as not to lack water in case of a siege.

This establishment, nine leagues distant from the port of Bodega, does not have a bay to accommodate ships. It was only founded by the Russians with the sole intention of facilitating their relations with the Spaniards of California. The latter were not aware of this object, being previously very displeased with their [i.e., the Russians'] proximity, and they [i.e., the Spaniards] did not fail to assert their rights to all of the American coast from Tierra del Fuego to Bering Strait. However, several years of uninterrupted possession having legitimized the right of the Russians to occupy Bodega, the Spaniards became loyal allies and good friends, although at the same time resenting all of the repercussions of such neighbors.

Within cannon shot of the fort the natives of New Albion have built a village, where they live peaceably. The lightest services that they render the Russians are generously rewarded, and the latter never show the least desire to make them recognize their dominion. The savages' huts, built of reeds [tule], are conical in shape and arranged fairly orderly. Having very few passions and lacking courage, they have only in mind to be able to end their lives peacefully. Acorns, ground into flour, are the basis of their subsistence; rarely do they hunt or fish. They wear almost no clothing, and very few of them are tattooed.

With the intention of returning by sea to San Francisco, I took three umiaks[10] with seven "Aleuts" from the establishment, and after six hours I entered the port of Bodega to give the paddlers some rest. It is open to winds from the southern quarter and is suitable for small ships only. The Russians have built a dwelling and a bathhouse here; the latter is indispensable to a Russian settlement. After having safely doubled Point Reyes, I visited the bay of Sir Francis Drake [Drake's Bay]; it is poorly suited to anchorage, and its name is all that makes it remarkable. On the third day I reached San Francisco.

---

[10]The original has "umiaks" but may well have meant "kayaks"; it is uncertain from the context.

In taking the three umiaks I had in mind to travel in them up the San Francisco [Sacramento] River, which flows into the bay of the same name, and to probe the cause of the light that we had noticed to the ENE of our anchorage in the port. It could not be attributed to fires, as the time when the Indians burn the grass to get their seeds had already passed. I assumed that this light stemmed from the burning of naphtha or was due to the eruption of some volcano in the Sierra Nevada, but the desire to satisfy my curiosity encountered major obstacles in the suspicions of the Spaniards, who did everything possible to dissuade me from my plan, and I was forced to abandon it.

On 27 March 1823, aided by a strong current, and despite a contrary wind, we left San Francisco Bay and directed our course toward the channels of the Northwest Coast of America to find foreign vessels. . . .[11]

[11]The rest of Shabelsky's account, which describes the *Apollon*'s return to New Archangel and homeward voyage from there via the Horn in company with the *Ladoga* (including another but shorter stop at San Francisco at the end of 1823), is omitted here.

DOCUMENT 14

Excerpt from Andrey Lazarev's Journal of a Visit to Alta California, 1823–1824

EDITOR'S INTRODUCTION

One of the unfamiliar problems encountered by the Russians in the North Pacific sphere of international rivalry was mercantile competition (in Siberia Russia had a free hand, thanks to Chinese and Japanese isolationism). Their principal competitors on the Northwest Coast were American fur trading vessels (until the 1830s, at least, whereupon they were supplanted by the ships and posts of the Hudson's Bay Company). The Yankee skippers did not hesitate to exchange firearms and spirits to the coastal natives, especially the Tlingits, thereby rendering them less tractable and more dangerous to the Russians, who, moreover, unlike the transient Americans, had to cope with the natives perennially. However, the American "coasters" also brought provisions and goods, which they traded not only to the natives (for sea otter skins) but also to the undersupplied Russians at New Archangel (for fur seal skins). This dilemma was resolved by Tsar Alexander I's decree of 4/16 September 1821 whereby foreign vessels were excluded from Russian coastal waters on both sides of the North Pacific on pain of confiscation (and Russian sovereignty was extended down the Northwest Coast as far as 51° N latitude). To enforce this decree, Russian warships were dispatched from the Baltic to patrol coastal waters (and defend New Archangel against the Tlingits), while the round-the-world shipment of goods from St. Petersburg and the purchase of provisions from Alta California, by then open to foreign trade, replaced the embargoed American vessels.

This situation did not last long, however, as pressure from the United States and Great Britain resulted in conventions in 1824 and 1825, respectively, that lifted the embargo for ten years, provided that weapons and spirits were not sold to the natives. In the meantime, however, Russian warships did cruise the North Pacific coast, beginning with the *Ayaks* (*Ajax*) and *Apollon* (*Apollo*) in 1822, thereby raising the profile of the navy in Russian America's affairs. The warships commonly refreshed and restocked during the winter at San Francisco. In 1823–24 they were the sloop *Ladoga* and the frigate *Kreiser* (*Cruiser*), which were scheduled to be relieved in 1824–25 by the sloop *Predpriyatie*.

CAPTAIN-LIEUTENANT ANDREY LAZAREV,[1] AN EXCERPT FROM A JOURNAL OF A VISIT TO CALIFORNIA DURING THE ROUND-THE-WORLD VOYAGE OF THE SLOOP *LADOGA* IN 1822–24,[2] [SLOOP *LADOGA* IN SAN FRANCISCO BAY?], 1 DECEMBER 1823–12 JANUARY 1824 . . . .[3]

Chapter VII
California.

Port of San Francisco. Festivities of the inhabitants. Work on the sloop. Presidio of San Francisco. Mission. Priests, or fathers. Population, and Planting and Harvest of Grain. Horseback riding. Catching of wild bulls. Change in form of government. Instructions of Mr. Khlebnikov, Manager of New Archangel Counter. Advantages of this port. Remarks on vegetation and air temperature, information on animals and minerals. Departure.

In the morning of 30 November we sighted the coast of New Albion, and we estimated that we were 35 miles away; at midday, according to the bearing of the western island of the Farallon group and the known latitude, we were about 42 miles off the entrance to the port of San Francisco, while our chronometers (35 days after their last check) showed us 13 miles farther west than the map did.*

The gradually dying wind slowed our entrance into the said port; at half past 10 o'clock in the evening, owing to the absence of wind and a contrary current, we

---

*On Arrowsmith's map this coast is located in accordance with Captain Vancouver's determination.

[1]Andrey Petrovich Lazarev (1787–1849), a prize-winning graduate of the Naval Academy, distinguished himself in naval operations against the French during the Napoleonic Wars and was promoted to lieutenant in 1810. In 1819 he commanded the brig *Novaya Zemlya* [*New Land*] in an unsuccessful attempt to round the archipelago of the same name. In 1821 he was promoted to captain-lieutenant, and the next year on the *Ladoga* he undertook his sole round-the-world voyage. After his return to Russia he served in the White and Baltic Seas and rose steadily through the ranks, becoming vice admiral in 1842. See Bolgurtsev, *Morskoy biografichesky spravochnik*, 111; and Pierce, *Russian America*, 297.

[2]Lazarev, *Plavanie vokrug sveta*, 177–99.

[3]The description of the voyage of the *Ladoga* from Kronshtadt through the Atlantic, around the Cape of Good Hope, and through the Indian and Pacific Oceans to Petropavlovsk and New Archangel is omitted here. The sloop left the colonial capital on 14 November 1823.

dropped anchor in a shoal four miles from the port. Here the depth ranged from 7 to 4 sazhens, and the bottom was silt with fine sand. The turbulent breakers in many places frighten navigators who do not have accurate knowledge of them beforehand, and the strong current of up to 6½ knots activating the outgoing and incoming tides directly through the entrance demands close attention on the part of the helmsman.

The next day (1 December) we sighted the frigate *Kreiser* standing at anchor; it had arrived just a few hours before us. At two o'clock in the afternoon with a favorable current we raised anchor and began to tack toward the port; just before 7 [o'clock] we passed the fort abeam and slowly dropped anchor in a depth of 5 sazhens, with the fort WSW⅓W at 1½ miles. At this roadstead we found the sloop *Apollon*, which had come from the port of New Archangel for repairs and the Russian-American Company brig *Golovnin*, which had been sent to buy wheat.

The entrance to San Francisco's roadstead is about 2½ miles wide, and on both sides there are rocks along the shore; at the time of passage it is best to keep to the northern side and come to anchor at a distance of ½ a mile from the southern side, nearing a building whose roof only is visible from the roadstead. I do not advise passing closer to shore, because there is a small rock in the shallow water. The bottom is generally very good; only the current is troublesome, with frequent settings of the hawsers.

The boom of cannon fire from the fort, over which a completely new (to us) flag* was flying, signalled a great festival on the part of the local residents in honor of the Madonna [Our Lady] of Guadalupe (the protectress of this whole region), who undergoes a long pilgrimage annually. The secular calendar at this place was one day later than ours because we reached it from the east and the local Spanish settlers from the west.

The day after our arrival, after having double anchored, we saluted the fort with seven guns, and it answered us with the same number. Towards evening we took a tent ashore and began to arrange a place for checking the chronometers and setting to work the next day. We started to mend the sails and to repair the water barrels, many iron items, and the rigging. The thought of returning to our beloved fatherland intensified our operations; the clear and warm weather that prevails constantly here at this season was also very favorable. Only the procurement of fresh water and firewood, which we had to stock in substantial quantities, slowed us, owing to the long distance and the strong currents; however, the common effort and the assistance overcame these difficulties, and within 40 days we were ready to leave, although we were detained by a SW wind, which lasted for two days and nights.

---

*Three horizontal stripes—red, white, and green— constitute the flag of the new Mexican empire [*sic: republic*]; in the center on a white field is a one-headed eagle sitting on a rock in a lake and killing a snake.

On the S shore there is a quadrangle [i.e., plaza] enclosed by dirty and partially collapsed dwellings; in one of them lives the commandant of the fort and the head of this place, and so it is called the presidio of San Francisco. The garrison, and the total force defending this coast, comprises about 25 ragged soldiers, who for a long time have not received any pay from the government. Mission San Francisco is found 7 verstas from the presidio, and there are four more like it within a radius of 100 verstas. These missions are administered by priests and comprise savage, nomadic Indians, caught by lasso and received against their will into the Catholic faith without any prior explanation of the dogmas of the religion and even without the slightest study of the language. They are treated severely by these fathers, who, supported by a few soldiers, compel them on festive days to go to church, where, not understanding the sermons or the liturgy itself and following the external ceremonies with their eyes only, they have to imitate them willy-nilly, and the rest of the time they work the land without rest or relief to satisfy the self-interest of their mentors, who, having fattened themselves with sloth and satiated themselves with greed, within a few years under the pretext of disease retire with piasters to the tranquility of their homeland. They not only do not try to spread Christianity among the various tribes but also [do not try] to accustom them—even those used to their way of life—to civic duties. The long stay of the Spaniards on this coast has taught some of the [native] Americans (Catholics) to learn the Spanish language and to serve as tools of the designs of their mentors; for this the priests maintain a number of bodyguards, or followers, called *vaqueros*.[4] The church and the adjoining bleached stone dwelling, which accommodates the clergymen and their storehouses, constitutes the principal building of each mission; the quadrangle, composed mostly of a dwelling of unfired brick [adobe] without [window] glass, a floor, or a ceiling, serves as the residence of the oppressed and naturally feeble-minded [native] Americans. The filth and stench of this structure are extreme and are probably the main cause of the premature death of those living there. Corn, peas, beans, and on holidays meat (which abounds on account of the propagation of feral bulls) are issued moderately at dinner from the common kitchen and constitute their usual food; cloaks [serapes], which they themselves make from she[e]p's wool and which serve to cover their nakedness, form their meager clothing.

The vicinity of this place is rather variegated and pleasant; two lakes with fresh water, replete with wild ducks and loons,[5] often induced us to stroll and afforded tasty food. The moderate temperature of the air, the clear weather, and the abundance of different wild birds—of which the [California]

---

[4]Literally "herdsmen."
[5]Russ., *morskie kuritsy*, literally "sea hens."

quail* differs from the others in its beauty and taste—enticed our hunters fairly far afield, and fatigue often forced them to turn aside for repose at the nearest mission, the road to which was easily recognizable from the heads of bulls and the bones and carcasses of dead horses scattered everywhere; the foul smell from them and the flocks of crows, seagulls, and various hawks devouring all of this carrion usually means the proximity of habitations. I think that this province is indebted solely to the feathered kingdom for protection against infectious and epidemic diseases.

Having taken part repeatedly in rambling and hunting, I sometimes stopped at the missions, and I was always thankful for the general hospitality of the priests. A table, wine, and fresh milk were freely offered to travelers, and our conversations, despite the secretiveness of the missionaries, always led to more knowledge of these places. I do not consider it superfluous to mention here the closest mission to us, Mission San Francisco, because it was built before the others on the coast; this place was the most suitable for a landing for our ships during the return voyage from New Archangel to Russia. Two priests, José [Altimira] and Tomás [Esténaga], administered the mission and had separated before our arrival; the very hard-working preacher José obtained permission to establish a new congregation. This mission was founded in 1777; it is nearly surrounded by water, and the floodtide from the W comes so close that with a moderate rise in the water level our longboat easily reached it.

The land within a radius of about 9 miles belongs to Mission San Francisco; although not all of it is equally suitable for grain growing, it is always sufficient to sustain 6,000 persons. In addition, there is extensive pasturage. Unfortunately, this place is not watered by rivers, and so the residents do not have good water, and they fetch water (neither very tasty nor clean) from wells.

According to information collected by me, there are 958 residents of Mission San Francisco, including 490 adult Indians, 286 women, and 182 children of both sexes, plus 4,049 cattle, 8,830 sheep, and 820 horses.

Herewith I attach a table of plantings and harvests of crops in 1823.

	Planted	_harvested_
Wheat	300 fanegas*	2,800 fanegas
Barley	20	386
Peas	4	100
Beans	4	103
Haricots	5	110
Corn	5	600

*La Pérouse calls it a Perdris [_Perdix,_ the partridge genus].
*A fanega is a measure of grain used throughout California; it contains about 4 puds in weight.

Without disputing the data on the yield of crops and without doubting the care and the skill [expended] in the local economy, I grant myself the right to make a few comments here. More than once I happened to visit Mission San Francisco on holidays and to hear the liturgy. The church is fairly well appointed and on these days was filled with local Indians; judging from their number, it was impossible to agree with the aforesaid large population. The yield of grain in the table is also unusual, for the shoddy working of the land, the innumerable birds nesting in the fields after sowing and right up to the harvest, and the threshing of the ears of grain by horses' hoofs give cause to doubt such a high productivity, which in a few years would fill all of the granaries, in which there was a small stock at the time of our stay. The sale of grain is very negligible, despite its recent export to Lima on the occasion of a complete harvest failure there (stemming from domestic revolts) and its annual delivery to New Archangel. These circumstances cannot apply to just the mission of San Francisco and its extensive environs, for the very same [amount] was stocked at most of the missions adjoining Monterey and other coastal places. Apart from the priests, [at the missions] the Indians themselves do not know the taste of grain.

The abundance of horses afforded us more than a little pleasure and benefit; not only I and all of the officers but also even the lower ranks, being ashore on holidays, hired them for a very cheap price and dared to ride at full gallop for 15 verstas without fearing any harmful result from not knowing horsemanship, for the stirrups and saddle are so well made that it is impossible to fall during the roughest ride, and the horses are so surefooted that they never stumble. Their natural caution while descending hills and avoiding dangerous places always vindicated our boldness, so that nobody could complain of any misadventure.

Such gallops always ended with another, no less amusing spectacle. Every two or three days for provisions we were supplied with several [feral] bulls, which, having been lassoed, were usually bound very firmly by the horns to farmyard bulls, and, escorted by mounted vaqueros, they [i.e., the wild bulls] were brought to our tents with much labor. Here a tame bull, stabbing the ground with his horns and detaining the others, gave the horseman time to toss a lasso around the front legs of the wild bull and throw him to the ground; then they untied the former, which was bound to the other by the horns with a rope up to 5 sazhens in length [weighted] with bal[l]ast of 8 or 10 puds, and freed its legs. It is surprising that such a strong animal in the heat of its rage always stood its ground—even upon the approach of humans, whom it always charged with fury—despite the fact that the place was insignificant to its predicament. Upon the resting of this wild captive our sailors amused themselves by lassoing it and, having entangled its legs, brought it to the ground and then killed it, thereby ending the favorite spectacle of the Spaniards.

Upon the replacement of the lawful government in Mexico, the people chose as emperor [in 1822–23] Don Agustín Iturbide, who had served as a general[6] in the Spanish army. From the beginning of his reign he was called Augustino Primo [Agustín the First], and subsequently, at the will of the same electoral authority, he was dethroned, and he managed to flee [the country] with a lot of treasure, after having enhanced his royal title with the designation Ultimo [the Last].[7] Then the government passed to the authority of a junta, and because of its weakness and internal discord each [Mexican] province is seeking independence. During our stay at Monterey, the seat of the governor of Upper California, at the will of the people a junta was chosen, consisting of the surrounding missionaries and several old retired Spaniards who had settled in the territory. It decided to separate completely and make this part of California independent of the other regions that once constituted a vast and rich possession of Spain. Now California is governed by its former laws and Don Luis Argüello, an army captain and the province's provisional governor, who has appropriated the right to rule from the clergy.

During our stay at the port of San Francisco the brig Golov[n]in, having obtained some wheat for goods, set off for Santa Cruz, where it had been proposed to get the rest of its cargo. Meanwhile, Mr. Khlebnikov, the manager of New Archangel Counter, presented with the opportunity to put all of the wheat on the brig Ryurik and guided by correspondence with the governor of the colonies, Mr. Muravyov, sent the brig Golov[n]in to the Sandwich Islands to buy rum, sugar, and other items greatly needed by the colonies. He himself came to the port of San Francisco with the brig Ryurik. Mr. Etolin,[8] commander of the brig Golov[n]in, had to make this purchase after the example of former years, i.e., by

---

[6]Actually, he had reached the rank of colonel (1813), and just before the proclamation of independence in 1821 he was promoted to brigadier.

[7]In fact, Iturbide simply abdicated and went to Tuscany to live, and he called himself Agustín Primero, not Primo and never Ultimo.

[8]Adolf Karlovich Etolin (Arvid Adolf Etholén) (1799–1876), captain of the Golovnin, was one of several Swedo-Finns who served the Russian-American Company with distinction. He was born in Helsingfors (Helsinki) when Finland was still part of Sweden. After graduation from St. Petersburg's Naval Academy, he was seconded to the company and posted to New Archangel, where he arrived in 1818 aboard the Kamchatka. He made several voyages in colonial waters before finishing his five-year term and returning to Kronshtadt in 1825, whereupon he was promoted to the rank of midshipman. In 1826 Etolin was again assigned to the company and returned to New Archangel via Siberia. Again he made numerous trading and exploring voyages throughout the colonies, and he also served stints as assistant governor, acting governor, and captain of the port of New Archangel. In 1837, after serving two consecutive five-year terms in the colonies, he returned to Russia.

In 1838 Etolin was promoted to captain of the second rank and appointed governor of Russian America. As governor he improved and expanded facilities, consolidated settlements, bettered relations with the natives and the Hudson's Bay Company, and helped to suppress the native liquor traffic. In 1845, he returned to Russia and officially transferred his gubernatorial duties to his Alaska-bound successor, Captain (of the second rank) Mikhail Tebenkov. Upon his return to St. Petersburg in early 1846 Etolin was decorated and elected to the company's board of directors, serving until 1859.

trading fur seals to ships of the United States that now stop at these islands with various goods.*

The usual price of a fur seal is 1¾ Spanish piasters. This hunt now constitutes the chief branch of the trade of the [Russian-]American Company; the [sea] otter hunt is very insignificant, so that Mr. Khlebnikov for the Company's benefit has taken advantage of the confusion in the government of California and succeeded in making terms with its governor for unrestrained permission to hunt [sea] otters in San Francisco Bay. For this [purpose] 25 umiaks[9] with "Aleuts" are sent from the settlement of Ross and, boating around the bay in parties, catch [sea] otters, and at the end of the agreed period the catch is divided equally. Mr. Khlebnikov in 2 months here has managed to hunt up to 300 [sea] otters, one-half of which have to be given to a schooner—sent by the governor under the American flag—for sale at Canton. It is worth noting that both the [sea] otters and the schooner belong to the present governor [Luis Argüello] of New Albion [Alta California]; this accords with the saying "to catch fish in troubled waters."

The port of San Francisco is, so to speak, the only place in this region for repose for a seafarer wearied by a long stay on the Northwest Coast of America, for besides the security from winds and the tranquil anchorage, for the most part the clear weather affords every opportunity for the safe repair of one's ship for new undertakings. The abundance of cattle, the fresh grain, and the complete liberty of men ashore (restoring their strength) renew the mariner's former cheerfulness, and he sets out again in the wide sea fully prepared to endure new difficulties. Throughout our stay here, through dealings with the commandant, Don Ignacio Martínez, we obtained plenty of fresh meat, paying 4 piasters for a feral bull weighing about 9 puds, and we bought wheat from the priests for 3 piasters a fanega (about 4 puds). We baked delicious and healthful bread in stoves installed on the shore through the solicitude of Captain Vasilyev (the leader of the expedition sent to Bering Strait), who was here in 1820, and the commander of the sloop *Apollon*, Lieutenant Khrushchov.[10] Now it only remains for visiting seafarers to

---

*In accordance with rules set by His Majesty, naval cruisers are now sent annually to our colonies on the Northwest Coast of America, and the trading vessels of the United States have almost abandoned their trade with the Tlingits. After arriving at the Sandwich Islands, they expressed a desire to the shipmasters of the [Russian-]American Company to exchange their goods for fur seals, and they even proposed to exchange the ships themselves.

[9] The context suggests kayaks, not umiaks.

[10] Stepan Petrovich Khrushchov (1790–1865) graduated from the Naval Academy in 1806 and saw active duty during the Napoleonic Wars in the Mediterranean and North Seas, for which he was promoted to midshipman in 1809 and lieutenant in 1813. He sailed on the *Apollon* as senior lieutenant but succeeded to its command in the spring of 1822 in the Indian Ocean upon the death of Captain Tulubyev. Upon his return to Russia, Khrushchov rose rapidly through the ranks to first captain-lieutenant and then captain of the second rank in the same year (1824), captain of the first rank in 1829, rear admiral in 1834, and vice admiral in 1843. See Grinëv, *Kto yest kto*, 577; and Pierce, *Russian America*, 233.

wish that the missionaries would abandon their indifference to the propagation of poultry, which on account of their extreme scarcity here can be obtained with much difficulty from only the priests themselves, and by their own example attempt to rouse industrious settlers to grow garden vegetables, for despite all of the conveniences they still do not have any green vegetables, except pumpkins.

Here it is fitting to give Mr. Ogiyevsky's[11] remarks about the vegetation, air temperature, fauna, and minerals:

"The vicinity of the site of the port of San Francisco comprises mountains and hills of medium size with broad summits, terminating in lovely slopes and interrupted by picturesque valleys crossed by streams and clear little lakes. Small trees and bushes cover the slopes, and the valleys are filled with a variety of grasses turning green. There is no construction timber near the port, except [coast] redwood, whose thickness exceeds that of our one-hundred-year-old pines; however, it is very soft and weak. Of the small bushes, only one [poison oak] is worth a mention; its size and bark are similar to those of the guelder rose.[12] It grows in abundance and causes an unusual effect: a careless touching of the wood produces an unbearable itch, pain, and strong swelling in that part [of one's body] that has come into direct contact with the wood, as well as in all other parts touched by the first part. The inhabitants spare themselves this effect by using a poultice of cow's milk with white bread or corn flour. The Russian doctors who witnessed frequent trials on our suffering Russian sailors found that a lotion of Goulard water [i.e., cerate] was very helpful, and a poultice decocted from linseed and the like even more effective, but hardly better than the best remedy of all—lamp oil [i.e., low-grade olive oil] with camphor. The ailment lasts two to three weeks. The Spaniards call this tree *Hydra;* during our stay it was bare, and for that reason we could not acquire enough information about all of its parts.

From November, i.e., when the sun shifts to the southern hemisphere, the temperature of the air here changes noticeably; the nights become cold, although no lower than the freezing point of 0° Réaumur. Delicate plants wither, and the weakest trees and shrubs defoliate, and the reason is not so much the cold as the lack of rain, which does not begin to dampen the dry soil until the return of the sun at the end of December, imperceptibly awakening nature so that in early January the blossoms of the currant bushes[13] and field violets[14] can be seen. Such is winter here! The ungrateful residents complain of its severity, but the Russian seafarers consider this season the most pleasant; however, the Spaniards living here have neither stoves nor fireplaces in their homes, and only the priests and the military officials have glass windows.

---

[11]Pyotr Ogiyevsky, the ship's physician.

[12]Or snowball tree, or cranberry tree (or bush), *Viburnum opulus.*

[13]Possibly the wild black currant, or flowering currant (*Ribes americanum*), with greenish yellow blossoms, or the buffalo currant (*Ribes odoratum*), with yellow blossoms.

[14]Possibly the dogtooth violet (*Erythronium americanum*), with yellow blossoms, or the adder's tongue (*Erythronium albidum*), with white blossoms, or even the snow lily (*Erythronium grandiflorum*), with yellow blossoms.

Besides cattle and horses, both tame and feral, there are many sheep here; pigs are very rare. Of animals, there are numerous bears, wolves [coyotes], wolverines, foxes, wildcats [cougars?], and others; of reptiles, lizards and various snakes are known. Nothing can be said about aquatic fauna because the abundance of cattle, which afford their best food, diverts the lazy residents from fishing.

The mineral realm here has not been investigated. It is known only that the mountains of California, especially in the vicinity of Monterey and Santa Cruz, abound in silver ore, which they began to work in 1820, but this undertaking proved unprofitable to the Spaniards and thus was abandoned. Around the port of San Francisco there are various kinds of serpentine, soapstone, asbestos,[15] variegated sandstone, jasper, hornblende,[16] and others."

On 31 December the men were freed from all work and were allowed to go from ship to ship. Separated for a long time by service, compatriots and friends were reunited, and they talked pleasantly about the past, and toward evening the convivial fellows devised carousels [i.e., merry-go-rounds] and various games and enlivened their reunion with songs; midnight of 1 January was testimony to the tender parting of fine sons of the fatherland.

In the morning of 1 January 1824 with emotion we expressed our gratitude to the Lord God for preserving us from the past dangers of the voyage, and requesting His blessing and protection for our future success in fulfilling the will of our Great Monarch, we made haste to accelerate the moment of our return to our beloved fatherland.

On 10 January 1824 we were completely prepared to depart, having removed the tents from the shore and stocked all of the provisions for the sloop, and we awaited only a favorable opportunity for getting under sail. We left as testimony to our visit a sorrowful memorial to Midshipman Tulubyev,[17] who served on the sloop *Apollon* and died here last year; Lieutenant Kyukhelbeker,[18] a shipmate and friend of the deceased, took upon himself the fulfilment of this duty and erected a four-cornered pyramid atop a hill opposite our ships and surrounded it with a rather attractive railing.

The clear weather gave us an opportunity to check properly chronometer 991,

---

[15]Russ., *amiant*.

[16]Russ., *rogovy kamen*.

[17]Aleksandr Vsevolodovich Tulubyev (17??–1823), possibly a relative of the *Apollon*'s initial (and deceased) captain, had died on 4 February and had been buried on what was to become known as Russian Hill.

[18]Baron Mikhail Karlovich fon Kyukhelbeker (Wilhelm Karlovich von Kuchelbeker) (1797–1852) was a romantic poet, critic, and translator. He served as a midshipman on the *Novaya Zemlya* under Lieutenant Andrey Lazarev in 1819. An ardent patriot, Kyukhelbeker became a member of the secret Northern Society and took part in the abortive Decembrist uprising at the end of 1825, whereupon he and his brother Vasily (Wilhelm) were arrested; Mikhail was sentenced first to prison and then to twenty years of hard labor at the Nerchinsk mines in Siberia, where he died. He was one of several young liberals who took a keen interest in the Russian-American Company and its colonies. See Pierce, *Russian America*, 239.

which on the last day of observations (11 January) had been 5° 46' 40" behind the [1]23rd meridian of San Francisco and was losing 22' 19" daily; the tabulation of 237° 51' 30" E was used to determine the longitude of the place. It differed from Arrowsmith's map by 7 minutes to the W.

On the 12th at 8 o'clock in the morning a NW wind crowned our expectations and the two sloops, the *Ladoga* and the *Apollon*, raised anchor and began to tack out of the bay. Our former comrades on the cruise came to bid us farewell.[19] Happy to reach the fatherland soon, we tried to demonstrate our readiness for new assignments, and they boasted of impending labors; this contest did not last long, as our duty and zeal to serve quickly reconciled us and forced us to part with mutual wishes for success.

During our departure from the port of San Francisco I had to change some nighttime signals, on account of the small caliber of our cannons, and I ordered Lieutenant Khrushchov, commander of the sloop *Apollon*, in case of a sudden separation from me to sail into the wind and cruise for two days with small tacks to the spot where the last signal had been seen. . . .[20]

---

[19]Lazarev is referring to the sailors of the *Kreiser,* which remained at San Francisco for a while.

[20]The description of the voyage of the *Ladoga* and *Apollon* through the Pacific and Atlantic Oceans and around Cape Horn and of their long stay at the Brazilian island of Santa Catarina and their return to Kronshtadt in October 1824 is omitted here.

DOCUMENT 15

Excerpt from Dmitry Zavalishin's Journal of a Visit to Alta California, 1823–1824

EDITOR'S INTRODUCTION

Dmitry Irinarkhovich Zavalishin (1804–92), a midshipman on the *Kreiser*, was one of Russian America's most interesting protagonists. The precocious son of a military governor, he was schooled in St. Petersburg's Naval Academy. He had a broad education and diverse interests, including the frontier regions of the Russian Empire, where he had been born. But he was unable to indulge these interests until he was invited to join the round-the-world voyage of the *Kreiser;* he accepted eagerly, intending to return overland via Okhotsk to study Siberia firsthand.

He spent six weeks in Alta California, and in his capacity of purchaser of the *Kreiser*'s provisions he traveled widely and conversed with numerous Californios. So the cocky radical was able to become acquainted with the precarious situation of both Russian and Mexican California and to conceive some bold plans. He concluded that California, with its political instability and agricultural and mineral potential, should be annexed by Russia to enhance Russia's Pacific position. He cultivated the Californio authorities, advising them to secede from Mexico, in the belief that an independent province could be more easily annexed by Russia. Zavalishin even envisioned himself as the Grand Master of a knightly "Order of Restoration," modelled on the Knights of Malta. This amorphous institution, which he had conceived in early 1822 with the aim of spreading the Enlightenment, supporting human rights, and purging Europe of "troubled minds," was to be based in Alta California and to serve as a vehicle for Russian expansion.

His machinations were interrupted by the *Kreiser*'s return to New Archangel, and because of a letter he had written to Tsar Alexander I, he was recalled to

St. Petersburg to speak to the emperor. Alexander had time for only a hurried audience, so his proposals—which by that time included not only the occupation of Alta California but also the seizure of Sakhalin, the Amur River valley, and even the Hawaiian Islands, all to safeguard and develop Russian America and to enhance Russia's naval power—were submitted in writing and examined by a special committee chaired by the notoriously reactionary Count Alexis Arakcheyev. The committee essentially rejected Zavalishin's proposals; he was told that the tsar found his "Order of Restoration" to be a fascinating but impractical concept. Thereupon he secretly founded his order anyway and converted it into a republican and "masonic" (subversive) society but retained its international and semimystical flavor.

The Russian-American Company, whose "chief protector," Count (and admiral) Nikolay Mordvinov, had been a member of the special committee, was much more sympathetic to Zavalishin's scheme. At Mordvinov's urging the company decided to adopt his proposals for reorganizing the colonial administration and rejuvenating agriculture in Russian California through free colonization by Russian peasants. The company asked Zavalishin to facilitate the implementation of these proposals by becoming manager of Ross Counter for two years and then governor of the colonies for five. However, the tsar refused to release him from his naval duties, for fear that his actions would provoke a conflict with Great Britain or the United States.

At this point the Decembrist revolt intervened to deprive Zavalishin of any audience. A year before this manifestation of disaffection in the imperial capital on the part of radical officers and intellectuals, he had been persuaded by the poet Kondraty Ryleyev, the company's chief clerk at its headquarters, to assist the "Northern Society," an underground political circle that had been formed in 1822 with the goal of abolishing autocracy and serfdom. Following the abortive coup d'état at the end of 1825, Zavalishin was arrested in Kazan Province. He was returned to St. Petersburg for trial and initially condemned to death, but his sentence was then reduced to hard labor in Siberia for life. In 1839 he was freed from hard labor and allowed to settle in Chita in Transbaikalia. There he continued to study and write, becoming an authority on Siberia. In 1856 he declined an amnesty from the new tsar, Alexander II, but seven years later was deported from Siberia for slandering the local administration. He spent the last thirty-five years of his life in Moscow, promoting popular education and scientific societies and writing copiously, including an account of his round-the-world voyage and a study of the Russian-American Company. When he died in early 1892 at the age of eighty-eight, he was known as the "last Decembrist," having outlived all of his fellow conspirators.

Dᴍɪᴛʀʏ Zᴀᴠᴀʟɪsʜɪɴ,[1] Aɴ Exᴄᴇʀᴘᴛ ғʀᴏᴍ ᴀ Jᴏᴜʀɴᴀʟ ᴏғ ᴀ Vɪsɪᴛ ᴛᴏ
Aʟᴛᴀ Cᴀʟɪғᴏʀɴɪᴀ ᴅᴜʀɪɴɢ ᴛʜᴇ Rᴏᴜɴᴅ-ᴛʜᴇ Wᴏʀʟᴅ Vᴏʏᴀɢᴇ ᴏғ ᴛʜᴇ
Fʀɪɢᴀᴛᴇ Kʀᴇɪsᴇʀ,[2] [Mᴏsᴄᴏᴡ?], 1 Dᴇᴄᴇᴍʙᴇʀ 1823–12 Jᴀɴᴜᴀʀʏ 1824
. . . .[3]

On 1 December [1823] we dropped anchor in San Francisco Bay not far from
the presidio (fortress) of the same name; at the anchorage we found the sloop
Apollon and two ships of the Russian-American Company, and within several
hours the *Ladoga* arrived, too. Thus, a considerable (for that time) Russian naval
force assembled in San Francisco Bay, for the Russian-American Company ships
had cannon, and the naval forces of neither England nor the United States were
represented by a single vessel. In fact, Russia then dominated the northern part
of the Great [Pacific] Ocean, but the time to reap [the] benefit of this position
was already being lost.

As my health had still not fully recovered, and meanwhile I had to occupy
myself with the buying of wheat and the getting of fresh provisions for the frigate, the next day a room was allotted to me in the house of the governor [i.e., the
commandant], who had become the president [i.e., the governor] of the province
and was moving to Monterey.[4] Because in these houses there are no glass windows, no wooden floors, and no stoves, our joiners and carpenters made window
frames and floors, and in place of a stove a spare copper fireplace from the frigate
was installed. The aristocracy of San Francisco liked all of this [improvement]
very much, and my room became a gathering place for the ladies and maidens of
the presidio, considerably constraining me and hampering my work.

In my articles "A Recollection of California" [actually, "California in 1824"][5]
and "The Case of the Colony of Ross," published in *Russky vestnik*,[6] I have already
mentioned many things relating to the political situation and social life of [Alta]
California, and therefore I intend to limit this account mainly to those circumstances that directly concern the frigate *Kreiser*.

To have any business then in California was extremely difficult because everything there was still in a primitive state, with respect to not only the Indians
but also the ruling Spaniards [Californios]. Notwithstanding the abundance of
wheat, it was impossible to get flour, even in an amount sufficient for preparing
at least fresh bread for the command; it was fortunate that I had brought a hand

[1]See Zavalishin, *Vospominaniya*, 66–77, 79–93, 93–103, and 103–14. Also see Mazour, "Dimitry Zavalishin,"
552–54.
[2]Zavalishin, "Krugosvetnoye plavanie fregata *Kreiser*," 210–17.
[3]Zavalishin's description of New Archangel and of the *Kreiser*'s voyage from there to San Francisco is
omitted here.
[4]Zavalishin is referring to Luis Argüello.
[5]See Zavalishin, "California in 1824."
[6]See Zavalishin, "Delo o kolonii."

millstone from Russia just for the purpose of milling on the frigate: the Spaniards did not have mills driven by water, wind, or horses or even hand mills, and every grain grower prepared a small amount of flour for himself for unleavened flatcakes [tortillas], grinding the grain with a stone on a slab, as we grind dyes.

The method of transporting purchased grain was also extremely laborious. Although part of it was bought at the nearest mission, the fields belonging to it and the farmstead where the granaries were found lay on the left [northern] side of the bay, and if we had had to transport the grain by land we would have had to travel more than a hundred verstas around the entire bay, and with the lack of vehicular roads and carts it would have been necessary to haul it [i.e., the grain] on packhorses. Meanwhile, for water transport, which was much closer and easier, the Spaniards had only clumsy barges of the most primitive construction that barely moved, and in this way for every round trip we had to spend twice or four times as much time as with a good longboat, but our longboat was constantly employed in other tasks for the frigate and we could not use it to transport wheat. And the Indians also had no means of transport whatever, such as could be found, for example, among the "Aleuts" and Koloshes [Tlingits] at Sitka. Nowhere had we ever seen river navigation, let alone ocean navigation, in such primitive condition, and this [state] was perhaps explained by the fact that San Francisco Bay is closed on all sides and so there is no necessity of struggling with the element of water.

We had seen a variety of savages in different situations, and all of those who had to strain their mental powers and their energies to struggle with the natural elements were able to invent various kinds of vessels in accordance with local conditions. The Koloshes have canoes [*baty*] that can accommodate a large number of people and that in contests with our rowing vessels are as fast as our best gigs and whaleboats; the "Aleuts" have excellent skin kayaks and umiaks that are equally capable of traveling the open sea or crossing the shallowest shoals; and the dugouts [*odnoderevki*] of the inhabitants of the islands of the Great Ocean [i.e., the Polynesians] are so skillfully constructed that they cannot be overturned (for this they position a small tree a certain distance from the boat and fasten it firmly crosswise to each end of the boat with lengths of wood, and this [outrigging] does not let the boat overturn because on the one hand it keeps the boat pressed to the water, and on the other hand the lengths of wood act as levers that lend enough weight to the small tree to keep the craft level; to haul loads they join two boats to form a common deck). But the Californian Indians have devised nothing better than two bound bundles of reeds [tule] that they fasten to themselves and, parting the bundles in the middle, wriggle into them and float thusly, submerging half of their bodies and employing a thick stick in place of an oar.

The slowness of the delivery of wheat was very inconvenient to us. We had to return to Sitka by March, when the herring fishery there drew several thousand savages and always created not a little danger to the colony; besides, it would not be possible for us to embark until all of the needed amount of wheat had been delivered to the frigate.

Regarding meat, however, there was no difficulty at all; it was always abundant and cheap. For a live bull we paid two Spanish piasters, which were strictly for the labor of catching it and bringing it to a spot where we had built a workshop. The owner kept only the hide for his own use, since hides then constituted California's sole item of export besides wheat. We issued a double ration of fresh meat daily to the command and, in addition, salted not a little meat for use at Sitka so as to conserve for the return voyage to Russia that corned beef that had been brought from Russia and prepared in such a way as to last three years; we also took some corned beef from the sloops *Apollon* and *Ladoga*, which had economized theirs considerably. We did not even buy game but killed it ourselves. Besides the daily hunts of the officers, every day we sent ashore a very skillful hunter, a sailor who bore the name "huntsman"; he was given two helpers, and every day they brought a whole cargo of the most varied game—geese, ducks, snipe, quail, and rabbits. In order to give an idea of the abundance of game, I can cite the following anecdote. One of the *Apollon's* officers, M[ikhail] K[arlovich] Kyukhelbeker, a very good and tolerant man, went hunting with his batman, a great knave who had, of course, to carry everything that his master shot. In a very short time the batman, seeing that he was already carrying a dozen and a half geese and that his master was continuing to hunt, suddenly fell to the ground and moaned, saying that he must have stumbled and could not walk because of a pain in his leg. The good master took the catch himself to carry and ordered him to walk slowly and lean on a stick that he [i.e., Kyukhelbeker] broke off a bush. Of course, the medical assistant who examined the batman's leg did not find even a trace of an injury, but the master did not want to believe him and confirmed that he [i.e., the batman] really had stepped awkwardly and stretched a tendon.

Fresh butter and milk were likewise abundant and were especially agreeable to those officers who liked to drink tea and coffee with milk and for whom the want of milk was a great hardship. Three times, it is true, we tried to bring cows onto the frigate, and each time during the first prolonged storm and strong rocking we lost them; at Sitka there was no milk, because for want of pasture it was impossible for the residents to keep cows, so that it was not until California that the frigate was able to enjoy milk for the first time since Tasmania. Of course, the hunters tried to substitute either condensed or powdered milk for fresh milk, but it was always very expensive and insufficient. In California milk was a commonplace beverage and was of excellent quality, owing to the superior grass; only cream was impossible to get from the inhabitants, who did not use it, and we had to skim it ourselves.

Because of the purchases of wheat, we had to travel throughout the northern part of California, at first on horseback to purchase it and then by water to transport it; thus did I visit all of the places that later became famous with the discovery of gold. I visited the missions of San Rafael and San Francisco Solano [Sonoma], the only ones built on the northern side of San Francisco Bay, the latter with the very aim of impeding the expansion of the Russian colony of Ross, which I visited on this occasion, too. I was also at San Pablo [Bay] and on the banks of the Sacramento River, where I proposed that a new Russian colony be established (it was here that gold was first found).[7] I was at San José and Santa Clara [Missions] repeatedly; I crossed [the Santa Cruz Mountains] to Santa Cruz [Mission] by the most difficult, dangerous, and desolate direct route; and I was at the Mariposa [River] and the canyons of the Calaveras [River]. I examined the abandoned silver mines, and I may say that after the discovery of gold, when much began to be written about California, for a long, long time I did not read the name of a single place where I had not set foot; in one day I made more than 150 verstas on horseback, and on one trip I traveled 600 verstas in four days.[*]

In the meantime, while I was spending so much time on travel, my comrades were not deprived of diversions, especially while the ships were still at San Francisco. There was no shortage of opportunities for festivities, because all holidays were repeated twice, not only because they were reckoned according to the Old Style [Julian calendar] among the Russians and the New Style [Gregorian calendar] among the Spaniards but also because the Spaniards had come to America from the east and we from the west, with the result that we differed by one day from them, so that when it was still Saturday to them, it was already Sunday to us, and on our Monday it was still only Sunday for the Spaniards. Before the celebrations the hunters could make merry two Sundays in a row, the Russian and the Spanish. It must be said, however, that our officers furnished the chief means of merrymaking for the Spaniards ashore; always there was our music, our wine and dessert, our plates and dishes, our servants, our cook. The Spaniards provided only the premises and ordinary victuals, which were nothing there, and they invited the female society. To this it must be added that the officers preferred

---

[*]The horses in California were excellent and were of Andalusian stock, which, as is well known, are derived from Arabian horses. For frequent changes while traveling I took three or four more horses than the number of riders.

---

[7]Actually, east of New Helvetia at Sutter's Mill on the site of the Indian village of Koloma on the American River, a left-bank tributary of the Sacramento, on 24 January 1848.

to have such festivities ashore because to arrange them on the frigate was very troublesome, given the necessity of bringing and returning guests, especially females, in our rowing vessels.

The sloops *Apollon* and *Ladoga,* whose sole purpose in stopping at San Francisco was the necessity of letting their commands rest and recuperate, were soon, of course, ready to leave, and on 12 January 1824 they set out on their return voyage to Russia. I cannot help recalling the honorable and sensitive behavior of our frigate's officers on that occasion. Knowing that our former senior lieutenant, K[----],[8] who had been transferred from the frigate, would be coming to delicately bid the frigate's officers farewell, all of them—in sight of the command that had demanded his removal—approached him to say goodbye, although few of them had not been seriously mistreated by him. None was himself personally and directly to blame for the clashes with him, having generally avoided dealings with him, but he had found the means of provoking conflict with us in various devious ways. It is true that he never dared to address me rudely or to interfere directly with my orders, knowing that I reported every day to Lazarev and would not fail to openly recount his disagreeableness; but I often had to take the part of the young officers and his subordinates and therefore not infrequently had also confronted him.[9]

It would be superfluous, of course, to go into a detailed description of California after what has occurred and been discovered there recently, but it should be said that the chief value and importance of California was even then already fully known and frequently proclaimed officially. The working of mineral wealth has its limits, and we see that not even thirty years have passed since the discovery of gold (whose existence, however, had long been known there),[10] and its extraction has decreased substantially, and other countries have already surpassed California in the amount and value of extracted minerals. But the superior climate, rich soil, and capital location on the Great Ocean, with one of the best ports in the world, constitute the unalterable and inalienable advantages of California, and from this [fact] naturally sprang the desire to expand our colony of Ross at least as far as the northern shore of San Francisco Bay and the Sacramento River, and to that extent it was then still possible. For that reason—keeping in mind such an expansion of our colony—I took advantage of my official travels throughout

---

[8]Probably Ivan Kupreyanov, then a lieutenant (since early 1820) on the *Kreiser* and later (1835–40) a governor of Russian America. The other possibility is Ivan Kadyan, also a lieutenant on the *Kreiser* but most likely junior to Kupreyanov.

[9]Zavalishin was also critical of the lieutenant in his memoirs, recalling that "Kupreyanov was not without abilities but with evil propensities and insufficient education" and adding that Kupreyanov was Lazarev's favorite and his informer (Zavalishin, *Vospominaniya,* 70).

[10]Zavalishin, as was his wont, is exaggerating here; the presence of gold was most likely suspected by a few individuals rather than generally known, and even then not for long.

California in order to make every possible inquiry and to collect the necessary information for reaching the said goal. It is well known that as a result of the legend preserved at the settlement of Ross about the places that I examined on the Sacramento River, the manager of the colony of Ross, Mr. Rotchev, who knew this legend, had been prompted to show the Swiss Sutter places on the Sacramento River that were suitable for the establishment of an agricultural colony [New Helvetia], and that it was precisely there that during the construction of a water mill traces of gold were found.[11] But its presence was known earlier, and it had even been secretly worked in California, as I have shown in the article comprising my reminiscences of California (see "California in 1824" in *Russky vestnik,* November 1865). Only security and laborers were not forthcoming, and the Franciscan friars, who held sway in California, did not tolerate foreigners, fearing an excessive influx of them and thus the loss of their power.

This fear was also the main reason why they stopped working the silver mines, which had been started under the Spanish government and stopped with the defection of Mexico from Spain, when California became completely defenseless, as was demonstrated by the attack of a freebooter [the insurgent Hipólito Bouchard], who pillaged Monterey [in 1818]. There also existed the opinion that the Jesuits, who had owned the missions before the Franciscan friars, mined gold surreptitiously and that this [mining] explained the richness of their churches, which was inexplicable in view of the lack of trade and of the possibility of making money from the province's other products.

It is known that at present the value of California's agricultural output has for a long time exceeded the value of its gold output,[12] and it was always possible to foresee this turnabout because the rich productivity of California's soil was even in our day already an indisputable fact that is now more glaringly evident than it was when the friars worked the land less perfectly. I myself saw at San Francisco Solano Mission that in place of a harrow they dragged a felled laurel tree over the fields. And what of it? Wheat yielded ten-fold, barley twenty-fold, and corn one hundred and twenty–fold [the seed]. For that reason when our government declined to make an effort to expand the colony of Ross, and the Russian-American Company wanted to assume the responsibility for doing so and proposed my assistance in the matter, in a note that I submitted at that time I advised the Board of Directors to exert every effort in grain growing and at the same time to caution some directors against rushing to search for valuable minerals (to which they were attracted by knowledge of the former mining of silver

---

[11]In fact, the first traces were discovered on the American River at the site of Sutter's sawmill.

[12]This assertion is questionable, although Zavalishin was writing three decades after the gold rush, by which time the heyday of gold mining had ended and farming had revived.

there), since this would readily attract a throng of adventurers (who were already rushing there), whom we would be powerless to restrain. Grain was already at that time in demand everywhere, but its production was insufficient even in California itself, which did not have its own trading vessels for hauling it. Needless to say, there was stock rearing at that time in California; the herds were so large that the owners did not keep count, and they determined the ownership of this or that herd according to the place where they grazed; dairying was quite unknown, and they kept only as many cows as were needed to give milk for domestic use.

With the declaration of Mexican independence, California became independent of Spain, but its personnel in government remained the same. After the ephemeral Emperor Agustín (Iturbide) was deposed, Mexico became a federal republic; in California the only change consisted of the fact that the former governor, Don Luis Argüello, was transformed into the president of the province of Upper, or New, California (Alta, or Nuevo, California). Only the friars, the leaders of the missions, felt the change in that with the cessation of dependence upon Spain aid from there also ceased; now they had to maintain the guardian soldiers, who likewise stopped receiving salaries from Spain. This [deprivation], however, induced the friars to engage even more in grain growing as their chief source of income and to slacken the overly frequent religious exercises of the Indians. The arrival of our frigate and two ships of the Russian-American Company to buy wheat afforded the missionaries unexpected revenue because while meat was very cheap, wheat, in view of our great need of it for the colonies, was sold to us very dearly by the missionaries—about four paper rubles per pud. Apart from the generally small output, the shortage of wheat at that time stemmed partly from its export to Peru, for which a small American cutter was hired. It was more to our disadvantage than anyone else's to buy wheat at this price, because the supply of a large amount required hard cash, whereas part of the [grain] cargos of the Russian-American Company's ships was bought for goods, and what the company did pay in money it soon recouped with interest because—given the gaining of money by everybody, the issuing of salaries to everybody, and the generosity of our officers—it sold all of the goods that it had brought.

Two places were allotted for the work of the frigate: one opposite the frigate's anchorage, where workshops were established and the chronometers were checked, and the other on the northern side of San Francisco Bay, where firewood was cut, charcoal was made, seamarks were made, and linen was washed.

Upon the completion of all of the work the sailors had to be given a rest in order to prepare for a monotonous anchorage of a whole year, and perhaps longer, at Sitka if they were not relieved or for some reason mail did not arrive from Okhotsk and orders to return were not received. The enormous number of horses and the cheapness of hiring them gave the sailors the opportunity of trying an unknown or long-forgotten pleasure—riding on horseback. The Spaniard here does not take a step on foot; having taken his seat on a horse, he reluctantly dismounts, so that not infrequently he even rides into a room (through a high—by custom—doorway) in order to request something.[13] Therefore, every Spaniard in the presidio has at home a great many horses that he exchanges in his herd. At the landing all of the officers had saddled horses always at the ready day and night, besides some for special dispatches. For the sailors, however, the chief pleasure consisted of the ride itself, although various adventures that befell them served as a source of merriment and endless storytelling.

Before our departure we were visited by the governor of the province and the head of the missionaries, the Father President (Padre Presidente), as he is called. The latter's visit caused me a lot of trouble. Our hiermonk ought to have conversed with him, but he was an uneducated man from the family of a Cossack captain in the Don Army who retained an old liking of horses but was not at all versed in theology, and against my will I acted as an intermediary between them in conversations. Imagine my difficulty when the Father President began to ask our hiermonk questions about the Graeco-Russian [Russian Orthodox] Church, about dogma, rites, and the position of the clergy, and about the morals of the people and our hiermonk asked him only about horses and everything concerning them. To satisfy both of them I had to write both the questions and the answers. The sailors, too, almost put us in difficulty. They organized a theatrical performance for the governor and began to act some sort of disgusting [?][14] play in which the protagonists were a pope and a deacon uttering a very indecent ektenia.[15] It was just as well that our doctor sensed [the satirical intention] and told the Father President that it was a medieval mystery play, but the play ended, of course, after the first act.

Understandably, the liveliness that the presence of our ships—especially our frigate with its large number of officers and its music—brought to the little society of San Francisco's residents caused it [i.e., the society] to part from us with difficulty. The constant pleasure and benefits that we afforded them and the generosity of the officers, who rewarded every paltry service, made us the most desirable guests of the Spaniards continually and everywhere, and for that

---

[13]In a similar vein, two decades later newcomer John Bidwell wrote, "It is a proverb here (and I find a pretty true one) that a Spaniard will not do anything which he cannot do on horseback . . . for they did almost everything on horseback"; he added, "I doubt if their horsemanship is surpassed by the Cossacks of Tartary" (Gillis and Magliari, *John Bidwell and California*, 92).

[14]The original has the apparently concocted adjective *pregadky,* which may mean "disgusting" (from *pre* ["very"] and *gadky* ["vile"]).

[15]A part of the Orthodox liturgy comprising versicles and responses.

reason they saw us off with genuine tears and reminded us afterwards with letters. The Indians liked us no less—for our gentle treatment of them, for our
presents (which we gave to their children), and for our intercession to save them
from punishment, and for a long, long time we dreamt that we would come to
free them from the power of the Spaniards. The leader of one independent tribe,
who gave me a "chief's belt" as a symbol of his rank, said that if only we were to
expand our colony to the north [*sic:* south?], he with his whole tribe would relo-
cate on our territory; and the outlaw Pomponio[16] did not bother me, although I
was accompanied by an important Spaniard (who was hated by him) while we
were twice found in the most dangerous place in sight of the hidden band of this
brave Indian.

It was not without regret that we left California, where we had found a hearty
welcome, rest, an abundance of everything that we needed, and pleasure. After
celebrating Christmas and the New Year twice (according to the Russian and the
Catholic reckonings) and bidding a sincere farewell to the residents for wishing
us a safe voyage and a return to them, we sailed from San Francisco Bay; for a
long time we were able with the telescope to see all of our acquaintances among
the populace, which had assembled on the southern point of the entrance to the
bay in order to see us off as long as possible. Our return passage to Sitka was quite
safe and presented nothing remarkable.

. . . .[17]

---

[16]Pomponio was a runaway neophyte from San Rafael Mission who after four years of marauding was
captured and executed in early 1824 (see Brown, "Pomponio's World," 217–34).

[17]Zavalishin's description of events at New Archangel during his absence is omitted here.

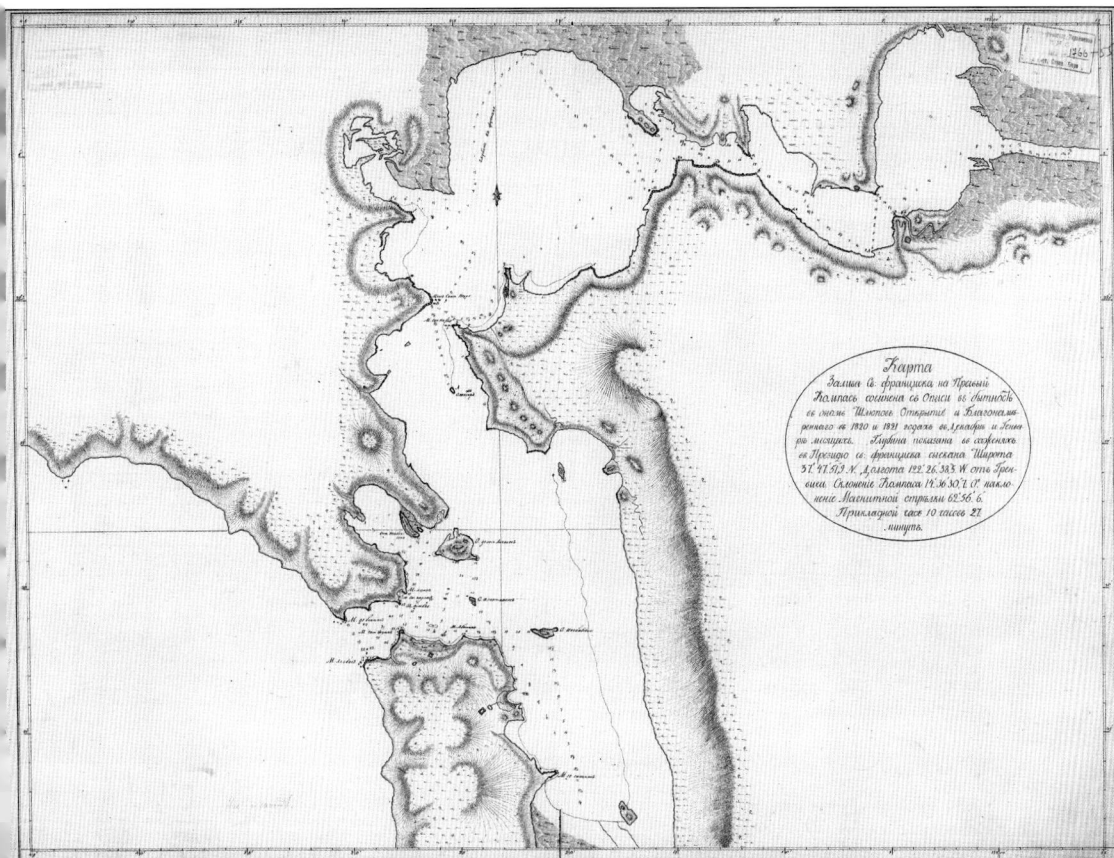

Anonymous, *A Map of San Francisco Bay*, 1820–21, ink. *Courtesy of the Russian State Naval Archive, St. Petersburg, f. 1,331, op. 4, d. 189.* The caption adds, "Composed from notes made during the stay of the Sloops *Otkrytie* and *Blagonamerenny* in 1820 and 1821 in the months of December and January. Depths shown in sazhens."

(*Above*) Mikhail Tikhanov, [*Coast Miwok*] *Inhabitants of Rumyantsev* [*Bodega*] *Bay in New Albion*, 1818, watercolor and pencil. *Courtesy of the Scientific Research Museum of the Russian Academy of Fine Arts, St. Petersburg, no. P-2090.* The caption adds, "The woman is pounding kernels plucked from wild rye." Tikhanov was the artist aboard the three-masted sloop-of-war *Kamchatka*, which is visible through the dwelling's entrance.

(*Opposite, top*) Mikhail Tikhanov, *A* [*Coast Miwok*] *Inhabitant of California by the Name of Baltha-zar*, Port Rumyantsev (Bodega Bay), 1818, watercolor and pencil. *Courtesy of the Scientific Research Museum of the Russian Academy of Fine Arts, St. Petersburg, no. P-2096.*

(*Opposite, bottom*) Mikhail Tikhanov, *A* [*Coast Miwok*] *Inhabitant of Rumyantsev* [*Bodega*] *Bay in New Albion*, 1818, watercolor and pencil. *Courtesy of the Scientific Research Museum of the Russian Academy of Fine Arts, St. Petersburg, no. P-2097.*

Индѣйцы Новаго Альіона

(*Above*) Louis Choris, *Indians of New Albion*, 1818, sepia. From [Kotzebue], *Puteshestvie v Yuzhny okean*, facing p. 12. *Courtesy of the Alaska and Polar Regions Collections, Rasmuson Library, University of Alaska–Fairbanks.*

(*Opposite, top*) Louis Choris, *Jeu des habitan[t]s de Californie*, watercolor. From Choris, *Voyage pittoresque*, plate IV. *Courtesy of the Alaska and Polar Regions Collections, Rasmuson Library, University of Alaska–Fairbanks.*

(*Opposite, bottom*) Louis Choris, *Habitants de Californie*, 1818, watercolor. From Choris, *Voyage pittoresque*, plate VII. *Courtesy of the Alaska and Polar Regions Collections, Rasmuson Library, University of Alaska–Fairbanks.*

Jeu des Habitans de Californie.

Habitants de Californie.

Bateau du port de S.ⁿ Francisco.

(*Above*) Louis Choris, *Bateau du port de San Francisco,* 1818, watercolor. From Choris, *Voyage pittoresque,* plate X. *Courtesy of the Alaska and Polar Regions Collections, Rasmuson Library, University of Alaska–Fairbanks.*

(*Opposite, top*) Louis Choris, *Canis ochropus* [*latrans*] *(Coyote),* 1818, watercolor. From Eschscholtz, *Zoologischer Atlas,* plate XI. *Courtesy of the Alaska and Polar Regions Collections, Rasmuson Library, University of Alaska–Fairbanks.*

(*Opposite, bottom*) Louis Choris, *Jeune lion marin de la Californie,* 1818, watercolor. From Choris, *Voyage pittoresque,* plate XI. *Courtesy of the Alaska and Polar Regions Collections, Rasmuson Library, University of Alaska–Fairbanks.*

Canis ochropus.

Prof.V. Guimpel sc.

Lith. de Langlumé

Dess. et lith. par Choris

Jeune lion marin de la Californie

Ilya Voznesensky, *An Indian Vaquero of New Albion*, 1841, pencil drawing. *Courtesy of the Peter the Great Museum of Anthropology and Ethnology (Kunstkamera), St. Petersburg, catalogue no. 1142-4.*

Ilya Voznesensky, *The Spaniard [Californio] Don Garcia in National Costume*, 1841, pencil drawing. *Courtesy of the Peter the Great Museum of Anthropology and Ethnography (Kunstkamera), St. Petersburg, catalogue no. 1142-31.*

DOCUMENT 16

Dmitry Zavalishin, "[Alta] California in 1824"

DMITRY ZAVALISHIN, "CALIFORNIA IN 1824,"[1] [MOSCOW?],
[FIRST HALF OF THE 1860s?]

Part I

In early 1824 several sailors, mostly musicians, deserted the frigate *Kreiser* in San Francisco Bay in California. There were some grounds for suspecting that the desertions had not occurred without the connivance of the Franciscan friars who were in charge of the missions and who had long been in sore need of musicians. Capture of the deserters was very difficult because with the assistance of the Spaniards [Californios], especially the heads of the missions, the deserters were easily concealed somewhere nearby until an opportunity arose to send them farther away. Correspondence with the local authorities would evidently have resulted in a loss of time and only have made it still easier for the deserters to hide themselves. So the famous commander of the frigate, Mikhail Petrovich Lazarev (later an admiral and the commander of the Black Sea Fleet), decided to act on his own and to take forthwith decisive measures for quickly capturing the deserters. He entrusted me with this mission. For various reasons a plan that I had suggested was adopted; it involved the immediate dispatch at night of an armed party to Mission San Francisco, following a route such that nobody would meet us and warn the mission of our coming. [On the one hand,] after having taken the head of the mission unawares and shown him the basis of our suspicion of collusion by the missionaries in the desertion of the musicians, I hoped to persuade him to clear himself by giving me immediate and active assistance in the capture of the deserters, promising in that event to drop the matter completely if the deserters were to admit complicity on the part of any Californios.

---

[1] *Russky vestnik* [Russian herald] 60 (1865): 322–68. This translation was first published in *Southern California Quarterly* 55, no. 4 (Winter 1973): 369–412. It has been slightly revised here.

I wanted to add that in case the deserters were captured solely as a result of my orders and were to make the same admission, the head of the mission would be left to have only himself to blame for the unpleasant consequences of the affair. On the other hand, in appearing at the nearest mission without delay I hoped to intercept the deserters, who could not have gone far anyway, since their desertion had occurred only the previous evening. The route that I chose was very difficult; it mostly followed damp sand exposed along the beach by the outgoing tide. But our party spared no effort, not even stopping for a moment's rest, and before dawn, hardly able to distinguish nearby objects, we entered Mission San Francisco and approached the gates of the main building. However much we had tried to proceed quietly, some noise from the passage of an armed party was unavoidable. As a result of this noise—and perhaps quite accidentally—only when we passed the *casa** of the sergeant, who commanded a detachment of Californio soldiers guarding the mission, was the window opened and did this sergeant, whom I knew well and liked, show himself. I had been coming to the mission almost daily, partly to study Spanish with the head of the mission, and as I passed his house the friendly sergeant never failed to exchange greetings and a few words with me, and sometimes he persuaded me to drink some buttermilk without dismounting. Having now seen me entering the mission with an armed party and myself armed from head to foot (there were no revolvers then, and I had perforce taken two pairs of pistols), he was dumbfounded with surprise, and the only words that he could utter were "*Ajá! Don Demetrio!*" Then the window slammed shut. Meanwhile, we approached the mission's main building. I ordered a gentle knock on the gates; a commotion was heard inside, but there was no answer. We knocked again; a side window opened slightly, but then it slammed shut. Running was heard, but there was no reply to my request for admittance, and a dead silence ensued. Then we began to knock loudly at the gates with our gunstocks. This time the window was opened wide, and the head of the mission's leader, the fanatical Father Tomás (Father Foma) [Esténaga] appeared. His face, minus the usual sternness and seeming anger, expressed the greatest degree of amazement and indignation. "*¿Qué quieres hombre?*" (literally, "What do you want, mister?"—a familiar expression corresponding to our "*Chto ugodno?*" ["What can I do for you?"]), he shouted in a voice expressing vexation but at the same time something like tender reproach, as it were, for he liked me very much. Not hearing my answer, he gave vent to a whole stream of personal reproofs— that I had deceived him for so long, with him believing that the conjunction of

---

*Casa in Spanish means a house in general, although the term "house" was not very suited to the mission structures, which corresponded more to simple cob houses [crude cottages made of clay, gravel, and straw in southwestern England].

such a number of Russian ships in San Francisco Bay[2] was accidental and that we did not have the slightest intention of taking California by force, whereas my present appearance with an armed party finally betrayed our long-held design, etc., etc. It cost me much effort to stem his swift flow of words and to convince him that I had no intention whatever of making him a martyr or giving him an opportunity for heroic resistance (he spoke rashly to me of martyrdom and resistance in the manner of Saragossa,[3] which was still well remembered then, and the like). I declared that it was only necessary to render me speedy assistance in the capture of the runaway musicians if he wanted to clear himself of suspicion of complicity in their desertion and even, perhaps, of inducement.

I added that if the deserters, who were known to have taken firearms, were to offer armed resistance* and it became necessary to use force, then I would shoulder [the responsibility for] everything myself so as not to expose the Californios to danger. I asked only that I now be given some chocolate** to drink and that my men be fed and allotted a place where they could rest quietly (not the place that he had given us once in order to make us agree that there is a purgatory*). I promised to pay all of the expenses. Although my words greatly annoyed him and evidently affected him because of the ready sureness I exhibited about the participation of the Californios in the desertion, he nevertheless reassured himself of the principal but imaginary danger and, although not much in favor of

---

*In another case during my circuit of California a runaway sailor from a previous expedition who was being hidden by the Californios shot at me when I encountered him by chance on a trip to a rancho on the Sacramento River belonging to Mission San José at a spot where he had not at all expected to meet me; I demanded that he follow me, and I chased him when he decided to flee.

**This was the only drink in use there that was very good in quality and that was well prepared, whereas coffee and tea were very badly made.

*This refers to an incident when, after a heated argument with him about purgatory, Father Tomás allotted us (me and the late Nakhimov and Butenev, who accompanied me by rowboat to Rancho San Pablo for the transport of wheat that I had bought) a room for the night that was filled to an incredible degree with certain insects [fleas?], and having locked the door with a key, he did not want to release us until we had agreed that there was a purgatory, which obliged us, of course, to force the door. [JRG: The Crimean War hero Pavel Stepanovich Nakhimov (1800–1855) had been serving in the Baltic Sea Fleet when he was assigned to the *Kreiser* as a midshipman. Upon his return to Russia he rejoined the Baltic Sea Fleet, and in 1834, right after the outbreak of the Crimean War, by then a vice admiral, he commanded the squadron that destroyed the Turkish fleet at Sinope, the last major engagement between sailing vessels. In 1854 he was put in charge of the defense of Sevastopol, where he was mortally wounded. See Grinëv, *Kto yest kto,* 370; and Pierce, *Russian America,* 375. Ivan Petrovich Butenev (1802–1836) was a midshipman on the *Kreiser.* After his return to Russia he served with distinction in the Baltic Sea Fleet; at the Battle of Navarino (1827) in the Peloponnesus against the joint Turkish-Egyptian fleet he lost his right arm. He was promoted to the rank of captain, second class in 1834. See Grinëv, *Kto yest kto,* 82–83.]

---

[2]The sloops *Apollon* and *Ladoga* and the Russian-American Company's *Baikal* and *Kyakhta,* besides the frigate *Kreiser.* Little wonder that the Californios were apprehensive.

[3]The Aragonese city of Saragossa (Sp., Zaragoza) in northeastern Spain had heroically resisted two French sieges in 1808 and 1809, commemorated in the "The Maid of Saragossa" in Lord Byron's *Childe Harold.*

capturing the musicians, became very compliant about everything else, having rid himself of the fear of a forcible seizure of California by us.

It was clear that he had tried to trick me and that he could easily catch the deserters, whom he probably had [concealed] somewhere nearby, certainly not far away. He now ordered the assembling of all available *vaqueros*,** i.e., horsemen, and having whispered something to them and his majordomo (*mayordomo*— properly speaking, a steward who supervises housekeeping at the mission), he issued a loud order in my presence to ride in different directions—in one direction to seek the deserters and in another direction to the nearest *aldea* (village) to announce the desertion, informing all herdsmen encountered on the way. The deserters, of course, were soon found and delivered to us.

I relate this story at the beginning of my article on the condition of California in 1824 in order to indicate our relations then with the Californios. The following story will show how we were regarded by the Indians, who together with the Californios formed the two main groups of California's population at that time.

Once in the presidio (fortress) of San Francisco I and my late friend, Feopemt Lutkovsky,***[4] passed the prison, where the Indian Pomponio, who had terrorized all of California before our arrival, was then held under close guard in dreadful irons; he was one of those people who are called marauders (as the Californios call him) by conquerors but who in the eyes of the conquered people or tribe are important as national heroes in the manner of Robin Hood and the like. This sympathy on the part of the population explained Pomponio's successes and the difficulty of catching him, for he had connections everywhere and obtained news and warnings from every quarter. When he was finally confronted with the Indians who had lived with him in one of the missions and who therefore must have known him well, none of them indicated that they knew him; all of them stubbornly disavowed him and denied that he was the real Pomponio. The fantastic notion that it was impossible to capture Pomponio could, of course, have contributed to this [attitude], but it is more likely that the main motive for

---

**"Vaquero" comes from the Spanish word *vaca*—"cow." These vaqueros were chosen from converted Indians, mostly those born on the missions who spoke Spanish well. Although their main occupation was guarding the herds, they were also important as mission police, so to speak, being considered the most trustworthy and faithful [of the neophytes], and in this capacity they were hated by the [other] Indians as executors of sentences, instruments of their punishment and coercion, and spies for the missionaries.

***The Californios called us two volumes of the same book; besides myself, he alone among all of the officers spoke Spanish fairly well.

---

[4]Feopemt Stepanovich Lutkovsky (1803–52), who had also voyaged around the world on the *Kamchatka*, was a midshipman on the *Apollon*. Upon his return to Russia he served with distinction in both the Baltic Sea and Black Sea Fleets, taking part in a total of twenty-seven naval campaigns in thirty-four years of service. He retired as a rear admiral. See Grinëv, *Kto yest kto*, 316.

their disavowal was an unwillingness to betray him by revealing their relations with him. I should say that during my initial travels throughout California I was often threatened by the danger of falling into Pomponio's hands; indeed, there were occasions when not one Californio dared to accompany me anywhere Pomponio might be hiding, and I had to travel to those places alone, guided only by the general directions that had been given to me. There were even occasions when because of a liking for me they [i.e., the Californios] simply obstructed me and hid the horses. It was impossible for me, however, to heed such danger, since on account of my duties and the continual missions that the head of the expedition assigned to me, I could not be absent long from the frigate, and I had received permission from Lazarev to travel always with the least delay. In order to save time I almost always had to lessen the distances by taking the shortest but most dangerous and uncomfortable routes; for example, on the direct road to Santa Cruz, which shortened the journey by a dozen miles, we had to crawl along a jagged mountain ridge, straddling it with a precipice on either side, having let the horses go ahead on their own. But to return to the aforementioned event—when we passed the prison where Pomponio was held, as I said before, he was sitting by the door on the outside, where he was allowed to warm himself in the sun (the sole source of heat in the prison even in winter, which, of course, is generally not bad in California, although it is noticeable in a dwelling without a stove in San Francisco, where the thermometer approaches the freezing point). Pomponio greeted us politely and affably, and a minute later one of the guarding soldiers overtook us and told me that Pomponio wanted to ask me something. Knowing that it was the custom among the prisoners to request rather than beg a cigarette or a cigar, I said that I did not smoke and therefore did not carry such things; but as Lutkovsky had found a cigar, we were glad to have an opportunity to see Pomponio more closely and to talk to him, so we returned and approached him, and my companion gave him the cigar. He took it and thanked us in clear Spanish but said that he had not called us for that. "I wanted to talk to you, Don Demetrio!" he said to me. "I wanted to say to you: do you know me? Why, twice you were within my grasp. What a temptation it was! And what made me want to kill that Californio, José de la Cruz, who was your guide then? Ah! I would have destroyed all of them. But because of you I spared him!" Thereupon he related in detail all of the circumstances of one such occasion, namely, during my passage along a road that had been abandoned for a dozen years and that the family of this José de la Cruz, my guide, could barely recall having been passable. Pomponio added that when José and I descended to the bottom of a gully to drink from a stream flowing there and, alighting from the horses, sat under a huge sequoia and discussed the unusual size and straightness of the California pine [redwood], he was several steps from us behind some bushes, so that he heard our conversation. He said that at first he wanted to show himself and talk to me about what interested him the most, but he was afraid that we would have misunderstood and fired and then his gang, having been aroused, would have come running and attacked us before the misunderstanding had been explained. "But why," I asked him, "did you spare me, who simply fell into your hands, when, as is well known, you never spare anybody?" "Because you alone have always been affectionate and kind to the poor Indians; why, you are fairly well known everywhere, including the missions and rancherías. But, in addition, we know that you have come to take this land from the accursed Californios and to free the poor Indians! Then the Indians will be all right!"

The foregoing incidents typified our relations with the Californios and the Indians, however impossible it is to attest the relative situation of California and Russia's possessions in America at that time. On the one hand, the occupation of California by the Russians, which was proposed by the inhabitants of that province themselves, seemed very natural and very feasible to those most concerned. It only remained to find a form of agreement that would firmly link Russia's interests with the interests and desires of the population and thereby form a strong force from the very beginning. I hoped to resolve this question very simply by talking to both sides without misreading or exaggerating the reasonable desire for mutual benefit and fairness. I add that a good knowledge of Spanish, and some Latin, made me generally necessary as an intermediary in all relations with the inhabitants, and supervision of the expedition's stores—in accordance with my official duties and missions—put me in direct contact with all classes of California's population. I also had access to a domestic circle of many families, and I was accepted as a kinsman in the home of the sister of the governor of the province.[5] On the other hand, because of my official assignments and my own wishes I succeeded in traveling throughout much of California and becoming personally acquainted with the peculiarities of the country and the position of places, so that I could justifiably think that hardly anyone then could have known California's situation or foreseen its future better than I.

Part II

California was not one of those possessions of Spain that she considered important on political grounds or that she valued for material benefits. In California the Spaniards acted solely "for the greater glory of God" (*ad majorem gloriam Dei*), as they had earlier in Paraguay. Intending only to convert the pagan Indians

---

[5]Presumably Governor Luis Antonio Argüello and his youngest sister, Dolores.

to Catholicism, the Spaniards cared little about the welfare of the country, which had been placed by nature in the most favorable conditions.

First the Jesuits and then the Franciscan friars were the chief figures in California;[6] hence, they were not only predominantly but also exceptionally important. A military force was stationed there solely for the maintenance of their activities by force in case they did not have to or want to use persuasion. It [i.e., the army] could not have had any other purpose, owing to both its general negligibility and its dispersal over a vast area. I mentioned this in 1824 to the Californios themselves, and experience proved me quite right when Monterey (Montreal), the chief town in Upper, or New, California, was sacked by a few pirates several years in a row, despite the fact that it was the residence of the province's governor. The military force was situated in four presidios, which, however, in no way deserved the name fortresses, as others have sometimes incorrectly called them. The northernmost presidio on San Francisco Bay was the most important politically and commercially because that bay was larger than all of the other places frequented by foreign ships. To the south Monterey served as the province's seat of government; the two remaining ones were called Santa Bárbara and San Diego. In its original form a presidio comprised a large, quadrangular, one-story building of unfired brick [adobe] whose outside was blank and hence had to be replaced by a wall or rampart to form the main defense against the attacks of the savages. Inside, around the entire building, ran a gallery or ledge that connected all of the quarters. In front of the single gate on the inside stood two cannons; in San Francisco's presidio there was a special commander of this artillery. He also commanded the battery that had been erected on a promontory at the entrance to the bay, and ships had to pass under its line of fire. In the event of danger, livestock and fowl were driven into the spacious interior courtyard, and all belongings were brought there, since in such cases the residents of all of the surrounding settlements and missions withdrew to the presidio. But as the danger of attack from the savages diminished or, at least, came to affect only the more remote missions, they began to permit outside buildings at the presidios, and as a result it became necessary to make passageways through the heretofore blank outer wall. Lately even Russian expeditions have had bakeries attached to the outer wall for the baking of both fresh bread and extra rusks for a cruise. This is how San Francisco's presidio became a rather formless pile of half-ruined dwellings, sheds, storehouses, and other structures. The floors, of course, were everywhere of stone or dirt, and not only stoves but also fireplaces were lacking in the living quarters. Whatever had to be boiled or fried was prepared in the

---

[6]Zavalishin is oversimplifying here; the Jesuits operated in Baja California only (until they were expelled and replaced by the Dominicans) and the Franciscans in Alta California only.

open air, mostly on fired bricks; they warmed themselves against the cold air over hot coals in pots or braziers. There was no glass in the windows; some people had only grating in their windows. The entry doors to some compartments (for example, to the governor's room) were so large that one passed from the interior courtyard to the outside through the wall on horseback. Because my duties required permanent quarters ashore where all who had to do business with me could present themselves, one room in the governor's residence was renovated for me by our frigate's craftsmen in the European style with a wooden floor, glass-paned windows, and European-style furniture. A spare copper hearth from the frigate was installed in it. During my off-duty hours this room became a meeting place for female company, who came there with work. Generally the governor's room was occupied after his move to Monterey (he was formerly the commandant of San Francisco) by his married sister, who lived here with her husband and daughter, and furthermore it served for the balls that the Russian officers gave for Californian society. I mention all of this [improvement] in order to show that then the local residents knew very well how to appreciate the comforts that were provided by another way of life but that they themselves had no chance or means of providing. This [appreciation] was not the only reason why they favored me with their plans for the disposition of California's future. In their [i.e., the plans'] fulfilment they saw the sole possibility of achieving much that was precious and desirable without, however, paying such a high price as they later had to pay the Americans, about whom I will warn in due course, as we will see below.

Another type of settlement in California was the mission, which served the main object pursued by Spain in this land and where the converted Indians lived, just as it had earlier in Paraguay and still does in many former Spanish and Portuguese possessions in America; but the method of converting the Indians to Christianity in California differed considerably from that of Paraguay and other provinces and countries. In California there was really no preaching; the savage Indians were conscripted. The captives were put in irons, forcibly baptized, and kept in irons until they had been tamed. This [coercion] explains the peculiar construction and layout of the missions. In these respects they naturally had in mind primarily security against outside attacks by hostile Indians, whose closest relatives had been abducted, and subjection of the captured Indians. The main building, which served as a citadel, as it were, was mostly on the northern side, occupying one side of a large square [plaza] whose other three sides constituted the compact quarters of the Indians, with the outside wall blank, as in the presidios. The main building was also a closed square, to which a passage led through the building itself with large gates. The main front wall, which faced the interior of the large square that formed the entire mission, that is to say, faced the quarters of the Indians, contained a church and the quarters of the friars, who managed the mission; only one of their rooms had a window on the outer wall. In the other three sides of the main building, which was not quite correctly termed a monastery, there were compartments for all boys and girls of more than 6 or 7 years of age (who were rarely abandoned by their parents before the age of 8), converted but untrusted Indians, and unconverted Indians, and, in addition, workshops, storerooms, etc. Trustworthy Indians, or those whose children were hostages, lived in outside buildings. Some houses, or *casas,* served as quarters for the soldiers who guarded the mission.

The third type of settlement was the so-called *aldea;* in form and type of construction it was simply a small village, although it sometimes bore the grand name of town, as, for example, Los Angeles, San José, and others (wherefore it was amusing to me during the war between the United States and Mexico in 1846–1847 to read, for instance, that the Americans had taken such and such a town in California, whereas basically the fact was that a party of soldiers or even hunters—20 men—had entered a village of several houses that could not even have been defended against a dozen ordinary hunters armed with good rifles!). Retired soldiers were settled in these aldeas. Naturally the dispatch of soldiers from Spain must have been incredibly expensive, especially since married ones were requested and received—a condition that the missionaries particularly demanded, fearing that otherwise the soldiers would be their opponents rather than their supporters in their dealings with the Indians. With this in mind the missionaries encouraged early marriages among the Spaniards (males from 16 years and females from 13 years of age). Ships from Spain reached Acapulco in nine or ten months, no earlier, and overland communication from Mexico was not only more difficult but also quite unthinkable for a family. The route to California went via Sonora, through which there was almost no passage whatever, even for small military parties. For this reason the Spanish government tried all kinds of different privileges to encourage servicemen to remain in California and become settled, so that it would be possible to recruit from subsequent generations for military service, which, however, was generally advantageous under Spanish rule because for service, which was relatively light, even an ordinary private received [annually] from 140 to 160 Spanish piasters, or from 180 to 210 of our silver rubles.

There was another small settlement like a farm or farmstead with fields; it had huge storehouses, where grain, hides, wool, etc. were stored. The living quarters, for both guards and temporary visitors, were arranged in the storehouses themselves, and in case of a large visitation the guests slept unceremoniously on piles of grain spread in separate heaps, since there were no bins whatever for storing grain. Horses were put in the same storehouses; here they lit fires and actual bonfires, both for cooking food and warming the night [air] during the cool season.

Two or three trustworthy Indian families usually lived beside the storehouses. This farm was called a *rancho;* such was the Rancho San Pablo, which belonged to Mission San Francisco and which lay on the north[east]ern side of the bay of the same name. All of these settlements, which in themselves were insignificant (there were about 1,000 people in the missions and about 500 in the presidios), were scattered over a vast area in Upper California. Mission Santa Clara, for example, was 90 verstas distant from Mission San Francisco, with only one rancho about halfway between them.

Regarding the natives, or so-called Indians (*Indianos* [*sic:* Indios]),[7] being neither warlike nor united for resistance they lived in separate huts, and only recently have they grouped several huts together. These Indian settlements are called *rancherías;* however, they were not permanent habitations. Sometimes they were moved from one place to another for various fortuitous reasons. The huts were made mostly from rushes [tule].

The sedentary population of California was very small. In Upper, or New (*Alta o Nueva*), California the highest estimate has never exceeded 10,000 by any exaggeration; others have lowered this to 6,000. Naturally this sedentary population consisted of converted Indians living in the missions and Californios. Regarding the free Indians, it was impossible to determine their number, and it was not attempted; in any case they could not have been numerous. No foreigners were allowed to settle in California, not even those who agreed to adopt Catholicism.[8]

Compared with the other Indians of North America glorified in the novels of [James Fenimore] Cooper and other writers, California's Indians were a meek lot. Of course, they were sometimes driven to ferocity by brutal treatment, and then they committed atrocities on Californios who fell into their hands, especially missionaries; but as among other tribes, there was some severity and fierceness in their mutual relations. Undoubtedly with good treatment and proper upbringing they were capable of development; this was proven by numerous examples in the missions. Even in the wild state they displayed remarkable abilities in many respects. They made many artistic and very durable articles. Their root baskets and hats were waterproof and combined unusual lightness and durability with resilience; head ornaments, belts, the outsides of baskets, and other articles, which were minutely decorated with the different and multicolored feathers of local birds, were splendid examples of art and patience. They gave me a belt* that by

---

*It goes without saying that the usual gifts from savages, if we consider their material value, cost much more than purchases from them, since it was necessary to give presents in return; but there were some things that they would not sell for any price.

---

[7]*Indianos* were Spaniards who had come to the New World and then gone back to Spain.

[8]This is an overgeneralization; some exceptions were made.

tradition had been passed from generation to generation in one tribe from one chief to the next as one of the tokens of their esteem, and it had not lost any of its freshness, despite long use. Regarding weapons, their bow, strung with sinew, was usually so taut that the strongest among us could not pull it without practice and skill. Their arrows were made from rushes with stone heads daubed with poison; wounds from them, regardless of the poison, were very dangerous, for they had a rough finish and a jagged edge. In only one occupation were the Indians completely unskillful. Nowhere, even among wild tribes, have I encountered such an infantile state of boating as among the Californian Indians; they had not even achieved the invention of the raft. At a time when the Kolyuzhes, or Koloshes, in our colonies had dugout canoes whose speed was not inferior to that of the best rowboats or even whaleboats and gigs of English construction, and the "Aleuts" even plied the ocean in their kayaks and boats, or skin umiaks, the Californian Indians had not devised any other means of navigation than two bundles of rushes tied end to end. Parting the middle, a man squeezed between them, keeping the lower part of his body below water, and navigated with a paddle or short oar like a spade. These rush bundles supported him in the water and were his boat or raft.

The Indians living at the missions, especially those who had been born and raised there, were quite different. If most of them, dispirited by a rather inquisitorial political system of upbringing, proved to be obtuse, as if having been deprived of natural and even common sense and having lost the good qualities of savages and at the same time not having adopted the good qualities of the Californios, then sometimes there emerged among them both brave and clever vaqueros devoted to the missionaries and fierce enemies of the Californios in the manner of the courageous and resourceful Pomponio. The runaways were all the more dangerous in that they spoke Spanish well, were familiar with all Spanish ways and with all of the circumstances of the missions, and maintained secret connections and relations (especially through the women) with those living in the missions. Nevertheless, experience showed that the devotion of the vaqueros was sometimes only a clever ruse; during an uprising at Mission Santa Cruz the missionaries were betrayed by the vaqueros and were put to agonizing deaths. One cannot be surprised by such treachery; the Jesuits' inquisitorial political system of upbringing bore the same fruit here that it did everywhere.[9] The suppression of all free, independent, candid thinking, feeling, and action by incessant exhortation and observation, under the pretense of not letting anything evil become established in a person, drove all mental powers inward, gave rise to dissembling and pretending, and naturally resulted in either the complete stifling of inner strength or the occurrence of a more dangerous and more

[9]In fact, the Jesuits did not missionize in Alta California.

violent outburst, as, for example, the uprising in which the head of Mission Santa Clara was tortured. Incidentally, these missionaries really did act sternly and arbitrarily, and they contributed greatly to the uprisings; but as regards the allegation that secretly they morally abused those Indians who were dependent upon them, especially the children living in the main building, I cannot judge its veracity. I just think that at least those mission heads with whom I most often had dealings—namely, Father Tomás, head of Mission San Francisco on the southern side of the bay of that name, and Father José Altimira, head of the new Mission San Francisco Solano [Sonoma] on the northern side of the bay—were both above such reproach, which can be partly explained, however, by the peculiar character of each. The first was a true fanatic. I called him Torquemada;[10] he did not resent the comparison, and he warranted the name. Once during our religious discussions he told me that if he were certain that to save my soul it would be necessary to throw me into a fire right then, he would do so without a moment's hesitation; and I was sure that he would have indeed done so. He was not meek in front of anyone, even his padre-presidente (all of the missions were subordinate not to a bishop but to a head of the missionaries who bore the title of padre-presidente) or the governor of the province, whom he reproached in my presence for "yielding to the spirit of the times." The second, Father José Altimira, was more a politician and a soldier than a friar or missionary. He always carried, like all lay Californios, a knife or dagger under the leather that was wrapped around the calves of his legs and that was substituted for boot tops, since they wore shoes, not boots. Life's circumstances redirected Altimira from a brilliant career that was promised by his high birth and led him to the obscure career of a missionary in a then-unknown corner of the world. It seems that he always secretly cherished the thought of politics, as if he were constantly asking himself what bitter mockery of fate had cast him into the most unsuitable and most lonesome field of activity. His efforts to find some favorable result of this outlook explain why he so zealously pursued the organization of a new mission as an activity that still included at least some kind of political thinking and why later he sympathized so deeply with my views on California's brighter future, views that I told him and that promised him a more prominent role in the affairs of this world. It must be said that because he did not burden the Indians with a strict performance of rites and generally did not nag them, he was almost the only missionary who was liked by them.

In conclusion, with regard to the Indians I will say a few words about their relations with the Russians. Whoever has studied the Russian national character

---

[10]After Tomás de Torquemada (1420–98), a Spanish Dominican and onetime confessor to Ferdinand and Isabella, who became infamous as a fanatical and cruel inquisitor.

knows very well that Russians, if they have not been aroused by some special external circumstance, are very good-natured and well-disposed toward everyone, despite differences in religion, nationality, and social status. A Russian disdains neither a savage nor a heterodox; we have seen, for example, in Siberia how [Russian] Orthodoxes lived in the same house as Jews and to some degree even imparted their tolerance to the latter. Just as the Russians left the house during Jewish holidays in order to give the Jews more space, so did the Jews in turn vacate the house on major Orthodox holidays. We have seen how in this joint living of Russian and Jew their books of worship, and other books, stood on the same shelf, and how in the absence of the Russians on common business the Jewish girls tended the icon lamp in front of the cross of the Savior. Thus did the Russians also treat the nomadic, half-savage, and savage tribes. "It means such according to their faith" or "Such is their custom," a sailor would say, and without disdain or mockery he would watch the strangest things and perhaps sometimes merely add, "Wonderful people, really wonderful!" The sailors believed that if we were to read comments or some sort of magazine—which the more literate of them sometimes followed—nowhere would we find a hint of derision, except perhaps occasionally condescending regret about the inability of the natives to make anything or to use something. Usually the observations went like this: "We reached the town of Abrasil, a possession of the king of the Portuguese. Here all are Araps, which means slaves; the Portuguese are the masters. But the Portuguese are no better than the blacks; the people are dirty, although there is water nearby and there is no winter, so it would seem that everyone could bathe," or about Tahiti: "We were in an Anglican church, and the English have converted the savages to their faith; but the church is quite empty, with nothing to venerate. Little wonder that the savages secretly go to pray to their idols, which they still erect in their cemeteries," etc. No wonder that the [Californian] Indians liked the good-natured Russian sailors, especially the generous and affectionate officers. I know that all of my arrivals at the mission were festive occasions for them. However much the missionaries grumbled or argued with me, I would still ask somebody to pardon or reduce their [i.e., the Indians'] punishments for disciplinary infractions. The Indians always liked to hear my explanations of various ways of making their work easier; when the time came to apply them, one after the other would eagerly try to show that he had heard and understood me well and profitably. Thus, I have a full right to say that the Indians expected the best from the Russians.

Regarding the Californios, they were all military personnel, with the exception of a small number of missionaries. However, it is very difficult to characterize them and to find the right term for them. They were not officers in the noble sense of that word, and they were not conscripts, for a certain nobility of spirit and seriousness, inherent in all Spaniards, did not let them become vulgar. Looking at their knightly armor of thick hide—sufficient protection against Indian arrows—and their helmets and cuirasses with shields—adorned with the emblem of Spain (this was already after the secession)[11]—they could be taken for Don Quixotes, people out of place and out of time (*deplacés et declassés*) who continued to live in an imaginary realm, and consequently it was sometimes necessary to act in a correspondingly artificial manner.

Part III

The secession from Spain, which had the immediate and direct effect of stopping its subsidies and protection, placed both the Californios and the other groups of California's population not only in a difficult position but also on completely new terms with each other. I found them just at this crisis, and I must go into some detail about the inclinations, customs, ideas, and situation of the Spanish population in order to clarify the response that contains my proposals and the sympathy that is expressed by the measures cited by me as the best means for the most advantageous disposition of their future.

Provided with a good salary by the Crown, the Californios lived in comfort, although the utter lack of trade made all articles that were impossible to obtain locally terribly expensive. Naturally, with the cessation of subsidies from Spain everyone on salary was immediately impoverished. They suffered for a while, but the time finally came when they were forced for their necessary support to demand salaries from the missionaries. This immediately changed their relations with the missions. On the one hand, the missions themselves lost their stipends and had to worry not only about the pay demanded by the military but also about finding some new source and means for covering expenditures on their own needs, which were sometimes urgent. Because they had hitherto received the necessary utensils, clothes, and similar articles readymade from Spain, with the discontinuation of this source much fell into disrepair and decay—for example, everything relating to the church service; there were no iconostases [reredos?] and no images or statues for new churches and chapels. There were not enough musicians or musical instruments (they used organs), and for me it was very strange to see that in the new mission of San Francisco Solano* some old, jingly clavichords (virtually abandoned by Rezanov, our emissary to Japan), set inside a shed that substituted for a church, served as an altar and an organ, and that

---

*This mission was founded not long before our arrival on the northern side of San Francisco Bay for political reasons, namely, to block expansion inland by our colony of Ross, as will be explained below.

[11]The secession of the colony of New Spain (Mexico) from the Spanish Empire in 1821.

Father José Altimira celebrated the rites and played the piano simultaneously, performing the duties of a priest, organist, reciter, and chorister. [On the other hand,] it became necessary to curtail the Californios' religious practices and to think more (as before) about work for getting income from the sale of products, forsaking all thought of new recruitments of savage Indians by means of raids and battues. These circumstances generated attempts at working silver ores. Because California has recently gained fame primarily from the extraction of metals and because it is precisely this circumstance that has made us Russians regret the loss of our colony of Ross in California, here, I think, is the most proper place to examine the degree to which California's wealth in this respect was known at that time and what significance it had then to my plans for this land.

Of course, it would have been most advantageous for me—and easier and simpler, besides—to cite various notes and documents about this subject that were communicated to me by the then director of the Russian-American Company, I. V. Prokofyev,[12] at a time when the development of the company and the implementation of some of my plans for California mattered (as far as this was possible without the direct participation of the government). Because of misplaced apprehension all of these papers were burned by the aforesaid director in 1825 at the time of a well-known situation, as I discovered from an official notice;[13] although this notice gave me some hope that copies of these notes could still be found with other persons, I will, not, however, refer to them. I will cite evidence of another kind that, I hope, will suffice to prove that California's mineral wealth was very well known at that time, that major obstacles to its exploitation existed then, and that there were even stronger reasons for concealing this wealth or at least for not publicizing it.

I will not dwell on the legend and conjecture that the Jesuits had already secretly engaged in the working of California's goldfields or, more truthfully, the extraction and collection of *pepitas,** that is, small nuggets of gold;[14] but it is impossible not to notice the richness of the ornaments in the churches in the old missions, a richness that did not correspond to anything else in California at that time. Let us cite more recent proof. It is known that there has long existed a whole class

---

*This comes from the Spanish word *pepita*, which properly means a fruit pit. Thus were called small nuggets of gold, whose shape was like that of nuts or the pits of plums, peaches, etc. In the state of Sonora, according to eyewitnesses, they were found in the sod and sometimes even on the surface of the ground. They were eventually found in California, too.

---

[12]Ivan Vasilyevich Prokofyev (17??–1845) was a Moscow merchant who served on the Russian-American Company's board of directors from 1822 until 1844. See Grinëv, *Kto yest kto*, 441; and Pierce, *Russian America*, 413.

[13]Here Zavalishin is referring to the company's panicky reaction to the Decembrist uprising, whose fomenters had direct links with the firm, and the subsequent official inquiry.

[14]Perhaps in Baja, but not in Alta California.

of gold seekers who even bear the special name of *gambusinos*,[15] and published evidence about them can be found long before 1848, that is, before the announcement of the latest discovery of gold on the Sacramento River. The main field of these gold seekers was really the state of Sonora, but it is known for certain that they sometimes penetrated adjoining California. When I went to Mission Santa Cruz—precisely with the aim of examining the silver mines, whose working had begun to be abandoned—they introduced me to a man at that mission whom they considered half mad and who constantly talked about rich sites of gold allegedly known to him. He said that he often went to collect it and always returned not only with empty hands but [also] almost without everything that he had taken with him, even what he had worn, adding that the Indians, who always watched him and followed him back and forth, robbed him and took his gold. According to him, they even laughed at him and in releasing him said, "Be off, Pepe! (Joseph, a common name like our Oska[16]) and take a rest, but come again soon!" This is why he was always pleading for someone to take him elsewhere by sea and thereby help him to hide from the watchful neighboring Indians, who, he asserted, followed all of his movements on land. Nobody believed him, of course, and they mocked him. It should be said, however, that stories and legends about various places rich in metals did not have much impact then in America, and even positive indications were unable to cause such activity as is caused by similar hearsay stemming from special circumstances. It goes without saying that such wealth was assumed to exist everywhere in America, and everyone felt that the question was not whether it existed but how to exploit it and not risk losing everything. Regarding the tales of the aforementioned old *gambusino* (he was a tall, lean old man with wild, roving eyes, covered with hair that was still very black, almost naked and barefoot, in a threadbare cloak and friar's sandals, but he gave very definite answers to my questions and displayed no insanity at all), in view of recent events the places that he mentioned were in all probability Mariposa and Calaveras Canyon,[17] which I had visited. At the latter occurred the incident related to me by Pomponio, who for some time lurked in this canyon with his gang.

Speaking of the fact that the discovery of gold in California was known before its final divulgence to the whole world and the exciting activity of 1848, I think that here, as a parenthetical episode, I will incidentally relate a completely analogous incident in Siberia that proves that every discovery has its historic period, before which not even the most reliable and definite indications have enough power to arouse general activity.

---

[15]Sp., prospectors or fortune hunters.

[16]Russ., a diminutive form of "Iosif" ("Joseph").

[17]Both of these places in the foothills of the central Sierra Nevada were the sites of gold strikes in 1849 (and Calaveras County was the scene of Bret Harte's short story "Outcasts of Poker Flats").

It was long rumored in Siberia that gold nuggets existed there. I will not mention the significance of the popular saying "Siberia is a gold mine!" because it could obviously have another meaning ["soft gold," i.e., furs]. Not only the meaning of the adjective "gold," which is attached to various names in Siberia, but also the eventual confirmation of conjecture about Siberian gold (owing to discoveries in the Urals) attests the possibility and even the probability of the existence of gold nuggets in other parts of Siberia. I am speaking here of rumors that directly concern Eastern Siberia and that arise from definite indications; sometimes they have even prompted official activity and decrees, which unfortunately never persisted, however. Of these indications, I will mention one that I personally reported to the former Governor-General of Eastern Siberia [1822–33], Aleksandr Stepanovich Lavinsky, having obtained firsthand information directly from the persons involved. Here is what happened. Aboard the Russian-American Company ship *Volga*, which we took from Sitka to Okhotsk [in 1824], there were many who had served and even re-served their terms as *promyshlenniks* with the Russian-American Company. Being then engaged in the collection of all possible information about Siberia and the [company's] colonies, I often invited these old hands to my cabin and elicited testimony from them, recorded it, listened, and supplemented it. It was found that these men were mostly Tomsk and Yeniseisk *meshchanins*,[18] as well as natives of other parts of former Tomsk Province, which then included present Yeniseisk Province and hence the rich goldfields of Biryussa, Uderey, Pit,[19] and others. Before joining the Russian-American Company these promyshlenniks had been engaged in trapping, and here is what they swore to me, some of them even agreeing to sign a written statement.

Having been sent to remote places to trap (mainly, it goes without saying, to wild, unbroken forests, which have lately become better known under the name of *taiga*[20]), these hunters usually assembled sizable parties or artels [co-ops] and took enough supplies for the entire hunt. Arriving at the spot where they were to be divided into small groups, they dug a deep pit in which they cached all of the supplies needed for their return, as well as everything necessary for wrapping and carting or carrying their catch. They left two or three men at this main pit to hunt and trap nearby by various means (traps, snares, or bows and arrows) and occasionally to see that the pit had not been touched. Then they formed small groups that proceeded farther, the only difference being that the subsequent pits served as caches not only for provisions and supplies but also for pelts, which were difficult to carry very long. Naturally, for better identification these pits were dug in spots that were easy to notice and find afterwards—somewhere on the bank

---

[18]Russ., lower-class to middle-class townsmen, or petits bourgeois.
[19]These rivers in central Siberia were the sites of gold strikes in the late 1830s.
[20]Properly speaking, the northern coniferous forest.

of a river or creek or near a spring, which was marked with a special sign on a large boulder, if such were available, or a pile of rocks or slashes on a tree. And so, in penetrating the taiga the promyshlenniks usually advanced by a system of rivers and streams, marking the way that they turned at the rivers' mouths. To safeguard the caches—to save the provisions from animals and the precious catch of furs from the elements—the pits were made very deep. In digging them the hunters happened to find repeatedly (in their words) not only sparkles, or grains, but even nuggets of gold. But it is remarkable that for various reasons such finds not only did not arouse joy but even incurred an irresistible and partly superstitious fear, so that the find was thrown into the pit, which was immediately filled, or into the water, and the promyshlenniks swore a fearful oath to each other not to tell their leader or even any member of their own families. It was even rumored that there had been instances of fur hunters killing a comrade who, despite the sworn oath, had surreptitiously taken evidence of their discovery that had somehow been accidentally found thereafter in his belongings. It is interesting that the motives of the promyshlenniks in rejecting such unexpectedly discovered opportunities for enrichment were very diverse. Some frankly admitted to me that they simply considered it a satanic ploy that helped the devil to divert them from the immediate and profitable hunting of precious furs. "Why, have you been listening to their stories, your lordship[?]" they would say to me (almost always in unison) when they heard how others had contended that it had been real gold; "From what devil came the gold? Perhaps there are mines in the mountains there! It was simply the devil's temptation! What sense was there in it? What use was it to us? Like getting a nice pelt—that's your gold!" But others laughed at the imaginary devil's ploy, knowing that it really was gold and that the real reason for the concealment and oath was more substantial and natural, namely, the fear that in case they told their leader of the gold discovery, state exploitation by convicts and perhaps peasants would occur without fail. "They might conscript nearby peasants for mining," they said (examples of assignments of peasants to factories, which formerly occurred not infrequently, were then still fresh in their memories), "and then people would worry and complain about us and curse us, and if convicts were settled there the vicinity would be deprived of peace by runaways." In addition to this [concern], in their view there were the usual [obligations] in the vicinity of all state institutions and establishments—the delivery of provisions, cartage, posses for seeking fugitives, etc. Finally, and I should think primarily, secrecy was prompted by the complete certainty that the discovered gold would never be their own; if they secretly took some and sold it, the state would learn of it somehow and would then seize all that had been found and demand still more. "They would say that we had hidden it somewhere, and they would take us to court," for all metals were then considered to belong exclusively to the state.[21] For this reason they said that it was better to be as far as possible from sin. I will add that the truthfulness of these accounts of such finds of gold was subsequently confirmed by the fact that when the general gold mining movement ensued, in many cases the guides were nonlocal runaways who, as everyone knows, led the search parties unerringly to the gold deposits.

All of this was told to me by A. S. Lavinsky. Later he received similar reports from others; incidentally, there is the story of the famous case of the discovery of grains of gold in the entrails of a slain wood grouse. It seems that several searches were even undertaken on behalf of Lavinsky on the basis of information received by him. Lastly, Vice-Governor Pestov's memoirs of Yeniseisk Province[22] mention the making of a definite and announced discovery; but thereafter all was quiet for several years until the general gold mining movement, which began in the 1820s in the Urals and gradually reached Western Siberia in the early 1830s and Eastern Siberia in the second half of the century.

I have cited this story about Siberia in order to make more understandable how it could happen that despite the absolute certainty of the existence of gold in California, nobody undertook its regular extraction. At that time not only the Californios and Indians but even we ourselves did not at all doubt California's mineral wealth. I will show below why we put this wealth in second place, how the possibility of its premature development filled us with misgivings, and what precautions we wanted to take before anyone began to search for metals. Regarding the Californios, the reasons why they concealed California's mineral wealth— which was undoubtedly known to them—and did not use it themselves consist partly of fears like ours but mainly of the inadequate security, the small Californio population, and the animosity of the Indians, who made even simple trips to remote places unsafe. It was absolutely impossible to have used the Indians themselves to mine gold because, firstly, there would then have been nobody to cultivate the land, what with the shortage of hands and the crude methods of cultivation, and, secondly, and more importantly, in that case it would have been difficult to prevent the Indians from fleeing, and it would have been quite impossible to keep the mining secret. And most of all, the Californios feared the publicity, foreseeing (as was later justified) that this would be the best way of attracting self-interested foreigners to the country, especially English and American adventurers.

In speaking of the existence of precious metals in California there is no need to base our [conclusions] on suppositions and fragmentary information only; we can

---

[21]There was a state monopoly on gold mining in Siberia until 1826.

[22]Ivan Semyonovich Pestov (17??–1840) was a noted jurist who served as president of the Yeniseisk Provincial Treasury in 1827–34. His account of Yeniseisk Province was published first as an article entitled "Svedeniya o Yeniseiskoy gubernii" and then as a book entitled *Zapiski ob Yeniseiskoy gubernii*.

turn to absolute facts. In 1820 the Californios, who were obliged by dire necessity to find some way of replacing the lost subsidies from the former motherland, decided to begin working silver mines near Santa Cruz, but not after 1824, the time of our visit, when exploitation had already been stopped on the grounds of unprofitableness. But with my close relationships with everyone it was not possible to hide from me that the reasons for halting extraction were quite different, namely, the imperfect methods of exploitation, the unskillfulness of the workers, and the weakness of the machinery. The Californios did not derive the anticipated profits from this exploitation, and they requested good masters and workers from Mexico and Peru but were hampered by the lack of means and the disarray that were then plaguing all of the former colonies in America. There remained only the admission of foreigners—Englishmen and Americans—who would extract it themselves, but this [influx] would have meant a complete takeover of the country by them. This [fear] was the real reason why (as some of them frankly admitted to me) they hurried to conceal their initial exploitation of the silver ores.

The failure to exploit the metals, with the continuing necessity to somehow replace the former subsidies, led, on the one hand, to the conclusion of an accord with the manager of the Russian-American Company's chief factory at Sitka, Khlebnikov, on the Company's right to hunt sea otters (sea beavers) in Californian waters at the cost of half the catch, and, on the other hand, to the strengthening of grain cultivation. The proposal to have one or two Russian warships permanently in the colonies [in the first half of the 1820s] raised the hope of a regular and profitable sale of grain to both our ships and our colonies. We bought whole wheat at three Spanish piasters per fanega, a weight of about four puds—hence at about a silver ruble per pud, a very advantageous price at that time. In addition, the buying of cattle was begun, which was very advantageous to us. We paid from three to four piasters for a steer, with most of the cost going for catching, since for this we paid two mounted Californios from two to three piasters, depending upon the distance to the owner's wild herd, from which the bulls were selected for slaughter. The owner's chief income consisted of the hides, which they always kept for themselves. These hides were sold on the Sandwich Islands by American vessels, although they did not arrive every year. In conclusion I will say that California bought European goods primarily from visiting ships of the Russian-American Company. This was a very important circumstance for my hopes and proposals.

Part IV

I have already said that my main task with regard to California was to find a formula for an agreement that would firmly connect Russia's advantages with the population's advantages and wishes. Consequently, it is understandable how important it was for me to preserve and to develop an even better disposition toward the Russians on the part of both segments of the population and how necessary it was for me to study closely the way of life of both the Spanish and the Indian population. Spanish society in the colonies at that time embodied many interesting features, an account of which will not, I hope, be without interest.

Like all other Spaniards in America, the Californios retained the good qualities and the shortcomings of their European compatriots but with a special flavor because of their peculiar situation. The Spaniards in America were everywhere the ruling class, the conquerors (*conquistadores*), as they called themselves; as a result, a very peculiar cast to their aristocratic origins was manifested in their character and manner, without class differences. The realization of this quality, the resultant simplicity of mutual relationships (despite differences in official and social positions), a certain inborn nobility of bearing and manner, a special grace among women in the most ordinary endeavors, and so forth—these were the qualities that involuntarily attracted attention. There was nothing common in their occupations and amusements. I never happened to witness drunkenness, hand-to-hand fighting, or vulgar swearing. I never even had occasion to hear shouts or boisterous conversation, even during heated arguments. The women were especially distinguished by their propriety. During my trips to the missions I sometimes happened to pass a place where the women washed their laundry— like Princess Nausicaa[23]—all together in a group, beginning with the sister of the governor of the province, the wife and daughter of the commandant, down to ordinary soldiers' wives. I would be riding behind some bushes and come right up to them and still think that there was nobody there. Neighbors held quiet conversations (*pláticas*) between themselves and never outshouted each other. If women were washing alone, it was possible to spot their presence even more quickly, for in that case a song would be heard, usually some sort of spiritual song. Especially familiar to my ears was the following song, or cantata, of Our Lady:

Quiero seguir	I want to follow
A ti flor de las flores!	You, flower of flowers!
Siempre decir	And always proclaim
Cantar a tus loores	And sing your praises.
Non me fallar	I will never cease
De te servir	Serving you,
Mejor de las mejores!	Best of the best!
etc.	etc.

---

[23]In Homer's *Odyssey,* Princess Nausicaa makes a point of washing her own and her brothers' clothes to improve their marriage prospects.

Despite their poverty, the Californios were very haughty. Memories of Spanish exploits in America and of the heroic struggle against Napoleon naturally aroused in them a high opinion of themselves. "Nothing is impossible for them to attain," Altimira said to me, speaking of the Californios, "provided they always remember that they are the descendants of Cortés and Pizarro and belong to the breed that struck the first mortal blow to Bonaparte!" Fairness demands that it be said that this high opinion of themselves prompted them more to the good than to the bad. They were very considerate and even overly tactful. I do not recall a single example of begging, imploring, or importunate service with the aim of getting something, and I recollect several instances of quite disinterested service that they rendered to me—for example, serving as guides in very dangerous places. Generally they bore their scarcity—even absolute poverty, it can be said—with great dignity, ennobling themselves in tatters (thus had their clothes sometimes to be called, literally and truthfully). Only remnants of certain metallic items (for example, cinches for a silver saddle, silver edging for bridles, scraps of silver saved by someone, crude Mexican forging, and the like) indicated their former prosperity and their habit of using silver articles. They were very frugal with food, especially if they happened to be traveling or hunting, when they usually contented themselves with several strips of sun-dried meat [*charqui*, or jerked beef (beef jerky)] and fried cornmeal, sometimes mixed with granulated sugar and sometimes with plain cold water. Social relations among different classes of society were very equable; because a large part of even the lowest class had claims to better origins (ordinary soldiers had such names as de la Cruz, Mercado, and de Rocafuerte), from the outside society did not exhibit that sharp cleavage among different classes that we see in other countries. External official relations always seemed to be on an equal footing, and even the lowest class behaved with dignity before high officials. At parties given by Russian officers or Spanish authorities, everyone entered the dance hall without differences in rank and without a special invitation, except a general announcement that there would be a *fandango* (the name of a certain dance). Single girls of all classes straightaway joined the circle of dancers equally with the highest members of society; married women and widows sat in the first unoccupied seats, and the men placed themselves in the corners and at the door, standing or sitting unceremoniously on the floor. If not everyone was regaled (they expressed no pretensions to entertainment), they nevertheless took part in the festivities, either joining in the singing (for the dances were always accompanied by songs) or playing a guitar or mandolin, which many of them had brought.

Spanish dances, especially in America, included many dramatics; the combination of the dramatics, the music, the singing, and the improvisations made them more like excerpts from a theatrical performance than proper dances. The dancers' favorite, the fandango, which expresses changes of emotion, requires the continual improvisation of verses (*seguidillas*) on the part of everyone. It begins with fast music and movement, which gradually makes everyone more gentle, languid, and quiet, and then suddenly everyone stops completely as a lady and her partner gradually approach each other and finally stand against each other. Then begins—now singly, now altogether—the singing of verses, which have to be improvised and appropriate to the situation of the dancers. Thus, for instance, if the dancer were a Russian officer, the lady would often ask him whether he would forgo some "blond or brunette and blue-eyed beauty whom he had left in the faraway and frigid north and who was awaiting his return with impatience," and the like. There was one dance that dated from the initial plight of the Spaniards in America when the arrival of a ship was a rare event and was especially greeted by the settlers. The unmarried girls in the next room are assigned the names of various gems. Then they enter the ballroom and stand in a semicircle. A single dancer, who represents the captain of a newly arrived ship, approaches them, and they all sing together:

> *¡Señor Capitán!*
> *¡Qué busca Usted aquí?*

This means:
Mr. Captain,
What do you seek here?

He replies:
> *Jo busca mi china,*
> *Que aquí la perdí.*

This means:
I am seeking my gem
That I lost here.

Then they ask him to identify this particular gem. He begins to describe it with praise but in evasive, indefinite language, meanwhile trying to catch some sign that will help him to guess the name taken by the girl with whom he wants to dance. Now there sometimes occurs, of course, a little trickery—previously arranged signs and deftly asked questions that help him to guess what he wants. For example, a ruby will apparently accidentally display a red ribbon, a pearl will ask if he bought his jewels in Ceylon, and the like. Finally, the captain names the gem and dances with the girl who represents it, and another dancer appears in the captain's role.

There was also a dance that represented the fight of two girls over a prisoner condemned to death, each girl wanting to save him from death and to free him from captivity by escape on the condition that he marry her. Craving a speedy deliverance, the prisoner, of course, thoughtlessly makes promises to each of them in the hope of being freed by either one or the other. Unfortunately for him, both arm themselves and come at the same time. At first the rivals resort to persuasion, sometimes proving their prior right by the strength of their love and sometimes trying to persuade their opponent to yield him to her. Finally, they decide to end the argument by fighting, using the arms that they have brought (during our visit, our officers' sabers replaced the heavy Spanish ones); they fight to the sound of music and singing above the prisoner, who kneels blindfolded. The steps of the dancers express the various maneuvers of the fight. At last, neither being able to win, and prompted by jealousy, they suddenly accost the prisoner—as if obeying the same thought—and stab him so that neither rival will win him. The prisoner falls and sprawls full length. At the sound of unusually sad music, another girl dancer appears, lifts the prisoner, and carries him to the door.

There was yet another presentation with two choruses singing—one about cavaliers going to war and the other about girls restraining them. The girls wind and form a circle, which encloses the cavaliers. Among the convictions that are expressed humorously in verses are the following:

¿Pensaréis que en la guerra juegan al burros?

That is, "Do you think that in war they play the fool" (literally, the donkey, in Spanish)?

Moreover, the minuet was still fully preserved, although it was danced mainly by elderly people, and the commandant of the presidio of San Francisco, Don Ignacio Martínez, never missed dancing the minuet at every ball with his spouse, to the great pleasure of the Californio audience and his own satisfaction.

There was always general animation, especially with dramatic dances presented as if they were excerpts from operas. Everyone, even the old men and women, joined in the singing and followed the course of activities with the greatest interest. Now they would jump up, then they would sit down—approving, reproaching, pointing. "*¡Bueno, hombre!*" ("Well done, fellow!"). "*¡Más a derecho, muchacha!*" ("More to the right, lass!"). Et cetera. During the intervals between dances they sang songs and verses; very poetic images were evoked, such as the following:

> *Cuando el corazón se abrasa*
> *Echo luego*
> *Por las ventanas de casa*
> *Vivo fuego, etc.*

That is:

> When my heart catches fire,
> It soon casts
> A bright blaze
> Through my eyes, etc.

Very often they also sang the following song:

> *Madre! la mi Madre!*
> *Guardas me ponéis!*
> *Que si yo no me guardo*
> *No me guardaréis, etc.*

That is:

> Mother! Oh, Mother!
> You have put a guard on me;
> But if I do not save myself,
> Nobody will save me, etc.

Or:

> *Cuatorce años tengo*
> *Ayer los cumplí:*
> *Que fue el primer dio,*
> *Del florido Avril*
> *Y chicos y chicas*
> *Me suelen decir:*
> *'Porque no te cazan*
> *Mariquilla, di?'*

That is:

> I was fourteen years old yesterday,
> The first day
> Of flowering April.
> And that is why the boys and girls
> Say to me:
> "Why do you not marry
> Mariquilla, eh?"

In general the Californios were very poetic. Almost all of the women were beautiful, such as María Antonia, the commandant's daughter, whom the Russian officers nicknamed Madonna, María Josefa, a niece of the governor, María del Carmel, also called Mariposa (Butterfly), and María Francisca; the last two were daughters of ordinary soldiers and would be considered first-class beauties by us. Their dress was old-style Spanish, which lasted longest of all in the colonies. It usually comprised a skirt, mostly knitted and always dark colored, a very thin chemise without multicolored embroidery, and a shawl, which on weekdays was usually white and blue striped and on holidays was black with crepe or lace, which they could drape very artfully and gracefully. They were very witty by nature and especially adept at what the French call *sailles et reparties* [sallies and repartees]. I should mention their relative ability for improvisation, which is greatly facilitated by the very nature of the Spanish language (it is like Italian in this respect and, moreover, permits blank verse, rhyming verse, and assonance) and, finally, by syllabification, so that the half of a word ending a line rhymes with the ending of the second or third line, and the other half begins the next line; for example:

> *Y mientras miserable-*
> *mente. . . . .*
> *. . . . . . insatiable, etc.*

This property of the language that facilitates improvisation and versification in general was undoubtedly one of the reasons why some Russian officers began to write Spanish novels and especially verses (*seguidillas*) needed for the fandango. At one time, the following one was greatly in vogue and very well known in California:

> My breast is full of new feelings;
> I grieve and pine;
> I long for someone's soul,
> With a mysterious, sweet yearning!
>
> My blood surges faster!
> Is it love?
> The idol of all tender hearts,
> The crown of earthly bliss! etc.

The Californios were very courageous. The former governor and then president of the province, Don Luis Argüello, would stalk bears alone without any other weapon than a short iron lance or spear attached to a rope, with which he tried to wound the beast mostly in the groin or the hind legs, and his hunting was always successful. Fusing, so to speak, with their Arabian horses, they were fearless horsemen; their most common pastime—catching wild bulls for slaughter—required incredible courage. Having tracked a herd and chosen a bull, they chased the galloping herd, which dashed up steep slopes and through river

torrents. The flushed horses (of the superb Andalusian breed with long, beautifully flowing tails) flew straight over rocks, ruts, stumps, and bushes and under
drooping branches that forced them [the riders] to crouch continually. Having
overtaken the bull, the riders positioned themselves on each side of him and at a
signal suddenly threw lassos from both sides around his neck, continuing, however, to gallop for a while, and then abruptly turning around; the lassos checked
the bull and snubbed his hind legs. If the bull were very strong and difficult to
hold, one of the riders dismounted and hobbled the stunned animal's legs with a
lasso. I should add, incidentally, that since there were no vehicular roads in California all of the women usually traveled on horseback, and they rode superbly.

Male dress comprised short trousers, sandals with leggings of stamped or
gilded hide that they wrapped around their calves, a jacket with braid, and to
crown everything instead of a cloak a poncho, a kind of blanket with a slit in
the middle through which they thrust their head, plus a black kerchief on their
head, sometimes with a round hat above it and sometimes without a hat, and,
finally, a large spur with an eight-pointed star with very sharp points—all of this
formed their customary off-duty garb. It should be mentioned that they wore the
spur on one foot, which they literally stuck into the horse's body; our little spurs,
whose small and dull wheel tickles rather than pains a horse, did not cow the
Californian horses, and they reared.

Despite the ardor of the predominantly acrimonious temperament, quarrels
among the Californios were fairly rare, and the chief causes of them were love
and jealousy; then the matter was often settled by a knife fight. In this fight two
main systems were known: the Andalusian and the Navarrian. The short and
deft Andalusian is more suited to striking blows from below; the tall and strong
Navarrese strikes from the shoulder and inflicts blows from above. There was,
however, another special and very dangerous way of fighting with knives, namely,
throwing a knife with unusual sleightness and strength from a sleeve. During our
stay a soldier was wounded by this method whereby a very long knife penetrated
his body up to the hilt.

The most remarkable among them in intellect and education were the Franciscan friars who ran the missions; most of them were quite intelligent and very
erudite men. There were almost no fanatics (with the exception of Father Tomás)
or ignoramuses among them, although it would be easy to think otherwise after
hearing their sermons in which they tried to adjust to the limited comprehension of the Indians. Thus, I remember how one of them, Father Narciso [Durán],
wanting to portray Christ's suffering in the dungeon, said to the Indians, "You
think that He cried like you, that He shed two or three tears! No, in one night
He filled a whole tub with His tears! Do you grow many fingernails in one year?

In one night from Him they got a whole vara!" (about three feet; with this he showed them the dimension with his [outstretched] hands).

But there was a complete lack of practical knowledge on the part of the Californios. Having heretofore been provided with everything, they did not think to engage in anything except service, and in order to avoid boredom from idleness they occupied themselves with card playing and cock fighting in their free time. It is impossible, however, to say that they were not inquisitive. They read my former Spanish books avidly, and some youngsters even expressed a wish to follow me to Russia in order to study and earnestly asked me to take them with me (two of them were already married); but they had no books at all or other means of education. Some old textbooks that I happened to find offered rather strange statements. In astronomy, for example, an author in expounding the Copernican system[24] used this dodge: "Speaking of the planetary system, it is impossible for us not to warn believers against one heretical opinion that is, unhappily, generally accepted by heretics and others," and then there followed a full exposition of the Copernican system. In the use of labor-saving devices the local Californios had not yet even surpassed the simple hand millstone, and the women prepared flour by grinding the kernels on a slab with a pestle, just as paints are pulverized. It is because of this [toil] that whereas a pud of whole wheat cost a silver ruble, flour (albeit of excellent quality) cost from 20 to 24 rubles [per pud], and it could be obtained only in small amounts—two or three pounds—for pastries. The Californios were unable to derive household benefits from the most lavish gifts of nature. Despite the unusual abundance of cattle, fowl, and game, they were quite unable to prepare meat in salted, smoked, or dried-broth form as a domestic reserve or for sale to visiting ships. All preparation of meat consisted of cutting it into thin slices, heavily rubbing both sides of the slices with a mixture of salt and ground cayenne pepper, and drying it in the sun. Despite the strict observance of fasts, they not only did not care about salted or any other useful preparation of fish but did not even engage in fishing at all, for want of the necessary gear. Notwithstanding the climate, which greatly favored the production of all fruits, especially grapes, wine was made by primitive methods and was very poor in quality; and dried fruits, berries, and jams were unknown to them. Nutritious and fragrant grasses in the hills and uplands afforded cattle excellent feed, and for that reason it can be said that milk in California was superb and uncommon in quality; but they never pondered or knew how to make butter, which could

---

[24]The Polish astronomer Nicolaus Copernicus (1473–1543) held that the earth rotated daily on its axis and that the planets revolved in orbits around the sun at the center of the universe; this heretical view, which was subsequently corroborated by the Italian astronomer Galileo Galilei (1564–1642), was opposed to the orthodox view of Claudius Ptolemy of Alexandria, who posited in the second century A.D. that the sun and the stars revolved around the earth as the fixed center of the universe.

have been sold in quantity to ships. In order to build boats they had to let an Englishman, one Richardson,[25] live in the presidio; however, he had to adopt Catholicism beforehand. In order to explain how they cultivated the soil, I will relate what I myself saw at the newly founded mission of San Francisco Solano. For want of agricultural implements they felled laurel trees with very crooked and strong branches. The ends of the branches were sharpened; several brace of oxen were hitched to the trees, which they dragged all over the field that had been dried by the usual autumn drought, with all of its grass having been burned beforehand. This was the extent of plowing! Of course, only the usually favorable pedologic and climatic conditions could triumph over the shortcomings of such a barbaric or, perhaps, infantile method of cultivation. Nevertheless, it was really so. During my stay, sowing occurred at the end of December [i.e., beginning of January], at the start of the second rainy period; around the middle [i.e., end] of January, when I visited the mission a second time, I found all of the fields covered with dense and high green shoots. Wheat sometimes yielded seventy-fold [the seed] and corn, which grew twice a year, a hundred-fold and more each time.

Vegetables, mostly chickpeas, black beans [frijoles], and string beans, a little meat, and milk constituted their main food; whoever had more means obtained chocolate from Mexico and partly from southern [Baja] California, and although it was apparently very plainly and crudely prepared in ordinary pans or griddles, it was of the best quality. They did not use tea or coffee and did not know how to make either. I remember how Father José Altimira, having noticed during his visit to the frigate that I drank coffee after dinner, decided to surprise and treat me when I visited him. He bought some coffee from a Russian-American Company supercargo, burnt it almost to coals, brewed it in a teapot like tea, and triumphantly presented it to me; afterwards, when I thanked him for his thoughtful attention, I could not but laugh and let him taste what he had given me, but he could not understand at all why the wish-wash that he had made with his own hands and with such diligence and care was not in the least like the tasty beverage that we had served him on the frigate.

However few Californios were inclined to commercial labor and economic activities, necessity had finally to assert itself. Later, after they had broken with Spain and when they could not rely upon Mexico for support, they were put at the worst disadvantage. There remained one remedy—to ask foreigners for help

---

[25]William Richardson (1796–1856) was an English sailor who, while serving as mate on the whaler *Orion*, jumped ship at San Francisco in 1822 and received permission to settle in Alta California, provided he instruct Californios in navigation and carpentry. He changed his first name to Antonio and converted to Catholicism in 1823, married María Antonia Martínez (the daughter of the commandant of San Francisco) in 1825, and obtained Mexican citizenship in 1830. He was active in trade, and he owned a small ship and several ranchos. He served as captain of the port of San Francisco in 1837–1844 and 1846–1847. See Miller, *Captain Richardson*.

and to learn from them. But to whom, if not the Russians, would it have been most advantageous for them to turn in order to obtain their wants without injuring their pride and losing the advantage of their current and partly independent position to which they were accustomed? This consideration finally persuaded them to heed my proposals, whose acceptance offered them the opportunity to gain everything necessary without undergoing the consequences that threatened them—as I indicated and as they themselves believed—in the event that they were subordinated to some other power, especially the United States, which obviously was already gnashing its teeth.

To supplement this story of the Californios I will say a few words about their relations with the officers of our squadron. These relations were most friendly. If there was sometimes unmannerliness in small things as a result of the usual simplicity of the relations, there was never any importunity on our part. The officers had incomparably more means than the local residents. Besides, the frigate had its own music. So it was very natural that the officers would offer evenings of dancing or balls much more frequently than the Californios, who at their balls could not even afford music and entertainment without the assistance of the officers. From early morning (the Californios rose very early and then slept after lunch), the musicians came with their instruments to the beach and went around the presidio via an interior corridor or an open gallery under an awning playing their music. This [serenade] signified that the officers were giving a ball. At that moment, dispatch riders galloped in all directions to notify nearby places. The officers usually held the ball in the quarters of the governor or the commandant. In the first case the household arrangements were managed by the governor's sister, Doña Antonia, and her married daughter, Doña María Josefa de la Cruz, and in the second case (which was more frequent) by the commandant's second daughter, María Incarnación, whom we usually called "Miss Coronation" and whom we liked for her affability. Wine, candy, tidbits, dishes, table linen, and servants were furnished by the frigate; provisions were supplied by the Californios, and the food was cooked on the beach through the joint efforts of their and our cooks. With such arrangements, naturally each time we had to be concerned about the safety of the supplies on the beach; when we would ask the buffet attendant and the aides-de-camp if everything had been safely provided, they usually answered, "And how! Everything has been safely delivered by the hands of Miss Coronation herself." The Russian officers pressed the Californio dancers throughout our sojourn in California, but our attempts to teach the Californios our common dances utterly failed. Some found them meaningless and stiff; others found them to be "confused congestion." Needless to say, the Russian officers were always happy wherever they went, and they were regaled and served like moguls. The Californios were also very amicably disposed toward the sailors, although it was noticeable that they considered themselves above them. Because there was no general drunkenness, fights did not occur; the Californios were even very lenient toward trouble, which was sometimes caused by drunken sailors, and they never answered insult with insult on the excuse that people in that condition did not know what they were doing. In extreme cases they put them to sleep in some closet or informed the duty sergeant, who was always on the pier by the sloop. The Californio women behaved very prudently, with much tact and dignity, and they did not initiate any romantic intrigues with either the officers or the sailors, even in jest, despite the fact that talk of love was the most common topic of conversation. Many girls, however, would have been inclined to marry Russians if they would not have had to change their religion and leave California, and they were amused to hear that mixed marriages, which were unprecedented among them, were not at all rare among us.

Such were the people with whom I had to deal, for whom there was the prospect of a considerable role in case my proposals were realized, and upon whom the success of these proposals greatly depended. I did not conceal my proposals from the population, and I thought then and think now that in joining the Russians they would have contributed many good qualities and that jointly we could have formed a new and splendid people.

Part V

California's subjection to Russia would have brought mutual and considerable advantages.

Although the Amur River had long been part of all of our colonial plans, everyone knew that not the Amur's mouth, Sakhalin Island, or even possession of the so-called Tatar Coast [the western shore of Tatar Strait] could provide domination of the Pacific Ocean or even of its northern part. Everyone who understood the matter knew the reasons why the key to sway over the Pacific or at least to predominant influence over it ought to be sought not on its Asiatic coast but on the western coast of North America. Only on this coast, even far to the north, could there be found harbors that never froze and that permitted unrestricted coming and going at all times, for it is known that western coasts are warmer than eastern ones, and whereas the Gulf of Pechili [Chihli, or Po Hai, the northwestern arm of the Yellow Sea], which lies around 40° of [northern] latitude on the eastern coast of Asia, is sometimes covered with ice, the bays lying around 57° [N] on America's Northwest Coast never freeze.

Regarding the possibility of subjection, although by a treaty [the Adams-Onís, or Transcontinental, Treaty of 1819] concluded between Spain and the United

States* the boundary between the possessions of those powers on the Northwest Coast of America was defined as the 42nd parallel of North latitude, any pretension by Spain to sovereignty north of San Francisco Bay, even after this treaty, was nevertheless questionable; the very name of California was given only to the territory up to this bay, and the name "New Albion" was widely applied to the upper part. Whereas the United States in order to justify the seizure of Indian lands concluded treaties with the Indians and made fictitious purchases, the Spaniards did not do so and the Indians did not want to do so. To us, however, they [i.e., the Indians] offered agreements of this kind, and such an act could have served as an incontestable argument for us vis-à-vis the United States, that is, the sole power that had a basis for seriously opposing us. Spain never had any settlements on the northern side of San Francisco Bay, except the minor mission of San Rafael, and did not undertake any operations against, or negotiations with, our colony of Ross, as far as is known. The only action that had political overtones, and that was intended to halt the spread of the Russian colony inland (after having surrounded it with a series of missions), was the establishment at the end of 1823 of the new mission of San Francisco Solano [Sonoma] on the northern side of the bay, but this [act] occurred independently of the local administration.

We had nothing to fear on the part of Mexico. Despite the transfer to Mexico from Spain of the rights to California, the latter during our visit was in fact independent and could decide its own destiny the same as Yucatán—another province of Mexico at its other extremity—finally did. It is true that the short-lived emperor Agustín I, Don Agostino [sic] Primero, sent his agent, but California, instead of paying taxes for the benefit of Mexico (which had previously never paid them to Spain), conversely demanded from Mexico first of all the payment of overdue salaries (l'arriéré) and mission subsidies for several years. Mexico, however, was unable to defend California, for it had no naval power of its own. When finally in the early 1830s a single pirate plundered the main town of Monterey and California demanded protection from Mexico, the then president of Mexico, [General Antonio López de] Santa Anna, sent only three hundred convicts, who, of course, merely increased the confusion and disorder. But if Mexico was helpless to defend California from a pirate, it was even less able to hold it in the face of conflict with some naval power, especially with its utter lack of warships.

Such was the state of affairs. Its outcome was easy to foresee. It is true that for some time the Californios labored under the delusion that European intervention in 1823 in the internal affairs of Spain[26] would extend to the return to Spain of its

---

*It seems that this was in 1818 [sic], but in any case already after our occupation of Bodega Bay and the founding of the settlement of Ross.

[26]Here Zavalishin is referring to the suppression in 1823 of the Spanish revolution of 1820 by the French army acting for the Holy Alliance.

colonies and that they would then enter into their former relationship with Spain and receive subsidies, etc., but it was not difficult to show them that all of this was an unfounded hope and also to make them understand and realize that they faced one future—falling prey to either England or the United States, and most likely to the latter. It should be said that they feared this most of all. In their eyes the Americans were heretics, and the specimens of United States citizens that they had come to know—adventurers and petty traders—had done little to recommend their nation. Furthermore, it was rumored that neither in Louisiana nor in Florida, which had recently been unfairly taken from Spain, had the United States recognized Spain's former rights to its landed possessions. As they themselves realized, almost the only means of deliverance from the terrible danger and at the same time from their disastrous situation was union with Russia. Everything that they could have reasonably wanted would have been secured. Russia's several million Catholics were proof to the friars of her tolerance; the soldiers could be put in active service, and the permanent stationing of ships would increase the means of the inhabitants and stimulate the economy, making it more profitable, and so on.

In case our government did not agree to annex this province, there still remained a way for it to defend itself against encroachment by the United States. For this there had only to be an expansion of the territory of the Russian-American Company's colony of Ross so as to position it between California and the boundary of the United States and make it an obstacle to the complete merger of California with the territory at 42° already ceded to the United States. It should be said that such a deal would have been liked more by the Californios than a complete annexation of the whole province. This [prospect] flattered them with the hope of preserving some degree of independence with the attendant advantages and without at the same time undergoing the disadvantages of defenselessness against the attempts of the Americans of the United States.

To the credit of the Californios it must be said that all of the conditions, or, more correctly, current desires, that were voiced by the most influential of them in their conversations with me could not have been more practicable and reasonable. This [assessment] was admitted at the time [i.e., 1825] by the late N. S. Mordvinov[27] and the directors of the Russian-American Company, who even agreed to the addition of much that was not included in the stated desires.

---

[27]Count Nikolay Semyonovich Mordvinov (1754–1845) was a longtime public figure in Russia, serving as a member of the advisory State Council (1801–1816) and minister of the navy (1802). He became an admiral (1797), as well as the owner of vast estates and many serfs. During his three years of naval training in England in the middle 1770s he became a convert to the principles of British liberalism and Adam Smith, which made him popular with young radicals in Russia, including the Decembrists, although after their abortive revolt in 1825 he became one of the judges of the conspirators. He was also an influential shareholder in the Russian-American Company, serving for many years on the tsar's oversight committee for the company. He helped to organize the first Russian round-the-world voyage (in 1803–1806). See Grinëv, *Kto yest kto,* 354–55; and Pierce, *Russian America,* 63–64.

Of course, if our government had agreed to the annexation of all of California, a formally authorized agent would have been sent to settle the matter. But in case our government left the matter solely to the Russian-American Company, it was proposed to act in the following way.

The Californios would have pledged not only to refrain from hindering the occupation of territory and the establishment of new Russian settlements on the northern side of San Francisco Bay as far as the Sacramento River and from attracting the attention of the Mexican government, which could obtain information through them only, but also to render full assistance in everything to the Russians and to act jointly with them on the northern side of the bay, in exchange for which the Russians would have been obliged to defend and fully assist them.

In the agreement between the Russians and the Indians about the cession and sale of territory to the Russians—which the Indians repeatedly requested—it would have had to be mentioned formally that all hostile acts of the Indians against the Californios, against both missions and individuals, would have to be considered tantamount to hostile acts against the Russians themselves.

The two missions of San Rafael and San Francisco Solano, which had already been founded by the Californios on the northern side of San Francisco Bay, presented the main difficulty. They would have had to be abandoned so as not to damage the economy of the [other] missions, for they were the only ones that did not exceed one-tenth of the annual complement of able-bodied workers (although the Indians would not have been permitted to transfer from the missions to the Company's service).

The Californios would have had to be given the right to reside in our settlements and to undertake economic activities there.

At Ross or some other settlement in California, a school would have had to be established where the children of the Californios could have been sent and where a certain number of Indian children from the Californian missions could have studied trades [or] music and [received] vaccination free of charge. In no cases would these children have been sent to Sitka or Russia to complete their studies, and the school in California would have had to be given the necessary means for their adequate education.

The Company would have had to have a doctor who would have regularly toured California to offer help and advice.

Our government or the Company would have been obliged to station permanently on the coast of California a ship that would have been strong enough to defend it.

Then there followed various conditions for individuals: the granting of extraordinary stipends, life pensions, and sundry privileges, an obligation to supply certain articles, etc. All of these [terms] would not have constituted too much expense for the Company, which would have been handsomely rewarded by the innumerable benefits that it would have unquestionably derived from the development of Russian colonization in California.

Upon my return to California or upon the arrival of some other authorized person, a written agreement would have had to be concluded on the basis of the above conditions. This agreement, which would have been similar to the pact that the governor had independently concluded with Khlebnikov, would have had to have been approved by only the Californian junta, not needing approval or ratification at all by the Mexican government.

Of course, the development of grain cultivation and various other economic activities would have had to be the main goal of the Company's efforts and of Russian colonization. The magnificent port of San Francisco Bay, the favorable climate, and the rich soil—all eternal and immutable conditions—these, not the exhaustible mineral wealth, were the chief assets of California in my eyes. How favorable these conditions were was best of all revealed later by the experience—besides the terrible ordeal—that California underwent economically during the crisis caused by the feverish gold mining. It is known that when everyone pursued gold, grain cultivation and all branches of agriculture in general were utterly neglected and abandoned; with the sudden influx of newcomers, cattle rearing was almost completely destroyed in order to feed them. Even orchards and vineyards were felled in many places for joinery. And what then? Before a decade had passed, the population of nearly half a million not only was able to provision itself from local output but was even able to begin the export of butter, salted beef, and flour ([including] to us, by the way, at Nikolayevsk on the Amur and at lower prices than those from the nearest Siberian sources), and wine making had already begun.

For the development of secure colonization in California, the Russian-American Company proposed to recruit experienced agriculturalists, mainly with families; in order to find volunteers more easily, it was proposed to redeem them among serfs, and by no means were exiles to be sent as settlers. These volunteers would be contracted for seven years, counting a stay of five years on site. It was proposed that they be supplied with all necessities by the Company. If at the end of seven years they wanted to leave, they would be returned without delay; [but] if they wanted to settle permanently in California, everything that they had received would be given to them, and they would also be given a certain amount of land. Eventually, when girls from the Indian tribes were raised and taught in the girls' school, it was proposed to seek permission to let a certain number of our discharged and unmarried sailors settle in California.

In addition, the Company's directors, who were captivated by the information on silver mining (which the Californios had begun but then abandoned) and on the supposed existence of gold, wanted from the very beginning to commence mining, but I restrained them, deferring it to the time when agriculture had been organized and sufficiently established. Like the Californios, I feared that any discovery and publicizing of mineral wealth would inevitably draw a multitude of adventurers whom it would be quite impossible to keep in check.

Closely connected with the development of agriculture in California were the provisionment not only of our colonies [in Alaska] but also of Kamchatka, Okhotsk, and other coastal places on the Asiatic seaboard, the possibility of maintaining a large number of Russian ships in these waters and the resultant development of Russian navigation, and, finally, the current plans regarding the Amur, De Castries Bay (where it was proposed to winter the Okhotsk Flotilla instead of at Okhotsk), and the Tatar Coast.

The Russian-American Company did not demand any assistance. Its sole request was to release me for its service; twice it made an urgent representation about this [secondment].

I was not allowed to do so [i.e., to be released to the company], and with that the affair ended, since its realization was closely connected with my presence in California and depended mainly upon my personal relations with local influential figures. As far as could be understood from official and unofficial reports, the reasons why our government did not agree to give the Russian-American Company permission to implement my proposals with its own means and on its own responsibility were the same ones that kept the government from direct participation in the matter—the danger of a clash with England and the United States.[28]

Later the colonial administration [i.e., Governor Wrangell in 1835] also tried to secure permission to expand the territory of the colony of Ross* and to strengthen the development of agriculture there in accordance with my earlier proposals, but those attempts were unsuccessful. It is noteworthy that in the colony of Ross the old tradition of selecting sites for new settlements[29] was preserved and that it served as a guidepost for the Swiss Sutter in founding the establishment [i.e., Sutter's Fort] [near] where gold was to be discovered.

*See my article "Delo o kolonii Ross" in the next number of this journal.

---

[28]Zavalishin neglects to mention (or was prevented from doing so by the censor) that his sympathy with the Decembrists rendered him a pariah and that his involvement in the uprising—and especially that of the ringleader, the poet Kondraty Ryleyev, who worked in the Russian-American Company's headquarters in St. Petersburg as chief clerk—placed the company under suspicion of disloyalty.

[29]The nature of this "old tradition" is unclear.

When Americans from the United States seized California, the mission Indians scattered and perished or were annihilated.[30] The Californio population disappeared in the massive influx; the Americans, as is known and as was envisioned beforehand, did not recognize the land rights of the Californios, and if any of them with whom we had relations and talks is still alive, I am sure that in the light of everything that has happened, they often remember how much better it would have been if, instead of the events that occurred, our mutual proposals and desires had been realized at that time.

---

[30]Actually, the Indians had already scattered with the secularization of the missions in the middle 1830s.

DOCUMENT 17

Otto von Kotzebue, "Alta California and the Russian Colony of Ross," 1824

EDITOR'S INTRODUCTION

After his return in 1818 from his abortive attempt to find a northern passage through the Arctic Ocean from Bering Strait, Kotzebue had been promoted to captain-lieutenant. In 1823 on the newly built sloop *Predpriyatie* with 118 men, he embarked on his third and last round-the-world voyage (his second as commander). It was undertaken in order to deliver freight to Kamchatka and to enforce the tsar's 1821 decree. Originally it was also intended to explore Bering Strait, but this object was deferred, and instead Kotzebue was instructed to undertake exploration and scientific research. After arriving at New Archangel, Kotzebue was told by Governor Muravyov that he would not be needed until March 1825, so he sailed south to winter in Alta California and Hawaii. This time he spent a month longer at San Francisco than in 1816, so he was able to travel and observe more and even make a trip to Fort Ross. After returning to New Archangel he was informed by Chistyakov, Muravyov's replacement, that the 1821 embargo had been nullified by a convention with the United States, so he was free to return to Russia via the Cape. His health broken by twenty-seven years at sea, Kotzebue retired from the navy in early 1830 to his estate near Reval.

CAPTAIN-LIEUTENANT OTTO VON KOTZEBUE, AN EXCERPT FROM
A NEW VOYAGE AROUND THE WORLD IN 1823–1826,[1] [SLOOP *PREDPRIYATIE*
IN SAN FRANCISCO BAY?], 10 SEPTEMBER–25 NOVEMBER 1824

Chapter Eleven
California and the Russian Colony of Ross

As I have already mentioned in the preceding chapter, I was permitted to spend the winter of 1824–25 in [Alta] California and on the Sandwich Islands. Captain Lazarev, whom I relieved [on coastal patrol], also intended to run into San Francisco Bay on his return voyage in order to stock fresh provisions before sailing around Cape Horn. However, he had to await the post from [St.] Petersburg that comes only once a year to such remote points of our huge empire. Via impassable Siberian roads it reaches Okhotsk in the spring, and from there in the autumn it is forwarded by sea to New Archangel.

After having made all of the necessary preparations for our forthcoming sojourn at New Archangel [next spring and summer] and readied the ship for sailing, we put to sea on 10 September 1824. A favorable north wind carried us quickly southward toward the fertile coast of California. The voyage passed safely. It was not marked by any interesting happenings, except the fact that below 40° North latitude we for the first time happened to observe a rare spectacle—the struggle between two opposing winds.

A south wind blew fairly briskly for several days. Suddenly clouds appeared in the north, and from the movement of the water it was noticeable that an equally fresh wind was approaching from the north. The waves, rushing toward each other, raged furiously, but between them lay a neutral belt of some 50 sazhens

---

[1]Kotsebu, *Novoye puteshestvie vokrug sveta*, 204–40. The journal of Kotzebue's round-the-world voyage of 1823–26 in the sloop *Predpriyatie* was published in two variants. The first appeared in Russian in St. Petersburg in one volume in 1828; the second variant, excerpted here, was published in German in Weimar in two volumes in 1830 (and in an English translation in London in two volumes later the same year). For a long time the German edition was thought to be a translation of the Russian edition, but in 1956 the Russian scholar Daniil Tumarkin ascertained that it was an independent work written in Kotzebue's native language (see Tumarkin, "Zabyty istochnik"). Tumarkin's translation into Russian (second edition) of the German edition was published in Moscow in one volume in three different years (1959, 1981, and 1987), and recently it was reprinted in a one-volume edition of both of Kotzebue's voyages (Kotsebu, *Puteshestviya vokrug sveta*, 527–950). As he notes, the German edition of 1830 is more than three times as voluminous as the Russian edition of 1828 and substantially different in content. "The 1828 book," he writes, "is a dry report by the ship's captain, compiled in strict chronological order in the form of a journal, whereas the German edition, addressed to a broad circle of readers, is a collection of essays about visits to the islands of Oceania, Kamchatka, Russian America, Alta California, and elsewhere that contains extensive geographical and ethnographical material and more fully reflects Kotzebue's personal opinions about current events" (see Tumarkin, "Zhizn i puteshestviya"). The English translation of Kotzebue's voyage (Kotzebue, *New Voyage Round the World*) is marked by occasional infelicities and even embellishments, as well as archaic language. The natural science results of the voyage were published in Lenz, *Physikalische Beobachtungen angestellt*. Eschscholtz's twenty-five color plates of fauna were published in five parts as *Zoologischer Atlas*.

in width that stretched from west to east as far as the very horizon. Here it was absolutely calm, and even a faint breeze did not ripple the ocean's surface, which was as smooth as glass. After a while the north wind was victorious, and it drove the neutral belt toward our ship.

Hitherto we had been in the zone of the south wind, but now we found ourselves in the calm belt; our ship could not continue its course, although very high winds raged behind and before us. This uncommon phenomenon lasted about four hours. Finally, the north wind overtook us and carried us quickly to our destination.

On 25 September we were already very close to the cape called King's Cape [Point Reyes] by Spanish seamen. Not far from it is found San Francisco Bay. However, the thick fog that prevails at this time of year on the Californian coast hid the shore from us. Only in the morning of 27 September did the fog lift, and we saw the desired cape. It is a fairly high hill without any vegetation that falls toward the sea as a black rocky wall. The said hill's appearance does not warrant its name at all. At ten o'clock in the morning we rounded this royal cliff at a distance of three miles. Here we noted very strong breakers, generated by the rapid succession of two swift ocean currents. With blind rage the waves beat the foot of the monarch, who was indifferent to their fury.

The width of the strait [Golden Gate] leading to the large and beautiful bay of San Francisco is only half a cannon shot wide. The fortress [presidio] of San Joaquín, situated on a high cliff on its left [southern] shore, commands the strait. We saw that the republican flag was flying above the presidio. It meant that this, the northernmost colony of Spain, no longer recognized the authority of the motherland. We also noticed several cavalrymen and a throng of people; all of them, it seemed, were following the rapid approach of our ship with close attention.

When we had come within gunshot range, a sentry grasped a long hailer with both hands and demanded to know our nationality and whence we had come. His harsh bellow, the cannons aimed at the channel, the small force of armed soldiers, including cavalrymen ready for battle, and, finally, a demand made of us to salute the presidio—all of this [display] could have created the impression that the commandant had the power to prevent even a warship from entering the harbor. However, we had to some extent been informed of the true situation. The fact is that the presidio of San Joaquín lying atop the cliff is the most peaceable in the world. Not one of the cannons is fit for accurate firing, and its garrison can conduct only a verbal battle. Nevertheless, out of courtesy I ordered that the presidio be saluted, hoping thereby to secure us a more cordial welcome. What was my surprise when there was no reply whatever to our salute! A representative of the commandant soon arrived from the presidio and explained this mystery to me: he asked me to give him a little gunpowder so that they would be able to answer my greeting in the proper manner.

As soon as we dropped anchor, all of the garrison came from the presidio—having, as usual, left it quite undefended—and made themselves comfortable on the beach together with the other curious people. Ships entered this harbor very rarely, and so our ship aroused almost as much surprise and delight here as on the islands of the South Sea. I sent Lieutenant Pfeifer[2] ashore, enjoining him to officially report our arrival to the commandant and at the same time to appeal to him with a request to assist us in replenishing our stock of fresh provisions.

The commandant himself, Don Ignacio Martínez, holding the rank of cavalry lieutenant, had been summoned to the council at Monterey, the capital of California. His deputy, Second Lieutenant Don José Sánchez, received my envoy very cordially. He retained very friendly memories of me from the time [i.e., 1816] when I visited this harbor on the brig *Ryurik*. Don Sánchez was then a worthy and gallant noncommissioned officer, but now he had attained officer rank under the republican government. He extended his favor to me, promising to render us the utmost assistance, including troubling himself with the immediate sending of fruit, vegetables, and fresh meat.

Here I will interrupt the narrative of our sojourn in California. In this beautiful land nature herself has created all of the conditions in order for an industrious and energetic population to be able to enjoy life peacefully. However, until quite recently California was the most neglected of Spain's colonies. There was only unimportant and scant information on it. So I hope that a brief survey of the history and system of government of California will not appear superfluous to readers. Perhaps it will induce them to relate to the narrative of our stay in this little-known land with great interest.

At first only the narrow peninsula on the western coast of North America stretching 150 German miles [675 English miles] from San Diego Bay (32° N latitude) to Cabo San Lucas (22° N latitude) was called California. Subsequently, however, after the Spaniards had discovered the mainland coast to the north, they extended the same name to it. Thereafter they began to call the peninsula Old California and the seaboard as far as San Francisco Bay at 37° N latitude New California. So-called New Albion was located farther to the north.

[Hernán] Cortés, the tireless conquistador, did not content himself with the seizure of Mexico. He ordered the construction of a ship on the coast of the Great [Pacific] Ocean so as to extend Spain's possessions even farther. As a result, in

---

[2]Nikolay Fyodorovich Pfeifer (d. 1835), a Baltic German, later (1827) took part in the Battle of Navarino (Pylos) against the Egyptian fleet and was awarded a gold saber for bravery. He was promoted to captain-lieutenant in 1831. See Grinëv, *Kto yest kto*, 446.

1534 Spanish navigators saw the coast of California for the first time, and in 1537 Francisco de Ulloa[3] visited it.[4] When the news of this discovery reached the Spanish government, it considered it expedient this time to reject the methods they had used in the conquest of Mexico and Peru. It was decided to take possession of this land peaceably by converting the population to the Christian faith. This devout purpose was declared the sole reason for the annexation of California. Indeed, Jesuits, protected by only a small military detachment, were sent there [i.e., to Baja California]. They were ordered to found a settlement in the new territory and to begin the spread of Christianity. The purpose of this expedition, entailing substantial expense, appeared to be quite unselfish. Actually, however, this undertaking was dictated by a secret fear: in Madrid they were afraid that the new lands, which were located near Mexico, would be seized by another power, which would then have the opportunity of threatening the Spanish gold mines.[5]

The Jesuits arrived in [Baja] California and immediately set to work. After them [i.e., their expulsion] came the Dominicans and, finally, the Franciscans. At the present time the Dominican settlements, called missions here, are found in Old California and those of the Franciscans in New California. All of these friars have applied themselves earnestly and continue to convert the local population to Christianity. We will see below how they do so.

The first missions appeared on the coast of Old California and were able to communicate with Mexico by sea. They were founded in those localities that seemed more suitable for cultivation. The military detachments that accompanied the friars chose for their settlements those points from which the security of several missions could be immediately guaranteed. Thanks to this arrangement, the soldiers were always ready to come to their defense and to render the missionaries support in their activities. Such a military post bears the name "presidio" here.

The friars were unable to make themselves understood to the extremely timid and artless local inhabitants, who were not far removed from a brute state and who probably in general had no concept of religion. In these conditions it was useless to even think of spreading the Christian dogma, and the holy fathers had to propagate Catholicism—more accurately, on their own by force of arms. Such "conversion" succeeded so well that the number of missions, which were built by the Catholic converts, multiplied rapidly. Here in New California the first mission

---

[3]In 1539 Ulloa, on the orders of Cortés, explored the Gulf of California as far as its northern end, thereby proving the peninsularity of Baja California.

[4]Kotzebue is more or less correct here. Cortés conquered Aztecan Mexico in 1519, and three years later conquistadors reached the Pacific Coast of New Spain. In 1533 the mutinous crewmen of one of two ships outfitted and dispatched northward by Cortés in search of fresh riches encountered Baja California, and in 1539–40 Ulloa probed as far as the head of the Gulf of California and rounded Cabo San Lucas.

[5]Actually, New Spain's rich silver mines were much more lucrative than its few gold mines.

was founded in 1769 at San Diego, and now the missionary settlements already number twenty. Twenty-five thousand Indian converts are subject to these missions. The small army, consisting of 500 dragoons, keeps them obedient and also watches them so that they do not flee. Sometimes some of these Indians succeed in evading their guards and returning to their tribe. But the dragoons find them there and forcibly return them to the missions and, moreover, at the same time with their sabers recruit new Christians among the tribesmen of the runaways.

The lot of these Indians, so-called Christian Indians [neophytes], merits all kinds of pity. Even the situation of Negro slaves cannot be worse. The Indians are subject totally to the unlimited arbitrariness and tyranny of the friars. While suffering they do not even have the possibility of finding comfort in religion, for their spiritual shepherds appear in the role of doormen to the kingdom of heaven and do not admit those who to them are unfit. The Indians do not have anything of their own and pass their whole lives in prayer and work for the friars. Three times daily they are driven to the church, where they listen to the mass in Latin. The rest of the time they work in the fields and in the gardens, using only the most crude and primitive implements, or they perform some other work. At night they are locked in a barracks with a dirt floor. These barracks do not have windows and resemble cattle sheds more than they do human dwellings. There are no beds at all in them, and in addition they are so crowded that it is hardly possible to find a place to sleep. All of their clothing consists of a coarse woolen shirt. They themselves make these shirts, and then receive them as gifts from the mission.

This is the happiness that the Catholic religion brings to the poor Indians, this is the joy that awaits them at the missions! And those who dare to quit this "paradise" in order to try to return to their former life among their free fellow tribesmen are caught and put into irons as punishment.

The devout priests seized large tracts of arable land. These lands are worked by their congregations and planted mainly to wheat and legumes. The harvest is kept in special storehouses. That which is in excess of local needs is sent whenever possible by sea to Mexico, where it is exchanged for those articles that are not produced at the missions. The leftover sizable surplus is thereby converted into cash for the mission coffers.

The friars and the local soldiery, which is strongly dependent upon them, continued to manage quietly in California while the other Spanish colonies declared themselves independent. They remained faithful to the king even when rebellion gripped Mexico and new governments offered them favorable terms to unite in common cause; they stayed loyal, despite the fact that for many years the Spaniards neglected California and did not send to either the churchmen nor the soldiers the salaries owed to them. As usual they strictly observed the royal order to close harbors to all foreign vessels. But ships no longer arrived from Spain, and the ships of the new republics were also deemed foreign. As a result, both the missions and the presidio began to feel a keen want of the many goods that were not produced locally. All of the soldiers, right up to the commander in chief, walked around in rags and, moreover, not receiving any salary, were forced to solicit sustenance from the friars. The latter, too, experienced considerable difficulties in connection with the shortage of agricultural and other implements, for with characteristic Spanish carelessness they had not taken any measures earlier for their [i.e., the tools'] manufacture in California itself.

Thus, the source of income of the missions threatened to run dry. However, the friars continued to remain loyal to the king, which would have done them honor if such a policy had not been dictated by their own interests. In fact, any other form of administration would only have led to the limitation of their power. Meanwhile, the soldiers had already evinced discontent that jeopardized the sway of the friars. An event that occurred two years before our arrival suddenly turned this spark of discontent into a real flame.[6]

As their sole comfort, the Indians from time to time received knickknacks from the friars similar to those that sailors bring from the islanders of the South Sea. The receipt of these knickknacks also ceased, of course, whereupon the Indian converts felt truly unhappy. Their despair turned into revolt. In a fury they broke free of their imprisonment and attacked the dwellings of the friars, but soon they had to yield to the power of firearms. The garrison inflicted a decisive defeat upon the rebels, incurring only minor losses, and the unfortunates had to return to their former bondage. But now the dragoons realized that the friars would fare badly without their courageous intervention. Intoxicated with victory, henceforth they [i.e., the soldiers] began to regard the holy fathers as their wards in need of their protection. Despite the protests of the friars, the soldiers declared themselves the first estate in the country and distanced themselves from Spain, which, it seemed, had already abandoned them many years ago. The same events occurred in Old California, too. Both of these lands, which had earlier considered themselves different provinces, are now separate republics.

Spain could have kept these fertile lands entirely to itself. If it had shown them the slightest support, in all probability they would not have separated from the motherland. And how convenient it would have been to conduct a struggle from here for the restoration of the rebellious colonies to the motherland, especially Mexico, which is contiguous to California and which in the past was an important center of gold extraction! The wealth of the Philippine Islands, which have

---

[6]Kotzebue may be referring to the Chumash revolt, although it occurred in the same year as his visit. See Sandos, "Levantamiento!" 8–11.

remained loyal to Spain, could have provided the means for the fulfilment of this task. However, probably Providence itself had seen to it that Spain had forgotten its Californian possession and that new states could emerge and flourish here.

When California became independent, its harbors were opened to the vessels of all nations, and at first trade grew. The first to take advantage of this change were the ships of the North American [i.e., United] States. At present grain, steer hides, tallow, and valuable sea otter furs are exported from California. An attempt was even made to launch, at the Californios' own risk, trade with China, but it failed. The fact is that a ship with a rich cargo was entrusted to a North American captain. He sold the cargo in China but reckoned that it was more profitable to appropriate both the ship and all of the money earned, and so he did not return.

During our sojourn in New California its head was Don Luis Argüello, the very young man with whom I had become acquainted during my voyage on the *Ryurik*. Then he held the post of commandant of the presidio of San Francisco. Now his residence is in Monterey. There Argüello has considered new laws that could facilitate the establishment of order in this state, which consists of such diverse elements as dragoons, friars, and Indians. One would like to believe that the fate of the last will be safeguarded. At the time of our visit the country still did not have a constitution, and besides, Argüello himself probably did not have either the power or the abilities necessary to achieve the implementation of the project that he had developed. Apparently in both parts of California major changes would have to occur before it was transformed into a thriving and happy country, for which [condition] nature had afforded them every opportunity.

The morning after our arrival I visited old Sánchez at the presidio. He received me with sincere pleasure and recounted in detail all of the events that had occurred here in the eight years that had elapsed since my visit to this harbor on the *Ryurik*. Sánchez told me, incidentally, that Don Luis had become a very important person and that he himself [i.e., Sánchez] had been promoted to the rank of lieutenant, which is highly rated here. He nevertheless condemned the current customs and predicted that they would lead to no good. In his words, he would rather be a humble subject of the Spanish king than a republican officer.

The presidio is in the same state as that of eight years ago. Nothing indicates any important changes in the administration of the country, if one does not count the appearance of the republican flag. It seemed to me that life at the presidio passed, as before, carefreely and indolently.

Sánchez promised to supply our ship daily with fresh meat. Moreover, for vegetables he advised us to send the sloop[7] to Mission Santa Clara, where they were

---

[7] A sloop (Russ., *shlyupka*) was a larger ship's small sailing vessel with a single mast and a single lugsail—as distinct from the larger (two-masted and three-masted) naval sloop (Russ., *shlyup*), a warship of the seventeenth through nineteenth centuries used mainly for auxiliary naval duties.

had in abundance. At the presidio itself, owing to an unconcern understandable only here, they grow fewer vegetables than are needed to feed the garrison.

At the time of my first visit to California I did not have an opportunity to see Mission Santa Clara, and so I resolved to set off there the next morning in our large sloop. Sánchez was so obliging that he provided us with a good pilot, and he also immediately dispatched a rider to the mission to give advance notice of my visit.

San Francisco Bay has a circumference of no less than 90 miles. Islands divide it into two almost equal parts—a southern and a northern [San Pablo Bay]. Three missions—San Francisco, Santa Clara, and San José—are located on the shores of the southern part, which protrudes eastward. I will recount the northern part later.

In the morning of 28 September the longboat was supplied with everything necessary for a short voyage and prepared for departure. We took advantage of the flood tide and the favorable breeze and set out toward the east along delightful shores, capes, and islets. The voyage's destination—Mission Santa Clara—was found approximately 25 miles away from our ship in a straight line. Everywhere we looked, the locale seemed picturesque and fertile. Nowhere were bare cliffs to be seen here: the low shore was covered with lush verdure, a little farther from the shore arose undulating hills in an amphitheater, and on the horizon forested mountains were visible. Over the hills were scattered small groves of oak, separated from each other by beautiful meadows. These groves form the loveliest clusters, such that even the most expert gardener is unable to create.

In this area it is possible without much effort to gather bumper harvests. But you would search in vain here for people making use of these gifts of nature. A dead silence, broken only by the cries of wild beasts, reigns everywhere over the beautiful meadows. As far as the horizon not one hut is visible and no trace of man in general is noticeable. Not a single boat plows the surface of these waters, although large ships—for which there are several good harbors—could sail here. Only large white pelicans with huge pouches under their beaks exploit the rich local fishery, for the Spaniards after two centuries in California have been unable to acquire even nets for catching fish.

Here thousands of families could live carefreely and contentedly. So how much more sensible it would be to enlist Europeans who are now sent as colonists to Brazil, provided they preferred to settle in California! In Brazil they encounter great difficulties and do not always meet with understanding and support on the part of the government, and in the end they perish, not enduring the unfamiliar heat. In California these colonists would find a climate like that of southern Germany,[8] and nature would reward their slightest efforts lavishly.

---

[8]In fact, the climate is rather warmer, sunnier, and drier than that of southern Germany.

After having sailed about two hours, we noticed on our right a deeply indented bay on whose shore, among wooded hills, sprawled the mission of San Francisco. Meanwhile, the ebb tide commenced, the wind died, and we had to advance slowly with the oars. Because of this [slowness], after going about 15 miles, we decided to make camp on a small, comfortable island. It was already time to replenish ourselves. We made a large campfire, and because every sailor had some knowledge of cooking, dinner was soon ready. Taking advantage of the fine weather, we composed ourselves in the fresh air under a shady oak tree. That [repose] is likely [the reason] why the dinner seemed so tasty to us.

While the sailors rested, we investigated the island. Its high northern shore dropped nearly vertically into the bay. Here, as everywhere in the vicinity of San Francisco Bay, variegated slate[9] was deposited under the layer of black earth. We did not notice any signs on the island that people had ever visited it. Probably man had never trod here, for only recently have boats existed hereabouts, and even now each mission has only one barge. In these flat-bottomed vessels the pious friars navigate the rivers flowing into the northern half of the bay. They undertake such voyages with the aim of converting to Christianity the Indians roaming the banks of these rivers, i.e., in order to recruit new workers. The Indians themselves likewise have no ships, if one does not count the boats made of sheaves of reeds. They sit in these boats nearly up to the waist in the water. In a region abounding in construction timber nobody knows how to make even a simple wooden boat! This [lack] clearly attests both the inertia of the Spaniards [Californios] and the stupidity of the Indians.

Wild ducks and other waterfowl swam around our island. Baldheaded eagles soared over the tops of the oaks. They were hunting small rabbits, as well as the graceful partridges [California quail] that are often encountered here. For about two hours we took pleasure in resting on land, so agreeable for seafarers, and then we again set off, taking advantage of a rising fresh breeze.

The sun was already setting when we approached the eastern shore of the bay. Here it was deep enough for large sloops only, and the locale had a different appearance. The mountains receded into the background. Before us stretched a wide plain that became lower and lower toward the shore, ending in a marsh. The marsh is dissected by meandering but fairly deep channels, along which one can reach dry land in boats. It had already grown dark when we entered these channels. Without a good pilot here it would be possible to lose one's way even in daytime, for both sides of the channels were densely overgrown with high reeds [tule], over which only the sky was visible. Our sailors rowed with much difficulty. Gradually the passages narrowed and the locale became drier. Soon

---

[9]Or shale or schist.

beyond the wall of reeds a human voice was heard, and at midnight we finally reached the landing. Here a large bonfire had been lit. Around it stood two dragoons with two saddle horses intended for us, as well as several half-naked Indians sent from the mission to meet us.

I decided to overnight, for it was still another hour to the mission, and the night was very dark; in addition, I did not want to disturb the night's rest of the friars. Immediately our small tents were pitched, several new campfires burst into flames, and the cook again set to work. During the day we had sailed fewer than 40 miles, for we had been obliged to change course often. After such a long voyage in the boat a sleep in a tent in this lovely night seemed very agreeable to us. Although it was already the end of September here, the breeze blowing around us was as warm as our hottest summer nights at home.

Around our camp some sort of barking was heard repeatedly, as if we were surrounded by many young dogs. It was the barking [yipping] of a small, fox-sized local breed of wolves [coyotes], which are encountered abundantly throughout California. These animals are extremely daring and cunning. They often sneak up to dwellings during the night and try to steal something, and it is with difficulty that one manages to drive them off. In this matter we had to learn from our own experience; having left our supply of meat insufficiently guarded, in the morning we found only empty gnawed bags.

The rising sun announced the advent of a fine morning and gave us an opportunity to examine the neighborhood of our camp. Around us stretched a boundless plain on which the friars grow wheat. The crop had already been harvested, and large herds of cattle, flocks of sheep, and bands of horses were grazing the stubble. Mission Santa Clara possesses great riches. It has more than 14 thousand head of cattle, a thousand horses, and 10 thousand sheep. Most of the cattle graze without supervision in the woods and, running wild, multiply rapidly.

I ordered the horses saddled, and we galloped to the mission, the horizon visible beyond extensive fields. The reaped fields that we passed were literally covered with flocks of wild geese, ducks, and snipe. They allowed us to come so close that with a little skill it would be possible to throw a stick and kill many birds. These migratory birds winter in California, and in summer they go north, where they hatch young. We fired several shots and killed a dozen geese. Some of them were totally white and in size did not differ from our domestic geese.

After about half an hour in the saddle we arrived at Mission Santa Clara [de Asís]. The friars received us very hospitably and exerted every effort to make our stay here pleasant. Mission Santa Clara was founded in 1777. It is situated on the banks of a small river [Guadalupe River] with miraculous water in the middle of extensive and extremely fertile plains. The mission buildings were surrounded by shady oaks. Adjoining them were orchards and gardens, which are cultivated very carelessly but nonetheless supply the friars abundantly with every possible fruit and vegetable, including fine grapes.

Mission Santa Clara has the same buildings as all of the other missionary settlements: a large stone church, a spacious dwelling for the friars, a capacious storehouse for the grain and various implements, and, finally, barracks for the Indians, the so-called ranchería, which I have already mentioned. These barracks consist of long rows of squat, narrow huts, more like stalls, with sections for each family, where with difficulty one can be accommodated for the night.

We were also struck by a large building constructed in the form of a closed quadrangle and without a single window on the outside. One can enter this building only through a small, carefully locked door, such that it is very reminiscent of a prison for state felons. Here the missionaries, those strict guardians of chastity, keep under special supervision the young unmarried Indian women. The prisoners engage in spinning, weaving, and other such work. The prison's door is opened only when the young recluses go to church, two or three times a day. Several times I happened to observe that when the door is flung open, the poor girls literally burst outside and, intoxicated with joy, inhale the fresh air. However, an old ragged Spaniard with a cane in his hand immediately drove them to the church, treating them like a flock of sheep, and at the end of the Mass the young Indian women had to return immediately to their quarters. The girls are found under the very strict supervision of the holy fathers. Nevertheless, sometimes they manage to evade the vigilance of their guards, as attested—I was told—by the shackles that I saw on the legs of some of these plain local beauties. Only after marriage do these young novices move again to the common barracks with their compatriots.

Three times a day a bell summons the Indians to eat. Their food is prepared in large cauldrons, and then portions are distributed among individual families. Meat is given rarely to the Indians. Usually they eat a broth of millet flour, corn, peas, and beans, cooked in water. It is not possible at all to call this [fare] the most healthful food.

At Mission Santa Clara live 1,500 Indian males, about half of whom are married. This human mass is managed by three friars; it is guarded by four soldiers under a noncommissioned officer. Since such negligible protection is quite sufficient, it must be assumed that the Indians live better at the mission than at liberty, or they are so bound by habit that, like animals, they are attached to the place where they are fed.

The first of these suppositions does not, evidently, correspond to reality. The hard work every day except Sunday, which is passed almost solely in prayer, the corporal punishment, imprisonment, and shackles for unpunctual fulfilment of the friars' demands, the poor food, the squalid quarters, the deprivation of everything of their own and of nearly all of the joy of life—all of this [privation], of course, cannot in any measure satisfy even the most undemanding human existence. Consequently, many Indians try to save themselves by fleeing. However, the soldiers quickly find the runaways, even if they manage to hide themselves among their savage compatriots, and force them to return, as I have already said. Severe punishment awaits them at the mission.

Only extreme backwardness can explain the fact that the Indians patiently endure their cruel treatment at the missions. This stupid and plain people, it seems to me, rank even lower in development than the inhabitants of Tierra del Fuego and Van Dieman's Land [Tasmania]. Essentially, these creatures bear only a remote similarity to humans. The Christian religion, or more accurately what the friars call religion, does not promote their cultural development at all. And how can notions of Christianity penetrate such limited minds if the holy fathers do not know the local languages and thus have almost no opportunity to explain themselves to their flock! On the contrary, contact with the missionaries depreciates these stepchildren of nature even more. Subsequently I chanced to observe the free Indians. They did not seem as stupid and were, evidently, more developed than those under the care of the "thinking people" (*gente de razón*).

If they wanted to make the Indians into real people, not imaginary Christians, then they should teach them house building, grain growing, and stock rearing on the lands remaining in their possession, as well as allow them to freely dispose of the output of their own labor. In that event human culture would spread among them of its own accord, and then, perhaps, the "barbarians" (*los bárbaros*) would compare to "thinking people."

A great many Indian tribes, who speak different languages and are frequently completely unlike each other, inhabit California. In the single mission of Santa Clara, for example, the Indians speak more than twenty languages. Representatives of all of these tribes are equally stupid, dirty, and ugly. They are, as a rule, of medium height and very weak build, and their skin is of a very dark shade. The faces of the Californian Indians are flat with thick, outturned lips, broad noses of the Negro type, very low foreheads, and thick, black hair. Their spiritual development is rudimentary. La Pérouse probably did not exaggerate when he asserted that any of them who is able to understand that two fours make eight is considered a Descartes or Newton by his countrymen. For most of the local Indians this deduction is too complicated.

All of the savage Indians here lead a nomadic way of life. Hunting is their sole occupation; only it affords them a means of existence. So the bow and arrow is the only skill at which they excel. This skill has cost the lives of many Spaniards. The Indians roam the forests and mountains naked in pursuit of a kill. If they want to stop somewhere for a while, they build a wretched shelter of thatch that they burn upon leaving the site.

As I have said, crop growing is a source of great income to the local clergy, and they cultivate very large expanses. In the mission of Santa Clara only the yearly harvest of wheat exceeds 3,000 fanegas, i.e., about 620 English quarters [4,960 English bushels] or 3,400 Berlin *chetveriks*.[10] Thanks to the exceptional fertility of the soil, the average yield in these places is forty-fold [the seed], although European agriculturalists would find that the land is worked unsatisfactorily here. They till the soil with a very primitive plow and then sow and till again. At this point all work ends, and not a little of the seed dies under the hard clods of soil. With good tillage these fields would yield crops that are unknown in Europe. The friars themselves admit that they know little about cultivation, but they are quite satisfied with the present bumper harvests. What is completely inexcusable, however, is their unconcern with respect to the making of flour. Heretofore not a single flour mill has existed in California, and the unfortunate Indians with much labor have to grind the kernels of wheat between two flat stones.

We made an excursion to a pueblo a half hour's walk from the mission. This [i.e., a pueblo] is what in California is called a village where families of invalids and retired presidio soldiers with their offspring live. The said pueblo is located in a very picturesque locale. Comfortable stone houses surround fruit orchards, from the fences of which clusters of grapes droop temptingly. The residents emerged to meet us hospitably, and with the courtesy and ceremony typical of Spaniards they invited us into their simple but clean homes. All of the pueblo's residents have a healthy and content appearance. And they are really happy. Free of any exactions, these people own all of the land that they want to occupy, and they live carefreely on the prolific returns of crop growing and stock rearing.

In California there are many such pueblos, and their population is increasing considerably each year. At the same time the number of Indians living at the missions is rapidly decreasing as a result of their high mortality; often death removes up to one-third of the neophytes in one year. So in general the holy fathers could not exist here if it were not for the constant enrolment by force or cunning of new recruits among the savage Indians. In Old [Baja] California, several missions have already closed, for the Indians living thereabouts were completely annihilated. In the northern part of New [Alta] California there are still populous reserves of people, but if in the future they are treated as wastefully, then

---

[10]The meaning of "Berlin chetveriks" is uncertain; there are eight chetveriks to one chetvert, which in turn equals 6 English bushels, so that 3,400 chetveriks equal only 2,550 English bushels.

the time will come when this source, too, will run dry. Meanwhile, the number of pueblo residents will increase steadily; it is they who are forming California's new population.

We passed three days at Mission Santa Clara, whose friars, in any case, it is impossible to fault in one virtue—hospitality. We set off on our return route with a load of fruit and vegetables, purchased fairly cheaply. They conducted us to the shore in very clumsy and heavy two-wheeled carts,[11] drawn by oxen. The wheels of these carts were solid disks of thick boards attached to each other. These disks did not have a totally correct shape, and in addition they were not bored precisely in the center, so that they turned with difficulty, and the axles constantly jerked up and down. From this our fine muskmelons, watermelons, peaches, apricots, figs, and grapes, as well as remarkable apples (such as Europe does not have), suffered greatly. On the launch everything had already been prepared for receiving the cargo. The sailors told us that at night large white wolves had troubled them.

Taking advantage of the outgoing tide, we sailed away from the shore and soon saw a narrow bay, resembling a river, stretching toward the east. At its end, in a very fertile locale, was situated Mission San José, founded in 1797. At present it is one of the richest in California. A pueblo has also arisen near it. This pueblo and the pueblo near Mission Santa Clara are to this day the only pueblos on the shores of San Francisco Bay. A road was built long ago between the missions of San José and Santa Clara. One can cover it in two hours on horseback.

Soon after we had returned to the boat, a friar appeared ashore riding in the company of one dragoon. Swinging his big hat, he gave us to understand that he wanted to come aboard. We immediately sent the sloop for him, and a thin Spaniard of medium height, extremely lively and talkative, appeared before us. He was called Father Tomás [Esténaga][12] from Mission San Francisco, and he offered for a goodly payment to supply us daily with fresh provisions, even including two bottles of milk. The friar owned countless cows and boasted greatly that he was the only man in the San Francisco area who had finally succeeded after long effort to obtain some milk from them. Because they could not supply us from the presidio, and Mission Santa Clara was too distant, I had to accept his offer. Upon his departure Father Tomás invited me to dine with him.

The next day I set off on horseback to Mission San Francisco, accompanied by several officers. I have already described it in the account of my previous voyage. Since then the mission has virtually not changed. The merry and cheerful Tomás was now the only friar there, so he was the sole manager. He received us very

---

[11]Sp., *carretas.*

[12]Tomás Eleuterio Esténaga (1790–1847), a native of Spain's Basque Country, arrived in Alta California in 1820. He served at Mission San Francisco from 1821 until 1833. He did not take the oath of allegiance to Mexico until 1843. See Geiger, *Franciscan Missionaries,* 78–81.

hospitably and treated us sumptuously. Innumerable dishes, heavily seasoned with pepper and garlic, were served at dinner. He also zealously poured us the local wine, which was not bad and which he stored in his cellars. At the same time we were entertained with music. Little naked Indian boys strummed on bad violins, and the worthy friar himself twirled the barrel organ standing beside him. The fruit served for dessert had been sent from Mission Santa Clara, for hereabouts it ripened poorly because of the sea fogs that not infrequently come right up to the mission.

One morning we heard cannon fire. It was done with the help of the very gunpowder remaining from the salute that had been given in honor of our ship. With this firing the presidio welcomed the arrival of its commandant, Don Ignacio Martínez, who was returning after fulfilling his duties upon the conclusion of the [provincial] congress at Monterey. With him on business came the commandant of the presidio of San Diego, Don José María Estudillo,[13] with whom I had become acquainted during my previous stay in this country. Both commandants, accompanied by Sánchez, visited me, and we dined on the ship. They liked it so much aboard that they did not return ashore until nighttime.

Pressing official business called me to the settlement of the Russian-American Company called Ross, located about 80 miles north of San Francisco. For some time already I had been thinking about going there by land. However, such a journey was attended with great difficulties, which could be overcome only with the assistance of the governor. So I decided to take advantage of his friendly disposal, and he readily satisfied me. We requested riding horses, as well as a military escort, who had to show us the way and at the same time protect us in case of an attack by the savages. Both were given to us by the governor. Don Estudillo decided to take part in this adventure and took upon himself the command of the escort assigned to us.

[The naturalist] Doctor Eschscholtz, [the mineralogist] Gofman,[14] two of my officers, two sailors, Don Estudillo, and four dragoons had to go with me. So our entire detachment consisted of twelve men. A day of rest was set. In the evening of the day before [our departure,] Don Estudillo came to the ship with his four dragoons. They were well armed and tightly fitted in leather armor. Estudillo himself in old Spanish dress with an enormous sword and even more impressive spurs, with pistols and a dagger in his belt and a carbine in his hands, presented

---

[13]José María Estudillo (1772–1830) was a peninsular who had left for the New World at the age of fifteen. He arrived in Baja California in 1795 and enlisted as a soldier the next year. In 1806 he was transferred to Monterey, where he was promoted to lieutenant and appointed commandant, serving until the end of 1827, whereupon he was promoted to captain and transferred to San Diego. See [Bancroft], *California Pioneer Register*, 134.

[14]Ernst Karlovich Gofman (Ernst Karl Hoffmann) (1801–71) was a naturalist and geologist of German origin. From 1833 to 1863 he taught geology and mineralogy at Dorpat (Tartu), Kiev, and St. Petersburg Universities. See Grinëv, *Kto yest kto*, 135.

an even more picturesque appearance and resembled an adventurer of the past. He was certain that it was necessary to observe the utmost caution, for we had to cross areas where "unpeaceable Indians" (*los indianos* [*sic: Indios*] *bravos*) held sway. So we, too, provided ourselves with plenty of arms.

Early in the morning, when the first rays of the sun were only beginning to gild the mountain peaks, our small but well-armed party took its seats in the longboat. We set off northeastward through San Francisco Bay, for our land trip had to begin only at the mission of San Gabriel [*sic:* San Rafael],[15] situated on the northern shore of this bay. The weather was fine, the air unusually agreeable. We rowed in a dead calm. Our pilot was the Indian Marco, brought by Estudillo. Either the local Spaniards are unable to remember the route by sea, even in the event that they have made the same voyage several times, or they consider the duties of a pilot too onerous. So they always take an experienced Indian with them as a helmsman.

Despite his middle age, Estudillo was very merry company. He proved to be the most educated of the Spaniards met by me in California. Estudillo strutted his literary knowledge somewhat, and he named three books that he had read, not counting *Don Quixote* and *Gil Blas*.[16] As he told me confidentially, none of the other Spaniards here had hardly ever seen any other book, except the Bible.

Marco had grown old at the mission. For the friars he was a very valuable man, and so they treated him considerably better than they did the other Indians. Marco spoke Spanish fluently. Estudillo tried to make him the butt of his jokes but found a worthy opponent in the old Indian. Sometimes he was stumped by Marco's responses. The example of Marco demonstrates that under favorable conditions the mental capacity of the Californian Indians can be fully developed. However, this happens very rarely at the missions.

Don Estudillo spoke very openly about the situation in California, where he has already spent thirty years.[17] Like most of the soldiers, he is unfriendly to the missionaries and calls them egoists who care only about themselves. Estudillo explained that the holy fathers enrich themselves at the expense of the brutal exploitation of the Indian converts, and then depart with their wealth for Spain. He also described how this treatment occurs. In Estudillo's words, not infrequently the friars send dragoons into the hills to catch free pagans, intending

---

[15]The reason why Kotzebue confuses these two missions is unclear, for San Gabriel Arcángel lay several hundred miles to the south, in today's Greater Los Angeles area; perhaps he was befuddled by the fact that both missions were named after archangels. Hereafter I have identified his San Gabriel Arcángel as San Rafael Arcángel.

[16]*L'Histoire de Gil Blas de Santillane,* a picaresque novel by Alain-René Lesage, published several times between 1715 and 1735.

[17]Estudillo, however, was born in 1798, so by 1824 he would have lived no more than twenty-seven years in Alta California.

to convert them into Christian slaves. This hunt is done with a lasso—a strong leather rope ending in a noose; the other end of the rope is tied to a saddle. A dragoon deftly throws this lasso a distance of 7–8 sazhens and almost always without missing. Having sneaked up to a group of Indians, in an instant he throws the noose of the lasso over the head of one of them, and spurs his horse and gallops to the mission with his catch. Sometimes he delivers only a corpse. I must say that I have never chanced to meet more skillful and daring horsemen than the local dragoons. It is not surprising that several of these cavalrymen together actually succeed in lassoing even bears and feral bulls. For catching Indians a single dragoon suffices.

Estudillo asserted, too, that not one Indian, in spite of the protestations of the friars, has come to a mission of his own free will. All of them either are caught in the aforesaid manner or are slyly lured. For this purpose several Indians like our pilot Marco [i.e., decoys] are kept at each mission and treated very well. They are sent traveling through remote areas, where they must employ all of their eloquence in order to persuade their savage compatriots to visit a mission. Upon those Indians who visit, even if only once, they immediately perform the ceremony of conversion, and they [i.e., the converts] remain forever in the power of the friars. When an Indian tries to flee, he is pursued by a horseman with a lasso. The lash and shackles await the runaway.

I suggested that now probably much is changing, since the sway of the clergy has ended and the soldiers are no longer so heavily dependent upon them. To this Estudillo replied as follows.

"California could become a powerful state, for nature has endowed it with an abundance of everything that is necessary for this [development]. However, we must be guided by a strong person. Don Luis Argüello is not capable of putting our utterly ruined finances in order and implementing a system of seniority, without which no state can exist. He is unable to give us a constitution, which could be safeguarded by peace and general satisfaction. All of the soldiers hold the opinion that whoever pays them their salary that is still owed by Spain can command them! Such statements are often repeated for all to hear. On this basis Mexico has begun talks with us that are at the center of attention of the council in Monterey. It is still not known whether California will become an independent state or fall under the control of another power."

I confess that I could not but think how happy this land would be under the protection of our great empire and what benefits Russia itself would receive. California would be a granary for Kamchatka, Okhotsk, and all of the settlements of the Russian-American Company. Its annexation would breathe new life into these areas, which not infrequently experience a want of necessities.

By this time, when the sun was shining in all its splendor over the mountain-tops, we had already rowed between the islands separating the southern part of the bay from the northern part [San Pablo Bay]. Soon a smooth surface of water unfolded before us. Beyond it lay the nearest destination of our journey—the mission of San Rafael Arcángel, which can be identified only by the mountains rising at a distance from the shore, for the unfolding plain was so low that it did not appear on the horizon. To the northwest we saw another recently founded mission, San Francisco Solona [sic: Solano].[18] These two establishments still remain the only missions on the shores of the northern part of the bay.

Here are found the same charming landscapes as on the shores of the southern part of the bay. Sloping hills, whose height gradually increases with their distance from the shore, woods resembling parks, and lovely meadows were visible everywhere. This time the northwestern shore stayed on our left, and later I visited it repeatedly. Here there are several small but safe natural harbors. Their depth at the shore is so great as to allow the largest ships to anchor. It was right here that our ship stocked very tasty drinking water, for the water in the vicinity of the presidio is poor in quality.

The whole of San Francisco Bay is a capital harbor in which a thousand ships could anchor. There are more suitable small coves [in which] to repair them located along the northwestern side, since there ships can almost come right up to the shore, and nearby there is superb shipbuilding timber, including large trees [coast redwoods] for masts.

Strictly speaking, all of the northern side of the bay is not regarded as California but seen by geographers as part of New Albion. This coast has not yet been explored by a single navigator and is little known even to the local Spaniards. Two large navigable rivers, one [the Sacramento] from the north and the other [the San Joaquín] from the east, fall into the northern part of the bay. Later I had the opportunity to examine them. The region seems fertile everywhere, and its climate can perhaps be called the finest and most salubrious on earth. However, the destiny of this territory is like that of a mute virtue or a humble merit: like them, it remains unnoticed. Our descendants will do it more justice and thereby at some time recognize the value of California. Towns and villages will appear in this empty region, the ships of all nations will come to anchor in the local waters, which now are furrowed only rarely by a solitary boat, and the prosperous and happy population of this area will with thanks enjoy the generous gifts of nature and deliver the local treasures to all parts of the world.

---

[18]Here again Kotzebue's geography is confusing. From his boat's position Mission San Rafael would have lain to the northwest and Mission San Francisco Solano (commonly called simply Sonoma Mission) to the north, not the northwest, and moreover at a distance of up to twenty miles, which would have put it out of sight.

A favorable fresh wind helped us to overcome the opposing current generated by the ebb tide. The steep banks of the common mouth of both aforesaid rivers stayed on our right. And when the sun was about to set in the blue sky behind the tops of the mountains [Coast Ranges] in the west, we passed through a narrow channel crossing a marshy riverside plain and reached a landing place.

From here a good nautical mile [1.15 land miles] remained to the mission of San Rafael Arcángel, visible at a distance amid some old oak trees.[19] Numerous horses belonging to the mission grazed a lovely meadow stretching along the riverside. Alongside them a herd of small deer, abundant in these parts, nibbled the grass peacefully. Our dragoons, not wanting to go to the mission on foot, grasped their lassos and caught as many horses as they needed. We had saddles with us, so we were soon being borne at a gallop over the plain past the oak trees growing singly here.

The mission of San Rafael Arcángel is now managed by one friar [Juan Amorós], who met us very hospitably. This mission, founded in 1816,[20] is apparently situated more advantageously than the mission of Santa Clara. A high range of hills protects it from the cold north winds. However, in the friar's words, "unpeaceable Indians" live beyond this natural barrier. Once they even succeeded in attacking the mission and burning its buildings, so that they [i.e., the Californios of the mission] have to be on their guard constantly. Actually, Mission San Rafael Arcángel seems to be an outpost defending all of the other missions. Its garrison, comprising six dragoons, is ready for battle at the least alarm.

At night insects prevented me from falling asleep, and I took a walk in the direction of the hills. Here I saw two sentries, fully armed. They had made campfires, and every ten minutes they rang a bell hanging between two poles, evidently in order to demonstrate their vigilance. Each time the sound of the bells was answered by the cries of wolves [coyotes] that roam about the mission. These small beasts are rather similar in external appearance to foxes. The mission has hardly anything serious to fear from other enemies, as attested by both the small number of dragoons and the absence of defensive structures, although the mission is located in the middle of an open field. The bravery of the "unpeaceable Indians" apparently consists of their not wanting to submit willingly and of concealing themselves from pursuit, and sometimes, perhaps, of even stealing toward the mission in order to torch it. Here we saw several such "heroes." They worked patiently in shackles, and nothing distinguished them from the Indians living at the missions of San Francisco [de Asís] and Santa Clara.

---

[19]It is not definite from Kotzebue's hydrographic, topographic, directional, and distance references (in terms of both time and miles) here and later that this mission was indeed San Rafael (his "San Gabriel"); it may well have been Mission Sonoma, although it was located at least a dozen miles inland.

[20]In fact, at the end of 1817.

With the first rays of the rising sun we were already on our horses. After the valley of the mission had been left behind and we had crossed the height bordering it, our guide turned to the northwest. We moved even farther inland. Our horses trod the virgin soil as if it were lacking unevenness. Trees with dense shading leaves grew in it in picturesque separate stands. It seemed as if they had been planted by expert gardeners who still continued to tend them lovingly. How easy it would be to cultivate these fields in which there were no stones whatever! How fertile this soil must be, judging from the lush grass growing here!

All of the time we came across innumerable herds of small deer. These [black-tailed] deer were so bold that they allowed us to come almost right up to them, and only then would an arrow move them to a distance. More infrequently we saw deer [*sic:* elk] of another kind, the size of a horse with beautiful spreading antlers. They usually grazed on heights from which it would be convenient to survey the vicinity, and they seemed much more cautious than the small deer. Nevertheless, the Indians hunt them successfully. They attach to their heads the antlers of dead elk, cover themselves with elk skins, and, moving on all fours, sneak through the high grass toward a herd, accurately imitating the movements the elk make while grazing. The elk continue to take the hunters for their kind until the arrows begin to whistle and the first victims fall.

Toward noon the heat was so unbearable that we had to halt. We settled ourselves on a hillock in the shade of an oak tree, and [after] releasing our horses to graze, we began to eat. At this time a group of Indians appeared at a distance beyond some thickets, so that our dragoons immediately grasped their guns. But the savage Indians soon disappeared without daring to approach us. After resting for two hours, we again set off on our route. I was not a little astonished by the ability of our guide to find his bearings easily in the area, where he had been but once before and where there were no special landmarks from which it would be possible to find one's way.

We were witnesses to the pursuit of a herd of small deer by two large and shaggy white wolves [coyotes]. This time these graceful creatures were saved, for the wolves fled upon seeing us. In many places we saw small cylindrical huts built of boughs. They had likely been very recently deserted by the Indians, and twice we even came across recently extinguished campfires with the ashes still smoldering. Apparently we often came close to the Indians. However, thanks to their sharp eyesight the latter spotted us before we saw them, and so quickly did they hide from the dreaded soldiers with their lassos that we did not succeed in seeing them.

In the evening we approached a small river [Estero Americano] that flows through a mountainous ravine and enters the sea at Port Rumyantsev, or Bodega. The sea was not far, but a good ten miles still remained to the colony of Ross. It was already growing dark, and so we decided to overnight here. The night was foggy and cool; we passed it quite badly.

In the morning we forded this shallow stream. Now we advanced through an area that was very different from that through which our route had run the day before. The difference became more appreciable the nearer we approached the coast. The gently sloping hills and the valley's delightful appearance were replaced by a bleaker landscape. High, sharp cliffs overgrown with thick decidu-ous woods alternated here with steep precipices. We made many detours, but still it was impossible to avoid numerous steep ascents, which we had to climb with great difficulty. By midday we had reached a considerable height, from which a delightful view unfolded. The ocean, whose shore forms Port Rumyantsev here, was visible to the west. Only small vessels can enter it. Owing to its location, there is an insignificant Russian settlement here that will probably never become as important as it would if circumstances had permitted its founding on San Francisco Bay. To the east a valley, which, Estudillo told me, the Indians call the Valley of White People, extended deeply into the mainland.

Among the Indians there exists an old legend according to which one day a ship was lost on the local shore. The white people saved from it settled in this valley and lived in friendship with the Indians. Nothing is known about what happened to them afterwards.

To the northeast rises a large mountain overgrown with a thick spruce forest. It has an impregnable appearance, as a result of which mainly Indians live on it. Their presence there was attested by a column of smoke. Our soldiers said that on this mountain there lives an Indian leader who is respected by both the Spaniards and his fellow tribesmen for his bravery. According to the soldiers, this entire tribe belongs to a completely different race. All of its members are distinguished by courage and prefer death to subjugation by the missionaries. So none of them is found in the power of the priests. The higher level of development of these Indians is possibly explained by the fact that they derive from intermarriage with the white survivors of the shipwreck.

Now in places we had to ride along the ocean's sandy beach, so that the waves of the breakers poured over the hoofs of our horses and here and there forced their way to the meadows and heights. Soon, after having left Port Rumyantsev behind, we forded a shallow river [the Russian River] that the Russians call the Slavyanka. Its depth increases with distance from the ocean, and it even becomes navigable. The Russians have ascended its course for a hundred verstas. The Slavyanka flows from the northeast. Its banks are apparently very fertile but are populated by numerous warlike tribes.

The area through which we were passing looked very romantic, although it continued to be very bleak. Lush grass grew everywhere, attesting to the fertility of the soil. After having found ourselves again atop a high mountain, we were glad to see Fort Ross below. A fairly decent road ran down a slope. We spurred our tired horses and to the considerable surprise of the fort's residents galloped to its gates. The manager of the settlement, Shmidt,[21] received us very amicably and ordered the firing of several cannons in honor of our arrival on Russian-American Company land. Then he very hospitably invited us to his comfortable and clean house, built of thick logs in the European style.

Fort Ross is situated on a high marine terrace by the mouth of a small stream [Fort Ross Creek] at 38° 33' North latitude. It was founded in 1812 with the consent of the native inhabitants, who willingly helped to bring construction materials and even to take part in the erection of buildings. The Russians settled here in order to expand the hunting of sea otters along the Californian coast, for these animals had been completely extirpated at our more northerly settlements. The Spaniards, who do not engage in this hunt,[22] willingly permitted the Russians in return for a fixed indemnity to settle the local coast, where at that time there was still an abundance of sea otters. At the present time these animals have become rare here. Nonetheless, on the coast of California, where hunting is conducted from the colony of Ross, more sea otters are still caught than anywhere else in the world.

The fort is a quadrangle surrounded by a palisade of high, thick logs. It has two watchtowers provided with 15 cannons. At the time of my visit to the fort its garrison consisted of 130 persons, of whom only a few were Russians and the rest "Aleuts."

At first the Spaniards had no objection to the presence of Russian settlers here and supplied them with bulls, cows, horses, and sheep. However, after having noticed that the colony of Ross, despite its less fertile soil and worse climate, was flourishing more than their own settlements, they began to envy the colonists and to fear for their own future, and so they demanded that the Russians leave. The Spaniards asserted that their possessions on the western coast of America reach as far as the North Pacific Ocean, and they threatened to support their

---

[21]Karl Ivanovich Shmidt (Carl Johan Schmidt) (1796–1863) succeeded Ivan Kuskov as manager of Ross Counter in late 1821. A native of Sveaborg (Suomenlinna), a fortress in the harbor of Helsinki, Finland, he was trained in navigation. In 1817 as a civilian navigator he sailed to Russian America as a passenger on the *Kamchatka*. At New Archangel he was hired by the company to supervise the colonial capital's arsenal and artillery, as well as its library. In 1820 Governor Yanovsky appointed Shmidt manager of Ross Counter. He continued shipbuilding and expanded farming at Ross, but his management of the counter proved unsatisfactory to the company, and at the end of 1824 Governor Muravyov replaced him. A year later he was released by the company, and he returned to Russia aboard the *Yelena* in 1826. The rest of his career was spent in naval service in the Baltic Sea until 1861, when he retired at the rank of captain, second class. See Grinëv, *Kto yest kto,* 613; and Pierce, *Russian America,* 447.

[22]This is not totally correct, as not a few were taken by Baja California's natives under the aegis of the missionaries in the late 1700s.

demand with force of arms. Kuskov, the founder and then manager of Fort Ross, a sensible and fearless man, gave them a very firm answer. He said that he had founded the colony on the orders of his superiors and, moreover, in a locality that had not been occupied earlier by any other power. He stressed that really only the native inhabitants could lay claim to the land in question, but they had willingly ceded it to the Russians. On these grounds Kuskov rejected such a baseless demand and warned that force would be answered with force. The Spaniards understood that they could not best the Russians, and so they dropped their ridiculous claims and again launched amicable relations with the settlers. At present these two nations live here in complete harmony.

Meanwhile, the settlement of Ross brought much benefit to the Spaniards. Neither a single locksmith nor a single blacksmith is found in all of California. So all of the iron implements of the Spaniards are manufactured or repaired in the Russian colony for a handsome payment. The dragoons accompanying us brought many broken rifle bolts with them to be repaired.

In order that the Russians could not extend the boundary of their colony to the northern shore of San Francisco Bay, the Spaniards hurriedly built the missions of San Rafael Arcángel and San Francisco Solano there. It is a great pity that we did not forestall them. Indeed, a settlement on the shore of this fine bay could bring us innumerable benefits, especially if one considers that in this region we possess only the poor harbor of Bodega.

The residents of the settlement of Ross live in peace and harmony with the local [native] population. Many Indians come to the fort and work there for daily payment. They usually pass the night outside the fort. The Indians willingly give their daughters in marriage to the Russians and "Aleuts." As a result, numerous family ties have emerged that facilitate the further cementing of friendship and mutual understanding. The residents of Ross, hunting deer and other game alone, range far from the fort. They often pass the night among Indians of various tribes, and nothing bad ever happens to them. The Spaniards would never bring themselves to do so. The more striking the contrast between the oppression of the Indians in the missions and their treatment in our settlement, the more must every human being rejoice upon entering Russian territory. The Orthodox Church does not propagate its doctrine by force. It is free of fanaticism and preaches love and tolerance. This church does not strive at any cost to attract people of another faith but allows them to accept Orthodoxy only in accordance with sincere inner conviction. For those whom it admits to its bosom it forever remains a loving mother. How different this is from the policy of the Catholic priests and Protestant missionaries!

The locality of the settlement of Ross is distinguished by a mild climate. Only rarely does the mercury in the [Réaumur] thermometer fall below zero here.

Unfortunately, the frequent fogs hamper the development of horticulture and vegetable gardening. However, at a distance of several verstas from the coast, in those places where the fogs do not penetrate, nearly all southern plants grow very well. Vegetables here reach an extraordinary size. Radishes weighing up to 50 funts and pumpkins weighing 65 funts are to be found; and other vegetables are correspondingly enormous. Potatoes yield one hundred– or two hundred–fold [the seed] here and, moreover, are harvested twice a year. So famine is scarcely possible at the settlement of Ross. The fort is surrounded by fields of wheat and barley belonging to individual inhabitants of the settlement. Owing to the fogs, cereals do not grow as well here as at Santa Clara [Mission], but the colonists nevertheless have the opportunity of eating white bread and kasha daily. Usually the "Aleuts" leave their homeland very reluctantly, but they like this area so much that they are pleased to stay here and do not miss their islands.

The Spaniards should study farming at the settlement of Ross under Shmidt. He manages the economy here with astonishing and praiseworthy perfection. All of the agricultural implements are made here under his direction and are not inferior to the best European models. Our Spanish companions were likewise staggered by all of this. But what amazed them most of all was the windmill; they had never seen such a perfect and useful machine.

Around the settlement of Ross there is a lot of construction timber that the company exploits. Two ships have already been launched from the stocks here. The sea abounds in very tasty fish, and an inexhaustible number of the best game is found on land. Possessing all of these merits, the settlement suffers only from the want of a good harbor. However, given the skillful management of its economy, it can nevertheless eventually supply our more northerly settlements with all necessary supplies.

The local Indians [Pomos and Miwoks] are very like those who live at the missions. It is possible to say that they all belong to one race, although they speak different languages. Here, however, they are not as dull and look more cheerful and contented, whereas at the missions their faces have the stamp of profound gravity, and their eyes are always fixed on the ground. These differences are explained by their dissimilar lot.

The Indians here also go naked and lead a nomadic way of life. Apart from their daily work with the Russians, their sole occupation is hunting. They are very undemanding in their choice of food. They will eat any trash heartily, including various insects and worms, making an exception for venomous snakes only. In winter they stock acorns and the seeds of wild rye, which grows here abundantly. When the rye ripens, the Indians set fire to it. The straw is burned off, and the scorched kernels are left on the ground. They gather it in piles and mix it with acorns. In such form this dish is used as food. The local Indians have devised several games of chance that they adore. They indulge in them passionately and not infrequently lose everything that they own.

If at some time the blessings of civilization are disseminated among the backward inhabitants of this region, then the Russian settlements, not the Spanish missions, will deserve them. Having been introduced to culture, the local peoples will come to thank the Russians for their awakening to a life of reason. Such an awakening has already begun among the "Aleuts."

Having spent two days at the settlement, we said farewell to the estimable Shmidt and returned by the same route. Nothing remarkable happened to us on our way back. Professor Eschscholtz stayed at the settlement in order to conduct some investigations in the realm of natural history. He intended to return by sea in an Aleut kayak,[23] taking advantage of the fact that many of them had soon to be sent to hunt sea otters in San Francisco Bay.

Since the Spaniards themselves do not engage in the hunt for sea otters, they willingly allow the Russians to hunt along their shores and receive a fixed share of the catch. I was very glad that the kayaks from the colony of Ross would come to the bay during our stay here. The fact is that I intended to devote some time to the exploration of the rivers flowing into San Francisco Bay, for which these small craft would be very suitable. This is [the reason] why I waited for them to come [to San Francisco Bay] before leaving [California].

All summer the northwest wind, which is never accompanied by rain, prevails here. But now it was already the end of October, when south winds often blow, bringing with them foul weather and heavy downpours. It was because of them that we had for some time to await the return of Professor Eschscholtz and the arrival of the kayaks.

Once, to our great surprise, a six-oared sloop entered the bay from the open sea, and soon it approached our ship. It had been launched from an English whaler that had already been tacking several days off the bay's entrance, not having an opportunity to enter it on account of a contrary wind. Most of the crew suffered from scurvy, and the captain had decided to send the sloop ashore to get fresh meat for the sick. I immediately ordered an abundant supply of meat and vegetables for them, and the sloop set out on its return. The next day the ship itself entered the bay and anchored alongside us. From the way they furled the sails it was evident that few able-bodied men remained among them. The captain, who soon visited me, was also quite wasted, and his mates lay in bed. This ship had passed seven months on the coast of Japan without once coming to anchor or going ashore for

---

[23]Throughout his account Kotzebue confuses umiaks with kayaks, perhaps because of the close similarity of their names in Russian (*baidaras* and *baidarkas*, respectively). Hereafter I have identified his umiaks as kayaks.

support. Despite such prolonged hardships, the crew had not succeeded in catching a single whale, although the animals abound along the shores of Japan.

I can only ascribe the crew's scurvy to poor food as a result of inexcusable economy, as well as uncleanliness. The latter quality is generally uncharacteristic of the English, but with such a protracted and uninterrupted voyage it is difficult, of course, to avoid [filth] aboard ship. During the entire voyage of our ship not the slightest trace was observed of this terrible disease, from which so many seafarers have died in the past.

The captain told me that a large number of whaling vessels hunt along the shores of Japan, and that many of them leave there after a short time with rich catches. All of these ships suffer much from frequent storms. Another substantial inconvenience is the strict prohibition against landing on Japanese soil.

As is well known, the Japanese do not want to have any dealings with other nations, with the exception of the Chinese and the Dutch, and treat foreigners as lepers; it is forbidden there on pain of death to supply foreigners with food. The Japanese see in this a reliable means of preserving the purity of their ancient customs, with which they are content. Having spent seven months in Japan during my first voyage with Admiral Kruzenshtern, I can attest that anyone who has had an opportunity to become acquainted with its people cannot but respect them. By their own efforts the Japanese, without any foreign influence whatever, have attained a high level of civilization. It is possible, too, that such isolation is the result of the policy of their very despotic government, which fears the spread of ideas unfavorable to them.

. . . .[24]

Toward the end of our stay in California, real winter began there. Storms, accompanied by rain, occurred frequently. And a southwest wind that blew on 9 December could compare in force with the typhoons of the East Indies and the hurricanes of the West Indies. It tore the roofs from houses, uprooted trees, and generally caused much destruction. One of our thickest anchor cables broke, and if we had not been held by another, more durable cable, we would have been driven onto the rocky shores of the strait connecting the bay with the open sea. In the strait the swift current struggled with the storm's wind, with the result that exceptionally powerful breakers were formed. Fortunately, after only a couple of hours the storm began to weaken, but even in such a short time it managed to cause substantial damage in the vicinity. Even flooding occurred. Water rapidly submerged all low-lying places so rapidly that our men barely had time to move the tent and the astronomical instruments to a safe site.

---

[24]The rest of Kotzebue's digression about whaling and Japan—the fate of the two whalers that landed there—is omitted here.

Carefully comparing the time differences between St. Petersburg and San Francisco and taking into account their latitudinal differences, we established that the great flood in St. Petersburg, which caused so much distress, not only occurred on the same day but also began at the same hour as the flood in California.[25] To the west, on the Sandwich Islands, an equally severe storm raged. And hundreds of miles farther west, on the Philippine Islands, the storm was accompanied by an earthquake, and many houses were destroyed. In Manila Bay, usually such a safe harbor, the force of the wind was so terrible that a French corvette there under the command of Captain Bougainville (son of the celebrated navigator) had all of its masts broken. The inhabitants of Manila and the Sandwich Islands themselves [subsequently] told us of these events. Thus, the storm struck much of the Northern Hemisphere simultaneously. That the cause of its appearance was found beyond the limits of the earth's atmosphere can therefore be posited.

In winter, with such storms, our anchorage was not safe enough. So the next day we took advantage of the nascent fair weather and moved several miles to the east. Here we dropped anchor in a small bay with picturesque shores, quite safe at any time of year. Vancouver had also stopped in this bay. The Spaniards call it Yerba Buena in honor of a fragrant grass growing on its shores.

Because the kayaks with Doctor Eschscholtz had still not arrived from the colony of Ross, I began to fear that some accident had befallen them during the storm. So much the greater was my joy when on 12 November twenty kayaks arrived. They were completely undamaged, and our friends were alive and well. This small flotilla had actually left the colony before the commencement of the hurricane. But before it broke, the voyagers had reached the coast at Point Reyes. There they calmly waited until the storm had passed.[26] They had to spend this time on a high bare cliff, where taking shelter against the foul weather was impossible; they suffered much from the want of food. But the difficulties endured by Doctor Eschscholtz did not deprive him of his cheerfulness, and he was prepared immediately to undertake with me the trip to explore the aforementioned rivers.

Now everything was ready for our sailing. The pilot Marco had again to be sent with us, as well as one soldier from the presidio who had volunteered to accompany us. And so on 18 November, taking advantage of the favorable weather, we took our seats in the sloop and the longboat and set off on our route in the company of a flotilla of "Aleuts." Our detachment was well armed and supplied with a sufficient stock of provisions.

---

[25]The worst flood in St. Petersburg's history occurred on 19 November 1824, when the level of water in the Neva River rose 13½ feet above normal and flooded most of the city, drowning up to 569 people and destroying 462 houses. Exactly a century later, incidentally, in 1924 a comparable inundation occurred.

[26]While there, Eschscholtz found a new species of beetle, the American black tiger beetle, with large mandibles. Altogether during this Californian visit he collected nearly 200 beetles, all but one of them a new species (Beidleman, *California Frontier Naturalists*, 59).

At first we proceeded on the route already known to us toward Mission San Rafael. Our vessels crossed the southern part of the bay, passed among the islands, and came upon the northern part. Here we turned to the east, leaving Mission San Rafael considerably to our left in the northeast.[27] Toward midday we reached the common mouth of both rivers [Sacramento and San Joaquín], 30 miles distant from our ship. This mouth is one and a half miles in width. Both of its banks are high and steep and covered with trees here and there only. The mouth is crossed by a sandbar with a depth of no more than 2–3 feet. However, a channel runs through its eastern part that is deep enough for fully laden vessels of medium size. The opposing current here was so swift that our oarsmen had to strain every nerve in order to cross this shallow place.

We landed on the left bank of the mouth, wanting to determine its geographical position. According to our measurements, its latitude equals 38° 2' 4" N and its longitude 122° 4' W. After completing this task, I climbed one of the highest coastal cliffs, composed of alternating layers of slate and quartz. Before me opened a wonderful vista: to the south stretched the immense bay of San Francisco with its numerous inlets and islands, and to the north meandered a beautiful, wide river, formed as the result of the convergence of the two said rivers. Here in places it flows among high cliffs, and in others among picturesque meadows on which trees are scattered and large herds of deer of various kinds graze. Everywhere one looks, delightful landscapes enlivened by luxuriant vegetation are to be seen.

Our "Aleuts" dispersed on all sides in their small kayaks and hunted the wildfowl, which were extremely numerous here, both on water and on land. Nowhere else had these ardent hunters ever encountered such an abundance of wildfowl. Shots rang out constantly, and sometimes they even succeeded in killing birds with their spears.[28] The "Aleuts" handle their small skin boats as deftly as our Cossacks do horses. They pursue game with great speed, turning the kayaks easily in all directions, so that the prey rarely manages to escape.

White and gray pelicans twice the size of our geese are met here in large numbers. One of the "Aleuts" in his kayak rode into the very center of a flock of pelicans and killed one of the birds with a spear. This angered the others so much that they threw themselves upon the hunter and beat him unmercifully with their wings before the other kayaks could come to his aid. The numerous pelicans on the river attest the fact that many fish run here. This [abundance] was confirmed by our pilot. However, we ourselves noticed that large fish were breaking the surface.

After having rested the sailors for a couple of hours, we resumed our route upriver. But the outgoing tide began, and the tidal current in combination with

---

[27]This is undoubtedly a slip for "northwest."

[28]Russ., *drotiki,* which could also mean, instead of spears, the short harpoons that the "Aleuts" used for hunting sea otters.

the river's greatly hindered our subsequent progress. So, after going several miles, we put ashore at six o'clock in the evening and settled ourselves for the night on a picturesque meadow. Here the river flowed as before from the north, its width approximately equal to a mile and its depth sufficient for the largest of vessels.

The next morning it was barely dawn when we quit our camp, and taking advantage of the incoming tide and favorable wind, we quickly set out almost directly northward. Now the river often changed its appearance, and its width varied from one to two and even three miles. En route we sometimes came upon large round lakes with picturesque shores, many miles in circumference. We also sailed passed charming islands overgrown with tall trees with luxuriant leaves. Everywhere the depth was sufficient for large vessels. The steep banks alternated with charming plains on which herds of deer grazed in the shade of oaks. Even at this time of year it was a very pleasant voyage.

After having gone 18 miles from our last night's camp and 23 miles from the mouth, we reached the site of the confluence of the two rivers. One of them flows from the east and the other from the north. The Spaniards call the first of these rivers the Pescadores. Upstream two more rivers enter it that are as wide and deep as it is, according to our pilot. The missionaries have named them in honor of San Joaquín and Jesús María. The banks of these rivers are extremely fertile and were formerly densely populated. The holy fathers made trips right up to the said rivers, converting the Indians in their own way to the Christian faith in order to supply the missions with workers. Now some of the Indians are baptized, and the rest, having saved themselves from conversion, have fled farther into the interior, as a result of which the banks of these rivers have been deserted. A populous tribe of indigenes[29] used to live in the locale where we found ourselves. For the same reasons no traces of them remain here now.

Because the Pescadores River had been investigated earlier, we set off along the other river, which flows from the north and bears the name Sacramento. We sailed on it for only several miles, for around noon a strong contrary wind forced us to land on its banks. At this time we were located at 38° 22' North latitude.

The wind grew stronger, and so this day there was nothing to do but think about the continuation of the voyage. We had to remain here overnight, and we made camp on a picturesque meadow stretching along the western bank of the river. I again climbed a height to examine the surroundings. To the west, low hills, on which solitary trees grew here and there, were visible. To the east and southeast on the horizon rose the snowy summits of the Sierra Nevada range, which crosses all of America from north to south.[30] These mountains are at least

---

[29]Russ., *korekiny*.

[30]Kotzebue is mistaken here, of course; the Sierra Nevada run from the Klamath knot in the north to the Mojave Desert in the south; no range, not even the Rockies, crosses the length of North America, let alone the Americas.

40 miles distant from us, and half of them seem to be covered with snow and ice. A very low plain, overgrown with dense forest, stretches between the river and the mountains. It is cut by a great many large and small rivers that divide it into separate islands. We had yet to meet one Indian, but many columns of smoke rose over these marshy islands in the direction of the Sierra Nevada. They attest the fact that the Indians who have saved themselves from conversion to Christianity have fled there, where the dragoons with their lassos cannot overtake them.

It is possible to say with certainty, of course, that the sources of the Pescadores River, as well as those of the San Joaquín and Jesús María that enter it, are found in the snowy mountains, for these rivers begin in the east and flow across the lowland, absorbing many small rivers en route. As regards the Sacramento, it flows from quite another area situated to the north. According to some Indians living at the missions, this river flows from a large lake.[31] I suggest that the Slavyanka, which enters the sea near the colony of Ross, is one of its tributaries.[32]

Numerous small and large rivers water this fertile region, and they will bring great benefit to future settlers. The lowland is perfectly suitable for the growing of rice, and the higher lands, which are fertile everywhere, could yield the richest harvests of the best wheat. Grapes, too, would grow very well, for nature has already seen to it that they will spread here. They are encountered in a wild state everywhere along the banks of the rivers and are propagating like weeds. Their clusters reach a large size, but the grapes themselves are the size of peas, very sweet, and agreeable to the taste. We treated ourselves to them in large quantities without injuring our health. The Indians also eat the wild grapes with gusto.

In order to kill time we went hunting. Herds of large and small deer grazed everywhere, and geese, ducks, and cranes thronged the riverbank. The wildfowl were so numerous that even those of us who had not been keen on this sport before grasped muskets and became ardent hunters. The sailors, who entertained themselves mainly by hunting deer, managed to kill several such animals.

When it grew dark, we made a large campfire in order to ease the return to camp of the hunters who had lost their way. At night we were bothered by a bear, which hunted deer right outside our tents. The moon shone brightly, and we saw the deer leap into the water and begin swimming to the opposite bank. The bear rushed after them and also swam—but then we lost sight of them.

At sunrise we moved farther, as the wind had died a little. On the bank we noticed a small [Northern Pacific] rattlesnake, which could easily cause us serious trouble. We killed the snake, and it was added to Professor Eschscholtz's collection. Now the river flowed from the northwest. Its width here was 250

---

[31]The Sacramento rises in the Klamath knot in the vicinity of Mount Shasta.

[32]Kotzebue is mistaken again; the Slavyanka (Russian) River, which rises in the Coast Ranges, does not lie in the drainage basin of the Sacramento River.

to 300 sazhens, and narrower tributaries joined it from the east to form many islands. The river's western bank remained hilly and the eastern bank low lying. The current hereabouts was so strong that we advanced very slowly, despite the efforts of our rowers. After the sun had risen above the horizon, the north wind again strengthened, hindering our progress even more. So already by noon we had to land on the western bank after going only 10 miles. We reached a point at 38° 27' of North latitude and 122° 10' of West longitude.

This [point] was the culmination of our short voyage. The unfavorable weather forced us to abandon further attempts to sail upriver against the current. However, our pilot confirmed that at this time of the year, it was generally impossible to penetrate much farther, since because of abundant rainfall there is so much water in the river that the current becomes insurmountable. Let our explorations be continued by voyagers who happen here in the summer, when these obstacles do not exist.

Indians had evidently stopped near the site of our landing. Here we found a pole with a pennant of feathers stuck in the ground, two Indian boats made of reeds, and the remains of several campfires; the coals were still covered with a thin layer of unscattered ashes. The pilot named two tribes, the Chupukans[33] and the Khulpuns,[34] who formerly lived here and possibly sometimes visit these places. Now columns of smoke from their campfires were rising above the marshy islands, on the higher parts of which they build their dwellings.

The majestic mountain chain of the Sierra Nevada was visible from here in all of its splendor. Along all of the eastern edge of the horizon stretched this high, ice-covered massif, and in front of it, like a green sea, extended the low-lying plain. In San Francisco Bay it is not possible to see the Sierra Nevada. But as soon as the traveler passes the site of the confluence of the Pescadores and Sacramento Rivers, part of this mountain range opens before him.

The rest of the day we again devoted to hunting, and we shot several deer. Their meat seemed very tasty to us. During the night small wolves [coyotes], which are encountered here in abundance, disrupted our sleep. They stole several pieces of venison from us.

Early in the morning we set off on our return route and soon left this fertile region, where many thousands of families could live in prosperity. How luxuriant and splendid is the vegetation here! But because of the complete absence of inhabitants this territory produces an oppressive impression that is intensified by the knowledge of the sad lot of the local Indians.

---

[33]Apparently a tribelet of Bay Miwoks (see Heizer, *California*, 401).
[34]Unidentified.

On our return route we made careful soundings and ascertained that in the middle of the river its depth is everywhere 15, 17, or 20 sazhens, whereas at its mouth it does not exceed 4–5 sazhens.

On 23 November we returned to the ship with a supply of venison for the entire command. During our absence Captain Lazarev had arrived here with his frigate. He had to combat storms nearly all of the way from New Archangel to San Francisco.

I had not wanted to quit California before his arrival, since we could send letters home on the frigate. Now nothing more detained us, and so our ship was prepared forthwith for departure; our camp ashore was razed, and all of the equipment, including the astronomical instruments, were transferred to the sloop. On the last night ashore our men killed a skunk that had stolen into one of the tents to steal something. This animal, whose size and build are reminiscent of a cat, emits such an awful stench that it is literally impossible to endure. Dogs, which sometimes attack skunks, are unable to rid themselves of this smell and in a frenzy rub their noses on the ground until they bleed. Skunks occupy the same place in the animal kingdom as Koloshes [Tlingits] do among people.

In the morning of 25 November, as the outgoing tide commenced, we took advantage of a northwest wind—which usually brings good weather here—to leave San Francisco Bay. The sea had still not quieted after the recent frequent southwesters, so there were still high waves in the passage connecting it with the bay. Under the influence of the strong current, our ship, meeting the waves in the passage, answered the helm poorly, so that we were nearly dashed upon a cliff. So I advise all mariners to leave the bay only when the strait is calm. It is usually thus, provided that for several days the northwest wind has been blowing constantly.

According to our repeated observations, the presidio of San Francisco is situated at 37° 48′ 33″ North latitude and 122° 22′ 30″ West longitude. The variation of the magnetic compass is 16° to the east.

The high-tide time in the bay, calculated as an average of our observations, proved to be equal to the new moon and the half moon of 11 hours, 20 minutes. The greatest difference in the water level reached 7 feet. The rivers entering the bay exert much influence on the duration of the incoming and outgoing tides, as a result of which the latter lasts eight hours and the former only four hours.

Matvey Muravyov's Report about a California Indian Uprising and the Desertion of Russian Employees, 1825

EDITOR'S INTRODUCTION

The Russians at Fort Ross had to cope with a chronic problem: the desertion of contracted (and usually indebted) employees, just as sailors on Russian vessels at San Francisco (like sailors in all exotic ports, particularly in the tropics and subtropics) not infrequently jumped ship. Alta California, like the Hawaiian Islands, offered a balmy clime and a carefree lifestyle, especially by comparison with cool, damp Sitka and the low pay and hard life of company service, both ashore and afloat. Usually the runaway sailors were captured by the Californio authorities and returned; the runaways from Fort Ross, however, ran less risk of capture, as they were much more likely to know the province's geography and some of its residents, both natives and Californios, who might hide and help them. The following document reports one such case of desertion, with one of the deserters helping to lead the Chumash Indian uprising and another becoming Alta California's most notable Russian renegade.

GOVERNOR MATVEY MURAVYOV,[1] A REPORT TO THE
BOARD OF DIRECTORS OF THE RUSSIAN-AMERICAN COMPANY
ABOUT AN INDIAN UPRISING IN ALTA CALIFORNIA AND THE
DESERTION OF SIX EMPLOYEES FROM FORT ROSS,[2] NEW ARCHANGEL,
17 FEBRUARY 1825

Regarding the Indian uprising [i.e., Chumash rebellion][3] in [Alta] California,
Manager Khlebnikov of New Archangel Counter tells me that total order has
now been restored everywhere. The governor [Luis Argüello?] told him that the
uprising was initially plotted by the Indians of the missions of La Purísima [Con-
cepción], Santa Inés, and Santa Bárbara. At the first two missions the Indians
united and acted in concord and, it seems, under the leadership of a runaway
from Ross, the employee Prokhor Yegorov. The rebellion was discovered at Santa
Bárbara a day later than at the first two. Mission Santa Inés was razed to the
ground, and all of its buildings were torched, and of its supplies 3,500 fanegas
of wheat, 1,200 fanegas of corn, and 350 bags of tallow and lard were burned,
according to the assurances of the governor. After destroying these missions,
the Indians fled to an island in the middle of a large lake in the vicinity of Santa
Bárbara, where they held fast for a long time; with them, too, was our Russian,
Prokhor Yegorov, who was killed there by the Indians. A military detachment
was sent there twice by the Spanish [i.e., Californio] government but without
any success. Finally, the padre president [of the missions] was sent with a detachment, and with his exhortations he succeeded in reducing them to obedience,
promising at the same time that they would remain unpunished. Under these
terms the Indians returned to the missions. At the outset of the uprising, 8
Spanish soldiers were killed in various skirmishes. These events were not taken
as a lesson by the Spaniards, who did not protect the [Russian] runaways; of the
six men who fled from the settlement of Ross in December 1821, they soon sent
to Fort Ross the employee Rodion Shabanov, who is now at New Archangel.
Of his other comrades in flight, Fyodor Vagin was brought here on the *Apollon*,
Prokhor Yegorov was killed by the Indians in the said uprising, [Pyotr] Malyavin

---

[1]Matvey Ivanovich Muravyov (1784–1836) had participated in Captain Vasily Golovnin's round-the-world
voyage of 1817–19 in the *Kamchatka* as a lieutenant, and upon his return he was promoted to captain-lieutenant and appointed to a five-year term as governor of Russian America (1820–25). There he had many new
buildings erected in the colonial capital, and he forged better relations with the neighboring Tlingits. After
his return to St. Petersburg, he served first (1826–27) in the company's headquarters and then (1832–36) on
the company's special committee on political questions, despite his broken health. See Grinëv, *Kto yest kto*,
359; and Pierce, *Russian America*, 368–71.

[2]RRAC, roll 29, doc. 74, fols. 206–207.

[3]See Sandos, "Levantamiento!" 8–11.

and Stepan Kornilov went to Mexico, and [Osip] Volkov[4] is on a whaling vessel—which I have the honor to report to the Board of Directors.

[4]Osip Volkov (José Antonio Bolcof) (ca. 1795–1866) was a native of Kamchatka and a seaman on company
ships. In 1815 while hunting sea otters from the *Ilmena* he either jumped ship or was captured by a Spanish
patrol. He settled in Monterey and worked variously as an interpreter, a sailor, a shoemaker, a smuggler, a
farmer, and a gold miner. See [Bancroft], *California Pioneer Register*, 63; Grinëv, *Kto yest kto*, 104; and Pierce,
Russian America, 532.

DOCUMENT 19

Kirill Khlebnikov, "About a Change in Government and [Other] Events in [Alta] California," 1825

EDITOR'S INTRODUCTION

On behalf of the Russian-American Company's board of directors, its colonial governor at New Archangel dutifully monitored happenings in Alta California, either through the manager of Ross Counter or through its trade agent in the province (as in the case of this document). To do so was vitally in the company's interest, for Alta California served as Russian America's breadbasket from the opening of foreign trade in the early 1820s until the secularization of the missions in the middle 1830s, so awareness of any economic setbacks—such as harvest failures, higher tariffs, and cheaper and better imports from competitor—was essential. Also, any political disarray among the Californios could enable the Russians to consolidate their foothold of Ross Counter by expanding it eastward to the agriculturally more productive valleys of the interior and southward to the northern littoral of the superior harbor of San Francisco Bay.

Manager Kirill Khlebnikov,[1] A Report to the
Board of Directors of the Russian-American Company
"About a Change in Government and Various Events in
[Alta] California,"[2] San Francisco, 15 December 1825

I have the honor to most humbly report to the Board of Directors the situation in [Alta] California following a change in government there in the course of 1825:

The crew of the 74-gun Spanish ship *Asia*, which had been sent by the royalists from Lima to Manila, mutinied. They landed the officers and passengers on one of the Ladrone Islands and turned to the coast of California with two brigs. After reaching Monterey in May, they declared themselves on the side of the patriots[3] and demanded fresh provisions. At this port all of their demands were met out of fear; nevertheless, much impertinence and unruliness occurred, and one of the Californio soldiers was killed. At Santa Bárbara, instead of paying for supplies with money, a brig began firing but caused no damage. The governor of California, Don Luis Argüello, sent an aide with reports by sea to the Mexican government, and the ship reached Acapulco and stopped there. Its crew consisted of various nationalities, most of whom had come from trading vessels.

A new governor, Lieutenant-Colonel Don José María Echeandía, arrived in California from Mexico with the title and rights of Commandant General of both Californias. He halted at the port of San Diego on the border of these provinces. For the most convenient management of both he will reside in Monterey, where he is expected in January or February. Comptroller[4] Don José María Herrera has arrived to do business with foreigners and is located in Monterey. Having had occasion to become acquainted with him through the usual channels, I found him to be a good and intelligent man who at the first opportunity rendered me much assistance and favor, and he promised to be of service in the future.

With the arrival of the governor, the new enactments of the Mexican government were announced, such that foreigners [may] trade at the ports of San Diego, Santa Bárbara, Monterey, and San Francisco, but trade is prohibited at remote missions. Mexico has established a congress after the example of the United States of North America, and Don Guadelupe Victoria, a native of the

---

[1]Kirill (or Kiril or, diminutively, Kirilo) Timofeyevich Khlebnikov (1784–1838) had joined the Russian-American Company in 1801, acting as its agent first in Okhotsk and then (1808–13) in Kamchatka. He arrived in Russian America in 1817, and he served as the manager of New Archangel Counter, the governor's assistant, and the company's agent in Alta California from 1818 until his departure from the colonies in 1832, whereupon he became the company's chief clerk at its headquarters in St. Petersburg. In 1835 he was appointed to the board of directors, and in 1837 he was named a corresponding member of the St. Petersburg Academy of Sciences. See Grinëv, *Kto yest kto*, 573; and Pierce, *Russian America*, 229–30.

[2]ARGO, raz. 99, op. 1, d. 27, unpaginated (copy).

[3]The *independistas*, the revolutionaries seeking independence from Spain.

[4]Sp., *comisario*.

state of Guanajuato, has been chosen as president for 4 years. The vice-president has been sent as plenipotentiary ambassador to England to solicit recognition of the republic's independence.

The missionaries in California have refused to swear an oath to the constitution, and so at present disagreement continues between them and the government. It is thought that all of them will leave for Mexico, and from there those who so wish will be dispatched to Europe and their places taken by white clergy.[5]

Foreign trade is increasing greatly on the coast of California; this year more than 10 trading vessels arrived from Canton, Calcutta, and North America, including that of Mr. Hartnell,[6] who conducts regular trade and always obtains his goods from Liverpool and Lima. The exports by foreign vessels comprise uncured hides and tallow but primarily hard cash, up to 30 t[housand] piasters of which have been brought to Alta California from Mexico.

[signed] Manager of New Archangel
Counter Kiril[l] Khlebnikov.

---

[5]Meaning, in the terminology of Russian Orthodoxy, married priests, as opposed to unmarried ("black") clerics. Apparently Khlebnikov had heard a rumor to this effect, as improbable as it may seem, although the Mexican revolution exhibited a marked anticlerical dimension.

[6]William Edward Petty Hartnell (1798–1854), a native of England, arrived in Alta California in 1822. He became a Catholic, married a colonial, and was naturalized. Fluent in Spanish, French, and German, Hartnell engaged in a variety of pursuits, and in 1833–36 he acted as Californian agent for the Russian-American Company. See [Bancroft], *California Pioneer Register,* 180–81; also see Dakin, *Lives of William Hartnell.*

Kirill Khlebnikov, "Notes about [Alta] California," 1828 [?]

Editor's Introduction

Kirill Khlebnikov, who for fifteen years (1817–32) served as the Russian-American Company's agent in Alta California, came to know the province well, visiting it thirteen times, learning to read, write, and speak some Spanish, and making many friends among the authorities, missionaries, and businessmen (with some of whom he continued to correspond after his return to Russia). Given his predilection for chronicling, it is not surprising that he would write the following document. Originally it was intended to be part of his authoritative and voluminous "Notes" on Russian America;[1] instead, it was published in 1829 in Moscow in a weekly literary, political, and historical journal for the edification of the reading public (a very small percentage, incidentally, of the country's population).

[Kirill T.] Khlebnikov, "Notes about [Alta] California,"[2] [New Archangel?], 1828 [?]

Table of Contents

---

[1] These "Notes" were finally published in Russian in two volumes in Leningrad in 1979 and in Moscow in 1985 (but without the part on Ross Counter) and were translated into English and published as Khlebnikov, *Notes on Russian America*. Khlebnikov's accounts of three of his trips to Alta California have been published in English as [Khlebnikov], *The Khlebnikov Archive*.

[2] *Syn otechestva i Severny arkhiv* 2 (1829), no. 11, pp. 208–27, no. 12, pp. 276–88, no. 13, pp. 336–47, no. 14, pp. 400–10, no. 15, pp. 25–35. The manuscript (first variant), which has been edited (but was not written) in Khlebnikov's own hand, is found in ARGO, raz. 99, op. 1, d. 112. The first page states that it was intended to accompany part 6 of his "Zapiski o koloniyakh v Amerike" [Notes about the colonies in America]. A second variant with fewer and different emendations in pencil (not in Khlebnikov's hand) is found in ARGO, raz. 99, op. 1, d. 109; the emendations are not included here, because they are inconsequential *(continued)*

About Spanish America in General

From the time of the discovery of America by Columbus, i.e., since 1492, Spain has had absolute possession of much of the New World for more than 300 years. A small number of native inhabitants remain here and there, enslaved and scattered throughout the colonies; those who were not subjugated had hidden themselves in caves in the mountains, protected by nature itself. New generations have appeared, and having been born into ignorance, they have blindly imitated the customs and manners of their conquerors. Their ties with Europeans have been cut, and the inhabitants of America of European blood have in the course of three hundred

---

attempts to improve the document's language, not its content. The article was first published in an English translation by Anatole G. Mazour as K. T. Khlebnikov, "Memoirs of California." It is an indifferent rendition, containing many errors, omissions, and infelicities. Another translation—incomplete—appeared as doc. 68 in Dmytryshyn, Crownhart-Vaughan, and Vaughan, *Russian-American Colonies,* 386–98. Both the published Russian and English versions omit several addenda in Khlebnikov's handwriting (including a table of contents and an appendix) that have been retained here.

years not changed the customs of their forbears. Even at the beginning of the 19th century Spanish Americans were true replicas of those who had lived at the end of the 15th century; looking at them one could, it seems, imagine Cortés, Pizarro, and others who are famous in the history of the conquest of this part of the world.

When Napoleon placed the Spanish crown on the head of his brother Joseph[3] and, contrary to national law, kept Ferdinand VII[4] in captivity, in [Spanish] America revolution erupted in 1808. Many unsuccessful actions were taken; enterprising men emerged, but they perished for lack of understanding and assistance.

In Mexico the clergy took command of the rebels. Hidalgo[5] in 1810 and then Morelos[6] lost their heads and, after dying, left only their followers. In 1816 Mina[7] astonished Mexico more than all of his precursors, but he also fell victim to his efforts.

In the province of Caracas an uprising flared in 1810; there Miranda[8] distinguished himself, but he lost his head, too. Finally, in 1813 Simon Bolívar,[9] a native of the province, appeared and became famous for his successes.

---

[3]Joseph Bonaparte (1768–1844) was Napoleon Bonaparte's oldest brother. He became king of Spain in 1808 but reluctantly abdicated in 1813 after unsuccessfully defending his throne in the Peninsular War (1808–14).

[4]Ferdinand VII (1784–1833) ascended to the Spanish throne in early 1808 after a palace revolt and was enthusiastically acclaimed by his subjects. But he was soon forced by Napoleon to renounce his throne, and he was imprisoned in France. In his name the nationalist and liberal elements of Spain resisted the French invaders during the Peninsular War, and in 1812 the Cortes proclaimed a liberal constitution. Throughout the Spanish Empire Ferdinand's name was the rallying cry of revolutionists, but upon his restoration in 1814 he promptly abolished the constitution and revealed himself to be a thoroughgoing reactionary. See Bridgwater and Sherwood, *Columbia Encyclopedia*, 667.

[5]Miguel Hidalgo y Costilla (1753–1811), a national hero of Mexico, was a parish priest of Dolores and a creole (*colonial*) intellectual who was profoundly influenced by the French Revolution. He ran afoul of the authorities by championing his Indian parishioners. In 1810 he issued the *grito de Dolores* ("cry of Dolores"), which launched the revolt against Spain. He attracted many natives to his cause and adopted the banner of Our Lady of Guadalupe as his standard, promising freedom for all and free land. He was defeated by royalist forces and executed. See Bridgwater and Sherwood, *Columbia Encyclopedia*, 893.

[6]José María Morelos y Pavón (1765–1815), like Hidalgo both a liberal priest and a national hero, assumed Hidalgo's fallen mantle. But he, too, was defeated by royalist forces and executed. See Bridgwater and Sherwood, *Columbia Encyclopedia*, 1,321.

[7]Francisco Javier Mina (1789–1816) was a Spanish soldier and revolutionist who after the failure of the revolt against Ferdinand VII fled to England. There he organized a group of supporters of the Mexican revolution and proceeded to the United States and then Mexico, where he was likewise defeated and executed. See Bridgwater and Sherwood, *Columbia Encyclopedia*, 1,286.

[8]Sebastián Francisco de Miranda (1750–1816) was a Venezuelan soldier and adventurer who succumbed to revolutionary ideas and became the apostle of Venezuelan liberty. After the outbreak of the revolution in 1810 he returned to his homeland and became prominent in the patriot forces but soon alienated Bolívar and other leaders and was jailed. Then he was seized by the royalists, who put him in prison for the rest of his life. See Bridgwater and Sherwood, *Columbia Encyclopedia*, 1,291–92.

[9]Simon Bolívar (1783–1830), known as the Liberator, was the son of a wealthy creole family of Caracas. After the defeat of the rebel forces in 1815, he fled to the West Indies but returned at the end of 1816 and engineered a series of victories against Spanish armies, culminating in the triumph of the revolution in South America. But his dictatorial power and highhanded methods created dissension among the liberated colonies and eroded support for his vision of a united Spanish America, which collapsed. He resigned the presidency in 1830 and, disillusioned and impoverished, died of tuberculosis. See Bridgwater and Sherwood, *Columbia Encyclopedia*, 220–21.

The Present Division of Spanish America

Spain's great empire in America collapsed from this unrest, and upon its ruins there arose seven republics and one province, as follows:

(1) *Mexico.* It is limited on the north by Cape Francis Drake [Point Reyes], including California, and on the west by the Pacific Ocean and the Gulf of California; it is bordered on the east by the possessions of the North American United States in Louisiana, the Gulf of Mexico, and the Gulf of Honduras, and on the south by the Republic of Guatemala.

(2) *Guatemala.* It is, as before, divided into 12 provinces: Soconusco, Suchitepéquez, Sonsonate, San Salvador, San Miguel, Tegucigalpa, Chocoteca [Choluteca?], Honduras, Nicaragua, Costa Rica, Verapaz, and Chiapas.

(3) *Colombia* includes the former Caracas, consisting of the provinces of New Andalusia, Barcelona, Venezuela, and Maracaibo and the coast of the Caribbean Sea, and later the province of Santa Fe de Bogotá was added.

(4) *Peru,* which is known by the same name as before.

(5) *Chile.*

(6) *Río de la Plata,* or *Buenos Aires.*

(7) *Bolivia,* named in honor of Bolívar. This republic consists of a detached part of Upper Peru and comprises the provinces of La Paz, Chuquisaca, Potosí, Cochabamba, and Santa Cruz de la Sierra.

(8) *Paraguay* has not been added to any of these republics, and it is administered in accordance with the customs and decrees of the Jesuits who were introduced there earlier. The protector of this territory is Doctor Francia.[10]

California

California is a province of Mexico. It is divided into two parts: Lower and Upper, or Old and New, California. Old California is a peninsula as far as Cabo San Lucas in latitude 22° 55' N. New California stretches from Cape Francis Drake in latitude 38° as far as the mouth of the Colorado River. The Mexicans, however, now consider the boundary of California to be 42° N latitude.

Old California was discovered by [Hernán] Cortés in 1536 but New California not until the end of the 16th century. Admiral [Sebastián] Vizcaíno described its coast and a bay that he named Monterey in honor of the Mexican viceroy. The Jesuit [Eusebio] Kino in 1684 crossed it and found that Old California is a peninsula. In 1769 two ships were sent there from Mexico to build forts.

The territory of California is bordered on the north by the Russian settlement of Ross in 38° 30' N latitude and on the east by Indian habitations and the Colorado River, and on the south and west it is washed by the Pacific Ocean.

---

[10]José Gaspar Rodríguez Francia (1766–1840) participated in the bloodless revolution against Spain in 1811 and declared himself dictator ("El Supremo") in 1814, ruling until his death. See Bridgwater and Sherwood, *Columbia Encyclopedia,* 711.

In Old California there is one fort, Loreto, on the eastern coast of the peninsula. In New California four forts, or *presidios*, have been built, [each] under the direction of a commandant; they contain a garrison and some cavalrymen. These presidios are as follows:

San Francisco at 37° 48' N latitude, founded in 1776.

Monterey at 36° 48' N lat. and est. in 1770.

Santa Bárbara at 34° 22' N lat. and est. in 1786.

San Diego at 32° 39' N lat. and est. in 1770.

Monterey was formerly the chief town of both Californias and the seat of the governor; but the head who arrived from Mexico in 1825 as general commandant of both territories established himself at San Diego for the greater convenience of command. All of the artillerymen and the commissioner of both territories are still found at Monterey.

Missions

Here by the word "mission" is understood an establishment for the conversion of Indians to the Christian faith. These establishments were founded initially by the Jesuits, but afterwards they passed to the friars of other orders. It should be noted that forcible measures have not always been used to convert the savages; many of the Indians voluntarily came to the missions, sometimes [to see] their relatives and sometimes out of hunger, staying there and adopting Christianity.

The missions are under the control of the Franciscan friars in New California and of the Dominican Order in Old California. The Padre,* [Padre] President, and Padre Prefect [i.e., Commissary Prefect] are the principals. Herewith is affixed a reckoning of all of the missions and their division into districts in New California, with an approximate indication of the number of Indians living at each of them.

NEW CALIFORNIA

District	mission	number of Indians
the district of San Francisco presidio	San Francisco Solano [Sonoma]	600
	San Rafael [Arcángel]	1,000
	San Francisco [de Asís]	400
	Santa Clara [de Asís]	1,400
	San José (St. Joseph)	1,700
	Santa Cruz (Holy Cross)	500

Padre denotes a father and is applied to clerics in general. We [Russians] used the plural *padri*, taken from the Italian, which is grammatically more similar to the plural in Russian than to the Spanish *padres*.

the district of Monterey presidio	St. John the Baptist (San Juan Bautista)	1,100
	San Carlos [Borromeo] de Monterey	370
	[Nuestra Señora de] La Soledad	500
	San Antonio [de Padua]	500
	San Miguel [Arcángel] (St. Michael)	500
	St. Ludovik the Bishop (San Luis Obispo [de Tolosa])	400
[the district of Santa Bárbara presidio]	The Pure (La Purísima [Concepción])	500
	Santa Inés [Virgen y Mártir]	400
	Santa Bárbara	500
	San Fernando [Rey de España]	600
	San Gabriel [Arcángel]	1,000
[the district of San Diego presidio]	St. John (San Juan Capistrano)	800
	St. Ludovik the King (San Luis Rey [de Francia])	2,800
	San Diego [de Alcalá]	1,750

Note. The number of Indians at many of these missions is indicated very approximately, not precisely. As a foreigner, the compiler was unable to personally verify the data, which were given to him by the Spanish missionaries.

MISSIONS IN OLD CALIFORNIA
1. San Miguel [Arcángel de la Frontera][11]
2. Santo Tomás [de Aquino]
3. Santa Catalina [Mártir]
4. San Vicente [Ferrer]
[5.] [Santo Domingo]
5. [6.] [Nuestra Señora de] el Rosario [de Viñadaco]
6. [7.] San Fernando [de Velicatá]
7. [8.] San Francisco de Borja [Adac]
8. [9.] Santa Gertrudis
9. [10.] San Ignacio [Kadakaamán]
10. [11.] La Purísima [Concepción de Cadegomó] (The Pure)
11. [12.] San José [de Comondú] (St. John)
12. [13.] Santa Rosalía [de Mulegé]

---

[11]San Miguel was a *visitas* (outlier) of Mission San Javier.

13. [14.] San Francisco Javier [de Biaundó]
14. [15.] [Nuestra Señora de] Loreto [Conchó]
Note. To the south, near Cabo San Lucas, are founded the missions of
15. [16.] San José de San Lucas [del Cabo]
16. [17.] San Domingo [Santiago el Apóstol Aiñiní?]
17. [18.] All Saints (Todos Santos)
Note. The missions in Old California contain very few Indians, and some of them are quite deserted.

The friars who manage the missions are appointed by the Padre President. Before Mexico separated from Spain they were sent from Europe, and there were two at each mission; now that the sending of them has ceased and many of them have died, barely one friar remains at a mission. They are sometimes transferred from one mission to another, but many live permanently at their missions.

Father Felipe Arroyo [de la Cuesta] has been at Mission St. John the Baptist (S[an] Juan Bautista) continually for 18 years; he has learned two Indian languages perfectly and compiled a grammar of them. He explains Christian dogma to the Indians in their own language and has thereby gained their special love and respect.

After the overthrow of the ephemeral Emperor Agustín Iturbide the restored republic demanded an oath of allegiance to the constitution from the friars; but the Padre President, Padre Prefect, and many of the friars refused to do so, and it was impossible to force them. The governor of California in 1825 reported this to the Mexican government, which has now ordered that the Padre President be removed from office and deported. Rumor has it that the government intends to appoint secular clerics to the missions in place of the Franciscan friars. Because of this [rumor] now the friars have neither the zeal to improve the economy nor the desire to enlist the savages. All of them want heartily to leave for Europe or Manila. Many of the missionaries have saved a sizable amount of hard cash, but as the government—under various pretexts—has demanded money from them, and they have had to render it, they have now decided to have no cash at the missions or to have it in gold so that in case they leave, it will be more convenient to carry it with them. In 1825 two friars[12] from southern California left for Europe on whaling vessels.*

---

*In 1827 [*sic*: 1828] two friars who headed the missions of S[anta] Bárbara and S[anta] Inés [*sic*: San Buenaventura] fled on the American trading vessel *Harbinger,* Capt. [Joseph] Steel. The latter was Father José Altimira, who left a letter for the governor explaining why he had found it necessary to flee.

[12]Khlebnikov is presumably referring to Antonio Ripoll of Mission Santa Bárbara and José Altimira of Mission San Buenaventura, who secretly departed Santa Bárbara together on the Boston trader *Harbinger* at the end of January 1828. See Geiger, *Franciscan Missionaries,* 9, 208.

At the missions there are from 500 to 3,000 Indians of both sexes.

Formerly, under Spanish rule, the governors outfitted the military commands partly with Indians who knew the hideaways of their tribesmen, and such detachments, which sometimes comprised up to a hundred men, would unexpectedly attack a habitation of savages, and capture and abduct Indians for settlement at the missions. It repeatedly happened that the Indians desperately defended themselves, and both sides left behind some dead and wounded. I saw Spanish soldiers with the stone heads of Indian arrows in their corpses, and they [i.e., the arrows] had been the cause of their [i.e., the Spaniards'] premature deaths.

The layout of the missions is uniform: it comprises a quadrangle with an interior square. In some missions all of the buildings are of brick, and in others they are of earth bonded with clay [adobe], and in still others the foundations and struts are made of stone that is suitable for building. The church and the many large rooms connected to it are under one roof with neither floors nor ceilings; the best rooms are floored with bricks and very rarely with wood. In the foundations of all of the buildings, except the living quarters, storerooms are built for keeping grain and other supplies. All of the buildings are usually tiled and whitewashed inside and outside. At each mission there are from 2 to 6 soldiers, and the one who merits more trust is given the title of *mayordomo* ([i.e., majordomo,] manager), who, following the Padre's orders, commands the Indians, manages the livestock, and maintains all supplies.

From the mission the majordomo receives a salary of 12 piasters a month, two bulls, lard, and grain. The rules of the Franciscan Order forbid the friars to accumulate wealth, especially silver and gold, and so one can see some of the missionaries, when they receive money, declaring their inability to count it and directing the majordomo to count and store it as mission property; but he himself meticulously counts the sacks of piasters again upon the payer's departure and assiduously stores them in his bedroom.

At each mission there are orchards with fruit trees suited to the climate; the trees are planted in the same order, and a system of water supply is installed in the orchard. Many orchards, as at S[anta] Cruz, Santa Bárbara, and S[an] Gabriel, are very well arranged.

Earlier the upkeep of the Indians was very meager, but with the declaration of independence [from Spain by Mexico] the mode of administration of the Indians and their maintenance were bound to change. At present they are issued the following provisions at each mission for daily consumption: frijoles, corn, barley, and dried meat, and on Sundays fresh beef, wheat, lard, and fruit. Married Indians and those with families live in houses or grass huts built at the missions, but single adults [live] in communal quarters, with the men separated from the women. Every evening the rooms or sheds for the women are locked, and in the morning they are opened.

The seizure of free Indians has also ceased, and the elderly [mission] Indians are even being freed, but being unaccustomed to a nomadic life, they seldom return to their native wilds. The government's plan to make them citizens and to settle them throughout California will probably not be fulfilled for a long time or ever. Now those who have been freed from the missions in accordance with the governor's order and are living at the presidios do not want to work at all, not being forced to do so, and they maintain themselves through theft. Generally all of the Indians at the missions have converted to Catholicism. The missionaries make musicians of them, and almost every possible instrument is in use, even if there are no superior virtuosos among them. At the better missions various workshops have been established, and although they are not perfect, they meet all household needs without exception.

According to the testimony of all officials, the best mission in all of California is St. Ludovik the King (San Luis Rey). Every laudable trait is attributed to its friar[13] as the most enlightened and energetic of his brethren.

It should be noted that without additions of savage Indians the mission population has appreciably decreased from diseases, and although the women bear from 8 to 10 children, most of them die in infancy. Many women, it is asserted, deliberately abort the fetus in the womb and miscarry.

Venereal disease has spread to a great degree throughout California. Father Felipe Arroyo [de la Cuesta] asserted that it is transmitted from the savage Indians to those living in the interior of the continent.

The missionaries have titles: *Reverendo* and *Ministro Apostólico,* i.e., "reverend" and "Apostolic Minister." They enjoy the respect of foreigners, and many of them are noted for their civility and hospitality.

Fortresses and Settlements

The aforementioned four presidios are populated by soldiers on active service and retired soldiers; the most populous of them, Monterey, numbers no more than 700 souls, and the others fewer.

In 1826 Monterey's military command was reckoned at up to 70 men: 30 infantrymen and up to 25 artillerymen [and the rest cavalrymen], but the female population was supposed to be up to 400 souls.

---

[13]Antonio Peyrí (1769–18??), a Catalán, left Cádiz with twenty other friars in 1795 and, after five months of training at Mexico City's San Fernando College, reached Alta California in 1796. He was assigned to Mission San Luis Obispo, but in 1798 he founded Mission San Luis Rey, which he developed into the province's largest mission. He remained there until the end of 1832, when, upset about the recent expulsion of Spaniards from Mexico, he secretly quit the province. See Geiger, *Franciscan Missionaries,* 192–96.

Besides these establishments, there are three other settlements in New California where retirees or those who have never served—descendants of California's first settlers or subsequent migrants from various parts of Mexico—live. The 1st is called the village of St. Joseph (Pueblo de San José) and is located at the mission of San José in the district of the port of San Francisco; the 2nd is the town of Branciforte (Villa de Branciforte); and the 3rd is the village of St. Ángeles (Pueblo de los Ángeles), lying not far from Mission San Gabriel and in the vicinity of San Pedro Bay. It is populous, comprising more than a thousand souls of both sexes. It is located on a plain about two miles from the mountains and about 20 miles from the sea; the district's climate is said to be the best in all of California, for fog occurs there no more than five or six days of the year, on account of the distance from the sea. This village is under the direction of an elder (*alcalde* [magistrate]) elected by the citizens, who resolve all petty cases themselves, while criminal offenders are forwarded to the presidio, where they are tried by deputies and presidio commandants, whose decisions are confirmed by the governor.

In the last 10 or 15 years [since the middle 1810s], when foreign vessels began to come to California—first for contraband trade and then with rightful permission, a number of sailors of various European nations and Negros have deserted from them, and all of them have settled at the missions or at other establishments. Some of these men, having accepted Catholicism and married, engage in crop growing and stock rearing and live better than the native Californios; but the indolent and the shiftless barely earn a living.

From our settlement of Ross several Russians deserted in the beginning and subsequently, too; but not one of them has remained, all of them leaving, one for Mexico and the others on various trading vessels for Europe and the North American [United] States.

Climate

The climate of New California is temperate and consists of two seasons, summer and winter. Summer begins in April or May and lasts until November and December. In summer, northwest winds blow almost constantly, and in the vicinity of San Francisco and Monterey the coast is covered with thick fog. A beautiful picture presents itself from the summit of a high mountain in the shade of green laurel [i.e., bay] trees when the sun is hot and the air is fresh—and dense fog covers the surface of the land and undulates like the sea along the entire horizon. The mountain summit rises like an island in the mass of gray fog.

In November or December, winds begin to blow from the southeast to the southwest, with heavy rain, which sometimes floods the land, washes away buildings, and carries away sown grain. In summer there is no rain at all, but dew occurs and moistens the soil. During cold winters, snow falls at San Francisco but soon melts. On the northern coast there is no hot weather, but places distant from the sea are not subject to winds and fogs and are therefore quite hot. It does happen that little rain falls in winter, and this is as harmful to crop growing as [is] excessive rain. In that event, grain is lost to the drought and the soil is deprived of its fertility. In all of the province there are neither stoves nor fireplaces in the houses, although in the northern parts the cold is appreciable.

The air is salubrious everywhere, but during seasonal transitions it is sometimes unhealthful and causes sickness. During a new moon the air becomes noticeably thin, and in the morning one can see a faint circle around the old moon and in the evening the same around the new moon, and usually the new moon is visible the next day. The mildest and most agreeable climate extends from Santa Bárbara to San Diego. Fogs are very rare there, and the sky is almost always clear, and although it is rather hot during the day, the transition to nighttime is not as sensible as in the north of the province. As the day ends, people are deprived only of the intense heat, the warmth of the air changing very little. At Monterey, by contrast, if the day is hot, then by the evening the humidity is appreciable and the cold is penetrating; a heavy dew falls that can soak one to the skin. With any change in temperature one can quickly catch a cold or a fever. In winter severe thunder and lightning occur with the southwest winds. There are earthquakes almost yearly in the Santa Bárbara area but rarely elsewhere. In the same area there are two volcanos that now emit only smoke; across the mountains to the east of the port of S[an] Francisco a glow is visible at night at a great distance, so it can be concluded that a volcano is burning there, a fact that is also known from the Indians. In February 1827 during a strong earthquake at night distant noises like thunder claps were heard, and probably said volcano was the cause of this phenomenon. Mineral hot springs are found near Mission San Juan at Santa Cruz and near Mission San José. To the first is attributed great power in the treatment of chronic diseases, but nobody has tested them. Mineral resin flows from the ground near Mission San Miguel and beside Pueblo de los Ángeles. Salt lies in many lakes throughout California.

Character of the Country

A chain of fairly high mountains parallels the coast from S[an] Francisco to the port of S[an] Diego and beyond. Most of them have sharp peaks that are covered with snow in winter. The coast is high and steep wherever the ground is clay or limestone, as at Cape Drake [Point Reyes], Point Año Nuevo near Santa Cruz, Point Conception, Cape [Santa] Bárbara, and Famine [Point Fermin?] at S[an] Pedro. The sandy slopes have cliffs, as within Monterey Bay. In calm weather the surf (or breakers) is audible up to 5 or 6 miles seaward. In many places the high mountains abut the sea, and in accordance with their position they sometimes form a sloping shore and sometimes a steep shore, as in S[an] Francisco Bay and beyond at Santa Cruz.

Inland from the coast there are the most beautiful valleys of rich dark soil, extremely fertile and abounding in succulent pasture. One of them lies in the vicinity of Missions Santa Clara and San José, there is a fairly extensive one at Mission San Juan Bautista, and there are many between Mission San Gabriel and S[an] Diego. The hills, or knolls, and places near the sea are sandy and uncultivated; grass grows on some of them and thereby affords sustenance for livestock. The summits of the mountains are stony and barren, but these drawbacks pale by comparison with the advantage of the other places. The location of Mission S[anta] Clara on a broad plain is very interesting; about 20 years ago the head of the mission, Father Magín [Catalá], built an avenue from this mission to the pueblo of S[an] José, a distance of about 3 miles, or one league. The level surface of the terrain did not require human exertions; in summertime the trees afford dense shade to travelers. The width of the avenue is about 4 sazhens.

There are no large rivers along the entire coast, except the Colorado, but small rivers and streams, and in some places lakes, supply the inhabitants with enough water. The ports of Monterey, S[an] Pedro, and S[an] Diego do not have any running water except that from wells.

The best harbor is the port of S[an] Francisco, although there is no fresh water nearby, it being necessary to cross the strait [Golden Gate] to find a mountain stream [at Sausalito], from which all ships get water. Besides S[an] Francisco, it is possible to anchor safely at any season of the year at S[an] Diego and Monterey; other roadsteads are more or less sheltered from the northwest winds but exposed to the southerlies and therefore suitable for the mooring of ships in summer, but in winter they do not dare to anchor there without being exposed to great danger.

The ocean current in the entrance to S[an] Francisco is up to 8 knots and in the harbor from 2 to 4, and at S[an] Diego it is up to 6 knots in the entrance and from 2 to 3 in the harbor. At the latter port at the time of the new and full moons with south winds great amounts of seaweed are torn from the reef and carried by the current into the harbor and deposited on almost the entire length of the hawsers of ships, and if they are not removed in good time the ships will drift and be pulled by the current.

The rise of the tide during a full moon is 7 feet at Monterey, 7 at S[an] Francisco, 12 at S[an] Diego, and 7 at Bodega. High tide at S[an] Francisco and Monterey begins at 11 o'clock in the morning and at S[an] Diego about 9 o'clock; at Bodega it starts about 10 o'clock.

Products

Northern California—that is, the districts of S[an] Francisco and Monterey—is fairly wooded, the most important trees being oak, pine, alder, laurel, and redwood; in addition, there are various kinds of shrubs, willows, nut trees, and a species of small willow [*sic:* sumac] called *yedra* [*hiedra*] *ponzoñosa*, that is, poison willow [*sic:* oak (*Toxicodendron diversilobum*)]. It is found in abundance on the shores of S[an] Francisco Bay and at Monterey. This plant's poison is transmitted through contact with its sap or its leaves or even through smell; it causes swelling in one spot, accompanied by itching that spreads over the whole body, but within two or three months it disappears on its own accord. In the southern districts there are no trees whatever close to the sea, except in remote mountainous places; but elsewhere there are small groves of oak, alder, and other shrubs, plus the ubiquitous plant *junas*[14] (cactus), whose stalk bears wide, thick leaves covered with sharp needles. Its fruit in appearance and taste is similar to that of dried figs; it is gathered and dried, forming one of the chief stores of the savage Indians. Trees of various species grow in the mountains, including a kind of cedar [pinyon pine] that produces nuts very similar to those of the Siberian cedar [stone pine], except twice as large.

In April and May all grasses flower, and they spread a fragrance through the valleys; in June and July plants wither, and the land loses its charm. Fruit is grown abundantly throughout New California. Apples of various kinds, pears, peaches, and figs are characteristic of the whole country, but in the southernmost parts, beginning at Santa Bárbara, a lot of grapes are grown, as well as lemons, [sweet] oranges, sour oranges, pomegranates, citrons, and platans.[15] Fruit orchards are adorned with rose bushes, pinks, and stocks [gillyflowers]; many medicinal plants are cultivated, and of garden vegetables there are muskmelons [cantaloupes], watermelons, pumpkins, garlic, onions, potatoes, various cabbages, lettuce, and other greens. But these crops can only be seen at the missions.

Of cereal grains, wheat, barley, peas, beans, frijoles, garbanzos [chickpeas], lentils, and corn are grown. There are fertile valleys everywhere. In a good harvest, wheat yields 60-fold and 70-fold the seed. There have been instances when a single measure (a fanega) produced more than a hundred [fanegas]. But bumper years do not occur often; sometimes heavy winter rain, sometimes drought, and sometimes fog interfere, in which case the harvest is 10-fold and 15-fold [the seed]. It even happens that barely the seed is returned. The usual harvest is 20-fold, 25-fold, and 30-fold the seed. In 1823 at Mission San Diego 11 t[housand] fanegas of wheat and 4,000 of barley were reaped from a sowing of about 400 fanegas. And in the next four years there was no harvest at all. In 1826 at Mission S[an]

---

[14] *Tunas,* the fruits of the prickly pear, also known as the cochineal fig.
[15] Plane trees, or sycamores.

Luis Rey 1,000 fanegas altogether were planted but only 700 were harvested. In the same year all grain was injured by rust. Maize, or corn, yields 300-fold, 400-fold, and 500-fold the seed, and it constitutes the main food of the inhabitants.

For wheat the land is plowed after the first rains in November or December, usually by oxen. They plant in December and January and sometimes even in February; they reap in July and August. They thresh with horses on swept ground, so that a lot of sand usually remains in the grain.

Throughout California crops are severely damaged by rodents—gophers.[16] They move underground and eat the roots of plants, greatly impeding their growth.

Of all the fruits, only grapes yield much profit. At each of the missions from Santa Bárbara to S[an] Diego about 100 barrels (*barriles*) of spirits (*aguardiente*) and wine are made; in a good year Pueblo de los Ángeles produces up to 150 barrels of spirits, which is similar to Russian vodka and—according to the assurances of many—very harmful to one's health.

Red and white wine are made, sometimes fairly well—mainly at Mission S[an] Luis Rey—but generally inferiorly. A barrel of spirits sells locally for 40 to 50 piasters and wine for 15 to 20 piasters; foreign vessels buy apples and other fruits for 2 piasters and onions for 3 piasters per arroba. At the southernmost missions many olives are pickled, and they sell for 18 to 20 piasters a barrel. At Mission S[an] Diego a lot of cotton of good quality is grown; at some missions flax and hemp are cultivated but not regularly.

Animals

Innumerable herds of domestic livestock are reared at all of the missions, as well as by many individuals, and they constitute the chief local [source of] wealth. Horned livestock[17] number from 20 to 30 thousand head at many missions. The foremost stock-rearing missions are S[an] Luis Rey, S[an] Diego, S[an] Gabriel, S[an] Luis Obispo, and S[an] José, the first having from 25 to 30 t[housand] and the last from 18 to 20 t[housand] head. But in addition to these [livestock], many have run off to the mountains and become feral. There is a goodly number of horses and mules, and a great many sheep; pigs, by contrast, are very few. The Californian dogs are of a very good breed; they are numerous everywhere and very placid.

Of wild animals, there are bears, lynxes, American [mountain] lions, small wolverines, wild goats and sheep, deer, real wolves and a small breed here called *coyotes*,* which frequent settlements, come close at night to steal carrion or

---

*Jackals?—[*Auth.?*]

[16]Russ., *khomyaki*.

[17]Russian terminology distinguishes between horned (cattle, sheep, goats) and hornless (horses, mules, donkeys, pigs) livestock.

garbage, and howl like Kamchatkan dogs. Wildcats [bobcats] more than twice the size of domestic cats attack passersby. They have a beautiful coat like that of a snow leopard. Numerous marmots and gophers live in burrows everywhere; there are hares and rabbits in some parts.

Throughout the province there are a great many snakes, and in the south there are venomous snakes with rattles, 3 inches thick and up to 5 feet long. In the marshes live frogs, lizards, and scorpions. In the north there are small turtles that quickly become tame.

Geese arrive from the north in great numbers. They winter throughout Upper California from October to March and April and then leave. There are cranes and white and gray herons in summer and winter, as well as ducks and sandpipers of various kinds. But the tastiest dish of local game is the *codorniz* [California quail], a bird similar to a partridge and about the size of a dove; although it [i.e., the word] translates as "quail," it is not like one at all. It is found throughout the province.

Of raptors, there are eagles, hawks, various kinds of kites[18] (which have bald heads covered with red flesh, like an Indian chicken), common crows (which feed on litter and carrion around settlements), and magpies with white heads (somewhat smaller than European magpies). Sparrows of various kinds with beautiful feathers abound; but there are whole flocks of black birds called *chanates* [redwinged blackbirds]; some of them [males] have red feathers under their wings with which the Indians decorate the baskets that they plait from tree roots. These birds are a little larger than swallows and frequent plowland, and they cause much damage to grain and fruit. In summer hummingbirds appear in large numbers.

Of domestic fowl, there are common chickens; at a few missions there are Indian chickens. Many pigeons are kept at various places, but there are no wild ones.

Of marine animals, sea otters, sea lions, sea elephants [elephant seals], and harbor seals inhabit the entire coast. During fish runs a great many whales appear, and killer whales usually follow them. Sea pigs [porpoises and dolphins] also inhabit the sea.

The sea has a great abundance of fish of various kinds. A kind of herring (sardines) and mackerel approach the coast periodically, and others occur year-round. The most remarkable of them are sharks, sunfish, skates [rays], and hogfish with large teeth. In addition, there are sea perch [bass], which the Russian promyshlenniks call Kuzma's fish. In S[an] Francisco Bay there are many sturgeons, which are also found in the Slavyanka [Russian] River and the Río del Pájaro [Bird River].

There are various kinds of round crabs with long tails like lobsters; the latter abound in S[an] Diego Bay near Cape Famine, but it is remarkable that they do

---

[18]Either turkey vultures or California condors.

not have any large claws. Oysters are found in the vicinity of S[an] Diego, and there are a great many shells along the whole coast; one sort[19] has a beautiful blue color and is prized by the savages of the Northwest Coast, and at Canton Americans sell them for 10 piasters per *picul*.[20] In Old California the gulf [Sea of Cortez] has many pearls, which are not inferior in quality to those of Ceylon.[21]

Of sea birds, there are pelicans—here called *alcatraces*—everywhere, various kinds of gulls, albatrosses, common murres (guillemots),[22] puffins,[23] and many others.

Population

The inhabitants of Spanish extraction who settled in Upper California long ago, as well as the soldiers and civilians who were transferred [there] later from various Mexican provinces, number no more than 2,000 males and up to 4½ thousand souls of both sexes in 4 presidios and 3 villages and towns. There are no more than 50 genuine Europeans, even including friars. The Indians [i.e., neophytes] at all of the missions of Upper California are reckoned at a little more than 20,000 of both sexes. Foreigners—Englishmen, Americans, Negros, and others—number up to 100 persons. The total population of this province can be put at no more than 25,000 souls, excluding independent Indians, who are very numerous in the interior.

The Californian women are surprisingly fecund; nearly every couple has a family of no fewer than 10 children, and many have from 15 to 18. Opinions of their fidelity vary, and the following anecdote is even told. At S[an] Francisco a certain foreigner called at the home of a resident acquaintance with a large family and, after looking at the children, with surprise asked why it was that some of them had blonde, some had light brown, some had red, and some had black hair. "That is not surprising," answered the poised father of the family; "You know that this is a port. Ships of various nations come here, and Englishmen, Americans, Russians, and Frenchmen visit our homes." The mother of the family, who was present, wrapped herself tightly in a shawl and hung her head. But I repeat that this is an anecdote about only one family.

Way of Life

The Californios are generally indolent, untidy, and lacking in foresight, and their simple manner attests their childlike state. Now the Mexican leadership is trying

---

[19]Monterey, or abalone, shells.

[20]A *picul* was a commercial measure of weight in Southeast and East Asia of varying poundage but usually equal to 133⅓ pounds.

[21]See Gerhard, "Pearl Diving."

[22]Russ., *urily*.

[23]Russ., *toporki*.

to introduce European customs, beginning with dress, dances, and food. Young people often dress in the European fashion and use tea, coffee, table settings, and other things. Older people still keep the former customs; their dress consists of short trousers with codpieces and undone buttons on the knees, and gold braid an inch wide is sewn on the bottoms. A long camisole of particolored silk or cotton is fastened with two or three buttons at the bottom only. Over the camisole they wear a jersey of blue cloth with a red collar, lapels, and cuffs, and girded with a red silk sash, sometimes with tassels. Their boots of dressed deerskin are short, and those of the wealthy are embroidered with gold and silk. Over the boots, from the heels to the knees, they wrap their legs in ochered suede imprinted with various figures; usually their underwear shows under their short trousers, and under it stockings come down into the boots if the legs are not wrapped in suede. They wear a kerchief around their necks, but instead of tying it they wind it around once and run both ends through a ring, which glitters on their chests. On their heads they tie another kerchief of silk or cotton, and when they intend to go for a walk or a ride they wear a hat over it. Instead of a greatcoat they wear a fabric, a kind of blanket with a hole in the middle (serape*) that they put over their heads and wrap around themselves. Many of these serapes are made of fine blue cloth with a velvet rectangle in the middle and are fringed with tassels; usually the particolored woolen serapes made at the missions are rather plain, however.

Old-fashioned women wear skirts, and they cover their bosoms with a Mexican shawl of coarse cotton (*rebozo*). They usually throw this shawl over their heads and wrap it around themselves so that only half of their faces are visible. Fashionable ladies wear long dresses, mostly of muslin or silk; they curl their hair into ringlets and pin it with a comb, which is adorned with various artificial flowers. The shawl is left on their shoulders only. Commoners have neither floors nor ceilings in their houses, and because of the filth there are usually a great many fleas.

The food of the inhabitants of California consists of corn, frijoles, and meat. Corn is boiled in water, with some lime added so that it boils better, and then it is ground into flour on a stone, and, after having soaked it in water, they bake it in a pan into flatcakes like pancakes (*tortillas*), which are a substitute for bread for nearly all of the inhabitants. They prepare them just before they want to eat, for they are tastier when warmer. Frijoles are cooked in lard (*manteca**), but meat is usually cooked in a sauce with a great amount of red pepper until it begins to break into pieces, and they eat it with chili sauce. Of vegetables, they love pumpkins [or squash] (*calabazas*) and a ground fruit, called

---

*This seems to be the same thing as the *sar[r]au* ["smock"] of French settlers, a kind of outer shirt.—*Ed.*

*The inhabitants of California call beef [?] fat *manteca;* in many cases it is a substitute for butter for them. In particular, they always use this fat, or *manteca,* for frying.—[*Auth.*?]

*tomate*** in Spanish and love apple in English, that they make into a sauce. At the table, even if there are 10 persons, no more than one or two knives are provided and there are no forks at all. Men of all ages smoke hand-rolled cigarettes, and many older women do so, too. The men drink vodka [spirits] (*aguardiente*) at the table, but the women, even girls, like to drink wine. Many women of the lower classes readily drink vodka and rum but not a lot. One should generally say of Californios that they are temperate, and drunks are to be seen very rarely.

It was no more than 10 years ago that the missionaries began to have table settings, and the foremost officials linens, armchairs, and chairs. In the homes of longtime residents there is usually a divan or bed on which the mistress of the house always sits with her daughters, who wear shirts and skirts but no shawls; in the presence of strangers they sometimes wrap themselves in shawls. The children are very slovenly and extremely naughty.

Californios are excellent horse riders. They begin to ride horseback from childhood, and with age they become skillful horsemen. They throw lassos unerringly over the horns of bulls and heads of horses when they have to catch them. They ride to hunt bears with lassos; after throwing one lasso over a bear's head and two over its legs, they lead it for a great distance. Often two men without any weapons and only lassos set out on this dangerous pursuit. Children also want to lasso, and they are trained in this pursuit from childhood, throwing lassos over pigs and chickens and—out of mischief—often over horses.

The men do almost nothing, and if they can get Indians from the missions for work, then they just walk about with their arms folded, having shown the Indians what to do. There is not one workman among them. Since the opening of free trade [1821] some inhabitants have begun to till the soil and sow wheat and become used to hard work, but they relinquish their idleness very, very reluctantly.

Meeting in the morning, they usually inquire about your health and are certain to demand three or four answers before starting to talk about the weather. It is strange to see the treatment of underlings by their superiors, for example, a soldier on duty approaching an officer takes him by the arm and asks about his health and, after receiving an answer, says that he is very glad to find him healthy, and then, after adding some sort of greeting and getting an answer, he—as if reluctantly—relates what has been done or asks what should be done. Taking his leave, he will without fail say "Goodbye" or "See you tomorrow," as circumstances permit. The officers themselves have often said that the present

---

**We call this fruit *tomata* [*pomidory* in modern Russian] and the English and the French, love apples (*pommes d'amour*).—*Ed.*

form of government, which has absolutely nothing that can satisfy the soldiers, cannot even force them into strict obedience. Only recently the commandant of a presidio, [after] listening to a soldier's nonsense, told him that he had observed a Don Quixote in him, and the soldier, folding his arms on his chest, replied that "it is no wonder that you have observed this similarity because I have long found in you a Sancho Panza." In accordance with the right to liberty, the officer could not say a word.

Californios always carry a large knife, which is wrapped in something and placed behind their suede leggings; they use it at the table. In arguments they become heated to the point of craziness; sometimes, being unable to prove something or to justify himself, one of them will instantly grasp his knife and without thinking stab his opponent. It has often happened, and still happens, that for little reason they have inflicted mortal wounds or left a body on the spot. Suicide among them is unknown. Theft among the lower classes is not rare; upon inviting them to a ship's cabin it is necessary to watch them or to remove alluring objects.

Californios are passionate card players, and one often happens to see two or three men meeting on the road, sitting down, spreading a serape, and playing cards, and then ending the game with a quarrel. Cockfighting is also one of the favorite pursuits of Californios. The game of lotto[24] is very popular, but they make the cards of different values, and what they put in the pot accords with their number, for example, 1 real for a card with five rows, 2 for ten rows, 3 for fifteen rows, 4 for twenty rows, and so on. During the game they spread the cards on the table, and because the game usually attracts so many enthusiasts, they—especially the women and children—sit on the floor with their cards. They place a kernel of corn on the number called. Those who want to win quickly pool some piasters until the first double [the same number called twice in a row] or triple occurs, but usually they win or lose on the next odd or even number (*pares o nones*). I have seen some soldiers bring 50 piasters each and lose them on two numbers.

Most Californios are tall and of strong build. Their skin is dark; their face is regular, with a straight or hooked nose; their hair is black and braided into a long pigtail; and they grow long side whiskers and rarely shave their beards. Their stern disposition, inherited from the conquerors of Mexico, is reflected in their faces.

Hospitality is an alien virtue to them, but they themselves like to be treated. When two or three persons are invited to dinner, they are sure to bring ten or more friends with them without considering whether or not there is room on the ship for receiving them.

---

[24]Lotto is a bingo-like game played with cards bearing five numbers in each line; the holder covers a number when it is called by someone who draws numbered balls from a bag, and the game is won by the first player to cover a line of numbers.

The slovenliness of the inhabitants is visible when approaching a settlement; everywhere around the houses are scattered the heads, horns, and hoofs of bulls, which usually every Saturday are driven to their yards and slaughtered, the meat and hide removed and the heads, hoofs, and innards discarded. Also, they never sweep away the refuse, not having the requisite place for it, and they spread it everywhere. After this [neglect] one can imagine what sort of air prevails in these settlements.

The principal exercise of the inhabitants is horse riding. The women have a special kind of saddle; they sit on one side and ride very deftly and fast. Carts have two wheels, each made of a single piece of wood 4 or 5 inches thick; but the axles are crudely made, and the body consists of poles tied with osiers. They harness two or four oxen to these carts in order to transport heavy loads, which consist of, for example, 12 or 20 fanegas of wheat, that is, from 50 to 80 puds. Almost none of the inhabitants has a carriage, except some of the missionaries, who use European wheels.

Most of these observations apply to the longtime residents, who are steeped in the old ways. The young people, especially those coming from Mexico (where education has been introduced), are very civil and affable and would perhaps be hospitable if only they were acquainted with housekeeping and thrift.

The primary expense of Californios is the attire of their wives and daughters. It is not my business to discuss the women's whimsies, which arise from various causes; women everywhere—in California, Kamchatka, and Europe and on the Northwest Coast of America—have their foibles and caprices. A blue shell in the ears of a Northwest Coast woman excites the envy of another to the same degree as a shawl does among Mexican women.

It seems that in accordance with the natural order of things the transition from youth to old age in a person can also be applied to an entire nation. I daresay that heretofore the Mexicans were in the youth stage. Mr. [Governor] E[cheandí]a once said that they were only machines that performed various actions. The present period is their adolescence; indeed, they are becoming familiar with the way of life and politics of Europe, or rather in the spirit of the times they are jumping with joy like children and with the innocence that fits this age. The artifices and intrigues of their elders in the formation of nations are still unknown to them. Their thoughts reveal a sort of natural artlessness, and if in this respect we take for comparison the natives of North America, then it must be said that the vengeance that is their main vice is also not alien to adolescent nations. It is impossible not to be surprised by their bitterness toward the Spaniards, whose blood flows in their veins, and in this instance it is impossible not to confirm the rightness of the Russian proverb that there is no greater hatred than that between kinsmen.

Englishmen, Frenchmen, Spaniards, and Italians—good men as well as scoundrels—are gradually multiplying in Mexico and other republics. From these teachers the new peoples will soon learn paths to cunning, but it will still be a long, long time before they can stand equal with educated Europeans. It is said that in Mexico academies of sciences and letters have opened, as well as various educational institutions, and that artists and writers have already emerged there. The local newspapers are filled with poems.

Communication with Mexico

Communication by water between Mexico and California is very negligible, for heretofore only one brig, the *San Carlos,* has been used, arriving in California every two or three years and bringing sometimes officials and sometimes some money and ammunition for artillery. In 1825 the Mexican government bought two English three-masted ships to use for communication by sea.

The usual route to Mexico is by land, for example, beginning from Monterey through all of the missions on the coast to S[an] Diego in Upper California, from there through Lower California, first to the northwestern coast and then crossing to the eastern coast to the town of Loreto. At that place there are small sailing craft and large rowing vessels in which—depending upon the season and the wind—they cross the gulf [Sea of Cortez] to Guaymas, Mazatlán, or San Blas. The usual express ride from Monterey to Mexico [City] is accomplished in 2½ or 3 months, but during the rainy season in winter it is much longer. At San Blas the worst season occurs from May to October because of the sultry heat and the resultant contagious diseases. Regular mail is dispatched to Mexico [City] every month; whenever necessary, special couriers are dispatched expressly.

The present government is trying at S[an] Diego to open a road overland around the [head of the] gulf, or Vermilion Sea, and across the Colorado River, which in summertime drops to the extent that fording it is possible; but the independent Indians living at its mouth have still not consented to its [i.e., the road's] establishment. However, [the government] hope[s] to persuade the Indians eventually and to build posting stations and thereby shorten the means of communication appreciably.

Trade

Given the present indifference of the inhabitants and the negligence of the missionaries, few of the country's products are exported. The main exports are uncured cattle hides, tallow, wheat, and a small number of [sea] otters. Free trade was opened to all nations in 1821, and thereafter up to 10 English and American ships arrived annually from Calcutta, Canton, Boston, and Liverpool. We [Russians] began to have regular intercourse with California in 1817 for the purchase of provisions and always with the special permission of the governor, as I have expounded in detail in the first part of my "Notes" about our colonies in America.[25]

During the revolution at Lima, from 3 to 5 t[housand] fanegas of wheat were exported thither from California in the course of three or four years, but now these shipments have ceased. From 1½ to 3 t[housand] fanegas are exported annually to our colonies. Wheat is sold locally for 3 or 3½ piasters per fanega.

From 25 to 30 t[housand] cattle hides are sold [yearly] at all of the missions; depending on size, their price is from 1½ to 2 piasters [apiece]. They are shipped to England and North America. For freight to England they [i.e., the sellers] pay 1 piaster per hide, which usually weighs 25 or 30 English pounds; there they are sold on the spot for about 6 piasters per hide, so that after expenses they [i.e., the sellers] make a certain profit of 100%.

From 5 to 8 t[housand] and occasionally up to 10 t[housand] quintals of tallow are exported from California to Lima and San Blas, and it is bought for 1 to 2 piasters per arroba. During the revolution at Lima it was sold for 24 piasters per quintal, but usually it went for about 14 piasters; sometimes it is cheaper, and in that case the sellers incur a loss.

Sea otters hunted by mission Indians are sold locally to Americans for 16 to 20 piasters for a large skin; but they are also shipped to Mexico, where they are now put to use. They make peaked caps from them [i.e., the skins], and they trim 1¾ inches of spencers [short woolen jackets] and collars [with the fur]. Those who do not have peaked caps of sea otter are considered ignorant of fashion. In Mexico a skin sells for 30 to 40 and even 50 piasters. From 100 to 200 large sea otter skins are exported from California annually.

The total export of various products from California reaches from 80 to 100 t[housand] piasters' worth yearly, including bulls that foreign vessels buy for eating and for salting. The price of a large bull is 8, and of a medium bull 7, piasters. The Americans buy cattle horns for 3 and 4 piasters.

Those with reliable and detailed information about the state of the province reckon that there are 180,000 cattle altogether, and they conjecture that ¼ of them are slaughtered annually; consequently, a total of up to 45 t[housand] hides could be collected, but of this number   [15,000?] are used domestically, that is, made into shoes, horse harness, straps, bags for tallow, lard, etc., leaving   [two-thirds?], or 30 t[housand] hides, for export abroad. But this figure cannot be viewed as invariable, for the usual exportation reaches from 20 to 25 thousand hides.

---

[25]See Khlebnikov, *Notes on Russian America*, 102, 108–15.

Whaling vessels hunting whales in the expanse of ocean between the coasts of Japan and California call at local ports to the number of 20–30 annually for refreshment. They buy fresh meat, potatoes, pumpkins, fruit, and greens. Duty of 10 piasters is exacted from every whaler and any other ship that arrives but does not trade; those coming to trade, however, are assessed heavy burdens. In accordance with a ship's tonnage, 2½ piasters is exacted for each ton, and for the sale of goods 25% was imposed before 1826 and 42% at present.

Lima [Peruvian] and Mexican ships come yearly, sometimes one from each place and sometimes in twos from Mexico; the latter bring tobacco in both raw and processed form (that is, as cigarettes) and various kinds of shawls of local manufacture. The Lima ships bring cacao and European goods, and sometimes money for the purchase of tallow.

In 1826 three ships under the Sandwich Island [Hawaiian] flag arrived in the name of Chief Kalanimoku. Their captains were Americans of the United States, and some of the sailors were also from there, but most of the crewmen were Sandwich Islanders.

Several of these ships put in to Guadalupe Island, where in the course of a year they bagged about 8 t[housand] fur seal skins. In California they also obtained horses and cattle for the Sandwich Islands, and they bought some wheat and other grains.

California's internal trade is very insignificant. At the southern missions of New California and Pueblo de los Ángeles they sometimes make from 3 to 4 hundred barrels of spirits and wine, some of which are conveyed to the northern districts for sale at various missions. The inhabitants make soap, candles, and crude blankets from sheep's wool, and they resell small wares; in the same way, horses and cattle enter into internal trade. The best horses sell for 80 to 100, good horses for 25 to 40, and ordinary horses for 9 to 15 piasters [each]. A brace of the best draft oxen sells for 25 or 30, and an ordinary pair for 10 or 15, piasters.

California abounds in a variety of products, and with proper organization it could export rather a lot of cattle hides, horns, tallow, lard, wheat, flour, frijoles, peas, barley, corn, dried fruit, salted olives, olive oil, cheese, butter, salt, flax, hemp, cotton, sheep's wool, suede, ham, salted beef, soap, sea otter skins, spirits, and wine.

Of minerals that could enter into trade, there are chalk and pitch; the former is found in the mountains near S[an] Diego and the latter flows from the ground in various districts.* The silver mines contain rich ore and even native silver; on

*Near Mission S[an] Juan Bautista, too, pitch flows from the ground. The best time for collecting it is June–July. Perhaps from 50 to 100 barrels of it could be obtained in one place. Coal of the best kind is found in abundance in the vicinity of [Missio]n Santa Cruz.

Catalina Island the silver ore is mixed with lead. But centuries will pass before these minerals are developed.

All European products are used in California, but they are primarily consumed by churches and missions; however, cloth, cotton, silk and linen goods, tableware, tea services, glassware, copperware, ironware, hats, stockings, tables, chairs, mirrors, watches, trunks, etc., sell well.

In accordance with a recent decree of the Mexican government, it is forbidden to import alcoholic beverages, tobacco, millet, coffee, sugar, readymade clothing and footwear, blankets, and some other things; but this prohibition is not observed very strictly, and officials themselves—who are charged to enforce it— buy up these goods from foreigners.

Army

The army consists of artillery, cavalry, and infantry. The artillerymen were sent from Mexico only recently, and the infantrymen—100 of them—were posted in 1820 from the province of Mazatlán. The cavalrymen are local inhabitants, who are recruited from the young men by lots; they serve for 12 years, and they can remain longer but only by choice. Their salaries, according to the latest regulations, are [as follows]: 17 piasters per month for a horse soldier, 15 for an artilleryman, and 9 for a foot soldier; from this salary they are required to provide their own provisions and ammunition, and the cavalrymen their horses. So as part of their salary the state issues them frijoles, corn, soap, lard, and tobacco. The government obtains the provisions from the missions, and the last is sometimes supplied from Mexico. It often happens that calico, cloth, stockings, and other things are bought and distributed to the soldiers as part of their salary, for there is not enough cash to satisfy everyone everywhere.

The soldiers who have recently been sent from Mexico are tolerably uniformed in the European fashion, but the uniform of the Californios consists of [only] the aforementioned clothing. Add to this [attire] a variety of hats, headbands, and neckerchiefs, and one can [only] be surprised at their [the Californios'] sufferance.

A commandant general receives a salary in accordance with his rank of 3 t[housand] piasters (up to 5 t[housand] with various extras), a commissioner [*comisario?*] 1,000 piasters, a commandant of a presidio and a captain of the artillery (in accordance with his rank) 860 piasters, a lieutenant (*teniente*) 500 piasters, and an ensign (*alférez*) 400 rubles. It is generally believed that the expenses of both provinces [Alta and Baja California] reach 100 t[housand] piasters.

Money is rarely provided by Mexico, and revenue is insufficient, so the government is in arrears to all of its employees. Under the Spanish government before the outbreak of the revolution in Mexico no funds had been sent for about 12 years, and the lower officials received nothing (save provisions as part of their salaries), and they were deprived of all of their possessions, for the republican government did not assume any responsibility for these payments. I have seen from the accounts that from 1821 to 1827 soldiers were each to be paid from 400 to 800 piasters [annually].

Revenue

From all products of the land, the government receives 1/10 in kind, which it supplies to the soldiers as part of their salaries. The missions usually provide the presidio annually with an inventory of their harvest and livestock for the payment of the tithe (*diezmo*). The presidio's commandant takes these products at a fixed price, for example, a calf at 2½ piasters, a fanega of wheat at 1¾ piasters, and so on, and he keeps an account of the amount of supplies received (and from whom) that are necessary for the maintenance of the garrison. However, these accounts always leave the missions in the red, the commandant [actually] taking much more [than what they state], and these amounts accumulate from year to year in the state's account. The revenue from foreign trading vessels, as noted above in the section on trade, reaches 40 to 50 t[housand] piasters annually in Upper California. From the dealers who buy spirits at the mission and retail them at the settlements, 8 piasters per barrel are exacted. But these sources are insufficient to meet the salaries of both the higher and the lower officials, and so only the former are fully paid while the latter receive chits, and this not infrequently causes grumbling and disorder. With respect to proposed duties on imported goods in 1820, herewith is enclosed an excerpt from a decree of the Mexican government composed in English for foreigners.

["]Duties that ought to be paid by foreigners. Vessels of any nation for goods imported & exported in the ports of the Mexican Republic.
the 25 p. Cent of introduction over the Valuation that be made according to the prices that the book of rated [rates?].[26]
the 15 p Cent of importation over the Value of the book of rates increased in one fourth part.
the 2½ p Cent of damage regulated over the principal sales: [that] is to say over the same that produce the Valuation Without the increase of the fourth part.
the 3½ p Cent over the Exportation of Coin money and 2 p Cent the Gold
    Worked Silver . . . . 3½ p Cent
        "   Gold 2   p Cent
Duties in tons 20 Reals p[r] ton
All the rest of this Country goods With Exception of none they Will be absolutely free of Duties.["][27]

---

[26]Illegible word.
[27]Either this decree was published in broken English or the excerpt was transcribed imperfectly.

Indians

Many travelers compare the Indians of New Albion and California to cattle on account of their [i.e., the Indians'] marked stupidity. But it seems to me that they do not have to be intelligent, of course, because firstly, comprising countless tribes and completely different languages, they do not lead social lives wherein from necessity understanding is developed rapidly and language for expressing themselves is perfected. Secondly, the climate and the country afford them sufficient sustenance. Oak provides acorns, which constitute their chief staple; they gather the grain of wild rye, which grows in many places; and many gophers, marmots, mice, frogs, and such—all of which enter their diet—live in or on the ground. Those living on the coast collect crabs, shrimp, shells, and the carcasses of various sea animals. They are able to catch geese and other birds expertly, as well as mountain sheep, goats, and deer. Thirdly, they have neither houses nor any kind of permanent settlements; rather, they find shelter in the hollow trunks of large trees, in the clefts of mountains, or in huts made of branches, huts that they do not begrudge leaving when moving from one place to another. Usually they obtain fire by rubbing dry wood, pieces of which they keep when they move. Fourthly, the climate allows them not to muffle themselves against the cold in some animal skin or fabric. Men and women go quite naked; a few women wear a scrap of hide of some animal fastened to a grass belt to cover the loins. Fifthly, neither barter nor trade of any kind is conducted between them. Nature produces everything that is necessary for everyone equally. And sixthly, many of their tribes are not at all warlike. Their weapons consist solely of bows and arrows, which are quite skillfully made, but even these they use mostly against birds and animals only.

Since in the savage state of man his chief needs—food and shelter—are found everywhere, there is consequently no reason for exerting mental capacities to invent the means for improving his condition; it seems to him that he is more blessed than all of the world's other inhabitants, who are known to him from their proximity or from hearsay. Perhaps it is just such a way of life that is to blame for their profound ignorance. However, one cannot deny that they are clever in their own way. Their bows are very skillfully made and are strung with deer sinew, and they set heads of obsidian, jasper, or stone in their arrows with much care; from roots they plait neat, strong baskets, adorning them with red and pale blue feathers and dark blue shells. Their headdresses are also beautifully made from feathers. The Indians living on the islands opposite Santa Bárbara have wooden boats (canoes), but they must have been introduced at the behest of the Spaniards, for the other Indians living near the sea—for example, at S[an] Francisco or in Great Bodega [Tomales] Bay and Little Bodega Bay—have none whatever, and in the event of a crossing they use reeds [tule] tied into something like a dug-out or kayak, and in such sheafs they cross very swiftly, sometimes through breakers, and at S[an] Francisco they not infrequently convey soldiers in them [i.e., the reed boats] to the missions. The Indians living at the missions even include artists and artisans of all kinds, albeit imperfect ones, but that is perhaps because they do not have models and systematic training. Many of them understand Spanish and learn to read and write.

The Indians who have been settled at the missions, having been baptized and placed under the strict supervision of the missionaries, become accustomed to communal living. They share huts, in each of which two or more families live. The artisans and the servants of the priests are dressed in heavy, coarse cloth or frieze, but the laborers usually have woolen blankets that they wrap around themselves. The women wear shirts and skirts. On Sundays all of them go to church and are dressed fairly neatly. On all holidays both sexes are freed from work, and they are given better food than that issued on other days. Then they usually play outdoors in particular groups. The males—adults and children—and the women, too, form special circles near or facing the mission. The oldsters sit in a circle, and the playful youngsters chase a ball. Many of the Indians are worthy of trust and have their own cattle, pigs, and chickens and cultivate gardens. It is strange to see one or two thousand savages abjectly obeying a friar attended by 5 or 6 soldiers who are hardly better than the Indians themselves. However, there have been examples of missionaries falling victim to their excessive strictness. One of them[28] was hanged in the garden on a fruit tree at S[anta] Cruz.

In 1806 the Indians of Mission Santa Bárbara undertook a revolt, but it was soon discovered and the culprits were punished. Then Chilean insurgents under the Frenchman Bouchard looted Monterey and several missions in California in 1818. For the Indians this [event] afforded solid grounds for convincing themselves of the weakness of their masters. Thereafter they had designs, and they held secret talks at many missions. In 1822 an uprising erupted at Missions Santa Inés, La Purísima Concepción, and Santa Bárbara; the first two were torched, and several soldiers were killed but the missionaries were spared. The Indians hid the looted property in the bush, and they positioned themselves on an island in a small lake, taking all precautions. A military detachment was sent against them but returned unsuccessful; finally, with exhortations the padre presidente persuaded them to return to their former abodes. All of their misdeeds were consigned to oblivion, and the plundered property of the missions was left in their possession.

The Indians living at the missions are no longer savages, and so their way of life cannot be compared with that of those who roam the mountains and deserts, as

---

[28]Andrés Quintana in 1812.

some travelers, such as the following, say: . . .[29] This description cannot be applied to all of the savage tribes, but as far as is known it probably does in most respects.

Information about the Colorado River

The Colorado River empties into the Vermilion Sea, or Gulf of California. It flows from the Green Mountains (Sierra Verde) [Rocky Mountains] and runs a distance of about 200 leagues (600 miles); its banks have been settled by numerous tribes of independent Indians. Because of the nearness of the port of San Diego, they not infrequently go there. In 1825 the governor sent an official to chart the river in order to establish a post road. At the beginning of 1826 some Indians came to S[an] Diego; their leader called himself a general and his two subordinates captains. All of these mighty individuals arrived naked, except for a breechcloth hanging from a belt in front. The commandant general of California was cordial, entertaining them and giving them clothes in the hope of establishing lasting friendship with them; but upon their departure they drove away from the environs of S[an] Diego all of the horses belonging to the residents of that port. A posse that was sent after them returned unsuccessful. These Indians were tall, stately, and sturdy. The general, or their leader, was distinguished by a long staff with a silver knob. Both men and women were naked. They have many cattle, and they ride horses bareback adroitly and swiftly. In the rainy season the Colorado River is deep, but in summer it can be forded. The governor is determined to build a post road across it to Mexico.

The Indians related at S[an] Diego that in the summer of 1826 a foreign ship arrived at the mouth of the river, but the government did not know its nationality. Finally, at the end of November 14 well-armed Americans of the United States came from across the mountains to Pueblo de los Ángeles; they said that they had left a ship at the mouth of the river, and they described the place where it lay and drew maps.[30] It is to be hoped that this expedition will eventually furnish the world with trustworthy information about the course of the river and the peoples living along it.

Observations[31]

1. ABOUT THE ROUTE TO MEXICO. It is from 12 to 20 days by sea from Monterey to San Blas or Acapulco.

---

[29]This excerpt has not been translated here, because it is extraneous. It was taken from Bonnycastle, *Spanish America*, beginning on page 79; Khlebnikov was arbitrary in his choice and order of passages and approximate in his translation.

[30]Khlebnikov is presumably referring to the Southwest Expedition of Jedediah Smith. See Brooks, *Southwest Expedition*; and Weber, *Californios versus Jedediah Smith*.

[31]These remarks are appended in Khlebnikov's handwriting to the end of the first variant of the edited manuscript without any interruption in pagination, so presumably he intended to include them in the published version. They obviously constitute commercial intelligence for prospective entrepreneurs.

It is 80 leagues from San Blas to Guadalajara, and the road is good; it is 250 leagues from Guadalajara to Mexico [City] on a good road (see the itinerary).

It is 90 leagues from Acapulco to Mexico [City], and the road is mountainous, suitable for riding on horseback and for mules. The usual crossing is no more than 20 days [but can be] much faster if necessary.

It is 110 leagues from Mexico [City] to Veracruz, and the road is excellent in European carriages. There are inns all along the route, and all supplies are cheap. The usual drive is no more than ten days; express is faster.

2. About the Islas Tres Marías. They lie opposite San Blas and abound in salt, which can be obtained for very little duty, which must be paid at San Blas, whence a man is taken who can find the salt lakes. It is possible to avoid paying duty if one comes to an arrangement with the officials.

On it, besides salt, there are sea turtles, called *carey* [tortoiseshell], whose shell is the very best for making articles. Crews come expressly from San Blas—as well as American ships—to catch them.

On these islands there grows a lot of guaiacum wood [lignum vitae] that is in demand for ships' pulleys and other tackle.

3. About the port of Loreto. It lies on the Californian peninsula on the Vermilion Sea. Nearby there is a large island [Isla del Carmen] with many salt lakes. The salt can be obtained from them at little expense.[32]

Many turtles are caught in the sea there, as well as pearls, which Americans come there to buy.

4. About the port of Guaymas. It is located in the province of Mazatlán on the coast of the Vermilion Sea that separates it from California. At this port for about 3 or 4 piasters per quintal one can buy flour that is brought by the inhabitants on mules from the interior provinces that abound in wheat; but wheat itself is not brought.

This port conducts considerable trade with foreigners, who receive silver bullion for their goods.

5. About timber and planks. At all of the aforesaid places one can import sawn planks of 1¼, 2, and 3 inches [in thickness], squared beams of 8 and 10 inches, and thin poles of 3 to 4 inches in diameter, used in very ordinary houses. The boards should have a length of 3 and, if possible, more sazh[ens]. Squared beams of 4 to 6 sazh[ens] are sold by the foot at great profit.

6. About the port of Realejo [Fonseca Bay?]. It lies in the republic of Guatemala in the province of Nicaragua in 12° 12' 48" N latitude and 87° 30' W

---

[32]The salt was not only low in cost but also high in quality.

long[itude]. It has a good harbor. It is located near the city of León in Nicaragua, and there it is possible to profitably obtain mahogany of good quality, timber, hemp, sugar, yew wood, pitch, and indigo dyestuff.

7. ABOUT THE GALAPAGOS ISLANDS. Here there are many sea turtles. From the mussels found on this island they obtain a purple dye.

8. ABOUT [SEA] OTTERS ALONG THE COAST OF CALIFORNIA. Not far from Seros Island [Isla Cedros] is the small island of [Isla San] Benito; there are many [sea otters] on it. They abound on the coast [of Baja California] near Mission San Fernando [de Velicatá], and there are also many near Mission El Rosario [de Viñadaco].

DOCUMENT 21

Peter Chistyakov's Report about the Condition of Alta California, 1830

EDITOR'S INTRODUCTION

The following two documents describe Alta California in late 1829, a year marred by a meager harvest and military rebellion. Both events loom large in the dispatch to the Russian-American Company's St. Petersburg headquarters by Governor Chistyakov; his remarks are based on the observations of his assistant and agent for California, Kirill Khlebnikov, who was sent there in the company brig *Okhotsk* to buy wheat and to negotiate an agreement for the joint hunting of sea otters. Khlebnikov failed on both counts. The other report was penned by Yevgeny von Berens (1810–78), who as a midshipman on the sloop *Krotky* (*Gentle*) under Captain-Lieutenant Hagemeister was making the first of his three round-the-world voyages to Russian America (the other two were those of the naval transport *Amerika*, Captain-Lieutenant von Schantz, in 1834–36 and the company ship *Nikolay I*, which he himself commanded, in 1837–39).[1]

[PETER CHISTYAKOV,] A REPORT FROM
GOVERNOR PETER CHISTYAKOV TO THE BOARD OF DIRECTORS OF
THE RUSSIAN-AMERICAN COMPANY ABOUT THE CONDITION OF
ALTA CALIFORNIA,[2] NO. 70, [NEW ARCHANGEL], 4 MAY 1830

The brig *Okhotsk*, which I sent on 18 October of last year [1829] to California, returned safely to New Archangel on the 5th of this month.

---

[1] See Grinëv, *Kto yest kto*, 62; and Pierce, *Biographical Dictionary*, 53.
[2] RRAC, roll 32, doc. 70, fols. 67v–71v (copy).

The Board of Directors of the company will deign to see from my report for 1829, which I am now submitting, that in accordance with the instructions of 16 October, no. 292,[3] which I gave to Mr. Khlebnikov, in sending him to California the aim of his voyage there was not only the purchase of grain but also the benefit to the company arising from [sea] otter hunting along the coast of California, and so I provided him with a letter[4] to the then governor [José Echeandía], but because of my uncertainty about the present situation of this province and particularly its present administration I took the precaution of furnishing Mr. Khlebnikov with another letter[5] to the presumed new governor [José Padrés] so as not to halt the operations that I prescribed there; for his own consideration of this matter I added a copy of this letter in Russian.

The rapid, unexpected return of the brig *Okhotsk* forced me to doubt the success of his [i.e., Khlebnikov's] mission, and indeed to my extreme regret this time our ship returned from California without any wheat; and given the present circumstances there it was impossible to think of hunting [sea] otters! That land is impoverished on account of a harvest failure for several years in a row, whereby it is deprived of almost all means of provisionment, and its unfortunate inhabitants are again subject to physical and moral temptation; it is now found in a most grievous situation and is close to utter ruin. What remains of niggardly nature is being destroyed by internal strife and violent anarchy!

From Mr. Khlebnikov's report of 30 November to me from Monterey, it is evident that the deplorable state of this province has reached an extreme. Last year's drought is the reason why there was no grain harvest anywhere in California. Some were fortunate enough to be able to reap sufficient [grain] for seed, but most were deprived of all that was sown; all of the grass withered, and in many places a full one-third of the livestock died. A general discontent has arisen from the shortage of food for provisioning the army, and two days before the arrival of the brig *Okhotsk* at Monterey an insurrection erupted there. At night armed soldiers seized the commandant and the company's officers and put them under guard. The next day they chose as commandant Captain Don Solís,[6] who had been sent from Mexico by the party of the former emperor, Agustín Iturbide, and they promulgated a plan of revolution. In this document they asserted that General Commandant de Echeandía in collecting duties from trading vessels had been keeping all of the money for the benefit of himself and his officials,

---

[3]See GAPK, f. 445, op. 1, d. 22, fols. 1–2v.

[4]See RRAC, roll 31, doc. 292, fols. 539v–42.

[5]See RRAC, roll 31, doc. 292, fols. 542–44v.

[6]Joaquín Solís was one of the leaders of the army revolt of 1829. He had been deported to Alta California from his native Mexico in 1825 as a convict, and in 1830 he was returned to Mexico. See [Bancroft], *California Pioneer Register,* 335.

while the soldiers had not received any salary for several years, and that they had starved during the recent harvest failure, and so on.

Soon after the arrival of the brig *Okhotsk* the new commandant, Solís, went with some soldiers to San Francisco and replaced Commandant Martínez there with Ensign Sánchez. A detail of soldiers was sent to Baja California to stop all communication with that province. Now Don Solís and some soldiers with a cannon intend to go to Santa Bárbara and to San Diego and replace Mr. De Echeandía and other officials. The newly appointed governor is expected from Mexico no sooner than January, and he must go to San Diego first.

The harvest failure is the reason why throughout California it is not possible to buy even a hundred fanegas of wheat or other grain; it is extremely expensive, the inhabitants buying corn among themselves for 4 and 5 piasters per fanega, and in the summer they paid half a piaster for Boston biscuit [hardtack].

This province's political changes and their consequences did not allow Mr. Khlebnikov to learn Governor de Echeandía's position on [sea] otter hunting, and so, having found it impossible to fulfil my orders in the usual way, he sought various other means in order that the brig *Okhotsk* would not return to New Archangel in vain; but they all proved questionable or exposed him to risk and useless expense, and for that reason he decided to send the brig *Okhotsk* back without any cargo.

With respect to my letter to the newly expected governor, Mr. Khlebnikov tells me that he decided to leave it at Monterey with a Mr. Herrera, a respectable resident of the territory and well-known for being well-disposed toward the Russians; he for his part [i.e., Herrera,] has promised to solicit permission for [sea otter] hunting, and in case of the governor's authorization of it he has promised to send Mr. Khlebnikov's dispatch to Mr. Shelikhov [manager of Ross Counter] who has been told to prepare up to 15 kayaks for dispatch with an aide to San Francisco for hunting between there and Monterey.

As no trade or barter whatever was undertaken this time in California by the brig *Okhotsk,* anchorage fees and other port charges were not paid there. All of the cargo on board was brought back to New Archangel.

At Monterey Mr. Khlebnikov transferred to the sloop *Baikal,* which under the command of Mr. Etolin left there safely on 2 December for Chile. I have the honor to report this [information] to the company's Board of Directors.

DOCUMENT 22

Excerpt from Yevgeny von Berens, "Notes Kept during a Round-the-World Voyage," 1829

[YEVGENY ANDREYEVICH VON BERENS,] "THE NOTES OF
MIDSHIPMAN YEVGENY ANDREYEVICH [VON] BERENS, KEPT
DURING A ROUND-THE-WORLD VOYAGE IN THE SLOOP *KROTKY* IN
1828–30,"[1] [SLOOP *KROTKY* IN SAN FRANCISCO BAY?],
24 NOVEMBER–12 DECEMBER 1829

Finally, on 24 November at 9 o'clock in the morning we saw to the SE 40° at a distance by eye of 15 to 20 miles the Farallon Islands,* which lie 20 miles from the coast and almost in front of the entrance to the port of San Francisco. They are nothing more than bare rocks disposed in two groups and even more conspicuous for their white color, derived from the bird dung that covers them. On [Captain George] Vancouver's maps they are situated in three groups, which, however, is incorrect, for three groups are quite unknown to the promyshlenniks of the Russian-American Company who now live on these islands.**

---

*Great [Southeast] Farallon Island is a crag lying in latitude 37° 42' N and longitude 122° 59' W.

**The value of guano was undoubtedly not known at that time. P. A. Tikhmenyov on p. 210 of pt. 1 of his [officially commissioned] *Historical Survey of the Formation of the Russian-American Company and Its Operations up to the Present Time* (1861) says: "Another food of the Russians (living in the colony of Ross near San Francisco) consists of the meat of sea lions and local murre eggs. They are conveyed salted and dried from the rocky isles of the Farallones, which are found to the west of the entrance to San Francisco Bay. There is a party of several Russians and Aleuts on the largest of these islets." On p. 356 [he writes]: "fur seals have also been completely extirpated on the Farallones (in 1833 there were only 54 animals), and for that reason hunting has ceased." Tikhmenyov has no information on the guano deposits of the Farallones.

---

[1] A. Kr., "Zapiski michmana Berensa." This is chapter 5 of Berens's serialized account in the journal. For the spare logbook of the navigator on this voyage, Second Lieutenant Dmitry Ivanovich Yakovlev, see RGAVMF, f. 870, op. 1, d. 3, 947b.

Soon a cape revealed itself to us, whereupon we trimmed the sails and began to keep to the coast, whose proximity completely becalmed us, and we moved quietly ahead. The stillness continued until 1:30, when with a squall coming from the SW a fresh wind arose; taking advantage of the squall, we approached the entrance to the port of San Francisco, but no sooner had we entered the narrows [Golden Gate] than we met a strong adverse current, which, despite the fact that the sloop was making from 5 to 8 knots, began to push it back. Keeping to the right shore, we noticed that the current lessened appreciably, and very soon we rounded Fort Point and saw the ship *Yelena* [*Helena*] of the Russian-American Company,[2] and after passing it we dropped anchor and let out up to 60 sazhens of cable. No sooner had the men managed to reach the top and furl the sails than we felt the ship's stern gently bump the bottom; upon measuring the depth we indeed found only 14½ feet, whereupon after again raising anchor we immediately moved to deeper water, and the next morning we set the ship on two anchors.

San Francisco Bay was discovered about 1602 and named in honor of St. Francis Assisi; the latitude of Fort Point, which forms the southern limit of the entrance to this bay, is 38° 48' 48". The bay is completely sheltered and very extensive; its width at the entrance is no more than ¾ of a mile but more than 30 miles in its midst, where there are rather many large coves and bays that are safe for ships. But the most advantageous anchorage is found opposite the presidio, where in a depth of 10 sazhens a ship will be completely unexposed to ocean winds and will not be bothered by waves.

In winter here very strong winds blow from the SE, and for that reason at this time of year it is necessary to use double anchors [starboard and port] and to put one of them to the SE. The water in San Francisco Bay is subject to the strong effect of the tides. This [effect] was observed by us in the course of our 19-day stay here. On 29 November there was a new moon with gentle breezes and light winds, and high tide occurred in the morning.

At the port itself the wind blows mostly from the NW and NNW, i.e., directly from the coast. The fresh water here is fairly good, but it is conveyed from a great distance and with inconvenience. We verified our chronometers here against the corresponding heights of the sun. A revolt was under way when we arrived here.

It is known that the first Europeans to settle in [Baja] California were the Jesuits, who tried to convert the inhabitants to Christianity, and at the same time to establish their own authority.

---

[2]The Russian-American Company's ship *Yelena* under the command of Lieutenant Vasily Khromchenko had set out on its round-the-world voyage in the same year of 1828. Its voyage was very successful; Khromchenko sailed around the Cape of Good Hope to Sitka and returned to Kronshtadt around Cape Horn. Not only did he not lose a single crewman but there was not even any damage to the ship or its equipment. See Grinëv, *Kto yest kto*, 577.

In order that nothing about California would be divulged, the Jesuits published the most extraordinary descriptions of this land, but as soon as the deception was noticed they were expelled, and the Dominicans moved here in their place. The Dominicans acted just like the Jesuits, founding many missions under the protection of a garrison that now comprises 21 men; each soldier receives an annual salary of 200 piasters.

Thus did this blessed province prosper until 1812, receiving every possible assistance from Spain; but not having received not only their due pay but even per diem provisions for 6 years, the residents of California overthrew the yoke of Spain and voluntarily placed themselves under the protection of Mexico, which sent them a governor to put everything in order again. At the governor's discretion the soldiers were assigned a new salary payment, which they received punctually at first, but now it has been more than 4 years since they have received any assistance from Mexico. A rebellious group of 25 men has united under the leadership of a very brave young Spaniard [Joaquín Solís, a Mexican] at the chief presidio of Monterey. The rebels, incidentally, possess two cannons; their plan, which they have begun to implement in the northern part of the presidio [*sic:* province], is to replace all former officials with appointees chosen at the will of the soldiers of the presidio of Monterey. Thus, during our visit they came to the port of San Francisco, and [upon] learning that there were two Russian vessels* here and fearing the rumor that we had landed a force of 200 men to defend the commandant, they stopped at San Francisco Mission, where the doctor from the ship *Yelena*, Mr. Vebel,[3] happened to be at that time, and for his part he completely reassured them. Two days later they appeared at the presidio, whose discontented soldiers met them joyfully and demanded that the old commandant, Don Martínez,[4] be placed in a dungeon; however, the leader of the group [of rebels] indignantly refused, saying that they must not do so, that Don Martínez was their former commandant, and that the first who dared to occasion him the slightest insult would be shot on the spot.

The soldiers elected to install as commandant Don Sánchez,[5] who was already

---

*The *Yelena* and the *Krotky*.

[3]Anton Bogdanovich (Khristianovich) Vebel (1800–49) served as the *Yelena*'s doctor during its round-the-world voyage of 1828–30, and during the ship's sojourn at Sitka (July–October 1829) he treated the colonial capital's sick. See Grinëv, *Kto yest kto*, 93.

[4]Ignacio Martínez (1774–185?), a native of Mexico, was a veteran soldier, Indian fighter, and public servant. According to Bancroft, he was "haughty and despotic" as an officer but "very courteous and hospitable" as a ranchero ([Bancroft], *California Pioneer Register*, 241).

[5]José Antonio Sánchez (17??–1843) was a native of Mexico and a veteran soldier, a courageous Indian fighter, and an intrepid explorer. He served as commandant of San Francisco's garrison in 1829–33. In Bancroft's opinion, "he was a good man, of known honesty and valor, but very ignorant and unfit for promotion" ([Bancroft], *California Pioneer Register*, 318).

a very old and foolish Spaniard and an officer of the first rank, which he had received from the Mexican government. From here the group went to Monterey in order to replace the governor, who, of course, had had time to conceal himself; as soon as they fulfilled their plan, they intended to send a delegation to Mexico so as to explain their action to the Mexican government.

Their principal displeasure with the governor is the fact that while receiving duty from American and other ships coming here he paid the soldiers nothing, and they did not even receive their per diem sustenance and were reduced to a most wretched state. The duty constituted a sum absolutely sufficient to pay for the upkeep of a very small number of soldiers—if not for complete maintenance, then at least for one-half of it. The soldiers are unable to till the soil, for they do not know how to do so, and they cannot make amends with the help of the Indians, as formerly happened, because this year the Indians under the leadership of the somewhat educated Estanislao,[6] withdrew into the province's interior, where they are rather well fortified and enjoy complete freedom. The Spaniards tried to attack them but were strongly repulsed and returned with substantial casualties.

I happened to be at San Francisco Mission. It is now found in the most tumble-down condition; over time the buildings have gone to ruin, and repairing them is not possible, on account of the very small number of neophytes. Father Tomás,[7] the head of the mission, was at that time in very straitened circumstances, for he was in fear of losing everything at any minute upon the slightest displeasure or shortage of sustenance on the part of the group of rebellious soldiers. Some missionaries like him from the other missions,[8] having collected enough piasters, saw fit not to remain here any longer under such disruptive circumstances and managed to conceal themselves aboard American ships bound for Europe. The Indians left at the missions have continued as before to live in mild bondage. A ring of the bell calls them to church, work, and dinner. They are under the watchful supervision of their spiritual and physical shepherd; each neophyte must spend 7 hours a day at work and 2 hours at prayer.

The work is done under supervision; the women perform domestic tasks (spinning wool, sewing clothes, cooking barley, grinding flour with hand mills) and

---

[6]Estanislao (17??–1833), a member of the Lakisamne tribe, was a literate magistrate (as well as a vaquero and a mule trainer) at San José Mission and, when he refused to return on furlough from his *ranchería* (native village) to the mission after the 1828 harvest, a renegade neophyte. His rebel force defeated two Californio expeditions before being atrociously suppressed by Lieutenant Mariano Vallejo in 1829. He escaped to return to his mission, where he was pardoned, eventually becoming a hunter himself of fugitive neophytes. He died of smallpox. See Gutiérrez and Orsi, *Contested Eden*, 212–13; Orsi, "Estanislao's Rebellion"; and Orsio, *History of Alta California*, 89–94.

[7]Tomás Eleuterio Esténaga (1790–1847), a peninsular from the Basque Country, went to Mexico City's San Fernando College in 1810 at his own expense, and in 1820 he was assigned to Alta California, where, not in robust health, he served at various missions, including San Francisco in 1821–33. He did not take the oath of allegiance to Mexico until 1843. See Geiger, *Franciscan Missionaries*, 78–81.

[8]José Altimira of Mission San Buenaventura and Antonio Ripoll of Mission Santa Bárbara in early 1828.

the men weave blankets, work coarse cloth, till the soil, and grow vegetables and greens in the mission gardens.

Except for poultry, they do not have any possessions; all of the output of their labor belongs to the missionaries, who then clothe and feed them, however.

As regards their mental ability, the Indians are still at this time at a very low level—anything that they cannot feel is beyond their understanding.

At a distance of 5 or 6 verstas from the mission there is an extensive valley surrounded by low mountains and reaching on one side to the shores at the end of the bay. Huge flocks of sheep belonging to the mission graze in this valley, and in the middle of it stand three wretched Indian shacks, conical in shape and 6 feet high and as many feet wide. They are built in the following way: round poles as thick as an arm are stuck in the ground, and the top ends are tied together and interwoven with branches and then covered with dry leaves and grass; an opening above serves in place of a window and a vent. Here live three poor Indian families, whose slovenliness and indolence beggar description. Many cattle graze right around the shacks, causing a strong stench, which is not only unbearably fetid but also very unhealthful; the Indians, however, are unable to overcome their idleness so as to bury it [i.e., the filth], even on the same spot. For two months here before our arrival there was a severe drought, from which numerous cattle died, and during our 19-day stay here we could not get a single bunch of any sort of greens.[9] Harvests here, however, are [usually] quite good, wheat yielding 30-, 80-, and often 120-fold [the seed].

There is no construction timber at all in the vicinity of the bay; farther to the north a lot of fir, cypress, oak, beech, elm, and other trees grow.

On 12 December (Thursday) at midday with a fresh NNE wind we began to raise the double anchors, standing at that time on the starboard cable; after having raised the main anchor, we raised the other [port] cable to 30 sazhens. When we began to hoist the topsail halyard, the ship started to drift very fast, and within ¼ of an hour the current had drawn it out of the bay, whereupon we found ourselves very close to the underwater rocks at Fort Point, and indeed it was thanks only to Providence that we did not pay dearly, for on account of the dead calms that can occur suddenly here it would have been impossible to steer the ship. As soon as the danger had passed, we answered with 7 guns the salute of the Russian-American Company ship *Yelena,* which intended to raise anchor right after us. After [we] had passed the fort, the current continued to carry us SE along the coast, where we saw enormous rookeries of sea lions, some of which lay atop rocks 4 sazhens high. Our captain told us that earlier he had happened to see these animals on rocks up to 12 sazhens in height.

---

[9]The sloop *Krotky* called at San Francisco to buy provisions but was unable to obtain them on account of a harvest failure as a result of drought.

DOCUMENT 23

Excerpts from Ferdinand von Wrangell's Diary of a Journey from New Archangel to St. Petersburg, 1835–1836

Editor's Introduction

The principal proponent of the expansion of the Russian-American Company's colony of Ross eastward and southward at the expense of the *frontera del norte* of the Californios was Governor Ferdinand von Wrangell (1830–35). St. Petersburg allowed him to return to Russia in 1836 via Mexico and to hold talks with Mexican officials about such an expansion. His attempt failed, however, for his prospective intermediary, Alta California's Governor Figueroa, had just died, and President Santa Anna was absent from Mexico City. Besides, Wrangell did not have plenipotentiary authority, for reactionary Tsar Nicholas I refused to recognize the Mexican Republic. Wrangell's journal of his trip from his departure from New Archangel until his departure from Monterey follows.

GOVERNOR FERDINAND VON WRANGELL,[1] DIARY OF A JOURNEY FROM
NEW ARCHANGEL TO ST. PETERSBURG VIA MEXICO:
FROM NEW ARCHANGEL TO MONTEREY,[2] [ST. PETERSBURG?],
13 OCTOBER 1835–1 JANUARY 1836

With the coming of October 1835 the five-year term of my service in the colonies expired, and a rank holder should have arrived in my place on the company

---

[1]Baron Ferdinand Petrovich fon Vrangel (Ferdinand Friedrich Georg Ludwig von Wrangell) (1796–1870) was born in Estonia to a Baltic German family. After graduating in 1815 from the naval cadet corps at the head of his class, he persuaded Captain Golovnin to include him as a midshipman in the 1817–19 voyage around the world of the sloop *Kamchatka*. Upon his return to Russia, Wrangell was appointed leader (*continued*)

sloop *Sitkha* [*Sitka*]. On the naval transport *America,* which sailed from N[ew] Arch[angel] on 13 October, I had already dispatched most of my belongings to Russia, leaving only what was necessary for my return journey with my family. If, after a six-year separation from the fatherland and a long stay in such a place as Sitka, anything could further increase the yearning and impatience to finally find oneself homeward bound, then it was, of course, our situation upon the departure of the *America;* we remained with our suitcases in a temporary apartment, as if at a station, and watched the governor's house in the expectation that the new residents would soon gladden us with their appearance and free us from the heavy uncertainty. The autumn cold had already come, the usual time for the return of the transport from Okhotsk had long since passed and hope of seeing it at Sitka this year had disappeared, and the many inconveniences of station life were added to the tedium of futile waiting—in short, we finally decided to again occupy the house in which we had spent five years, and against our will we reconciled ourselves to the cruel notion of postponing our return to Russia a whole year, and perhaps longer!

On 25 October a ship appeared on the sound's horizon—it was the sloop *Sitkha,* and it flew the conventional standard proclaiming the arrival of the new governor of the colonies. In a rowing vessel I hurry to welcome him, and I recognize my close friend and comrade from the [naval] academy, C[aptain] of the 1st r[ank] Iv[an] Ant[onovich] Kupreyanov;[3] I descend with him into the cabin, and

---

of an expedition to explore the northeastern coast of Siberia in 1820–24; there he dispelled the notion of the existence of a land mass north of Bering Strait and demonstrated the occasional viability of the northern sea route. Upon his return he was promoted to captain-lieutenant and given command of the round-the-world voyage of the brig *Krotky* in 1825–27.

Wrangell was promoted again upon his return and offered the governorship of Russian America; he accepted, and during his five-year term, he energetically reformed the somnolent colony.

After his return to Russia Wrangell was promoted to rear admiral but soon retired from the navy to his wife's estate, although he continued to serve the Russian-American Company, sitting on its board of directors from 1840 until 1849. The blow of his wife's death in 1854 prompted him to reenter public life, becoming minister of the navy with a promotion to the rank of vice admiral and then admiral. In 1864 poor health forced him to retire once more to his estate at Tartu (Ger., Dorpat or Russ., Yuryev). See Grinëv, *Kto yest kto,* 108–109; and Pierce, *Russian America,* 543–48; also see O'Grady, *Baltic to Russian America.*

[2]EHAT, f. 2,057, op. 1, d. 353, fols. 1–6 (original). Wrangell's diary of his homeward journey, written mostly in Russian but also here and there in French and German and even in Spanish, was published in a censored and abridged version in 1836 in St. Petersburg, first in the journal *Severnaya pchela* (nos. 240–46 and 259–64) and then as a book as Vrangel, *Ocherk puti iz Sitkhi v S.-Peterburg,* more recently published in Spanish as Wrangel, *De Sitka a San Petersburgo.* The complete manuscript was finally published under the editorship of Shur in *K beregam Novovo Sveta,* 190–259. For recounting of Wrangell's crossing of Mexico, see Richardson, *Mexico through Russian Eyes,* 32–46; and Richardson, "Wrangell's Journey of 1836."

[3]Ivan Antonovich Kupreyanov (1799–1857) served in the Baltic Sea Fleet after graduation from St. Petersburg's Naval Academy. In 1819–21 he sailed as a midshipman on the *Mirny* under Lieutenant Mikhail Lazarev during its round-the-world voyage of Antarctic exploration with the flagship *Vostok* under Captain Bellingshausen. In 1822–25 he again voyaged around the world, this time with Lazarev on the *Kreiser.* Afterwards he returned to duty in the Baltic Sea Fleet and was promoted to the rank of captain-lieutenant in 1828. In 1834 he was appointed governor of Russian America, which he and his wife reached in the autumn of 1835. Five years later they returned to Russia on the *Nikolay I* via the Horn. During the remainder of his naval career Kupreyanov commanded frigates in the Baltic Sea, becoming a vice admiral in 1852. See Grinëv, *Kto yest kto,* 281; and Pierce, *Russian America,* 277–79.

the young spouse of my successor receives me! The transition from unpleasantness to joyfulness—I will say from despair to an abundance of pleasure—could hardly be more striking than that which we felt on this occasion: suddenly the lost hopes that had occupied us for many years in our remoteness are restored to us; I embrace my friend as a joyful messenger, and my wife greets his cultured, amiable lady. The new arrivals were no less gladdened than we, having seen the end of the anxieties and difficulties of a fatiguing journey through all of Russia and Siberia and a crossing from Okhotsk to Sitka lasting 60 days in late autumn—unprecedented in the annals of colonial navigation.

A whole month was passed in final preparations of the ship, which was intended to take us to one of Mexico's ports; very foul weather delayed the work, and finally contrary winds detained us several more days, so that we moved to the sloop *Sitkha* under the command of C[aptain]-L[ieutenant] Pr[okopy] Pl[atonovich] Mitkov[4] no earlier than 24 November, and the same day we left the harbor and the sound.

Who has not felt the feeling of sadness that possesses us when we quit a place where we have passed a large part of our life, when we are ready to part with people with whom we have shared both sorrow and joy? For us Sitka is blessed with memories; there lies a dear babe—the joy of an anxious mother on the difficult journey from Siberia, her comfort during the first years of our life at New Archangel! All of the residents and officials here and their families, bidding us farewell, expressed their most sincere wishes to us, and far from leaving these good people with indifference, we were moved to tears. My colleagues on this occasion gave me a precious (to me) token of their sincere and noble feelings for us, and all of our life, of course, we will remember with gratitude our Sitkan friends and our final parting from them.

A light favorable breeze distanced the sloop from Sitka's shores, which we still saw the next day, however. The temperature of the air was fairly high, and the Réaumur thermometer did not fall below +7° as far as latitude 50° [N], and to the south it indicated 9° with a southeast wind and intermittent rain. On 4 December we found ourselves on the parallel of the Columbia River, where company ships usually encounter severe southeast winds in autumn and winter during their sailings from Sitka to the Californian coast; we caught a strong NW [wind] and went at 8½ knots, making for the settlement of Ross. In the evening of the next day we passed through a dark cloud, from which electricity burst with a severe

---

[4]Prokopy Platonovich Mitkov (1799–1866) was a native of Novgorod Province and the son of an army ensign. He devoted his life to the navy, beginning as a cadet in 1811 and attaining the rank of vice admiral in 1855. He entered the company's service in 1831 and commanded various colonial ships. In late 1836 he succeeded Etolin as assistant to the governor of Russian America. He was discharged from the company in 1842 and spent most of the rest of his naval career in the Baltic Fleet. See Grinëv, *Kto yest kto,* 349; and Pierce, *Russian America,* 359.

squall and large hailstones, St. Elmo's Fire[5] lit up the two yardarms, summer lightning flashed around the ship, and gusts with hail recurred throughout the night, but with less force. On Sitka's coast, thunder occurs in winter and always with west and southwest winds, with which atmospheric electricity occurs in more southerly latitudes in these waters. The air became noticeably colder under the influence of the northwest wind, and the thermometer stood at $7°$ [R] in latitude $44½°$ [N].

On 11 December with a favorable NW [wind] and in a thick fog, finding ourselves in the latitude of Ross, we went along the parallel straight to the coast and expected to raise it no earlier than the next morning: the longitude, according to a determination by chronometer after midday (albeit with a very unsteady mercury level), indicated a direct distance to the coast of 62 miles; after the observation we went 25 miles, whereupon the horizon cleared completely of fog and unexpectedly revealed the coast ahead of both catheads. Although on account of the evening darkness we could not recognize the shore, judging from the last bearing we were no fewer than 8 miles from the nearest cape, so there was an error in the longitude [reading] of $40°$, relating undoubtedly to the position of the coast, not to that of the ship. However, the determination of this error required observations under more favorable conditions than those that accompanied ours. . . .[6]

Wanting to approach the settlement of Ross for a meeting with the manager of the counter, Mr. Kostromitinov, and for other necessities, we kept to the coast for two days, [but] because of the gloom and the adverse light wind we were not able to fulfil our intention. On the 14th there arose a strong swell from the NW with light breezes from the SW quarter, forcing us to leave the coast and finally on the 16th to take a course for Monterey in order not to waste our precious time.

The 17th [passed], and on the 18th at midnight we dropped anchor at Monterey in 12 sazhens; at sunrise the next morning two ships appeared under the flag of the Nor[thern] Un[ited] States and entered the bay, one of them from S[an] Francisco, from which we received news of the company brig *Polifem* [*Polyphemus*], which had obtained nearly a full load of wheat and was ready to set sail within 5 days; the other ship was the brig *Diana* from Sitka, which it had left 5 days after us and in passing between latitudes 51 and $40°$ [N] had withstood a severe storm from the N with which it ran under foresail to the south, fearing that a huge wave would take them into the wind and finding themselves at the same time in danger of being inundated from the stern. We received letters from our friends in Sitka.

---

[5]An electric discharge that sometimes occurs at the mastheads and yardarms of a ship under certain atmospheric conditions.

[6]Here are omitted the calculations of the longitudes of Cape Mendocino, San Francisco, Monterey, and New Archangel by Captains Vancouver, Beechey, Malaspina, Kotzebue, and Mitkov.

The port and customs officials brought us the unpleasant news of the death of General Figueroa;[7] his position is occupied by Lieutenant-Colonel Don Nicolás Gutiérrez.[8] With this event my stop at Monterey became quite unnecessary, and I could foresee that with the change in governor my relationship to him also changed; the friendly correspondence between General Figueroa and me must remain fruitless, and for my part it would be unwise to trust an official unknown to me and one who, undoubtedly, must soon yield his position to another from Mexico. At his first meeting with me Don Nicolás put his services and his home at my disposal; however, at the same time he took the precaution of not shaving his beard, complained of illness, and apologized for the impossibility of not paying me a visit: all of this acted as a correct, crushing rejection and saved him the trouble of receiving a guest invited by his predecessor. Don Nicolás limited his attention to assistance with the dispatch of a passenger to Ross; and I, in order not to remain in his debt, offered to take aboard the sloop and carry to San Blas an official who had been posted there and a commoner.

For other necessities I preferred to apply to Mr. Spence,[9] a Scotsman who had settled here and who obliged me greatly, affording us the possibility of seeing the nearest mission San Carlos, stretch our legs on horseback, and admire the pleasant surroundings along the road to S[an] Carlos [Borromeo]; for my family Mr. Spence found a barouche,[10] which was pulled by a skinny mule with a vaquero in the lead. After an hour's ride and without any particular adventures we reached the mission.

Remembering this establishment from 1818, when the missions flourished under the management of the Spanish friars, I was astounded by the sight of destruction, destitution, and indifference that struck us at every step and on all sides; on the spot where a large building stood to accommodate the Indians and their masters we now saw a ruin—outer walls a few feet high and a pile of

---

[5]An electric discharge that sometimes occurs at the mastheads and yardarms of a ship under certain atmospheric conditions.

[6]Here are omitted the calculations of the longitudes of Cape Mendocino, San Francisco, Monterey, and New Archangel by Captains Vancouver, Beechey, Malaspina, Kotzebue, and Mitkov.

[7]José Figueroa (1792–1835) was a native of Mexico, where he had a successful military and political career. Appointed governor of Alta California in 1833, he oversaw the secularization of the missions and, like most Californios, opposed the Híjar-Padrés colonization project of 1834, an abortive attempt to settle indigent artisans, teachers, and farmers from Mexico on the former mission lands. See [Bancroft], *California Pioneer Register,* 141.

[8]Gutiérrez came to Alta California in 1833 with Figueroa as a captain and was promoted the same year to lieutenant colonel. He supervised the secularization of Mission San Gabriel in 1834–36. Twice in 1836 he served as acting governor. See [Bancroft], *California Pioneer Register,* 175.

[9]David Spence (1798–1875) came to Alta California in 1824 via Lima, started his own business in 1827, and became active in both mercantile and political affairs. See [Bancroft], *California Pioneer Register,* 338–39.

[10]A four-wheeled carriage with a folding top and two seats facing each other.

stones; the beautiful fruit orchard was neglected, open to livestock and lacking the high stone wall that at that time [had] protected it from the cold winds off the sea; the good and noble friar, a native of Castile,[11] who then received guests heartily and was able to engage them in interesting conversation, had now been replaced by a Mexican who was a picture of apathy to everything around him and of displeasure with the world and himself.

We wanted to see the well-known picture of the arrival of La Pérouse at S[an] Carlos that had been painted by one of the artists of that unfortunate expedition; unfortunately, however, we heard that this picture, after many unsuccessful attempts by several foreigners to steal it, had been removed by the Padre President to another mission, and with the strong disposition of the current missionaries to turn everything into money this valuable memorial to the visit of the celebrated navigator had likely succumbed at some time to the temptations of a devout follower of Saint Francis. They showed us one old Indian woman who, being already about 30 years [of age]) when she had been brought from the woods to the friar (the first to be placed in this mission [est. 1770] and the first to be baptized by him), remembers this event well, being more than 100 years old, and she has kept her memory, eyesight, and hearing, walks fairly steadily, gathers firewood in the forest herself, and, stooped, leans on a staff, and carries her heavy loads to her hut. It is remarkable that of the 200 Indians thought to be at this mission she is the only one who does not speak Spanish and does not even understand when they speak this language. The old Indian woman was a witness to the building of the mission and will perhaps even live alive until its abolition, for it is rumored that a town, or rather, a pueblo will rise on the ruins of the mission—the village of San Carlos [Carmel]; and eventually, too, all of the missions in California will become pueblos.

My wife's maid, an Unalaskan Creole,[12] did not believe her eyes, seeing in the orchard two trees (an olive and a pear) in blossom and with fruit at the end of December at a time when on Unalaska and at Sitka it is frightful to shed a warm parka.

In order to show the cause of the utter decline of the well-being of the missions in California it is enough to recall the change after 1834 in the management of these establishments: the old friars, natives of Spain, were replaced by uneducated and self-interested Mexicans and their economic direction passed to the government, which for this [purpose] appointed civilian *administradores;*

---

[11]Neither of the two friars stationed at Mission San Carlos in 1818, Juan Amorós or Vicente de Sarría, was in fact a native of Castile, the former having been born in Catalonia and the latter in the Basque country; however, Wrangell may have used "Castile" to connote Spain, not to denote one of its kingdoms.

[12]In Russian America a Creole was the offspring of a non-native (usually Russian) father and a native mother, comparable to a Métis in British North America.

freedom was proclaimed to the Indians, lands were allotted to them, the necessary assistance in livestock and implements was given to them for their initial
undertakings, and no obligation was imposed on them other than the cultivation
of the so-called common lands, whose output was designated for the maintenance of public institutions—hospitals, schools, churches, and seminaries. All
of this [benevolence], one would think, is very good and in accordance with
philanthropic intentions; unfortunately, however, neither the executors nor the
Indians were ripe for these intentions. The administrators, lacking the power and
the ability to manage the savages, an idle and at the same time free people, find
the sole reward of their labors in the search for the means of securing their own
fortune; the Indians, for whom freedom has no meaning other than the carefree
life of a sponger, have given themselves up completely to this delightful *far nientes*
[doing nothing] and have partly withdrawn to their former woods and valleys,
and those who have remained, from having become either unaccustomed to a
nomadic life or accustomed to liquor at the missions or pueblos, do not find a
better use for their earnings than to spend them on drink. Such are the fruits of
the sudden transformation of the political and civil state of a people and of the
instantaneous transition from childhood to adulthood, a transition so contrary
to the immutable law of nature—gradualness.

Monterey, too, has changed since 1818 but in an opposite sense to that of the
missions. The opening of California's ports to all nations for trade and the allowing of foreigners to settle in the province have drawn many people here, businessmen and adventurers, mostly Englishmen and citizens of the Northern United
States, who with their customary ingenuity have built many quite decent houses
here, opened shops, and enlivened Monterey. The buildings are scattered over a
broad expanse without order or symmetry, and the town, not yet having *streets*,
can boast of a large number of *squares;* the skeletons of slaughtered cattle lie
everywhere, and steer heads with horns are innumerable. The presidio and the
battery with cannons but without mounts are nearly in ruins; the governor's
residence and the barracks inside the presidio have not been noticeably improved
from time to time, whereas the private houses are improving and multiplying.
The modest means of the government for [the provision of] the most essential
assistance are noticeable. Its employees are rarely paid their salaries, and almost
never in cash, replacing it [i.e., money] with goods. For communication with
other parts of Upper California—S[an] Francisco, S[anta] Bárbara, and S[an]
Diego—there is no serviceable vessel, although a decked boat with a crew of 5
would answer the purpose; there are not even rowing vessels or yawls, and the
customs officials boat to arriving ships in yawls from those very ships. Before the
transformation of the missions the government received considerable financial

assistance from them, especially provisions for allowances for the army; now customs exactions constitute the sole source of income, and, given the inconstancy of duties and the frequent change[s] in the regulations concerning foreign trade, they do not reach that level of importance that would be enhanced under favorable conditions. Before, 10 piasters for anchorage were exacted from each arriving ship and 17 reals for each ton of capacity, or so-called *toneladas* [tonnage], and in addition duties on imports that are now paid in goods; now anchorage for money has been abolished, and instead tonnage is exacted for the right to stand at anchor, and duty is required to be paid on freight, even if none of it is to be sold in California, and, besides, this duty must be paid partly in cash. Under such constraints trade is declining noticeably, and in the course of 1835 only two ships with goods put in to Monterey, so that the collection of duties did not exceed 12 thousand piasters! The government, not being in a position for many years to meet the salaries of its employees, is deprived by the current year's harvest failure even of the means of feeding the soldiers; it summoned contractors and was prepared to consent to high prices, but, not enjoying the slightest credit, it has not yet had any success concluding a contract.

In Upper California the *army* comprises 3 companies, the chief of which is quartered at Monterey, and the commander-in-chief is the governor. The company of cavalry consists of 30 riders and 10 horses, and the infantry of 30 men, respectably uniformed. The artillery consists of 20 men and several field pieces, which, they say, are in good condition. Of this number, 5 men have been allotted to S[an] Francisco, 5 to S[anta] Bárbara, and 11 to S[an] Diego, besides mounted militiamen. In these three companies of 80 me[n] there are thought to be 20 army officers! Lower California is administered independently of the governor of Upper California and has its own governor at the rank of lieutenant-colonel, whose seat is [La] Paz.

The fertile lands and healthful climate of Upper California are so well known that they have virtually become proverbial. These fine lands await cultivators; the extensive plains grow succulent grass for feral cattle and horses, which are scattered countlessly throughout the province; the oak and coniferous forests do not bring the residents any benefit other than a supply of firewood in the short, mild winters; and the rivers still do not serve as routes of communication and the sea itself does not yield its riches to the carefree residents of this land: its ~~wealth~~ sources of industry are inexhaustible but still remain ignored.

Here every foreigner who has declared himself a Catholic and his desire to become a citizen of California is accepted as such without the slightest difficulty; as a citizen he is allotted land in accordance with his means—for which he must present evidence—to buy cattle and hire workers to cultivate the land. Such lands—ranchos (estates)—are considered inalienable property from generation to generation of the person in whose name they were originally registered, but they cannot be sold to others. Thus, with 1,000 piasters of cash capital it is possible here to enter the field of agriculture and expect to improve and expand one's holding. The biggest difficulty is the hiring of workers; an Indian is paid 4 reals (2½ rubles) per day but a white man 6 reals, and a joiner or a good carpenter 3 piasters per day. Horned livestock [cattle, sheep, goats], if bought by the herd or flock, cost 2½ piasters per head. Because hides and tallow constitute the chief export product, and they make 2½ piasters on each steer hide, the ranchero begins his turnover with the rearing of herds of horned livestock; he engages in no more grain growing and gardening than is necessary to feed his family and hired hands. Knowledgeable and industrious colonists from Europe would be of the greatest benefit to the province and undoubtedly not of a little benefit to themselves.

The interior of this beautiful land still remains *terra incognita* for the Californios; they know from the legends and stories of the Indians that across the [coastal] mountains in the parallels [of latitude] of S[an] Francisco and Monterey and even farther to the south there are very extensive lakes whose shores are populated by many beaver; the deep river of the Sacramento that empties into S[an] Francisco Bay probably flows from these lakes, which are called Tulares by the Californios. Hunters from the English [Hudson's Bay] company on the Columbia R[iver] and citizens of the North[ern] United States come [to] these places to trap beaver and buy horses from the Indians who roam the plains of the Sacramento River, [including] those [horses] that they have driven from the missions with not a little daring.

In 1833 under the influence of the vice president of the Mexican states, [Valentín] Gómez Farías, an officer [Lieutenant John Laighton] was sent here to explore the Sacramento River and its surroundings and to build a wharf and a naval dockyard on the superb bay of S[an] Francisco, which abounds in construction timber; but the provincial authorities in Monterey lacked the means of implementing this most useful proposal, and the officer from S[an] Blas, after spending 18 months doing nothing, finally was free to return (he was the very one whom I offered to take to S[an] Blas).

The proposal to build a naval dockyard formed part of a broad plan whose aim was to settle California with colonists from Mexico [the Híjars-Padrés colony] and to acquire the mission lands and all internal trade on behalf of a private company. A company [Cosmopolitan Company] was formed under the chairmanship of Gómez Farías himself; it was granted the right to take over all of the missions of Upper California and to appoint at each of them for management a special administrator, who was obligated to transfer all output to the company, which undertook to supply the Indians and the inhabitants generally with needed goods brought on its ships—thereby intending to take all of California's trade in its hands and make it a monopoly of a couple of individuals: one of California's deputies (Juan Bandini)[13] and the vice president of the Mexican confederation himself. Who does not marvel at the patriotic outlook of the head of the republic and the representative of one of its provinces! The implementation of this thievish project was begun immediately: spongers called colonists were recruited in Mexico, and the best of them—i.e., the literate ones—were raised to the rank of teachers, and it was intended to entrust them with the administration of the missions; wives and some skilled workers were added to this throng, and to the number of 400 persons the famous colony was conveyed to S[an] Blas, where a Mexican warship, the corvette *Morelos* (the republic's sole warship in these waters), and the leased merchant brig *Natalia* [*Natalie*] the very ship on which Napoleon left Elba in 1815) received this riff-raff and many officials for dispatch to California. At this time [i.e., 1834], General Santa Anna took the reins of government, removed Gómez Farías, and hastened to send a courier to Monterey with an order to cancel all arrangements made by former vice president Gómez Farías and particularly the rights and operations of the company. Fortunately, the courier reached Monterey in 36 days by land from Mexico, but the corvette *Morelos* had a long passage of 54 days, so that upon its arrival General Figueroa was already the plenipotentiary and did not permit the company's agents to implement the proposals of its founders; the brig *Natalia*, with a considerable load of goods belonging to the company, suffered a shipwreck in Monterey Bay with the loss of all of its cargo. In order to bring this history to an end it remains to mention that the participants in the collapsed company tried to overthrow General Figueroa, who discovered their scheme, sent the chief rebels to Mexico, and dispersed the other fraudulent colonists throughout California. The government allotted land to them near ~~the new~~ Mission [San] Francisco Solano [Sonoma] in order to draw new settlement toward Ross; however, not one of them agreed to take a plow in hand.

~~After spending three days at Monterey, we hurried to go to sea, and, taking advantage of the settled good weather, we went quickly southwards with a NW wind.~~ During the short time of our anchorage at Monterey the weather continued to be fine: in daytime, moderate breezes blew from the NW and N, and at nighttime and at dawn, light breezes from the coast; a heavy dew fell every night and the thermometer registered +4° before sunset and +10° during the day. I hurried to take advantage of the NW winds that were becoming established and went to sea early in the morning of the 21st—the New Year itself according to the reckoning ashore.

[13]Juan Bandini (1800–1859) arrived in Alta California in the late 1810s or early 1820s from Peru with his father and soon became prominent in government and politics. He represented the province in the Mexican congress in 1833 before returning as a leader of both the Híjars-Padrés scheme and the Cosmopolitan Company and an inspector of customs. See [Bancroft], *California Pioneer Register*, 49–50. Also see Bandini, *Description of California*.

Peter Kostromitinov, "About Turmoil in [Alta] California," 1836

EDITOR'S INTRODUCTION

From the middle 1830s, economic and political turmoil intensified in Alta California, arising from the secularization of the missions, the decline of the hide and tallow trade, the strife among Californios over their ties to Mexico, and the influx of foreign immigrants, especially Americans. These developments, which likewise affected the province's trade with the Russian-American Company and even the existence of its colony of Ross, were reported by the latter's last two managers to the company's board of directors, which duly reported the information to a cabinet minister.

MANAGER PETER KOSTROMITINOV,[1] A REPORT TO
GOVERNOR IVAN KUPREYANOV "ABOUT TURMOIL IN
[ALTA] CALIFORNIA,"[2] FORT ROSS, 25 DECEMBER 1836

To His Honor the governor of the Russian colonies in America, Guards Captain of the 1st rank and Cavalier Ivan Antonovich Kupreyanov.

An unexpected event has recently occurred in California, and as a result it has declared itself a free state belonging to the Mexican republic. It is almost

---

[1]Pyotr Stepanovich Kostromitinov (180?–18??) was the oldest of three brothers from a merchant family of Veliky Ustyug in the service of the Russian-American Company. He was probably hired in 1822 and reached the colonies in 1823. He succeeded Pavel Shelekhov as manager of Ross Counter in 1830 and stayed until 1838, when he became manager first of Kodiak Counter and then of New Archangel Counter. Governor Etolin had him negotiate the sale of Ross in the early 1840s. In 1847 he was replaced at New Archangel by his brother, Innokenty. Pyotr returned to Russia via Ayan after twenty years of colonial service. But *(continued)*

impossible without laughing to watch these ventures, which are grand and menacing in words but will likely end in nothing or in a new subjugation of California by Mexico. Here is how this upheaval occurred.

Upon the departure of Mr. Chico[3] for Mexico, his promise to ret[u]rn soon and commit reprisals greatly alarmed all of the inhabitants, who have had occasion to learn his character well. Taking advantage of the population's general fear of, and hatred for, the centralized system adopted in Mexico and proclaimed here by Mr. Chico, D[on] Ángel Ramírez,[4] the administrator of the Monterey customs house, made a pretense of devising a plan of revolution on the following basis. California would reject centralism, wanting to govern itself in accordance with the 1824 system, i.e., a federal system, and would not recognize the higher authority of the officials sent heretofore from Mexico and would have its own Californio authorities. It should be noted that actually the centralized [and] the federal system were absolutely the same thing for the Californios, because they did not understand the essence of one or the other; but the foreigners explained to them that centralism leads to slavery. Moreover, the Mexican government itself, sending mostly indigent and mercenary men to govern California—men whose sole aim was to make a fortune and return to Mexico—paved the way for an upheaval, which was rendered so much the more difficult to stop by force by the fact that nearly all of the Mexican soldiers, who had been sent to California for some sort of offense, received virtually no salary and lived from day to day somehow or other. The Californios knew about this [plight] and during the current upheaval took advantage of it, bribing the Mexican soldiers.

Thus did Mr. Ramírez, after having concocted a plan of revolution, win one of the junta's deputies and a customs house official at the time, D[on] Juan Bautista Alvarado,[5] to his side. All of the customs house personnel took part in the conspiracy; but as there were both Californios and Mexicans among them,

---

he rejoined the company in 1850, becoming its commissioner at San Francisco in 1851 and Russian vice-consul in 1852. He was replaced in these positions in 1862 by Martin Klinkovstrom, and Kostromitinov and his wife and six children returned to Russia. See Grinëv, *Kto yest kto*, 259; and Pierce, *Russian America*, 259, 262.

[2]ARGO, raz. 99, op. 1, d. 67, fols. 1–7v (verified copy).

[3]Mariano Chico (1796–1850), a native of Guanajuato, was appointed governor of Alta California at the end of 1835 and took office in the spring of 1836 but was expelled by the Californios three months later. See [Bancroft], *California Pioneer Register*, 99.

[4]Ángel Ramírez (17??–1840) was a onetime friar who had left his order around 1820 and taken part in the Mexican revolution. In 1833, the Mexican government appointed him the head of the customs house at Monterey, where he arrived overland the next year. Ramírez first supported and then opposed Governor Alvarado (1836–42), who dismissed him from his customs post at the end of 1836 and then had him arrested in 1837. Thereafter he lived under suspicion until his death from syphilis. See [Bancroft], *California Pioneer Register*, 295.

[5]Juan Bautista Alvarado (1809–82), a native of Monterey, led the revolt against Governor Gutiérrez in 1836 and himself served as governor until 1842. Subsequently he was appointed head of the Monterey customs house, where he had also served in the 1830s. See [Bancroft], *California Pioneer Register*, 33–34. Also see Miller, *Juan Alvarado*.

each of them participated in accordance with his own prospects and interests. These men, who receive a large salary, strongly influenced the other residents of Monterey and San Francisco. Mr. Alvarado succeeded in inciting another junta deputy, D[on] José Castro.[6]

Mr. Gutiérrez knew about the conspiracy's existence but, knowing at the same time the character of the chief conspirators, could not believe that they would undertake anything definite. Meanwhile, he had some sort of disagreement with Mr. Alvarado and wanted to place him under arrest; perhaps he intended to seize one of the first conspirators [so as] to halt further attempts.

Mr. Alvarado, who had served in the customs house and had done business with all of the merchants and the captains of ships visiting California, had occasion to borrow many new ideas from them, ideas that he himself was unable to grasp properly because he had not had any education; not understanding things in their true form, he imagined that he had been summoned by fate to be the savior of society, for the Americans had instilled in him [the notion of] the despotic administration of the Mexican governors. In his view the time had come when California could and should secede from Mexico. He began to act independently of Ramírez. Among the American traders Messrs. Hinckley[7] and Steel[8] even promised to help him revolt. Generally the Americans employ every measure to kindle hatred of the Mexicans by the Californios, and they seem to hope that a California independent of Mexico will at least come under the protection of the United States, if not join it.

On the eve of the day when Mr. Gutiérrez wanted to arrest Mr. Alvarado, he fled to San Francisco, and from there, in accordance with an agreement already struck with Mr. Castro, he went to see the commander of the frontier between Ross and California, D[on] Mariano Guadalupe Vallejo,[9] to confer with him

---

[6]José Castro (ca. 1810–60), a Californio, served as acting governor for four months after the death of Governor Figueroa in 1835. He participated in the resistance to both Chico and Gutiérrez in 1836 and again served as acting governor after the latter's expulsion. Castro also actively resisted the American takeover. He fled to Mexico in 1846 but returned in 1848. In 1856 he was appointed military commander of Baja California, where he was killed in a brawl. See [Bancroft], *California Pioneer Register,* 91–92.

[7]William Sturgis Hinckley (1807–46) was a native of Massachusetts. He arrived in Alta California in 1830 from Honolulu and became active in maritime commerce as a shipmaster and a supercargo. In 1842 he was naturalized and married, and in 1845–46 he served as captain of the port of San Francisco. See [Bancroft], *California Pioneer Register,* 188–89.

[8]Presumably Joseph Steel (18??–18??), a Boston trader and skipper who was active in Alta California with several vessels in 1826–40. See [Bancroft], *California Pioneer Register,* 341.

[9]Mariano Guadalupe Vallejo (1808–90), Alvarado's uncle, was a native of Monterey. He joined the army in 1824 and participated in several campaigns against the natives. He served as commandant of San Francisco in 1831–34 and military commander of Alta California in 1836–42. In 1835 he founded Sonoma and acquired nearly 300,000 acres with 51,000 head of livestock, becoming one of the wealthiest and most influential Californios. Vallejo did not oppose the American takeover of the province, whereupon he became one of the foremost advocates of cooperation with the new regime. He left an account of his visit to Ross in April 1833 (see Vallejo, *Report of a Visit;* also see Vallejo, "Ranch and Mission Days"). On Vallejo see [Bancroft], *California Pioneer Register,* 365–67; also see Rosenus, *General M. G. Vallejo.*

about the measures that had to be taken for the seizure of Monterey and the expulsion from California of Mr. Gutiérrez and all Mexicans; Castro for his part left abruptly to incite the inhabitants from Monterey to San Francisco. Mr. Vallejo, likewise a man without any education but with enough natural intelligence and sound common sense, clearly saw all of the rashness of their plans and told Mr. Alvarado that if they succeeded in expelling Mr. Gutiérrez, then they would not have the power to oppose the army that would undoubtedly be sent by the Mexican government; furthermore, not being certain of the success of their undertaking, he had not begun to help their side openly.

Thus, Alvarado left Mr. Vallejo without anything certain in mind and without knowing how he would act. Upon his [i.e., Alvarado's] arrival at the pueblo of San José he received news from Castro that he already had up to 20 rancheros (something like peasants but only partly indigent) on his side. The pueblo of San José and vicinity comprises up to 750 residents. Although Mr. Alvarado did not yet have a well-founded plan for attending somehow to business, he decided to summon the pueblo's *alcalde* [magistrate] and inform him that he already had most of the residents of Monterey and San Francisco on his side and that even the American ships at Monterey at that time had promised to help him. The alcalde, a simple and uneducated man who did not understand one system or the other, promised to assemble the residents so that he himself could speak to them. He assembled 20 villagers, and Alvarado told them that although Gutiérrez was not very severe, nonetheless the centralized system leads to slavery and that soon there would be neither deputies nor a junta, that all power is concentrated in the governor only, that the unlawful deeds of the Mexican officials had exasperated all of California, that at Mission San Juan [Bautista] he had a strong party that at the first sign from him was ready to go to Monterey, and that he was inviting them to take part in the great exploit of the liberation of the fatherland. But the residents received his words very coldly, and he resorted to another kind of oratory, his exhortations greatly affecting everyone. He sent to have drink bought, and with a warmer welcome he ignited their enthusiasm and patriotism so much that they began unanimously to cry, "Long live free California" and "May tyranny perish." But the next morning this enthusiasm had been quite forgotten, together with the wine fumes, and Alvarado again resorted to the same means in order to ignite their courage. Thus passed three days, during which the patriotism of these men was maintained only by the power of strong drink. Finally, seeing little profit in all of his efforts, Alvarado announced that, having received news from Castro, he had to go to Monterey immediately or forever lose the opportunity to capture the town. This [declaration] had an effect upon some, and about 12 men followed him to the mission of San Juan. Upon arriving there at night he joined Castro, assuring the residents that all of California had taken up arms and that it remained only to seize Monterey and expel Mr. Gutiérrez. Many of the residents took the side of the plotters. In the course of the several days spent by Castro and Alvarado at San Juan they mustered 120 men, to whom were added another 40 riflemen— American beaver hunters [mountain men] with their leader, whom they hired for 2 p[iasters] per man per day plus, in the event of success, the best rancho sites. Thus, the combined forces of the nearly unarmed defenders of the fatherland left San Juan and proceeded directly to Monterey. Mr. Castro was chosen the general of these soldiers. Before Mr. Gutiérrez learned of the advance of the plotters on Monterey they had already occupied the battery near the landing at Monterey, and they sent an envoy to him with a demand to surrender. Mr. Gutiérrez was resolved to defend himself, having up to 80 soldiers, but they repudiated him, having been bribed earlier. While Mr. Gutiérrez was thinking what to do, the valiant plotters fired one shot at the presidio, whereupon half of them fled, fearing that Mr. Gutiérrez would respond the same way. But he did not respond! Whereas only two shots were necessary to restore calm to all of California, Mr. Gutiérrez yielded to capitulation. The Mexicans, seeing the small number of plotters, came to their senses, but it was too late! Mr. Gutiérrez and the other Mexican officers and soldiers were captured and sent to Mexico on the English trading brig *Clementine;* with them were also sent up to 90 Mexican families living at Monterey. All of them were landed at Cabo San Lucas, however. The foregoing is all of the information that I was able to collect about the revolution in California. Here it should be mentioned that Santa Bárbara, San Diego, and Pueblo de los Ángeles have not yet recognized the authority of the new government. A civil war is expected. Herewith I have the honor to submit the decrees and proclamations of the new government in the original.[10] In them You will deign to see that the plotters, besides arrangements in various sectors of the administration, are making themselves president of the supreme council, commandant general, and civil governor. Having promoted themselves to the upper ranks, they are promoting others to colonels, captains, and lieutenants, so that now almost all of them are officers, but for the time being there are no soldiers. One of the decrees speaks of duties; for tonnage one has to pay 8 instead of 17 r[eals] per ton now, and the duty on goods has been reduced by half.

Mr. Vallejo did not take upon himself the title of commandant general, which is very flattering to him, but meanwhile he thinks that the Mexican government will not ignore such mischief and will send an army to subjugate California. He intends to build a fort toward Ross; to arm it he will move all of the cannons from San Francisco and elsewhere, and he will defend himself or perish in the ruins

---

[10]Not found.

of the new fort. For this purpose Mr. Vallejo has already arrived at his rancho, which lies 80 verstas from Ross. Mr. Alvarado, who is now the civil governor and colonel of the national guard, has gone to Santa Bárbara and beyond to administer the oath [of allegiance] to the residents of those places. Mr. Castro, president of the state council, has stayed in Monterey to govern. Mr. Ramírez, the onetime leader of the conspiracy at its inception, annoyed that the plotters had deceived him and expelled the Mexicans, fomented a counterrevolution, but they learned of it and put him under arrest, and he now lives under guard at Mission San José.

Finally, the residents of Monterey and San Francisco are beginning to understand the consequences of the revolution and the impotence of the new government. Many of them asked me whether or not they could hide themselves at Ross in the event of the arrival of a Mexican army. I avoided a definite answer, and I most humbly request that [you] provide me with guidance in this matter. I also consider it necessary to inform Your Honor that in the event of the arrival of a Mexican army for the subjugation of California (whether or not it makes an attempt on Ross) the leaders of the army, not having any idea of the rights of the people, during the subjugation of some of the provinces will more than likely treat residents and foreigners indiscriminately with the utmost brutality.

According to the latest information from Baja California, there is also a revolution there; the system of centralized government has been abolished and replaced by the federal system. In Mexico the army has been reequipped for the subjugation of the province of Texas, but the government does not have the cash for dispatching the army. Meanwhile, the Americans secretly assist the Texans [Tejanos] with men and money. In the latest American newspapers there is a great deal of talk about war between Russia, England, and France. Several weeks before the departure of Mr. Gutiérrez an American naval frigate arrived at Monterey with the admiral of a fleet that cruises the Gulf of Mexico. It is said that he demanded satisfaction for various oppressions against American traders here. It is not known how Mr. Gutiérrez responded. The frigate stayed at Monterey four days; it left for an unknown destination, and they expect it in California a second time. I have the honor to report this to Your Honor.[11]

---

[11]Six months later on 14 June 1837 Governor Kupreyanov at the beginning of a dispatch to the board of directors acknowledged receipt of apparently another report from Kostromitinov dated only five days later: "I consider it necessary to forward herewith [not in the file] for the information of the board of directors a copy of a report to me, no. 154, about the political revolution that occurred in that country at the end of last year. From this report the board of governors will deign to see that the present disorder there is unlike that to which [Alta] California has heretofore been continually subjected, not really having any consequences other than the replacement of some temporary governor, commandant, friar, or other [figure]. The current revolution under way there, [however,] has the aim of declaring California's independence of the Mexican government, dismissing all former authorities, and electing a government from California's citizens. The consequences of these disturbances have not been reported to me by Mr. Kostromitinov, who should know

Manager of the Counter, P. Kostromitinov.
[Verified by] Titular Counsellor [----].[12]

all of the circumstances of this matter by now. At the end of his report he expresses his fear of a probable attempt on Ross by Mexican soldiers; concerning this [possibility], however, it can be assumed that Mexico, which is about to disintegrate from its own rebellions, is hardly in a position to take active and strong measures to suppress the Californios, and if a small landing force were to be sent from Mexico, then upon seeing the complete absence of Russian involvement in this matter (which has always been observed and now even more strictly) they will not make an attempt to disturb Ross. Generally speaking, I do not have any sound reason to fear for that quarter [Ross Counter]. I will await with impatience further news from Mr. Kostromitinov on the sloop *Sitka,* which I intend to send at the end of June to Bodega Bay with a reinforcement of fifteen promyshlenniks for Ross. I have ordered Mr. Kostromitinov to act with the utmost caution and not to enter into any political relations with the rebels but instead to maintain our fortifications as much as possible in an appropriate condition, as well as due order in general. The bulletins and proclamations in Spanish [not in the file] that are enclosed with Mr. Kostromitinov's report were forwarded by me beforehand with a letter to Director K. T. Khlebnikov on the brig *Okhotsk*" (RRAC, roll 39, doc. 321, fols. 370v–72). On the basis of Kostromitinov's report of 25 December 1836, which was forwarded by Kupreyanov to St. Petersburg, the company's board of directors compiled a report to Minister of Finance Kankrin on 31 December 1837 (see Document 25).

[12]Illegible signature.

DOCUMENT 25

Russian-American Company's Report about a Rebellion in Alta California, 1837

THE BOARD OF DIRECTORS OF THE RUSSIAN-AMERICAN COMPANY,
A REPORT TO MINISTER OF FINANCE YEGOR KANKRIN ABOUT
A REBELLION IN ALTA CALIFORNIA AND THE CONDUCT OF THE
AMERICANS,[1] [ST. PETERSBURG], 31 DECEMBER 1837

The governor of the colonies in America, Captain of the Guards of the 1st rank Kupreyanov, in a dispatch of 14 June 1837 (no. 321)[2] forwarded a report from Manager Kostromitinov of Ross Counter about disturbances in California that states that the Mexican official Chico, who was at Monterey to inspect affairs, left there in fear of the Californios but soon returned in order to stop the [dis]turbances and punish the insubordinates. Knowing his [i.e., Chico's] cruel nature, some California-born officials incited hatred of the Mexicans in the residents, telling them that they [i.e., the Mexicans] wanted to enslave California, that the Mexican government was sending mostly indigent and mercenary men to administer California with the sole aim of enriching themselves, and that the Mexican soldiers who were being sent to California for some sort of offense would not receive any salary from the government and would live at the expense of the Californios. The American trading captains Hinckley and Steel, who were then at Monterey, strongly promoted the uprising of the Californios, even promising to help them during the coup d'état and seducing them with the hope that the government of the North American [United] States would take them under its protection.

---

[1]AVPRI, f. RAK, op. 888, d. 360, fols. 1–2v (original). The following sentence is written in pencil in the margin at the beginning of the document: "Correspond with Co[unt] Nesselrode." The following sentence is written in pencil at the end of the document: "[Ask?] Co[unt] Nesselrode [whether?] or not it would be useful [to report?] this to the envoy of the American [United] States [and ask him?] to explain the matter to him."

[2]See RRAC, roll 39, doc. 321, fols. 370v–75.

Governor of California Gutiérrez, who knew of the existence of a conspiracy, was also aware of the insignificant forces and means of the main plotters, and for that reason he could not believe that they were able to undertake anything definite. Meanwhile, one of the young Californio officials stole away from Monterey and, going to San Francisco, managed to muster there and in the surrounding settlements up to 120 inhabitants, and to them he added 40 American beaver hunters and their leader (who were roaming near California to trap beaver), promising to pay them each 2 piasters per day, and after having designated Sergeant Castro[3] from the rebels as general, he left for Monterey.

[Upon] arriving there, the rebels occupied the battery and sent an envoy to the governor with a demand to surrender. At first Mr. Gutiérrez was determined to defend himself, having 80 soldiers in the garrison, but they, having been bribed, refused to obey. Then the rebels fired a shot at the garrison, and the governor was forced to surrender. The rebels hired the English trading vessel *Clementine* and embarked the governor and other Mexicans (90 families), who were landed on California's southern extremity, Cabo San Lucas.

After having dispatched the Mexican officials, the Californios declared their independence, and the officers, who were no more than lieutenants, ensigns, and sergeants in the Mexican service, took upon themselves by decree the ranks of commandant general, governor, and president of the council and promoted the lower ranks to colonels and captains.

The inhabitants of Southern [Baja], or Old, California did not recognize the authority over them of the new government, and for that reason they are expecting a civil war.

This event took place in October 1836, and the residents of Monterey and San Francisco, understanding the impotence of the new government, expect that soon an army will without fail be sent from Mexico to punish them, and for that reason many of them are turning to the manager of Ross Counter with proposals to take them under his protection, wherefore the governor of the colonies has ordered Mr. Kostromitinov that he not enter into any relations with the rebels.

Meanwhile, some Americans of the United States living in California began to move their buildings closer to the settlement of Ross 3[0] verstas up the Slavyanka River, and they intend to establish economic pursuits at Cape Drake [Point Reyes], solely, it seems, with the purpose of constraining the sphere of our operations in that country. The governor, figuring that the Americans in the guise of Californian citizens will occupy the plains on the Slavyanka River (as the most favorable place for cultivation) before we do, has found it difficult

---

[3]Unidentified; quite possibly José Castro (1810–60), whom Bancroft rated "the most prominent of his name as a public man" in Alta California ([Bancroft], *California Pioneer Register,* 92).

how to act in these circumstances; but in order not to appear inattentive to the audacity of the new settlers, he ordered Mr. Kostromitinov to cultivate places surrounding Rumyantsev [Bodega] Bay and, after having established settlements there, to strengthen our possession of the bay itself.

In representing the events in California to Your Highness, the Company's Board of Directors dares to request a decision as to how the colonial administration should act in case the Americans of the Northern United States, taking advantage of California's anarchy, want to constrain the sphere of our operations at Fort Ross, where we have occupied all of the vicinity for twenty-five years without any hindrances on the part of the previous governments of Spain and Mexico and even with special respect on the part of the Californios.

Director Ivan Prokofyev.[4]
Director Nikol[ay] Kusov.[5]
[Verified by] Bazhenov as chief clerk.
[Sent?] 1 January 1838.
[Received?] 4 January 1838.

---

[4]Ivan Vasilyevich Prokofyev (17??–1845) was a Moscow merchant and one of the Russian-American Company's directors from 1823 to 1844. See Grinëv, *Kto yest kto,* 441; and Pierce, *Russian America,* 413.

[5]Nikolay Ivanovich Kusov (1780–1856) was a St. Petersburg merchant (and mayor of the city in 1824–33) and one of the Russian-American Company's directors from 1824 to 1856. See Grinëv, *Kto yest kto,* 284; and Pierce, *Russian America,* 285.

.

DOCUMENT 26

Alexander Rotchev's Report about the Political Situation in Alta California, 1840

MANAGER ALEXANDER ROTCHEV, A REPORT TO
GOVERNOR ADOLF ETOLIN ABOUT THE POLITICAL SITUATION
IN ALTA CALIFORNIA,[1] [FORT ROSS], 11 AUGUST 1840

Concerning the political situation of this province, I have the honor to report that it has not changed up to this point. In April 1840 the government of California imagined that a conspiracy against its authority had been formed on the part of the American and English settlers here. Not having enough facts at all for charging the foreigners, it sent patrols at night to various ranchos, where imaginary plotters were found; the soldiers forcibly caught and bound as many men as it could and took them to Monterey. Without any trial and clear proof 80 men were put in irons and sent forthwith like negroes on the chartered Mexican ship of Mr. Aguirre,[2] the *Joven Guipuzcoana* [*Young Guipuzcoana*] to Mexico. On this occasion many of the foreigners, having been taken unawares, were deprived of all of their property and were gravely wounded by bullets. One of them, a certain Mr. Graham,[3] who owned a distillery near Monterey, lost five thousand piasters in cash, his property, and his house; all of these [possessions] were looted by the soldiers. While the shackled foreigners were being held in the Monterey jail,

---

[1]ARGO, raz. 99, op. 1, d. 23, fols. 9–10 (original).

[2]José Antonio Aguirre (ca. 1793–18??), a Spaniard from the Basque country, became a wealthy trader at Guaymas, plying the California trade in several vessels and visiting Alta California frequently, finally making Santa Barbara his home about 1838. See [Bancroft], *California Pioneer Register*, 28–29.

[3]Isaac Graham (179?–1863) was a fur trapper from Kentucky who arrived in Alta California from New Mexico in the middle 1830s and settled at Natividad near Monterey. According to Bancroft, he was "unprincipled, profligate, and reckless," becoming involved in several scrapes. See [Bancroft], *California Pioneer Register*, 165–66.

the American trading vessel *Don Quixote,* with an American military officer as a passenger, happened to arrive here from the Sandwich Islands. In the name of his government the officer asked Mr. Alvarado to explain his conduct toward the foreigners; but the governor probably considered any satisfactory answer unnecessary and did not even want to favor him with a meeting. Despite this [rebuff], the American officer went to the jail and, after having collected the aforesaid prisoners, immediately raised anchor and sailed to Mazatlán, from which cruisers were being sent to meet the ship loaded with prisoners. At the beginning of last June three three-masted naval vessels—American, English, and French— arrived. These ships came with the intention of demanding a report on the insult to the foreigners and satisfaction for the losses incurred by them. After having gathered the necessary evidence from the remaining foreigners and having designated various amounts that California had to pay forthwith as satisfaction (these amounts reached up to 500 t[housand] piasters, according to rumors), the naval vessels left for Callao, where the commander of the squadron is found; their return here is expected daily. At this time Governor Alvarado fled to [Mission] San Juan [Bautista], and only now has he returned to Monterey. An American ship left a naval officer, plus a consul for further elucidation of the circumstances. The unrest and anxiety of the inhabitants are great, and every day they expect a genuine resolution of this affair.

I consider it my duty to report this [information] to Your Honor.

Manager of the Counter A. Rotchev.

DOCUMENT 27

Yegor Chernykh, "About the Seeds Sent from Upper California," 1841

EDITOR'S INTRODUCTION

On the initiative of Governor Wrangell, who inspected Ross Counter for six weeks in the summer of 1833,[1] the Russian-American Company attempted to expand and improve agriculture there as part of a final effort to make the colony viable. To facilitate this program it hired an agronomist, Yegor Chernykh, who spent five years trying to bolster farming, with some success. He, too, found Alta California interesting, particularly its productive agriculture but also its flora and fauna (he even collected a species of explosive bombardier ground beetles that was named after him, *Brachinus tschernikhi*), as can be seen from the following three documents, which offer a detailed portrayal of Californio farming on the eve of the American takeover by a professional and experienced specialist.

YE. CHERNYKH,[2] "ABOUT THE SEEDS SENT FROM UPPER CALIFORNIA*
(FROM A LETTER TO THE PERMANENT SECRETARY [OF THE
IMPERIAL MOSCOW AGRICULTURAL SOCIETY]),"[3]
CHERNYKH RANCHO, 16 JANUARY 1841

Of the varieties of bread grains, that which the Spaniards call *Espigin* [from *espiga*, "spike"] (bearded) merits special attention; it has a large bearded ear that

---

*In February of this year the society received from Corresponding Member Ye. L. Chernykh the seeds of various Californian cereals, trees, and flowers. The last were sent to the Horticultural Society and the first were distributed to the hon. members for planting. Here follows a description of the most remarkable plants.—*Ed.*

---

[1]For his findings, see Gibson, "Russia in California."

[2]Yegor Leontyevich Chernykh (1809–43) was, in Russian parlance, a Kamchatkan Creole, his father being a Russian priest and his mother a Kamchadal (Itelmen) woman. Upon the recommendation of Kamchatka's commandant, Captain Pyotr Rikord, he was sent to Moscow in 1823 to enroll in the Moscow Agricultural School. After graduating in 1827 as an agronomist, Chernykh returned to Kamchatka, where he (*continued*)

comprises seven small ears. It is very fruitful; last summer I planted 2 f[anegas] of this wheat in a field and obtained [a yield of] more than 76-fold [the seed]. Even more remarkable is the fact that white Chilean wheat without a beard grew alongside it and was damaged by rust, while Espigin remained unharmed. Other wheats have been obtained from the South American republics. Formerly almost exclusively Espigin wheat was sown in California, and a high yield was obtained; but now it has been supplanted by a variety of wheats.

Madreño [madrone, or arbutus (*Arbutus menziesii*)] is considered the hardest wood in California. The residents of Ross—and I don't know why—call it *yellow palm;* it has nothing in common with the palm family. The pronounced roughness of its evenly yellowish bark is lost yearly, and new bark forms in its place. The tree is very pretty and branchy, with limbs spreading from various sides but mostly the sunny side; I did not have occasion to see its diameter of 1½ arsh[ins]. It grows alone among oaks, redwoods, and spruces; its leaves are large and very green and shiny, and whitish underneath. This tree is always greening; when young leaves appear, the old leaves fall. It blooms in April and May; its berries, which resemble rowanberries in color and size, ripen in October and November. The Indians eat them but in small amounts, and they are fairly tasty.

Cypress seeds: this tree is called *cypress*[4] by the Spaniards and *juniper* by us; it is seldom found, and it has a thickness of ½ an arsh[in]. The wood is hard and the trunk is gnarled.[5]

Allow me to expand upon the [coast] *redwood tree*,[6] whose propagation in Russia could bring much benefit. It is called *palo colorado* (red wood) by the Californios and *kassyl* by the Indians to the north of Ross. The redwood [*Sequoia sempervirens*] is the largest of all of the trees growing on the coast of California. *Chaga* is named after its thick bark, which is very similar to the *chaga* that is used to make fire;[7] its bark is often 1½ quarter-arsh[ins] thick. The largest number grow to the north of the port of Bodega, beginning from the Slavyanka River

---

tried to improve farming but without much success. He then entered the service of the Russian-American Company as an agricultural specialist with the task of expanding and improving agriculture in Ross Counter. He arrived at the beginning of 1836 and remained as assistant manager until the sale of the counter in 1841; one of the new Russian ranchos was named after him in recognition of his efforts. He then accepted the position of inspector of New Archangel Counter with a promotion from collegiate secretary to provincial secretary. He died suddenly at the colonial capital in the summer of 1843 from "neural fever." See Grinëv, *Kto yest kto*, 586; and Pierce, *Russian America*, 86. Also see Gibson, "Kamchatkan Agronomist in California."

[3]Chernykh, "O semenakh, prislannykh."

[4]Sp., *ciprés.*

[5]Chernykh seems to be referring here to the Monterey cypress (*Cupressus macrocarpa*), one of ten species in California, each with a rather localized distribution.

[6]Russ., *chaga.*

[7]Here Chernykh seems to be referring to the Siberian meaning of *chaga* as birchbark tinder; the word also denoted a fungus (*Polyporus igniarius*) on a birch tree (Dal, *Tolkovy slovar*, 1279).

between Ross and Bodega, and they form a continuous dense forest. They grow in soils that are characteristic of other coniferous trees, excluding boggy soils. The largest trees occur along the banks of rivers; all of the mountains and ravines around Ross are overgrown with this tree. Mostly spruce, oak, madrone, laurel [bay], and small bushes grow among them. They bloom in April and May; their small round cones ripen in October and November. The redwood is very straight and soft, like our poplar; it has only upper branches, which are short and thin and covered with short, fine needles. Even the youngest trees have very thick roots. All buildings and articles at Ross are made from this tree.

The chief merit of redwood is its cleavability; the thickest tree can be split into the finest pieces. Without this quality, using redwood would be difficult, because of its extreme thickness. Not infrequently one tree affords up to 500 seven-arshin planks. Furthermore, the upper part is about ½ of the whole tree; because it is a bit dry, it is almost always discarded. From one tree here several plank houses are often made.

Here are the sizes of several redwoods that I measured: in November 1839 a redwood that was felled for planks had a length of 201 feet (of 7 feet to a sazhen) from the ground to the very top. On 18 February 1840 a redwood was felled 1½ arsh[ins] from the ground; it was 7 feet thick at the butt and 178 feet long. In May 1840 a redwood was felled for planks 2 arsh[ins] from the ground; it had a diameter of 11 feet, 9 inches at the butt, and 20 feet above the butt it was 7 feet, 6 inches thick. The top of this giant had been broken by the wind, so that its length was indeterminate. I did not chance to see a redwood thicker than this last tree or longer than 238 feet; I was assured that there were longer ones. The thickest redwoods are seldom tall.

I think that the redwood could grow successfully not only in our southern provinces but [also] wherever conifers grow.[8] For this purpose the seeds that I am sending are fresh and clean and in cones.

Among the various plants on the ship *Nikolay* [*Nicholas*] [*I*] bound for Kronshtadt I have sent seeds of the giant [sugar] pine (*Pinus lambertiana*)[9] to the hon. director of the Imperial Botanical Garden, O. B. Fisher, and I have asked Mr. Fisher to forward some to you in Moscow.* These seeds were collected by me personally on 1 September 1840 50 verstas north of Ross. The tree from which

*These have been received and distributed to the hon. members.—*Ed.*

---

[8]Chernykh (an agronomist, not a silviculturalist) was mistaken. Coast redwoods require specific temperature (mild winters), exposure, soil (non-ophiolites), and especially moisture (ample rainfall and fog drip) conditions.

[9]The sugar pine is the world's largest and tallest pine, with cones reaching 18 inches in length.

the cones were taken was 2 arshins in diameter, and its length from the butt (an arsh[in] above the ground) was 81 arsh[ins]; its branches began 20 arsh[ins] above the ground. It grows singly on the highest mountains and among redwoods, spruces, and oaks. The wood is straight and very sappy; it [i.e., the sugar pine] blooms in spring, and its nuts [seeds] ripen by 1 September. I did not see any young trees during my trip.

With the last post I had the honor to present to you the seeds of a tobacco that grows wild in California, and on account of circumstances I did not have time [then] to write anything about them; permit me to say a few words now. *Wild tobacco*[10] grows in sand along riverbanks; the seeds that I have sent were collected by me in the sand of the Slavyanka River. It does not grow high, but then its branches spread far to the side. It blooms in August and its seeds ripen in September; it has white florets (*flos*). It drops its seeds in winter, when the river overflows and carries them in the current, and thereby the tobacco propagates itself. The Indians gather its leaves and dry them in the sun and then smoke them. It is fairly strong.

Among the seeds are those in the black bag of the *bloating sapling* [poison oak (*Toxicodendron diversilobum*)], which the Spaniards call *Hyedra* [*sic: hiedra* ("ivy")]. Is any useful medicine derived from this shrub? One of my friends, an Englishman who had accompanied the famous traveler Douglas[11] in [Alta] California, told me that Douglas had hired him to collect whole bundles of *hiedra* for some sort of medicinal use. It was upon this basis that I decided to dispatch some seeds of this remarkable shrub. The residents of Ross call it *bloating sapling* because touching it produces a severe swelling [in a person's flesh] at the point of contact, accompanied by extreme itching. However, it does not affect everyone; on some—many Russians, for example—it has no effect at all, whereas others are affected so severely that even a wind blowing from this shrub produces swelling, especially when it is blooming. I know one American who is so sensitive to *hiedra* that if he passes by it he will become swollen and itchy; but the swelling always ends harmlessly. This shrub grows in abundance on all slopes facing the sun; horses and cattle eat its leaves with no ill effects. It blooms in May, and its seeds ripen in August and September.

---

[10]There were at least four species of *Nicotiana* in Alta California, all called "Indian" or "wild" tobacco. *Nicotiana* was used medicinally and ceremonially by the Indians, some of whom also cultivated it (see Mead, *Ethnobotany,* 271–75; and Strike, *Aboriginal Uses,* 95–97).

[11]The Scottish botanist David Douglas (1799–1834), after whom the Douglas fir (which is not a true fir) was named, visited Alta California in 1831. The English friend may well have been William Hartnell, whose home Douglas used as a base while botanizing in the province.

DOCUMENT 28

Yegor Chernykh, "About Cultivation in Alta California," 1841

YEGOR CHERNYKH, "ABOUT CULTIVATION IN ALTA CALIFORNIA,"*1
CHERNYKH RANCHO, 12 JANUARY 1841

On the Northwest Coast of America between Cabo San Lucas and the port of San Francisco lies the blessed land called California. It is divided into *Upper*, or *New*, and *Lower*, or *Old*, California. The stretch lying between the ports of San Diego and San Francisco is called Upper [Alta] California, and that between the port of San Diego and Cabo San Lucas, Lower [Baja] California.

Having the honor to serve in the colonies of the Russian-American Company, namely, at the settlement of Ross, I have succeeded in becoming familiar with the climate of Upper California and the economy of its inhabitants. In order to understand better the course of agricultural work in Upper California, it is necessary to become familiar with the seasons of the year.

Here it is possible to divide the whole year into rainy and *rainless* [seasons]; they call the former *winter* and the latter summer. The rains begin in October and last until April; the first rains usually occur in September and the last in May. In

*This interesting article was sent to the society by Corresponding Member Ye. L. Chernykh, who, having first been educated at the Moscow School of Agriculture, does honor to this institution with his knowledge of agronomy and, having been engaged for 10 years in the economy of the s[ettlement]. of Ross in California in the employ of the Russian-American Company, has several times submitted articles to the society on Californian cultivation that have been printed in the 2nd decade of the [existence of the] *Zemledelchesky zhurnal* [Agricultural journal].—*Ed.*

[1] Chernykh, "O zemledelii v verkhney Kalifornii." An unrevised version of this translation appears in Farris, *So Far from Home*, 175–82. For an earlier (and anonymous) translation of this article, see Chernykh, "Agriculture of Upper California."

April, May, and even June there are intermittent rains, but these rarely occur; as stated above, October–April can be considered the exclusive rainy season.

Verdure begins to appear after the first rains, but growth occurs slowly; the cause of this, apart from the lowness of the sun and the excess of moisture, is the strong and rather cold northwest winds. In February all wild grasses start to grow noticeably, some of them even blossoming, and trees bud. The largest number and the greatest variety of blossoms appear in April and May. In late May wild grasses begin to fade and the ground begins to dry out; in June most plants have faded, and July, August, and September present a picture similar to our winter: springs and all grasses have been desiccated by the heat, except in marshy places, and the ground has hardened and cracked, especially dark and clayey soils. Hills and open places dry up faster and deeper than valleys and low places that are less exposed to the winds and more capable of retaining moisture.

Hoar-, or white, frost occurs intermittently from November until the middle of April and sometimes even later.

There are two prevailing winds: the northwest and the south; the former is the most common, blowing almost constantly from May to October and always bringing fair weather and occurring with rain only sporadically after the prolonged, rainy south wind. Southwest and southeast winds blow strongly in winter, always bringing foul weather, and weakly in summer, producing fog. In winter the south wind often blows with strong gusts. East and west winds blow very rarely and not for long, sometimes only several hours but with extreme force. The northeast wind (*NEE*) blows from the land, mostly in the autumn in September and October, and it is always very warm, up to 22° R. Within a few hours it dries out not only the soil but even old, weathered buildings and wooden articles. During this wind the inhabitants are stricken with coughs and not infrequently chest pains. The west wind, blowing directly from the ocean, brings thick, black clouds with rain and sometimes with hail and thunder; it blows mostly in November and usually during the transition from south to northwest winds. Thunder rarely occurs.

Here is an extract of the temperature observations made partly by me and partly under my supervision in 1837, 1838, 1839, and 1840.[2] In 1837 the observations were made in Fahrenheit and converted into Réaumur, but they were made in Réaumur in the other years.

---

[2] These readings were republished in German in Erman, "Beiträge zur Klimatologie." Erman also published some general comments on the Russian and Californio settlements (see Erman, "Einege Bemerkungen").

1837	average temperature			rainy days	over[cast] & fog[gy days]	cloudy [days]	clear [days]	[days with] thunder	[days with] hail
	7 AM	2 PM	6 PM						
Jan.	6.3	9.4	7.3	10	12	4	5	1	0
Feb.	6.2	10.0	6.5	4	4	8	12	1	1
Mar.	7.9	12.1	8.5	6	3	10	12	0	0
Apr.	8.7	13.0	9.3	4	3	10	13	0	0
May	11.7	15.0	11.1	3	8	7	13	0	0
June	12.7	14.2	10.8	1	5	4	20	0	0
July	13.3	15.1	11.7	0	6	5	20	0	0
Aug.	13.1	15.9	11.6	0	4	2	25	0	0
Sept.	10.5	13.5	10.1	2	8	3	17	1	0
Oct.	8.8	11.5	8.8	4	3	4	20	0	0
Nov.	5.3	9.4	6.2	4	3	10	13	0	0
Dec.	6.2	9.4	7.1	18	5	5	3	1	0
	9.2	12.3	8.8	56	64	72	173	3	1

[Average] annual temperature = +10.2[° R]

1838	6 AM	2 PM	8 PM						
Jan.	4.64	9.70	5.51	4	3	3	21	1	1
Feb.	5.64	9.34	7.14	6	2	11	9	0	0
Mar.	6.09	10.67	6.83	7	7	3	14	0	0
Apr.	7.60	11.13	7.46	9	4	5	12	1	1
May	7.93	12.58	7.96	2	12	4	13	0	0
June	8.96	13.96	9.10	1	11	5	13	0	1
July	9.22	13.51	9.51	0	15	7	9	0	0
Aug.	8.77	13.87	9.87	0	11	2	18	0	0
Sept.	8.90	13.43	9.66	1	14	5	10	1	0
Oct.	8.16	13.74	8.90	1	5	3	22	0	0
Nov.	8.03	11.73	8.53	6	2	10	12	0	0
Dec.	5.67	9.87	6.38	12	5	7	7	0	0
	7.46	11.81	8.07	49	91	65	160	3	3

[Average] annual temperature = +9.11[° R]

1839

Jan.	6.09	10.80	7.29	0	7	11	13	0	0
Feb.	7.21	11.57	8.17	2	3	9	14	0	0
Mar.	7.22	11.00	8.00	8	7	10	6	1	0
Apr.	7.00	10.90	7.93	10	6	8	6	0	1
May	9.22	12.09	9.58	2	8	12	9	0	0
June	10.43	13.76	10.58	0	8	13	9	0	0
July	10.25	13.35	10.38	0	14	11	6	0	0
Aug.	11.03	14.38	11.12	0	3	21	7	1	0
Sept.	8.50	12.93	8.76	1	5	21	3	0	0
Oct.	7.45	11.83	8.29	6	2	17	6	0	0
Nov.	6.10	10.66	6.86	1	2	21	6	0	0
Dec.	7.12	10.38	7.80	13	8	10	0	1	0
	8.13	11.97	8.73	43	73	164	85	3	1

[Average] annual temperature = +9.61[° R]

1840[3]

Jan.	4.16	9.12	4.58	11	1	16	3	1	0
Feb.	3.03	9.41	4.56	8	4	16	1	1	2
Mar.	4.38	8.90	6.09	7	4	17	3	0	1
Apr.	6.36	10.93	6.86	2	2	10	16	0	1
May	9.77	14.22	10.29	1	1	17	12	0	0
June	10.53	14.20	10.16	0	6	19	5	0	0
July	10.93	14.90	10.54	0	13	8	10	0	0
Aug.	10.32	13.35	10.22	0	12	13	6	0	0
Sept.	10.10	14.06	10.46	0	4	19	7	0	0
Oct.	8.93	12.51	9.09	1	4	19	7	0	0
Nov.	9.86	12.60	9.56	8	1	16	5	0	0
Dec.	6.83	10.42	7.51	2	4	17	8	0	0
	7.93	12.05	8.32	40	56	187	83	2	4

[Average] annual temperature = +9.43[° R]

Not[es]. 1. The Réaumur thermometer was hung in the shade on a wooden wall facing N and was exposed to all winds, especially the prevailing NW [wind]. The difference between 1837 and the other years in [average] annual temperature arose from the difference in the hour when observations were made.

2. The observations were made at the settlement of Ross right on the coast; the difference in temperature between the coast and the interior is substantial:

---

[3]The 1840 data were copied by the French agent Duflot de Mofras (see Wilbur, *Duflot de Mofras*).

in winter, when it is +3–4° R in the morning *in [the colony of] Ross* at *Chernykh Rancho,* which is found 15 verstas from the sea, there are -1° or -1½° of hoarfrost, and the farther inland from the sea, the colder [it becomes]. In summer it is the opposite—the farther from the sea, the warmer [it becomes]; for ex[ample], when it is +18° at Ross, it is up to +22° at Chernykh Rancho, and so on. On the coast hoarfrost occurs very rarely, and in November and December on clear mornings; inland from the sea they occur almost every clear and calm morning. When it rains, snow is always visible on the distant hills, and then harder frost occurs.

3. The highest temperatures occurred in July and August in 1837, in 1838 on 26 November at 2 o'clock in the afternoon with a warm NEE [wind] (+22° in the shade), in 1839 on 29 June at 2 o'clock in the afternoon (+19° in the shade), and in 1840 on 22 July at 2 o'clock in the afternoon (+18° in the shade). The lowest temperatures occurred in November in the morning in 1837, in 1838 in January and February at 6 o'clock in the morning (+2°), in 1839 on 19 January in the morning (+3°), and in 1840 in February in the morning (+2°).

4. The number of clear and cloudy days also indicates the number of days when the NW and sometimes the NE [wind] blew; with a S [wind] it is rarely clear and usually overcast, foggy, and rainy. However, after prolonged south winds rain and fog not infrequently come from the NW.

[Although] I doubt the accuracy of the barometer, I nevertheless attach an extract of barometric observations for 1838, 1839, and 1840.

Month	mercury level					
	1838		1839		1840	
	high	low	high	low	high	low
January	30.4	29.7	30.4	29.8	30.0	29.7
February	30.3	29.6	30.3	29.9	30.2	29.7
March	30.1	29.7	30.1	29.8	30.0	29.6
April	30.1	29.7	30.1	29.7	30.3	29.8
May	30.1	29.7	30.1	29.7	30.1	29.8
June	30.2	29.8	30.2	29.9	30.1	29.8
July	30.1	29.8	30.2	29.7	30.0	29.8
August	30.1	29.8	30.1	29.8	30.1	29.8
September	30.1	29.8	30.1	29.9	30.0	29.8
October	30.2	29.8	30.3	29.8	30.1	29.8
November	30.4	29.9	30.3	29.8	30.2	29.8
December	30.3	29.5	30.3	26.5	30.2	29.8

The difference between the highest and the lowest mercury levels in the barometer was 0.9 in 1838 and 1839 and 0.7 in 1840.

The barometer was hung in an occupied room, which was never heated; the usual temperature in it at midday was 11–12° R in the summer and 9–10° in the winter, and in the summer it was generally colder in the room than in the open air. The room faced the N, and the sun's rays never penetrated it.

Having become acquainted with the temperature of Upper California, let us turn to the economy of its inhabitants, the Spanish Creoles [mestizos, i.e., Californios].

All of the missions and ranchos in California are located on the coast and on bays, especially San Francisco Bay. The coast is mountainous and often dissected by small but fertile valleys that are watered by pure springs; in the valleys and on the coast the land comprises deep, dark soil—silt mixed more or less with clay. The banks of rivers and streams are considered the most fertile places. The soil of the mountains consists mostly of gravel and clay. During the rains the broad valleys here are covered with water, and lakes are formed, but they dry up at the end of the rains. On the coast there are few spacious valleys suitable for cultivation.

In the valleys between the mountain ranges and not infrequently on the mountains themselves huge trees are encountered: redwood, pine, spruce, fir, laurel, oak, California palm (madrone), and others. Generally California is not rich in timber, and Lower [California], I am assured, can be called *treeless*. Upper California is rich in trees *here and there*. Extensive thick forests begin north of the port of Bodega.

Of agricultural implements, only the plow is used here; an oak or palm bough takes the place of the harrow. A primitive plow of the most simple sort is used; a curved tree is selected, and one end serves as the handle, and an iron wedge—from 1½ to 2 four[ths] of an arsh[in] long, 2 vershoks wide at the top, and pointed at the bottom—is fastened to the other end. A shaft is attached to the middle of this tree; the end of the shaft is attached by a harness to a yoke, which is secured to the horns of two oxen. Here they plow and harrow with oxen, despite the multitude of horses; this preference can be attributed more to the habitualness and simplicity of the ox harness than to the success of its performance.[4] During plowing the handle of the plow is held in the left hand and the oxen are driven with the right hand. They usually plow with a pair [of oxen]; in breaking virgin land they sometimes harness 4–6 oxen. It is obvious from the construction of the plow that it does not overturn the soil but merely plucks and tears it; nevertheless, it plows old land fairly deeply—from 2 versh[oks] to 2 four[ths] of an arsh[in] [deep] and sometimes deeper.

The grains grown in Upper California are [as follows]: wheat, barley, peas, corn, beans (*frijoles*), and garbanzos [chickpeas], and the vegetables include potatoes, watermelons, pumpkins (calabazas), and muskmelons (cantaloupes), as well

---

[4]As draft animals, horses did have the advantage over cattle of being able to walk backwards.

as cayenne peppers [capsicum], common onions, garlic, tomatoes (love apples [from the French, *pommes d'amour*]), and some cabbages. Formerly, during the sway of the missionaries [i.e., before the secularization of the missions], carrots, beets, and other vegetables were planted, but now they are rarely found. There are no cucumbers.

The crops grown here are divisible into frost-*resistant* and frost-*intolerant:* the first [category] applies to wheat, barley, oats, peas, and garbanzos and the second to frijoles, corn, watermelons, pumpkins, muskmelons, and common onions. Potatoes belong to both categories. Of the latter, frijoles are the most sensitive to frost.

With the first rains—from November onwards—they begin to cultivate frost-resistant crops. They usually plant barley first in order to have fresh bread sooner.

Old land is planted twice to *wheat* and *barley,* and new land several times. The prepared land is sown slowly, then it is tilled with a plow at right angles to the furrows of the first plowing, and finally it is fenced with tree branches. Unless it is necessary, the Californios never let the sown land lie fallow, fearing the evaporation of the slime mold of the dark soil.

Peas and garbanzos (*pois chiche*), or chickpeas, are sown side by side. The land assigned to them is tilled deeply and very thoroughly several times, and then furrows are made in it with a plow 3 four[ths] of an arshin, one arshin, and more from each other; the planter follows the plow and drops 2–3 peas together through his fingers into the furrow every half arshin, and as many garbanzos every 1–2 arsh[ins]. In order to simplify the determination of the distance during planting, the sower usually measures with his steps: with every small step he throws 2–3 peas together, and as many garbanzos with every two steps. The more widely spaced garbanzos are planted, the more luxuriantly they grow. I have not had occasion to see them in Russia; the appearance of its stalk resembles that of the fern: in the very same way ears studded with utricles containing the seeds extend along the sides of the stalk. It is very tasty, and in California highly esteemed. While throwing peas into the furrow the planter at the same time very skillfully and rapidly covers them with soil with his right foot. After sowing, some farmers immediately harrow without spreading soil on the seed with their foot; others, having covered the seed during sowing, do not harrow until weeds appear and until it is necessary to heap soil around the plantings. They sow peas in winter at the same time as wheat and in spring at the same time as corn in order to have them fresh at any time. Spring-sown are more tender and sweeter than winter-sown peas.

The sowing of frost-resistant crops usually continues until the 1st of March; then they begin to prepare the land for frost-*intolerant* crops—corn, frijoles, watermelons, and others. The planting of these crops is done from April until 6 June, especially if late rains occur. Not infrequently frost occurs in May, whereupon the sowing of frijoles is almost certainly affected, and they are replanted. I succeeded in testing that a light frost does not harm corn, although its foliage yellows.

CORN (maize) is, after meat, the most common food of the Californios. For it they plow the land thoroughly several times; then they level the whole surface of the plowed land with heavy oak or palm boughs. If a lot of butts [of trees] or clumps [of earth] are found in the plowland, they sometimes eradicate them [i.e., these obstacles] in the following way: they drag very heavy branches over the plowland, and their [i.e., the branches'] weight presses the clumps into the soil; each clump, after being pressed into the soil, is crumbled and softened by the soil moisture. It goes without saying that the clumps can be easily subsumed only in soil that has been well worked and—most importantly—deeply plowed. After having leveled the surface of the plowland designated for corn, they make shallow furrows with a plow, 1½ vershoks [deep] and 1¼ to 2½ arsh[ins] and sometimes more from each other [but] usually two paces [apart]; then in each furrow at the same distance [apart] they put 2–4 corn seeds together, so that if half of the seeds do not sprout, then as many are left. If the land designated for maize is dry, then for a day before sowing they soak the seed in fresh water; otherwise they sow it dry. When the corn sprouts and reaches a height of ¼ of an arsh[in], they uproot the worst plants and leave only the two healthiest and most promising in each hill. At this time offshoots—here called "baby corn"—emerge from the soil on both sides of the corn stalks. They likewise leave 1–2 of these, provided there is no more than one corn stalk in the hill; otherwise they uproot all of them. In general the fewer the plants they leave in one hill and the greater the distance between them, the more abundant the harvest and the larger the kernels. Corn roots are not deep, but they spread laterally, and that is why they [i.e., the Californios] leave a lot of space between plants.

After this operation, consisting of the eradication of excess plants, they loosen the soil around the maize and heap it around the plant. Some loosen and mound the soil by hand with a spade,[5] provided the acreage is not large; others—if the sown area is sizable—plow thoroughly between the rows of corn and mound soil around it with the plow. Afterwards the corn grows noticeably faster. They heap soil around the maize a second time at the beginning of blossoming; in this case good farmers rake the upper dried soil away from the corn beforehand and then heap fresh, moist subsoil around it and pile the dry soil on top. This action takes the place of watering. Sometimes they happen to see some maize stalks starting to yellow, sicken, and grow very slowly in good soil; this is relieved by raking the dried soil away from the plant and raking up fresh, moist subsoil; within two days it is impossible to recognize the ailing plant, which has turned green and come alive.

---

[5]Russ., *koparul.*

Only on sandy and stony soil do they water corn; on all other soils they plow deeply instead. In California deep plowing is the primary condition of good land preparation. In winter, when at times it pours for several weeks in a row, deep plowing protects the plantings against washouts,[6] which are inevitable on soils that have been lightly plowed. In summer, when at +12–25° R the constant clear weather is only rarely interrupted by fog, deep plowing of the soil serves to preserve moisture during the 4–5 months of the *rainless* period. Deep plowing of the soil greatly facilitates the preservation of moisture: in the months of May, June, July, and August all weeds wither and unplowed land dries out to a depth of 1–1½ arsh[ins]; dig up deeply plowed soil and you will be surprised to see that only the uppermost one or at most two vershoks of the soil have dried out! Dew falling on such soil moistens its surface and combines with the moisture [already] in the soil and thereby takes the place of watering. Without testing it, it is difficult to check the degree to which deep plowing is beneficial. In California they always try to plant and to seed frost-intolerant crops after the end of the rains, so that during planting often no rain at all falls, and this is one of the wishes of the farmers because after rain the soil surface dries out and hardens. I repeat that here watering is seldom employed, despite the fact that there is no rain for *five* months, which is the same as *drought lasting five months every year*. Thorough working of the land, especially deep plowing, takes the place of watering.

They dig around and rake around the corn only twice; if the land has been poorly worked, they rake three times. In a hot summer the corn grown here ripens in August; in a cool, foggy summer it ripens in September, so that rain catches it still in the fields, as in 1839, for ex[ample]. The ripeness of corncobs is easily recognized and so well known to everyone engaged in its cultivation that it is not necessary to talk about this.

Sometimes up to 6 cobs, but usually 2–4, form on each stalk of corn here. With the ripening of the corn they break off the cobs, and they leave the stalks themselves in the fields, not making any use at all of them, [although] sometimes they use them for huts. The core of the stalk is very sweet, and they give it to children and Indians as a delicacy. Cornstalks, which are readily eaten by livestock, rot slowly, especially their stubble.

They dry the harvested cobs in the sun; for this [purpose] they either hang them on poles, tying them together with the husks* that cover the cobs, or they

---

*These husks are in much use in California; after having cut them into large square pieces, they wrap cut tobacco in them and smoke them. I am assured that smokers find these *papelitos* ["little papers"] more agreeable than [real] paper.—*Comp[iler's] n[ote]*.

---

[6]Russ., *vymochki*.

simply spread them over a level spot. Then, for want of granaries, they store them in attics for safekeeping, first shucking the said husks. After drying the cobs, if the corn is intended for sale, they thresh them with sticks; for domestic use they keep the corn on the cob. For seed corn they prefer the lower part of the cob, i.e., its bottom half. Corn kernels intended for seed are separated from the cobs by hand in order not to damage the kernels, such damage being easily done when the maize is very ripe and well dried.

FRIJOLES. This is what they call all beans in general in California, but they cultivate mostly yellow [wax, or butter] beans. They [i.e., beans] are the favorite food of the Californios.

Having properly prepared the land, they make shallow furrows from 1 to 2 arsh[ins] apart and put 2–3 seeds together in plantings 1½ arsh[ins] apart. The sower, having cast the seeds, pushes loose soil over them with his foot; after some time, before the frijoles sprout but after weeds appear, they harrow. While the frijoles are growing they plow thoroughly between the rows and pile soil around them. This has a great effect on the harvest.

After sprouting the frijoles send long branches, studded with pods, in all directions; these branches spread over the ground and keep it shady, despite the fact that the frijoles are planted far apart. Their roots go deep into the soil, and for that reason they [i.e., the Californios] plow deeply for it [i.e., bean planting]. The chief inconvenience of frijole growing is harvesting. Not all of the pods ripen at the same time; some are ready [to pick] while others are just forming. With a small sowing they pick the ripe pods as they mature and leave the green ones to ripen. If the field is large, then after having waited until most of the pods have ripened, they pull out the frijoles by their roots and leave them in the field to dry; afterwards they haul them to the threshing ground.

POTATOES are planted to a small extent; for the most part each grower plants them for his own consumption only. They cultivate mostly red potatoes, which grow more abundantly and larger than white potatoes, although they say that the latter are tastier. The potatoes grow well; very often I happened to see here a perfectly round red potato with a diameter of ¼ of an arsh[in], and it was an ordinary red potato, not some special sort.

On prepared land they plant potatoes either in furrows made with a plow or in pits (holes) made with a spade. They make the furrows and holes in which they place the potatoes 2–3 arshins apart. For planting they cut the potatoes in two and place both pieces in the same spot. When the potatoes blossom, they cut off all of the foliage within 3–4 vershoks of the ground and pile fresh soil around them. They do nothing special to the potatoes; mainly they try to have looser soil around their roots.

WATERMELONS, MUSKMELONS, AND PUMPKINS. For these vegetables[7] they prepare the soil in the best way, removing all roots and lumps; then they make shallow furrows, usually 2–3 steps apart, and at the same distance apart they put 3–5 watermelon and muskmelon seeds together. For pumpkins they leave more room, 3–4 steps (about 4 arsh[ins]), and put 2–4 seeds in one spot. When the young plants sprout, they leave the two healthiest and pull out the others. They watch these vegetables while they are growing in order that they are not choked by weeds and the soil around their roots stays moist and loose; they do nothing else to them.

They grow the largest watermelons and pumpkins here, but the former lack the taste of our European watermelons. I had occasion to receive some seed from Astrakhan: the first year excellent watermelons were grown from them, but they were poorer in the second year, and in the third year they changed such that it was impossible to tell them from the local watermelons.

COMMON ONIONS AND *CAYENNE PEPPERS* are much in use. At first they grow the seedlings, which they plant in January and February after the *full moon;** then, when frosts can no longer be expected they transplant them to a spot where they should bear fruit. When they transplant the onions from the seedbed, they cut off the roots but not right up to the bulb, leaving about an inch of root; half of the tops are also torn off, and then they plant them shallowly. A shallow onion produces a larger head, of course, in loose soil with thorough watering. The onion is one of the plants that requires frequent watering; they recover very quickly after being transplanted. During its growth it is wholly a matter of weeding, watering, and loosening the soil around the roots; sandy dark soil, given its suitability for watering, is considered the best for onions. After the bulbs (heads) have fully formed, the tops fall off by themselves; at this time the onions are tamped into the soil in order that the roots can conduct sap to the heads only. Not infrequently I happened to see onions whose heads were 3 versh[oks] in diameter.

The *ripening periods* of grains are nearly the same as our Russian periods. Barley ripens the earliest of all grains—by 20 June to 1 July, wheat and peas by 10–20 July, garbanzos in August, and watermelons, muskmelons, pumpkins, onions,

---

*The full moon plays an important role among the Californios, especially when they plant onions, watermelons, pumpkins, muskmelons, potatoes, and others. They are convinced that an onion planted at the *new moon* will never head, by contrast with one planted at the *full moon* or later, that many crops which are transplanted and many trees which are grafted at the *new moon* will die and the grafts will not take well, and so on. Thus, the gelding of bulls, stallions, roosters, and such is always done after the full moon.—*Comp[iler's] n[ote]*.

---

[7]Russian does not distinguish between "vegetables" and "fruits" in the same way as English; in Russian a vegetable is any edible plant grown in a garden.

and cayenne peppers in late August and later, generally depending upon the degree of warmth in the preceding months.

They reap with sickles; for easier threshing they usually cut only the ears off grain crops. The straw is left in the field and is burned or destroyed by livestock. The pared ears are hauled in large, clumsy carts to the threshing ground; here these carts are called *carretas,* and their wheels are nothing but the wide crosscut sections of thick, whole logs.

Threshing is done with horses. For this purpose they construct two sorts of threshers (threshing floors): *earthen* and *stone.** For an earthen threshing floor they select a level, smooth spot on clayey ground; they encircle it with a fence, and during the winter they drive livestock into it in order that they [i.e., the animals] completely trample and level the irregularities. When the rains finish and the heat begins, this patch of clayey ground becomes as hard as stone. For a stone threshing floor they also select a level spot; they make the floor and walls of brick or flagstone. The diameter of the threshing floor depends upon the amount of grain and the number of horses and ranges from 8 to 12 sazhens. A long pole is sometimes erected in the very center of the threshing floor. They bring the harvested grain to the threshing floor built in this way and either strew it *all over* the floor to a depth of two arshins or stack it in the center of the floor around the pole, leaving a small space of 4 arshins [in width] between the sides of the stack and the walls of the threshing floor for circling by horses. After having stacked the grain in this way, they drive in from 50 to 180 horses, depending upon the size of the threshing floor.

After the grain has been strewn *all over* the threshing floor, the driven horses wallow in it until it is trampled; for an hour or an hour and a half they are driven by whip over the threshing floor so that they are in constant motion, knocking the grain out of the ears. Then the horses are driven out; after having overturned the straw, they drive them in again, and so on. When they see that the grain has been separated from the straw, they carefully remove and discard the top layer of straw; after having turned all of the straw several times, they continue to drive the horses in and out until the ears lying on the threshing floor are turned into chaff. After sifting this chaff, they obtain pure grain. The hapless animals, bounding in the crowded enclosure, injure themselves; pregnant mares abort and not infrequently die. In order to thresh 1,000 sheaves per day by this method of threshing, it is necessary to have 100–200 horses and 20–25 Indians, who take turns driving the horses with whips. The Indians leap about the threshing floor

*It seems that there are only wooden ones at Ross.—*Comp[iler's] n[ote].*

with the horses and sing over and over in time the two words: "Yevva! Kamya! Yevva! Kamya!"

The second method of threshing is preferred to the first. The stack of grain [around the central pole] is gradually lowered from the top down by a man sitting there; with the horses it is not difficult to thresh the thin[ner] layers. They assure [me] that with this method 8–10 men with 150 horses thresh more than 1,000 puds per day; in this case it is not necessary to turn the straw constantly, as in the first case, and for that reason not as many men are needed. Despite the imperfection of the method of threshing with horses, on account of its rapidity it merits attention, especially for threshing the hard wheat that is cultivated in California. The said threshing floors are found only at the missions and among prosperous farmers with sizable sowings.

Poorer farmers have small threshing floors for threshing their own grain with 10–30 domestic saddle horses. For threshing they always use droves of mares, which are pastured separately and almost never used for riding; their use is limited solely to threshing.

Many impurities and damaged kernels are left in the grain that is threshed by horses.

The *amount of sowing* is generally inconsiderable. Each farmer, or rancher, mostly sows only enough for his own provisionment, if he does not have profitable marketing in mind.

The *amount of the harvest* is likewise difficult to determine accurately. None of the Californios will state his actual harvest: if he sells grain, then he complains of a meager harvest, and if he does not sell it, then he exaggerates the harvest out of boastfulness.

Despite my desire, I have not yet been able to obtain a single tally of the *sowing* and *harvest* of various grains in Upper California in recent years. Instead, I have taken the liberty of extracting from V. M. Golovnin's *Voyage** a table of the sowing and harvest of various grains in Upper California in 1818.[8]

Puteshestvie vokrug Sveta, [Po poveleniyu Gosudarya Imperatora sovershennoe,] na voyennom shlyupe Kamchatka, v 1817, 1818 i 1819 godakh, Flota Kapitanom Golovninym, Pt. 1, Supp., p. xviii, Table B [see Golovnin, *Around the World,* appendix 6, pp. 308–10].

---

[8]Chernykh reproduced only part of Golovnin's original table, omitting the columns of data on the missions (dates of founding and latitudinal and longitudinal locations), the Indians (number of converted, married, deceased, and living Indians), and livestock (number of cattle, sheep, goats, pigs, mares and colts, tame horses [stallions?], and hinnies and mules). Also, Chernykh failed to check Golovnin's totals, almost all of which were added incorrectly.

*Mission sowing and harvest in 1818 (in fanegas**)*

		wheat	barley	corn	beans	small beans[9]	peas	oats
San Diego [de Alcalá]	sow.	250	134	6	7	0	0	0
	har.	2,800	1,800	600	68	0	0	0
San Luis [Rey]	"	361	201	10	3¾	½	0	4
	"	1,500	2,000	800	60	30	0	12
San Juan [Capistrano]	"	150	3	12	4¼	7/24	11/12	3¹³/₄₈
	"	2,296	16	1,663	55¹/₁₂	5¼	3	10
San Gabriel	"	280	4	26	5	⅙	⅙	⅙
	"	110	40	6,500	310	1	2	2
San Fernando [Rey]	"	200	0	3½	3	1½	0	0
	"	4,000	0	400	60	41	0	0
San Buena ventura	"	200	90	8	5	½	1	½
	"	3,800	230	1,200	50	0	30	0
Santa Bárbara	"	144	40	9	3	5/12	1	1
	"	5,098	534	540	50	2	12	29
Santa Inés	"	60	4	3	4	0	1	0
	"	1,200	60	300	160	0	100	0
San Luis [Obispo]	"	130	0	2	4	¾	1	2
	"	1,060	0	100	100	3	19	27
[La] Purísima [Concepción]	"	123	18	8	5	½	6	10
	"	2,500	600	1,000	120	4	500	540
San Miguel	"	95	18	¾	1	0	0	0
	"	1,650	200	127	5	0	0	0

**A *fanega* is a Spanish measure containing 3 puds, 20 funts of our wheat. It is divided into 12 *almudes*, or *celemines*.—Comp[iler's] n[ote].

---

[9]Chickpeas?

San Antonio								
[de Padua]	"	181	6	1	¾	0	½	½
	"	1,890	22	162	19	0	52	6
Nuestra Dama								
de Soledad	"	100	12	3	5	⅓	½	6
	"	100	290	400	24	6	36	110
San Carlos								
[Borromeo]	"	61	61	2	7	0	8	10
	"	642	900	8	70	0	120	238
San Juan								
Bautista	"	60	1	2	2	⅙	9	4
	"	1,600	14	200	4	9	13	0
Santa Cruz	"	14	0	1½	½	0	0	0
	"	700	0	700	200	0	0	0
Santa Clara	"	205	12	5	3	⅓	2	3
	"	3,450	150	800	170	3	130	190
San José	"	61	3	2	2	0	1	2
	"	3,000	107	170	78	0	16	76
San Francisco								
[de Asís]	"	210	180	½	3	½	3	9
	"	2,800	1,500	20	24	½	100	400
total sowing		2,875	787	105⁷⁄₁₂	69¼	5¹⁷⁄₂₄	43⁷⁄₁₂	55¹¹⁄₂₄
total harvest		42,089	10,533	15,690	1,627¹⁄₁₂	104¾	1,133	1,640

From this table it is evident that the yield of wheat was approximately 14½-fold, barley 13½-fold, corn 149-fold, beans 21-fold, peas 29-fold, and oats 29-fold [the seed].[10]

The highest yield of *wheat* was 50-fold at [Mission] Santa Cruz and 49-fold at [Mission] San José. The highest yield of *barley* was 33-fold at Mission Purísima, of *corn* 466-fold at [Mission] Santa Cruz and 160-fold at [Mission] Santa Clara, of *beans* 400-fold at [Mission] Santa Cruz, of *peas* 104-fold at [Mission] San Antonio and 100-fold at Mission Santa Inés, and of *oats* 45-fold at Mission San Francisco.

Even now Missions San José and Santa Cruz are considered the most productive.

Such was the harvest twenty-two years ago, at a time when the Indians, it can be said, worked under the lash for the missionaries; now, on account of the

---

[10]By comparison with Chernykh and Golovnin, De Roquefeuil reported an 1817 harvest at Alta California's missions of 52,001 fanegas of wheat, 22,354 of corn, and 18,895 of other crops, with an average yield of 23-fold (Rudkin, *Camille de Roquefeuil*, 72–73).

decline of the power of the latter, each Californio* owns the land that has been allotted to him and works it *for himself,* and for that reason the harvest should be more plentiful than before. In fact, not infrequently now it is possible to hear of harvests of wheat of 60-fold to 100-fold and of corn of 100-fold to 500-fold. It goes without saying that such harvests occur yearly among good farmers. The usual harvest of wheat can be safely put between 10[-fold] and 70[-fold].

The longtime Spanish settlers who came from Europe and Mexico are considered good farmers here. The latest generation pays little attention to cultivation.

The chief causes of harvest failures in Upper California are *rust,* which annually damages wheat, and *grasshoppers,* which sometimes eat standing wheat, frijoles, and other [crops]. Not infrequently in July and August *fire* set by the Indians destroys not only sown grain but all wild plants, so that there is no feed for livestock; the fires occur every year. It also happens that on rich soils grain lodges from overgrowth and becomes damp; this occurs seldom, however, because rain does not [usually] fall either during or after ripening.

How much is sown on a given amount of land? Not a single local farmer can answer this question satisfactorily. It should be noted that here they plant grain seeds far apart, so that when the field is covered with grain it is possible to walk through it without fear of trampling the sown grain. It is estimated that here no more than 4–6 puds of wheat are sown per desyatina.[11] Some farmers sow wheat by hand in plowed furrows and obtain a bumper harvest.

One is curious to know, of course, under what system of agric[ulture] do the Californios reap such plentiful harvests? If you ask a Californio this question, he will not understand what you have asked him; the time has not yet come for these fortunates to consider systems of agric[ulture]. Perhaps their distant descendants will be able to answer the proposed question?

In California they sow the same land until weeds prevail, and the harvest is always excellent. When the weeds proliferate, they leave it in pasture, provided there is something to take its place; if not, they assign the infested field to crops that are usually tilled frequently—corn, frijoles, peas, garbanzos, and others. The weeds among these crops are destroyed because several times during the summer the soil is plowed thoroughly and hilled [around the crops]. This [practice] resembles intercropping.

It has been said that in California the same land is sown several years running and not just two or three years and then fallowed; no, here they sow the same

---

*The Spanish Californians [Californios] call themselves *razónes* or *hombres de razón,* "thinking people," and the savage Indians *gentiles* ["gentiles" or "pagans"].—*Comp[iler's] n[ote].*

---

[11] I *desyatina* = 2.7 acres or 1.1 hectares.

land 5–10 years and more [in a row], and to wheat only, and they always obtain an excellent harvest, provided something unusual does not occur to harm growth. And besides, they never manure the fields. How does slime mold seem to have time to develop from dark soil* in order to yield so much? This is easily explained: one has only to remember that under the annual temperature here slime mold develops from dark soil uninterruptedly year-round, and for that reason it serves as an inexhaustible storehouse of plant food. This [process] is, in fact, what has been found.

The *chief market* for wheat from California has heretofore been our [Russian-] American colonies, which annually bought 3–4 thous[and] fanegas of wheat; the farmers turn the rest into flour and sell it here to American traders, who take it to Lower California, where the lack of water, the heat, and the frequent droughts do not favor cultivation.

After having achieved independence, Mexico allowed anyone to settle freely in California on land grants; one has only to become a citizen of the Mexican republic and a Catholic. Now, however, they are paying less attention to the latter condition. This freedom of settlement has attracted many Americans and Irishmen and some Germans and Frenchmen. Land 2 leagues* in length and 1 league in width is given to each settler. More than this amount is given to whomever has wealth. The granted land is called a *rancho*. Every rancho owner (ranchero) has the right to grow or rear anything on it that he finds profitable: grain and other crops, fruit trees, various livestock.

With the multiplication of ranchos, a way was opened of acquiring grain otherwise than from the missionaries, and at the same time the price of grain fell. One cannot suppose that sowings in general increased with the proliferation of ranchos; on the contrary, they must have declined. Now they plant almost nothing at the missions, where formerly 100–300 fanegas were sown, because all of the Indians, upon having their freedom proclaimed, left the missions and now engage in raiding; they rustle herds of horses from the *thinking people* and steal. With the multiplication of ranchos, only the monopoly of the missionaries was destroyed; it revived trade in grain and brought more benefits to all of the residents of the country. Formerly, when almost only the missionaries sowed and sold grain, wheat cost 3–4 Span[ish] piasters per fanega and then 2 piasters, and recently—namely, since 1838—the price has fluctuated constantly and has finally come to a halt at 1½ piasters per fanega.

Kurs s. kh. professora M. Pavlova [The course in agric. of Professor M. Pavlov], vol. 2, pp. 13 ff.—*Comp[iler's] n[ote]*.

*A league contains 5,000 Span[ish] varas or 1,986¾ Russ[ian] sazh[ens].—*Comp[iler's] n[ote]*.

Most of the rancheros, especially the less prosperous ones, refused to plant grain for sale at this price.

Of course, the price of 1½ piasters per fanega—i.e., 2 rub[les] per pud—is rather high, judging from the bumper yields; but the harvesting of grain, namely, reaping and threshing, is very dear because of the shortage of hands. It is possible to reconcile the Indians to working voluntarily but only for high pay—a piaster (5 rub[les]) a day—and despite this [rate], they will quit over the slightest discontent or compulsion. It often happens that a farmer, having lost hope of finding workers for the harvest, removes only the amount of grain that he needs for himself and discards the rest. Often a ranchero here will offer you a field of luxuriant wheat if you will gather it and give him only half of it!

Orcharding is undertaken in Upper California on a small scale. There are small orchards of fruit trees and vineyards at the missions only. When the orchards were under the control of the missionaries, they were properly maintained; but now, under the administrators, everything has been neglected and in some places destroyed. Whenever private individuals have orchards and vineyards, they are so insignificant as not to merit attention.

Here apples, pears, peaches, apricots, quinces, plums, and other [fruits] reach a considerable size. The fruit is generally coarse. Blue grapes—very tasty—are grown, and they yield abundantly. Grapevine cuttings are stuck into the ground, and some of them bear fruit in 3–4 years. The local grapes make good wine but in a small amount, and it does not keep well.

Many wild grapes are found along the banks of rivers and streams; their vines climb trees to a considerable height.

In this year of 1841 the prices of local output are as follows:

			piasters	*reals*
1	fanega of	wheat	1	4
1	"	barley	—	—
1	"	frijoles	2	4
1	"	corn	2	0
1	"	peas	2	0
1	"	garbanzos	2	4
1	Arroba* [of]	wheat flour	1½–2	4
1	"	cow's butter	12	4
1	"	dried meat	0	4–6
1	"	tallow	1	4

*1 Span. arroba = 28 of our fun[ts].— *Comp[iler's]* n[ote].

1	"	lard	2	0
1	"	Calif. Soap	12–14	0
1	"	onions	2	0
1	"	apples	2	0
1 large bull (12–20 puds)			5–8	0
1 raw cowhide			2	0
1 tanned cowhide			6–8	0
1 raw deerskin			1	0
1 raw goatskin			0	4
1 ordinary horse			8–10	0
1 " "per day [to hire]"			1	0
1 large pig			6–8	0
1 hen			0	4
1 ram			2	0
12 eggs			0	2
1 gallon of Calif[ornia] gra[pe] wine			3	0

The prices of local products change very seldom because of [unchanging] quality and quantity, as well as demand. If the above products are bought for goods, then they cost much less, especially if they are bought at the ranchos.

The small population is the reason why there are still no ranchos in the interior. The fear of attacks by the Indians forces the Californios to settle close to one another. In 1839 the first attempt at settlement on the Sacramento River, which flows into San Francisco Bay, was made. The Swiss Sutter, a retired captain in the French service, with several hired Hawaiians and Americans settled on the said river, and the settlement is called *New Helvetia*. It seems that this settlement was established mostly with a view to the Hudson's Bay Company, whose energetic trading parties roam constantly in all directions south of the Columbia River and now have frequent contacts with Sutter.

It ought to be regretted that this blessed country of California, which pampers a carefree people, is sparsely populated. The anarchy that prevails here under the guise of a republic and the excessive dearness of all goods because of high duties frighten a prudent man against deciding to settle here. Despite all of this [disincentive], many poor Irishmen, Englishmen, and Americans have found happiness in California, and many, many more unfortunates are anticipating it here!

Society Correspondent Ye. Chernykh.

12 January 1841.

Chernykh Rancho of the Russ. Amer. Comp. in Upper California.

DOCUMENT 29

Yegor Chernykh, "About Stockbreeding in Alta California," 1842

Yegor Chernykh, "About Stockbreeding in Alta California,"*[1] New Archangel, 8 April 1842

All along the coast to the south of the port of *Bodega* at different distances are scattered missions and *ranchos,* whose extensive surroundings, dissected by small rivers, sustain large herds of various domestic livestock.

The animals reared here are [as follows]: cattle, horses, mules, sheep, pigs, and a small number of goats.

Cattle

In California, cattle are the main basis of the wealth of the sedentary inhabitants. Here, in order to judge the wealth of a resident of California, they ask, *"How many thousand cattle does he have?"* Those who have more than three thousand head are considered wealthy.

---

*This interesting article, which acquaints us with the semicivilized state of our neighbors in North America, was sent to the editor with the following letter of 9 May 1843:

"In the summer of last year, together with our honorable superior [Governor Etolin], I was on Kodiak Island and in Kanar [Kenai] Inlet, with which I am hoping to acquaint you more closely in the future. Upon my return here I was sent on business to California, whence on the return route I nearly perished at sea 200 miles from the coast during a fierce *storm* in the dark night of 27 September. Our ship was swamped; four men were swept from the deck, and one was killed, and the captain [Nikolay Kadnikov] drowned or, more correctly, perished in the cabin, where we were both floundering in the floodwater, and only God's special mercy delivered me from the same fate. I wanted to die quickly; but God in His mercy saw fit to save me. In this pitiful state we arrived at New Archangel on 4 October."—*Ye. Chernykh.*

The editor is placing this letter in the *Journal of Agric[ulture].* with thanks to merciful Providence for preserving a valuable contributor.—*S. M[aslov].*

---

[1]Chernykh, "O skotovodstve."

Every local resident, after having accumulated the necessary amount of money for acquiring several cows for propagation, tries to establish a *rancho,* i.e., he asks the government for land for stock rearing and crop growing. A citizen owning a *rancho,* however poor he is in the beginning, ensures the future of his family; for a good farmer the establishment of a *rancho* is a sure means of enrichment. A favorable climate, land with succulent pasture, and hilly terrain with small valleys watered by streams of wholesome water greatly facilitate stockbreeding. In winter during the rains, cattle feed more in the hills, and in summer in low-lying places; wild clover [*Trifolium pratense*], which grows abundantly throughout California in the hills and lowlands, where it often reaches a height of 2 arsh[ins], wild oats [*Avena fatua*], bluegrass [*Poa pratensis*], timothy [*Phleum pratense*], and other grasses constitute the nutritious feed of cattle. During heavy rains most of the valleys here are drenched, the water draining only with the passing of winter; in these valleys, with the end of the rains, tall grasses grow, and they constitute an enormous supply of feed for cattle. Snow does not fall here; cattle are pastured year-round. They never stock hay, not even for calves; only at *Ross* do they make hay for calves, and this greatly astonishes the semicivilized Californios. Add to everything that has been said that here there are no mosquitoes, no midges, and no gadflies, except in a very few places, and you will have an idea of the comforts of this climate.[2]

The most abundant and succulent feed for cattle occurs from February until the middle of June, whereupon the grass withers. September, October, and November are the leanest months. Although some verdure occasionally occurs in November, provided rain falls in early October, the cattle attack it greedily and suffer from bloody flux. The cattle are really plump in June, *when the grass begins to dry out;* in October, November, and December they are at their thinnest.

When establishing a *rancho,* each farmer considers his first duty to be the making of a shelter: a hut of branches roofed with straw; in accordance with his enrichment, he afterwards builds a stone or wooden house. Then he drives home the cattle that he has bought; but they do not become used to their new locale quickly, and they always try to escape to their old one, however far away it is, and for that reason during the first months and even for a whole year the farmer watches the cattle closely. At first he rounds them up every day at a certain time; when the cattle become used to the locale, he rounds them up every one or two days and then once a week. They call the place [where the cattle are assembled] a *rodeo* [corral]. In order to accustom the cattle to the *rodeo* more quickly, there they sometimes erect knotty posts on which the cattle can rub themselves, and they become so used to this place that with the first call from the herders at the

---

[2]Chernykh was a native of Siberia (Kamchatka), where *gnusy* (various and myriad biting insects) were commonplace.

appearance of an animal and with each alarm they run bellowing toward the *rodeo,* crowding together and milling around.

When establishing a new *rancho* the most difficult matter is accustoming the cattle to the *rodeo,* and it is always necessary to persevere in this. Cattle that do not know the *rodeo* consider themselves lost; they become wild, and at the first appearance of anybody they run and hide, so that it is almost impossible to catch them. Here they judge a *ranchero*'s diligence by the degree to which his cattle are used to the *rodeo.* Disreputable is the farmer about whom they say, *He has cattle that do not know the rodeo!*"

I am assured that cattle, even after the lapse of several years, do not forget their native fields. The cattle make more effort to escape to their birthplace with the appearance of new grass; then, as it were, they recall the home grass on which they were reared. Cattle here multiply very fast; heifers almost always calve before the age of two years (at 18 months). The local cows bear twins fairly often; during my 6 years at Ross this happened three times among 500 cows.

Epidemics, or cattle plagues [murrain], never occur here. Cattle die more from a lack of feed after *fires,* especially young calves, which are [also] killed in considerable numbers by wolves and coyotes (jackals); only in places where bears are accustomed to [eating] meat do they also prey somewhat on cattle.

The principal supervision of cattle consists entirely of the above. They build neither barnyards nor cowsheds; the cattle pass their whole life under the open sky. In heat and in rain they take shelter under a tree, and where there are no trees they all move to an open field. One has only to buy several cows in the beginning, watch them in order that they do not become wild, and *live;* nature does the rest: the cattle multiply, and the ranchero soon grows rich. For his part he needs only to do a little tending; the cattle feed themselves and breed.

One poor ranchero, who had betrothed his daughter, gave her a cow as a dowry, and she had 11 head from it in 5 years. Experienced local farmers assure me that if one buys 100 cows, then after 5 years under favorable conditions one can have an increase (inclusive) of 1,000 head, or 800 head under unfavorable conditions, for an average, therefore, of 900 head. There is no fixed ratio between the number of studs (bulls) and cows; some keep 30 for 100 cows, others keep 20, still others keep 10, and a few keep only 5. It has been noticed that more bulls are born when many bulls are kept, and vice versa.

At the end of the rains, usually in May, they brand, castrate, and count the cattle; they sear the brand onto the hind leg, and if they sell the cattle, then they usually put the brand of the former owner on the front legs of the sold stock. After two years, bulls designated for draft are castrated, whereupon they develop thick, strong necks; others are castrated a year earlier.

The products of livestock in California are [as follows]: hides, tallow, lard, and beef.

The hide is flayed from a slaughtered animal in the usual way, and then it is stretched with small stakes and dried in the sun; it is sold in this form. The backbone with the head, neck, horns, hoofs, and guts of the slaughtered animal are discarded; for food they keep only the front and hind legs, ribs, breastbone, and tongue, and everything else is thrown away to rot in a field.

Usually they obtain up to 3 arrobas (2 puds, 4 f[unts]) of tallow from each animal, provided it is killed at the right time; the fattest animal yields 5 and 6 arrobas (3 p[uds], 20 f[unts] to 4 p[uds], 8 f[unts]). I do not know whether our butchers distinguish internal from external fat. Here external fat [lard] is called *manteca* and is used in place of butter in all kitchens. Actually, good, pure manteca differs little from kitchen butter. In all of our colonies, manteca is much in use and takes the place of butter; many promyshlenniks eat it like butter with bread. They usually obtain from ½ to 1 arroba of manteca and sometimes more from one animal.

Both tallow and manteca are kept in bags of cowhide and deerskin. A bag, irregularly sewn from a whole hide, is filled with melted tallow or manteca and then stitched tightly and put in a cool place in order for the tallow or manteca to harden. In this form they keep the tallow and manteca and put it on the market. Formerly, bags of tallow were accepted by buyers without inspection, but now one must be vigilant: dishonest rancheros have begun to put sand in the middle of the bags to increase their weight.

Because the bulls live constantly with the cows, calving occurs irregularly; but most cows calve in February, March, and April, the very best time because of the abundance of feed.

The best time for *slaughtering cattle* (*tiempo de matanza*) for tallow, manteca, and hides is June, when they are plump; the Californios kill cattle in other months only out of necessity and for the home. For them, slaughtering, branding, and castrating times are benchmarks; they often say, "[T]his happened at slaughtering time, branding time, etc." The branding and castrating of cattle usually occur earlier than slaughtering because, firstly, then there are fewer flies and, secondly, the cattle, being in better condition then, more easily endure all operations. Most cattle designated for slaughtering are old, castrated bulls and barren cows, as well as old, castrated studs called *toruños* [?]. Cattle designated for slaughtering are separated from the herd and locked in a pen or pastured near the *rodeo*. Most rich owners slaughter their cattle in the *rodeo* itself, and, despite the wildness of the cattle, the animals do not scatter but run around the *rodeo*.* Then the vaqueros

*How foolish!—[*Ed.?*]

catch them with lassos, throw them onto the ground, and cut their throats. From the slaughtered animals they take the hides, tallow, and manteca; and they take only the very best parts of the beef, leaving the rest to whomever wants it. As much as their time and strength allow, they at the same time dry the beef in the sun; beforehand they cut it into thin strips, which, after having been dipped in brine, are hung in the sun.

Annually up to 10 trading vessels—almost exclusively American—ply the Californian coast and buy up all of the hides and tallow and part of the manteca; for everything they pay the residents in goods at the highest prices. The usual price of a large cowhide is 2 piasters; but an American always pays for a hide in goods, never in piasters. Piasters are rarely given as cash for hides. The price of tallow is almost always 2–3 piasters per arroba, and of manteca 2 piasters. The Americans improve the collected hides, cleaning them of bits of meat and then salting them, i.e., immersing them in a vat of brine for a while; after having been removed, the hides are dried in the sun and loaded onto a ship.

In 1842 the price of a cow and a large bull was 5–7 piasters, and of one- and two-year-old heifers and bullocks 2–4 piasters.

In a few places in California many tame domestic cattle have gone wild [feral], especially in forested and mountainous localities. A few indolent farmers have whole wild herds, from which it is impossible to derive any profit. They reckon that the cattle that are at risk of going wild are old studs and cows, which are always trying to separate and not infrequently take a considerable part of the herd with them, and for that reason they [i.e., the Californios] always kill old studs, as well as in general cattle that often leave the herd; they do the same to cattle that bolt during drives to the *rodeo*. I know one family in California that has up to 4 t[housand] cattle but suffers from hunger; their cattle have gone wild.

The local cattle are handsome and strapping, with huge horns [i.e., longhorns].

Three-year-olds usually weigh 8–10 pud[s] and old bulls 15 and even more than 20 pud[s] (of beef only, of course). Some cows live more than 30 years.

Horses

It is difficult to determine the actual breed of horses reared here. It has been written that all of the horses reared in America are of the Spanish breed. In California one often encounters horses that differ little from stud horses not only in beauty but also in build [points] and size; of course, they are not as well broken as our stud horses. Their lightness and strength can be judged from the fact that with all of their harness, plus heavy saddles and riders, they [can] overtake wild deer, bears, and even goats. Very often 70–90 verstas are covered in one day on the same horse. It is remarkable that here almost every horse always runs at a gallop; one encounters many amblers but very few trotters. The color of most of the local horses is bay, generally reddish.

Just like the cattle, the horses rear themselves; the tending is identical. Usually the herd is divided into two groups: mares with several stallions, and geldings, or saddle horses. Mares and stallions are almost never used for riding; the whole purpose of their existence is breeding. Only they, too, thresh grain. By contrast, the hapless riding horses bear the whole burden of service. Ordinarily hay is not made for either cattle or horses; only saddle horses are occasionally fed barley in summer by some farmers.

Good farmers in both the New World and the Old take care of their animals. Unfortunately, either cheapness or simply negligence is the reason why in California the saddle horses of most farmers are in pitiful condition, especially during the heat of summer; the unfortunate horse is almost always saddled the whole day, and sometimes even during the night, and it must stand tethered in the sun without feed or water. It is frightful to speak about their backs; the cruel vaqueros look without pity at the wounds made by the nasty saddle to the animal's back, and they continue to torment it until it dies. And the better the horse, the more torment it suffers; everyone wants to ride a good horse—rest assured!

For a Californio a horse is the first necessity, after food; without a horse, he is not himself. Being accustomed from childhood to horseback riding renders him incapable of even a short journey on foot; if he has to go a versta from his home, a Californio will mount a horse without fail.

The value of a horse depends upon its quality and beauty. The usual price of a good horse is 10–30 piasters; middling ones sell for 5–9 piast[ers]. The best horse costs from 100 to 150 piast[ers]; but a buyer will always pay in goods and rarely agree to pay in cash, so that a horse that costs 100–150 piast[ers] in goods is worth 50–75 p[iasters] [in cash].

Horses were never exported from California. Only recently have a few been shipped to Manila; at first they are hauled to the Sandwich Islands, where they are fattened after the ocean voyage, and forwarded to Manila. I am assured that a good Californian horse is worth from 200 to 400 piasters in Manila. Manila's own horses are small. The Hudson's Bay Company also sometimes buys horses and cattle here and drives them along the coast to its possessions on the Columbia River.

During the last decade [i.e., the 1830s] the number of horses in California declined considerably. The emancipated Indians, fully aware of the weakness and impotence of the Californios, withdrew to their primeval dwellings; they began to raid the *ranchos* and drive away the horses. Along the southern side of San Francisco Bay the Indians drove off almost all of the horses; where thousands once grazed, now not a hundred are seen. At present it is even difficult to pass along the coast from San Francisco to Monterey, on account of the shortage of horses.

The Indians partly sell the stolen horses to Hudson's Bay Company [fur] traders, and partly they themselves eat them. I am assured that these horses even go as far as the United States.

The main aim of the raids of the Indians, by their own admission, is the following: they know very well that all of the opposing power of the Californios consists of horses. From the beginning the savages decided to drive away their horses and [thereby] weaken them. When the Californios have no horses, then it will be easy to take away and drive off their cattle, too. Thus, after having deprived the Californios of all of their livelihood, the Indians hope to dominate them. This policy is fairly sound.

The Indians who formerly lived at the missions are generally all excellent riders: half naked, without saddles, and with bows and arrows on their backs and lassos in their hands they race rapidly after their prey! The word *vaquero* properly means a herder, a cowboy, from the word *vaqua* [*sic: vaca*], "cow." But it is much closer in meaning to "express rider"; whether he has to catch a horse, drive cattle, kill livestock, or go somewhere—a vaquero will do so without fail. The vaquero breaks young horses and trains young bulls. He watches cattle, and for that reason his duty is the hardest; daily, and often at night, he is in the saddle. The Indian raiders are almost all former mission vaqueros. The cruel treatment of the Indians by the Spaniards and their violence have revived the extreme hatred of the former for the latter.

There are many wild—more correctly, feral—horses in California. For a long time, runaway herds of horses have gone quite wild, and they have now multiplied to a large number, especially opposite Monterey, far from the coast on open, level expanses. The shortage of tame horses now forces the Californios to make trips to catch wild horses. The wild horses are very strapping but slim and wiry. While hunting them the Californios greatly fear the stallions, which attack their pursuers. The wild horses try to unite with the herds of tame horses, and when they have mingled, the Californios drive them to an enclosure built for this purpose; then they capture them with lassos.

They make pretty reins here from horsehair; and they make lassos from cowhide.

[Other Livestock]

Besides horses, *mules* are reared in considerable numbers in California, and they are used almost exclusively for hauling heavy objects. The price of a mule or hinny is higher than that of an ordinary horse; they sell for 12–15 piasters.

SHEEP. The sheep reared here have fairly coarse wool;[3] with the abolition of the missions, i.e., missionary ownership, sheep breeding nearly disappeared. Formerly the missionaries forced the Indians to make serapes and blankets from wool and then sold them; now serapes are made in only a very few places. Nobody buys wool and sheepskins here; American ships buy only an insignificant amount of wool, strictly for their own needs. From sheepskins the Californios make suede. (?[—*Ed.*])

The sheep graze year round, and all winter here they are under the open sky; during the day they are killed by coyotes (jackals), and at night they are locked in a pen. Their most dangerous enemy is the coyote. The usual price of ewes and rams is a piaster.

GOATS are kept for enjoyment only. The Californios cover their legs with goat fleeces [chaps] while riding in muddy conditions. I am assured that a goat, when put in a herd of sheep, will not mingle and that goats always keep an orderly herd, not letting it scatter, etc., and for that reason goats here always graze and live with sheep.

VERY FEW *PIGS* ARE REARED; they cause more harm than good. I doubt that there is a more carefree place in the world for pigs than California; here they eat primarily the beef that is discarded in the fields after cattle are slaughtered, watermelons, pumpkins, muskmelons, potatoes, and various wild roots. The pork is very tasty but extremely fatty. Here almost nobody at all eats pork; they keep pigs to sell to ships. The usual price of a pig is 4–10 piasters.

[*Stockbreeding*]

These are all of the four-legged animals that are reared in California.

Everyone will note from this description what little benefit is derived from stockbreeding in California; only tallow, manteca, and hides have any value. How much butter could California sell in the United States and elsewhere! Because of its small population, of course, California cannot make much butter for sale now; but on account of the indolence of the Californios, they do not even have butter for themselves. They have always pressed us to sell them butter from Ross for 4 reals a pound! Many will not believe that when you pass through a *rancho*, which has more than a thousand cows, and ask for milk or butter, you will be told with a smile of surprise, ["W]e *do not have these items, we do not milk cattle*!["]

The excellent pasture, the location, and the favorable climate offer every convenience for sheep breeding and viticulture; but it will hardly occur to us to open a vessel of Californian wine or to wear cloth made from the wool of Californian

---

[3]The Alta California breed of sheep was the *churro,* a small animal that provided inferior lamb and mutton and thin, coarse wool.

sheep. This uncommon, blessed land will not reach its fitting degree of well-being for a long—very long—time yet, especially under the present sway of a vainglorious and half-educated people. We must wish it a better fate! . . .

It is certainly difficult to determine the number of livestock in California; one can only say that it has decreased greatly since the time [i.e., 1821] of Mexico's independence from Spain. The self-interest of the administrators and governors sent from Mexico and the anarchy—these are the main causes of this decrease. There have been many examples recently of the governors out of cupidity ordering the slaughter of thousands of cows solely for their hides and tallow. Thus, at Mission Santa Clara recently up to 1,000 pregnant cows were slaughtered! There were plenty of cattle at Mission San José last year, when all vaqueros were invited for the slaughter, and out of every three slaughtered animals two had to remain the property of the mission and the third was given to a vaquero for his work. The vast fields were covered with the carcasses and awash in the blood of the hapless animals! Of course, if the number of cattle has decreased at the missions, and they have disappeared completely from some, then in exchange private cattle breeding [at the ranchos] has increased at the expense of the missions, but not nearly in the same proportion as mission cattle breeding has decreased.

(To be continued).[4]

Ye. Chernykh.
8 April 1842.
New Archangel.

---

[4]The translator has not found any sequel in subsequent issues of the same journal: perhaps it was never written (Chernykh not having had time to do so before his death sixteen months later), or it was written but not accepted or even dispatched, or it was written and published elsewhere.

DOCUMENT 30

Excerpt from Alexander Markov's Recollections of California, [ca. 1845]

EDITOR'S INTRODUCTION

Most Russian accounts of Alta California were impersonal official documents. A very few, such as the following memoir by a Russian-American Company employee, were travel accounts written in a light, informal style for the general public, whose attention had been attracted to recent tumultuous events in California, which had gone from a Mexican province to a Bear Flag Republic to an American state in just a few years (although the turmoil is rather belied by the memoir, which describes pastoral tranquility). The interest of Russian readers was further aroused by their awareness of the longtime presence of the Russian-American Company in California (and the belief on the part of some of them that in withdrawing the firm had overlooked a golden opportunity).

Markov's account describes his overland journey across Siberia to Okhotsk and his voyages from there to Sitka, from Sitka to the Californias, from there back to Sitka, and from Sitka back to Siberia via Ayan, with ethnographic sketches of the "Aleuts" and Tlingits, descriptions of life at Sitka and in the Californias, and the prospects of Russia's Pacific trade. The California section is apparently based upon his experiences there in the late summer–early autumn of 1845, for he identifies himself as a member of the crew of the company ship *Naslednik Aleksandr* [*Alexander's Heir*], which visited San Francisco at that time—and at the same time, moreover, as the company brigs *Veliky Knyaz Konstantin* [*Grand Duke Constantine*] and *Baikal*—in order to fetch the wheat that had been acquired for the company by its Californian agent and to collect the debts owed the company by sundry Californios, notably General Sutter for the purchase of Fort Ross; they were also to go to Baja California to buy salt. The attempts to collect Sutter's debt and to purchase salt were both unsuccessful. However, Markov also recalls that he visited Alta California "several times," so his impressions may be partially composite, too.

AL. MARKOV,[1] RECOLLECTIONS OF CALIFORNIA,[2] [MOSCOW?], [1854–55?]
The Eastern [Pacific] Ocean

How unexpected was my happiness when we learned that the ship [i.e., the *Naslednik Aleksandr*] was going to California [from New Archangel], to the land which has been recounted so glowingly and which on the gloomy island of Sitka—inhabited by coarse, ignorant people—I imagined to be an earthly paradise.

The day came when we had to go to sea. Joy was written on each of our faces. How fast and well did the work aboard ship go! Each sailor consoled himself with the thought that his labor would be rewarded at the first tavern in California.

The ship's command consisted of 25 sailors from the navy and another 5 employees of the Russian-American Company, 30 men altogether. We unfurled the sails and gave the fort of New Archangel a seven-gun salute, and under our pennant with a full breeze our ship bore to the south. In the evening from the ship's stern we took a parting look at our former dismal abode, which appeared as a black streak in the distance. It was dark there, and menacing clouds hung over the island that we had left.

. . . .[3]

---

[1]Aleksandr Ivanovich Markov (18??–1853?) was evidently a Moscow *meshchanin* (lower-to-middle class burgher) on his mother's side and a serf from the village of Antipin in the Galich District of Kostroma Province on his father's side. In 1838 he entered the employ of the Russian-American Company and was assigned to its fleet as a supercargo, serving chiefly on the *Nikolay I* plying the "Kolosh trade" in the "straits" of the Alexander Archipelago. Aleksandr was sent back to Russia in the spring of 1846 at the request of his peasant father. However, he seems to have soon rejoined the company and returned to Russian America, where he stayed until, presumably, the expiration of his contract in 1853, when he was scheduled to leave. See Grinëv, *Kto yest kto*, 332; and Pierce, *Russian America*, 342. Also see RRAC, roll 15, doc. 400, fol. 403, doc. 523, fol. 532v., doc. 540, fols. 603–03v; roll 48, doc. 328, fols. 294v–95; roll 50, doc. 512, fol. 193v, doc. 160, fols. 311v–12; roll 51, doc. 222, fol. 129; roll 59, doc. 349, fols. 365–65v.

[2]Markov, *Russkie na Vostochnom okeane*, 102–81. This account was first published in Moscow in 1849, three years after the author's return from his first spell in Russian America. First it was serialized in the periodical *Moskvityanin* and then issued as a monograph. His book was republished in St. Petersburg in 1856 (and again in 1876) in a second, revised and enlarged, edition. The California section, which is twice as long in the second and third editions as in the first edition, was originally translated by the notorious Ivan Petroff, a discredited translator and researcher for H. H. Bancroft and the U.S. government in the late 1800s (see Owens, "Magnificent Fraud"; Pierce, "Note on 'Ivan Petroff'"; and Pierce, "New Light") and published with a foreword by Arthur Woodward in Los Angeles in 1956 in a limited edition of 300 copies by Glen Dawson as volume 27 of his Early California Travel Series, now long out of print. Petroff's translation is excessively figurative and frequently imaginative, with infelicities and embellishments—and sometimes outright mistranslations (or falsifications).

[3]An extraneous conversation among the sailors about boozing is omitted here.

Evening fell; the weather was fine, the wind was steady and favorable, from the cloudless sky the moon reflected its languid face in the rippling waves, and the loud songs of the sailors, mixed with the muted noise of the sea, reminded each of them of his homeland; my dreams carried me far away, and imperceptibly I fell asleep on deck.

By morning our ship was already 160 miles from the island of Sitka, and every day found us closer to California. The air became warmer and balmier. On the fourteenth day of our voyage the navigator reported to the commander that a sailor had died.

They put the body in sailcloth, tied two cannon balls to its feet, and pushed it overboard.

"Well, mate, you were just sick of hardtack," said one sailor, perched on the railing of the ship so as to receive the body; "Good lord, how he has put on weight; it'll be four puds. Well, say farewell to this world. Ooh, how smartly he plunged to visit Leptune,* it seems he smelled the vodka.

"The time will come, lads, when we will plunge there, too.

"What's to be done! . . . but then there's room . . . . Ugh, lads, what a fog is coming; I suppose Spain is nearby; a wall of fog always stands by its coast."

Actually, we were 80 miles from San Francisco, the northernmost settlement of the Californios in New [Alta] California.[4] But, not seeing the coast because it was covered with an impenetrable fog, we did not dare to proceed to the harbor by dead reckoning alone; in addition, we were afraid of the strong current on this coast carrying the ship irresistibly into a bay that would be difficult to exit. Not having even taken a midday observation, we were forced to tack impatiently for a whole week in the thick fog.

Finally, to starboard the Farallon rocks were [now] seen and then again covered with fog, but we succeeded in taking a bearing from them and determined the position of the harbor. We decided to attempt it; we put out extra sail and after more than 6 hours found ourselves in a very critical position, hearing how the breakers roared in striking the rocky faces of the shore, but it was not visible to us. The commander's courage and experience guaranteed our success from the beginning; he ordered that the anchor be readied just in case, measured the depth, and heard which side the waves struck harder. Suddenly a broad harbor opened ahead of us with many ships of various nations. With the innate bravery of Russians, in sight of all of the foreigners we went under two sails with a fresh

---

*Thus was Neptune called by the sailors. When a ship crosses the Equator, the sailors make a presentation in honor of this mythological divinity.

---

[4]In fact, at this time Sonoma (est. 1835) was the province's northernmost town.

breeze straight through the middle of the strait [Golden Gate] into the long bay of San Francisco, leaving the unsteady wall of the fog behind us, made a turn among the ships, and dropped anchor.

"Well done, Russians!" shouted someone from an American brig.

It was clear in the harbor, but the sun was already starting to set and with its weak rays was illuminating a grove of laurel trees on the right shore. The aroma of fragrant grasses and flowers spread throughout the extensive bay; distant from each other in the picturesque landscapes around the bay were scattered the ranchos of the Californios, and between them stretched green meadows and valleys with grazing sheep, cattle, horses, and mules, and somewhere in the distance wild geese honked.

On the left shore of the bay stood handsomely built little wooden houses; from them, I noticed with a telescope, peeped the pretty faces of Californian women. Beyond the settlement a high green mountain with small bushes was visible; on it was running a pronghorn,[5] and an adroit Californio was lassoing a bull.

After a long stay on a barren island [Baranof Island], in the midst of savages, where everything was dead, monotonous, and lifeless, how agreeable it was to me to find myself in this lush land, lavishly endowed with all the gifts of nature.

Long did I feast my eyes on the shores of California; finally I noticed that a small boat with three Californios was sailing directly to our ship from the settlement of Yerba Buena, where the captain of the port and the American consul live.

We had anchored not far from the left shore close to the new mission,[6] or the settlement of Yerba Buena, which is found six verstas from San Francisco; the boat approached us, and from it came two men in striped serapes and patent leather black hats with broad brims, with *pajitos*[7] in their teeth. They looked pompously at the ship and spoke in Spanish, which none of us understood except a few sailors, but they were busy doing necessary work in the bay. There was a silence, which turned into laughter; finally one of us said in English, "What would you like?" They answered in English, too, and we invited them to the captain's cabin, where they tried to display their smartness[8] with scraping and bowing and courteous movements, as was their custom.

---

[5]Here and later Markov uses the term *zebra*, which is likely a misprint for *zubr*, the European bison. The North American bison was widespread on the continent at the time of European contact, although it is unlikely to have been found in the vicinity of San Francisco Bay in the middle 1840s. The word *zub* means "tooth," but it can also mean "horn" or "prong," so Markov may have been referring to the pronghorn, which also boasts a couple of zebra-like white stripes on its neck. Another possibility is the elk.

[6]Presumably Markov is referring to Mission San Francisco de Asís (also known as Mission Dolores), although it was then an old (est. 1776), not a new, mission. It had been secularized in 1835 and ordered to be sold in 1845. Markov implies that it had just been renovated or rebuilt or even relocated closer to Yerba Buena.

[7]Cigarettes rolled with corn husks instead of paper.

[8]Russ., *lovkost*.

Our captain[9] was a young and educated man; he received them very cordially and asked them to explain what they required of us. "We are customs officials," said one of the Californios, "sent by the captain of the port in accordance with the regulation here to inspect your ship, [to determine] its dimensions and goods, and [to see] whether or not you have from our governor, who resides in Monterey, written permission for the right to trade, for without that permission you cannot trade here. For this reason one of us must stay here."

"Gentlemen, I allow you to examine the ship," answered the captain; "We have no goods whatsoever, except those brought for the command on the voyage, and I do not have permission for the right to trade from your governor, because I did not stop at Monterey, for very good reason. As security for the fact that until the governor permits it we will not commence any trade here, my word only is sufficient. So I do not permit you to be here as inspectors, because that would be an insult to our Russian honor."

The Californios, after having listened to this monologue without saying a word, took their leave respectfully and went ashore.

The next day the commander and I [as supercargo] went to the Californios' settlement for talks with the captain of the port [William Richardson].[10] His house was built on a knoll and enclosed by a palisade. [As we were] approaching the captain's house, we saw a very pretty, lively, smart girl of fifteen years of age leaving it. She met us as if we were longtime acquaintances, took the commander by the arm, and talked to him in Spanish. We did not understand Spanish, but from her gestures we guessed what she had said; the sailor walking behind us who knew Spanish interpreted that she was inviting us to the home of the captain, her father.[11]

We purposefully went somewhat quietly; it was pleasing to us to look at our pretty companion, especially after those horrible painted [Tlingit] faces that had constantly surrounded us at Sitka. She noticed our attention and began with a smile to say something in Spanish, and with a wagging finger she warned the sailor walking behind us not to interpret.

Finally, we found ourselves at the very threshold of the captain's house and went straight into a large room, where at first glance we were presented with a richly ornamented bed.

[9]Either Lieutenant Pyotr Velichkovsky (1844) or Lieutenant Aleksandr Rudakov (1845) (see RRAC, roll 48, doc. 605, fols. 441v–443v and roll 51, doc. 56, fols. 261v–263v).

[10]William Antonio Richardson (1795–1856), an Englishman, arrived in Alta California in 1822 aboard a whaler. He became a trader and a pilot. From 1841, he lived at Sausalito, where ships commonly watered, and served as port captain until 1844. See [Bancroft], *California Pioneer Register,* 302. Also see Miller, *Captain Richardson.*

[11]Here Markov is presumably referring to Captain Richardson's daughter, Mariana, who would have been eighteen years old in 1844.

For Californios a bed is the principal adornment of a house. In their houses, dry clay is in place of a floor, but to compensate for it one's attention was attracted to the splendid bed with long, superbly adorned pillows.

There was fine furniture in the port captain's house; he himself was sitting on a divan behind a large red table and reading some thick book.

When we entered, he arose smartly, bowed to us, and asked us in English to seat ourselves in the armchairs standing near the divan, and he himself went into the opposite room, which was more like a summer house [lanai?].

After a minute he returned with a book in English in his hands and began to read the regulation on the right to trade within the limits of San Francisco.

We ourselves knew very well that a ship did not have the right to enter San Francisco Bay without first having stopped at Monterey and obtained permission for the right to trade from [Alta] California's governor, who resided there permanently. But we did not want to go to Monterey by ship, because San Francisco lay closer to our course; moreover, it was surrounded by the settlements where we had to buy wheat, frijoles, peas, corn, meat, tallow, *manteca* [lard] (pure tallow, which can be eaten on bread instead of butter), etc., for the island of Sitka. Furthermore, it was possible to reach Monterey from San Francisco by ship in one day, but for the trip back to San Francisco from Monterey one had to spend three weeks or more on account of the usual contrary current and the constantly adverse NW winds.

Thus, in order not to go to Monterey we resorted to stratagem: we had deliberately lowered the main topgallant mast, as if it had been broken by a storm, and we told the captain of the port that without repairing the mast we could not go to Monterey and intended to mend it here, and we asked him to allow us to ride by land to the governor's in Monterey to obtain permission there for the right to trade and to pay the duty for anchorage, which for our ship in Russian money was 1,666 paper rub[les], 66 k[opecks].[12]

The reason for our coming [to talk to the port captain] was very valid. We paid the anchorage fee to the captain of the port; he wrote a report to the governor in which he stated that a Russian naval vessel had arrived in San Francisco Bay to buy provisions for the Russian colonies but could not proceed to Monterey without prolonged and significant repairs, so that, after having paid the anchorage fee at the port of Yerba Buena, it requested permission for the right to trade within the limits of San Francisco. The packet was sent by express to the governor in Monterey; we thanked the captain of the port for the kindness shown to us and went back to the ship.

---

[12]In 1845 1 silver ruble equalled 3½ paper rubles.

Within 2 days we received permission from the governor of [Alta] California, Don Castro,[13] to buy in cash but not to sell or barter any of our goods without paying a special duty.

California

Let us turn now to the land that is still so little known to us but that now occupies such an important place in the industrial world. I am speaking of California.

The first settlement, where our ship stopped, was Yerba Buena. *Yerba Buena,* or *New Mission,* consists of small houses arranged in various directions on San Francisco Bay, whose waters during high tide come quite close to the buildings.

Here there is no landing, and rowing vessels always approach the spot where the shore is somewhat steeper than elsewhere; nevertheless, it is inconvenient to land from jolly-boats[14] without deploying ladders, not to mention other, larger vessels, which, on account of the sandbank here, must remain some distance offshore.

The first building that struck our eyes when we went ashore and ascended the knoll was a tavern. Its keeper, a Frenchman, had once served in Napoleon's army. He began—very *mal à propos*—to tell us about his triumphant campaign in Russia.

"And what is this?" one of us asked, looking at a cheap popular print from Moscow stuck on the wall and showing a caricature of the French withdrawal from Moscow. This comrade of Napoleon had decorated the small room of his famous tavern as if to display his penchant for boasting. How unamusing was this occasion, and my thoughts carried me far, far across the seas and snowy steppes to white-stoned Moscow. Twenty thousand verstas separated me from it . . . and the Russian flag was waving proudly on the faraway coast of California!

[After] descending the knoll to a little hollow, we encountered another tavern, much larger than the first. Its manager was a Swede who, as he himself related, [had] left his homeland because of his wicked wife. Now he is content with his lot and his business is thriving, the clinking of glasses not ceasing from morning until late at night. In choosing this hollow as the site of his residence, as if in order that his tiresome helpmate would not disturb the peace and quiet of his life, the Swede had a purpose in mind: to have the opportunity to unite the calling of publican and the occupation of smuggler, for the first duty of the sailors coming ashore from the ships was to visit the tavern—and namely, this very one, being

[13]José Castro (ca. 1810–60) had been active in provincial politics from the 1830s as a staunch supporter of the aspirations of the Californios, opposing the outsiders appointed by Mexico City, as well as the foreign settlers, leading part of the military resistance against the American invaders. He fled to Mexico in 1846, returned in 1848, and went back to Mexico in 1853, becoming military commander of Baja California in 1856. See [Bancroft], *California Pioneer Register,* 91–92.

[14]Russ., *yalboty.*

hidden from the eyes of the shipping authorities and affording them complete freedom—to conduct the sale of the goods brought by them in their ships.

Across a small meadow in a straight line from the Swedish tavern stood a handsomely built house with a porch and a picket fence. Two friends, both Germans, lived here. They had once served as sailors on an American whaler, but the wandering seafaring life, too unsettling for their propensity for a sedentary life, had got on their nerves, and they had decided to settle permanently in California, marry Californias, raise children, breed ducks, chickens, and geese, and live in complete contentment. After having chosen a most profitable trade in this quarter, namely, tailoring, they made themselves known to all of the surrounding ranchos, and since there were only two of them among a fairly large number of inhabitants, our Germans were up to their ears in work and making a handsome profit from it. Thus, e.g., for embroidered trousers in the Spanish style one has to pay them 10 piasters, not to mention the heavy, coarse cloth that fetches a high price. Once I saw, namely, in the Swede's tavern, how one sailor sold a yard of dark blue cloth for 5 piasters; the cloth was rather coarse, and for Russians it would cost no more than 6 pa[per] rub[les] per arshin. This increase in prices is not at all surprising, judging how poor California is in manufactures.

Not far from the house of the tailors a mill was being built by an English settler. He has chosen an extremely beneficial industrial undertaking for these parts because the Californios have neither wind nor water mills with large millstones. Some very few have small hand mills, but most residents of California grind flour by means of two flat stones. Can you imagine how much flour one man [can] grind in this way in one day?—no more than is needed at one sitting for one Russian cabby in Kolomna. For this reason, in California, with the nearly legendary growing of wheat, flour is costly. There a small loaf, half the size of our French bread,[15] costs 1 real, that is, a piaster fetches 8 small loaves, and even then it is not readily to be had.

Here a certain American must also be mentioned. He came to California with 5 piasters and was an ordinary worker, but now he has a well-stocked store full of at least 20 t[housand] piasters' worth of sundry goods. He buys contraband cargo from arriving vessels, entertains various political opinions, and recently received the title of American consul![16]

Once I happened to do a little business with him. I sold 50 ar[shins] of white Flemish linen to him for 20 piasters, 2 puds of Virginia leaf tobacco for 40 piasters, and 5 pairs of calf-leather boots for 25 piasters.

---

[15]French, or German, bread was fine wheat bread from a bakery.

[16]Presumably Thomas Oliver Larkin (1802–58), who arrived in Alta California in 1832 and opened a general store in 1833 in Monterey. In 1845 he was appointed the first U.S. consul to California. See [Bancroft], *California Pioneer Register*, 214–15. Also see Hague, *Thomas O. Larkin*; and Hammond, *Larkin Papers*.

Incidentally, about tobacco and hides. The demand for smoking tobacco in California is the same as ours for tea. From the young to the old, even including the female sex, everyone there smokes tobacco, but then a very high duty is imposed on it. Some of the residents of California have tried to cultivate tobacco on their ranchos; it grows, but its quality—probably for some physical [environmental] reason—cannot at all compare to the tobacco grown on the eastern seaboard of North America.[17]

As to hides, on account of their abundance they constitute the primary and common enterprise in California, but only in raw form. The Californios do not have tanneries and cannot process the raw hides as well as we do, so our tanned leather is highly esteemed in California, especially anything sewn from it, such as boots, shoes, saddlecloths,[18] etc. The lack of skilled shoemakers can be considered another reason. During my time at Yerba Buena, San Francisco, and other surrounding places I did not chance to meet a single master boot maker in the full sense of this term. In some homes I occasionally saw someone engaged in sewing boots or shoes—rather flimsy and coarse—and lackadaisically and apparently for themselves only. Add to this the everlasting enemy of everything that is possible in the world of work—laziness.

The finest house of all has been built near the store of the American consul, who lives in it. He is punctual to the highest degree, serious, proud, and without equal in all of this new settlement. The rear of his house faces a kind of courtyard. In the middle of it stands an empty long, low, wooden barracks, and at its doors there are two small brass cannons that are turning a little green [from verdigris]. At this guarded place of the settlement of Yerba Buena you will never meet a single soldier.

On the left side of the barracks an English company is building a large stone trading house. It is impossible not to be surprised by the indefatigable and energetic enterprise of this nation. The English are prepared to settle anywhere commerce offers them profit. Look in any of the best ports in the whole world, and you will without fail meet an Englishman there. Thus, for example, the English are now settling in California. What draws them here across distant seas and lands? Is it not the premonition that California will sooner or later become the most flourishing and richest of lands[?] Actually, for a long time the small town of Yerba Buena was an uninhabited wilderness where only feral cattle roamed and geese walked freely; but now there are more than 60 handsomely built houses, and the settlement is gradually increasing, inevitably having to expand each year, judging by the current influx of people who in the hope of quick enrichment

---

[17]The southeastern United States has the humidity that central California lacks.
[18]Probably of suede.

rush from nearly every quarter of Europe to the shores of California. During my time at Yerba Buena, the number of the settlement's residents reached 300 souls of both sexes, comprising mostly immigrants who had quit their native lands forever and each of whom had found his most profitable and most suitable occupation here.[19]

Here there are neither orchards nor large gardens that could serve as objects of permanent enterprise for the residents of Yerba Buena. Only a few of them engage in orcharding or gardening; most fruits and vegetables are imported here at the town's port on boats from the nearby ranchos.

In the vicinity of Yerba Buena there are many *ranchos,* or estates, abounding in all of the gifts of nature. The closest rancho is found at a distance of no more than half a mile from the settlement. In it lives a Californio family, a cheese maker and the owner of a fairly large number of cows and the first purveyor of milk, which he brings to Yerba Buena for sale from a boat standing in the harbor. This is a long-time native of California. His rancho is a most picturesque tableau. The owner's dwelling rises in the middle of a lush green valley; on one side it is enclosed by a wattle fence that serves as a corral for horses, and on the other it is confined by a garden in which watermelons and pumpkins have been planted and here and there apple and pear trees are growing; beyond stretches plowland, planted in wheat, barley, corn, and peas. And everything is fragrant, blossoming, and ripening to the full, even, one can say, in legendary abundance. Would many people believe that in California 1 fanega (3½ puds) of wheat yields from 80 to 100 fanegas of large, plump grains? But this is not at all surprising in California, where it is not necessary for a man to toil, in the sweat of his brow, [while] manuring fields and where nature herself with a liberal hand lays bare in front of him all of the treasures of the vegetable kingdom. The rain so necessary for plantings rarely visits this land; but by way of compensation its place is taken by almost daily dew, which is so heavy that it forms puddles on the ground, and if one stands for a quarter of an hour in the open it is possible to become soaked to the skin. With the sunrise it all evaporates, but the morning frosts are fairly cold; but then the Californio, true to his natural disposition to idleness, does not leave his dwelling until the sun's rays warm the cold air. Then he goes out to his cornfield in a serape* and a straw hat with a wide brim; after him follow his wife and children. Meanwhile, a

---

*A woven patterned mat 4 arsh[ins] long and about 1½ arsh[ins] wide. A hole is made in the middle, and they thrust their head through it and wear it so instead of a cloak.

---

[19]According to the Russian naturalist Ilya Voznesensky, who visited Yerba Buena in 1841, the settlement was called Loma Alta de Gerba Buena by the Californios, who had begun to build houses there in 1831 or 1833, and by 1841 a square vara of land there cost two reals (I. G. Voznesensky, "Kalifornskie zametki," St. Petersburg Branch of the Archive of the Russian Academy of Sciences, f. 53, op. 1, notebook 1a).

worker lights a small fire in his hut and begins to make breakfast, i.e., grinds corn and from its flour bakes a kind of flatcake [tortilla], or rather, something like blini to us Russians, cooks some small pieces of beef in a pot, and adds butter, salt, and such a large number of chili peppers that for the unaccustomed it is impossible to swallow one bite without a strong pungent sensation. You will not find stoves here; you will encounter them among very few only, the reason being the shortage of bricks in California, for the inhabitants of this blessed land think that it is better to prepare food under the open sky. After breakfast the Californio takes the favorite instrument of both sexes, the guitar, and lies on a green velvet couch under a shady tree or mounts a horse and rides to his plowland to see how the hired Indians are working. These smart people are content with strings of black, white, or red beads of a sazhen in length. Beads serve as their chief adornment, for men as well as women, and so they are quite expensive in California. Thus, one sailor sold 5 *livres* [pounds] of beads for 10 piasters, whereas among us in Russia this amount would cost no more than 5 pa[per] rub[les]. In addition to this payment in beads, an Indian must also be fed wheat gruel without any flavoring, not because they do not want, or are unable to eat, better but because the Californio does not give him anything better, saying that his labor is not worth it. However, the Indian does not ask for tastier food, and if he takes it into his head to treat himself, then he tries to catch a field mouse, skewer it on a stick, grill it over a fire, and eat it with delight. They sometimes burn large fields in order to make it possible to catch the field mice more readily.[20]

There are those among them who are already accustomed to living in houses, and they perform all of the chores of domestic life. The Californios pay them a salary or clothe them and feed them decent food. If the Indian tires of this dependent life, he has the right to withdraw to his native hills, where a knife and a bow and arrow are his only riches. They can shoot well from a handgun or a rifle, but few use these firearms, which in this quarter require costly supplies, namely, lead and gunpowder. The latter serves the Indians, both men and women, for body decoration. They inscribe their chest, face, arms, and back with various figures and rub gunpowder into them; from this tattooing the figures become blue and appear clearly on their body. Among them this is a kind of vanity.[21]

But let's return to our estimable Californio; we will glance at the interior of his house, look at his family life, and become acquainted with some of the daily routine of the residents of California.

Entering the first room of his dwelling, you meet nothing of interest. A dry clay floor, a simple wooden table, surrounded by some benches, and bare walls, from

---

[20]The Californian Indians periodically set fire to grasslands and woodlands for a variety of purposes.
[21]Russ., *shchegolstvo*.

one of which hang saddlecloths, spurs, and generally all of the harness for a horse. This is a reception room for visitors. On the right is another room of the same size as the first but much more interesting. Here one's eye is struck first of all by the large double bed, adorned with such care and richness that even any of our European beauties would envy it—but meanwhile the floor is the same as in the first room. In one corner stands a barrel with rum for sale. Chests arranged along the wall serve as benches for visitors, and sometimes many gather here, especially on holidays, with the stoppage of ship work. Then you will meet here an Englishman with a serious air and a bottle, a Frenchman with his boastful phrases, as well as a bottle, and a Russian with his open, resourceful[22] mien and two bottles. There is yet a third room, perhaps more interesting than all of the others, but they curtain its entrance, and it is not accessible to all curious eyes. In it lives the daughter of the estimable Californio, a hospitable, lively, smart, charming, and—what is rather seldom encountered at the same time—very intelligent girl.

Thus does this rancho, supplied with all of the aforesaid comforts, attract a multitude of visitors seeking diversions in the valleys of California.

You need a riding horse—pay a piaster and ride all day wherever you like. You want rum—a whole bottle of it appears immediately in front of you, likewise for one piaster. Take your pleasure wherever you want: at a large table or in the open under a shade tree. If you like to quench your thirst with thick, sweet milk—drink to the full for one real. Perhaps you like to dream—before your eyes there is the roll of a bay's waves and a foggy, distant prospect, above which only the dreamer's imagination can rise. But you are a sailor, you see only the sky, and the sea, and the familiar faces of your friends; you would like to carry from this land the utterly pacifying memory of something beautiful—take a step and engage in conversation with the sweet daughter of the Californio, and an involuntary sigh will escape your breast when the duty of service again calls you to the ship, ready to sail from this blessed coast.

In short, here one's eyes and heart and stomach find food and rapture in equal measure. This rancho is still memorable to me from the story of an incident to which I was an eyewitness from a distance. A sailor from our ship came to the Californio's daughter and asked for milk. He explained his request with various signs, but she did not understand him, or perhaps as a joke she pretended that she understood nothing. What was the poor man to do? There was no interpreter, and to arrive at the ship without milk would mean angering the crew. Suddenly a happy thought flashed across his mind. The sailor went down on all fours, placed his hands to his head in the shape of horns, and bellowed like a cow. The California girl burst out laughing and brought the sailor 2 bottles of milk, taking no money from him as payment.

---

[22]Russ., *zamyslovaty*.

I suppose that she very much liked the ingenuity of the Russian. However, it should be noted that in contrast to other foreigners the Russians in that quarter enjoyed special respect for their cordial treatment of the natives; in the remote corners of the Eastern Ocean the Russian name serves as an emblem of amiability, cordiality, ingenuity, and resourcefulness.

To the left of the rancho that I have described, a road to San Francisco ascended a small sandy hill.

One fine morning I hired a horse from the owner of the rancho and set off to see San Francisco, the northernmost town in California. The road was rather hilly and mostly sandy; at times I came upon level, scrubby stretches where herds of wild [feral] horses or bulls roamed. The latter animals are incredibly numerous here, and they constitute the principal enterprise of the Californios. The largest bull or cow, about the size of one of our bullocks, costs 8 piasters here, and one of moderate size 6 piasters, including the hide, and without the hide it falls to 2 piasters. These prices are constant, never rising or falling.

Every herd has an owner, and, if he needs them, he unfailingly finds them wherever they may roam. Each year *vaqueros** [herdsmen] set out for the nearest herds and brand the newborn calves, slit their ears, or saw off their horns; so a vaquero knows immediately to which brand and owner the cattle belong.

More than once I happened to see the catching of wild bulls by courageous and experienced vaqueros.

Two daredevils on habituated horses, swinging lariats [*reatas*] of fiber or hair in the air, rush headlong into a herd of cattle. The animals, as if sensing their impending doom, look around with fright and emit a savage bellow, and in the hope of saving themselves by fleeing their implacable pursuers, scatter to all sides. But it is to no avail. The vaqueros lasso their victim from a distance; in an instant the unerring lariat fells the animal by a hind leg, another lariat snares a front leg, and the animal, no longer having the possibility of escaping, falls heavily to the ground. (The horses pull the lariat taut and do not move an inch from the spot.) The vaqueros tie the ends of the lariat tightly to their saddle horn, jump to the ground, and calmly cut off the head of the wild animal, furious but powerless in its rage. During all of this action the horses stand as if rooted to the ground until the lariats have been untied.

There is another kind of bull catching, and it appeared to me more interesting than the first. In this case a vaquero, with the help of a trained [i.e., broken] bull (for this purpose they always choose the largest and strongest bull), boldly sets out to catch wild bulls. He also dashes with a lariat on a swift horse at a herd of bulls

*In California the best horsemen are called *vaqueros*. They are entrusted with the cattle, and they catch them with lariats and bring them to the owner alive or dead, depending upon need.

and throws the lariat over a bull's foreleg, making it run, and then he suddenly stops; without fail the bull stumbles and falls. Then the vaquero leaps nimbly from the horse (which meanwhile does not slacken the lariat, pulling it backward and thereby preventing the bull from standing), approaches the animal, and as calmly as in the first kind of catching ties its feet and renders it completely immobile. Whereupon he leads the trained bull to the wild bull, ties them together by their horns, and finally unties the legs of the wild bull. The latter rises, but not having the strength to break away from its fellow creature, unwillingly follows the trained bull, which, on the vaquero's orders, pulls the doomed victim with all of its might to the slaughtering ground. The trained bull serves more to haul the meat. Sometimes it happens that the vaquero catches a bull so far from a settlement that it is difficult for the horse to haul a whole carcass weighing up to 20 puds; to pull a live bull with a single lariat is very inconvenient because it will become entangled incessantly in large bushes. The trained bull sometimes runs with the wild bulls, and they do not fight each other. Having caught sight of a horse rider in the distance, wild bulls will scatter, but a trained bull will stay, not moving from the spot. It knows that it will not be caught for slaughtering. But if the bulls meet a man on foot, then they will certainly charge him; it is especially difficult to save oneself from them when coming across them somewhere in a level place, so in California both men and women never go anywhere on foot.

Bulls are also used in California for transport. Some missionaries have [unsprung] carriages in which they haul various provisions. These carriages are rather like chicken coops; they have a flat wooden roof, and an opening is made in the rear through which passengers enter; instead of wheels they have thick, uneven, round slabs that make a terrible squeak when turning. To this contraption is yoked a pair of oxen, which with quiet, slow steps plod from one mission to another.

During my passage from Yerba Buena along the San Francisco road, I chanced to meet one of these ridiculous carriages. In it there were no supplies at all, however, only a very pretty California girl and her mother. The latter was knitting stockings, and the former, it seemed, was dreaming about something. In front sat a Californio, and he constantly prodded the oxen, which moved their hoofs a little.

I found myself already at the halfway point on the road to San Francisco. Surrounded by magnificent, sturdy vegetation, I slowly climbed a green, sloping hill, covered with small trees. All was quiet around me; only at times did a soft breeze rustle the leaves of the trees, and somewhere a grasshopper began its monotonous song, and again everything fell silent.

Suddenly on the right side of the road I heard the cracking of dry twigs and the rustling of falling leaves. Curiosity induced me to turn off the road; I peered into the grove . . . and there in front of me stood a young Indian girl. There was not a shred of clothing on her; she did not move from the spot, and with shyness but no shame she looked me straight in the eye.

"What a child of nature!" I thought to myself and rode closer to her.

The Indian girl was silent and as before stood on the same spot. I began to pity her and gave her a shawl; she took it but did not respond with a word or a bow. And when, after having ridden some distance away from her, I glanced back, the little savage was gone.

[After] descending the hill and passing some bushes, I found myself in an extensive empty clearing; here I took it into my head to test the speed of my horse. I gave him his head and my spurs, and the swift steed carried me over the level stretch with the speed of an arrow fired by a strong arm from a taut bow. Not even five minutes had passed before the plain was already behind me and I found myself at the foot of a high sandy hill. The flushed horse ran up to its summit at a gallop. . . . There I stopped him . . . and besides, it was the last hill on the road to San Francisco. From its summit the whole town loomed before me; it consisted of a mission and no more than twenty low, white, adobe houses, arranged in various directions.

I descended the hill, and at the bottom coursed a small stream; on the other side a ditch had been dug in the form of a little inlet for collecting water. Here I met three women; they were washing linens, and not far from them a little boy was lassoing a rooster. Beyond stood a long house, and by its door sat a Californio with a guitar in his hands. Seeing me, he rose, greeted me with a handshake, and asked me to sit in his place, constantly repeating in Spanish, "Russians are good people! good people!" I liked the cordiality of this stranger very much.

I entered his room; it was dark yellow and ran the length of the house, as if it were a corridor, and it was illuminated by two doors. In one corner stood an ordinary bed with a drawn silk curtain, and on the opposite wall hung a brown bearskin. Nothing else was to be seen.

"Where is your family[?]" I asked the Californio.

"I don't have a family."

"What do you do, then?"

"Nothing."

"You know, one can die from hunger, señor."

He smiled and said, "I have a horse and a strong lariat."

A strange man! I thought, I must learn a little more about his life. But there was no time to do so now because very soon I had to head back; and besides, curiosity drew me on, and I wanted to examine San Francisco more closely. And so, leaving my new acquaintance, I proceeded.

Directly in front of me stood another house in which, apparently, there was incomparably more activity and life than in the first. Nearby lay two Californios

(probably the owners of the house) on serapes. One of them was smoking a cigarette;[23] the other was playing a guitar. They also greeted me and suggested that I lie
on a serape spread on the ground. I thanked them and asked for a drink of water.

They directed me to the door of the house.

I entered. It consisted of one room with a partition; the floor was clay, swept
clean, and the corner, as usual, flaunted a bed, appointed with the greatest possible
refinement. Along the wall stood a large chest, and a fat California woman was sitting on it and smoking a cigarette. I told her I was thirsty, and the señora consider-
ately satisfied my request. After this favor I offered her a cigarillo, which she took,
thanking me and saying, as my first acquaintance did, "Russians are good people."

Through a side door near the exit of the house I noticed a courtyard, enclosed
by a wattle fence. In the middle of the courtyard a rack had been built. "Probably some sort of trade," I thought to myself, and I was not wrong. Two Indians
were cutting beef into thin strips, lightly salting them, and hanging them on the
poles, thusly preparing dried meat [beef jerky?], which in California constitutes a
not unimportant item of trade. Dried meat is prepared primarily at the missions,
which have more space. At Yerba Buena and San Francisco this activity engages
few people, and even then [the dried meat is] for their own use.

Opposite the aforesaid house, across a small square, stood a long, low, stone
building with large windows; at the end of it a monastery with a high bell tower
had been built in the name of St. Francis.

I wanted very much to see the interior of the monastery, but unfortunately it
was locked, and I found it necessary to return to the fat señora and find out from
her when the monastery was open and who was in charge of it.

When I crossed the small square I came upon the same little boy who had
been lassoing the rooster. I turned to him, hoping he would be able to tell me
what I wanted to ask the fat señora who loved cigarettes. The urchin actually led
me to the house with the large windows and said that his father lived there and
guarded the monastery but that he was not at home now because he had gone
to the priest's at the mission. There was nothing to be done; at least here I'll see
how the watchman lives. I opened the door and stepped onto a brick floor. The
spacious room very much resembled a hall; around it long benches stood against
its walls, and in the middle a table ran across the entire building. Everything
was covered in a thick layer of dust. On the right side of the room hung a small
curtain, through which a human figure was discernible, and on a windowsill lay
a bunch of keys, which attracted particular attention because of their huge size.
I took the keys and started to turn around. Immediately a woman came out to
me from behind the curtain and said that they were the keys to the monastery.

"You are likely the watchman's wife?" I asked her.

---

[23]*Papiroska*, or *papirosa*, a Russian-style cigarette with a short cardboard mouthpiece.

"Just so," she replied.

"Where is your husband?"

"He rode to the priest's. What do you want of him?"

"I would like to see the interior of the monastery."

"Allow me; I will show you. [I]t may be a long time before he comes—let's go. I will open the door of the monastery for you."

She took the keys, and we set off to the monastery.

"You are probably a Russian?" she asked.

I answered in the affirmative.

"Good people!" remarked the spouse of the estimable watchman.

Approaching the monastery, I noticed a small brass cannon; it was mounted on a bad gun carriage and in utter neglect.

"Why is this gun here?" I asked her.

"When the governor comes here from Monterey," answered my guide, "they meet him with a salute from this cannon."

Finally, the iron door opened on its hinges, and we entered under the high arches of the monastery. My attention was arrested first of all by a small room near the entrance on the left side; in it there was a coffin with an infant, and to the left something like a cupboard had been made in the wall behind an iron grille. This was a confessional, which the priest enters when he performs confession. The rich altar is the main adornment of the monastery's chapel; the paintings in it are rather old. The Evangelists, standing on a high pedestal, are distinguished by precise fretwork. The entire altarpiece [reredos] is covered with gold and silver, and the pulpit for preaching is enclosed by a gilded railing; the gallery for singing and playing music is arranged under the arches themselves. For want of an organ, violins are played here. The Venetian windows, six arshins above the floor, lend a gloomy air to the whole building, an air that inspires a kind of morbidly heavy feeling in one's soul.

"And is there often a service here?" I asked my guide.

"No, only on holidays," she replied.

Apart from this monastery, which alone can attract the attention of travelers, I found nothing especially interesting in San Francisco, except, perhaps, the fact that there is such a multitude of dogs here that each of the residents must have one, if not two, of them.

Not far from the monastery, on the road to Monterey, I could not help noticing one house. It was finer than the others and served as the dwelling of a widow who was engaged in the selling of rum and gin. Around it grew olive trees; under one of them sat an Indian woman, probably a worker of the owner, and she was plucking the feathers of California quails. These small birds are dark gray in color, with a black topknot of no more than three feathers; they have white, tasty, rather sweet meat and are often encountered in California and are used by the native inhabitants for food.

Plowland, sown to wheat and barley, was visible here and there behind the settlement, and on the right side lay the smooth surface of a small lake, and beyond it stretched a wood.

The time was nearing midday, and smoke rose from almost every house. It was a sign of the making of dinner.

On the Monterey road two riders were galloping full tilt. When they neared the settlement, I was able to see them properly. They were Californio soldiers, and they brought news of the arrival of the governor at San Francisco. Their clothing consisted of dark blue, coarse cloth jackets with red stripes and trousers of the same color with slits at the cuffs, not to mention the huge spurs that are the property of every Californio. A black patent-leather hat with a wide brim completed the outfit. A long lance with a small flag was attached to one leg, and a pair of pistols was visible under the saddle blanket.

The residents of the settlement, hearing of the arrival of [Alta] California's governor, began to bustle. A few of the citizens handled the monastery's cannon and loaded it so slowly and noisily that in watching them I could not keep myself from laughing. People gradually assembled at this spot, the cannon was ready, and the curious throng stood in anticipation of their leader. Then at the end of a clearing appeared a troop of horsemen, gradually approaching San Francisco.

A cannon shot resounded, announcing the coming of the governor. Then one could see all of the cavalcade, approaching at a slow trot. It comprised thirty men. The shakos of some of the officers resembled those of our uhlans [lancers] but were much more awkward, and those of the others had a round shape with a spike on top. The dark blue and dark green full-dress uniforms with tails were distinguished by their red or yellow lapels and the trousers by broad stripes. A bright saber was the sole weapon of the officers.

The governor himself, who was found in the middle of his military retinue, rode in a long, blue, velvet cloak with a small collar of the same color, similar to a woman's cape, and edged with a silk fringe; under the cloak one could see a *kazakin*[24] or rather, an *akhaluk*,[25] of green velvet with a silk sash, under which a fine dagger was visible. A black patent-leather hat and a long black moustache lent his face a stern military expression.

This was Don Carlos [Antonio Carrillo], the governor of California.

Seeing me standing above the middle of the gaping crowd, he asked who I was.

"A Russian, from the ship *Naslednik*," I replied.

The governor greeted me with a handshake, and together we went to the room

---

[24]A man's knee-length coat with pleated tails.

[25]Or *arkalykh,* a short caftan.

of the monastery's watchman. There a table had already been covered with a white tablecloth; on it were glasses, 2 bottles of rum, and several carafes of water.

I wanted to take my leave of the governor, but he asked me to sit and drink a glass of grog.

I did as he wished and drank to the health of all of those present.

The governor patted me on the shoulder, and we parted.

It was still rather early, and I rode to a rancho a quarter of a mile from San Francisco and near the bay itself. It belonged to a German who had recently settled here, the son of a Riga merchant, and he had formerly worked for the Russian-American Company.[26] After having served the period of his contract [five years] with the company, he married a Creole at Sitka, settled here to increase his capital, and passes for a Russian. The location of his rancho is very beautiful, but it is worked as plowland [rather than pasture]. He is energetic and enterprising—so he combines in himself the two most important qualities that point the surest way to rapid enrichment in thriving California.

His house is built on a small scale, with a chimney and a Russian stove, and it is enclosed by a garden, where cabbages, turnips, onions, and potatoes grow.

His rooms are light and clean; well-engraved pictures hang on the walls, and the furniture is redwood, but the traveler's attention falls most of all here on one object, namely, on a pianoforte. Mister Geppner (the surname of the rancho's owner) plays this instrument very well and attracts many listeners, in particular some of the natives who have never had an opportunity to see this musical instrument. Sometimes on festive days he hauls the pianoforte to the monastery, so that Mr. Geppner is becoming more and more known in these parts. The first duty of the governor himself, when visiting San Francisco, is to arrange to visit the artist, in order firstly to tender his favor to him as a Russian settler and secondly to hear him play the pianoforte. He does not have livestock and plowland yet because he is a recent settler; but these two things constitute the chief object of current industry, and Mr. Geppner will be of great service to the Russian-American Company, and perhaps to a much more distant region [Russian Alaska], by supplying wheat and mitigating to a great extent its need of grain.

During my visit to the *rancho,* or estate, of Mr. Geppner we often discussed fertile, rich California, which is to a high degree capable of multiplying the products of nature that are necessary to man, and we were carried mentally to places familiar to us in Eastern Siberia. What a striking contrast! Vast spaces covered with snow versus eternally green and luxuriant valleys; man, nearly frozen by

---

[26]Markov is referring to Andreas Höppner (Andrey Andreyevich Gepner) (18??–1855), who arrived in 1836 at New Archangel, where he served as a foreman and a conductor, staging theatrical productions and playing the organ in the Lutheran church. He married a Creole, Anna Klimovskaya, in 1842, and in 1844 they left for Alta California, where they settled first on the San Francisco rancho and then in Sonoma. In 1849 Andreas left his wife and went to Chile, where he died. See Grinëv, *Kto yest kto,* 123.

the cold, morose, unsociable, and inactive, since nature herself sets limits to his activity, versus man warmed constantly by the sun's rays, serene, cheerful, and stagnating in idleness, and in the bosom of nature, offering him its best gifts without any requital, and between these two different spheres of life the greedy, seething activity of industry—all of this forms a picture for the extremely animating and powerfully stimulating curiosity of a thinker.

The inhabitants are divided by an enormous distance into two lands, and they are alien to each other, whereas they could share the fruits of their labor and talents and beneficially exchange the products of their homelands.

After staying on Mr. Geppner's rancho several days, I wanted to return to my ship at Yerba Buena, but he suggested that we go by launch to San Pablo, a small pueblo located on the other side of San Francisco Bay at a distance of 2 miles from the shore. Leaving my horse at Geppner's, I set out with him in compliance with his invitation.

At San Pablo live no more than seven families, each in a special house surrounded by a fence and a garden, with pods of red chili peppers hanging on the walls that are dried for sale and for their own use in food. The Californios are ardent lovers of peppers. In one house they make soap, fairly strong and of good quality. In other houses they dry meat and render beef fat, which they pour into sewn oxhide bags. The best head fat they pour into ox bladders; they call it *manteca,* and it is very pleasant to the taste. All of this constitutes an object of trade of California of no small importance. An enclosure has been built not far from the pueblo; there they mill wheat. Two Indians were driving unshod horses over the sheaves spread on the bare, hard ground. From this poor milling, many kernels are lost, for they are trampled deep into the ground, and others are left in the ears. It can be assumed that from ten fanegas of pure wheat at least ⅓ is lost. In the distance stretched a broad, green valley, not settled by anyone. The beautiful situation unfolding before my eyes held me to the spot for a long time; I did not want to part with these charming vistas, but the time was already nearing evening and I had to return to Mr. Geppner's, where, after getting the horse that I had left, I rode to Yerba Buena.[27]

After reaching my ship, I learned that in two days there would be a fandango.

---

[27]The Contra Costa's San Pablo, which was perhaps the best known of Alta California's ranchos, was visited and described by Ilya Voznesensky in December 1840. It lay four and a half verstas from the bay shore landing and belonged to three brothers. The surroundings were "most picturesque . . . : fine fields, flat as a plate, which had just been sown after the first rains, and thousands of cattle had been driven to graze on a vast meadow . . . that would accommodate all of the cattle in California. The rancho itself was built near the foot of some low mountains (hills), with two streams flowing from either side—and shaded by trees—full of pure and tasty water. 2 houses were built on a small meadow with the requisite outbuildings. I encountered this style everywhere" (Voznesensky, "Kalifornskie zametki," notebook 1a).

And actually, the next morning, invitations were sent to some persons living in the neighborhood of Yerba Buena, especially families.

The day of the party arrived. It was impossible to recognize the ship's quarter-deck; one could not imagine that on this deck, over which the ocean's menacing waves had splashed, the delicate little feet of a California lady would glide. An awning was stretched over half of the ship, i.e., from the taffrail to the mainmast, and its side reached as far as the bulwark, which, starting from the deck and ending at the awning and around all of the quarterdeck rails, was draped with striped ticking. The cannons were positioned along the ship, and planks were placed on them and covered with heavy, coarse cloth, thereby creating a divan for the guests. The heads were curtained by a flag with the double-headed eagle, the drainpipes[28] had been taken from one side of the ship to the other and nets had been stretched over them, and the stays and masts had been entwined with bunting, and this outdoor ship's salon was illuminated by thirty lanterns.

The sailors in red shirts sat in the cutters, launches, and yawls, ready to transport the guests. Everything exuded gaiety, and with these rare guests aboard, everything assumed a festive air that was unusual for one not used to it.

Now the invited guests appeared on shore, and rowing vessels were sent to receive passengers. In the first cutter to come alongside the ship's main ladder were the captain of the port and his two daughters, the cheese maker and his daughter, and several other family members. From time to time guests gathered on different sides—both riding and walking on shore and in boats on the bay. Many of the Californios had guitars, and two violins besides completed the orchestra. Under the sounds of this rather pleasant harmony began an orderly dance known as the fandango. How graciously this motley group moved back and forth, and how pretty were the Californian women in their national dress! At this time a feeling of both sadness and gaiety overcame me; it seemed as if I were enjoying myself among my own family, but everything was alien to the eyes, ears, and heart, which were used to seeing, hearing, and loving something else that was closer to them but separated by an immeasurable expanse.

Tables, covered with berries and bottles, had been set in the cabin and the wardroom. The Californian ladies drank weak wine unabashedly, and the Californio men strong wine. About midnight the Russian dancing songs of the sailors resounded on the quarterdeck; some of the guests doffed their serapes and jackets and made themselves at home. It must be admitted that for a while we forgot about discipline, without crossing the bounds of decency, however. On the part of the fair sex we encountered friendly, joyful laughter instead of caprices.

---

[28]Russ., *kapy*.

Finally, the sun began gradually to overcome us, and almost at sunrise the guests departed with feelings of genuine thanks for the hospitality of the Russians.

The ships of the Russian-American Company visit California annually to buy provisions, and while at anchor the commander of every Russian ship deems it virtually his duty to hold a party, or locally a fandango. I had to go to California several times, and I never saw any of the foreign ships anchored there take it upon itself to give a party for the Californios; but then the latter, for their part, did not confer this honor upon any of the foreigners, except the Russians, who knew how to incur their trust and respect. I will never forget one evening when the Californios in gratitude for our treatment of them held a fandango just for the Russians at Yerba Buena in the very same barracks that I have already mentioned. The barracks were beautifully illuminated and furnished. There was an abundance of Californian wine and fruit; the cannons, hitherto standing forgotten, did not stop firing. The Californios in an outpouring of friendliness, pumped our hands and in Russian shouted *"Ura"* ["Hurrah"]! I do not know of any Russian heart that would not have begun to beat with joy at these brotherly words of greeting from the mouths of foreigners!

[After] arriving at our ship after the party given in our honor by the Californios, for a long time I was unable to part mentally from their joyful company. The noise of the evening's feast still rang in my ears; finally, little by little sleep overcame me, and I did not awaken until late next morning.

We needed garden vegetables, including fruit, for both our own use and the use of the governor of the Russian-American colonies at Sitka, so I was commissioned to buy them at the pueblo of Santa Clara near San Francisco Bay, 26 miles from Yerba Buena.

It [i.e., Santa Clara] also consists of a few houses situated not far from the bay. Each house stands some distance from each other; gardens are cultivated between them with cabbages, turnips, onions, cucumbers, and mustard, and there are also empty tracts planted with nothing. Behind the pueblo stretch orchards with apples, pears, bergamots, olives, plums, cherries, and grapes; there are also walnuts and acorns. Beyond the orchards lie clearings or fields of pumpkins, cantaloupes, and watermelons. The pueblo of Santa Clara is prettier than all others by reason of its locale. One's glance rests now on the small green hills overgrown with thickets, then on dense groves, where oaks and gigantic *chagas* [coast redwoods] grow, then on level valleys that merge with the horizon in the distance or meet the blue mountains, barely visible in the distance. The bright bay completes the picture; all around there is a profound stillness, and everywhere [is] that carefreeness that generally distinguishes all of the residents of this blessed land.

A sunburnt Californio, with a cigarette in his mouth and a silent guitar, was lying by the fence of his house and watching how the hired Indians gathered cucumbers in his garden and piled them in squeaky carts, harnessed to two oxen. This train set off via San Francisco to Yerba Buena. The Californio's wife, sitting alongside a cow and wanting to quench her husband's thirst, milked a glassful for him; there are no cellars here and nowhere to keep milk for a long time. The morning's milk is used for cheese, provided it is not sold; if someone takes it into his head to have a drink, then they go immediately to the cow and milk a glassful, or they steam the milk, which is drunk like water.

I approached the Californio, greeted him, and told him what I needed.

"I have everything that you need," he replied; "Order your men to pick out as much as you need from the basket[s], and then we will see how much it will cost. You will probably overnight here," continued the Californio, "because it is late, and also the wind is against you for leaving in the boat, so you can set to work tomorrow morning, but now we will drink tea."

And he ordered an Indian woman to heat the kettle. There are no samovars in this country, and copper kettles take their place.

The sailors dispersed wherever they liked, and I walked with the Californio into his house. The Californio's house was not as pretty as others, but to make up for it everything in it was plentiful; it even meant a good deal that Don José (the name of my host) drank tea, which few enjoy in California, on account of its dearness. Here one pound of tea costs 3½ piasters (17 rub[les], 50 kop[ecks]), so that this beverage is a special luxury in California.

Don José has five children; the oldest, a daughter, is 17 years of age. Unfortunately, she was sick and not receiving any medical treatment, because doctors are very rare in California, and the residents, in the event of disease, mostly entrust themselves to the mercy of fate.

The hostess began to make supper, i.e., to knead tortillas and to boil meat seasoned with pods of red peppers, as is imperative in nearly all Californian dishes. Her two small sons brought apples, pears, and watermelons. Now other Californios arrived; they formed a circle, and a rather interesting conversation began.

One of the talkers, a fairly elderly man, surprised me with his knowledge. In appearance he resembled a Californio, but later I learned that he was an English captain who had left his homeland forever and settled in the vicinity of Don José's house. He discussed the war that was erupting between the Americans and the Mexicans and said that the former needed California and that after capturing it they, as an enterprising people, would settle the western coast of America to a considerable extent, bring their fleet to the Pacific Ocean, become friends with the Sandwich Islands and China, expand their trade, and even, one can suppose, give heed to Japan, too: then both oceans, the Pacific and the Atlantic, would fill North America with the riches of Eastern Asia and Western Europe. "Then watch," he continued, "how trade between the coasts of the Pacific and Atlantic Oceans will accelerate. Without fail the Americans will establish warehouses at Acapulco or Mazatlán. Then their Pacific ships will not go to the Atlantic but store goods at those ports, whence the goods will be transported overland through Mexico to the Gulf of Mexico at the port of Veracruz, where, in that event, they will build a warehouse; from Veracruz the freight will be conveyed to Europe on their Atlantic ships. Freight from Europe or the eastern countries of America will be hauled back the same way through Mexico to the western coast of America at Mazatlán or Acapulco or across the ocean to the eastern seaboard of Asia."

All of these suppositions of the Englishman were very plausible and also accorded with my views. The other members of the company listened attentively to the villager's narrative, and although they did not understand much, they felt that California would not stay placid very long and that sooner or later Mexico's laws would change and they would become the slaves of the strongest.

"The Americans," added the Englishman, "having California in their possession, could also even serve Russia by supplying Kamchatka or Okhotsk with grain, provided the Russians accept their service and do not themselves want to enjoy these benefits, i.e., send their own ships from the port of Okhotsk to California for wheat, peas, and barley. Then the Americans would reduce their prices substantially on provisions, which, I hear, are very dear around the Okhotsk Sea."

"Yes," I commented, "rye flour brought to Okhotsk from Yakutsk regularly costs from 8 to 10 rub[les] per pud and groats from 10 to 12 rub[les] per pud."

"Why so much?" asked the Englishman with surprise.

"Because flour and groats brought from the vicinity of Irkutsk to Yakutsk sell there for 1 rub[le], 50 kop[ecks] to 2 rub[les], 50 kop[ecks] per pud; from Yakutsk these foodstuffs are delivered by caravans of pack horses to Okhotsk, with a payment of 30 to 40 rubles for each horse, and since no more than 5 puds can be packed on a horse, then after deducting the hauling from the buying price, we can see clearly that it is not possible to sell the grain for less than those prices. And besides, the provisions dispatched from Yakutsk to Okhotsk are packed in dressed leather bags, and they are conveyed sometimes a whole month over an expanse of more than 1,000 verstas. On this remote route, owing to the frequent fording of rivers, the grain packed in the bags is often soaked; in addition, from the transport on horseback it is permeated with horse sweat and loses its freshness."

"You see the inconveniences," said the Englishman. "Why, then do the Okhotsk merchants not bring their ships to California for grain, which would yield them substantial profits?"

"Because the Okhotsk merchants," I replied, "although they have enough capital to have their own ships, are still not intimately acquainted with California and therefore unable to enter into trade with this country with much self-confidence."

"Judging from all of these circumstances," continued the Englishman, "the residents of the eastern territory of Russia would be glad if the Americans were to begin to supply them with fresh, undamaged, healthful provisions and, moreover, at half the price of those that exist today around the Okhotsk Sea. The residents of California, counting upon a large demand for their products, would undoubtedly exert more effort to grow wheat and other supplies at their ranchos."

"But the Americans," I said, "might export furs if they were allowed to enter the Okhotsk Sea."

"They will have to take steps against this, the best being, I think, strict customs inspection."

"Now the Californios sell their products to the Russian-American Company only," remarked Don José.

"Is that why," I said, "it is difficult for us to obtain the amount of supplies that we need, and it sometimes happens that we encounter a shortage of them?"

"It is because," the Englishman continued, "the Russian-American Company leased the Stikine [territory] to the English, so that the English Hudson's Bay Company delivers various goods, including wheat, peas, and other supplies, to the Russian colonies on their ships around the world.[29] Meanwhile, the amount of provisions supplied to the English from the Columbia has proven insufficient for the Russian-American Company, especially since it has opened trade with Kamchatka in various goods, including flour. This has forced the Company to again come in its own ships to California and buy wheat from the Californios, who, not being accustomed to sizable plantings, have not hitherto paid attention to the sowing of their fields, sometimes contracting them for a fixed amount to foreign trading vessels. For this reason we are now facing difficulties in the harvesting of wheat, peas, barley, and other supplies; but, judging from all appearances, it can be assumed that for the present wheat will constitute the foremost business of the residents of California."

But now the teapot was brought and with it, supper. Throughout the conversation the Californios had sat with their hats on; while sitting at the table, too, they did not remove them. Don José's family sat at one table, which was laden with various dishes; but there was no bread, which was replaced by tortillas. The first dish, made from minced meat, was begun by the hostess; following her example,

---

[29]Actually, the wheat supplied by the Hudson's Bay Company under the terms of its 1839 ten-year contract with the Russian-American Company came from its farms in the Oregon Country, although, as Markov's interlocutor adds, this wheat proved insufficient for both Russian America and the Russian Far East.

we reached to the middle of the table with our spoons. There was so much pepper in this dish that two spoonfuls burned my mouth, whereas the Californios ate theirs with pleasure. When it was finished, the hostess partook of the next dish, consisting of fried mutton, cut into large, very thin slices; after it came frijoles (small beans) fried in sheep fat, likewise strongly seasoned with pepper, then fried new cheese cut into slices and resembling curd fritters,[30] and lastly baked apples, with tea at the end.

The Californios, after rising from the table, lit cigars and left to lie down in the fresh air, inviting me to go with them. Don José's wife and older children also began to smoke cigars and left the house.

Declining the invitation of the Californios and wishing them pleasure in resting in the fresh air, I walked alone to see the pueblo of Santa Clara. From some houses rose a little smoke, denoting supper-making time; all around a profound silence reigned, and even the frying of something was audible. Occasionally hens wandered between houses, sheep nibbled grass, and somewhere cows mooed or horses snorted; not far from the bay shore, boys ran barefoot, chasing one another, and at one house an Indian was making himself bedding in the shape of a carpet, weaving stalks of straw and docking their ends for evenness. Beyond on the right stretched orchards, fenced with poles; our sailors were there, sated after treating themselves to fruit. Not encountering anything interesting, I walked back to José's house, where a bed had already been readied for me. Suddenly in several places dogs that had been lying quietly erupted in barking and ran from the pueblo, and boys after them. The alarm aroused my curiosity, and I walked in the direction of the running dogs. Passing four houses, I saw a gully ahead of me; in it two vaqueros on horseback were leading a bear straining on a lariat. They had caught it in a grove of oaks and were bringing it alive to the pueblo for amusement. It was brown in color and at least an arshin in height. From time to time the ferocious animal looked maliciously at the dogs barking around him and at the boys, who dared to poke him with sticks, knowing that the beast, held taut by its fore and hind legs, was unable to cause them the slightest harm. The vaqueros were confident that they could release it in the gully and lasso it again; it would have been interesting to see such a brave feat, but it was impermissible, for the bear might throw itself upon the gathering throng of people. The Californios forced the vaqueros to kill the creature right there on the spot. One vaquero drew a wide knife from the top of his boot and plunged it hard into the back of the beast's head. The bear began to sway on its legs and with a terrible roar fell to the ground. The vaqueros untied the lariats and made the Indians skin it. I went to José's house to sleep. The weariness of the past evening soon lulled me to sleep, and I slept deeply until dawn, when I

---

[30]Russ., *pryazhenchiki.*

was unable to keep my eyes closed; *coyotes* (a kind of jackal), running around the pueblo, disturbed me incessantly with their howling. They are frightfully numerous throughout California. In the quiet of the night they gather at the pueblos to hunt, taking sheep, if they are not penned, but when a man appears they run off to the woods. [After] dressing quickly, I ordered the sailors to grab as many fruits and vegetables as were needed from the baskets and sacks, and I walked with them to the orchard. Passing the spot where the bear had been killed the evening before, I didn't find a trace of its entrails, which had been discarded by the Indians but scavenged by the *coyotes* during the night.

I never happened to see Californios eating bear meat. They only use the skin and fat of this animal and sell them to trading vessels. The Indians eat bear meat with gusto.

The baskets and sacks that we had brought from the ship were soon filled by the sailors with fruits and vegetables. It only remained to settle accounts with the owner and ride back to our ship.

We were ready, but the residents of Santa Clara were still sleeping quietly and the doors of the houses were still closed, for the morning fog had not fully lifted and the air was cold. Not wanting to disturb José, I began to wait for him to awaken. At last the sun rose fairly high in the blue sky, the fog lifted, and the air became warmer. At some of the houses the doors were opened, and people began to emerge from them; the cattle were driven from the corrals, and Indian men and women went to milk them. Then smoke rose from the houses, and breakfast began to be prepared in the same way as supper.

Finally, Don José came out of his house to attend to the business of his rancho. Seeing us ready to depart, he greeted me and asked me to stay for breakfast with him. Fearing a contrary wind and wanting to take advantage of the calm weather, I excused myself on the grounds that the men with me were needed for work on the ship; [I then] paid him for the fruits and vegetables with goods (namely, beads, tea, and calico, which in California are more needed than money) and took our leave of him and his family. On the road I came across the Englishman, who also tried to detain me, but I thanked him and proceeded to my ship.

By 2 o'clock in the afternoon we were already aboard; the rigging, which had slackened in the great heat, was tightened, for with loose rigging the topmasts can easily be lost, especially during the strong tossing of the ship.

Upon our arrival from Santa Clara I faced the prospect of complete liberty until our departure from San Francisco Bay. I resolved to take advantage of this interval, and I found an opportunity to visit Monterey, California's capital, a distance of 250 miles from the pueblo of Yerba Buena.[31]

---

[31]The actual distance would have been about 100 miles.

Early in the morning I set out on the road to San Francisco, taking with me as a guide and guard a vaquero with a gun and his inseparable lariat. After passing San Francisco, we found ourselves on a broad, green plain crossed by trails, scarcely noticeable but for the occasional rider. After having crossed about 10 miles of the plain, we came upon three houses, fenced with posts. In them lived two Californios with their families. Cows and horses were lying behind the dwellings, and wheat was growing here and there. Nobody was visible, and only the barking of a dog was heard. When we rode up to one of the houses, a Californio came out to meet us and invite us in; time did not permit us to stay here long. After changing horses, the vaquero and I again set out through a valley to Monterey. The fast horses took us in a trice to another small pueblo by the Monterey road. At each of the pueblos that we encountered it was possible to change horses for a modest payment. On the way to Monterey we came upon many picturesque places. We had continually to ride through small groves; in them grew oaks, lime trees, beeches, redwoods of awesome thickness, alders, and sometimes poplars and wild grapes. We also came across large forests of laurel [bay], but we tried to cross them as quickly as possible, fearing the headaches that can stem from the strong scent of laurel leaves. In the distance we saw mountains and foothills of various sizes, some covered with trees and bushes and others not, a lake in which wild ducks and geese were swimming, and streams and small rivers flowing from the mountains or the lake and running over sandy and perhaps gold-bearing ground. To the side of the road smoke often rose, telling us of the closeness of Indian rancherías [i.e., settlements].

In one place at the foot of a small mountain at a considerable distance from the road I noticed more smoke.

Here there was probably a large Indian ranchería, I thought, and never having seen the domestic life of the Indians, I decided to take a look at their huts, and therefore, turning off the road, I rode with my guide straight to the settlement.

Nearing the ranchería, I saw that it consisted of 12 huts, arranged in various directions; some of them were covered with the hides of horses, bison, elk, and other rawhides or reeds [tule]. An Indian was sitting at the first hut and making an arrow with a knife. Seeing us, he stopped his work and, without rising from the spot, looked at us with the knife in his hands. His face, with small, sharp eyes (common to all of the Indians), was brutishly ugly. I gave him a cigar and asked to watch him work. He quickly leapt to his feet, as if he wanted to throw himself on me, ran into his hut, and brought me a completely finished arrow with a bow. The arrow, made from redwood, was 2½ feet long; on one end of it was implanted an arrowhead of hard bone, 9 inches long, and on the other end three feathers were inserted lengthwise in the shaft in order that the arrow would fly unwaveringly to its target. A very strong sinew, five feet long, was stretched extremely tightly to the bow. Out of curiosity I wanted to see how high the arrow would fly, and through the vaquero, who knew the Indian's language, I asked him to shoot it skyward. The Indian did as I asked; the arrow soared, went out of sight in the twinkling of an eye, and then came down not far from me, sticking five vershoks into the ground. Soon a throng of Indians surrounded us. All of them were distinguished by identical brutish, sunburnt faces, which had been tattooed with various figures that to them constitute vanity; their long black, coarse hair was tied behind in a bun. Their clothes consisted mostly of thin scraps of leather; some wore cotton or woolen fabrics, probably obtained from the Californios for labor, or perhaps stolen, because the Indians, like all savages, are very prone to theft.

In the gathering crowd there was not one woman. Among the Indians, women perform nearly all of the work, whereas their husbands stay idle. In this ranchería I met many women, and all of them were busy with something but their husbands were lying or sitting idly. Very few of them were doing something, e.g., sharpening knives or fashioning arrows. Here at one hut the woman was hewing a stake with an axe for the hut, and the man, probably her husband, was grilling meat on a stick. In other huts the women were squeezing juice from wild grapes (used for making wine), plaiting *ishkaty* (tight, strong, and very beautiful baskets that take the place of pottery among them) from tree roots, or making bands from variegated bird feathers, which both the women and the men use for headdresses. In the very center of the ranchería, three women were skinning a bull, which had probably been rustled. The vaquero wanted to see whether it had a brand, but I restrained him, fearing that he [would] bring suspicion on us and perhaps cost us dearly. A high degree of repulsive slovenliness prevailed in the ranchería; more than anything, the brutish appearance of the Indians inspired a kind of fear—and by now night was falling, so I hurried to leave the Indian settlement for the road to Monterey.

More than half of the way to Monterey remained, and we had to find a rancho in which to overnight. In the distance the roofs of a Californio pueblo came into view. I was disposed to spending the night there. It comprised four houses with various outbuildings. Many olive trees grew in the pueblo, and here and there, apple and pear trees. I came upon nothing of interest here, because all Californio pueblos are much the same. I stayed with one of the Californio families, which received me very cordially. The fatigue of horseback riding put me to sleep, and I slept soundly on a bison hide. In the morning, after changing horses, which had been readied for us the previous evening, we hurried to continue our journey, despite a cold fog. On the road, apart from picturesque localities, we did not encounter a single object of interest. Sometimes we came upon wildcats [bobcats] in the woods, but they fled from us, and we did not succeed in shooting any of them.

There were no obstacles to our changing horses, so we soon reached Monterey. We ascended a mountain, and from its summit the cross of Monterey's monastery came into view. Finally, after passing a small thicket, we entered the town, situated on the slope of the shore of Monterey Bay. The houses in it are arranged in some order; in many of them there were shops and storerooms where the goods were very expensive, for the government, not having much revenue from California's towns, imposes a high duty on imported goods.

The governor's house is found in the center of the town. Its exterior was finer than that of the other houses. Not far from it there was a barracks—a long, one-story building with little windows, and dilapidated in many places. The cannons standing in front of the barracks were in a somewhat better state than those that I had seen at Yerba Buena. A hall had been built near the barracks, and behind the hall, a prison. Approaching the latter, I saw an Indian sitting behind the bars; he had been condemned to be shot. The criminal's countenance, even without the disfigurement by tattooing, was [rendered] even more frightful by the savage, fierce glances that he cast around himself. This was his crime: he stole a bull from a Californio, the owner of a rancho. While the thief was leading the animal to his ranchería, he met a vaquero. Knowing from the brand to whom the bull belonged, he lassoed the Indian, who had tried to save himself by fleeing, and led his captive with the bull to the rancho of the robbed owner. The latter flogged the Indian severely and let him go. With malice and revenge in his heart, he left, but not before noting the place in detail. The next night he carefully stole up to the house and, spotting an open window, sneaked into the Californio's bedroom and knifed him and his wife to death. Their son, sleeping in a nearby room, was awakened by the noise and cried out loudly; the Indian attacked him, but at his cry people came running. The Indian, with the cunning of a savage beast, again sprang through the window, thinking to save himself by fleeing, but they overtook and captured him.

In Monterey there was a tannery built by a small river; I entered it and looked at the leather, which was much inferior to ours. Closer to the bay lay a huge piece of shell, which, I learned, they calcine, and it serves in place of lime for whitewashing houses. The wide bay was filled with trading vessels that had come to sell goods or buy local products. Among them were many whalers that had put in for repairs or a supply of water. A French ship had hauled up to the landing. It had come for live cattle for the Sandwich Islands. I did not find anything else remarkable in the town, and I made haste back to my ship.

Three weeks after our anchoring at Yerba Buena, two more ships, the [*Veliky Knyaz*] *Konstantin* and the *Baikal,* arrived in San Francisco Bay from the [Russian-American Company's] colonies to load wheat and beef; we received a packet from the governor of the colonies [Adolf Etolin] with orders to go for salt to the island of Carmen in the Gulf of California, or the Vermilion Sea.

Because cash in piasters were necessary for the purchase of salt and the payment of anchorage (and we did not have enough of them, plus bills of exchange on the Russian-American Company to the value of 5 t[housand] piasters, or 25 t[housand] pap[er] rub[les]), we faced the prospect of having to enter some port close to our route where it would be possible without difficulty to exchange the promissory notes. At those places where we had to get salt and in general at all of the places around the Gulf of California, we would be quite unable to exchange such a sum of promissory notes, for the local inhabitants do not have a lot of money, and if they do, then very few of them do; and besides, they do not have major transactions with the brokerages at the prosperous ports where we might expend the notes. European ships come here very rarely, and even then only on some special occasion, e.g., the need to water or to make some repairs. They seldom enter the Gulf of California for salt, and even the Russian-American Company fetches this product on Carmen every three years only, and for such voyages it always outfits a more capacious vessel.

Because our ship, the *Naslednik,* is the largest of the company's ships that are suitable for the voyage, we were ordered not to load wheat in California but to go for salt; the wheat had to be delivered to the colonies by the newly arrived brigs *Konstantin* [*Constantine*] and *Baikal.*

What could be more agreeable than this news? Each of us was sick of gloomy Sitka, with its constant rain and fog, and each wanted to enjoy himself a little longer in foreign ports, to bask in a fragrant climate.

Now we had to find a port where we could definitely and profitably exchange our promissory notes. The atlas indicated Mazatlán to us, lying on the Pacific Ocean on the western coast of North America.

The experience of the commander and the customary smartness of the sailors did not keep us lingering long and awaiting a favorable wind. After having stocked the requisite provisions and water, and despite much difficulty in dragging the anchor off the silty bottom of San Francisco Bay, at 3 o'clock we went to sea, singing, and by 8 o'clock in the evening we were 70 miles off the coast.

DOCUMENT 31

Mikhail Tebenkov's Report about the Discovery of Gold in California, 1848

EDITOR'S INTRODUCTION

Very soon after Markov's departure, the army and navy of the United States, which was fighting a war with Mexico, invaded Alta California and rendered it American territory in 1848. Early the same year, gold was discovered at the site of a mill being built for John Sutter, who had bought the moveable property of the colony of Ross. The last two documents in this volume attest both events. Governor Tebenkov[1] during his five-year term (1845–50) energetically and successfully promoted exploration, trade, and reconstruction; he also supervised the preparation of an atlas of the coasts of Russian America and Far Eastern Siberia.[2] His report on the gold rush was derived from his trip to California to try to collect Sutter's outstanding debt for the purchase of Fort Ross, whose previous manager, Alexander Rotchev,[3] had been dismissed by the company for mismanagement. He then worked irregularly (chiefly as a newspaper editor) and traveled

---

[1]Mikhail Dmitriyevich Tebenkov (1802–72), a native of Tallinn (Reval), graduated from the Naval Academy at the beginning of 1821 and served in the Baltic Fleet as a midshipman before entering the company's service in early 1825. After reaching New Archangel via Okhotsk, he commanded various ships in colonial waters before returning in 1834 to work briefly at the company's headquarters in St. Petersburg. In 1835 he captained the company vessel *Yelena* on its round-the-world voyage to New Archangel. In 1840 Tebenkov returned via Okhotsk to St. Petersburg, leaving the service of both the company and the navy and joining the Ministry of Education as an inspector with the civil rank of collegiate assessor. In early 1844 he rejoined the navy and was promoted to captain, second rank and appointed governor of Russian America. Again he crossed Siberia (this time with his wife) to Okhotsk, before sailing to New Archangel from Ayan, soon to succeed Okhotsk as Russia's chief Pacific port. Upon his return to Russia in 1851 he resumed his naval career, becoming a rear admiral. In 1856 he was elected a director of the Russian-American Company. He retired from the navy in 1860 with the rank of vice admiral. See Grinëv, *Kto yest kto*, 524–25; and Pierce, *Russian America*, 500–504.

[2]See Tebenkov, *Northwest Coasts of America*.

[3]See Rotchev, "Letters of A. Rotchev"; Rotchev, "New Eldorado in California," 33–40; and Fainshtein, *Vospominaniya*.

extensively. In this memoir, Rotchev wistfully recollects his trip to Sutter's Fort seven years before American invaders were to overwhelm his beloved California. He also published an account of Sitka that was likely written by Khlebnikov and a travel account.[4]

Governor Mikhail Tebenkov, A Report to the Board of Directors of the Russian-American Company about the Discovery of Gold in California,[5] [New Archangel], 23 December 1848

I have the honor to report to the Company's Board of Directors that throughout the colonies entrusted to my management all is well. Following the sickness (measles), which marked us so grievously, the native (as well as the [non-]native) population again experienced a bilious rheumatic fever (febris rheumatico-beliosa) in the autumn. Thanks to God, with the diligence of the physicians this disease, after having soon been overcome, was in any case forestalled with [His] help. The number of deaths was virtually insignificant: only two died. The weather this autumn has so far not been as harsh as in previous years, but this [moderation] has not improved the means of sustenance. In the spring I will have the honor to report on this vital subject in more detail.

The brig *Okhotsk* (Captain Klinkovstryom),[6] which returned on 9 December from San Francisco in California, brought us the news that is probably already known to the Board of Directors: Northern [Alta] California has been transformed from a poor, sleepy, patriarchal country into one of the richest, with people flowing there from every country in the world to seek gold, whose deposits have been discovered in the streams entering the Sacramento River—fabulous wealth, it is said. According to the newspaper *The Californian*, up to 3,500 men are already working the goldfields. It is known to the authorities that up to 150 t[housand] piasters' [worth] of gold is extracted daily.

This poor-to-rich phenomenon has caused and will cause a frightful change in everyone and will probably have an impact on the colonies. The very low degree

---

[4]Rotchev, "Ocherki severo-zapadnavo berega Ameriki"; Rotchev, "Vospominaniya russkavo puteshest-vennika."

[5]EHAT, f. 2,057, op. 1, d. 377, fols. 44–48v (original).

[6]Martyn Fyodorovich Klinkovstryom (Martin Klinkofström) (1812–84 or 1892), a native of Latvia, was descended from Swedish nobility. After graduating from St. Petersburg's School of Commercial Naviga-tion, he served the Russian-American Company as a colonial navigator in the 1820s. He returned to Russia but entered the company's service again in 1837, sailing to New Archangel as assistant navigator of the *Niko-lay I* under Captain Yevgeny Berens. For the next quarter of a century Klinkovstryom commanded various ships in colonial waters. In 1862 he was appointed Russian vice-consul and company agent at San Francisco, succeeding Pyotr Kostromitinov. The latter position lapsed with the sale of Russian America to the United States in 1867, but Klinkovstryom remained vice-consul until 1875, when he returned to Russia. See Grinëv, *Kto yest kto*, 235; and Pierce, *Russian America*, 242–43.

of effort, such as existed in California as recollected by the former missionaries, has now completely disappeared. Everybody and everything have taken to
seeking gold. The same newspaper writes that nobody gathers grain from the
fields and that it is left standing to rot. The dearness of everything is inordi-
nate and unprecedented. An ounce of gold (one funt of 82 *zolotniks*[7] equals 12
ounces) is worth 8 piasters in cash or 16 piasters in goods, and it corresponds
ordinarily to our paper ruble but sometimes even less. A worker earns from 10
to 20 piasters a day. A bull or cow has risen from 6 to 24 piasters and a fanega
of wheat to 12 piasters; the former are nowhere to be had, and nobody rounds
them up and drives them to a port. In addition, at the present time California
suffers from a great shortage of other necessities of life, namely, dresses, shoes,
and the like. For this reason a partner in the firm of Starkey,[8] Janion,[9] and Co.,
Mr. Falkner,[10] whom I chose as our agent upon the death of Mr. Leidesdorff,[11]
asked me to hasten to send to him as soon as possible 20 thousand piasters'
[worth] of some essential goods, promising to pay us in gold at [the rate of]
16 piasters per ounce of 23½ carats. As a result, on 23 December I dispatched
the barque[12] *Knyaz Menshikov* [*Prince Menshikov*] (on it I have the honor to
submit this report to the Board of Directors) with a cargo of goods to the sum
of about 50 t[housand] piasters. In all human undertakings and activities, success generally enlightens the mind. What will come from this undertaking and
from all of my assignments to Messrs. Ivanov,[13] Klinkovstryom, Doroshin,[14] and

[7] *1 zolotnik* = 4.27 grams or 0.14 ounces.

[8] Starkey was an English merchant who arrived in Alta California in 1848, formed a partnership with
Janion, and died around 1850. See Bancroft, *California Pioneer Register,* 40.

[9] R. C. Janion, an English trader, arrived in Alta California in 1847 from Honolulu and became a partner
in the firm of Starkey, Janion, and Co., which functioned until 1849. See Bancroft, *California Pioneer Register,* p. 199.

[10] E. R. Falkner, a clerk of Starkey, Janion, and Co. in San Francisco, arrived in Alta California in 1848.
See Bancroft, *California Pioneer Register,* 136.

[11] William Alexander Leidesdorff (1810–48), a mixed-blood native of the Danish West Indies (Virgin
Islands), arrived in Alta California in 1841 as supercargo of the *Julia Ann* from New Orleans. In 1845 he was
appointed U.S. vice-consul at San Francisco, where he invested heavily in real estate and became a prominent businessman and politician. See Bancroft, *California Pioneer Registry,* 219.

[12] A barque, or bark, was a sailing vessel with three masts, square-rigged on the fore and main masts and
fore-and-aft rigged on the mizzen (aftermost) mast. Until the middle of the nineteenth century they were
relatively small ships.

[13] Vasily Ivanovich Ivanov arrived in Russian America in 1841 and served the company as a civilian navigator. He became assistant manager of New Archangel Counter in 1847 and manager in 1865. See Grinëv,
Kto yest kto, 192.

[14] The geologist Pyotr P. Doroshin (ca. 1823–75), a lieutenant in the Corps of Mining Engineers, was hired
by the company in 1847 to prospect for colonial mineral resources for five years. At the beginning of 1849 he
was sent with four Russians and six Tlingits on the *Knyaz Menshikov* to California, where they extracted 11
funts, 53 zolotniks of pure gold from the Yuba River. Part of the gold was used to buy a 234-ton, three-masted
ship in San Francisco for the company's fleet; the rest was shipped to New Archangel. Thereafter Doroshin
mostly prospected for coal around Cook Inlet for the Californian market; he recommended the development
of the beds at English Bay (Port Graham), but they were not mined until the last half of the 1850s (at much
cost). See Grinëv, *Kto yest kto,* 159; and Pierce, *Russian America,* 123–24.

Rudakov[15] will be reported beforehand to the Board of Directors by Mr. Ivanov from California. In his submission he will explain to some extent my assignment to him and its outcome. M[r.] Rudakov went to command the ship, Ivanov and Klinkovstryom to sell the cargo and to recover Sutter's debt, and Mr. Doroshin to get gold dust, whose acquisition is highly likely.

I directed that the cargo—which is quite unnecessary for the colonies (I will have the honor to report on this [matter] in detail to the Board of Directors in the spring)—not be sold for gold only. I ordered that, if possible, a sound three-masted ship of 500 tons for whaling be bought in exchange for the goods, for coastal whaling alone cannot answer the purpose (I will also have the honor to report on this [subject] to the Board of Directors in the spring). Perhaps M[r.] Ivanov will draw bills of exchange on the Company's Board of Directors for the ship, but only in case he does not have enough gold to exchange [for it]—which I will report to the Board of Directors at the first opportunity. There is no better time than the present to buy a ship. M[r.] Klinkovstryom in his report tells me that there are 16 ships lying at San Francisco at the command of Providence, and some do not have even captains; all are chasing gold. This situation greatly alarms me; at Sitka there are very few Russian sailors, and the Finnish sailors cannot be sent to any foreign port. This [risk] has already been ascertained and demonstrated by experience. I do not know what Mr. Garder[16] (on the brig *Baikal*) will do; one Finn has already deserted Klinkovstryom. In such a state of affairs the government of California is powerless to help.

There is some hope, too, of seeing a recovery of Mr. Sutter's debt.[17] It is said that he owns the richest gold deposits. He has up to 300 workers for his business, and he has already asked Klinkovstryom how much (what value of) gold dust we intend to receive from him [in lieu of wheat].

The ship *Knyaz Menshikov,* which will take a cargo to San Francisco, will proceed from there to the Sandwich Islands to the port of Honolulu for salt and with

---

[15]Aleksandr Ilyich Rudakov (1817–75) graduated from the Naval Academy in 1832 and served in both the Baltic Sea and Black Sea Fleets before entering the company's service in 1844 as a lieutenant and commanding several vessels in colonial waters. A year after returning overland in 1850 to St. Petersburg via Ayan, he was first promoted and then appointed assistant governor of Russian America. He reached New Archangel in the spring of 1852 via the Horn on the *Kadyak* (*Kodiak*) and served under Governor Nikolay Rozenburg until the latter's departure a year later, whereupon Rudakov served as acting governor until the arrival of Stepan Voyevodsky in 1854. He left the company's service in 1858 and rejoined the navy, becoming a rear admiral in 1865 and a vice admiral in 1870, when he retired. See Grinëv, *Kto yest kto,* 461–62; and Pierce, *Russian America,* 434–35.

[16]Leonty Fyodorovich Garder (Leonard Christian von Harder) (1808–18??), a Baltic German from Livonia, arrived in Russian America in 1837 on the *Nikolay I* as a civilian navigator and served on various colonial vessels. He returned to Russia in 1852. See Grinëv, *Kto yest kto,* 118; and Pierce, *Russian America,* 157.

[17]Fort Ross had been sold to Sutter in 1841 for $30,000, payable in wheat within five years, but he defaulted, secure in the knowledge that the Mexican authorities would not enforce the Russian claims because under Mexican law only the buildings and equipment, and not the land, could be sold.

other goods for Mr. Janion. Here I have also stipulated that all trade turnover occur within the limits of colonial output, that is to say, bills of exchange will not be drawn. Depending upon the circumstances—if a ship has been bought—Mr. Rudakov will proceed directly from the Sandwich [Islands] to New Archangel; if a ship has not been bought, he will call again at San Francisco to fetch Messrs. Klinkovstryom, Doroshin, and Ivanov, who will have stayed there until that time.

Soon after [the departure of] the ship *Knyaz Menshikov* I intended to dispatch the longboat that was built for the late Leidesdorff and that I named the galiot *Klinkit* [*Tlingit*] (the name of the people whom we call Koloshes). M[r.] Faulkner asked me for it and agreed to give 6 t[housand] piasters, a price that I myself set without knowing about rich-to-poor California. I will order its sale in accordance with a judgment of the proportionate expensiveness of supplies, which, I think, we will not have occasion to obtain from California for a long time, especially if we do not increase our means of counteracting the wealth of activity for which we do not at present have the manpower in the colonies; the workers are perceptibly smoldering and disappearing, and there are very few in Sitka. In California, coal, timber, transport vessels, houses, and depots are in demand. With gold there can be no low prices, as our Siberia demonstrates.[18] And with men (workers, of course) we can neither behave easily with our former equilibrium nor even, I think, turn the odds in our favor within several years. All of this [information] I hasten to submit for the consideration and deliberation of the Board of Directors so as not to lose time taking appropriate measures, which in my view consist chiefly of making the colonies as self-supporting as possible. Likewise, in representing to the Board of Directors the hopelessness of obtaining supplies from California for the colonies, I would suggest that it hasten to use the route that I prescribed in no. 349 of 1848[19] to the Board of Directors.

I have the honor to report this [news] to the Company's Board of Directors.

[signed] Captain of the 2nd Rank Tebenkov.
Secretary Vysotsky.[20]

---

[18]Gold mining increased dramatically in Siberia between the 1830s and the 1840s (from one-sixth to three-quarters of Russian output), thanks mainly to discoveries in south-central Siberia, and inflation resulted.

[19]Not found.

[20]Grigory Grigoryevich Vysotsky served as Tebenkov's secretary.

Alexander Rotchev, "A New Eldorado in California," 1849

A. Rotchev,[1] "A New Eldorado in California,"[2] [St. Petersburg?], 1849[3]

What an enchanting land is California! For eight months of the year the sky is always clear and cloudless, and during the remaining months, beginning with the last days of November, it rains periodically; the heat in the shade does not exceed 25 degrees Réaumur. In January everything comes to life—the flora is in full bloom, everything is fragrant, and iridescent hummingbirds flutter and sparkle on a stalk or quiver like precious stones over the blossoms. The virgin

---

[1]Aleksandr Gavrilovich Rotchev (1806–73), the last manager of Ross Counter, was born in Moscow. He attended Moscow University but did not graduate, owing to his elopement in 1828 with Princess Yelena Pavlovna Gagarina. To improve his precarious financial situation as a copyist and translator, Rotchev entered the service of the Russian-American Company in 1835, and in August of that year he and his wife and son sailed on the *Yelena* for the colonies. After reaching New Archangel in the spring of 1836, Rotchev undertook various special assignments for Governor Kupreyanov, including a mission to California on the sloop *Sitkha* in the summer of 1836. A year later he was appointed Kostromitinov's successor as manager of Ross. During his managership, visitors noted the hospitality and gentility of their hosts and the quality of their cuisine. In July 1838 Rotchev met Captain John Sutter and helped him to establish his settlement of New Helvetia on the Sacramento River, and three years later he persuaded Sutter to buy Fort Ross, which the company had decided to abandon. On 1 May 1842 the Rotchevs left Russian America for Okhotsk, whence they traveled overland to St. Petersburg. En route either at Irkutsk or upon their return to the capital, Rotchev's wife left him; she became a schoolmistress in Irkutsk in the 1850s and published a book for children. Meanwhile, her onetime husband had been investigated by the Russian-American Company for mismanagement while manager of Ross and dismissed from its employ. See Rotchev, "Letters of A. Rotchev"; Rotchev, "New Eldorado in California"; and Fainshtein, *Vospominaniya russkovo puteshestvennika*.

[2]Rotchev, "Novy Eldorado v Kalifornii." For an earlier translation of this memoir, see Rotchev, "New Eldorado in California."

[3]After quitting Fort Ross in 1841, Rotchev did not return to California until 1850, so this article had to have been based upon his impressions while serving as manager of Ross Counter in 1838–41. It was probably submitted to the journal while he was living in St. Petersburg at the end of the 1840s, to take advantage of the interest of readers in the Californian gold rush.

soil of California bears astounding fruit: I happened to see a wheat harvest of one hundred and fifty–fold [the seed] there! Corn and frijoles a thousand, one hundred and fifty–fold! And with what slight effort: a pointed, curved branch, the end of which is shaped into a kind of blade, is a plow, and after scratching one and half vershoks into the soil the plowman starts to sow; the bough of a laurel tree, fastened to an ox, serves as his harrow. You pick a peach from the tree and the discarded stone falls to the ground, and after three years on that same spot you will see a mature tree and watch them pick and use its fruit! A gigantic pine, the *chaga* (*pinus Californicus*) [coast redwood], grows in California; you look at this enormous tree: it has lived 8–9 centuries! A hollow burned out of its trunk serves as a dwelling for entire families! Before my very eyes [at Fort Ross] from one tree were built a granary and a house that accommodated a colonial district's office and two apartments for foremen. Its height from the butt to the top was from 180 to 200 feet and its thickness from 8 to 10 feet. You can imagine with what a deafening crash this colossus fell, hewn by the hand of man! The other trees of the forest of California are laurel [bay], chestnut, and oak and wild grape along the riverbanks. And long has man regarded this land with indifference and coldness; now, when gold has been found in the bowels of this land, people rush across the Rocky Mountains, out of New Orleans, across Panama, and around the Horn, and now natural scientists and mineralogists head there. Under the dissecting knife of science every vein of this land of beauty is beginning to tremble! I passed the best years of my life there, and I reverently carry the memory of those days in my soul; and now, seeing as we are on the subject, I want to recount two events from the diary of my life in California.

It was 1838. On one of those bright, splendid California days a man presented himself to me whom I at first took to be the leader of a party of beaver hunters (*castoreros*). I was already prepared to offer him the usual services that I was accustomed to rendering to short-term guests, but I was astounded by my discovery. "I have come to you," he said to me, "with a letter of recommendation. I am a Swiss and a captain in the French service. I quit Switzerland; you know that it is very crowded there. I settled on the banks of the Missouri, but there was little room for my activities there! I sold my land and everything on it. I crossed the Rocky Mountains via a system of lakes to Astoria, but the Columbia was not to my liking. I was in the Sandwich Islands and at your colonies on the Northwest Coast of America. Here perhaps it is better! I like this country. You live here and know these valleys; please give me your advice and help. If I come to know this land, I will settle near you." This candid speech touched my heart; I received him cordially, and the next day I set off with the captain to San Francisco. There, having been invited by him to his launch, I decided to go up the Sacramento River with him for a few days. I saw how his lively face lit up at the sight of the charming banks of the Sacramento. At its entry into northern San Francisco Bay [San Pablo Bay] the river divides into enormous reaches dotted with numerous low-lying islands. After a day's ascent the banks become steep, and the virgin chagas are so dense that the wind could barely fill the sails of the launch. Most of the time we ascended with oars. "C'est un beau pays!" ["This is a fine country!"], said the captain. "I suppose you will not go any farther," I replied. "This virgin soil will reward your labor generously. Ask the Mexican government for [a land grant of] 5 sq[uare] miles; I will gladly be your neighbor, and you will not fail to find a market—we will buy it readily. What more could you want? Man here is an obedient child; the Indian is your worker for a few strings of beads—be kind to him and do not just shoot him like a dog at every turn, after the example of the Californian creoles [mestizos]. I will say without any exaggeration that here the most venomous animals are not malicious and the beasts are not ferocious. Tarantula and scorpion bites are nothing, and the bear flees at the sight of man. There are rattlesnakes and jaguars [cougars?], but they are rare." Thus did we ascend the river for three days; finally, our Indian guide, whom we had taken from San Francisco, spoke: "Aquí [e]sta bueno! [H]ay arboles, [h]ay agua—hará sandias!" ("Here it is good, a lot of water and trees—watermelons will grow"). We went ashore, and one and a half verstas from the river we laid the foundation of an outpost, which they named "New Helvetia." The Indians carried ashore all of the supplies and goods on the launch, and we pitched a tent and for a long, long time talked about the plans and intentions of the new owner. I heard how colonists from the United States would come to him and how they would form large parties to hunt beaver, how the captain's wife and children would come to him at his new holding, how he would sell me an enormous number of bushels of wheat. . . . This happy immigrant was Mr. Sutter, the founder and owner of the fort that is now known by the same name, and the discoverer of gold in California.

Exactly a year later I had to leave this country,[4] sell everything that could be sold to whatever buyer could be found, and abandon everything that could not fit in the hold of the ship. For these commercial negotiations it was necessary for me to meet Mr. Sutter. I set off in a launch to my old acquaintance on the Sacramento River; this time a friend, a highly educated Frenchman, Mr. [Victor] P[rudón],[5] accompanied me. He had lived a long time in Mexico, knew this country well, and would be a godsend as a traveling companion anywhere. That was in August, i.e., at that time of year when the forests and valleys of California, set alight by the Indians, are the very picture of that drawn by the

---

[4]Rotchev's dating is incorrect; he left California in 1841, which is three years after 1838.

[5]Victor Prudón (originally Prudhomme) (1809–?) lived for seven years in Mexico before arriving in Alta California in 1834 as one of the teachers in the Híjars-Padrés colony. Fluent in Spanish and English as well as his native French, he served as secretary to Governor Alvarado in 1837–38 and became secretary to General Vallejo in 1841, when he was granted Rancho Bodega. See Bancroft, *California Pioneer Register,* 292–93.

talented [James Fenimore] Cooper[6] showing the fires in the virgin forests of America. Rain starts to fall intermittently in October and November and puts out these fiery streams running through boundless expanses. Once, while going from California to our colonies [in Russian Alaska], for several hundred miles from the coast in the open ocean I happened to see thick masses of smoke that obscured the sun, and this phenomenon lasted several days!

On the third day of our trip on the Sacramento River my French friend lost patience; he grew weary of the monotonous splash of the oars of the Indians working in shifts, day and night. During the day the heat was unbearable. "Commandant!" the Frenchman said to me; "Je veux essayer du bonheur!" ["I want to try my luck!"] "For a long time I have been sitting day and night in the launch; I will try my luck. I think I see Mr. Sutter's ranch. Look, there it is! While you ascend the innumerable bends of the river, I will cross directly, and after presenting myself to Sutter I will tell him to get ready to receive you. There it is; I see the flag flying above the roof!" "Muchacho!" he shouted to an Indian, "Mira! [H]ay [e]sta la casa!" ["Boy! Look! There's the house!"]. "No [e]sta lechos, S[eño]r!" ["It's not far, sir!"] he replied. In vain I tried to persuade my Frenchman, in vain I assured him that no ranch, no roof, no flag, nothing at all had appeared to him, that his tired eyes were depicting nonexistent things, that it was the very same as the fata morgana[7] at sea. Nothing helped! "I will mock you when you arrive at Mr. Sutter's place," he said. "Give me your pistols, some caps and shells, a few rusks, and flints and steels." "Take them, but mind that you aren't sorry afterwards!" I told him. "I am very sorry that I can't give you any of my men; the launch does not move fast with oars, I will weaken its manpower by letting you have an escort, and the river is rapid." Jumping nimbly from the launch, the Frenchman set off, taking long strides toward the Promised Land of Mr. Sutter's ranch. He quickly disappeared in the vines covering the river's bank. We continued upriver against the current and did not reach New Helvetia until midnight. We received a hearty welcome from our host and a throng of his Indians, who had settled nearby amicably for work. My first question was about my French friend: "Nobody has appeared," Mr. Sutter answered anxiously. "Mr. P. has acted recklessly! How could he have decided to leave you in these boundless valleys without a guide and not knowing the terrain!" Whereupon my anxiety increased, too. I prevailed upon Mr. Sutter to assemble some Indians and send them in every direction after the missing Frenchman. The Indians, accompanied by several Americans from a party of beaver hunters, set off in search. Wearied by the trip and the heat, I was glad to throw myself onto a bed that had been readied for me and fell asleep thinking that my Frenchman would escape with a little fright, that they would find him

[6]Cooper (1789–1851) was a popular American writer of historical romances of life on the Indian frontier.
[7]A mirage seen in the Strait of Messina between Calabria and Sicily.

near the fort, and that we would just laugh at his impatience. Morning arrived but the poor fellow did not. Thus did three days pass, and Mr. Sutter and I lost hope, and in our hearts we considered him dead; he could have been taken by a jaguar [cougar] for breakfast, a rattlesnake could have bitten him—who knows what came into our heads. Suddenly on the third day we heard a shout, and a throng of Indians carried Mr. P. nearly lifeless into Sutter's room. One can imagine our joy! In forcing his way through thorns Mr. P. had almost lost his clothing, which was in tatters. He had not eaten for three days! Little by little from a spoon I filled him with tea. When he recovered, this is what we heard. "You saw how I set off cheerfully for the object, shimmering in the heat, that I took to be Mr. Sutter's ranch. I walked a long time without losing heart, but my goal did not come closer and all of the shimmerings, it seemed, receded farther and farther away from me! Finally, everything merged in my eyes and then disappeared! There was no flag, no house! I felt weary! After sleeping a little, I decided not to go on and not to go deeper into the valley but to return to the river. By nightfall I reached the riverbank, and only then did I begin to realize my recklessness! The next day I again began to look for Mr. Sutter's house and flag, and it seemed that I saw them! I walked to them boldly, but the same thing happened to me as the day before! Tired and ragged, I returned to the river and passed a troubled, feverish night! A wild goat made a noise in the reeds, but I imagined that I saw the glaring eyes of a jaguar [cougar] or heard a band of Indians coming to kill me! Ready to fire the pistols, I sat up all night, trying to scare off my enemies. Wanting to show my imaginary foes that I was not alone, I cried out repeatedly: 'Muchachos aquí! Ellos tienen miedo!' ['Here, boys! They're afraid!'] Thus did I pass the night, cursing my recklessness! Weakened, nearly naked, hungry, I had already lost any hope of rescue, certain that you were returning from Sutter's after only a few days; and who could see me in this wilderness? However, supposing that fate would bring someone to this spot on the river where I lay exhausted, I found a piece of paper in my pocket and wrote in pencil, 'Qui que tu soit, passant! Sauve un pauvre malheureux Français, egaré dans ces lieux!' ('Whoever you may be, traveler! Save a poor, unfortunate Frenchman lost here!') I wrapped the paper in a handkerchief, which I tied to a stick that I stuck in the sandy riverbank. On the third day I could not set out and just tried with what strength I had to start a fire in the valley, figuring that I would be more visible, and if men had been sent in search of me, they would find me more easily. Nobody appeared, my strength left me, I was dying in this wilderness! Finally, your men noticed me, and here I am with you." I gave Mr. P. time to recuperate and set off on the return route to San Francisco Bay, where our ship awaited me. . . .[8]

---

[8]The epilogue, which is a description of California's gold resources on the basis of a report of 10 September 1848 by the military governor of California, Colonel Richard Mason, is omitted here.

Glossary

ankerok (anker)	a Russian cask with a liquid capacity of about 3 *vedros* (pails), or about 36 liters or 38 quarts (9–10½ American gallons)
arroba	a Spanish measure of weight equal in Alta California to approximately 25 pounds or 11.3 kilograms
arshin	an old Russian linear measure equal to 28 inches
baidara	an umiak, used for freighting
baidarka	a kayak, with one, two, or three hatches, used for hunting and fishing and personal transport
chaga	coast redwood
chervonets	a tsarist gold coin of three, five, or ten rubles' denomination
chetvert	an old Russian dry measure commonly containing 5.77 Imperial bushels (346.2 pounds of wheat) or 5.96 American bushels (357.6 pounds of wheat)
colonial	a resident of New Spain who was born in the colonies
desyatina	an old Russian measure of area equal to 2.7 acres or 1.1 hectares
fanega	a rather variable Spanish dry measure, generally equal in Alta California to approximately 1⅔ U.S. bushels or 125–35 pounds
funt	an old Russian measure of weight equal to one-fortieth of a *pud*, or 0.90 pounds or 0.49 kilograms
Italian mile	the equivalent of 1.15 English miles or 1.85 kilometers
lot	an old Russian measure of weight equal to 12.78 grams or 0.45 ounces
peninsular	a resident of New Spain who was born in the Iberian Peninsula
piaster	a Spanish silver dollar, consisting of 8 reals
picul	a measure of weight commonly equal to 133⅓ pounds
presidio	literally, a garrison; figuratively, a citadel, fortress, or fort

promyshlennik a Russian-American Company common worker, one without any supervisory authority

pud an old Russian measure of weight equal to 36.11 pounds or 16.38 kilograms and consisting of 40 *funts*

ruble the standard Russian monetary unit, a silver coin (and later a paper bill) consisting of 100 kopecks

sazhen an old Russian linear measure equal to 7 feet or 2.13 meters

shtof an old Russian measure of capacity equal to 1.30 quarts or 1.23 liters

vershok an old Russian linear measure equal to 1.75 inches or 4.4 centimeters

versta an old Russian linear measure equal to 0.66 miles or 1.06 kilometers

zolotnik an old Russian measure of weight equal to 4.27 grams or 0.14 ounce

Bibliography

ABBREVIATIONS FOR ARCHIVES

ARGO   Archive of the Russian Geographical Society, St. Petersburg

AVPRI   Archive of the Foreign Policy of the Russian Empire, Moscow

EHAT   Estonian Historical Archive, Tartu

GAPK   State Archive of Perm Kray, Perm

RGAVMF   Russian State Archive of the Navy, St. Petersburg

RGIA   Russian State Historical Archive, St. Petersburg

RRAC   "Records of the Russian-American Company, 1802–1867: Correspondence of Governors General," File Microcopies of Records in the National Archives: No. 11, Washington, D.C., 1942 (77 reels)

SOURCES

Alekseev, A. I. *The Odyssey of a Russian Scientist: I. G. Voznesenskii in Alaska, California and Siberia, 1839–1849.* Translated by Wilma C. Follette. Kingston, Ont.: Limestone Press, 1987.

Alekseyev, A. I., N. N. Bolkhovitinov, and T. S. Fyodorova, eds. *Rossiisko-Amerikanskaya kompaniya i izuchenie Tikhookeanskovo Severa, 1799–1815: Sbornik dokumentov* [The Russian-American Company and the study of the North Pacific, 1799–1815: A collection of documents]. Moscow: Nauka, 1994.

Andreyev, A. I., ed. *Russian Discoveries in the Pacific and in North America in the Eighteenth and Nineteenth Centuries: A Collection of Materials.* Translated by Carl Ginsburg. Ann Arbor, Mich.: J. W. Edwards, 1952.

Arima, Eugene Y. "Building Umiaks." In *The North American Canoe: The Living Tradition,* edited by John Jennings, 138–59. Buffalo, NY: Firefly Books.

Avdyukov, Yu. P., Olkhova, N. S., and Surnik, A. P., comps. *Komandor: stranitsy zhiznii i deyatelnosti kamergna Yevo Imperatorskovo Dvora, ober-prokura Senata, rukovoditelya pervoy russkoy krugosvetnoy ekspeditsii N. P. Rezanova* [The Commander: Pages from the Life and Work of Chamberlain of the Imperial Court, Assistant Procurator of the Senate, and Leader of the First Russian Round-the-World Expedition, N. P. Rezanov]. Krasnoyarsk: "Ofset," 1995.

[Bancroft, Hubert Howe]. *California Pioneer Register and Index, 1542–1848: Including Inhabitants of California, 1769–1800, and List of Pioneers.* Baltimore, Md.: Regional Publishing, 1964. Extracted from Bancroft, *The History of California.*

Bandini, Juan. *A Description of California in 1828.* Translated by Doris Wright. Berkeley, Calif.: Bancroft Library, 1951.

Barratt, Glynn. *Russia in Pacific Waters, 1715–1825: A Survey of the Origins of Russia's Naval Presence in the North and South Pacific.* Vancouver: University of British Columbia Press, 1981.

Bashkina, Nina N., Nikolai N. Bolkhovitinov, John H. Brown, J. Dane Hartgrove, Ivan I. Kudriavtsev, Natal'ia B. Kuznetsova, Ronald D. Landa, et al., eds. *The United States and Russia: The Beginning of Relations, 1765–1815.* Washington, D.C.: United States Department of State, 1980.

Beidleman, Richard G. *California's Frontier Naturalists.* Berkeley: University of California Press, 2006.

Black, Dawn, and Alexander Petrov, eds. *Natalia Shelikhova: Russian Oligarch of Alaska Commerce.* Fairbanks: University of Alaska Press, 2010.

Blomkvist, E. E. "A Russian Scientific Expedition to California and Alaska, 1839–1849: The Drawings of I. G. Voznesenskii." Translated by Basil Dmytryshyn and E. A. P. Crownhart-Vaughan. *Oregon Historical Quarterly* 73, no. 2 (June 1972): 101–70.

Bolgurtsev, B. N., comp. *Morskoy biografichesky spravochnik Dalnevo Vostoka Rossii i Russkoy Ameriki XVII–nachalo XX vv.* [A naval biographical handbook of the Russian Far East and Russian America of the 18th to the beginning of the 20th centuries]. Vladivostok: "USSURI," 1998.

Bonnycastle, R[ichard] H[enry]. *Spanish America; or, A Descriptive, Historical, and Geographical Account of the Dominions of Spain in the Western Hemisphere. . . .* London: Longman, Hurst, Rees, Orme, and Brown, 1818.

Bowman, J. N. "Weights and Measures in Provincial California." *California Historical Quarterly* 30, no. 4 (1951): 315–38.

Bridgwater, William, and Elizabeth J. Sherwood, eds. *The Columbia Encyclopedia in One Volume.* 2nd ed. Morningside Heights, NY: Columbia University Press, 1950.

Brinck, Wolfgang. *The Aleutian Kayak: Origins, Construction, and Use of the Traditional Seagoing Baidarka.* Camden, Maine: Ragged Mountain Press, 1995.

Brooks, George R., ed. *The Southwest Expedition of Jedediah S. Smith: His Personal Account of the Journey to California, 1826–1827.* Glendale, Calif.: Arthur H. Clark, 1977.

Brown, Alan K. "Pomponio's World." In *Native American Perspectives on the Hispanic Colonization of Alta California,* edited by Edward D. Castillo, 217–34. New York: Garland, 1991.

Castillo, Edward D., trans. and ed. "The Assassination of Padre Andrés Quintana by the Indians of Mission Santa Cruz in 1812: The Narrative of Lorenzo Asisara." *California History* 68 (Fall 1989): 117–25.

Chamisso, Adelbert von. *A Voyage around the World with the Romanzov Exploring Expedition in the Years 1815–1818 in the Brig* Rurik, *Captain Otto Von Kotzebue.* Translated and edited by Henry Kratz. Honolulu: University of Hawaii Press, 1986.

Chapman, Charles Edward, ed. *Expedition on the Sacramento and San Joaquin Rivers in 1817: Diary of Fray Narciso Duran.* Berkeley: University of California Press, 1911.

Chernykh, E. L. "Agriculture of Upper California: A Long Lost Account of Farming in California as Recorded by a Russian Observer at Fort Ross in 1841." *Pacific Historian* 11, no. 1 (Winter 1967): 10–28.

Chernykh, Ye. "O semenakh, prislannykh iz Verkhney Kalifornii" [About cultivation in Alta California]. *Zhurnal selskavo khozyaistva i ovtsevodstva* [Journal of agriculture and sheep-breeding], no. 3 (1842): 309–13.

————. "O skotovodstve v Verkhney Kalifornii" [About stockbreeding in Alta California]. *Zhurnal selskovo khoyaistva i ovtsevodstva,* no. 11 (1843): 110–26.

————. "O zemledelii v verkhney Kalifornii" [About agriculture in Alta California]. *Zhurnal selskavo khozyaistva i ovtsevodstva* [Journal of agriculture and sheepbreeding], no. 9 (1841): 234–65.

Choris, Louis. *Vues et paysages des régions équinoxiales, recueillis dans un voyage autour du monde* [Scenes and landscapes of the equinoctial regions recorded during a voyage around the world]. Paris: Paul Renourd, 1826.

Choris, M. Louis, and J. B. B. Eyries. *Voyage pittoresque autour du monde, avec des portraits de sauvages d'Amérique, d'Asie, d'Afrique, et des îles du Grand océan; des paysages, des vues maritimes, et plusiers objets d'histoire naturelle* [A picturesque voyage around the world, with portraits of the savages of America, Asia, Africa, and the islands of the Great Ocean, landscapes, marine views, and several objects of natural history]. Paris: Didot, 1822.

Dakin, Susanna Bryant. *The Lives of William Hartnell.* Stanford: Stanford University Press, 1949.

Dal, Vladimir. *Tolkovy slovar zhivovo velikorusskovo yazyka* [Explanatory dictionary of the living great Russian language]. Vol. 4. Moscow: Progress and Univers, 1994.

Davydov, G. I. *Two Voyages to Russian America, 1802–1807.* Translated by Colin Bearne. Kingston, Ont.: Limestone Press, 1977.

Dmytryshyn, Basil, E. A. P. Crownhart-Vaughan, and Thomas Vaughan, eds. and trans. *The Russian-American Colonies, 1798–1867.* Portland: Oregon Historical Society Press, 1989.

D'Wolf, John. *A Voyage to the North Pacific and a Journey through Siberia More Than Half a Century Ago.* Cambridge, Mass.: Welch and Bigelow, 1861. Reprinted in 1983 by Rulon-Miller Books, Bristol, R.I., in a limited edition of 225.

Dyson, George. *Baidarka.* Edmonds, Wash.: Alaska Northwest Publishing, 1986.

Engstrom, Elton. *Joseph O'Cain: Adventurer on the Northwest Coast.* Juneau: Alaska Litho Printers, 2003.

Erman, A. "Beiträge zur Klimatologie des Russischen Reiches, [Part] I, Ueber das Klima von Ross in Californien und Herrn Tschernychs meteorologische Beobachtungen an diesem Orte" [Contributions to the climatology of the Russian Empire, (part) 1, About the climate of Ross in California and Mr. Chernykh's meteorological observations there]. *Archiv für wissenschaftliche Kunde von Russland* 1 (1841): 564–65.

————. "Einege Bemerkungen über die Russischen und Spanischen Niederlassungen in Neu-Californien" [Some comments about the Russian and Spanish settlements in New California]. *Archiv für wissenschaftliche Kunde von Russland* 6 (1848): 426–32.

————. "Zusats-Bemerkungen über Neü Californien" [Additional remarks about New California]. *Annalen der Erd-, Volker-, und Staatenkunde,* series 2, vol. 8 (June 1833): 240–60.

Eschscholtz, Friedr[ich]. *Zoologischer Atlas, enthaltend Abbildungen und Beschreibungen neuer Thierarten.* . . . Berlin: G. Reimer, 1829–33.

Eschscholz, Johann Friedrich. "Descriptiones plantarum novae Californiae, adjectis florum exoticorum analysibus" [Descriptions of the Plants of New California, with an Analysis of Its Exotic Flora]. *Mémoires de l'Académie impériale des sciences de St. Pétersbourg* 10 (1826): 281–92.

Fainshtein, M. Sh., comp. *Vospominaniya russkovo puteshestvennika* [Reminiscences of a Russian traveler]. Moscow: Nauka, 1991.

Farris, Glenn J. "Otter Hunting by Alaskan Natives along the California Coast in the early Nineteenth Century." *Mains'l Haul: Journal of the Maritime Museum of San Diego* 43, nos. 3–4 (2007): 20–33.

————, trans. and ed. "The Russian Sloop *Apollo* in the North Pacific in 1822." *Sibirica* 1 (1993): 47–70.

————, ed. *So Far from Home: Russians in Early California*. Berkeley: University of California Press, 2012.

————, trans. and ed. "Visit of the Russian Warship *Apollo* to California in 1822–1823." *Southern California Quarterly* 75 (1993): 1–13.

Flynn, Dennis O., Arturo Giráldez, and James Sobredo, eds. *European Entry into the Pacific: Spain and the Acapulco-Manila Galleons*. Aldershot, U.K.: Ashgate, 2001.

Frost, Orcutt. *Bering: The Russian Discovery of America*. New Haven, Conn.: Yale University Press, 2003.

Geiger, Maynard. *Franciscan Missionaries in Hispanic California, 1769–1848: A Biographical Dictionary*. San Marino, Calif.: Huntington Library, 1969.

Gerhard, Peter. *The North Frontier of New Spain*. Rev. ed. Norman: University of Oklahoma Press, 1993.

————. "Pearl Diving in Lower California, 1533–1830." *Pacific Historical Review* 25 (1956): 239–49.

Gibson, James R. "A Kamchatkan Agronomist in California: The Reports of Yegor Leontyevich Chernykh (1813–1843)." In *Russkoye otkrytie Ameriki: Sbornik statey, posvyashchenny 70-letiyu akademika Nikolaya Nikolayevicha Bolkhovitinova* [The Russian discovery of America: A collection of articles dedicated to the 70th birthday of Nikolay Nikolayevich Bolkhovitinov], edited by A. O. Chubaryan, 425–36. Moscow: ROSSPEN, 2002.

————, trans. "Russia in California, 1833: Report of Governor Wrangel." *Pacific Northwest Quarterly* 60, no. 4 (October 1969): 205–15.

————, trans. "Russian America in 1833: The Survey of Kirill Khlebnikov." *Pacific Northwest Quarterly* 63, no. 1 (January 1972): 1–13.

Gibson, James R., and Alexei A. Istomin, comps. and eds. *Russian California: Imperial Russia in Native, Spanish, and Mexican California, 1806–1860*. Translated by James R. Gibson. 3 vols. London: Hakluyt Society, 2012–13.

Gillis, Michael J., and Michael F. Magliari. *John Bidwell and California: The Life and Writings of a Pioneer, 1841–1900*. Spokane, Wash.: Arthur H. Clark, 2003.

[Gillsen, Karl]. "Puteshestvie na shlyupe *Blagonamerenny* dlya izsledovaniya beregov Azii i Ameriki za Beringovym-Prolivom s 1819 po 1822 god" [A voyage in the sloop *Blagonamerenny* to explore the coasts of Asia and America beyond Bering Strait in 1819–22], part 2. *Otechestvennie zapiski* 66, no. 11 (November 1849): 1–24.

Golovnin, V. M. *Around the World on the* Kamchatka, *1817–1819*. Translated by Ella Lury Wiswell. Honolulu: Hawaiian Historical Society and University Press of Hawaii, 1979.

[————]. *Puteshestvie rossiiskavo shlyupa* "Diana" *iz Kronshtadta v Kamchatku v 1807, 1808 i 1809 gg*. [The voyage of the Russian sloop *Diana* from Kronshadt to Kamchatka in 1807, 1808, and 1809]. 2 vols. St. Petersburg: Admiralteiskaya Departamenta, 1819.

Golovnin, Flot Kapitan. *Puteshestvie vokrug Sveta, Po poveleniyu Gosudarya Imperatora sovershennoe, na voyennom Shlyupe* Kamchatke, *v 1817, 1818, i 1819 godakh . . .* [A voyage around the world, made by command of the tsar emperor, on the naval sloop *Kamchatka* in the years 1817, 1818, and 1819 . . .]. St. Petersburg: Morskaya Tipografiya, 1822.

Golownin, Captain. *Memoirs of a Captivity in Japan, 1811–1813*. 3 vols. London: Oxford University Press, 1973.

Grinëv, A[ndrei] V. *Kto yest kto v istorii Russkoy Ameriki* [Who's who in the history of Russian America]. Moscow: Academia, 2009.

———. *The Tlingit Indians in Russian America*. Translated by Richard L. Bland and Katerina G. Solovjova. Lincoln: University of Nebraska Press, 2005.

Gutiérrez, Ramón A., and Richard J. Orsi, eds. *Contested Eden: California before the Gold Rush*. Berkeley: University of California Press, 1998.

Hague, Harlan. *Thomas O. Larkin: A Life of Patriotism and Profit in Old California*. Norman: University of Oklahoma Press, 1990.

Hammond, George P., ed. *The Larkin Papers: Personal, Business, and Official Correspondence of Thomas Oliver Larkin, Merchant and United States Consul in California*. 11 vols. Berkeley: University of California Press, 1951–68.

Heizer, Robert H., ed. *California*. Vol. 8 of *Handbook of North American Indians*. Washington, D.C.: Smithsonian Institution, 1978.

Hussey, Roland Dennis. *The Caracas Company, 1728–1784: A Study in the History of Spanish Monopolistic Trade*. Cambridge, Mass.: Harvard University Press, 1934.

Istomin, A. A., Dzh. R. Gibson, and V. A. Tishkov, comps. and eds. *Rossiya v Kalifornii: Russkie dokumenty o kolonii Ross I rossiisko-kaliforniiskikh svyazakh 1803–1850* [Russia in California: Russian documents about the colony of Ross and Russian-Californian relations, 1803–1820]. 2 vols. Moscow: Nauka, 2005–12.

Ivashintsov, N. A. *Russian Round-the-World Voyages, 1803–1849, with a Summary of Later Voyages to 1867*. Translated by Glynn R. Barratt. Kingston, Ont.: Limestone Press, 1980.

Iversen, Eve. *The Romance of Nikolai Rezanov and Concepción Argüello: A Literary Legend and Its Effect on California History*. Kingston, Ont.: Limestone Press, 1998.

Jennings, John, ed. *The Canoe: A Living Tradition*. Toronto: Firefly Books, 2002.

Kan, Sergei. *Memory Eternal: Tlingit Culture and Russian Orthodox Christianity through Two Centuries*. Seattle: University of Washington Press, 1999.

[Khlebnikov, Kirill Timofeyevich]. *The Khlebnikov Archive: Unpublished Journal (1800–1837) and Travel Notes (1820, 1822, and 1824)*. Translated by John Bisk; edited by Leonid Shur. Fairbanks: University of Alaska Press, 1990.

———. "Memoirs of California." Translated by Anatole G. Mazour. *Pacific Historical Review* 9, no. 3 (1940): 307–36.

———. *Notes on Russian America*. Part 1, *Novo-Arkhangelsk*. Translated by Serge LeComte and Richard Pierce. Kingston, Ont.: Limestone Press, 1994.

[Khrushchev, Kapitan]. "Plavanie shlyupa Apollona v 1821–1824 godakh" [The voyage of the sloop *Apollon* in the years 1821–24]. *Zapiski Admiralteiskovo departamenta* 10, pt. 3 (1826): 200–272.

Kotsebu, O. Ye. *Novoye puteshestvie vokrug sveta v 1823–1826 gg*. Translated from the German by D. D. Tumarkin. 2nd ed. Moscow: Nauka, 1981.

———. *Puteshestviya vokrug sveta* [*Voyages around the world*]. Edited by G. V. Karpyuk, D. D. Tumarkin, and Ye. I. Kharitonova. Moscow: Drofa, 2011.

Kotzebue, Otto von. *Entdeckungsreise in die Süd-See und nach der Beringsstrasse zur Erforschung einer nordöstlichen Durchfahrt. Unternommen in dem Jahren 1815, 1816, 1817, und 1818 . . . .* 3 vols. in 1. Weimar: Hoffmann, 1821.

———. *A New Voyage of Discovery, into the South Sea and Beering's Straits, for the Purpose of Exploring a North-East Passage, Undertaken in the Years 1815-1818 . . . .* Translated by H. E.

Lloyd. 3 vols. London: Longman, Hurst, Rees, Orme, and Brown, 1821. Reprinted, Amsterdam: N. Israel; New York: Da Capo Press, 1967.

———. *A New Voyage round the World, in the Years 1823, 24, 25, and 26.* 2 vols. London: Henry Colburn and Richard Bentley, 1830. Reprinted, Amsterdam: N. Israel; New York: Da Capo Press, 1967.

[———]. *Puteshestvie v Yuzhny okean i v Beringov proliv dlya otiskaniya severo-vostochnavo morskavo prokhoda, predprinyatoy v 1815, 1816, 1817 i 1818 godakh izhdiveniyem Yevo Siyatelstva, Gospodina Gosudarstvennavo Kantslera, Grafa Nikolaya Petrovicha Rumyantsova na korable Ryurike pod nachalstvom Flota Leitenanta Kotsebu* [A voyage to the Southern Ocean and to Bering Strait to find a Northeast Passage, made in 1815, 1816, 1817, and 1818 at the expense of His Highness the Honorable State Chancellor, Count Nikolay Petrovich Rumyantsov, on the ship *Ryurik* under the command of Fleet Lieutenant Kotzebue]. Part 2. St. Petersburg: Tipografiya Nik. Grecha, 1821–23.

Kr., A., ed. "Zapiski michmana Yegeniya Andreyevicha Berensa, vedenniya v krugosvetnom plavanii na shlyupe *Krotky* v 1828–1829 gg." [The notes of Midshipman Yevgeny Andreyevich Berens, kept during a round-the-world voyage in the sloop *Krotky* in 1828–30]. *Morskoy sbornik* 316, no. 5 (May 1903): 47–53.

Kroeber, A. L. *Handbook of the Indians of California.* Berkeley: California Book Company, 1953.

Langsdorff, Georg Heinrich von. *Remarks and Observations on a Voyage around the World from 1803 to 1807.* Vol. 2. Translated by Victoria Joan Moessner. Kingston, Ont.: Limestone Press, 1993.

Lazarev, A. P. "Zapiski o plavanii voyennavo shlyupa *Blagonamerennovo* v Beringov proliv i vokrug sveta dlya otkryty, v 1819, 1820, 1821 i 1822 godakh, vedennie gvardeiskovo ekipazha leitenantom A. P. Lazarevym" [Notes on the voyage of the naval sloop *Blagonamerenny* to Bering Strait and around the world for discoveries in 1819, 1820, 1821, and 1822 undertaken by Lieutenant of the Guards A. P. Lazarev]. RGAVMF, f. 213, op. 1, d. 111.

———. *Zapiski o plavanii voyennovo shlyupa* Blagonamerennovo *v Beringov proliv i vokrug sveta dlya otkryty v 1819, 1820, 1821 i 1822 godakh, vedennie gvardeiskovo ekipazha leitenantom A. P. Lazarevym* [Notes on the voyage of the naval sloop *Blagonamerenny* to Bering Strait and around the world for discoveries in 1819, 1820, 1821, and 1822 undertaken by Lieutenant of the Guards A. P. Lazarev]. Moscow: Geografiz, 1950.

Lazarev, Andrey. *Plavanie vokrug sveta na shlyupe "Ladoge" v 1822, 1823 i 1824 godakh* [A voyage around the world on the sloop *Ladoga* in 1822, 1823, and 1824]. St. Petersburg: Morskaya Tipografiya, 1832.

Lenz, Emil. *Physikalische Beobachtungen angestellt auf einer Reise um die Welt unter dem Kommando des Capitains Otto v. Kotzebue in den Jahren 1823, 1824, 1825 und 1826.* St. Petersburg: n.p., 1830.

Lister, Kenneth R. "The Kayak and the Walrus." In *The North American Canoe: The Living Tradition,* edited by John Jennings, 120–37. Buffalo, NY: Firefly Books, 2002.

Mahr, August C., ed. *The Visit of the "Rurik" to San Francisco in 1816.* Palo Alto: Stanford University Press, 1932. Reprinted, New York: AMS Press, 1971.

Markov, Aleksandr. *Russkie na Vostochnom okeane* [Russians on the Eastern Ocean]. 2nd ed. St. Petersburg: A. Dmitriyev, 1856.

Mathes, W. Michael. *The Russian-Mexican Frontier: Mexican Documents Regarding the Russian*

Establishments in California, 1808–1842. Jenner, Calif.: Fort Ross Interpretive Association, 2008.

Mazour, Anatole G. "Dimitry Zavalishin: Dreamer of a Russian-American Empire." *Pacific Historical Review* 5 (1936): 26–37.

Mead, George R. *The Ethnobotany of the California Indians.* La Grande, Ore.: E-Cat Worlds, 2003.

Miller, Robert R. *Juan Alvarado, Governor of California, 1836–1842.* Norman: University of Oklahoma Press, 1999.

———. *Captain Richardson: Mariner, Ranchero, and Founder of San Francisco.* Berkeley, Calif.: La Loma Press, 1995.

Mornin, Edward. "Adelbert von Chamisso: A German Poet-Naturalist and His Visit to California." *California History* 78, no. 1 (Spring 1999): 2–13.

———. *Through Alien Eyes: The Visit of the Russian Ship "Rurik" to San Francisco in 1816 and the Men behind the Visit.* Bern, Switzerland: Peter Lang, 2002.

Morrison, Raymond Kenneth. "Luis Antonio Arguello: First Mexican Governor of California." *Journal of the West* 2, no. 2 (April 1963): 193–204 and no. 3 (July 1963): 347–61.

Narochnitsky, A. L., ed. *Vneshnyaya politika Rossii XIX i nachala XX veka: Dokumenty rossiiskovo Ministerstva inostrannyk del* [The foreign policy of Russia in the 19th and the beginning of the 20th century: Documents of the Russian Ministry of Foreign Affairs]. Series 1, vol. 3. Moscow: Izdatelstvo Politicheskoy Literatury, 1963.

Nikolyukin, A. N., comp. *Vzglyad v istorii—vzglyad v budushcheye* [A glance at the past—a glance at the future]. Moscow: Progress, 1987.

Ogden, Adele. *The California Sea Otter Trade, 1784–1848.* Berkeley: University of California Press, 1941.

O'Grady, Alix. *From the Baltic to Russian America, 1829–1836: The Journey of Elisabeth von Wrangell.* Kingston, Ont.: Limestone Press, 2001.

Okladnikova, Ye. A. "Etnograficheskie nablyudeniya russkikh moryakov, puteshestvennikov, diplomatov, and uchyonykh v Kalifornii v nachale i seredine XIX v. (obzor istochnikov)" [The ethnographic observations of Russian seamen, travelers, diplomats, and scientists in California in the early and middle 19th century (a survey of sources)]. In *Russkaya America Po lichnym vpechatleniyam missionerov, zemleprokhodtsev, moryakov, issledovateley i drugikh ochevidtsev* [Russian America according to the personal impressions of missionaries, landsmen, seafarers, explorers, and other eyewitnesses], edited by A. D. Dridzo and R. V. Kinzhalov, 255–343. Moscow: Mysl, 1994.

Orsi, Richard J. "Estanislao's Rebellion, 1829." In *The Elusive Eden: A New History of California,* edited by Richard B. Rice, William A. Bullough, and Richard J. Orsi, 53–68. 2nd ed. New York: Alfred A Knopf, 1996.

Orsio, Antonio María. *The History of Alta California: A Memoir.* Translated and edited by Rose Marie Beebe and Robert M. Senkewicz. (Madison: University of Wisconsin Press, 1996.

Owens, Kenneth N. "Magnificent Fraud: Ivan Petrov's Docufiction on Russian Fur Hunters and California Missions." *The Californians: The Magazine of California History* 8, no. 2 (July–August 1990): 25–29.

Pestov, Ivan Semyonovich. "Svedeniya o Yeniseiskoy gubernii (Iz zapisok Pestova)" [Information about Yeniseisk Province (from the memoirs of Pestov)]. *Zhurnal Ministerstva vnutrennykh del,* pt. 5, bk. 4 (1831): 75–113.

———. *Zapiski ob Yeniseiskoy gubernii Vostochnoy Sibiri 1831 g.* [Memoirs of Eastern Siberia's Yeniseisk Province in 1831]. Moscow: Universitetskaya Tipografiya, 1833.

Pierce, Richard A. "New Light on Ivan Petroff, Historian of Alaska." *Pacific Northwest Quarterly* 59, no. 1 (January 1968): 1–10.

———. "A Note on 'Ivan Petroff and the Far Northwest.'" *Journal of the West* 3, no. 4 (October 1964): 436–39.

———, ed. *Rezanov Reconnoiters California, 1806: A New Translation of Rezanov's Letter, Parts of Lieutenant Khvostov's Log of the Ship "Juno," and Dr. Georg von Langsdorff['s] Observations.* San Francisco: Book Club of California, 1972.

———. *Russian America: A Biographical Dictionary.* Kingston, Ont.: Limestone Press, 1990.

Pierce, Richard A., and Alton S. Donnelly. *A History of the Russian American Company.* Vol. 2, *Documents.* Kingston, Ont.: Limestone Press, 1979.

Pubols, Louise. *The Father of All: The de la Guerra Family, Power, and Patriarchy in Mexican California.* San Marino: Huntington Library; Berkeley: University of California Press, 2009.

Richardson, William. *Mexico through Russian Eyes, 1806–1940.* Pittsburgh: University of Pittsburgh Press, 1988.

———. "Wrangell's Journey of 1836: 'From Sitka to Saint Petersburg by Way of Mexico.'" *Pacific Historian* 24, no. 4 (Winter 1984): 42–54.

Rogers, Cameron. *Trodden Glory: The Story of the California Poppy.* Santa Barbara, Calif.: Wallace Hebberd, 1949.

Rosenus, Alan. *General M. G. Vallejo and the Advent of the Americans: A Biography.* Albuquerque: University of New Mexico Press, 1999.

Rotchev, Alexander Gavrilovich. "Letters of A. Rotchev, Last Commandant at Fort Ross and the Résumé of the Report of the Russian-American Company for the Year 1850–51." Translated by Frederick C. Cordes. *California Historical Society Quarterly* 39 (June 1960): 97–115.

———. "New Eldorado in California." Translated by Alexander Doll and Richard A. Pierce. *Pacific Historian* 14 (Winter 1970): 33–40.

———. "Novy Eldorado v Kalifornii" [A new Eldorado in California]. *Otechestvennie zapiski* 62, sect. 8 (1849): 216–24.

———. "Ocherki severo-zapadnavo berega Ameriki" [Sketches of the Northwest Coast of America]. *Syn otechestva* 1, pt. 3 (1838): 65–78.

[———]. "Vospominaniya russkavo puteshestvennika o Vest-Indii, Kalifornii i Ost-Indii A. G. Rotcheva" [Reminiscences of a Russian traveler, A. G. Rotchev, to the West Indies, California, and the East Indies]. *Panteon* 8, no. 1 (1834): 80–108.

Rudkin, Charles Nathan. *Camille de Roquefeuil in San Francisco, 1817–1818.* Los Angeles: Glen Dawson, 1954.

Russell, Craig H. *From Serra to Sanchez: Music and Pageantry in the California Missions.* New York: Oxford University Press, 2009.

Russell, Thomas C., ed. *Langsdorff's Narrative of the Rezanov Voyage to Nueva California in 1806.* San Francisco: Private Press of T. C. Russell, 1927.

———, ed. *The Rezanov Voyage to California in 1806: The Report of Count Nikolai Petrovich Rezanov of His Voyage to That Provincia of Nueva España from New Archangel.* San Francisco: Private Press of T. C. Russell, 1926.

Samarov, A. A., ed. *M. P. Lazarev: Dokumenty* [M. P. Lazarev: Documents]. Vol. 1. Moscow: Voyenno-morskoye izdatelstvo Voyenno-morskovo Ministerstva Soyuza SSR, 1952.

Sandos, James. "Levantamiento! The 1824 Chumash Uprising." *Californians: The Magazine of California History* 5, no. 1 (January–February 1987): 8–11.

[Schabelski, Achille]. "Prebyvanie v koloniakh Rossiisko-Amerikanskoy Kompanii, G. Shabelskavo." *Severny arkhiv*, nos. 14–15 (1826): 131–54.

———. *Voyage aux colonies russes de l'Amerique, fait à bord du sloop de guerre l'Apollon, pendant les années 1821, 1822 et 1823.* St. Petersburg: N. Grech, 1826.

Schurz, William Lytle. *The Manila Galleon.* New York: E. P. Dutton, 1939.

Shelikhov, Grigorii I. *A Voyage to America, 1783–1786.* Translated by Marina Ramsay. Kingston, Ont.: Limestone Press, 1981.

Shur, L. A., ed. *K beregam Novovo Sveta: Iz neopublikovannykh zapisok russkikh puteshestvennikov nachala XIX veka* [To the shores of the New World: From the unpublished memoirs of Russian travelers of the beginning of the 19th century]. Moscow: Nauka, 1971.

Sitnikov, L. A. *Grigory Shelikhov.* Irkutsk: Vostochno-Sibirskoye knizhnoye izdatelstvo, 1990.

Smith, Barbara Sweetland. *Science Under Sail: Russia's Great Voyages to America, 1728–1867.* Anchorage: Anchorage Museum of History and Art and the Anchorage Museum Association, 2000.

Strike, Sandra S. *Aboriginal Uses of California's Indigenous Plants.* Vol. 2 of *Ethnobotany of the California Indians.* Champaign, Ill.: Koeltz Scientific Books, 1994.

Tebenkov, M. D., comp. *Atlas of the Northwest Coasts of America from Bering Strait to Cape Corrientes and the Aleutian Islands with Several Sheets on the Northeast Coast of Asia.* Translated by R. A. Pierce. Kingston, Ont.: Limestone Press, 1981.

Thurman, Michael E. *The Naval Department of San Blas: New Spain's Bastion for Alta California and Nootka, 1767 to 1798.* Glendale, Calif.: Arthur H. Clark, 1967.

Tumarkin, D. D. "Zabyty istochnik (O knige O. Ye. Kotsebu *Neue Reise um die Welt*)" [A forgotten source (about O. Ye. Kotsebu's *New Voyage around the World*)]. *Sovetskaya etnografiya*, no. 2 (1956): 8–9.

———. "Zhizn i puteshestviya Otto Kotsebu" [The life and voyages of Otto Kotzebue]. In Kotsebu, *Novoye puteshestvie vokrug sveta*, 3–4.

Uhrowczik, Peter. *The Burning of Monterey: The 1818 Attack on California by the Privateer Bouchard.* Los Gatos, Calif.: CYRIL Books, 2001.

Unkovsky, S. Ya. *Zapiski moryaka, 1803–1819 gg.* [A sailor's memoirs, 1803–1819]. Moscow: Izdatelstvo im. Sabashnikovykh, 2004.

Vallejo, Mariano Guadalupe. "Ranch and Mission Days in Alta California." *Century Magazine* 19 (December 1890): 183–92.

———. *Report of a Visit to Fort Ross and Bodega Bay in April 1833.* Translated by Glenn Farris and Rose-Marie Beebe. Bakersfield: California Mission Studies Association, 2000.

Vrangel, F. *Ocherk puti iz Sitkhi v S.-Peterburg* [A sketch of a journey from Sitka to St. Petersburg]. St. Petersburg: N. Grech, 1836.

Weber, David J. *The Californios versus Jedediah Smith, 1826–1827: A Cache of Documents.* Spokane, Wash.: Arthur H. Clark, 1990.

Wilbur, Marguerite Eyer, trans. and ed. *Duflot de Mofras' Travels on the Pacific Coast.* Vol. 2. Santa Ana, Calif.: Fine Arts Press, 1937.

Wrangel, Ferdinand Petrovich von. *De Sitka a San Petersburgo a través de México: Diario de una Expedición (13-X-1835–22-V-1836)* [From Sitka to St. Petersburg via Mexico: A diary of an expedition (13 October 1835–22 May 1836)]. Translated by Luísa Pintó Mimó. Mexico City: SepSetentas, 1975.

Zavalishin, Dmitry. "California in 1824." Translated by James R. Gibson. *Southern California Quarterly* 55, no. 4 (Winter 1973): 369–412.

———. "Delo o kolonii Ross" [The case of the colony of Ross]. *Russky vestnik* 62 (1866): 36–65.

———. "Krugosvetnoye plavanie fregata *Kreiser* v 1822–1825 gg., pod komandoyu Mikhaila Petrovicha Lazareva" [The round-the-world voyage of the frigate *Kreiser* in 1822–25 under the command of Mikhail Petrovich Lazarev]. *Drevnyaya i novaya Rossiya*, vol. 2, no. 5 (1877): 54–67, no. 6 (1877): 115–25, no. 7 (1877): 199–214, and vol. 3, no. 10 (1877): 143–58, no. 11 (1877): 210–23.

———. *Rossiisko-amerikanskaya kompaniya* [The Russian-American Company]. Moscow: Universitetskaya Tipografiya, 1865.

———. *Vospominaniya* [Reminiscences]. 4th ed. Moscow: Zakharov, 2003.

Zimmerly, David W. *Qayaq: Kayaks of Alaska and Siberia*. Fairbanks: University of Alaska Press, 2000.

Index